ETERNAL RIGHTEOUSNESS

Living Before God

WILLEM J. OUWENEEL

AN EVANGELICAL INTRODUCTION TO
REFORMATIONAL THEOLOGY
VOL III/2

PART III: REDEMPTION:
THE CHRIST-CENTERED HEART OF THEOLOGY

AN EVANGELICAL INTRODUCTION TO REFORMATIONAL THEOLOGY

Part I: Scripture: The Revealed Source For Theology
    I/1 *The Eternal Word:* God Speaking To Us
    I/2 *The Eternal Torah:* Living Under God

Part II: God: The Personal Source Behind Theology
    II/1 *The Eternal God:* God Revealing Himself To Us
    II/2 *The Eternal Christ:* God With Us
    II/3 *The Eternal Spirit:* God Living In Us

Part III: Redemption: The Christ-Centered Heart of Theology
    III/1 *The Eternal Purpose:* Living In Christ
    III/2 *Eternal Righteousness:* Living Before God
    III/3 *Eternal Salvation:* Christ Dying For Us
    III/4 *Eternal Life:* Christ Living In Us

Part IV: Consummation: The Lived Shape of Theology
    IV/1a *The Eternal People:* God in Relation To Israel: Israel in the Tanakh and the New Testament
    IV/1b *The Eternal People:* God in Relation To Israel: Post-New Testament Israel
    IV/2 *The Eternal Covenant:* Living With God
    IV/3 *The Eternal Kingdom:* Living Under Christ

Part V: Method: The Comprehensive Foundation of Theology
    V/1 *Eternal Truth:* The Prolegomena of Theology

ETERNAL RIGHTEOUSNESS

Living Before God

WILLEM J. OUWENEEL

Eternal Righteousness: Living Before God

This English edition is a publication of Paideia Press (P.O. Box 500, Jordan Station, Ontario, Canada L0R 1S0). Copyright © 2023 by Paideia Press. All rights reserved. Except for brief quotations in critical publications or reviews, no part of this book may be reproduced in any manner without prior written permission from Paideia Press at the address above.

Unless otherwise indicated, Scripture quotations are from the ESV® Bible (The Holy Bible, English Standard Version®). Copyright © 2001 by Crossway, a publishing ministry of Good News Publishers. Used by permission. All rights reserved.

Scripture quotations or references marked as NKJV are taken from the New King James Version®. Copyright © 1982 by Thomas Nelson, Inc. Used by permission. All rights reserved.

Scripture quotations or references marked as NIV are taken from the Holy Bible, New International Version®, NIV®. Copyright © 1973, 1978, 1984, 2011 by Biblica, Inc.™ Used by permission of Zondervan. All rights reserved worldwide. www.zonderan.com. The "NIV" and "New International Version" are trademarks registered in the United States Patent and Trademark Office by Biblica, Inc.™

Book Design by: Michael Wagner

ISBN 978-0-88815-344-9

Printed in the United States of America

*Your righteousness is **eternal righteousness**,*
  and your Torah is truth.
                              Psalm 119:142 (CJB)

Seventy weeks are appointed for your people
  and for your holy city
to complete the rebellion,
  to end sins,
to cover over wrongdoing,
  *to bring **eternal righteousness**,*
to seal up prophetic vision,
  and to anoint the most holy place.
                              Daniel 9:24 (CEB)

Table of Contents

Table of Contents (Expanded)		
Series Preface		i
Author's Preface		v
Abbreviations		ix
Chapter 1	The Righteousness of God	1
Chapter 2	Justification in Judaism	59
Chapter 3	New Perspectives on Paul	111
Chapter 4	The Imputation Doctrine	163
Chapter 5	Justification in the New Testament	219
Chapter 6	Saving Faith	281
Chapter 7	Practical Faith	333
Chapter 8	Positional Sanctification	393
Chapter 9	Practical Sanctification	453
Appendix 1	The Time of Propitiation	515
Appendix 2	The Idea of Placation in the Doctrine of Propitiation	533
Bibliography		543
Scripture Index		571
Subject Index		597

Table of Contents Expanded

Series Preface	i
Author's Preface	v
Abbreviations	ix
1 The Righteousness of God	1
1.1 Centrality of the Justification Doctrine	2
1.1.1 Descriptions	2
1.1.2 Not So Central?	5
1.2 A Short History	8
1.2.1 The Reformation	8
1.2.2 The Revived Rome-Reformation Debate	11
1.2.3 The Declaration of 1999	13
1.3 New Questions	16
1.3.1 Imputation and Sanctification	16
1.3.2 Analytic and Synthetic Justification	17
1.4 Terminology	20
1.4.1 *Dikē, Dikaios, Dikaioō*	20
1.4.2 Three Nouns	23
1.5 Declared or Made Righteous	25
1.5.1 Turn Out to Be Righteous	25
1.5.2 Make Righteous	26
1.5.3 Declaring or Making?	27

1.6	The Righteous God	29
	1.6.1 Terminology	29
	1.6.2 Righteousness and Faithfulness	31
1.7	Righteousness from God or of God?	32
	1.7.1 The Debate	32
	1.7.2 God's Righteousness – Many Interpretations	35
	1.7.3 God's Own Righteousness	37
	1.7.4 Just in Justifying	39
1.8	Righteousness in the Old Testament	41
	1.8.1 "The Law and the Prophets"	41
	1.8.2 Righteousness in the Prophets	43
1.9	Divine Righteousness	45
	1.9.1 Saving Righteousness	45
	1.9.2 Two Kinds of Faith	48
	1.9.3 Convicting of Righteousness	49
	1.9.4 Christ Our Righteousness	50
1.10	A Divine Attribute?	53
	1.10.1 Retributive Justice	53
	1.10.2 Some More Biblical Aspects	55
2	**Justification in Judaism**	**59**
2.1	Regeneration	60
	2.1.1 The Life-Bringing Torah	60
	2.1.2 The Love of the Regenerate	62
	2.1.3 Do the Righteous Exist?	64
2.2	Good and Evil Works	67
	2.2.1 Good Works by Believers	67
	2.2.2 Evil Works by Mere Confessors	69

	2.3	Biblical Examples	72
		2.3.1 Faith Versus Works	72
		2.3.2 The Source of Life	74
		2.3.3 *Tsaddiqim*	75
	2.4	*Tsedaqah*	77
		2.4.1 Charity and Legality	77
		2.4.2 The Pharisee and Phinehas	79
		2.4.3 The *Tsaddiq*: Three Characteristics	80
	2.5	Further Characteristics of the *Tsaddiq*	82
		2.5.1 What He Is	82
		2.5.2 What He is Not	84
	2.6	The Faith of Abraham	86
		2.6.1 Abraham and His Predecessors	86
		2.6.2 Faith Counted as Righteousness	89
		2.6.3 The Content of Abraham's Faith	91
	2.7	The Faith of Habakkuk	94
		2.7.1 Living by Faith	94
		2.7.2 Application to Christ	96
	2.8	Eschatology and Righteousness	98
		2.8.1 The Messianic Kingdom	98
		2.8.2 The New Covenant	99
		2.8.3 Individual Versus Collective	101
	2.9	The Righteousness of the Torah	104
		2.9.1 Two Sides of the Torah	104
		2.9.2 Legalism: Augmenting the Law	106
		2.9.3 Legalism: Attenuating the Law	109
3	New Perspectives on Paul		111

3.1	Paul and Judaism	112
	3.1.1 A Proper View of Judaism	112
	3.1.2 The Picture Changes	114
3.2	Meaning of the Sacrifice	116
	3.2.1 No Covenantal Nomism without Propitiation	116
	3.2.2 *Tefillot*	118
	3.2.3 Conclusion	121
3.3	Judaism Lacks Christ	122
	3.3.1 The Shadows and the Reality	122
	3.3.2 The Bloody Sacrifice	124
	3.3.3 The Greater Light	125
	3.3.4 Three Groups	128
3.4	Further Developments	131
	3.4.1 Paul's Critics	131
	3.4.2 Sanders' Allies	132
	3.4.3 Pinchas Lapide	134
	3.4.4 Lapide, Bonhoeffer, Luther	136
3.5	The Wright–Piper Conflict	138
	3.5.1 The Position of Piper	138
	3.5.2 The Position of Wright	140
	3.5.3 Salvation	142
3.6	Three Groups of Jews	144
	3.6.1 Legalists	144
	3.6.2 The Faithful	146
	3.6.3 A Third Group	148
3.7	Again: The Two Polities	149
	3.7.1 "Closed Systems"	149

		3.7.2 Torah and Christ	150
	3.8	NPP Issues	153
		3.8.1 Linguistic Issues	153
		3.8.2 Theological Issues (1)	155
		3.8.3 Theological Issues (2)	158
4	The Imputation Doctrine		163
	4.1	Introduction	164
		4.1.1 Confessional Testimonies	164
		4.1.2 "Counting as Righteousness"	166
		4.1.3 Acquittal	167
	4.2	Imputation?	169
		4.2.1 "Counting as Righteousness"	169
		4.2.2 Imputing Righteousness	172
		4.2.3 *Iustitia Aliena*	174
	4.3	More About *Logizomai*	176
		4.3.1 No Transference	176
		4.3.2 Again: Imputation	178
		4.3.3 The Obedience of Christ	181
		4.3.4 Woelderink and Berkouwer	182
	4.4	Bestowed Righteousness	184
		4.4.1 Righteousness of God in Christ	184
		4.4.2 Christ Our Righteousness	186
		4.4.3 "Clothed" with Righteousness	187
	4.5	Righteousness of the Law?	190
		4.5.1 Evangelical and Reformed	190
		4.5.2 Calvin and Calvinists	193
		4.5.3 Imputed Obedience?	197
		4.5.4 More Recent Views	199

	4.6	Evaluation	203
		4.6.1 Obedience Beyond the Torah	203
		4.6.2 "Why Then the Torah?"	205
		4.6.3 The Use of Someone Else's Good life	207
	4.7	The Place of the Torah	208
		4.7.1 Active and Passive Righteousness	208
		4.7.2 The Righteousness That Comes From the Law	210
	4.8	Christ's Torah Observance	213
		4.8.1 The First and the Last Adam	213
		4.8.2 Conclusion	215
5	Justification in the New Testament		219
	5.1	Means of Justification	220
		5.1.1 Wrong Means	220
		5.1.2 The Grace of God	223
		5.1.3 The Blood of Christ	225
	5.2	Faith	227
		5.2.1 "Out of Faith"	227
		5.2.2 Prepositions	230
		5.2.3 Faith and Justification	233
	5.3	Life as the Goal of Justification	235
		5.3.1 "Righteousness of Life"	235
		5.3.2 Dying for Sin, Dying to Sin	238
		5.3.3 Justification Leads to Life	240
		5.3.4 Making or Declaring Righteous?	242
	5.4	Righteousness by Works	245
		5.4.1 The Confessions and Catechisms	245

		5.4.2 Fruit-Bearing	246

		5.4.2	Fruit-Bearing	246
		5.4.3	Justification by Works: Societal Aspects	249
		5.4.4	Justification by Works: Eschatological Aspects	251
	5.5	Practical Righteousness in the New Testament		253
		5.5.1	Living Righteously	253
		5.5.2	Slaves of Righteousness	255
	5.6	Practical Versus Positional Righteousness		257
		5.6.1	Instantaneous Justification?	257
		5.6.2	Abraham and Habakkuk Again	259
		5.6.3	Fulfilling the Law	260
		5.6.4	The One Commandment	262
	5.7	Peace with God		264
		5.7.1	Forms of Peace	264
		5.7.2	Peace Rooted in Righteousness	267
	5.8	Typology		269
		5.8.1	Esther	269
		5.8.2	Mephibosheth	271
	5.9	Sins and Sin		273
		5.9.1	Effects of One Sin	273
		5.9.2	Romans 5:18	275
		5.9.3	Romans 5:19	277
6	Saving Faith			281
	6.1	What Is Faith?		282
		6.1.1	Introduction	282
		6.1.2	Terminology	285

6.2	Levels of Faith	287
	6.2.1 Believing That . . .	287
	6.2.2 Believing In = Trusting Someone	290
	6.2.3 Entrusting Oneself to Someone	292
6.3	Forms of Faith	295
	6.3.1 Immanent and Transcendent Faith	295
	6.3.2 More on Intrinsic and Extrinsic Religiosity	297
	6.3.3 *Fides Qua* and *Fides Quae*	299
6.4	"Jesus Is Lord"	301
	6.4.1 The Gospel of the Kingdom	301
	6.4.2 Spiritual Growth	303
6.5	A Fierce Debate	305
	6.5.1 Charles C. Ryrie	305
	6.5.2 Zane C. Hodges	306
	6.5.3 Other Views	309
6.6	Obedience of Faith	311
	6.6.1 A Continuum	311
	6.6.2 Faith Is the Beginning	312
	6.6.3 Misunderstandings	314
6.7	Perseverance	316
	6.7.1 Perseverance according to the Creeds	316
	6.7.2 Unilaterality	317
	6.7.3 "If Indeed"	320
6.8	Assurance of Faith	321
	6.8.1 Certitude	321
	6.8.2 Underestimating Grace	323

	6.9	Knowledge of Faith	325
		6.9.1 Believing Is Knowing	325
		6.9.2 Five Objections	327
		6.9.3 Four Other Objections	330
7	Practical Faith		333
	7.1	Little Faith	334
		7.1.1 Introduction	334
		7.1.2 "Size" of Faith?	336
		7.1.3 Five Cases	338
	7.2	Growing Faith	341
		7.2.1 Practical Exercises	341
		7.2.2 The Measure of Faith	343
		7.2.3 Faith and Hyper-Calvinism	344
	7.3	A Great Faith	347
		7.3.1 The Blind and the Centurion	347
		7.3.2 The Apostle and the Canaanite Woman	349
		7.3.3 Faith That Overcomes	351
		7.3.4 Discouraged Faith	354
	7.4	The Strength of Faith	355
		7.4.1 Receptivity	355
		7.4.2 The Power of Unbelief	357
		7.4.3 Faith Essential, But Not Sufficient	358
	7.5	The Creativity of Faith	360
		7.5.1 Abraham	360
		7.5.2 Peter and Others	362
		7.5.3 The Human Aspect	364
	7.6	Doubt of Faith	366

		7.6.1 Two Kinds of Doubt	366
		7.6.2 Support from Others	367
		7.6.3 Conditions of Faith	370
		7.6.4 Can God Change His Mind?	372
	7.7	Once Saved, Always Saved?	375
		7.7.1 Remonstrantism and Dordt	375
		7.7.2 Perseverance	377
		7.7.3 God's Preservation: Exegetical	378
		7.7.4 God's Preservation: Theological	380
	7.8	Once Saved, *Not* Always Saved?	381
		7.8.1 Biblical Arguments	381
		7.8.2 Perseverance and Apostasy	384
	7.9	Evaluation	386
		7.9.1 Reconciliation Possible?	386
		7.9.2 The Two Sides	388
		7.9.3 Theological Versus Pastoral	389
8	Positional Sanctification		393
	8.1	Sanctification and Justification	394
		8.1.1 Terminology: Old Testament	394
		8.1.2 Terminology: New Testament	397
		8.1.3 Reformed Sources	399
		8.1.4 Collective Aspects	402
	8.2	Salvation as Spiritual Maturity	404
		8.2.1 Stages of Salvation	404
		8.2.2 Parallels	407
	8.3	Holiness as a Present Possession	409
		8.3.1 The Reformed View	409
		8.3.2 "You *Were* Sanctified"	411

	8.3.3 "Once for All"	413
8.4	Outward Sanctification	415
	8.4.1 "Set Apart"	415
	8.4.2 The Believers' Consecration	416
	8.4.3 Jesus' Consecration	418
8.5	Models of Sanctification	420
	8.5.1 Erroneous Models	420
	8.5.2 Again: The Reformed Model	421
	8.5.3 An Evangelical Model	423
8.6	The Holiness of God	424
	8.6.1 Holiness as Luster, Majesty, Glory	424
	8.6.2 Holiness in Judgment and Redemption	427
	8.6.3 "Sanctifying" God	429
	8.6.4 Holiness in the Theological Tradition	431
8.7	"Wretched Man That I Am!"	433
	8.7.1 Three Exegeses	433
	8.7.2 A Third Possibility	435
	8.7.3 A Pre-Stage?	437
8.8	A Hypothetical Situation	439
	8.8.1 A Rhetorical Aid	439
	8.8.2 Some Testimonies	441
	8.8.3 Five "Laws"	442
8.9	Humbling Oneself	445
	8.9.1 Poor Sinners or Perfect Christians?	445
	8.9.2 Loathing Oneself	448
	8.9.3 Living in Grace	450

9	Practical Sanctification		453
	9.1 "Be Holy!"		454
		9.1.1 Negative and Positive	454
		9.1.2 Be What You Are	457
		9.1.3 Striving for Holiness	459
	9.2 The Norm for Holiness		461
		9.2.1 The Messianic Torah	461
		9.2.2 Old Testament Holiness	463
		9.2.3 New Testament Holiness	465
	9.3 Holiness and Renewal		466
		9.3.1 *Theosis*	466
		9.3.2 Metamorphosis	468
	9.4 Union with Christ		471
		9.4.1 In Christ (Paul's Teaching)	471
		9.4.2 In Christ (John and Others)	473
		9.4.3 What Union Is Not	475
		9.4.4 Living and Walking in Christ	477
	9.5 Sanctification and Spiritual Growth		478
		9.5.1 Process or Decision?	478
		9.5.2 Sanctification is Dying Away?	480
		9.5.3 Ephesians 4:21-24	482
	9.6 Three Stages of Growth		485
		9.6.1 Fathers in Christ	485
		9.6.2 Young Men	487
		9.6.3 Five Characteristics	489
	9.7 Poor Sinners or Rich Sons?		492
		9.7.1 Reformed Testimony	492
		9.7.2 New Testament Testimony	493

	9.7.3 False and True Piety	495
9.8	Spiritual Warfare	497
	9.8.1 Poor Sinners or Overcomers?	497
	9.8.2 Warfare in the New Testament	499
9.9	Discipline	501
	9.9.1 Education, Not Punishment	501
	9.9.2 Dealing with Discipline	504
9.10	Perfectionism	506
	9.10.1 No More Sinning?	506
	9.10.2 Two Sides	509
	9.10.3 No Excuse	511

Appendix 1	The Time of Propitiation	515
1	When Was the Atonement?	515
2	Active and Passive Obedience	517
3	No Vicarious Torah Observance	521
4	Only on the Cross	523
5	God's Delight in Jesus	524
6	"With His Wounds We Are Healed"	527
7	Darkness	529

Appendix 2	The Idea of Placation in the Doctrine of Propitiation	533
1	God's Wrath Placated?	533
2	Enmity between God and Humanity	534
3	No Placation	537
4	Propitiation and the Wrath of God	539

Bibliography	543

Scripture Index 571
Subject Index 597

Series Preface

BY MEANS OF THIS PREFACE, the editor and publisher of this series wish to help the reader both understand and process the content of these volumes.

The capacities and erudition of Dr. Willem Ouweneel need no demonstration or defense from us. His voluminous work and prodigious writing stand as a testimony of his love for the Lord Jesus Christ, God's Word, and God's people.

But these volumes present ideas that will surprise some, anger others, and possibly confuse still others. Both the editor and publisher disagree with some of Dr. Ouweneel's assertions and conclusions, but this is not the place for offering our counter-arguments. That requires an altogether different venue. Nevertheless, discerning readers will legitimately wonder why this editor and publisher invested effort and resources in putting these volumes into print.

At least three reasons justify that investment. Each of them is very sensitive.

The first reason is: *self-examination*. Some of our readers may conclude that, in presenting his exegetical, doctrinal, and historical case, Dr. Ouweneel is "coloring outside the lines" of what they have come to believe. He challenges deeply and firmly held convictions and beliefs, like those associated with Israel, with the law of God, with election and reprobation, with infant baptism, with covenant theology, and with justification. At each point, his challenges call us readers to self-examination, regarding our love for Scripture, for the God of Scripture, and for the Truth revealed and incarnated personally in Jesus Christ. One of Ouweneel's challenges is for us believers in Jesus Christ who are Reformed and Presbyterian church members to recognize that there are millions, even billions, of Jesus-believers who disagree with us *and are nevertheless genuine Christians*. And they ought to be acknowledged as such.

The second reason is: *repentance*. Coming, as they do, from one who lives and teaches outside the orbit of many of our readers, Dr. Ouweneel's observations about the state of our (numerous) churches and of our (interminable) doctrinal squabbles ought to embarrass us Reformed and Presbyterian church members. Our incessant polemicizing, our cantankerous stridency, and our offenses against the unity of Christ's church seriously compromise the gospel's witness to the watching world. Brothers and sisters, we must repent of these, for the sake of the gospel, for the sake of the church's witness, and for the sake of our children.

The third reason is: *ecumenicity*. This reason may indeed strike you as strange, but one of the salutary outcomes of reading Dr. Ouweneel's arguments can be this: *not* that you surrender your commitments and convictions that are being challenged, but instead that you come to *respect* and *love* those Jesus-believers who don't share them with you. These Christians are those whose spiritual pilgrimage and gospel-guided history have not brought them to the same place on the road, but who nonetheless are walking the same road as we.

You may well be asking: How, then, is this different from advocating doctrinal relativism? If these distinctive features of Reformed confession and theology are biblical, then why is Dr. Ouweneel being given a microphone for proclaiming his criticisms and rejections of these distinctive emphases of Reformed teaching? The short answer is this: So that from this brother in Christ, this close cousin in the faith, this fellow pilgrim-soldier, we may learn how to lock arms with other Jesus-believers as we face unbelief in our day, even if we can't hold hands. So that we may learn what it means to be Jesus-believers *first*, Reformed or Presbyterian confessors *second*, and only then, *thirdly, theological advocates.*

So we leave you with this challenge: Why do you believe what you believe? What is your biblical warrant? Dr. Ouweneel presents the various positions prevalent in Christendom fairly. The reader will learn why others believe what they believe, and why they don't emphasize certain teachings in the same way that we do.

These books, then, are *not* for the faint of faith. But they *are* for those wanting to grow up and mature into the unity of faith in our Lord Jesus Christ (John 17: 20-23; Eph. 4:13).

Nelson D. Kloosterman, editor
John Hultink, publisher

Author's Preface

THIS BOOK IS A RE-WORKING and expansion of a part of Volume 6 of my *Evangelical Dogmatic Series*, which is published in Dutch by Medema, Heerenveen [the Netherlands] and comprises a total of twelve volumes.[1] Part of it was already introduced in the first volume of the present series, *The Eternal Torah*, and the second volume, *The Eternal Covenant*,[2] and is expanded here. This present volume marks the midpoint of the series.

My intention was, and is, to offer an Evangelical analysis of three subjects that traditionally have played a great role in Reformational—especially Reformed—thinking: the law, the covenant, and justification. By "Reformational" I mean all that refers to the sixteenth-century Protestant Reformation. "Reformed" refers to one specific brand of Reformational thinking, namely, Calvinist. Unless specified otherwise, the word "Reformed" also encompasses "Presbyterian," not as referring to a specific type of church government but to Calvinist thought of Scottish and English origins. "Reformed" in the narrower sense refers to Calvinist thought of German and especially Dutch origins.

In this book, "Evangelical" means little more than orthodox Protestant (in which "orthodox" refers to Protestants

---

1. Ouweneel (2010a, chapters 7–10).
2. Ouweneel (2015a; 2015b).

rooted in the Apostolic and Nicene Creeds, as well as in the sixteenth-century Reformation). I use the term Evangelical to indicate that I am neither a Lutheran, nor a Calvinist, and that I feel more at home with pre-scholastic Christianity. This Christianity apparently did not yet feel constrained to develop what I call an "inferential theology": an elaborate thought system built upon inferences from inferences from inferences (inferentialism). These matters have been explained in the second volume of this series.

I have written the present volume with essentially two purposes in mind. On the one hand, I wanted to emphasize the importance of justification by faith in both the Old and the New Testament. On the other hand, I wished to point out that Reformed theologians have often emphasized the notion of justification too unilaterally—there is more than justification—or have beset it with misunderstandings, especially the "imputation" doctrine. These errors are striking examples of the "inferential-theological" approach, in which theologians have invented and imagined elements of justification theology that are not backed up by Scripture. We learn from (Lutheran and) Reformed theologians about the importance of justification by faith; I am tremendously grateful to them for that. However, we also learn from them the consequences of not remaining as closely to Scripture as possible.

Bible quotations in this book are usually from the English Standard Version. When other translations are used, this is indicated. I have taken the liberty to sometimes substitute "Torah" for "law," or "Messiah" for "Christ." Unless otherwise noted, quotations from the Three Forms of Unity and the Westminster Standards are from *Reformed Confessions of the 16th and 17th Centuries in English Translation*, 4 vols., ed. James T. Dennison Jr. (Grand Rapids: Reformation Heritage Books, 2008–14).

I thank Dr. Nelson D. Kloosterman again very warmly for his expert editorial work on the manuscript of this book. And

Author's Preface

I am again deeply thankful to my publisher, John Hultink, for his constant encouragement in this entire project.

Willem J. Ouweneel
Huis ter Heide, Netherlands
Spring, 2015

Abbreviations

Bible Versions

AMP	Amplified Bible
ASV	American Standard Version
CEB	Common English Bible
CEV	Contemporary English Version
CJB	Complete Jewish Bible
DLNT	Disciples' Literal New Translation
DRA	Douay-Rheims 1899 American Edition
ERV	Easy-to-Read Version
ESV	English Standard Version
EXB	Expanded Bible
GNT	Good News Translation
GNV	1599 Geneva Bible
GW	God's Word Translation
HCSB	Holman Christian Standard Bible
ICB	International Children's Bible
ISV	International Standard Version
JUB	Jubilee Bible 2000
LEB	Lexham English Bible
MEV	Modern English Version
MSG	The Message

NABRE	New American Bible (Revised Edition)
NASB	New American Standard Bible
NCV	New Century Version
NET	New English Translation
NIRV	New International Reader's Version
NIV	New International Version
NKJV	New King James Version
NLT	New Living Translation
NRSV	New Revised Standard Version
RSV	Revised Standard Version
TLB	Living Bible
VOICE	The Voice
WE	Worldwide English (New Testament)
WEB	World English Bible
YLT	Young's Literal Translation

Other Sources

CNT	Commentaar op het Nieuwe Testament
EBC	Expositor's Bible Commentary
EGT	The Expostor's Greek Testament
ICC	International Critical Commentary
KV	Korte Verklaring
NICOT	New International Commentary on the Old Testament
NICNT	New International Commentary on the New Testament

Chapter 1
The Righteousness of God

I am not ashamed of the gospel,
  for it is the power of God
for salvation to everyone who believes,
  to the Jew first and also to the Greek.
For in it the righteousness of God
  is revealed from faith for faith,
as it is written,
  "The righteous shall live by faith."
                              Romans 1:16–17

But now the righteousness of God
  has been manifested apart from the law,
  although the Law and the Prophets bear witness to it—
the righteousness of God
  through faith in Jesus Christ
  for all who believe.
                              Romans 3:21–22

We implore you on behalf of Christ,
  be reconciled to God.
For our sake he made him to be sin
  who knew no sin,
so that in him

> *we might become the righteousness of God.*
> 2 Corinthians 4:20–21

Summary: *The question of righteousness and justification are of vital importance for Christians. Opinions differ whether it is* the *vital subject. At least it played an essential role in the conflict between Rome and Reformation. Today the question is whether the two parties really understood one another; today, many Catholics and Protestants are happy with a formula like this one: a person is justified by faith alone, but then a faith working in love. Many other questions have arisen, such as: Does justification consist of the imputation of the righteousness of Christ? What is the relationship between being declared righteous and leading a righteous life? What is the relationship between analytic and synthetic justification? Is* justification *declaring* someone righteous, *or* making someone righteous? *What do the relevant Hebrew and Greek terms actually mean? How does God's righteousness relate to God's love and faithfulness? Is "God's righteousness" of which Paul speaks an attribute of God, or is it a human righteousness according to God's criteria? Is God righteous when he declares ungodly people righteous? How does the New Testament relate to the Old Testament when it comes to God's righteousness? What does it mean that Christ is the believers' righteousness? This chapter begins our discussion of these and other questions.*

1.1 Centrality of the Justification Doctrine
1.1.1 Descriptions

THIS BOOK IS ABOUT the righteousness of God, and the righteousness of redeemed humans. The English language is occasionally somewhat plagued by the riches of its vernacular:[1] in the theological sense, being righteous is the same as being just, righteousness is the same as justice, and justification means making, or declaring, a person righteous. The great center of the biblical doctrine of justification is the One "who justifies

---

1. This is due to its dual origin: "righteous" is Germanic, "just" is Latin-Romanic.

the ungodly" (Rom. 4:5), that is, God turning the ungodly person into a righteous person. This is one of the marvels of the Bible.

Some would even say: *the* greatest marvel. According to the Lutheran and Reformed traditions, with the doctrine of justification we touch the "center of the Pauline message,"[2] even "the main pillar on which religion rests,"[3] not the preliminary matter but the highest matter,[4] the "cornerstone of Christian theology and the church."[5] It is "the essence of the New Testament, the matter proper of the gospel,"[6] "the heart of the gospel,"[7] "the foundation and the core of the salvation of sinners who were lost in their guilt";[8] "there is no facet more comforting in the gospel than that of justification."[9] Therefore, Martin Luther called "justification by faith alone" *articulus stantis et cadentis ecclesiae*: "the article by which the church stands or falls."[10] He even wrote that the "article" of justification is the master and prince, the lord, the ruler, and the judge of all kinds of doctrines. It preserves and guides all church doctrine, and arouses our conscience before God. Without this article, the world is total death and darkness, according to Luther.[11]

R. C. Sproul has sharpened Luther's words in an even more emphatic way.[12] He argued that *sola fide* ("by faith alone") is

---

2. See the title of Wendland (1935).
3. Calvin, *Institutes* 3.11.1.
4. Bloesch (1997, 177).
5. Schwarz (1998, title).
6. Lekkerkerker (1949, 16).
7. Van Genderen and Velema (2008, 607); Jüngel (2001, title: *Justification: The Heart of the Christian Faith*); White (2001, chapter 1: "The Heart of the Gospel").
8. Duffield and Van Cleave (1996, 234).
9. Van der Waal (1973, 78).
10. See his comment on Ps. 130:4, and further Plass (1959, 2:704n5); see also Bavinck (2008, 4:196); Berkhof (1979, 436); Braaten (1990, title); Demarest (1997, 345).
11. Plass (1959, 2:703).
12. Sproul (1995, 70).

important not only because the church stands or falls with it. It is important because *humanity* stands or falls with it. He said that the place where, and the time when, we either stand or fall with it is before the judgment seat of God.[13] In this argument, even eternal bliss is implicitly linked with the "right" justification doctrine: it must be justification "by faith alone," otherwise there can be no salvation.

Henricus Gravemeijer quoted someone who had called justification "the soul of Christianity, the source of all true consolation and of sanctification," and continued by insisting that it is "also the palladium (the protecting guarantee) of Protestantism."[14] Luther said of Romans 3:23-24 ("justified by his grace as a gift"): "Please note, this is the most important and central part of this epistle of all Scripture."[15] J. I. Packer wrote that the doctrine of justification by faith is like Atlas: it carries a world on its shoulders, the entire evangelical knowledge of saving grace.[16] He argued that when justification falls, then all true knowledge of the grace of God in human life falls with it, and then, as Luther said, the church itself falls. When Atlas falls, everything that was resting on his shoulders collapses as well, according to Packer.

As recently as 2001, Peter Stuhlmacher argued that justification is not merely an important Pauline concept but, more generally, one of *the Bible's* "essential themes."[17] His book shows that, just as federalists see covenants everywhere in the Bible,[18] Stulmacher sees justification everywhere in the Bible. And Cornelis Harinck wrote in 2007 that the doctrine of justification by faith is "the heart of Christian doctrine and of

---

13. God is the "righteous Judge" (2 Tim. 4:8; cf. Gen. 18:25; Ps. 9:8; 50:6; 67:4; 96:10, 13; 98:9; Eccl. 3:17; Isa. 51:5; Jer. 11:20; John 5:30; Acts 17:31; 1 Pet. 2:23; Rev. 16:5; 19:2, 11).
14. Gravemeijer (1892–94); quoted in Van der Waal (1973, 65).
15. Annotation accompanying his translation of this verse: WA Deutsche Bibel VII, 39.
16. Packer (1961, VIII–IX).
17. Stuhlmacher (2001, 11).
18. See Ouweneel (2015b passim).

Reformed theology.... A revival of this doctrine would bring about a revival of the church.... [It] is the core of the Gospel, yes, it *is* the Gospel! ... Furthering the confession, preaching and experience of this doctrine furthers all biblical truths. The doctrine of justification by faith in Jesus Christ gives the church its vitality and piety. The lack of this doctrine brings the church deadliness and spiritual poverty."[19]

It is no wonder that Husbands and Treier said about justification by faith that this doctrine concerning salvation is often considered to be the main cause of division within Western Christianity, that is, between Roman Catholicism and Protestantism.[20]

In 1975, the Lutheran authors of the Leuenberg Concord—today one of the confessional documents of the Protestant Church in the Netherlands—wrote in article 2.8: "The Reformers expressed the true understanding of the Gospel in the doctrine of justification." And in article 2.12: "With this understanding of the Gospel we take our stand on the basis of the creeds of the early church and reaffirm the conviction, common to the Reformation confessions of faith, that the unique mediation of Jesus Christ in salvation is the heart of scripture and that the message of justification as the message of God's free grace is the measure of all the Church's preaching."

1.1.2 Not So Central?

All these centralist, and even jubilant, descriptions of (the doctrine of) justification are rather strange, and quite exaggerated. No one can honestly deny that the doctrine of justification plays a relatively limited role in the New Testament, since it appears mainly in Romans and Galatians (at best, one might add Luke 18:14; 1 Cor. 6:11; 2 Cor. 5:21; Phil. 3:9; Titus 3:7; James 2:21–25). Therefore, Wilhelm Wrede, William Davies, and Albert Schweitzer claimed that the entire theology

---

19. Harinck (2007, 9–11).
20. Husbands and Treier (2005, 8).

of Paul can be thoroughly described with only collateral references to his doctrine of justification.[21] Herman Ridderbos does not go that far, but even he says of Romans and Galatians: "[T]hese epistles are governed by a definite interest and a definite antithesis, namely, by the relationship of the gospel and the Jewish-synagogical doctrine of redemption. In other epistles other points of view are dominant, and for that reason the one gospel of Christ has another point and application: . . . ."[22] John Macquarrie even argued that the doctrine of justification is neither indispensable, nor particularly clarifying, since it forms only one element in the Christian experience of atonement.[23]

What happened in some of the jubilant descriptions of justification mentioned in §1.1.1 is that the meaning of this doctrine is expanded to include the entire doctrine of salvation. Indeed, no one can deny that salvation — in the many meanings of the term — is a central topic in the Bible. However, justification is only one of the many aspects of salvation. Other aspects are regeneration (rebirth or new birth), propitiation, reconciliation, forgiveness, "quickening" (being made alive), being raised with Christ, redemption (deliverance), positional sanctification, union with Christ, and adoption as sons.[24] None of these terms is exactly identical with justification, as we will see, although, of course, they all touch upon each other. Moreover, these aspects concern only the individual, not the collective aspects of salvation (see §8.1.3), nor do they involve the theotic and the eschatological aspects of salvation. It is only a Lutheran-Reformed prejudice — purely historically determined — to make justification by far the most important of all these aspects.

Some theologians have endeavored, not so much to belit-

---

21. Wrede (1962, 123); Davies (1962, 222); Schweitzer (1968, 225–26); cf. Shelton (2006, 117).
22. Ridderbos (1975, 160).
23. Macquarrie (1966, 304).
24. Cf. Ouweneel (2010a, §§1.1 and 1.2).

tle the significance of the New Testament's doctrine of justification, but to assign a more important place to other Pauline subjects, as do, for example, James Stewart regarding union with Christ, and Archibald Hunter regarding salvation.[25] As far as being the "article by which the church stands or falls," cardinal John Henry Newman argued that, instead, the incarnation of the Son of God, and not any doctrine derived from a partial view of Scripture (no matter how true and important it may be), is the article of a standing or falling church.[26] In Eastern Orthodoxy, the doctrine of justification plays hardly any role, certainly not a central one. It is much more *theosis* ("deification") that occupies the central position there.[27]

In an average Roman Catholic catechism, the doctrine of justification does not occur either. We will have to honestly admit that it is Lutheranism and Calvinism that have elevated the doctrine of justification to the status of "heart of the gospel."

In my view, soteriological topics such as atonement and salvation, which are not identical with justification, play a more central and fundamental role in the New Testament. And beyond that, there are the vital subjects of eternal life (in the Johannine sense), the fullness of God (Paul: Eph. 3:19), the divine nature (Peter: 2 Pet. 1:4), and especially the church as the Body of Christ (Paul: Eph. 4:12; etc.), and the Kingdom of God, which played such a central role in the ministry of John the Baptist (Matt. 3:2), Jesus (4:17, 23; 9:35, and more times in Matt.; Acts 1:3), and the apostles (Matt. 8:12; 14:22; 19:8; 20:25; 28:23, 31; Acts 19:8; 20:25; 28:23, 31; Rom. 14:17–18; 1 Cor. 4:20; 6:9–10; Col. 1:13; 1 Thess. 2:12; 2 Thess. 1:5; James 2:5; 2 Pet. 1:11; etc.). The Kingdom of God "is of prime importance in NT theology," wrote Thomas Schreiner.[28] Many have wondered whether something similar could be said of the truth of

---

25. Stewart (2002, 204–72); Hunter (1966, 14).
26. Newman (1843, 35).
27. See extensively, Ouweneel (2015b, chapters 7 and 9).
28. Schreiner (2008, 41).

justification, no matter how important and precious this truth is in itself.

1.2 A Short History
1.2.1 The Reformation

Especially during the Reformation, the doctrine of justification occupied the center of the debate. But actually it was already Augustine, the *doctor gratiae* ("teacher of grace"), who placed the problem of sin and the accompanying doctrine of justification by God's grace high on the theological and ecclesiastical agenda of the Western church.[29] Before that time, the ethical aspects of Christianity, and the cross viewed as cosmic battleground, came to the fore far more than the forensic and propitiatory aspects of the Christian faith.[30] This can still be seen in the ancient creeds, such as the Apostles' Creed and the Nicene Creed, in which the soteriological aspects ("I believe the forgiveness of sins"; "who for us men, and for our salvation, came down . . . was crucified for us . . . we acknowledge one baptism for the remission of sins") play a minor role, and in which the word "justification" does not occur. The Apostles' Creed breathes more the sphere of victory (". . . was crucified, died, and was buried; he descended to the dead. On the third day he rose again; he ascended into heaven, he is seated at the right hand of the Father, and he will come to judge the living and the dead") than that of propitiatory sacrifice. It is still the same in Eastern theology.

According to Gerrit de Ru, with Augustine a new era began (that is, in Western theology), in which henceforth the relationships between sin and grace, predestination and justification, would occupy the central place.[31] In this way, with Augustine salvation received a far more individualistic character, which, according to Donato Ogliari, conflicts with the mystery of the church as a community, namely, the commu-

---

29. Cf. Ouweneel (2008b, §12.1.1).
30. Cf. Ouweneel (2009, chapter 8).
31. De Ru (1966, 10); also see Ogliari (2003, 262); Meijering (2004, 149).

The Righteousness of God

nity of the Body of Christ,[32] and, one may add, underrates the important biblical subject of the restoration of the world. Reformed theologian Klaas Van der Zwaag spoke of a "turn from the object to the subject,"[33] that is, from the objective aspects of salvation (what was accomplished *for* the believers) to the subjective aspects thereof (what is accomplished *in* the believers).

How did Augustine understand "justification by faith alone," the subject that we now view as typically Reformational? On this question there has been much discussion,[34] which partly presupposed the well-known misunderstandings between Rome and Reformation. At any rate, here and there in his doctrine of justification, Augustine surely placed quite different accents than Protestants do when, for example, he linked it strongly with infant baptism.[35] He does underscore justification "by faith," but then, a "faith working through love" (Gal. 5:6), as former pope Benedict XVI has done also on several occasions. I therefore imagine that Augustine would not have been all too unhappy with the declaration of 1999 (see the next §).

In the time of the Reformation, the question of justification, righteousness, faith, and grace was given such a central place that other aspects of salvation were neglected. Apparently, the crucial question of the Reformation can be formulated in the wording of Job: "[H]ow can a man be righteous before God?" (Job 9:2 NKJV; cf. 4:17; 25:4). This is the same as asking: How can a person possess a righteousness that can stand before God's judgment seat? Paul desired to be one who was "not having a righteousness of my own that comes from the Torah, but that which comes through faith in Christ, the righteousness from God that depends on faith" (Phil. 3:9). Now the question that was raised during the Reformation was this:

---

32. Ogliari (2003, 353).
33. Van der Zwaag (2008, 123–24).
34. See extensively, ibid., 214–23.
35. Cf. especially Lekkerkerker (1947); McGrath (2005, 1:30–32).

Does this righteousness, which is from God and depends on faith, exclude human good works in any and every form?

Today, many theologians feel that during the Reformation this question was answered in a less satisfactory way than people had believed for a long time. Did the Reformers indeed have a correct picture of the Roman Catholic view of the justification of the ungodly? Did they really think that the Roman Catholic Church flatly contradicted the ever so clear statements found in Romans 3:20 ("by works of the law no human being will be justified"), Romans 3:28 ("we hold that one is justified by faith apart from works of the law"), and Galatians 2:16 ("we know that a person is not justified by works of the law but through faith in Jesus Christ")? Can we actually accept Martin Luther as a source in this regard, seeing that he himself failed to do justice to James 2, as we will see? In this Bible chapter, justification by faith *and* works is clearly taught (apart from the question, for a moment, of how this is to be interpreted). Is it not a bad omen that, for this reason, Luther called the epistle of James an "epistle of straw"?[36] James Adamson wrote: "Luther's logic [in regard to James] was, if possible, further obfuscated by his slavery to words — those of James and Paul — without understanding them: only so could he, or any man, have said that the Epistle of James 'contradicts St. Paul and all other Scripture in giving righteousness to works.'"[37]

This is all the more remarkable because the Augsburg Confession (1530), on which Luther had a major influence, certainly does have a place for good works in the believer's life: "Our churches . . . teach that this faith is bound to bring forth good fruits, and that it is necessary to do good works commanded by God, because of God's will, but that we should not rely on those works to merit justification before God" (Art. VI). "Furthermore, it is taught on our part that it is necessary to do good works, not that we should trust to merit grace by

---

36. Quoted, e.g., in Locher (1903, 200).
37. Adamson (1976, 36).

them, but because it is the will of God. It is only by faith that forgiveness of sins is apprehended, and that, for nothing. And because through faith the Holy Ghost is received, hearts are renewed and endowed with new affections, so as to be able to bring forth good works. . . . Hence it may be readily seen that this doctrine is not to be charged with prohibiting good works, but rather the more to be commended, because it shows how we are enabled to do good works" (Art. XX).

1.2.2 The Revived Rome–Reformation Debate

In opposition to Martin Luther, Willem Van de Pol, who initially was Reformed but later became Roman Catholic, wrote defiantly about "the Catholic *sola fide, sola gratia*."[38] What he wanted to say is that *sola fide* (i.e., by faith alone) and *sola gratia* (i.e., by grace alone) were not discovered during the Reformation but go back to (the Catholic!) Augustine. These phrases fully cover the Roman Catholic doctrine on the points concerned, even though the Reformers were not willing or able to recognize this. Today, theologians are indeed grasping this much better, including Protestant theologians. Therefore, already in his time (the 1950s), the Jewish author, Hans-Joachim Schoeps, who looked at the discussion as an outsider, could observe a certain shift to the disadvantage of Luther, and spoke of the present-day "de-Lutheranizing" of Paul.[39]

Yet, on the one hand, in 1983 Lutheran Jaroslav Pelikan could still write that the doctrine of justification was not only the main doctrine of Christianity (!) — which in my view is clearly erroneous — but also that it was the main point of difference that separated Protestantism and Roman Catholicism.[40] And Evangelical Douglas Moo could still write in 1996: "Despite important and welcome moves toward reconciliation between Protestants and Roman Catholics, the divi-

---

38. Van de Pol (1948, 136; cf. 75, 159–60).
39. Schoeps (1961, 197).
40. Pelikan (1983, 139).

sion between the two groups over justification remains."[41] On the other hand, Hans Küng proclaimed already in 1957, in his dissertation on Karl Barth's justification doctrine, that a right understanding of justification could bring Protestants and Catholics together.[42] Barth wrote Küng a letter, which was included in later editions of the work, and in which he remarked: "I salute your book as a symptom of the fact that the flood of the times in which Catholic and Protestant theologians only wanted to speak with each other either in a polemic way, or, in non-binding pacifism, usually not at all, is indeed not yet over, but at least is diminishing."[43]

There have been more such declarations on both sides, including the claim that the doctrine of justification no longer represents a church-dividing antithesis,[44] in contrast to the doctrine concerning the church. And the Catholic theologian Otto H. Pesch, during the same time, replied to the question whether Catholics and Protestants are one on the doctrine of justification: "We say confidently: Yes!"[45] Similar voices are heard from the Catholic theologian George H. Tavard (member of several Protestant–Catholic theological committees),[46] and more recently from the Lutheran theologian David E. Aune (teaching at the Catholic University of Notre Dame, in Indiana, USA).[47]

---

41. Moo (1996, 243).
42. Küng (2004); cf. the comment by Berkhof (1979, 437); Spykman (1992, 492).
43. On the discussion about justification between Roman Catholics, Lutherans, Calvinists, Anglicans, and Evangelicals from about 1966 until 1996, see extensively, Brinkman (1996); also Lane (2002), until 2002. A real treasure chest for the entire history of justification doctrine is McGrath (2005; e.g., about Luther: 218–35; Calvin: 253–58; the recession of this doctrine since 1950: 406–20). For an anthology of older and newer texts on justification, see Sauter (1989).
44. Feiner and Vischer (1973, 644).
45. Feiner and Löhrer (1973, 913).
46. Tavard (1984).
47. Aune (2006).

1.2.3 The Declaration of 1999

In this connection, a highlight so far was Reformation Day in the year 1999. On this day, Roman Catholics and Lutherans came forward in Augsburg with a remarkably interesting *Joint Declaration on the Doctrine of Justification*.[48] This declaration had been sent to all member churches of the Lutheran World Federation, and thoroughly investigated by them. More than eighty percent of the replies had been positive. The Vatican had given its permission, too. Of course, there were differences on details, but it was noted that "the remaining differences in its explication are no longer the occasion for doctrinal condemnations" (Art. 5). Both parties testified that a person is justified *sola fide* and *sola gratia:* "By grace alone, in faith in Christ's saving work and not because of any merit on our part, we are accepted by God and receive the Holy Spirit, who renews our hearts while equipping and calling us to good works" (Art. 15). "[S]inners . . . are incapable of turning by themselves to God to seek deliverance, of meriting their justification before God, or of attaining salvation by their own abilities. Justification takes place solely by God's grace" (Art. 19; see also 20 and 21).

Back in 2007, pope Benedict XVI (Joseph Ratzinger) wrote concerning the bread of life in John 6: this bread "cannot be 'earned' by human work, by one's own achievement. It can only come to us as a gift of God, as God's work [in contrast with any human work]. The whole of Pauline theology is present in this dialogue [John 6:25-40].[49] The highest things, the things that really matter, we cannot achieve on our own; we have to accept them as gifts and enter into the dynamic of the gift, so to speak. This happens in the context of faith in Jesus, who is dialogue—a living relationship with the Father—

---

48. See on this, e.g., Lane (2002, 119–26); H. A. Blocher in McCormack (2006, 197–217); G. Hunsinger in Stumme (2006, 69–84).
49. I myself would never make such a statement because the Pauline and Johannine approaches are so different; but for the point I am trying to make right now this is irrelevant.

and who wants to become Word and love in us as well."⁵⁰

These developments are not viewed as purely positive by all Protestants, as we see, for instance, in the example of Leonardo de Chirico, a Reformed Baptist in Italy.⁵¹ On the one hand, he pleaded for a dialogue with Rome; on the other hand, he believed that so far this has occurred in too shallow a way, too little from the viewpoint of the entire Roman Catholic theology. He argued that Protestants and Roman Catholics cannot come to a real agreement on the doctrine of justification because this doctrine cannot be separated from many other notions in Roman Catholic thought. With Rome, it is never "faith alone," or "Christ alone," but only faith or Christ along with the (Roman Catholic) Church.

Other Protestant theologians have expressed their dissatisfaction with the Joint Declaration mentioned above, and have condemned it as being too Catholic.⁵² Moreover, we must take into consideration that, after all, the doctrine of justification does not have the central position in Roman Catholic theology that it has in traditional Protestant thought. For example, this is something for which Protestants blame the Catholic priest Henri Nouwen, who is also widely read in the Protestant world.⁵³

Nevertheless, justification does appear in the Catechism of the Catholic Church, namely in Part III: *Life in Christ*, Chapter 3: *God's Salvation: Law and Grace*, Article 2: *Grace and Justification*. Here are some quotations: "[1987] The grace of the Holy Spirit has the power to justify us, that is, to cleanse us from our sins and to communicate to us 'the righteousness of God through faith in Jesus Christ' and through Baptism.... [1989] The first work of the grace of the Holy Spirit is conversion, effecting justification in accordance with Jesus' proclamation

---

50. Ratzinger (2008, 268).
51. De Chirico (2003).
52. See, e.g., Beutel *et al.* (1998).
53. www.stichting-promise.nl/ schriftgezag/henri-nouwen-over-de-weg-tot-god.htm.

at the beginning of the Gospel: 'Repent, for the kingdom of heaven is at hand.' Moved by grace, man turns toward God and away from sin, thus accepting forgiveness and righteousness from on high. 'Justification is not only the remission of sins, but also the sanctification and renewal of the interior man.' [1990] Justification *detaches man from sin* which contradicts the love of God, and purifies his heart of sin. Justification follows upon God's merciful initiative of offering forgiveness. It reconciles man with God. It frees from the enslavement to sin, and it heals. [1991] Justification is at the same time *the acceptance of God's righteousness* through faith in Jesus Christ. Righteousness (or 'justice') here means the rectitude of divine love. With justification, faith, hope, and charity are poured into our hearts, and obedience to the divine will is granted us."[54]

There is much in these quotes with which Protestant Christians should be happy, even if they might wish to express certain things in a different way. The main problem here is that justification is linked with both faith and (infant) baptism (as Augustine had already done): "Justification is conferred in Baptism, the sacrament of faith. It conforms us to the righteousness of God, who makes us inwardly just by the power of his mercy. Its purpose is the glory of God and of Christ, and the gift of eternal life." Another problem, certainly for Reformed theologians, is the place assigned to human freedom: "Justification establishes cooperation between God's grace and man's freedom. On man's part it is expressed by the assent of faith to the Word of God, which invites him to conversion, and in the cooperation of charity with the prompting of the Holy Spirit who precedes and preserves his assent." No matter what Protestants may think of this, at any rate there is nothing essentially anti-Protestant in this entire article on "justification by works"; from God's side it demonstrates only grace, and from the human side it demonstrates only faith.

---

54. This and the subsequent two quotations are taken from www.vatican.va/archive/ENG0015/__P6Y.HTM.

1.3 New Questions
1.3.1 Imputation and Sanctification

Is there something like a Reformed doctrine of justification? There may be much difference between Rome and the Reformation, or between what Rome thought the Reformation taught, and *vice versa*. But there is also much difference between, for instance, the younger and the older Martin Luther, between Luther and Philip Melanchton, between Melanchton and his critic, Andreas Osiander, between Lutherans and Calvinists, between "orthodox" Calvinists and hyper-Calvinists, between Reformed and Presbyterian. To describe all of this here would require too much attention and yield too little profit. Some of the differences will be dealt with in later chapters.

In the nineteenth century, new issues arose, leading even Reformed theologians to begin to question some of the statements in their own confessions. For example, first, is it correct to say that justification involves the imputation of the "active righteousness" of Christ to the believer? What does this involve anyway? His Torah observance? And what is the relationship between this issue of imputation and the cross of Christ?

Second, is it correct to claim, as some church fathers and Reformers have done, that the "righteousness of God" (Rom. 1:17; 3:21-22) is a righteousness *of humans*, namely, a "righteousness that is acceptable to God"?

Third, is it correct to place sanctification *after* justification, as the Second Reformation in the Netherlands (seventeenth and eighteenth centuries) always emphasized, instead of emphasizing the organic coherence of the two, as Hermann F. Kohlbrugge did, in line with the Reformers?[55]

But fourth, conversely, was Kohlbrugge correct, in contrast with the Second Reformation, when he again placed justifica-

---

55. See extensively, De Reuver (1992, chapter VI); also cf. De Groot (1952, passim); Van Genderen (1988, 102–105).

tion at the center of the doctrine of salvation and at the center of the church's preaching?[56] This is certainly in line with the Reformation—but is it also in line with the New Testament?

The twentieth century produced first and foremost dialectical theology, in which Karl Barth with his *Römerbrief* ("The Epistle to the Romans") also reopened the debate on justification.[57] Not only did Barth have a high appreciation for Kohlbrugge,[58] but—amazingly to some—Dutch Protestant theologian Theodorus L. Haitjema saw the authentic line of Reformed justification theology proceeding through Kohlbrugge and Barth rather than through Abraham Kuyper and Herman Bavinck.[59] In Haitjema's view, this is where real renewal should come from: Barth laid the full emphasis on Christ as the One who restores the broken covenant relationship between God and humanity, and *not* on the imputation of the righteousness of Christ to believers, as the "classical" Protestant approach insisted.[60] For others, however, criticizing the traditional imputation theory—and thus opposing, for instance, the Westminster Standards—seems to be the demise of true Reformed thinking. All these matters will be discussed extensively in the course of this study.

1.3.2 Analytic and Synthetic Justification

At the same time (the 1920s), the Berlin theologian Karl Holl instigated a new investigation of Luther's justification doctrine, and pleaded for a distinction between an "analytic" and a "synthetic" view of justification, a distinction going back to Albrecht Ritschl.[61] In the summary of Adrio König: analytic justification means that God, so to speak, "analyzes" the

---

56. Cf. Berkouwer (1949a, 9–10; omitted from the English edition); Berkhof (1979, 437).
57. Barth (1968); see further especially Barth (1956, §61).
58. Barth (1927, VI, passim).
59. Haitjema (1926, 153–55); cf. Berkouwer (1949a, 9–10; omitted from the English edition).
60. See the summary by Demarest (1997, 356–58).
61. Holl (repr. 2002).

human being, and then finds *in* him sufficient good because he himself had made him righteous: justification is *declaring* the renewed person righteous, a person who first had been renewed by God, that is, is viewed by God as having died with Christ and as having been raised with Christ (cf. Rom. 6:7 ASV, "he that hath died is justified from sin").[62]

In opposition to this, the "synthetic" approach puts all the emphasis on the fact that God justifies the *ungodly* (Rom. 4:5): therefore, justification is thought to be, not *declaring* a person righteous, but *making* him righteous through a "synthesis" between the sinner and the righteousness of Christ. In the former case, allegedly the emphasis lies on the justified person, in the latter case on Christ. Karl Holl argued strongly in favor of the former approach, which he claimed to be more Lutheran; the Reformed tradition seemed to be more inclined to the latter approach.[63] R. C. Sproul even called the former view Roman Catholic, and the latter one Reformational, thereby discrediting the former.[64]

In my view, the entire distinction is basically false, as indicated by the passages just quoted: on the one hand, the ungodly is *made* righteous (Rom. 4:5, "synthetic"), on the other hand, the believer united with Christ in his resurrection is *declared* to be righteous (cf. 6:7, "analytic"). There is nothing wrong with an "analytic" approach as long as this definitely does not involve any righteousness that humans have in themselves by nature, but only the righteousness that they have through union with Christ in his death and resurrection.

Underlying this kind of question are other questions like the following. First, can Luther's view of the believer as *simul iustus et peccator* ("simultaneously righteous and sinner") be accounted for theologically? Even if a believer still possesses the "flesh" (sinful nature), can that person still be called a

---

62. König (2006, 229).
63. Sproul (1995, 108–09).
64. Thus already implicitly Berkouwer (1954, 93-94, 105–07); cf. Ridderbos (1975, 171); Van Genderen and Velema (2008, 620-21).

"sinner" (cf. Rom. 5:8, "... while we *were* still sinners")? (Only the backsliding Christian is still called a "sinner," James 5:20.) Second, should we speak of the believer's "own" (new) righteousness as having died and risen with Christ? Or is this a righteousness imputed "from outside," that is, the "righteousness of Christ," "active" or "passive" or both?

Other classical as well as contemporary approaches could be mentioned:[65] justification as a process of moral development (liberal theology); justification as an "infusion" of righteousness (Roman Catholics); justification as a restoration of the moral order of the universe (Remonstrants and many other Arminians); justification as political and social emancipation (liberation theology[66]); justification as forensic acquittal (the classical Protestant approach).[67] Not to mention typical hyper-Calvinist—and Scholastic—thought products such as "justification from eternity"[68] and "justification in the court of conscience."[69]

Amid all these discussions, the so-called "New Perspective on Paul" arose: a new view of how Paul viewed the Judaism of his day and, concomitantly, how he viewed the Torah. Did first-century Judaism indeed teach that a person could be righteous before God through works of the law? Did *Paul* think that Judaism taught that? On what points did he resist the Judaism of his time? And how does his view relate to that of the Reformers, who claimed similar things with respect to the Roman Catholic Church of their day? What does this all

---

65. See the summary by Demarest (1997, 347–62); also cf. Van Genderen and Velema (2008, 631-39).
66. See, e.g., González (2005).
67. In justification doctrine, the term "forensic" (from Latin, *forum*, "market," but also "tribunal") goes back presumably to Melanchton, who said that God declares the sinner to be righteous in *foro divino*, "in the divine tribunal" (McGrath, 2010, 458–59).
68. See Berkouwer (1954, chapter 6); Van Genderen and Velema (2008, 621-22).
69. See Kersten (1983, 2:426); Van Genderen and Velema (2008, 622-23); Van der Zwaag (2003, 451–72).

mean for a theologically defensible view of the Torah?[70] Many of these questions will be taken up in the following chapters.

1.4   Terminology[71]
1.4.1   *Dikē, Dikaios, Dikaioō*

Let us now enter into some of the lexicographical and theological aspects of the terms that will occur most frequently in this study: just/righteous, justice/righteousness, justify (make/declare righteous), justification (the act of making/declaring righteous).

The root noun that is relevant here is Greek *dikē*, derived from *deiknymi*, "to show, to point to, to indicate, to posit, to establish." Originally *dikē* meant "indicating, establishing, the thing indicated or established," and from there, "attitude, state, mode, manner," and subsequently, "tradition, custom, usage, normal course," etc. From there the term came to mean "what is proper to someone, what is normal, what is right," that is, "right conduct, right treatment." As such, it corresponds with Hebrew *tsedaqah*, "righteousness." After this development, it was only one step to "jurisdiction, court session, lawsuit," and finally "execution, verdict" in the sense of "punishment." The word occurs with this latter meaning twice in the New Testament: 2 Thessalonians 1:9 ("They will suffer the punishment of eternal destruction") and Jude 1:7 ("a punishment of eternal fire").

In Acts 28:4 ("Justice has not allowed him to live"), *Dikē* is a name for the goddess of revenge, Nemesis, punishing justice (cf. Latin, *Iustitia*, the Roman goddess of justice). Here again, the punitive aspect of *dikē* comes to the fore.

The words derived from *dikē* include, in the first place, the adjective *dikaios*, corresponding with Hebrew *tsedeq*; the person who is *tsedeq* is a *tsaddiq*. The term *dikaios* originally referred to persons observing certain customs and rights; hence:

---

70. See extensively, Ouweneel (2015a).
71. Kittel *et al.* (1964, 2:174–219); Brown (1992, 3:352–77); Morris (1955, chapters VII–VIII); Moo (1996, 79–90); Pop (1999, 419–26).

"righteous." It occurs many times in the New Testament, and is used for God, for Christ, for people, and for concrete things (such as blood) and abstract things (judgment, act, commandment, ways). In Romans 3:8 and Hebrews 2:2, we find the related word *endikos*, which refers to the maintenance of justice in rendering a verdict. The connotations of these terms are: "fair, honest, impartial, unbiased, appropriate, according to good practice."

Second, the verb derived from *dikē* is *dikaioō*, "to show to be right, establish as just" (cf. the mentioned verb *deiknymi*), hence: "declare to be right, consider to be right, justify," corresponding with the Hebrew root *ts-d-q*. In the New Testament, *dikaioō* is used in two quite distinct senses, each of which possesses great theological importance (cf. §1.3.2):

(a) Prove or declare someone or something to *be* righteous (e.g., Matt. 11:19; Rom. 3:4; 1 Tim. 3:16; also cf. Gen. 44:16; Job 13:15; 36:3; Ps. 35:27). Thus, the people "justified God," that is, "declared God to be just" (Luke 7:29; cf. Ps. 51:4 = Rom. 3:4). Or people "justify" themselves, that is, declare (wish to show) themselves to be righteous; see Luke 10:29 ("But he, desiring to justify himself...") and 16:15, "You are those who justify yourselves before men...," that is: "pretend to be righteous" (cf. Job 32:2; Prov. 17:15). Wisdom is "justified," that is, shown to be righteous, by her deeds (Matt. 11:19), and a person is "justified," that is, shown to be righteous, by one's words (12:37). The doers of the Torah will be "justified," that is, shown to be righteous (Rom. 2:13). See more extensively §1.5.1.

(b) Make something righteous that was not righteous before; *the* New Testament example is again the ungodly who is made righteous by God (Rom. 4:5). Compare Isaiah 45:25, "In the LORD all the offspring of Israel shall be justified" (but also see EXB, ICB, NCV: "found to be good"; CJB: "find justice"). In the parable of the Pharisee and the tax collector, the latter "went down to his house justified" (Luke 18:14). Through his confession of sin, he had become a righteous man, something he had not been before (cf. 7:34; Matt. 21:31). Sinners "are justified by his [i.e., God's] grace as a gift, through the redemption that is in Christ Jesus" (Rom. 3:24), so that they are no longer sinners (cf. 5:8).

Formally speaking, "justification" is the juridical verdict of a judge: it is complete acquittal and rehabilitation (see the next chapter on *ts-d-q*, "to procure justice, to acquit"), as in 1 Kings 8:32 (NKJV), "[J]udge Your servants, condemning the wicked, bringing his way on his head, and justifying the righteous [Heb., *hatsdiq tsaddiq*] by giving him according to his righteousness [*tsedaqah*]." Later, we will see how it is fundamentally possible for God to justify (acquit) the ungodly in this way. In the summary of Douglas Moo: "As scholars now generally agree, it [i.e., justification] connotes the judicial decision of God to regard a sinner as 'just' or 'right' or 'innocent' before him."[72]

The term "rehabilitation" does not suggest that the accused has been proven innocent. It *is* appropriate, however, for expressing the thought that the traces of the penitent sinner's sinful past have been obliterated, and that the person has been fully accepted again in the favor of God. The most beautiful illustration of this is in the parable of the prodigal son, who was guilty, and yet rehabilitated: "But while he was still a long way off, his father saw him and felt compassion, and ran and embraced him and kissed him. And the son said to him, 'Father, I have sinned against heaven and before you. I am no longer worthy to be called your son.' But the father said to his servants, 'Bring quickly the best robe, and put it on him, and put a ring on his hand, and shoes on his feet. And bring the fattened calf and kill it, and let us eat and celebrate. For this my son was dead, and is alive again; he was lost, and is found.' And they began to celebrate" (Luke 15:20–24).[73]

---

72. Moo (1996, 147).
73. Duffield and Van Cleave (1996, 236–37).

1.4.2 Three Nouns

From the verb *dikaioō*, three nouns have been derived. The first noun is *dikaiosynē*, "that which is *dikē* (right)," the common word for "righteousness." In the New Testament, this is in particular a characteristic of God, pointing to the consistency in his actions. These are always in perfect correspondence with his being, which is light and truth. See, for example, how Christ uses the word at the beginning of Matthew: that which is indicated by God as something to be done (3:15); that which is "right" in itself, according to the will of God (5:6, 10, 20); religious duties (6:1); the sum of God's demands (6:33). In short: that which is to be done according to what is right and truthful, as measured according to God's criteria and being.

The second noun is *dikaiōsis*, which ties in best with the verb *dikaioō*; it is "declaring someone/something to be right(eous)." This is the common word for "justification." Originally it had the more general meaning of "defense before the judge," and conversely, "judicial verdict," even in the sense of "condemnation, punishment" (cf. *dikē*). In the New Testament, the word occurs only twice: Romans 4:25 ("raised for our justification") and 5:18 ("one act of righteousness [*dikaiōma*, see next paragraph] leads to justification [*dikaiōsis*]"). The emphasis is here on justification as a righteous judicial verdict by a righteous Judge.

The third noun is *dikaiōma*, which is "a certain expression of what is right," in three different ways:

(a) a righteous decree or demand: "statute" (Luke 1:6), "regulation" (Heb. 9:1, 10), God's "righteous decree" (Rom. 1:32), "precept" (2:26), "righteousness" (5:18), "righteous requirement" (8:4);

(b) "justification" as a fulfillment of God's righteous requirement (Rom. 5:16);

(c) a "righteous act" (Rom. 5:18; Rev. 15:4; 19:8).

It is interesting that words that, like these, have been derived from the perfect passive of a verb, receive their meaning from the suffix. The suffix *-ma* refers to the objective matter or act. The suffix *-sis* refers to the acting itself. The suffix *-tēs* refers to the one who is acting. To begin with the latter: *dikaiōtēs* (which does not occur in the New Testament) means "judge" (someone applying what is right, acting in a judicially right way),[74] and *dikaiōsis* means "declaring righteous." *Dikaiōma* refers to the objective sum of "what is right," that which a person has to accomplish in order to obtain some measure of righteousness; hence the connection with the law, but also "fulfillments" of it by God or the saints (Rev. 15:4; 19:8).

Similarly, Romans 5:16 tells us that the "free gift following many trespasses" is "unto *dikaiōma*," that is, fully answers to what is required of a person to be righteous before God. It is not the act of justification, then, but the sum of what is right that had to be fulfilled if one were to be righteous before God. *Dikaiōsynē* is what the matter is in itself, in an abstract sense; it is what a person possesses if one has been justified, that is, has become righteous.

In order to sharpen the distinction, let us look again at the four terms used in Romans 5:16-18:

(a) Verse 16: *dikaiōma*: the sum of righteous requirements that have to be fulfilled in order that a person can be declared righteous.

(b) Verse 17: *dōrea tēs dikaiosynēs*: "gift of righteousness," an epexegetic genitive: "gift, namely, righteousness," or perhaps a subjective genitive, that is, referring to what God gives us according to his righteousness, on account of what we are in Christ.

(c) Verse 18a: *dikaiōma*: an act in view of the fulfillment of God's righteous requirements.

(d) Verse 18b: *dikaiōsis zōēs*: "righteousness of life": the act of justifying, which, as the believer is in a new position beyond death, is characterized by the "life" of the resurrected

---

74. The common New Testament noun for "judge" is Greek *kritēs*, or the verb *krinō*, "to judge."

Christ.

1.5 Declared or Made Righteous
1.5.1 Turn Out to Be Righteous

From the technical discussion just provided, it may be clear, at least lexicographically, what "justification" means. The first meaning is *to turn out to be righteous* (analytic justification). In this case, "to justify" does not mean "to *make* someone righteous," but to declare that someone or something *is* righteous: "wisdom is justified [i.e., turns out to be just, is proven righteous] by her deeds" (Matt. 11:19), that is, by the deeds of the wise; or, "by all her children" (Luke 7:35), that is, by the wise.

Here the term "declare" is somewhat ambiguous, since "declaring" can sometimes mean the same as "making" (see §1.5.3). In the statement, "I now declare you husband and wife," it is not declared that two people *are* married, but they *become* so through this declaration. In the *declarative* view of justification, the point is precisely that of *making* a person righteous. Tradition has often debated the question whether justification by faith involves a declaring someone to *be* righteous, or *making* him righteous.[75] This is related to the difference between an "analytic" and a "synthetic" justification (see §1.3.2). I hope to show that, theologically speaking, in effect there is no basic difference between the two (§1.5.3).

The example just quoted from Luke 7:35 clearly involves declaring what someone or something *is*. In this meaning, the word can also be used for God: "When all the people heard this . . ., they declared God just," that is, they testified or confirmed that God is just/righteous. In Romans 3:4, Paul quotes a phrase from Psalm 51:6: "That you may be justified [i.e., may turn out to be righteous, your righteousness may become apparent] in your words." Compare Job 40:8 (NKJV): "Would you condemn Me that you may be justified [i.e., be proven righteous]?" (Job 40:8b). Something similar is said of believers: "[B]y your words you will be justified [i.e., proven

---

75. See, e.g., Kersten (1983, 2:409–410).

righteous]" (Matt. 12:37). It is said of a lawyer: "[H]e, desiring to justify himself, said . . ." (Luke 10:29), that is: prove himself righteous, or simply: prove that he was in the right.

Paul says, "[I]t is not the hearers of the law who are righteous before God, but the doers of the law who will be justified" (Rom. 2:13), that is, will be declared to be righteous, will turn out to be righteous because they observe God's commandments. And elsewhere: "I know of nothing against myself, yet I am not justified [ESV: acquitted] by this" (1 Cor. 4:4 NKJV), that is: yet this does not prove that I am righteous. We read of Christ that he was "justified in [ESV: vindicated by] the Spirit" (1 Tim. 3:16 NKJV), that is, by the Holy Spirit Christ's righteousness was manifested. In all these cases, the texts speak of persons (God, Christ, believers) who *are* already righteous — or think they are (Luke 10:29) — and whose righteousness is brought to light.

1.5.2 Make Righteous

The situation is very different with the second meaning of justification: *making* righteous, namely, someone who was not righteous before (synthetic justification). In fact, this is the literal meaning of Latin *iustificatio*, from *iustus*, "righteous," and *facere*, "to make." Making a person righteous means: release him of his guilt, or of the indictment that exists against him. Thus, Jesus says of the tax collector in the parable: "[T]he tax collector . . . beat his breast, saying, 'God, be merciful to me, a sinner!' I tell you, this man went down to his house justified, rather than the other" (Luke 18:13–14); that is, when he came to the temple, he was not yet righteous, but when he left the temple, he was, due to his confession of sin. This is a very specific meaning: *becoming* righteous (acquitted of sin) by confessing one's sins because this confession is followed by forgiveness (acquittal; cf. 1 John 1:9).

Paul says that "by Him [i.e., Jesus] everyone who believes is justified from all things from which you could not be justified by the law of Moses" (Acts 13:39 NKJV); that is, you *are* not righteous, as is clear from the many times you trespassed the Torah, but through Jesus you can *become* righteous. Paul even speaks of the person who "believes in him who justifies the *ungodly*" (Rom. 4:5). Through the divine act of justification, the ungodly person is *made* something that he was not before: righteous. Thus also: "the free gift [that came] from many offenses [resulted] in justification" (5:16 NKJV); "he that hath died is justified from sin" (6:7 ASV), that is, is judicially free from sin.

In these cases, being justified always means *becoming* a righteous person, that is, something one was not before: "Or do you not know that the unrighteous will not inherit the kingdom of God? Do not be deceived: neither the sexually immoral, nor idolaters, nor adulterers, nor men who practice homosexuality, nor thieves, nor the greedy, nor drunkards, nor revilers, nor swindlers will inherit the kingdom of God. And such were some of you. But you were washed, you were sanctified, you were justified in the name of the Lord Jesus Christ and by the Spirit of our God" (1 Cor. 6:9–11). Formerly, you were defiled, unholy, unjust fornicators, idolaters, etc., now you are the cleansed ones; the "sanctified," that is, holy ones; the "justified," that is, righteous ones. In Hebrew this would be the *tsaddiqim*, with the beautiful connotation of the "godly," the "pious" ones. They not only do what is right, but they are also devoted to God.

1.5.3 Declaring or Making?

Whereas in the first mentioned case (§1.5.1), justification means declaring someone righteous who was already righteous, in the second case (§1.5.2) it means declaring someone righteous who was *not* already righteous, that is, *making* someone righteous. The ungodly (unrighteous person) is made righteous by God. This is one way to describe what is taking place here. However, in fact the difference between the two cases is not as large as it may seem. In a certain sense, justification is *always* a turning out to *be* righteous; this pertains to the person who

(a) has been united with Christ in the latter's death and resurrection (Rom. 6:3-6);

(b) in this quality is "judicially free" (lit., "justified," Greek, *dedikaiōtai*, perfect tense[76]) from sin (v. 7);

(c) and, as a consequence of this, produces the fruits of the new life (*genuine* faith becomes manifest through the works following from it: James 2:21, 24-25).

All these things illustrate how important it is to always carefully define the terms we are using. In summary, "declaring" (or "pronouncing") righteous can mean:

(a) Declaring (openly stating, confirming) what a person *is* already, namely, righteous; compare expressions such as declaring/pronouncing one's guilt (i.e., to be guilty), declaring one's loyalty (i.e., to be loyal) (cf. §1.5.1).

(b) Declaring in the sense of *making* a person righteous; compare "declaring war" (declaring that from now on — not before — there is war); "declaring open" a certain session, that is, opening a session that was not open before (§1.5.2).

(c) Declaring in an anticipatory sense, in the sense of the distinction that Philip Melanchton made between the instantaneous *declaration* ("imputation") of righteousness, and the process-like *making* righteous, which he calls "sanctification" or — confusingly — regeneration.[77]

In other words, in the first case (a) it is declared what one *is* already, in the second case (b) what one *becomes* at the same moment, in the third case (c) what one gradually *will* become, and in the ultimate bliss perfectly will *be*. In my view, there can hardly be any doubt that there is truth in all three descriptions:

(a) The person who has been united with Christ in his death and resurrection cannot be declared anything else

---

76. The perfect tense in Greek refers to an act that took place in the past and whose effects still continue.
77. See McGrath (2010, 458).

than to *be* righteous, not in himself—that is, the "old self"—but in Christ. That is, it is not the "old self" that is declared righteous, but the "new self," the renewed person as he is in Christ, "created after the likeness of God in true righteousness and holiness" (Eph. 4:24; this is the "new creation," cf. 2 Cor. 5:17; Gal. 6:15).

(b) In the justification of the ungodly (Rom. 4:5) the point is that, at this very moment of justification, the ungodly *becomes* a godly person, the wicked becomes a righteous person, the unclean becomes a holy person. In essence, this is no different from (a).

(c) In practical justification, the believer learns to live in an ever more righteous way; the godly *becomes* more and more what he in principle already *is* since the moment he was saved: righteous. "[L]et the one who is righteous, still practice righteousness; and the one who is holy, still keep himself holy" (Rev. 22:11 NASB). "Whoever is steadfast in righteousness will live" (Prov. 11:19); "[T]he righteous shall live by his faith" (Hab. 2:4; cf. Rom. 1:17; Gal. 3:11; Heb. 10:38). "He [i.e., Christ] himself bore our sins in his body on the tree, that we might die to sin and live to righteousness" (1 Pet. 2:24). This will be explained further in chapter 5.

1.6 The Righteous God
1.6.1 Terminology

Generally speaking, "being righteous," whether stated of God or of humans, means doing the right (correct, fair, just) thing, especially toward others (see, e.g., John 5:30; 7:24; Rom. 2:5; 3:5; 2 Thess. 1:5-6; 2 Tim. 4:8; cf. Col. 4:1; cf. "dishonest" [lit., "unjust"] in Luke 16:8, 10; 'unrighteous" in 18:6). This *doing* right is rooted in *being* right; true righteousness is the *nature* of the person concerned. The "righteous one" (Heb., *tsaddiq*) is the truly godly person, living according to God's commands and norms, and doing so from within, with an upright heart: a really right walk requires a right heart (Matt. 1:19; 5:45; 10:41; 13:17, 43, 49; 23:29, 35; 25:37, 46; Mark 6:20; Luke 1:6, 17; 2:25;

14:14; 23:50; Acts 10:22; 24:15 [in fact also Rom. 1:17 = Hab. 2:4]; Rom. 5:7 [cf. 1 Cor. 6:1, 9 "unrighteous" = unbelievers]; Heb. 11:4; 12:23; James 5:16; 1 Pet. 4:18; 2 Pet. 2:7–8).

Jesus Christ is the Man who perfectly exhibited these features; he is *the* "Righteous One" (*tsaddiq*; Matt. 27:19, 24; Luke 23:47; Acts 3:14; 7:52; 22:14; 1 Pet. 3:18; 1 John 2:1; some expositors also mention James 5:6 DRA, "You have condemned and put to death the Just One, and he resisted you not").

In opposition to these are not only the explicitly wicked and ungodly, but also the falsely so-called (pretended or hypocrite) "righteous" ones; their heart is not right, or their walk is not right, or probably both (Matt. 9:13; 23:28; Luke 15:7; 16:15; 18:9; 20:20).

We now concentrate on the fact that God is the righteous God, and that his acts are righteous. Scripture expresses this many times: "righteous" is often used as an adjective or predicate of God (for example in Exod. 9:27; Deut. 32:4; 2 Chron. 12:6; Ezra 9:15; Neh. 9:8; Ps. 7:9, 11; 11:7; 112:4; 116:5; 119:137; 129:4; 145:17; Lam. 1:18; Dan. 9:14; Zeph. 3:5; John 17:25; Rom. 3:26; 2 Tim. 4:8; 1 John 1:9; 2:29; 3:7; Rev. 16:5).

Gottlob Schrenk describes it as follows: God is "the One who is infallibly consistent in the normative self-determination of His own nature, and who maintains unswerving faithfulness in the fulfillment of His promises and covenant agreements."[78] In this description, Schrenk refers not only to what is the meaning-kernel of the juridical modality but also to several analogies within this modality, such as the retrocipation upon the historical-formative modality ("self-determination") and the anticipation upon the pistical modality ("faithfulness").[79] Where Schrenk speaks of God's "normative self-determination" he apparently means that God in his own being is himself the norm for what is righteous and unrighteous, since he does not stand *under* a norm.[80] If the Hebrew

---

78. Kittel *et al.* (1964, 2:185).
79. See for this terminology Ouweneel (2014a).
80. Kittel *et al.* (1964, 2:195).

word *tsedeq* refers to "the state of a law-abiding person,"[81] it is particularly important to emphasize this, since God stands above all laws and norms. If anywhere, then surely here we see how important it is to emphasize that, although we can speak about God only in creaturely terms, we can do this not by using them in a formally conceptual way, but only in the way of associative ideas.[82] Every conceptual usage falls flat immediately since God's acts of justice cannot be measured according to any "right" (Greek, *dikē*) whatsoever, except the supernormative *dikē* of his own being.

1.6.2 Righteousness and Faithfulness

It is eminently important to grasp the biblical connection between God's righteousness and his covenant faithfulness (cf. Schrenk in the previous §). The reason for needing to emphasize this is that already Judaism in the New Testament period[83] as well as the Apologists (Justin Martyr) viewed God's righteousness unilaterally as "distributive" righteousness.[84] This is righteousness in the Aristotelian sense, which is that of a God who, as Supreme Judge, "distributes" (apportions) to each that which he or she deserves. We find the same view of justice in Roman law; in Latin: *ius suum cuique tribuendi*, "assigning to each his right (what is due to him)," as Roman lawyer Domitius Ulpianus formulated it around AD 200. Thomas Aquinas stated that God's righteousness can be recognized in that he gives to each what he deserves.[85]

It was this view that formed the large stumbling block for Martin Luther in his early adult years. After a long struggle, the Reformation set off with a man who discovered that God's righteousness does not only involve that God gives to each what he deserves, but primarily that God acts righteously ac-

---

81. Bavinck (2004, 2:221).
82. See Ouweneel (2014a; 2014b).
83. Cf. Eichrodt (1961, 240).
84. Cf. Pannenberg (1971, 339; 1988, 469–70).
85. Summa Theologiae II-II qu. 61.

cording to the promises of the gospel.[86] This was a profound and rich insight; God's righteousness is inseparable from his faithfulness (cf. Neh. 9:33; Ps. 89:14; 96:13; 119:138; Isa. 11:5; 16:5; Zech. 8:8; 1 John 1:9). However, we must make two comments here. First, it is striking that God used Romans 1:17 ("in it [i.e., the gospel] the righteousness of God is revealed") for Luther's conversion, even for the Reformation, whereas, in my view and that of many others, Luther never properly understood the core expression "righteousness of God" in this verse (see §1.7). Second, the early-Protestant Lutheran theologians, for example, Johann Gerhard, soon returned to the traditional view.

Yet, even some of the church fathers, such as Ambrosiaster, saw the true key to especially the meaning of God's righteousness in Romans 1:17 and further (3:21 in particular), which we will discuss in the next §§. Of course, the epistle to the Romans will play a great role in our considerations, and in this entire book. It is Romans that makes known to us the righteousness of God (1:17), which manifests itself in opposition to our own *un*righteousness (3:5), apart from the law (3:21-22), and in the justification of the sinner (3:25-26). The epistle shows how righteousness is counted to those who have come to faith (4:3-13, 22), tells us about the one righteousness of Christ (5:17-18), how the many are being made righteous (5:19), how grace reigns through righteousness leading to eternal life (5:21), how we have to "present . . . our members to God as instruments for righteousness" (6:13, 16), how we many function as "slaves to righteousness" (6:18-19), and "the Spirit is life because of righteousness" (8:10), to limit myself to the first eight chapters.

1.7 Righteousness from God or of God?
1.7.1 The Debate

The church father Augustine saw in the Greek expression *dikaiosynē theou* ("righteousness of God," Rom. 1:7; 3:5, 21-22,

---

86. Berkhof (1979, 126-27); Van Genderen and Velema (2008, 184-88).

25-26; 10:3) a *genitivus auctoris*, meaning that the expression refers to the righteousness *of the (justified) person*, a righteousness that comes from God. Martin Luther adopted this idea, and translated in Romans: *die Gerechtigkeit, die vor Gott gilt* ("the righteousness that is valid before God").[87] To him, this was an existential discovery.[88] Formerly, he had learned that the "righteousness of God" is God's own *punitive* righteousness, until he discovered that what matters is the righteousness of the believer before God, that is, a *given* righteousness. Unfortunately, he did not discern the third, in my view most wonderful possibility, namely, that the expression refers to God's own *redemptive* righteousness.

John Calvin's view was similar to that of Augustine and Luther; commenting on Romans 1:17, he said: "By the righteousness of God I understand such a righteousness that which is approved at His tribunal, ..."[89] Standing in the Reformed tradition, the Annotation to the Dutch *Statenvertaling* ("States' Translation," 1637) says on the same verse, "That is, the righteousness through which we can stand before the judgment of God, which is alone the righteousness of *Christ*, which is given to us by God, and imputed by faith." This is a sentence full of misunderstandings, as I will try to show below: (a) the "righteousness of God" is *not* the righteousness of the believer, but of God himself (these §§); (b) it is therefore not the righteousness of Christ either; (c) Scripture does not know such a thing as a righteousness of Christ that is "imputed" to us (chapter 4).

Jean Roozemeijer, too, speaks of "the righteousness that is valid before God," and appeals for this to Romans 10:3, "For, being ignorant of the righteousness of God, and seeking to establish their own, they did not submit to God's righteous-

---

87. Cf. *Neue Genfer Übersetzung* (note): *die Gerechtigkeit, die von ihm gewirkt ist* ("the righteousness that is worked by him"), or, *mit der wir vor ihm bestehen können* ("with which we can exist before him").
88. See the quotation in McGrath (2010, 454–55).
89. Calvin (1973, 28).

ness."[90] However, Paul is speaking here of the Jew not submitting to *God's* righteousness. This just underscores that we are really dealing here with God's own righteousness, and not some human righteousness that is valid before God. On the contrary, Paul means to say that the majority of the Jews did not recognize the special way in which God today, through the gospel, acts righteously toward the sinner who believes. Instead, they tried to find a way in which they could build up their own righteousness, which would be "valid before God."

Other expositors think along the same lines as the previous ones, from Augustine to Roozemeijer[91] (but many others do not, as we will see). Herman Ridderbos appealed to the additions "from faith for faith" (1:17) and "through faith in Jesus Christ" (3:22),[92] but in my view these mean simply that God's righteousness benefits people through faith. Moreover, the entire passage Romans 3:20–26 is dominated by the undeniable fact that "God's righteousness" in verses 25 as well as 26 apparently is his own righteous acting, as Ridderbos must recognize as well.[93]

Also note some very free English translations of Romans 1:17: "For in the Gospel a righteousness which God ascribes is revealed" (AMP). "For in it is revealed how God makes people righteous in his sight" (CJB; cf. ERV, GNT, ICB, NCV, NIRV, NLT). In all these cases, the text is thought to refer to the righteousness of people before God. But also compare: "You see, in the good news, God's restorative justice is revealed" (VOICE).

In his commentary on Romans, Karl Barth speaks in a rath-

---

90. Roozemeijer (1911, 28–29).
91. E.g., besides many early-Protestant expositors, Strack and Billerbeck (1928, 3:29, 163); Meyer (1876, ad loc.); Philippi (1878, ad loc.); Zahn (1925, 81–82, 174–75); Nygren (1978, 75–75); Oepke (1953, 257–64); Ridderbos (1975, 163–64); Murray (1968, 1:30–31); Young (1972, 389); Cranfield (1975, 202); Denney (1979, 590–91); Demarest (1997, 370–74); Stern (1999, 330).
92. Ridderbos (1959, 36).
93. Ibid., 85–87.

er different way: God's righteousness is the "consistency of God with Himself. . . . Where the faithfulness of God encounters the fidelity of men, there is manifested His righteousness. There shall the righteous man live."[94] A bit later he explains the expression "God's righteousness" as follows: "The word of God declares that He *is* what He is. By committing Himself to men and to the world which has been created by Him, and by His unceasingly accepting them and it, He justifies Himself to Himself. . . . He justifies himself for himself in that he makes himself known to humans and their world in that he does not stop showing mercy to them. . . . God's righteousness is His forgiveness, the radical alteration of the relation between God and man . . . ."[95] And on Romans 3:26: "Only through Him [Christ] is the righteousness of God clearly seen to be the unmistakable governance of men and the real power in history. . . . Believing in Jesus, to us the righteousness and justification of God are manifested and displayed."[96]

1.7.2 God's Righteousness — Many Interpretations

The genitive in the expression *dikaiosynē theou* ("righteousness of God") has been variously understood as:[97]

(a) a *genitivus relationis* (a genitive indicating a relationship): "righteousness before (or, in relationship to) God" (in effect: humans' righteousness);

(b) a *genitivus auctoris* (a genitive indicating an author): "righteousness coming from God" (in effect: humans' righteousness);

(c) a *genitivus causae* (a genitive indicating a cause): "righteousness (brought about) by God" (in effect: human's righteousness);

(d) theoretically even a *genitivus obiectivus* (a genitive indicating an object): the righteousness of which God is the object

---

94. Barth (1933, 40–42).
95. Ibid., 92.
96. Ibid., 106–107.
97. Ridderbos (1975, 163); Berkhof (1979, 434).

(God being justified by his acts);

(e) a *genitivus subiectivus* (a genitive indicating a subject): righteousness as an activity of God (God himself being righteous);

(f) a *genitivus possessivus* (a genitive indicating a possessor): the righteousness that is God's own possession (God himself being righteous).

In the first four instances, the righteousness is in effect that of redeemed humans, as we've been seeing; this was the view mentioned in the previous section. In the last three instances, the righteousness is God's own righteousness, which is manifested in the gospel, a merciful righteousness, which loyally fulfills God's promises to the sinner on account of Christ's redemptive work.

It is striking to see how many expositors since the nineteenth century have chosen this second, or a strongly related, interpretation.[98] There are also expositors who have tried to take a middle position;[99] God's righteousness would then be both God's righteous acting and the result thereof in humans: God both *being* righteousness and *giving* righteousness.

---

98. Kittel *et al.* (1964, 2:203–04); Brown (1992, 3:364–65); Darby (n.d.-a, 21:127–28; n.d.-b,6:291–94); Kelly (*Bible Treasury* 6:230–31; 20:263 etc.); Brockhaus (n.d., 28–30); Häring (1896); Grant (1901, 191); Kühl (1913, 39–40); Brinkman (1916, 123–24); Bavinck (2008, 4:211–12); Barth (1933, 40–42, 92, 106–107); Coates (1926, 20–25); Dodd (1932, 9–10); Greijdanus (1931, 106; 1933, 96–97); Wendland (1935, 26); Barth (1956, 2/1:118–19, 375–406; 4/1:392–93, 514; cf. Brown [1967, 130–39]); Jager (1939, 58); Brunner (1949, 275–77); Sevenster (1946, 178); Berkouwer (1954, 92–93); Van Leeuwen and Jacobs (1952, 34–36); Althaus (1952, 283–85); Schlatter (1995, 19–20, 92; 1962, 14–15); Weber (1981, 428–38); Müller (1964, 65–72, 109–14); Stuhlmacher (1966, 11, 21, 98); Kertelge (1967); Gaebelein (1970, 12–13, 22–24); Budiman (1971, 24–32); Ziesler (1972, 170–71, 187–88); Käsemann (1996, ad loc.); Harrison (1976, 19–20); H. Seebass in Brown (1992, 3:364); Beker (1980, 263–64); Vine (1985, 1:374); Medema (1985, 25–26); Hultgren (1985, 31); Wentsel (1987, 414–28); Berkhof (1979, 434); Van Genderen and Velema (2008, 614); Shulam (1998, 42–44, 135–38, 346–47); Pop (1999, 240); König (2006, 228); Shelton (2006, 112–17).
99. Scott (1939, 63); Sanday and Headlam (1950, 24–25); Morris (1955, 252); Wiersinga (1971, 76); Moo (1996, 70–75); White (2001, 148).

In my view, the fact that, at least primarily, Paul speaks of *God's own* righteousness and righteous acting follows immediately from the important parallel in Romans 1:17 and 18. God's righteousness is placed in juxtaposition with God's wrath. The opponents of this view see a different parallel: human righteousness that is from God (v. 17) *versus* human unrighteousness (v. 18).[100] As I see it, we could put this in the following way: God's righteousness in verse 17 is placed in juxtaposition with both God's wrath and human unrighteousness in verse 18. As Charles Coates explains it: "On the ground of the death of Christ, God is as righteous in justifying the ungodly sinner who believes in Jesus as He will be righteous in condemning everyone who has not 'faith in his blood.' We must learn God's righteousness either in grace or in judgment."[101]

One argument undergirding the claim that verse 17 refers to the righteousness of redeemed humans that is valid before God, is that in the second half of the verse Habakkuk 2:4 is quoted: "The righteous shall live by faith." It is argued that, if human righteousness is meant in the second half, then it is also meant in the first half of the verse. However, Paul clearly does not quote this verse to shed light on the meaning of "righteousness," but on the meaning of "faith": "For in it the righteousness of God is revealed from faith for faith, as it is written, 'The righteous shall live by faith.'" If wrath in verse 18 is a characteristic of God, then righteousness in verse 17 is too. It is the righteousness *of God* that makes the *ungodly* righteous in response to the latter's faith in the person and the accomplished work of Christ. And it is the righteousness *of God* that forever condemns the ungodly if the latter prefer to remain in their unbelief (cf. John 3:36).

1.7.3 God's Own Righteousness

In Romans 3:5, we again have to do unmistakably with an

---

100. Denney (1979, 590).
101. Coates (n.d.-c, 30).

attribute of God: "But if our unrighteousness serves to show the righteousness of God, what shall we say? That God is unrighteous to inflict wrath on us?" The "righteousness of God" is about God being righteous.

Verses 24-26 are equally clear: ". . . the redemption that is in Christ Jesus, whom God put forward as a propitiation by his blood, to be received by faith. This was to show *God's righteousness*, because in his divine forbearance he had passed over former sins. It was to show *his righteousness* at the present time, so that he might be just [or, righteous] and the justifier of [i.e., the One who makes righteous] the one who has faith in Jesus." There is no doubt that here God's righteousness refers to the righteousness that God possesses. Would it then be different in verse 21 (which refers back to 1:17): "But now the righteousness of God has been manifested apart from the law"? Should we really accept that here Paul is referring to a "righteousness [of humans] that is valid before God," and suddenly (in vv. 24-26) moves to righteousness as an attribute of God himself?

No, Romans 1:17, speaking of the core of the gospel, makes clear that the Christian gospel is not just or primarily about the *love* of God, as some might have expected (cf. 5:8; 8:35-39; John 3:16; 1 John 4:9), but about some other attribute of God's being: his *righteousness*. Apart from Romans 1:7, the love of God is not mentioned before Romans 5:5, 8 and 8:35-39. Paul's primary subject is not God's love but God's righteousness. It is God's own righteousness that, on the one hand, condemns the sinner who persists in his wickedness (Rom. 3:5) and, on the other hand, justifies (makes righteous) the sinner who repents and turns to Christ (Rom. 4:5).

As Peter T. Forsyth put it: we can understand any justification of humans only as rooted in the self-justification of God, that is, we can only understand God *declaring* humans righteous if we understand that God *declares* (shows, manifests) himself as righteous.[102] Elsewhere, Forsyth argued that God could justify humans before him only by justifying himself and his holy law before people.[103] That is, God declares humans righteous not *in spite of* his own righteousness—as if justifying the ungodly were an infringement on his own righteousness—but by *vindicating* his own righteousness. God does not turn a blind eye to his own righteousness when he declares ungodly people to be righteous. On the contrary, he is *righteous* when he does so, as Paul emphasizes in Romans 3:26; he is *righteous* when he forgives the penitent sinner, for— reverently speaking—he owes this to the accomplished work of Christ (1 John 1:9).

To be sure, it is the *love* of God that is capable of bringing the sinner to repentance and confession of sins. However, this event does not furnish the sinner with a new foundation on which to be able to stand before God. The love of God can *break down* the sinner's heart, bring it to repentance, but only the righteousness of God can *lift up* the sinner, since it is this that supplies people with a foundation for a "new man," the person renewed in Christ. It is the love and grace of God by which he grants the sinner forgiveness; it is the righteousness of God by which he justifies the sinner. The penitent sinner's heart longs for forgiveness, and that sinner's conscience longs for justification. Through the blood of Christ the sinner possesses both: one has forgiveness, and that consoles a person; one is justified, and that delivers a person from fear of judgment. We find the two together in 1 John 4:17: "By this is love perfected with us, so that we may have confidence for the day of judgment, because as he is so also are we in this world," namely, holy and righteous.

1.7.4 Just in Justifying

Handley Moule, too, rightly sought the key to the expression "righteousness of God" in Romans 3:26, "It was to show

---
102. Forsyth (1948a, 214).
103. Forsyth (1948b, 136).

his [i.e., God's] righteousness at the present time, so that he might be just [or, righteous] and the justifier of [i.e., the One who makes righteous] the one who has faith in Jesus."[104] As Moule put it, here we see the righteousness of God in action, confirmed by its effects. Because God is righteous, he *acts* righteously; it is an act of his righteousness when he declares the Jesus-believer righteous. It is this that wonderfully makes possible the mighty paradox that God acts this way: the thoroughly holy, eternally truthful, eternally righteous God is infinitely zealous in maintaining his Torah, which in its many precepts brings God's own nature to expression. *Yet*, it is this same God who can say to the penitent sinner: I, your Judge, acquit you legally, accept you legitimately, embrace you judicially. This is not because God turns a blind eye to the sinner's sin; on the contrary: in justifying the sinner, he acts thoroughly *righteously*. To put it even more strongly: God would not be righteous if he would refuse to justify the penitent sinner, since the redemptive work of Christ has laid a righteous foundation for this act of justification, a foundation intended for all those who in faith would appeal to it.

Here we see the beauty of the gospel of God's righteousness for poor sinners gloriously brought to light. It consists in God's righteousness becoming manifest here in an entirely new, even seemingly contrary way, namely, in this righteousness not condemning the sinner, but acquitting the sinner, notwithstanding the clear proofs for the sinner's sinfulness. God is here not the Judge but the Justifyer, not the One condemning in justice, but redeeming in justice (Rom. 3:24–26). One could also say: God *is* Judge here, but then a Judge acting in justice by justifying the repentant sinner on account of the work of Christ. Redemption is not in conflict with God's righteousness, but the opposite: it is a fair and just consequence of it. That is, when he justifies the believing sinner God is not only gracious and merciful, but also *righteous* (Rom. 3:26).

---

104. Moule (1893, 32–33).

Leander Keck therefore interprets God's "righteousness" as his "moral integrity."[105] How is it possible that a righteous God declares an unrighteous sinner to be righteous? How can such an act be "righteous"? This is the very secret of God's righteousness and of justification. It shows that a righteous God must have a very special foundation and reason to be able to do this. This can only be a moral "obligation" on his behalf toward a certain merit on behalf of something or someone else. God received this foundation in Christ, first, in the power of the blood—that is, of the *death*—of Christ (Rom. 3:25; 5:9); second, in the *resurrection* of Christ: ". . . Jesus our Lord, who was delivered up for our trespasses and raised for our justification. Therefore, since we have been justified by faith, we have peace with God through our Lord Jesus Christ" (Rom. 4:24–5:1; cf. 6:7). At a later stage, we will enter into this vital matter more deeply.

1.8 Righteousness in the Old Testament
1.8.1 "The Law and the Prophets"

Already in the Old Testament, particularly in the Psalms, God's own righteousness becomes manifest in his redemptive acts, as Paul says: "But now the righteousness of God has been manifested apart from the law, although the Law and the Prophets bear witness to it—the righteousness of God through faith in Jesus Christ for all who believe" (Rom. 3:21-22). We find here a striking contrast: it is a righteousness not *rooted in* the Torah, to be sure—yet *witnessed to by* the Torah. As we know, "the Law and the Prophets" is a reference to the *entire* Old Testament, including the Psalms (cf. Matt. 7:12; 22:40; Luke 16:16; John 1:46; Acts 13:15; 24:14; 28:23; cf. also the tripartition in Luke 24:44: beside the Law and the Prophets also the Psalms, i.e., *Ketubim*, of which Psalms is the first and largest book).

Sometimes even only "the Law" is a reference to the *entire* Old Testament. Jesus said, "Is it not written in your *Law*, 'I

---
105. Keck (1979, 118–23).

said, you are gods'?" (John 10:34), in reference to Psalm 82:6. In Romans 3:19, the quotations in verses 10–18 (mostly from the Psalms) are ascribed to "the Law" (the Torah, here in the sense of Tanakh).

Paul is saying in effect, then, that the Tanakh in its entirety witnesses of a coming manifestation of the righteousness of God that would *not* be based upon works of the Law. William E. Vine believes that this is why, in Romans 1:17, the article before *dikaiosynē theou* is lacking:[106] this fact would point to a different kind of manifestation than the one given at Mount Sinai. Vine argued that God's character is unchangeable but manifests itself in different ways, and particularly in the two contrasting manifestation modes of law and grace. The gospel is given on an equally righteous foundation as that of the law, and the righteous character of God is equally confirmed in each, but his righteousness is displayed in different ways. Gerrit C. Berkouwer argued "that in the cross of Christ we behold simultaneously God's justice and his love," and he referred to Isaiah 1:27, "Zion shall be *redeemed* by *justice*, and those in her who repent, by *righteousness*."[107]

If "the Law and the Prophets" do include the Psalms, let us see how this book bears witness to the righteousness of God apart from works of the law. It is full of references to the righteousness of God, that is, his own righteousness (not some "righteousness that is valid before God"). Time and again, the godly and righteous appeal to it (Ps. 4:1; 5:8; 7:17; 24:5; 31:1; 35:28; 36:5–6, 10; 48:10; 51:14; 71:2, 15–16, 19, 24; 85:10–13; 89:15–16; 98:1–2; 103:17; 119:40, 123; 145:7–8; also cf. Isa. 45:21; 46:12–13; 50:8; 51:5–8; 53:11; 56:1; Dan. 9:16; Micah 6:1–5). That is, they expect their deliverance not only from God's love and grace, but from his *righteousness*, connected with his covenantal loyalty (Heb., *hesed*) (see the combination of the latter two terms in Ps. 33:5; 36:10; 85:10; 89:14; 103:17;

---

106. Vine (1985, 1:374); others see in this omission only a style of definition (Moo [1996, 70]).
107. Berkouwer (1965, 279).

Isa. 16:5; Jer. 9:24; Hos. 2:19; 10:12).

In general, though, the emphasis is not on a sacrifice that supplies God with a righteous foundation for redemption, but on God's judgment upon the enemies of the godly, thereby avenging them. This seems to be different in the two cases that the righteousness of God is connected with the sufferings of the Messiah. Psalms 22 and 40 each begin with the agony of Christ under the judging hand of God, and end with the proclamation of God's righteousness to the new generation of God's people (22:30-31; 40:9-10). Again, what is proclaimed is not a "righteousness that is valid before God," but God's own righteousness, which expresses itself in God's redemptive acts. In the term "righteousness," a summary is given of the atoning sufferings of Christ as the ground for blessing all nations of the earth.[108]

1.8.2 Righteousness in the Prophets

In his "lawsuit" with Israel, the LORD calls upon his people to acknowledge God's *tsidqot*, "righteousnesses" ("righteous acts"), which here refers to his *redemptive* acts toward Israel and his revenge upon their enemies: "O my people, remember what Balak king of Moab devised, and what Balaam the son of Beor answered him, and what happened from Shittim to Gilgal, that you may know the righteous acts of the LORD." CEV therefore renders the last phrase as: "the LORD saved you many times," and MSG: "Keep all God's salvation stories fresh and present" (also cf. GNT and TLB). The "righteous triumphs of the LORD" (Judg. 5:11) are again his saving acts. God's righteousness involves that he deals with his people in a righteous way, both in delivering his people and in judging their enemies.

That is exactly what Paul is seeking to say in Romans. Paul is not following Greek or Latin ideas of righteousness, but Hebrew ideas. He writes in line with the Old Testament, not in line with Roman justice.

---

108. Coates (1926, 21).

We find a similar picture in 1 Samuel 12:7, "Now therefore stand still that I may plead with you before the LORD concerning all the righteous deeds of the LORD that he performed for you and for your fathers." CEV renders "all the righteousnesses of the LORD" as "how often the LORD has saved you." GNT: "all the mighty actions the LORD did to save you." God intervened many times to save and bless his people, but the word *tsidqot* indicates that he was *righteous* in doing this, and in the way he did it. God has found a righteous foundation for his benefits to Israel. In the New Testament we learn for the first time that he ultimately found this in the atoning work of the Messiah. Again, that is exactly what Paul is seeking to say in Romans.

John Ziesler has argued that, in early and late Hebrew tradition, God's righteousness is the way in which God acts, especially in the maintenance of the covenant.[109] When God redeems his people, this is an act of righteousness, because it happens within the framework of his covenantal loyalty. Ziesler shows that the way Paul speaks of God's righteousness is in line with this Hebrew tradition, and is very different from the way this happens in Greek thinking. Especially Psalm 98:2 is significant here: "The LORD has made known his salvation; he has revealed his righteousness in the sight of the nations." First, the text speaks unmistakably of God's own righteousness, as a characteristic of himself. Second, "righteousness" is here parallel with "salvation": it is essential for divine salvation that it manifests not only God's love but also his righteousness. This is in contrast with verse 9: "He will judge the world with righteousness." Again we conclude that God's righteousness comes to light both in judgment, because of the wickedness of people, and in redemption, because of the excellence of the propitiatory sacrifice.

Another remarkable example is Isaiah 45. Verse 8 says, "[L]et the clouds rain down righteousness; let the earth open,

---

109. Ziesler (1972, 19).

that salvation and righteousness may bear fruit." There is here again a parallelism of "righteousness" and "salvation." When God announces redemption he says, "I the Lord speak the truth [lit., speak righteousness], I declare what is right. . . . And there is no other god besides me, a righteous God and a Savior; there is none besides me" (vv. 19, 21). Here "speaking righteousness" is nothing less than announcing redemption. The "righteous God" is here the same as the "Savior"; to save his people is an act of righteousness. Again, that is exactly what Paul is saying in Romans.

Finally: "By myself I have sworn; from my mouth has gone out in righteousness a word that shall not return: 'To me every knee shall bow, every tongue shall swear allegiance.' 'Only in the Lord,' it shall be said of me, 'are righteousness and strength; to him shall come and be ashamed all who were incensed against him. In the Lord all the offspring of Israel shall be justified [i.e., declared to be righteous] and shall glory'" (Isa. 45:23–25; cf. §5.5.4). First, God's righteousness implies here again that *all* people, including the wicked, will have to acknowledge the Lord one day (alluded to in Rom. 14:11; Phil. 2:10). Second, the redeemed will praise the Lord for his acts of "righteousness," which for them are redemptive benefits. Third, they receive a share in this righteousness in that they themselves are made righteous (justified). It is an expression of God's righteousness that he makes his people righteous; again, this is precisely what Paul states in Romans 3:26.

1.9 Divine Righteousness
1.9.1 Saving Righteousness

We have seen that God manifests his righteousness in various ways. He is righteous when, after all his revelations and warnings, he inflicts wrath on the sinner (Rom. 3:5). But he is also righteous when he grants to the believer what he beforehand had put in store for such people; they are "those who have obtained a faith of equal standing with ours by the righteousness of our God and Savior Jesus Christ" (2 Pet. 1:1). Here again, the text deals unequivocally with God's own being righteous, and not with some righteousness "that is valid before God." Reformed theologian Seakle Greijdanus therefore states: "[W]e have to take 'righteousness of God,' in the sense of Rom. 1:17; 3:22; Phil. 3:9, and other places, also cf. Rom. 5:1, as that righteousness of God through which he has ordered forgiveness and salvation in Christ, so that he justifies that ungodly person for the sake of Christ and out of faith in him, Rom. 4:5."[110]

How meaningful and clear Romans 1:17 and 3:21 become when we think here of God's own righteousness, just as in Romans 3:5, 25-26, 2 Peter 1:1, and 1 John 1:9. This does not imply that this is the meaning in *all* New Testament passages that speak of God's righteousness. In Matthew 6:33 the expression "his righteousness" allows several interpretations; in 2 Corinthians 5:21 Paul speaks unequivocally of the believers becoming righteous; and in James 1:20 the text refers to righteous acts of humans according to God's criteria. Especially in Romans, however, it is very important to see that in the relevant passages it is always God's own righteousness that Paul is referring to. We do not need here the rather priggish distinction invented by the Council of Trent: "[T]he only formal cause [of justification] is the righteousness of God, not that through which he is himself righteous but that through which he makes us righteous."[111]

The good message is this, that the believer's salvation is not due to God's love in such a way that his righteousness, which rages against sin, would be shunted aside. On the contrary, this salvation is due not only to God's love but also to his very righteousness: it is *righteous* of God that he makes sinners righteous. As quotations from several authors have indicated: the fact that God justifies sinners forms a justifica-

---

110. Greijdanus (1931, 106).
111. Decree about Justification 7.

tion of himself, that is, proves his righteous character.[112] What is it that makes the gospel such a divine force? It is the fact that God reveals his righteousness in it. If Romans 1:17 would have mentioned God's love or mercy, we might always have wondered whether his righteousness—which cannot stand sin (Hab. 1:13)—would not be damaged if he saved sinners. Without the cooperation of God's righteousness, God's love and mercy cannot act; every act of God must be justified by all his attributes, so to speak.[113]

Let me now summarize the answer to my initial question: What is "the righteousness of God" in Romans 1:17 and 3:21? Is it a human righteousness that meets God's criteria, or is it God's own being righteous? I have defended the latter view. However, I now have to add that there is also some truth in the former view. These verses in Romans do not refer to an attribute of God only. Paul's speaking of God's righteousness is not to be separated from the righteousness that a person receives by faith in the gospel. It is a *providential* righteousness of God;[114] that is, it is God's *own* righteousness, but a righteousness in view of the justification of the ungodly (Rom. 4:5). This is precisely what Paul expresses in Romans 3:26, "It was to show his righteousness at the present time, so that he might be just [i.e., righteous] and the justifier of [i.e., the One who makes righteous] the one who has faith in Jesus." God shows his righteousness in declaring the believing sinner to be righteous. God is justified in justifying the ungodly.

This is comparable with what we find in 1 John 1:9, even though this text speaks of forgiveness, not of justification: "If we confess our sins, he is faithful and just to forgive us our sins and to cleanse us from all unrighteousness." In his holy being, God owes it to Christ to impute to each person, coming in faith and appealing to the atoning work of Christ, the effects of this work, which Christ accomplished precisely for

---

112. D.M. Kasali in Adeyemo (2006, 1357).
113. Grant (1901, 191).
114. Cf. Harrison (1976, 19).

such persons. God would be unrighteous if he would not forgive and justify the person who comes pleading on the basis of this work. As Jesus said himself, "[W]hoever comes to me I will never cast out" (John 6:37). The foundation presented to God in the work of Christ is so powerful and encompassing that God does not merely *allow* the sinner to come near to him, but *implores* the sinner to come: "[W]e are ambassadors for Christ, God making his appeal [NKJV: pleading] through us. We implore you on behalf of Christ, be reconciled to God" (2 Cor. 5:20).

1.9.2 Two Kinds of Faith

Allow me a little technical digression here. The expression "the one who has faith in Jesus" is in Greek, *ton ek pisteōs Iēsou*, that is literally, "him [who is] out of faith of Jesus," and in Romans 3:22 we find *dia pisteōs Iēsou Christou*, that is literally "through faith of Jesus Christ." Some expositors read a subjective genitive here, "the faith with which Jesus believed," or a possessive genitive, "the faith that Jesus possessed," and often render *pistis* then as "faithfulness."[115] They point to Romans 4:12 and 16, where *pistin Abraam* unmistakably means "the faith that Abraham had." The adherents of this view argue that linguistically it is most obvious to read Romans 3:22 and 26 in the same way.

Others have argued that the genitive in these verses must be an objective genitive.[116] That is, here "Jesus" is not the subject of faith (he who believes) but the object of it (he in whom others believe). The "faith of Jesus" is here the "faith in Jesus." We have a good example here of the way so-called "literal" translations can lead the reader astray. In English, "Jesus" in the expression "the faith of Jesus" can only be subject; in Greek, he can be either subject or object. Douglas Moo points to "the consistent use of *pistis* throughout Romans 3:21–4:25

---

115. Shulam (1998, 137,144); Stern (1999, 347–350); also cf. Karl Barth in §1.7.1 and see the older references in Moo (1996, 224n25).
116. Grosheide (1959, 83); Murray (1968, 1:111).

to designate the faith exercised by people in God, or in Christ, as the sole means of justification."[117]

1.9.3 Convicting of Righteousness

What we have discussed so far does not imply, of course, that there is no such thing as a human righteousness that is "from God" (Phil. 3:9; cf. 2 Cor. 5:21). However, reading this into the expression *dikaiosynē theou* in Romans is missing the point. Paul emphasizes in this epistle that God is *righteous* when he justifies a repenting sinner, because he owes this to the redemptive work of Christ. In this connection, it is of interest to pay attention to what Jesus himself said, "[W]hen he [i.e., the Holy Spirit] comes, he will convict the world concerning sin and righteousness and judgment: concerning sin, because they do not believe in me; concerning righteousness, because I go to the Father, and you will see me no longer; concerning judgment, because the ruler of this world is judged" (John 16:8–11).[118]

In this passage, the Holy Spirit gives a threefold judicial proof, which is as it were a "review" of the trial of Jesus (which at that moment was still to come).[119] First, the fact that the world refused to believe in Jesus was the proof of its sinfulness. Third, through the cross the definitive sentence was executed upon Satan, thus giving a proof of God's righteous judgment. Let us now look at the second point: the Holy Spirit gave a proof of "righteousness" in that Jesus would return to his Father. There are two ways to view this "righteousness":

(a) It is the righteousness of Jesus, which he had displayed on this earth and for which he was rewarded by being glorified at God's right hand (cf. John 17:4-5, "I glorified you on earth, having accomplished the work that you gave me to do. And now [i.e., Therefore], Father, glorify me in your own presence with the glory that I had with you before the world

---

117. Moo (1996, 225).
118. See Ouweneel (2007a, 161–62, 169n121).
119. M. F. Berrouard, quoted in Congar (1997, II, 122).

existed").

(b) It is the righteousness of God, who rewarded Jesus for his wonderful life and work by glorifying him at his right hand (cf. John 17:25, "O *righteous Father*, even though the world does not know you, I know you, and these know that you have sent me").

It is not easy to establish the correct interpretation here. With others,[120] I am inclined to the latter one, because it seems to me that in the context it is not so much the life of Jesus that stands out but rather his return to the Father, and the concomitant glorification.

The point of Jesus' statement is not how a person can be justified, or can receive righteousness from God, but rather what *is* true righteousness. In line with exegesis (a) one could argue: as much as the world needs a proof of what is sin, it needs a proof of what is a righteous life, which forms the absolute contrast with a sinful life. In line with exegesis (b) one could argue: the world needs a proof that God's righteousness knows how to reward such a righteous life, as well as such a righteous redemptive work (John 19:30). It is not an appeal to God's grace but to his righteousness that Jesus can pray the words just quoted from John 17:4–5. God showed his righteousness in that he covered the One who had been cast out by the world with the highest glory (cf. Acts 3:14–15, "But you denied the Holy and Righteous One, . . . and you killed the Author of life, whom God raised from the dead"; cf. John 7:52). Christ had a *right* to this place in the glory. As the Son of Man he glorified God (John 13:31); therefore, it was God's righteousness to glorify *him* (v. 32).

1.9.4 Christ Our Righteousness

Christ glorified God on earth. He did this for God, but he did it also in view of those who would believe in him: he was "delivered up for [*dia*, here: because of] our trespasses and raised for [*dia*, here: in view of] our justification" (Rom. 4:25).

---
120. Grant (1897, 592–93); Kelly (1898, 332); Gaebelein (1980, ad loc.).

Therefore, God is also righteous when he takes up believers in glory, just as he took up Christ: "Through him we have also obtained access by faith into this grace in which we stand, and we rejoice in hope of the glory of God" (Rom. 5:2; cf. 3:23). Believers are God's righteousness in Christ (2 Cor. 5:21) because, when God justifies them, he acts according to the rights that Christ has acquired for them. Toward them, this is of course pure grace, and yet it is at the same time pure righteousness (Rom. 4:24–26). The entire value of the work of Christ is counted to them as righteousness: Christ is their righteousness (1 Cor. 1:30).

As to this latter point: Joseph Shulam[121] associates the expression "God's righteousness" closely with the person of Christ in reference to Jeremiah 23:5-6, "Behold, the days are coming . . . when I will raise up for David a righteous Branch, and he shall reign as king and deal wisely, and shall execute justice and righteousness in the land. In his days Judah will be saved, and Israel will dwell securely. And this is the name by which he will be called: 'The LORD is our righteousness.'" The Messiah is the "righteous Branch" (lit., "Branch of righteousness," see NKJV), who "shall execute justice and righteousness in the land" (33:15).

Here Joel 2:23 is of special interest, even though the translations differ greatly: "[H]e has given the early rain for your vindication," says the ESV (cf. NIV), but the NKJV (margin) says, "He has given you the teacher of righteousness" (cf. NASB margin; Heb., *hammorē litsdaqah*). The Hebrew word *morēh* comes from a root *y-r-h*, which means either "to let reign," or "to show, teach" (e.g., 2 Kgs 17:28; Isa. 9:15; *torah* also comes from this root). Hence, *morēh* means either "early rain" (Ps. 84:6), or "teacher" (Job 36:22; Isa. 30:20). The Vulgate reads *doctorem* but the New Vulgate *pluviam*. Jewish sources, such as the Targum, Rashi, and Ibn Ezra, read "teacher," but the Talmud tract Taanith (6a) takes it as "rain."[122]

---

121. Shulam (1998, ad loc.).
122. Lehrmann (1957, 71).

If the rendering "teacher" is the right one, the text refers to a teacher who would teach God's people (the road of) righteousness. According to the rabbis just mentioned this is the Messiah. The "teacher of righteousness" who founded and led the Qumran community understood his office in the light of this and many other Messianic prophecies.[123] The members of this community had "faith in" this teacher, just as Romans 3:22 speaks of "righteousness of God through faith in Jesus Christ": "The explanation of [Hab. 2:4b] concerns all those who observe the Torah in the house of Judah. God will deliver from the house of judgment because of their oppression and their faith in the teacher of righteousness."[124]

Two special passages in the Old Testament reflect something of the activity of this teacher with respect to righteousness. It is said of the Messiah, "[B]y his knowledge shall the righteous one, my servant, make many to be accounted righteous, and he shall bear their iniquities" (Isa. 53:11). The Hebrew links "righteous one" (*tsaddiq*) with "make righteous" (*yatsdiq*) to underscore the connection between the two terms (*yatsdiq tsaddiq*): the Messiah will do justice to many, and is *able* to do so because he himself is the just one. This has to do in particular with the *positional* righteousness of his people: through his atoning work he has done away with their iniquities; as righteous ones they stand before him (cf. Isa. 45:25; 60:21).[125]

The second passage tells us that the Spirit that works in the Messiah will also manifest itself in the *maskilim* ("the wise"; NKJV: "those of understanding"; NASB: "those who have insight") of Daniel 11:33, 35; 12:3, 10. It is said of them, "And those who are wise shall shine like the brightness of the sky above [cf. Matt. 13:43]; and those who turn many to righteousness, like the stars forever and ever" (12:3). The phrase "turn many to righteousness" has been rendered as follows:

---

123. Shulam (1998, 42–43, 136–37).
124. 1QpHab 8:1–3; cf. Ziesler (1972, 103).
125. Oswalt (1998, 404–05).

"has led others to please God" (CEV); "put others on the right path to life" (MSG); "taught many people to do what is right" (GNT), etc. There is a clear similarity between this statement and the Pauline idea of justification. It might be argued that Paul's idea is more that of a formal declaration of being righteous, whereas Daniel speaks of the practical pathway of doing righteousness. But as we will see later, the difference between the two is only relative (cf. 1 Pet. 2:24, Christ "himself bore our sins in his body on the tree, that we might die to sin and live to righteousness").

1.10 A Divine Attribute?
1.10.1 Retributive Justice

"Righteous(ness)" implies relationship;[126] this concerns the social analogy in the juridical modality (in the Dooyeweerdian sense).[127] A person is righteous if he answers to certain claims that another has on him under the terms of their relationship. Likewise, the righteousness of God involves primarily his covenantal loyalty in regard to his people.[128] But this is not all; if righteousness involved only God's righteous attitude toward his creatures, in what sense could we then speak of God's righteousness before the world came into being? In other words, is righteousness really an attribute of God's eternal being?

I see two answers. First, there was in eternity absolute righteousness in the relationships between the divine persons in the Trinity, that is: a giving to the Other what is due to him as far as love, respect, faithfulness, fairness, reasonableness are concerned. Second, in past eternity, God's righteousness came to expression also in his counsel and promises. God is faithful not only in keeping his promises but also in the very giving of these promises. Titus 1:2 speaks of the eternal promise of "eternal life" (cf. 1 John 2:25). Of course, God's promis-

---

126. Cf. Eichrodt (1961, 241).
127. See Ouweneel (2014a).
128. Kittel *et al.* (1964, 2:195).

es from before the foundation of the world are a gift of pure grace (cf. 2 Tim. 1:9), but also of righteousness, namely, as that which God *a priori* owed to the atoning work that Christ one day would accomplish. This work was finished in the fullness of time (cf. Gal. 4:4), but predestined—and thus *a priori* absolutely sure (cf. Rev. 13:8)—before the foundation of the world (1 Pet. 1:19-20).

The legal-juridical element in God's righteousness clearly comes to light in Scripture passages such as Job 9:14-15, 19-20, 32-33 and Isaiah 43:9, 26, and 50:8-9, where the situation of a courtroom is depicted. God is the Judge, who adjudicates, condemning some and acquitting others (Ps. 75:7-8; Dan. 7:9-10; cf. Gen. 18:25; Ps. 94:2; James 4:12). As such he is the perfect example for all earthly judges (Exod. 23:7; Deut. 1:17). We have a remarkable example of this in Deuteronomy 25:1, "If there is a dispute between men and they come into court and the judges decide between them, acquitting the innocent and condemning the guilty . . . ." "Acquitting the innocent" is literally "they justify the righteous (person)" (NKJV, NASB, GNV, etc.; Heb., *wehitsdiqu et-hatsaddiq*), that is, the judges declare the "righteous" (i.e., here the person who turns out to be the innocent party) to be "righteous." He is not *made* righteous, but *found* to be righteous, and thus acquitted, just like the wicked is *found* to be wicked, and thus condemned (v. 1b; Heb., *wehirshi'u ha rasha'*).

Besides this judicial use, "righteousness" in a more general sense is "being (in the) right" in a dispute, that is, having justice on one's side in a certain case (Gen. 30:33; 38:26; 1 Sam. 24:18). This is true of God in a universal and absolute sense. He is always "(in the) right," both when he condemns the wicked and impenitent sinners (justice *in malam partem*) and when he saves the penitent and believing sinners (justice *in bonam partem*). Herman Bavinck mentioned many biblical examples of this.[129] They are important over against the many

---

129. Bavinck, (2002, 2:224–25).

modernist theologians who reject the notion of a retributive divine justice.[130]

1.10.2 Some More Biblical Aspects

The Hebrew root *ts-d-q* means "to be (in the) right" (Gen. 38:26), "to be put in the right" (Job 11:2), "to be righteous" (Ps. 19:9). The hiphil means "to do justice to, to acquit," especially in lawsuits (Exod. 23:7; Deut. 25:1; 2 Sam. 15:4; 1 Kings 8:32; Prov. 17:15; Isa. 5:23; 50:8). Actually, *ts-d-q* never means "to make righteous" a wicked person; in Isaiah 53:11 it is rather "to do justice to." That is, it means to do justice to the *righteous* one, let him go unpunished, acquit him.[131]

In the New Testament sense, where Greek *dikaioō* ties in closely with *ts-d-q*, this means acquittal of the person who is "in (the dead and risen) Christ." Already in Luke 18:13–14, the sinner who comes pleading on the basis of the *atonement* (Greek, *hilasthēti moi tōi hamartōlōi*, "be propitiatorily inclined to me, the sinner") goes home "justified" (*dedikaiōmenos*, perfect tense: once justified, and hence forever righteous). This is new: the reconciled person "is in the right." That which comes closest to this in the Old Testament is precisely Genesis 15:6, the famous verse quoted in Romans 4:3, Galatians 3:6, and James 2:23: Abram "believed the LORD, and he counted it to him as righteousness." That is, *not* because Abram in and of himself would be righteous, but because of his confidence in the LORD he is counted as a righteous person.

In opposition to John Murray,[132] I would like to emphasize the juridical element in this "righteousness" (although this certainly is not the only element that counts in Paul's justification doctrine). God is righteous, not only loving, gracious, and merciful, when he redeems penitent and believing sinners. He owes this to Christ's atoning work in a judicial sense. The point in God's righteousness is that God is *righteous* — not

---

130. Ritschl (1900), and many after him.
131. Morris (1955, 234).
132. Ibid.

only loving and gracious—when he justifies "the one who has faith in Jesus" (Rom. 3:26; cf. 1 John 1:9). *Dikaiosynē* is certainly an expression of grace, but of such a kind that the righteousness of God is displayed as well.[133]

However, we must remember again that we are not dealing here with forensic *concepts*.[134] Otherwise, an expression such as "judicially owing to" could be easily understood wrongly, as if God would be subject to a law that he has to obey. This "duty" of God is not placed upon him from "above"; he took it implicitly upon himself when he did not spare his own Son but gave him up for penitent sinners unto death (Rom. 8:32). We are dealing here with forensic terms referring to "ideas" rather than "concepts," especially in opposition to, for example, the conceptual approach of Anselm's forensic doctrine of justification. Only in emphasizing that this use of forensic terms is associated with "ideas" rather than "concepts" can we be kept from the senseless discussion between a more "forensic" and a more "ethical" doctrine of justification.

In a similar way, if we view the term "law" too much as a juridical concept, we will view the entire law-order under which God has placed his creation[135] too unilaterally as a juridical order. Thus, Herman Bavinck indeed speaks of an "order of justice,"[136] although he himself warns that not too many divine attributes should be reckoned to God's righteousness.[137] All the other elements in this law-order, which we can approximate through a use of other modally qualified terms as referring to "ideas," are then easily neglected. Conversely, the juridical and the ethical should not be identified either, as Bavinck does in a certain sense by calling the former a "piece" of the latter.[138] In this respect, a careful distinction

---

133. Kittel *et al.* (1964, 2:204).
134. Ouweneel (2014a).
135. See extensively, Ouweneel (2012b, chapter 3).
136. Bavinck (2004, 2:227–28).
137. Ibid., 226–28.
138. Ibid., 228.

between the various irreducible modalities (and their modal analogies) and a use of modal terms as referring to "ideas" may keep us from many dangers.

Chapter 2
Justification in Judaism

*Who among us can dwell with the
consuming fire?
   Who among us can dwell with
everlasting burnings?
He who walks righteously
   and speaks uprightly, . . .*
Isaiah 33:14–15

*In the L<small>ORD</small> all the offspring of Israel
   shall be justified and shall glory.*
Isaiah 45:25

*And those who are wise
shall shine like the brightness of the sky above;
 and those who turn many to righteousness,
like the stars forever and ever.*
Daniel 12:3

Summary: *The first difference between the* **tsaddiq** *and the non- or pseudo-***tsaddiq** *lies in "regeneration," the renewal of the heart by the Holy Spirit. One of the most conspicuous features of the regenerate is their love for God and his Torah. Love leads to observance; there is no* **tsaddiq** *who is not proven to be a* **tsaddiq** *(i.e., who is not "justified") by works of the Torah. This is why the good works* *of believers are rewarded, and why the evil works of merely religious confessors descend upon their own heads. The whole juxtaposition of faith and works, so common in Reformed theology, is often based on a superficial reading of the New Testament. People are justified by works resulting from a genuine faith (confidence in God), rooted in regeneration. Moreover, the* **tsaddiq** *acts out of God's power, acts in obedience to the Torah, and acts out of love to God and his people. The* **tsaddiq** *is not perfect, but when he fails he confesses his sins, and lives anew out of God's forgiveness. Abraham and Habakkuk are two Old Testament* **tsaddiqim** *living by their trust in God. It is not just in good works, but in this basic trust, that their righteousness came to light. Both in Abraham and in Old Testament prophecy we see that this trust focused on a person: the Man in and through whom God would not just save his own, but would ultimately fill the whole world with his righteousness. Justification, then, is not just a present and individual matter, but an eschatological and collective matter. The Torah, seen from its positive side, is the measuring-rod for the* **tsaddiq**; *his opposite is the "legalist," the pseudo-***tsaddiq**, *who in fact betrays God's idea of righteousness.*

2.1   Regeneration
2.1.1   The Life-Bringing Torah

IF WE WISH TO UNDERSTAND what righteous/just and justification mean in the Old Testament, or more precisely, in the pre-Easter era, we must start with the place and the meaning of the Torah.[1] This requires first and foremost that we take seriously the biblical datum that whosoever observes the commandments of the Torah will "live" through them: "You shall therefore keep my statutes and my rules; if a person does them, he shall live by them: I am the LORD" (Lev. 18:5). "I gave them my statutes and made known to them my rules, by which, if a person does them, he shall live. . . . But the house of Israel rebelled against me in the wilderness. They did not walk in my statutes but rejected my rules, by which, if a person does them, he shall live" (Ezek. 20:11, 13).

---

1. See extensively, Ouweneel (2015a).

This Tanakhic testimony is quoted with approval by the apostle Paul: "Moses writes about the righteousness that is based on the Torah, that the person who does the commandments shall live by them" (Rom. 10:5); "[T]he Torah is not of faith, rather 'The one who does them shall live by them'" (Gal. 3:12). Paul even says explicitly that the "doers of the law," that is, those who faithfully observe the Torah, "will be justified," that is, will be recognized and accepted by God as righteous (Rom. 2:13). We will have to figure out how such a statement relates to other statements in the same epistle, such as: "[B]y works of the Torah no human being will be justified in his sight. . . . [W]e hold that one is justified by faith apart from works of the Torah" (3:20, 28; cf. Gal. 2:16). But also how it relates to James' statement: "Was not Abraham our father justified by works when he offered up his son Isaac on the altar? You see that faith was active along with his works, and faith was completed by his works. . . . You see that a person is justified by works and not by faith alone" (James 2:21-24). We will come back extensively to these statements.

What precisely does it mean that those who observe the Torah "shall live"? In the first place, here "life" is the elongation of earthly life, as we see in the Fifth Commandment: "Honor your father and your mother, that your days may be long in the land that the Lord your God is giving you" (Exod. 20:12; cf. Deut. 5:16; 6:2; 11:9; Eph. 2:2-3). God told young king Solomon: "And if you will walk in my ways, keeping my statutes and my commandments, as your father David walked, then I will lengthen your days" (1 Kings 3:14).

Already the rabbis presumed that in the "life" that accompanies Torah observance, much more is at stake than just a long life on earth. When Moses said, "And now, O Israel, listen to the statutes and the rules that I am teaching you, and do them, that you may live, and go in and take possession of the land that the Lord, the God of your fathers, is giving you" (Deut. 4:1), the rabbis believed that Moses meant more than just living in the promised land. Here "living" refers also to life in the "world to come," the Messianic Kingdom.[2] This is what Psalm 133:3 speaks about: "life forevermore," that is, the life of Messiah's "age [to come]," "when brothers dwell in unity" (v. 1). "[M]any of those who sleep in the dust of the earth shall awake, some to everlasting life" (Dan. 12:2); again, this is fulfilled in the Messianic Kingdom. It is also the life of which Jesus speaks: "If you would enter life [v. 16, 'eternal life'], keep the commandments" (Matt. 19:17; in 25:34, 46, the Kingdom and eternal life coincide).

We see, then, that the Old Testament knows not only of a long physical life but also of life in the spiritual sense. God's commandments "will be life for your soul" (Prov. 3:22; cf. Ps. 19:7, "The law of the LORD is perfect, reviving the soul"). Also the statements, "your promise gives me life" (Ps. 119:50) and "I will never forget your precepts, for by them you have given me life" (v. 93), and the phrase "give me life" in verses 25, 37, 40, 88, 107, 149, 154, and 159, all point rather to life in some spiritual sense than in some physical sense. In the profoundest sense, God is known as the "fountain of life" (Ps. 36:9).

2.1.2 The Love of the Regenerate

In Scripture, we do indeed find persons who have experienced this life-changing, regenerating work of God in their souls. Apparently, they are those who can say in all uprightness: "Oh how I love your Torah! It is my meditation all the day. Your commandment makes me wiser than my enemies, for it is ever with me" (Ps. 119:97-98). Notice how often the writer of this psalm uses the word "delight": "In the way of your testimonies I delight as much as in all riches. I will meditate on your precepts and fix my eyes on your ways. I will delight in your statutes; I will not forget your word" (vv. 14-16;

---

2. See, e.g., Cohen (1983, 1010): Ibn Ezra on Deut. 4:10: true "living" will be possible only after Israel has returned to its land to live there as free people again. Ibid., 1021: Nachmanides on Deut. 5:33 (Heb. text: 30): if Israel were to prolong its days in the land, this could mean only that the land would remain in Israel's possession forever. This is life extending into the Messianic age.

cf. vv. 24, 35, 47, 70, 77, 92, 143, 174). Moreover, David can say, "[T]he precepts of the Lord are right, rejoicing the heart; the commandment of the Lord is pure, enlightening the eyes; the fear of the Lord is clean, enduring forever; the rules of the Lord are true, and righteous altogether. More to be desired are they than gold, even much fine gold; sweeter also than honey and drippings of the honeycomb" (19:8-10). Only the regenerate can speak in such a way.

The ardent love for God's Word is evidence of regeneration. John wrote, "[L]ove is from God, and whoever loves has been born of God and knows God" (1 John 4:7). And Jesus said, "If you love me, you will keep my commandments. . . . Whoever has my commandments and keeps them, he it is who loves me. . . . If anyone loves me, he will keep my word" (John 14:15, 21, 23). One of the most excellent ways to discover the righteous among Israel is to look at their attitude toward the Torah: "Blessed is the man who walks not in the counsel of the wicked, nor stands in the way of sinners, nor sits in the seat of scoffers; but his delight is in the Torah of the Lord, and on his Torah he meditates day and night. He is like a tree planted by streams of water that yields its fruit in its season, and its leaf does not wither. In all that he does, he prospers" (Ps. 1:1-3). Saying "regenerate" is here the same as saying "righteous": the righteous love the Torah. It is said of Zechariah and Elizabeth: "[T]hey were both righteous before God, walking blamelessly in all the commandments and statutes of the Lord" (Luke 1:6). The people who "know righteousness" are those "in whose heart is my Torah" (Isa. 51:7; cf. v. 4).

"Walking" blamelessly, that is, walking with God, is a common expression for the truly righteous in the Old Testament. "Enoch walked with God" (Gen. 5:22, 24). "Noah was a righteous man . . . [he] walked with God" (Gen. 6:9). "When Abram was ninety-nine years old the Lord appeared to Abram and said to him, 'I am God Almighty; walk before me, and be blameless, that I may make my covenant between me and you, and may multiply you greatly'" (Gen. 17:1-2). Abraham himself spoke of "[t]he LORD, before whom I have walked" (Gen. 24:40). And Jacob spoke of "[t]he God before whom my fathers Abraham and Isaac walked, the God who has been my shepherd all my life long to this day" (Gen. 48:15). And the prophet says, "He has told you, O man, what is good; and what does the LORD require of you but to do justice, and to love kindness, and to walk humbly with your God?" (Micah 6:8).

Luke presents even Jesus as "walking" (going, traveling, journeying) for the greater part of his gospel (since 9:51, "he set his face to go to Jerusalem"), going the way of God to the cross. In the book of Acts, he uses the phrase "the Way" for the young Christian movement (9:2; 19:9, 23; 24:14, 22).[3] The righteous is always "on the move," until he arrives in the Messianic Kingdom.

2.1.3 Do the Righteous Exist?

Do the truly righteous indeed exist? This idea seems to be in conflict with other Scripture passages. Already the Old Testament testifies: "[T]here is no one who does not sin" (1 Kings 8:46). "Can mortal man be in the right before God? Can a man be pure before his Maker?" (Job 4:17). "What is man, that he can be pure? Or he who is born of a woman, that he can be righteous?" (Job 15:14). "How then can man be in the right before God? How can he who is born of woman be pure?" (Job 25:4). "If you, O LORD, should mark iniquities, O LORD, who could stand?" (Ps. 130:3). "Enter not into judgment with your servant, for no one living is righteous before you" (Ps. 143:2). "Surely there is not a righteous man on earth who does good and never sins" (Eccl. 7:20).

The same apostle Paul who says that the doers of the Torah are justified (Rom. 2:13) says in the same letter that by observing the Torah no one can be justified, that is, be recognized and accepted as righteous by God (3:20, 22, 28; 4:2, 5;

---

3. Cf. Green (1997, 65n10).

cf. 4:6, 11, 13; 9:30; Gal. 2:16; 3:11; Eph. 2:8-9; Phil. 3:9; 2 Tim. 1:9; Titus 3:5). To put it even more strongly, no human can be justified on account of his own efforts whatsoever, including descent, denomination, and religious zeal (Phil. 3:4-6). Peter said of the Torah that it was a "yoke" that natural man ("neither our fathers nor we") had been able to bear (Acts 15:10).

In (seeming) opposition to this, the apostle James says, "You see that a person is justified by works and not by faith alone" (James 2:24; cf. vv. 14-26), clearly referring to works *of the Torah* (vv. 8-12). How can we explain this apparent contradiction, which we find throughout the Bible? Can a person be justified — that is, recognized and accepted as righteous by God — by his own effort or merit, or can he not?

The key to understanding this riddle is *regeneration*.[4] Purely by one's own effort, from an *unregenerate* heart, no justification and salvation are ever possible. What is needed is the renewal of the heart, that is, regeneration (re-birth, new birth): "[U]nless one is born again [*gennēthē anōthen*, or "born from above"] he cannot see the kingdom of God. . . . [U]nless one is born of water and the Spirit, he cannot enter the kingdom of God" (John 3:3, 5). "[H]e saved us, not because of works done by us in righteousness, but according to his own mercy, by the washing of regeneration [*palingenesia*] and renewal of the Holy Spirit" (Titus 3:5). "[H]e has caused us to be born again [*anagennēsas*, from *anagennaō*]" (1 Pet. 1:3).

This "regeneration" was not a New Testament invention. Jesus blamed Nicodemus for not understanding "these things" (John 3:10) because he could and should have known from the Tanakh what it is to be "born of water and the Spirit": "I will sprinkle clean water on you, and you shall be clean from all your uncleannesses, and from all your idols I will cleanse you. And I will give you a new heart, and a new spirit I will put within you. And I will remove the heart of stone from your flesh and give you a heart of flesh. And I will put

---

4. See extensively, Ouweneel (2010a, chapter 3).

my Spirit within you, and cause you to walk in my statutes and be careful to obey my rules" (Ezek. 36:25-27). To be sure, this is said to those Israelites who are about to enter into the Messianic Kingdom. But Jesus said that regeneration is needed in order to be able to even *see* the Kingdom of God (John 3:3), to spiritually *discern* it. Therefore, all the godly people in the pre-Easter era who *saw* the Kingdom from afar—were spiritually aware of it in their hearts—must have been born again (cf. Heb. 11:10, 13-16). Think of the psalm writers and the prophets, or John's father Zechariah (Luke 1:68-75), and so many more *tsaddiqim* in the pre-Easter era.

Regeneration is the work of God in a person's heart, its counterpart being the faith of the person who entrusts himself to God and his promises. It is the *regenerated* (re-born, born again) person who is justified by God, that is, recognized and accepted by him as righteous. It is also the *regenerated* (re-born, born again) person who can truly serve God in the power of the Holy Spirit, can observe his commandments, can and will produce good works "in keeping with repentance" (Matt. 3:8; Acts 26:20).

In §2.1.1, we saw that doing works of the Torah produces life. But we just saw that the person that is "made alive" (cf. Eph. 2:5; Col. 2:13) produces works of the Torah. We would think that both statements cannot be true at the same time: either Torah works produce life, or life produces Torah works. However, the reality is that both statements are perfectly true. Doing works of the Torah leads into everlasting life: "to those who by patience in well-doing seek for glory and honor and immortality, he will give eternal life. . . . There will be . . . glory and honor and peace for everyone who does good" (Rom. 2:7-10). But it is equally true that no one *can* truly do works of the Torah without having been "made alive" (regenerated, born again). Such doing works of the (Messianic) Torah is, in fact, the only true *evidence* of having been regenerated. In conclusion, this is the order: regeneration – works of the Torah – everlasting life (i.e., the life of the Messianic Kingdom).

2.2 Good and Evil Works
2.2.1 Good Works by Believers

It is striking that Scripture speaks time and again of good works, but only in reference to believers: "[L]et your light shine before others, so that they may see your good works and give glory to your Father who is in heaven" (Matt. 5:16). "God is able to make all grace abound to you, so that . . . you may abound in every good work" (2 Cor. 9:8). "For we are his workmanship, created in Christ Jesus for good works, which God prepared beforehand, that we should walk in them" (Eph. 2:10); ". . . so as to walk in a manner worthy of the Lord, fully pleasing to him, bearing fruit in every good work and increasing in the knowledge of God" (Col. 1:10). "To this end we always pray for you, that our God may make you worthy of his calling and may fulfill every resolve for good and every work of faith by his power" (2 Thess. 1:11).

"All Scripture is . . . profitable . . . for training in righteousness, that the man of God may be complete, equipped for every good work" (2 Tim. 3:16-17); ". . . our great God and Savior Jesus Christ, who gave himself for us to redeem us from all lawlessness and to purify for himself a people for his own possession who are zealous for good works" (Titus 2:13-14). "I want you to insist on these things, so that those who have believed in God may be careful to devote themselves to good works. . . . And let our people learn to devote themselves to good works, so as to help cases of urgent need, and not be unfruitful" (3:8, 14). "And let us consider how to stir up one another to love and good works" (Heb. 10:24). "Who is wise and understanding among you? By his good conduct let him show his works in the meekness of wisdom" (James 3:13). "Keep your conduct among the Gentiles honorable, so that when they speak against you as evildoers, they may see your good deeds and glorify God on the day of visitation" (1 Pet. 2:12; cf. Matt. 26:10; Acts 9:36; 1 Cor. 15:58; 16:10; Eph. 4:12, 28; Phil. 2:30; Col. 3:23-24; 1 Thess. 1:3; 2 Thess. 2:17; 1 Tim. 2:10; 5:10, 25; 6:18; Rev. 2:2, 19; 3:8).

We begin to see more and more clearly that it is false to suggest that a person is justified by faith *alone,* as if the good works of the believers would be just an *extra* that is merely interesting but unnecessary for salvation. Not only is the New Testament constantly underscoring the importance and necessity of the good works of believers, but believers are even assured that they will be judged—not just on account of their regeneration but—according to their works: "God will bring every deed into judgment, with every secret thing, whether good or evil" (Eccl. 12:14). "For you will render to a man according to his work" (Ps. 62:12). "For the Son of Man is going to come with his angels in the glory of his Father, and then he will repay each person according to what he has done" (Matt. 16:27).

In case someone may think that this holds only for unbelievers, let me quote this: "Why do you pass judgment on your brother? Or you, why do you despise your brother? For we will all stand before the judgment seat of God; for it is written, 'As I live, says the LORD, every knee shall bow to me, and every tongue shall confess to God.' [Isa. 45:23] So then each of us will give an account of himself to God" (Rom. 14:10-12). "[E]ach one's work will become manifest, for the Day will disclose it, because it will be revealed by fire, and the fire will test what sort of work each one has done" (1 Cor. 3:13). "Therefore do not pronounce judgment before the time, before the Lord comes, who will bring to light the things now hidden in darkness and will disclose the purposes of the heart. Then each one will receive his commendation from God" (1 Cor. 4:5). "For we must all appear before the judgment seat of Christ, so that each one may receive what is due for what he has done in the body, whether good or evil" (2 Cor. 5:10). "Do not be deceived: God is not mocked, for whatever one sows, that will he also reap. For the one who sows to his own flesh will from the flesh reap corruption, but the one who sows to the Spirit will from the Spirit reap eternal life" (Gal. 6:7-8). "And if you call on him as Father who judges impartially according to each one's deeds, conduct yourselves with fear throughout the time of your exile" (1 Pet. 1:17). "And all the churches will know that I am he who searches mind and heart, and I will give to each of you according to your works" (Rev. 2:23; cf. Isa. 40:10; Zeph. 2:3; Matt. 25:31-46; Rom. 2:5-10; Rev. 14:13).

In this sense, Scripture can also speak of rewards for the good works that believers have done:[5] "Rejoice and be glad, for your reward is great in heaven, for so they persecuted the prophets who were before you" (Matt. 5:12). "And your Father who sees in secret will reward you" (Matt. 6:4; cf. v. 6, 18; 10:40-42). "If the work that anyone has built on the foundation survives, he will receive a reward" (1 Cor. 3:14). "Therefore do not throw away your confidence, which has a great reward" (Heb. 10:35). "[W]hoever would draw near to God must believe that he exists and that he rewards those who seek him" (11:6). "Watch yourselves, so that you may not lose what we have worked for, but may win a full reward" (2 John 1:8). "[T]he time for the dead to be judged, and for rewarding your servants" (Rev. 11:18).

As the Belgic Confession (Art. 24) puts it: "In the meantime we do not deny that God rewards good works, but it is through His grace that He crowns His gifts." This is true—in spite of Jesus' word in Luke 17:10, "[W]hen you have done all that you were commanded, say, 'We are unworthy servants; we have only done what was our duty.'"

2.2.2 Evil Works by Mere Confessors

Some confessing Christians have *lived* consciously and perniciously in serious sins (idolatry, blasphemy, murder, robbery, greed, conceit, adultery, etc.), that is, as unrighteous persons. If they have not repented and have not turned from their evil ways, they may claim that they have been justified by faith, but they will be condemned because of their evil works: "For if we go on sinning deliberately after receiving the knowledge

---

5. Cf. Bavinck (2008, 4:234, 236–37, 265–66); Berkouwer (1954, 112–29); Wiersinga (1952, 117–22); Van Genderen and Velema (2008, 665–67).

of the truth, there no longer remains a sacrifice for sins, but a fearful expectation of judgment, and a fury of fire that will consume the adversaries. Anyone who has set aside the Torah of Moses dies without mercy on the evidence of two or three witnesses [Deut. 17:6; 19:15]. How much worse punishment, do you think, will be deserved by the one who has trampled underfoot the Son of God, and has profaned the blood of the covenant by which he was sanctified, and has outraged the Spirit of grace? For we know him who said, 'Vengeance is mine; I will repay.' [Deut. 32:35] And again, 'The Lord will judge his people.' [v. 36] It is a fearful thing to fall into the hands of the living God" (Heb. 10:26–31; cf. 3:14; 6:4–6).

"For if, after they have escaped the defilements of the world through the knowledge of our Lord and Savior Jesus Christ, they are again entangled in them and overcome, the last state has become worse for them than the first. For it would have been better for them never to have known the way of righteousness than after knowing it to turn back from the holy commandment delivered to them. What the true proverb says has happened to them: 'The dog returns to its own vomit, and the sow, after washing herself, returns to wallow in the mire' [Prov. 26:11]" (2 Pet. 2:20–22).

The situation just described is essentially different from that of born again Christians, who have pursued righteousness as the fundamental guideline for their lives (cf. Prov. 15:9; 21:21; Isa. 51:1; 1 Tim. 6:11; 2 Tim. 2:22), and have repented and confessed their trespasses that still have occurred during their Christian lives, and have lived out of the forgiveness of their sins. They have the privilege of knowing that the Judge on God's judgment seat is none less than their own Redeemer. Therefore, the Heidelberg Catechism (Q&A 52) explains the believer's comfort from Christ's coming to judge the living and the dead to be "[t]hat in all my sorrows and persecutions, I, with uplifted head, look for the very One, who offered Himself for me to the judgment of God, and removed all curse from me, ..."

This is not the place to deal extensively with the subject of the perseverance of the saints (the "once saved, always saved" doctrine). *Theologically* speaking, I am entirely on the side of the Dort fathers who "teach that those who truly believe and have been born again" can never "forfeit justifying faith as well as grace and salvation." For teaching the opposite "nullifies the very grace of justification and regeneration as well as the continual preservation by Christ, contrary to the plain words of the apostle Paul: 'If Christ died for us while we were still sinners, we will therefore much more be saved from God's wrath through him, since we have now been justified by his blood' (Rom. 5:8-9); and contrary to the apostle John: 'No one who is born of God is intent on sin, because God's seed remains in him, nor can he sin, because he has been born of God' (1 John 3:9); also contrary to the words of Jesus Christ: 'I give eternal life to my sheep, and they shall never perish; no one can snatch them out of my hand. My Father, who has given them to me, is greater than all; no one can snatch them out of my Father's hand' (John 10:28-29)" (Canons of Dort V, rejection of errors III).

However, from a *pastoral* point of view, it is equally important to tell those who claim to have been born again and justified by faith but who perniciously continue living in gross sin that they are on the way to eternal perdition. Here is where *works* again come into the picture: "I will give to each of you [in the church of Thyatira] according to your works" (Rev. 2:23). To the church in Sardis: "I know your works. You have the reputation of being alive, but you are dead. Wake up, and strengthen what remains and is about to die, for I have not found your works complete in the sight of my God. Remember, then, what you received and heard. Keep it, and repent. If you will not wake up, I will come like a thief, and you will not know at what hour I will come against you" (3:1-3). To the church in Laodicea: "I know your works: you are neither cold nor hot. Would that you were either cold or hot! So, because you are lukewarm, and neither hot nor cold,

I will spit you out of my mouth" (vv. 15-16). Can *Christians* be lost? Unfortunately, yes. Can *regenerate believers* be lost? Thank God, no.

2.3 Biblical Examples
2.3.1 Faith Versus Works

The psalm writer who loved God's Torah, Zechariah and Elizabeth, and so many other faithful in Israel, were regenerate people (§2.1.2). The persons to whom James 2 refers are as well. In other words, they are people who have a genuine faith in God, that is, faith producing fruit in the good works that follow from it.[6] As Gerrit C. Berkouwer says in line with the Belgic Confession (Art. 24): "Good works, it says, must proceed from 'the good root of faith.'"[7] If James 2:26 says, "[F]aith apart from works is dead," we can equally say, "[W]orks without faith are dead."[8] Therefore, Hebrews 6:1 and 9:14 speak of "dead works" (Phillips, "deeds of death"; CEV, "things that lead to death"; GNV, "sins which proceed from death, and bring forth nothing but death"; MSG, "dead-end efforts"). Conversely, Paul speaks of the "work of faith" (1 Thess. 1:3), that is, work that proceeds from faith.

In the latter verse, Paul speaks of "your work [*ergon*] of faith and labor [*kopos*] of love and steadfastness [*hypomonē*] of hope." It is striking that we find precisely these same nouns in Revelation 2:21, "I know your works [*erga*], your toil [*kopos*] and your patient endurance [*hypomonē*]," but this time without the proper motivation: faith, love, and hope. Either this means that these motives were never there, which it is the same as saying that they had never been born again. Or it means that these Christians had lost them, and that they had to repent and convert as soon as possible. Compare verses 4-5: "I have this against you, that you have abandoned the love you had at first. Remember therefore from where you

---

6. See more extensively, Ouweneel (1981, 42–53).
7. Berkouwer (1952, 41).
8. Stern (1999, 354, 734).

have fallen; repent, and do the works you did at first. If not, I will come to you and remove your lampstand from its place, unless you repent."

In summary, it is very important to state that, strictly speaking, in Scripture the issue is never a matter of faith versus works as such. On the one hand, we have unbelief or pseudo-faith *without* God-pleasing works, which are only dead works, and on the other hand, genuine faith *with* good (God-pleasing) works. In other words, on the one hand, we are dealing with "works of the Torah" without genuine faith (Rom. 3:20, 28; Gal. 2:16; 3:2, 5, 10). On the other hand, we are dealing with "works of faith," though not apart from the Torah.[9] This is comparable with what Paul calls "works of the flesh" and the "fruit of the Spirit" (Gal. 5:16–23). As Calvin has rightly put it: we are not justified *per opera* ("through works"), but not *sine operibus* ("without works)" either.[10] Or, as it has been said, there is a *iustificatio peccatoris* ("justification of the sinner"), which is found more with Paul. But there is also a *iustificatio iusti* ("justification of the righteous"), which is found more with James.[11] Paul and James complement each other: on the one hand, faith is a prerequisite for salvation; on the other hand, works confirm the authenticity of faith.[12]

In summary, we find four possibilities:

(a) Unbelief without works: this is the common condition of the wicked. There is no justification, neither by faith nor by works.

(b) Unbelief with works: these can only be dead works (pseudo-good works); no one is justified by such works, or he is at best justified (proclaimed righteous) by other sinners.

(c) Faith without works: this can only be pseudo-faith; no one is justified by such an empty, dead faith, that is, a faith that does not produce good works.

---

9. Berkouwer (1954, 108–09).
10. *Institutes* 3.16.1.
11. Bavinck (2008, 4:222); Demarest (1997, 361).
12. S. Andria in Adeyemo (2006, 1509).

(d) Faith with works: if it is a genuine faith, it will produce good works; a person is justified by faith, that is, faith producing good works. In this sense, James would say, such a person is also justified by works, namely, works produced by a genuine faith.

2.3.2 The Source of Life

Psalm 1 offers us an excellent Old Testament example of the true Old Testament *tsaddiq*. We find here a man who is called "blessed" (more accurate: blissful, happy) because he does not seek the company of the wicked but finds his delight in the LORD's Torah. That is, he finds joy not just by meditating on it but especially by observing it, as we read of Ezra: "Ezra had set his heart to [a] study the Law of the LORD, and to [b] do it and to [c] teach his statutes and rules in Israel" (Ezra 7:10). Now the point is this: the *tsaddiq* finds the power to do this not in himself. Rather, he is "like a tree" that draws its life juices from the "streams of water" (Ps. 1:3). In the New Testament, such "rivers of living water" turn out to refer to the Holy Spirit (John 7:38–39). It is in this way that the tree "yields its fruit in its season" (cf. John 15:1–8). It is truly a "fruit of the Spirit" (Gal. 5:22). This is what the Bible expresses through the term regeneration (re-birth, new birth): the true *tsaddiq* observes the Torah, but not by one's own power but by the power of God, in whom one's life is "rooted" (cf. for this metaphor Eph. 3:17, "rooted and grounded in love"; Col. 2:7, "rooted and built up in him").

A second, similar example is Jeremiah 17:7–8: "Blessed is the man who trusts in the LORD, whose trust is the LORD. He is like a tree planted by water, that sends out its roots by the stream, and does not fear[13] when heat comes, for its leaves remain green, and is not anxious in the year of drought, for it does not cease to bear fruit." Here, the emphasis is more

---

13. Literally, "see"; notice the word play with v. 6: the shrub in the desert "shall not see" (does not notice) any *good* coming; the tree at the water does not notice any *evil* coming because it is safe.

on faith (trust), and for the rest it is the same metaphor: the tree is strong, not because of its own power but because it is nourished by the stream. In Psalm 92, the tree is not at some stream but in the temple, that is, near God: "The righteous flourish like the palm tree and grow like a cedar in Lebanon. They are planted in the house of the LORD; they flourish in the courts of our God" (vv. 12-13). In all these cases, the meaning is the same: the righteous lives *by God*, or *out of God's life power*.

Such life metaphors are directly related to "regeneration" and "quickening" (the KJV term for "being made alive" or "making alive"). The fruit and leaves are produced by the tree, but the life force that is needed for this does *not* come from the tree as such: as the tree lives by its water source, thus the believer lives by the power source that is called God. With him "is the fountain of life" (Ps. 36:9). The Old Testament *hasid* is the person who yields fruit *for* God — but he can only do this by living *out of* God. It is the tree that yields the fruit, but it is the stream that yields the power (cf. Ezek. 47:7-12; Rev. 22:2). In the words of Jesus' parable of the vine: "Every . . . branch that does bear fruit he prunes, that it may bear more fruit. . . . Abide in me, and I in you. As the branch cannot bear fruit by itself, unless it abides in the vine, neither can you, unless you abide in me. I am the vine; you are the branches. Whoever abides in me and I in him, he it is that bears much fruit, for apart from me you can do nothing" (John 15:2-5).

2.3.3 *Tsaddiqim*

At the beginning of the New Testament, that is, before the redemptive work of Christ and the outpouring of the Holy Spirit, we encounter several such godly people, in Hebrew: *hasidim* ("saints," "godly ones") or *tsaddiqim* ("righteous ones"). I already mentioned the example of Zechariah and Elizabeth, who walked according to God's commandments. In this way, Luke presents a positive image of the Torah as the expression of God's will (cf. 18:20; 23:56). This is all the more striking when we take note of the contrast between Luke 1:6 (Zechariah and Elizabeth's obedience) and verse 7 (their barrenness), since the Mosaic Torah presents fruitfulness as a consequence of Torah observance: "Blessed shall be the fruit of your womb. . . . And the LORD will make you abound in prosperity, in the fruit of your womb and in the fruit of your livestock and in the fruit of your ground" (Deut. 28:4, 11).[14]

Such Torah observance did not at all exclude the necessity of redemption, as Zechariah apparently fully realizes (even though he probably thought primarily of the physical deliverance from Israel's enemies): "Blessed be the Lord God of Israel, for he has visited and redeemed his people and has raised up a horn of salvation for us in the house of his servant David . . . that we should be saved from our enemies and from the hand of all who hate us . . . to grant us that we, being delivered from the hand of our enemies, might serve him without fear, in holiness and righteousness before him all our days. . . . [John the Baptist is sent] to give knowledge of salvation to his people in the forgiveness of their sins, because of the tender mercy of our God, whereby the sunrise shall visit us from on high" (Luke 1:68–78).

Other examples, specifically in the Gospels, of Jewish *tsaddiqim*, still living entirely within the boundaries of Judaism, are:

(a) Joseph, Mary's fiancé, who is called "a just [or, righteous] man" (Matt. 1:19), which in Hebrew would be a *tsaddiq*.

(b) Mary, who speaks these words of faith: "Behold, I am the servant of the Lord; let it be to me according to your word" (Luke 1:38); see further her song of faith (vv. 46–55).

(c) Simeon, of whom we read: "[T]his man was righteous [cf. *tsaddiq*] and devout [cf. *hasid*], waiting for the consolation of Israel, and the Holy Spirit was upon him" (2:25); hear his song, too (vv. 29–32).

(d) Anna, of whom we read: "And there was a prophetess, Anna . . . a widow. . . . She did not depart from the temple,

---

14. See Green (1997, 65).

worshiping with fasting and prayer night and day. And coming up at that very hour she began to give thanks to God and to speak of him to all who were waiting for the redemption of Jerusalem" (vv. 36–38).

(e) Nathanael, of whom Jesus said, "Behold, an Israelite indeed, in whom there is no deceit" (John 1:47). Of course, the other disciples were *tsaddiqim*, too, except Judas Iscariot (John 6:70–71).

(f) Nicodemus, the Pharisee, had the courage to publicly appeal to righteousness with regard to Jesus, thus showing himself to be righteous (John 7:50–51; cf. 3:1–21; 19:39).

(g) Joseph of Arimathea is called a "good and righteous man" (Luke 23:50).

Above all, Jesus himself is the true *tsaddiq*. The wife of Pilate said, "Have nothing to do with that righteous man" (Matt. 27:19). Pilate himself said, "I am innocent of the blood of this just [or righteous] Person" (v. 24 NKJV). Peter blamed the Jews: "But you denied the Holy and Righteous One" (Acts 3:14). Stephen did the same: "[Y]our fathers . . . killed those who announced beforehand the coming of the Righteous One, whom you have now betrayed and murdered" (7:52). Ananias said to Saul of Tarsus, "The God of our fathers appointed you to know his will, to see the Righteous One and to hear a voice from his mouth" (22:14). Peter says, "Christ also suffered once for sins, the righteous for the unrighteous" (1 Pet. 3:18). And John says, "[W]e have an advocate with the Father, Jesus Christ the righteous" (1 John 2:1). Several translations suggest that the "righteous one" in James 5:6 also refers to Christ: "You have condemned and put to death the Just One, and he resisted you not" (DRA). "You have condemned and murdered The Righteous One and he has not opposed you" (Aramaic Bible in Plain English).

2.4 *Tsedaqah*
2.4.1 Charity and Legality
The British chief rabbi Jonathan Sacks has given a remark-

able description of the Hebrew idea of *tsedaqah*, "justice" or "righteousness."[15] He stated that in this one term two notions come together that normally are opposed to each other, namely, charity and legality. If I give money to someone because he is entitled to it, it is a lawful act, an act of legality (Latin, *iustitia*). But if I give it without the other being entitled to it, if I give it "for free," it is an act of charity (Latin, *caritas*). Now the interesting thing is, says Sacks, that *tsedaqah* is both at the same time. This can be understood only if we realize that the Israelite's goods were his possession but not his property, because everything belonged to God: "The land . . . is mine. For you are strangers and sojourners with me" (Lev. 25:23). Thus, the Israelite was only a steward of his goods, and as such was bound to stipulations for managing them.

One stipulation was that the Israelite had to give part of his possession to people in need (e.g., Exod. 23:11; Lev. 19:10, 15; 23:22; Deut. 14:29; 15:11; 24:19-21; 26:12-13; 27:19). This giving, then, was not just an act of charity but also one of legality, which could even be judicially enforced. Another example is found in Deuteronomy 24:10-13: "When you make your neighbor a loan of any sort, you shall not go into his house to collect his pledge. . . . And if he is a poor man, you shall not sleep in his pledge. You shall restore to him the pledge as the sun sets, that he may sleep in his cloak and bless you. And it shall be righteousness for you before the Lord your God." Here we have *tsedaqah* in its most elementary form: doing what is right to your neighbor. It is not right to take from your neighbor a pledge that is of little value to you, but for him is of vital importance, since it is his covering during the night. Restoring the pledge before nightfall is a judicial act because you do it in obedience to the Lord's commandment. But it is also a charitable act because you do it as an act of love toward your neighbor.

Seen from this viewpoint, the *tsaddiq* is not only some-

---

15. Sacks (2005, 150-51).

one who, in an entirely voluntary way, does good things to people. A true *tsaddiq* does good as a servant of God, for the honor of God, as one submitting to his commandments. His giving, or his restoring the pledge, his saving a life, is an act of *charity* as well as an act of *obedience*. These two aspects are both indispensable to mark someone as a true *tsaddiq*. Not every altruist, not every generous and magnanimous person, is a *tsaddiq* in the biblical sense of the term, namely, when his deepest motivation is not truly Godward.

2.4.2 The Pharisee and Phinehas

The person who is charitable only because his religion obliges him to do so, or because he desires to be honored by other people, is no genuine *tsaddiq* either. Such a person rather resembles the hypocrite Pharisee: "Beware of practicing your righteousness before other people in order to be seen by them, for then you will have no reward from your Father who is in heaven. Thus, when you give to the needy, sound no trumpet before you, as the hypocrites do in the synagogues and in the streets, that they may be praised by others. Truly, I say to you, they have received their reward. But when you give to the needy, do not let your left hand know what your right hand is doing, so that your giving may be in secret. And your Father who sees in secret will reward you" (Matt. 6:1–4).

The genuine *tsaddiq* is righteous *both* because he wants to serve and honor God *and* because he has love in his heart for his fellow human being. What he does to his neighbor, then, is true charity—but it is also a judicial legality because, as one standing under the Lord's commandments, he is formally obliged to act this way.

Tsedaqah may also be an act of love toward *God*. We have a remarkable example in Psalm 106:30–31, "Then Phinehas stood up and intervened, and the plague was stayed. And that was counted to him as righteousness." It is the passive form here, but for the rest the terminology is the same as in Genesis 15:6, "[H]e [i.e., the LORD] counted it to him [i.e., Abraham] as righteousness." On account of Abram's faith (an *attitude*) and of Phinehas's zeal (a concrete *act*) both were declared to be *tsaddiqim*.

This is all the more remarkable because of the nature of Phinehas's act: "Phinehas . . . took a spear in his hand and went after the man of Israel into the chamber and pierced both of them, the man of Israel and the [Midianite] woman through her belly. Thus the plague on the people of Israel was stopped." Interestingly, there was no specific commandment of the LORD that Phinehas obeyed in this moment; some might even complain that Phinehas took the law into his own hands. At best, his act was one of obedience in a very general sense to Deuteronomy 6:5, "You shall love the LORD your God with all your heart and with all your soul and with all your might."

Nevertheless, in his act, Phinehas had the *approval* of the LORD: "Phinehas the son of Eleazar . . . the LORD was with him" (1 Chron. 9:20) — a striking characteristic (cf. Joseph, Gen. 39:3, 23; Samuel, 1 Sam. 3:19; David, 18:12, 14; 2 Sam. 5:10; 1 Chron. 11:9; Solomon, 2 Chron. 1:1; Asa, 2 Chron. 15:9; Hezekiah, 2 Kings 18:7; also cf. Jesus, Luke 1:66; 5:17). Phinehas was filled with indignation over the wickedness of Israel, not on legalistic grounds, but out of love for the LORD and his Torah. In this sense, he too manifested himself as a true *tsaddiq*.

2.4.3 The *Tsaddiq*: Three Characteristics

In summary, the *tsaddiq* exhibits at least three characteristics:[16]

(a) He acts out of *power*, that is, he is one who *is able* to do what he does because he draws from the power of God (Old Testament language: he is a tree by the brook; New Testament

---

16. Cf. Westminster Confession of Faith XVI.7: "Works done by unregenerate men, although for the matter of them they may be things which God commands; and of good use both to themselves and others; yet, because they proceed not from an heart purified by faith; nor are done in a right manner, according to the Word; nor to a right end, the glory of God, they are therefore sinful and cannot please God, or make a man meet to receive grace from God: and yet, their neglect of them is more sinful and displeasing unto God."

language: he is filled with the Spirit, which in John 7:38-39 is compared to "rivers of living water").

(b) He acts out of *obedience*, that is, he *must* do what he does because he stands under the Torah of his God. In the first volume of this series we have seen that there is no redemptive-historical era without some manifestation of the Eternal Torah. Man is always under the Torah of God.

(c) He acts out of *love*, that is, he ardently desires to do what he does because he loves God and his neighbor.

If any one of these three is lacking he cannot be called a *tsaddiq* anymore. If (a) is lacking, he will try to act out of his own strength, and fail (this is the message of Rom. 7). If (b) is lacking, he is basically a rebel, no matter how charitable and generous he may be. If (c) is lacking but (b) is there, he is a legalist, or even a hypocrite (see §2.8).

Israel's official memorial to the victims of the Holocaust is in Jerusalem, and is called Yad Vashem. One of its tasks is to honor Gentiles who risked their lives, positions, or property to save Jews during the Holocaust. Such people are called the "Righteous Among the Nations"; their names are commemorated at Yad Vashem in the Garden of the Righteous. The expression "Righteous Among the Nations" comes from rabbinic literature. In a compilation of Jewish oral law called the Tosefta, Rabbi Joshua claimed that the "righteous among the nations" have a portion in the "world to come."[17] In the Talmud, Rab Judah speaks of the "thirty righteous men among the nations of the world by whose virtue the nations of the world continue to exist."[18]

Yad Vashem's initiative is laudable. Yet, we should feel uncomfortable with its description of a "righteous" person. To be a *tsaddiq* it is not enough to be charitable, even if this charity would cost this person his life. At stake are the *motives* of the charitable person. Rabbi Eliezer said that all the charity

---

17. Tosefta Sanhedrin 13:2.
18. Talmud: Hullin 92a.

done by the heathen is counted to them as sin, because they only do it to magnify themselves.[19] Of course, this does not hold for *all* pagans, and it also holds for some Israelites, but the point is well taken. Charity has limited value if it is not done out of true love for the neighbor *and* out of obedience to God and to honor him. Therefore, Isaiah says that even "our righteous deeds" — "righteous" according to human-secular standards — may be "like a polluted garment" (Isa. 64:6).

This is the same as what Jesus expressed in the following way: "[W]hen you fast, do not look gloomy like the hypocrites, for they disfigure their faces that their fasting may be seen by others. Truly, I say to you, they have received their reward. But when you fast, anoint your head and wash your face, that your fasting may not be seen by others but by your Father who is in secret. And your Father who sees in secret will reward you" (Matt. 6:16–18). In other words, this is not the kind of righteousness that the Father desires.

2.5 Further Characteristics of the *Tsaddiq*
2.5.1 What He Is

Apart from the three general characteristics of the *tsaddiq* given in §2.4.3, the Old Testament knows several elaborate descriptions of the *tsaddiq*. Some of the best-known passages are the following six:

(a) "O LORD, who shall sojourn in your tent? Who shall dwell on your holy hill [i.e., in (the courts of) the temple]? He who walks blamelessly [*tamim*] and does what is right (*tsedeq*) and speaks truth [*emet*] in his heart; who does not slander with his tongue and does no evil to his neighbor, nor takes up a reproach against his friend; in whose eyes a vile person is despised, but who honors those who fear the LORD; who swears to his own hurt and does not change; who does not put out his money at interest and does not take a bribe against the innocent" (Ps. 15:2–5). Compare Psalm 24:3–4, "Who shall

---

19. Talmud: Baba Bathra 10b, referring to an exceptional translation of Prov. 14:34b ("the kindness of the peoples is sin").

ascend the hill of the LORD? And who shall stand in his holy place? He who has clean hands and a pure heart, who does not lift up his soul to what is false and does not swear deceitfully."

(b) The *tsaddiq* is "[h]e who walks righteously [*tsedaqot*] and speaks uprightly [*yesharim*], who despises the gain of oppressions, who shakes his hands, lest they hold a bribe, who stops his ears from hearing of bloodshed and shuts his eyes from looking on evil" (Isa. 33:15). Compare Isaiah 58:6-7, "Is not this the fast that I choose: to loose the bonds of wickedness, to undo the straps of the yoke, to let the oppressed go free, and to break every yoke? Is it not to share your bread with the hungry and bring the homeless poor into your house; when you see the naked, to cover him, and not to hide yourself from your own flesh?"

(c) "If a man is righteous [*tsaddiq*] and does what is just [*mishpat*] and right [*tsedaqah*] — if he does not eat upon the mountains or lift up his eyes to the idols of the house of Israel, does not defile his neighbor's wife or approach a woman in her time of menstrual impurity, does not oppress anyone, but restores to the debtor his pledge, commits no robbery, gives his bread to the hungry and covers the naked with a garment, does not lend at interest or take any profit, withholds his hand from injustice ['*avel*], executes true justice [*mishpat emet*] between man and man, walks in my statutes, and keeps my rules by acting faithfully [*emet*] — he is righteous [*tsaddiq*]; he shall surely live" (Ezek. 18:5-9). Compare Matthew 25:35-36, "I was hungry and you gave me food, I was thirsty and you gave me drink, I was a stranger and you welcomed me, I was naked and you clothed me, I was sick and you visited me, I was in prison and you came to me."

First, notice the various terms that express the idea of righteousness (besides *tsedeq/tsedaqah* these are terms such as *tamim*, *yesharim* and *mishpat*).

Second, notice the fact that virtually all of the Ten Commandments are implicitly referred to in these three passages.

Third, notice the strong emphasis on the person's horizontal relationships, that is, much more on "love your neighbor" than on "love God." Even where Psalm 15 speaks of "those who fear the LORD," the *tsaddiq* is not described as the one who fears the LORD but as the one who honors those who do so. Of course, this does not mean that the love and the fear of the LORD are not important. So why this emphasis on the horizontal dimension? There is a very practical reason for this. If we say we love God, how can we prove this? We can do so by worshipping him and diligently study his Word. But even if we say we *apply* this Word in a practical way, or if we say we serve the LORD, the *direction* of such application and service is mostly horizontal.

For example, we serve the Lord by being apostles, prophets, evangelists, pastors and teachers (Eph. 4:11), but in practice this always means equipping the saints (v. 12). He who serves only people, not the Lord, is not a *tsaddiq*. But he who loves the Lord will prove this best by serving God's people. In the New Testament, this is underscored by the apostle John: "If anyone says, 'I love God,' and hates his brother, he is a liar; for he who does not love his brother whom he has seen cannot love God whom he has not seen. And this commandment we have from him: whoever loves God must also love his brother. Everyone who believes that Jesus is the Christ has been born of God, and everyone who loves the Father loves whoever has been born of him. By this we know that we love the children of God, when we love God and obey his commandments" (1 John 4:20–5:2; cf. 2:9–11; 3:10, 14).

2.5.2 What He is Not

The Old Testament gives us a very high picture of the *tsaddiq*, but never suggests that he is to be perfect. Even where it describes a believer as "blameless," such as Noah (Gen. 6:9), David (2 Sam. 22:14; Ps. 18:23), Job (Job 1:1, 8; 2:3), Daniel (Dan. 6:22) or Saul of Tarsus (Phil. 3:6), or expects him/them to be "blameless," such as Abraham (Gen. 17:1) or Israel (Deut. 18:13), this never means "sinless, perfect." In Psalm 19:13, the term "blameless" is parallel with "innocent of great transgression," whereby David avoids the common weaknesses of everyday life. To be sure, these weaknesses are sins too, and they need divine forgiveness; but they are an illustration of James' practical wisdom: "we all stumble in many ways" (3:2). In §2.1.3, I gave a number of references showing that the Old Testament knows very well about the sinfulness of all people, including the righteous.

To mention some examples: the same David who says, "I was blameless before him, and I kept myself from my guilt" (Ps. 18:23), says at another occasion, "Wash me thoroughly from my iniquity, and cleanse me from my sin! For I know my transgressions, and my sin is ever before me. Against you, you only, have I sinned and done what is evil in your sight. . . . . . Behold, I was brought forth in iniquity, and in sin did my mother conceive me. . . . Purge me with hyssop, and I shall be clean; wash me, and I shall be whiter than snow" (51:4–7). The same Bible book in which Israel testifies: "All this has come upon us, though we have not forgotten you, and we have not been false to your covenant. Our heart has not turned back, nor have our steps departed from your way" (Ps. 44:17–18), also says, "If you, O LORD, should mark iniquities, O LORD, who could stand? But with you there is forgiveness, that you may be feared" (130:3–4; cf. 86:5). The same prophet Isaiah, who so strongly emphasizes doing practical righteousness (see, e.g., 5:23; 26:9–10; 33:15; 46:12; 48:1; 56:1; 58:2; 61:3, 10), once called out: "Woe is me! For I am lost; for I am a man of unclean lips, and I dwell in the midst of a people of unclean lips" (6:5), while the seraph replied to him: "your guilt is taken away, and your sin atoned for" (v. 7).

On the one hand, the emphasis on righteousness never implies sinlessness. On the other hand, the reference to sins even in the *tsaddiq* never implies an excuse for sinning. Not only the New Testament (1 Tim. 6:11; 2 Tim. 2:22) but also the Old

Testament knows about "pursuing" righteousness: the Lord "loves him who pursues righteousness" (Prov. 15:9). "Listen to me, you who pursue righteousness, you who seek the LORD" (Isa. 51:1). I mention here again the three characteristics of the *tsaddiq*: (a) he has the *power* to pursue righteousness because God makes this power available to him, (b) he *loves* pursuing righteousness because he has an "upright heart" due to regeneration (1 Kings 3:6; Ps. 36:10; 64:10; 94:15; 97:11; 119:7), and (c) he does so out of *obedience* to God's Torah—an obedience in which he can fail.

The *tsaddiq* is not perfect, just forgiven. Solomon makes this remarkable statement: "[T]he righteous falls seven times and rises again" (Prov. 24:16). It is not characteristic of the *tsaddiq* that he falls so often—not only into troubles but also into sins—but that he gets up again, repenting of his sins, accepting the forgiveness of the LORD, and picking up the trail of righteousness again. He may sin, but he still has his regenerate heart, he still loves the LORD and his people, he still loves to observe his Torah, and he may still appeal, not only to the forgiving heart of God, but also to his power to embark again on the pathway of righteousness.

2.6 The Faith of Abraham
2.6.1 Abraham and His Predecessors

In §2.4.1 I mentioned three characteristics of the *tsaddiq*: spiritual power drawn from God, obedience to the Torah, love for God and his people. To this point I have not mentioned faith in God. Readers may be amazed about that, especially because the *sola fide* ("by faith alone") is at the heart of Lutheran and Reformed theology. To go straight to the point: the *sola* is a bit exaggerated. If someone would believe in God, but (a) not exhibit the power of God, (b) not observe God's commandments, and (c) not exhibit the love for God and his people, *he is not justified*, that is, he is no *tsaddiq*. Genuine faith is always associated with the love and the power of God within believers, and with their true obedience. I do not object to saying that we are justified "by faith alone," as long as we hasten to add that this must be *genuine* faith. That is faith exhibiting (a) the power of God, (b) obedience to his commandments, and (c) the love for God and his people.

To be sure, the notion of faith in connection with righteousness and justification is not reserved for the New Testament. On the contrary, the apostles do refer to the Old Testament to lay this connection. The two great examples are Abraham and Habbakuk, apart from a few other references such as: "Open the gates, that the righteous nation that keeps faith may enter in" (Isa. 26:2).

Although in Romans 4 Paul refers to Abraham as "righteous" the latter certainly was not the first *tsaddiq*. Abel is the first who is described as such: "the blood of righteous Abel" (Matt. 23:35). "By faith Abel offered to God a more acceptable sacrifice than Cain, through which he was commended as righteous" (Heb. 11:4).[20] Although this reference is from the New Testament, Abel is the first one with whom the connection between faith and righteousness was explicitly made.

Of course, there were other pre-Abram *tsaddiqim*. Sirach 49:16 says, "Shem, Seth, and Enosh were highly honored, but Adam's glory was above that of any other living being." Then there was Enoch: "Enoch walked with God, and he was not, for God took him" (Gen. 5:24). As Sirach says, "Enoch pleased the LORD and was taken up into heaven. He became an inspiration for repentance for all time to come" (44:16). "No one else like Enoch has ever walked the face of the earth, for he was taken up from the earth" (49:14). Also Enoch was characterized by faith (Heb. 11:5).

Next was Noah: "Noah was a righteous man, blameless in his generation. Noah walked with God" (Gen. 6:9), and this again in connection with faith: "By faith Noah, being warned by God concerning events as yet unseen, in reverent fear constructed an ark for the saving of his household. By this he

---

20. Cf. Ouweneel (2009, 148–49).

condemned the world and became an heir of the righteousness that comes by faith" (Heb. 11:7). He was a "herald of righteousness" as well (2 Pet. 2:5).

Nonetheless, it is Abraham who is mentioned in Romans 4 as the great example of an Old Testament *tsaddiq* because he, not Abel, Enoch or Noah, has become the father of a family of faith (although Enoch and Noah were forefathers of his, and thus forefathers of this same family; Gen. 5; 11:10-26). Abraham became "the father of all who believe without being circumcised [i.e., Gentiles], so that righteousness would be counted to them as well," and he became "the father of the circumcised [i.e., Israel] who are not merely circumcised but who also walk in the footsteps of the faith that our father Abraham had before he was circumcised" (Rom. 4:11-12). "Was not Abraham found faithful in temptation, and it was reputed to him unto justice?" (1 Macc. 2:52 DRA).

In the deuterocanonical Prayer of Manasseh, the repentant king speaks of "the righteous," namely, "Abraham and Isaac and Jacob, who had not sinned against you." This may seem to be incorrect — all three committed sins — but it is just as true as God's words about "my servant David, who kept my commandments and followed me with all his heart, doing only that which was right in my eyes" (1 Kings 14:8). That is, when God looks back upon the lives of his saints, he sees only their righteousness; their unrighteousness is under the blood of the sacrifice.

Isaiah 51:1-2 refers those who "pursue righteousness" (cf. Rom. 9:30-31; 1 Tim. 6:11; 2 Tim. 2:22; also see 1 Thess. 5:15) to their father Abraham ("Look to Abraham your father and to Sarah who bore you; for he was but one when I called him, that I might bless him and multiply him"):[21] Here again, as with Abraham at first, the path to righteousness with God is through belief in the promises of God (Gen. 15:6).

---

21. Oswalt (1998, 335).

2.6.2 Faith Counted as Righteousness

Genesis 15:6 says, Abraham "believed the Lord, and he [i.e., the Lord] counted it to him [i.e., Abram] as righteousness." This verse plays a central role in Paul's argument concerning justification by faith (Rom. 4:3, 9, 18, 22; Gal. 3:6; see also James 2:23), and therefore also in the Protestant doctrine of justification. The expression "he counted it to him as righteousness" is not immediately transparent, and is therefore rendered in many different ways: "He accounted it to him for righteousness" (NKJV; cf. GNV), "he credited it to him as righteousness" (CJB, NIV, MEV; cf. WEB), "He reckoned it to him as righteousness" (RSV, NASB). Much more freely: "the Lord recognized Abram's high moral character" (CEB); "the Lord was pleased with him" (CEV); "because of this faith the Lord accepted him as one who has done what is right" (ERV); "because of this the Lord was pleased with him and accepted him" (GNT); "God declared him 'Set-Right-with-God'" (MSG); "God considered him righteous on account of his faith" (TLB).

If I may allow myself such a free rendering as well, I would prefer this last one (TLB). In my view, the CEB is simply wrong (Abram's moral character was not at stake). The CEV and GNT are too weak; the basic meaning of "righteousness" has disappeared here. The ERV is wrong because it suggests that faith itself is some "good work" — whereas Romans emphasizes that justification is not by works. Moreover, if this were the right approach, we would expect in the quotations not Greek *dikaiosynē* ("that which is right") but *dikaiōma* ("righteous claim" *or* "act") (see §1.4). However, this is not a simple matter. Take Phinehas, Aaron's grandson, who put an end to Israel's adultery (Num. 25:7–8): "And that was counted to him as righteousness from generation to generation forever" (Ps. 106:31). Here we definitely have to do with a righteous *act* that was counted to Phinehas "as righteousness" (cf. ERV, "He considered what Phinehas did a good work"). Is it possible to view Abram's faith in Genesis 15:6 analogously as a "righteous act"?

Before we move on, notice the remarkable "it" in our verse: "counted *it* to him as righteousness." In Hebrew, this is a feminine pronoun, which appears here as a suffix -*hâ* (*vayyahsebēhâ*) and does not seem to agree explicitly with anything in the passage.[22] It can only refer back to the verbal form *vehē'emin*, "and he believed," that is, to the noun that is enclosed in this: ēmunah: it was Abram's *faith* that was credited to him as righteousness, analogous to what we find in Habakkuk 2:4 (see §2.6). So we repeat our question: Is the point of Genesis 15:6 that "faith" itself is viewed as a "righteous act"?

Justin Martyr took the easy route out: he rendered verse 6b simply as *edikaiōthē*, Abraham was "justified" by God.[23] It cannot be denied that "counted it to him as righteousness" is correctly rendered as "justified him." This seems to be precisely the way that Paul read the verse: "For what does the Scripture say? 'Abraham believed God, and it was counted to him as righteousness'. . . . And to the one who does not work but believes in him who justifies the ungodly, his faith is counted as righteousness" (Rom. 4:3-5). And: ". . . just as Abraham 'believed God, and it was counted to him as righteousness'? And the Scripture, foreseeing that God would justify the Gentiles by faith . . ." (Gal. 3:6-8). And James says, "Was not Abraham our father justified by works when he offered up his son Isaac on the altar? You see that faith was active along with his works, and faith was completed by his works; and the Scripture was fulfilled that says, 'Abraham believed God, and it was counted to him as righteousness'" (James 2:23). In these three passages, the expressions "faith was counted to him as righteousness" and "he was justified (declared righteous) by faith" clearly seem to be identical.

The important word "to (ac)count, credit, reckon" (Heb., *ch-sh-b*, Greek, *logizomai*) will play a great role in chapter 4 below. Several misunderstandings in the Reformed doctrine of

---
22. Robertson (1990, 179).
23. Justin (*Dial.* 23.4).

justification are linked with it. But first we must enter into the question how we are to understand the connection between faith and righteousness in the case of Abraham. For the apostle Paul, faith must in no way be viewed as an achievement or a good work, as is obvious from his juxtaposition of faith and works in Romans 4:2-6 and 15-16. The expression "counting someone's faith for (or, as) righteousness" does not mean that the *value* (the strength, the contents) of faith as such is counted to someone as righteousness. Here it is *not*: "According to [the measure, strength, excellence of] your faith be it done to you" (Matt. 9:29). Paul's entire argument is precisely that our righteousness is not of human origin, but of God—the God to whom faith entrusts itself.

Gerrit C. Berkouwer rightly said, "But Abraham is at home in Romans 4 just because his righteousness was only that of faith, and thus exclusively the boon of divine promise. Lifted out of the cell of self by God's promise, abandoning himself to God's keeping, overpowered by the divine Word—that is how Paul sees Abraham, That is the believing man."[24] God declared Abraham to be righteous, not on account of any merit on his behalf, not even on account of the merit of his faith, but precisely because he expected nothing from himself but everything from God.[25] Even if unfortunately this was not always the case in his life, nevertheless it was the basic tenor of his existence.

2.6.3 The Content of Abraham's Faith

Usually people have realized insufficiently not only that Genesis 15:6 supplies us with a universal rule—justification by faith—but that the *content* of Abraham's faith corresponds remarkably with New Testament faith.[26] We just have to ask the question: *How* did Abraham believe? *What* did his faith expect from God, according to Genesis 15? This: that God

---

24. Berkouwer (1954, 83).
25. Cf. Verkuyl (1992, 309–10).
26. Vgl. Coates (n.d.-b, 34–35).

would make all his promises come true, not on account of Abraham's own merits, but on account of the "son of promise," Isaac, the son that had been promised *and* in whom God would make all his other promises come true. Likewise, New Testament faith is directed to the "Son of promise," Jesus, the Son who had been promised *and* in whom God would make all his other promises come true: "For the Son of God, Jesus Christ . . . was not Yes and No, but in him it is always Yes. For all the promises of God find their Yes in him. That is why it is through him that we utter our Amen to God for his glory" (2 Cor. 1:19–20). That is, in the Son of God all God's promises find their ground and fulfillment.

So much for Genesis 15. There is a subsequent point of equal importance in Genesis 17: Abraham and Sarah had become too old to bring forth children: "Shall a child be born to a man who is a hundred years old? Shall Sarah, who is ninety years old, bear a child?" (v. 17). Romans 4:19 speaks of Abraham's body being "as good as dead" (NKJV: "already dead"), where "dead" means "barren" (cf. Eph. 2:1 versus 4:17; 5:11). That is, Abraham needed God's strength to be able to father a child: "Sarah was not able to have children, and Abraham was too old. But he had faith in God, trusting him to do what he promised. And so God made them able to have children" (Heb. 11:11 ERV). This means concretely: the son can only be born as it were "through death," by the quickening power of God.

The third chapter of importance in this context is Genesis 22: Abraham had to give up his son unto death, "from which, figuratively speaking, he did receive him back" (Heb. 11:19). We can now refine the similarity we found: Abraham had to learn that God would fulfill all his promises, not just in and through the "son of promise," but through the son as having gone through death. God fulfills all his promises through the son as the one who had gone through death and God's resurrection power.

Today, believers have to learn precisely the same lesson, namely, that God will fulfill all his promises in and through the "Son of promise," that is, the Son as having gone through death and resurrection. This death is represented in:

(a) the peculiar sacrifice of Genesis 15:9–10 (which, like *all* sacrifices, points to that of Christ);

(b) the "death," that is, barrenness, of Abraham's body (Rom. 4:19), so that God only "through death" could make his promises come true;

(c) the figurative death and resurrection of Isaac (Gen. 22:1–18), which indicated anew how God realizes his promises.[27]

This is exactly the content of the New Testament faith: God makes his promises to humanity come true through the "Son of promise," who for us has gone through death and resurrection. The only thing that God asked of Abraham as well as of us is faith, that is, entrusting oneself to *that* God and to *that* resurrected Son.

This is the message of Romans 4. Abraham understood that everything depended on the "son of promise," and that in that respect nothing was to be expected from him or Sarah. Such a faith is not a merit in any way; it is a throwing oneself in God's arms, realizing that we have nothing to contribute but our own incapacity and sins, and that everything must come from God, who will act through this son/Son. Abraham and Sarah were not capable of producing life from death, but Abraham put all his confidence in God, deeply convinced that God was quite able to do so through him and Sarah. Abraham's faith originated from the profound consciousness of his own powerlessness and barrenness, and a complete and unconditional surrender to the life producing power of God. Thus, Paul could make a direct connection between the content of Abraham's faith and the content of our faith, of

---

27. See Mackintosh (n.d., 105–108); Grant (1890, 57; 1902, 93–94); Coates (n.d.-a, 123–26).

"us who believe in him who raised from the dead Jesus our Lord, who was delivered up for our trespasses and raised for our justification" (Rom. 4:24-25). Justification is not simply "through Christ," but through the dead and risen Christ.

Faith has here the root meaning of confidence (see more extensively chapters 6 and 7). Especially after his body was "already dead," and afterward when he had to sacrifice his son, Abraham did not see how God could ever realize his promises. But he trusted God, who afterward made his promises come true through death and resurrection, namely, the death and resurrection of his own Son. Confidence in God, even when we see no warrant for this and all possibilities seem to have been exhausted, is one of the most profound secrets and features of the true *tsaddiq*. In the words of Mother Basilea Schlink (founder of the Evangelical [Lutheran] Sisterhood of Mary in Darmstadt, Germany): "Say to God in your distress: my God, I do not understand you, but I do trust you."[28]

In summary, we can read Genesis 15:6 as follows: through his confidence in God — "all things are possible for one who believes" (Mark 9:23) — Abraham turned out to be a genuine *tsaddiq*, that is, God declared him to be a *tsaddiq*. He did not *become* this at this very moment, but he turned out to *be* one at this moment. The true *tsaddiq* comes to manifestation as such when all human possibilities are exhausted, and he can only entrust himself unconditionally to God, "in hope against hope" (Rom. 4:18).

2.7 The Faith of Habakkuk
2.7.1 Living by Faith

The characteristics of the true *tsaddiq* mentioned above are exactly the same as those that we find in Habakkuk 2:4b, "the righteous shall live by his faith."[29] The Septuagint reads here: "[T]he righteous shall live by *my* faith(fulness)" (Greek, *ek pisteōs mou*); some manuscripts also have this in Hebrews

---

28. See Schlink (2000).
29. See extensively, Robertson (1990, 175–83).

10:38. Possibly this means "faith *of* me" in the sense of "faith *in* me."³⁰ A similar construction is found elsewhere (Mark 11:22; Rom. 3:22, 26; Gal. 2:16, 20; 3:22; Phil. 3:9; James 2:1; Rev. 2:13; 14:12), whereby not all expositors agree that "faith of Christ" means "faith *in* Christ" (see §5.2.3).

The prophet Habakkuk could not understand anymore how God's righteousness could be maintained in the world, given the wickedness of Israel as well as the Chaldeans, who came to chastise Israel (Hab. 1). He had to learn that the true *tsaddiq*, that is, the one walking in the way of the Torah, is characterized by the fact that, even if all appearances are against God, he keeps trusting him. He says as it were: God, I do not understand what you are doing, or why you are doing (or allowing) certain things, or how you are going to put things back in order, but I trust you (cf. §2.6.3). In the words of Solomon: "Trust in the LORD with all your heart, and do not lean on your own understanding" (Prov. 3:5), that is, let your confidence in God not be proportional to the measure by which you can understand his doings, or by which you think you can handle the situation yourself. On the contrary, let it be proportional to God's own greatness.

The words of Habakkuk 2:4 are quoted three times in the New Testament: "For in it [i.e., in the gospel] the righteousness of God is revealed from faith for faith, as it is written, 'The righteous shall live by faith'" (Rom. 1:17). "Now it is evident that no one is justified before God by the law, for 'The righteous shall live by faith'" (Gal. 3:11). "[M]y righteous one shall live by faith, and if he shrinks back, my soul has no pleasure in him" (Heb. 10:38). Decades ago, I suggested that Hebrews 10:38 quotes the Habakkuk verse most closely to its original sense ("*living* as a righteous one"), whereas Paul rather quotes this verse to explain how one *becomes* a righteous person.³¹ Today I would not accentuate this alleged difference. When it comes to justification, faith (Greek, *pistis*) is hardly ever a sin-

---

30. Cf. Moo (1996, 76-77n65).
31. Ouweneel (1982, 2:48).

gle act at a single moment through which something happens at that very moment (justification). Rather, it usually refers to the more permanent attitude of faithfulness and confidence, as in the cases of Abraham and Habakkuk. Perhaps, the question in Romans is not: How do I *become* a *tsaddiq*? but rather: How do I learn to *live* like a *tsaddiq*? I return to this important point in the next chapter.

2.7.2 Application to Christ

It is quite remarkable that in Hebrews 10:37-38 this principle is also worked out in a Christological sense: "Yet a little while, and the coming one (Greek, *ho erchomenos*) will come and will not delay; but my righteous one shall live by faith, and if he shrinks back, my soul has no pleasure in him."[32] This is the Septuagint version of Habakkuk 2:3-4, in which this "he" must be the Messiah or God. Later Jewish expositors applied the passage to the Messiah. "The coming one" or "he who will come" (Heb., *habba*) was a well-known expression for the Messiah, as is evident from John the Baptist's question: "Are you the one who is to come (*ho erchomenos*), or shall we look for another?" (Matt. 11:3; cf. 23:39). Also compare the shout of the multitude: "Blessed is he who comes (*ho erchomenos*) in the name of the Lord" (21:9; cf. Ps. 118:26), and Jesus' own word: "He who comes (*ho erchomenos*) from heaven is above all" (John 3:31; cf. 6:33).

Once the Messiah will have come, there will be hardly any room left for faith in this form. As Paul says, "[W]e walk by faith, not by sight" (2 Cor. 5:7). Soon, God's people will walk by "sight," be it in the Messianic Kingdom on earth or in heavenly bliss. "For the earth will be filled with the knowledge of the glory of the LORD as the waters cover the sea" (Hab. 2:14; cf. Num. 14:21; Ps. 57:5, 11; 72:19; Isa. 11:9). Then, all things will be brought into harmony with God, and all evil will be bridled. In those days, it will not be hard to trust God. However, as long as the Messiah is delayed, the *tsaddiqim* must

---

32. Ibid.

live by the power of their faith—that is both faithfulness and confidence—which, though not yet seeing the full redemption, counts upon God, and with perseverance expects the end result from him (cf. Heb. 10:36, "For you have need of endurance, so that when you have done the will of God you may receive what is promised"; James 5:7-9, "Be patient, therefore, brothers, until the coming of the Lord.... Establish your hearts, for the coming of the Lord is at hand ... behold, the Judge is standing at the door"). The *tsaddiq* will save his life, and ultimately enter into "everlasting life."[33]

O. Palmer Robertson points out that the root meaning of Hebrew *emunah* ("faith") is "steadfastness" (from '*-m-n*, "to be sure, certain, steady, steadfast").[34] Habakkuk 2:4 is not about "coming to faith" but about a steadfast confidence in God, whatever the circumstances may be, through all possible troubles. The *tsaddiq* lives out of this confidence. This is expressed by the arguably superior rendering of Psalm 119:30 (Heb., *derek-emunah*), "the way of faithfulness" (ESV, NIV, CEB, RSV, etc.) or "the way of loyalty" (NABRE; cf. ERV), that is, the way of steadfast confidence.[35]

Faith in the sense of steadfast confidence is also found elsewhere in the Old Testament, sometimes in contexts where related terms are used. For example, the *tsaddiqim* are those "who take refuge in him" (Ps. 34:22). "The salvation of the righteous is from the LORD; he is their stronghold in the time of trouble. The LORD helps them and delivers them; he delivers them from the wicked and saves them, because they take refuge in him" (37:39-40). "Let the righteous one rejoice in the LORD and take refuge in him" (64:10). Full of expectation do they look out for him: "The hope of the righteous brings joy, but the expectation of the wicked will perish" (Prov. 10:28). "The name of the LORD is a strong tower; the righteous man runs into it and is safe" (18:10). And as to the term "steadfast":

---

33. See Ouweneel (2010a, §4.1).
34. Robertson (1990, 179); the word "Amen" is derived from '*-m-n*.
35. Ibid., 180.

"You will keep in perfect peace those whose minds are steadfast, because they trust in you" (Isa. 26:3 NIV).

2.8 Eschatology and Righteousness
2.8.1 The Messianic Kingdom

Many of the Old Testament passages about the righteousness of God mentioned before (§1.8.1) have an especially eschatological significance, that is, are related to the coming of the Messiah and the establishment of his Kingdom. This holds for Messianic-prophetic Psalm words such as Psalm 22:32 ("they shall come and proclaim his righteousness to a people yet unborn, that he has done it") and 40:9–10 ("I have proclaimed the good news of righteousness in the great assembly; indeed, I do not restrain my lips, O LORD, You Yourself know. I have not hidden Your righteousness within my heart; I have declared Your faithfulness and Your salvation; I have not concealed Your lovingkindness and Your truth from the great assembly"; NKJV) (actually also 24:5; 48:10; 89:14–16; 98:1–2).

It holds especially for various passages in the second part of Isaiah, such as 45:21, "[T]here is no other god besides me, a righteous God and a Savior," and verse 25: "In the LORD all the offspring of Israel shall be justified [i.e., declared righteous, *or*, shall be done justice] and shall glory." Also see Isaiah 46:12–13 ("Listen to me, you stubborn of heart, you who are far from righteousness: I bring near my righteousness; it is not far off, and my salvation will not delay; I will put salvation in Zion, for Israel my glory"); 51:5–8 ("My righteousness draws near, my salvation has gone out, and my arms will judge the peoples; . . . my salvation will be forever, and my righteousness will never be dismayed. Listen to me, you who know righteousness, the people in whose heart is my Torah . . . my righteousness will be forever, and my salvation to all generations"); 53:11 ("by his knowledge shall the righteous one, my servant, make many to be accounted righteous, and he shall bear their iniquities"); 56:1 ("Keep justice, and do righteousness, for soon my salvation will come, and my righteousness be revealed").

These passages are also of interest: Isaiah 58:8 ("Then shall your light break forth like the dawn . . .; your righteousness shall go before you; the glory of the LORD shall be your rear guard"); 60:21 ("Your people shall all be righteous; they shall possess the land forever, the branch of my planting, the work of my hands, that I might be glorified"); 62:1–2 ("For . . . Jerusalem's sake I will not be quiet, until her righteousness goes forth as brightness, and her salvation as a burning torch. The nations shall see your righteousness, and all the kings your glory").

In these and other passages, the two eschatological aspects of God's righteousness are clearly visible: judgment for the wicked, and redemption for God's *tsaddiqim*. Isaiah again: "For when your judgments are in the earth, the inhabitants of the world learn righteousness. If favor is shown to the wicked, he does not learn righteousness; in the land of uprightness he deals corruptly and does not see the majesty of the LORD" (26:9b–10). In other passages, the term "righteousness" is parallel with the term "salvation," or the term "righteousness" as such is to be understood in the sense of "deliverance" (see Isa. 40:9–10, where the ESV renders *tsedaqah* as "deliverance").

2.8.2 The New Covenant

As far as the eschatological significance of the notion of "God's righteousness" is concerned, we think particularly of the establishment of the New Covenant with the house of Israel and the house of Judah:[36] "[T]his is the covenant that I will make with the house of Israel after those days . . .: I will put my Torah within them, and I will write it on their hearts. And I will be their God, and they shall be my people. And no longer shall each one teach his neighbor and each his brother, saying, 'Know the LORD,' for they shall all know me, from the least of them to the greatest, declares the LORD. For I will forgive their iniquity, and I will remember their sin no more"

---
36. See extensively, Ouweneel (2015b, §9.5.2).

(Jer. 31:33–34).

In 2 Corinthians 3, this description of the New Covenant implicitly plays an important role.[37] Paul describes himself and his collaborators as "ministers of a new covenant" (v. 6). Just as Paul presents the "ministry of reconciliation" in chapter 5:18–20,[38] we could say that chapter 3 deals with the "ministry of the New Covenant." Apparently, Paul distinguishes two parts in this, namely, the "ministry of the Spirit" (v. 8) and the "ministry of righteousness" (v. 9), parallel with the relationship between the gift of the Spirit and the righteousness of faith in Galatians 3:3–14.[39]

These two ministries correspond precisely with the two parts in the establishment of the New Covenant:

(a) The ministry of the Spirit corresponds with the words: "I will put my Torah within them, and I will write it on their hearts," in which Paul replaces "Torah" by "Christ," who is the Eternal Torah:[40] "You . . . show that you are a letter from Christ delivered by us, written not with ink but with the Spirit of the living God, not on tablets of stone but on tablets of human hearts" (2 Cor. 3:3). It is the ministry of the Spirit, through God's preachers, to write Christ on the hearts of the believers.

(b) The ministry of righteousness corresponds with the words: "I will forgive their iniquity, and I will remember their sin no more." This is a remarkable description: God administers so to say *his* righteousness to us by forgiving us our *un*-righteousnesses. God is righteous when he justifies (declares righteous) the repentant unrighteous (Rom. 3:26; 1 John 1:9).

In Jeremiah 31:30, it is—under the Old Covenant—righteous of God that "everyone shall die for his own iniquity" (cf. vv. 14–15). Under the New Covenant, there will be no restoration without chastisement: "I will correct you in justice"

---

37. Ibid.
38. See Ouweneel (2009, §§10.2–10.3).
39. Coates (1926, 65–66).
40. See extensively, Ouweneel (2015a, §6.1.2).

(30:11 NKJV). Yet, the miracle will be seen that God will be *righteous* when he will forgive the iniquities of his people. The key to understanding this lies in him who is called "righteousness": "Behold, the days are coming . . . when I will fulfill the promise I made to the house of Israel and the house of Judah. In those days and at that time I will cause a *righteous Branch* [lit., a *Branch of righteousness*] to spring up for David, and he shall execute justice and righteousness in the land. In those days Judah will be saved, and Jerusalem will dwell securely. And this is the name by which it will be called: 'The LORD is our righteousness'" (33:14–16; cf. 23:1, 5). The God who chastised his people "in justice," will forgive his people "in justice," on account of the fact that "justice" (or "righteousness") turns out to have a name: Messiah, Son of David. Compare Paul's word: ". . . Christ Jesus, who became to us wisdom from God, righteousness and sanctification and redemption" (1 Cor. 1:30).

2.8.3 Individual Versus Collective

Reformed theology has often given the impression that justification by faith is a strictly individual matter. Notice the Heidelberg Catechism Q&A 56 (God "graciously imputes to *me* the righteousness of Christ"), 59 ("*I* am righteous in Christ before God"), 60 (God . . . grants and imputes to *me* the . . . righteousness . . . of Christ"), and 61 ("because only the . . . righteousness . . . of Christ is *my* righteousness before God"). This idea could originate by a unilateral emphasis on the individual aspects of salvation, and much less on the collective-eschatological aspects. Righteousness is not just a personal possession. God not only made his individual children to be the "righteousness of God" (2 Cor. 5:21), but one day the whole earth will be filled with God's righteousness: "Shower, O heavens, from above, and let the clouds rain down righteousness; let the earth open, that salvation and righteousness may bear fruit; let the earth cause them both to sprout; I the LORD have created it" (Isa. 45:8). "For as the earth brings forth its sprouts, and as a garden causes what is sown in it to sprout up, so the LORD God will cause righteousness and praise to sprout up before all the nations" (61:11; cf. 2 Pet. 3:13, "we are waiting for new heavens and a new earth in which righteousness dwells").

The Bible focuses not just on the salvation, the reconciliation, the regeneration, the justification, and the sanctification of certain individuals, but on that of all things: "The Father loves the Son and has given *all things* into his hand" (John 3:35; cf. 13:3; 1 Cor. 15:27-28; Eph. 1:22; 4:10; Heb. 1:2); ". . . Jesus, whom heaven must receive until the time for restoring *all the things*" (Acts 3:21). "For from him and through him and to him are *all things*" (Rom. 11:36). Jesus, "who will transform our lowly body to be like his glorious body, by the power that enables him even to subject *all things* to himself" (Phil. 3:21). "For in him all the fullness of God was pleased to dwell, and through him to reconcile to himself *all things*, whether on earth or in heaven" (Col. 1:19-20). "And he who was seated on the throne said, 'Behold, I am making *all things* new'" (Rev. 21:5).

This does not mean that all *people* will ultimately be saved, reconciled, justified and sanctified,[41] but it does mean that the whole *cosmos* will ultimately share in the blessings of salvation, reconciliation, regeneration, justification, and sanctification: "Behold, the Lamb of God, who takes away the sin of the *world!*" (John 1:29). Not the *sins* of the world—as it daily resounds in many Roman Catholic masses: *Agnus Dei qui tollis peccata* [instead of *peccatum*] *mundi*—but sin as the dirty smudge that has stained the cosmos. Not all *people* will be reconciled, but the *cosmos* will be reconciled. Therefore, to avoid creating any misunderstanding, it is better to translate 1 John 1:2 not as: "He is the propitiation for our sins, and not for ours only but also for the sins of the whole world" (ESV and many others), but as: "He Himself is the propitiation for our

---

41. Heidelberg Catechism (Lord's Day 7).

sins, and not for ours only but also *for the whole world*" (NKJV, Darby; Greek, *alla kai peri holou tou kosmou*).[42] Compare the distinction in Colossians 1 between *all things* on earth and in heaven that are reconciled (vv. 19-20) and the believers who are reconciled (vv. 21-22).

The actual point I am stressing right now is that salvation, reconciliation, regeneration, justification, and sanctification do not encompass all people—because many people have refused to embrace Christ in faith—but they do encompass the *cosmos*. God has loved the *cosmos* (John 3:16), Christ is the Savior of the *cosmos* (4:42; 1 John 4:14). The ultimate purpose of God's salvation can never be less than that. In the end, soteriology is always about the worldwide Kingdom of God as the embodiment of all salvation, peace, redemption, reconciliation, justification, and sanctification.

In the picture of the total renewal in Revelation 21:1-8 ("new heavens and a new earth in which righteousness dwells," 2 Pet. 3:13), we are struck by the great exception of verse 8: "But as for the cowardly, the faithless, the detestable, as for murderers, the sexually immoral, sorcerers, idolaters, and all liars, their portion will be in the lake that burns with fire and sulfur, which is the second death." It forms an absolute contrast with the blissful new heavens and earth of verses 1-7, except in one respect: in the lake of fire, too, *righteousness will dwell*. Also in the "eternal punishment" (Matt. 25:46; 2 Thess. 1:7-9), God's righteousness will come to light in a perfect way: "As I hear, I [i.e., Jesus] judge, and my judgment is just" (John 5:30), whether it concerns the righteous or the wicked. He judges the world "in righteousness" (Acts 17:31; cf. Rom. 2:5).[43]

In this context, the following words from Wisdom 12:15

---

42. Cf. the L in the well-known Reformed abbreviation: "Limited Atonement" (i.e., though Jesus' sacrifice was sufficient for all, it is efficacious only for the elect) ("for our sake," 2 Cor. 5:21; "our sins," 1 Cor. 15:3; Gal. 1:4; 1 Pet. 2:24; 1 John 4:10; Rev. 1:5).
43. See Van de Beek (2008).

are of interest: "You [i.e., God] are righteous, and you rule everything righteously. You have never used your power to condemn a person who does not deserve to be punished"; and verses 25-26, "[Y]ou punished them for their stupidity, and your judgment made them look like fools. It was a light punishment, but those who pay no attention to such warnings deserve to feel the full weight of God's judgment."

All in all, we may say in summary that God is righteous in condemning the wicked, and he is righteous in saving believers. Not because believers in themselves are any better than the wicked but because they have found refuge in God himself for their salvation — in New Testament language: they have found refuge in Christ, who in person has become their righteousness (1 Cor. 1:30).

2.9 The Righteousness of the Torah
2.9.1 Two Sides of the Torah

In order to understand how Scripture views the relationship between righteousness and faith, we must now enter into the question how Scripture views the relationship between righteousness and the Torah. At the beginning of this chapter, we saw that, on the one hand, justification by faith stands in opposition to justification by works of the Torah, while, on the other hand, the justified person observes God's Torah — the "Torah of Christ" (1 Cor. 9:21; Gal. 6:2) — and in James' terminology is even "justified" (proven to be righteous) by such works (James 2:24). These two apparently contradictory matters are true at the same time: the Torah stands in opposition to faith *and* it forms the extension of faith. There is no true faith that does not prove itself through good works, and these works are demanded by the Torah of Christ. In other words, divine justification by faith without works resulting from this faith is impossible. Divine justification by works without faith (and love) toward God is also impossible.

In the first volume of this series, I have extensively pointed out that Paul speaks about *nomos* (law, Torah) in roughly two ways.[44] In the positive sense, it is the *Torah of love* (Rom. 13:8-10; Gal. 5:13-14; cf. Matt. 22:36-40), the *Messianic Torah* (1 Cor. 9:21; Gal. 6:2); also compare James' terms: the *royal Torah* (James 2:8, the "Torah of the Kingdom") and the *Torah of freedom* (1:25; 2:12). Love, the divine *agapē*, is the sum and fulfillment of this Torah. In Jesus, this love of God has been revealed in its most perfect form. In believers, this love of God takes shape in their observance of Jesus' commandments: "If you love me, you will keep my commandments. . . . Whoever has my commandments and keeps them, he it is who loves me. And he who loves me will be loved by my Father, and I will love him [i.e., that person] and manifest myself to him. . . .If anyone loves me, he will keep my word, and my Father will love him, and we will come to him and make our home with him. Whoever does not love me does not keep my words. And the word that you hear is not mine but the Father's who sent me" (John 14:15, 21-24).

"We love because he first loved us. If anyone says, 'I love God,' and hates his brother, he is a liar; for he who does not love his brother whom he has seen cannot love God whom he has not seen. And this commandment we have from him: whoever loves God must also love his brother. By this we know that we love the children of God, when we love God and obey his commandments. For this is the love of God, that we keep his commandments" (1 John 4:19-5:3; cf. 2:3). "And this is love, that we walk according to his commandments" (2 John 1:6). This is the true *tsaddiq*: he lives by God's love, and for love (toward God, Christ, and God's people), as observing God's (or Christ's) Torah. One who loves (or claims to love) without obeying the Torah is not a *tsaddiq*. Nor is one who obeys the Torah without true love.

The other way in which the word *nomos* (law, Torah) is used especially by Paul is in the sense of legalism or ethnocentrism. Legalism is the polity that requires works that sat-

---

44. Ouweneel (2015a, §1.4).

isfy the Torah and through which one tries to earn points for heaven, or even endeavors to bring about one's own salvation, in one's own strength. This is the traditional view concerning the negative meaning of the Torah. Ethnocentrism is the polity that arrogantly boasts in Israel as God's covenantal people, and requires the circumcision of repenting Gentile males in order to join God's chosen people, and thus share their blessings (newer view of James Dunn).[45]

Now the point is that, sometimes, this legalistic and/or ethnocentric polity as such is briefly called *nomos* by Paul (cf. Rom. 2:12, 17, 23; 3:19, 31; 4:14–15; 5:20; 6:14; etc.). In the latter sense – *nomos* as "legalism" – *nomos* is the "ministry of death" and the "ministry of condemnation" (2 Cor. 3:7, 9), a polity that "brings wrath" (Rom. 4:15) and brings people "under a curse" (Gal. 3:10). This horrific effect of the law is a consequence of the fact that no one can observe the Torah in his own strength. Whoever still tries to accomplish this will undergo the consequences: death, condemnation, wrath, curse. In *this* sense, and in this sense alone – that is, in opposition to any form of antinomianism – the believer can say with Paul that he has been "released from the law" (Rom. 7:2, 6; 8:2), has "through the law died to the law" (Gal. 2:19; cf. Rom. 7:4), that is, has been released from, or has died to, *legalism*. The person concerned is no longer part of a polity in which it is expected that people accomplish the Torah in their own strength, with an unregenerate heart and without the power of the Holy Spirit (if such a polity ever existed; if it was, it was purely man-made). *Such a legalist can never be a true* tsaddiq *either*.

2.9.2 Legalism: Augmenting the Law

It is important in this context to get a clear view of what le-

---

45. See especially Dunn (1998, 128–61, 354–71, 631–58), and references to earlier literature. Dunn's interpretation of expressions such as "under the law," "works of the law," "released from the law," in the light of his view concerning Israel's ethnocentric arrogance is clarifying and fruitful, but seems to me equally as unilateral as the traditional view.

galism is.[46] I briefly mention its most characteristic features. First, the legalist is never a genuine *tsaddiq*, but in general he is not overtly wicked either. He could be best described as a *pseudo-tsaddiq*, a hypocrite (i.e., lit., an actor): he *plays* the *tsaddiq*, but denies the essence of it: "having the appearance of godliness, but denying its power" (2 Tim. 3:5).

The legalistic person is first of all one who places himself under all kinds of prohibitions and commandments about which Scripture does not express itself. Thus, the Pharisees had surrounded the Torah by a thick layer of man-made commandments. It is against this "tradition of the elders" (i.e., the forefathers) that Jesus utters a strong protest (Matt. 15:1-9; Mark 7:1-23). It is this *adding* to the Word that is one of the most conspicuous characteristics of legalism. Many denominations have rules that cannot be found in many other denominations, rules that cannot be derived from the Bible either. This in spite of false attempts to do so; as Shakespeare says in his *Othello* (Act 1, Scene 3): "The devil can cite Scripture for his purpose." As an example, I know Reformed denominations where alcohol is taboo but television sets are no problem—and Reformed denominations where it is the reverse.

It is also typical for the true legalist that he not only follows a narrow pathway for himself but that he loves to show off, not only toward other people but sometimes even toward God, because he is convinced that his strict legalism is pleasing to God: "God, I thank you that I am not like other men, extortioners, unjust, adulterers, or even like this tax collector. I fast twice a week; I give tithes of all that I get" (Luke 18:11-12). He feels elevated above other people because he is so much stricter than they are. If he gets a chance, he loves to put these same things also on the shoulders of others. He is someone who preaches Christianity primarily as a system of prescriptions and prohibitions, and continually bothers other people therewith. It is similar to what many religious leaders

---

46. Cf. Ouweneel (1994, 106–109).

in Israel did in Jesus' day: "The scribes and the Pharisees sit on Moses' seat. . . . They tie up heavy burdens, hard to bear, and lay them on people's shoulders, but they themselves are not willing to move them with their finger" (Matt. 23:2-4).

It is this attitude that Paul is fighting in Romans 14, regarding the question of what to eat and drink, and what not. In opposition to this, Paul says, "[T]he kingdom of God is not a matter of eating and drinking but of righteousness and peace and joy in the Holy Spirit. Whoever thus serves Christ is acceptable to God and approved by men" (vv. 17-18).

It is remarkable that very often such legalistic commandments concern purely external and trivial matters, such as drinking wine or not (cf. Rom. 14:21): "Woe to you, scribes and Pharisees, hypocrites! For you tithe mint and dill and cumin, and have neglected the weightier matters of the law: justice and mercy and faithfulness. These you ought to have done, without neglecting the others. You blind guides, straining out a gnat and swallowing a camel" (vv. 23-24). Here "justice" does not refer to the judgment of God, but to one of three characteristics of the true *tsaddiq*. Because of the Pharisees' meticulous approach to the Torah, they often lost sight of its essence: (1) practicing justice and righteousness, (2) love and mercy,[47] and (3) faithfulness. This explains the metaphor of gnat and camel. The Jews strain their wine through a sieve in order to remove tiny unclean animals from it, such as gnats (Lev. 11:20-23). But a camel floating around in their cup (v. 4) is easily overlooked and quietly swallowed. Forgetting to pay the tithes of dill and cumin is a "gnat"; forgetting love and faithfulness toward God and people is a "camel." This hilarious contrast is of the same order as that between speck and

---

47. Cf. Matt. 5:7 ("Blessed are the merciful, for they shall receive mercy") and Hos. 6:6 ("I desire *hesed*," i.e., steadfast love, mercy, quoted in Matt. 9:13 and 12:7). N.B. Luke 11:42 (lit., "the love of God") probably means "the love *for* God" (cf. CEB, CEV, ERV), so that the verse refers to justice toward our fellowmen and love toward God (Green, 1997, 472), whereas Matt. 23:23 rather seems to refer to justice and mercy toward other persons and faithfulness toward God.

log (Matt. 7:3), and between needle and camel (Matt. 19:24). In Aramaic, the word play is even more striking: you strain out the *qalma* but swallow the *gamla*.⁴⁸

2.9.3 Legalism: Attenuating the Law

One of the most peculiar features of legalism is that, on the one hand, it makes a very strict, severe impression, but on the other hand, it takes God's commandments far too lightly. Every legalist has his own strict framework of commandments and prohibitions, within which he behaves meticulously, but outside this framework he thinks he can do as he pleases.

Mark 7:9-12 gives a poignant example of this: "You have a fine way of rejecting the commandment of God in order to establish your tradition! For Moses said, 'Honor your father and your mother' [Exod. 20:12; Deut. 5:16; Eph. 5:2]; and, 'Whoever reviles father or mother must surely die.' [Exod. 21:17; Lev. 20:9; Deut. 27:16; Prov. 20:20] But you say, 'If a man tells his father or his mother, "Whatever you would have gained from me is Corban"' (that is, given to God) — then you no longer permit him to do anything for his father or mother, thus making void the word of God by your tradition that you have handed down. And many such things you do." The passage describes the situation that children officially identify their property as *corban*, that is, a gift consecrated to God. In such a case, according to the Pharisees, the commandment to honor one's parents — namely (in this case), by supporting them financially in emergency situations — came second. Thus, in many cases, the meticulously elaborate legislation surrounding the Torah had in fact become a hypocritical means to precisely *escape* the Torah.

Other examples can be given, especially from the Sermon on the Mount. Jesus said, "You have heard that it was said to those of old, 'You shall not murder; and whoever murders will be liable to judgment'" (Matt. 5:21). This probably means that the divine command, "You shall not murder," was robbed of

---

48. France (2007, 874).

its force by leaving cases of homicide to local courts. The command, "You shall not take the name of the LORD your God in vain" (Exod. 20:7), was robbed of its force by swearing not by the LORD, but by heaven, the earth, Jerusalem, or one's own head (Matt. 5:33–36). The command, "You shall love your neighbor," was robbed of its force by understanding "neighbor" as referring only to one's compatriots or friends, but not to one's enemies (vv. 43–44).

Perhaps this is the most characteristic feature: the legalistic person commands not to do certain things, or to do certain things, because the law prohibits or requires them, while deep in his heart he would love to do these very things, or omit doing them, respectively. The *tsaddiq*, however, omits doing certain things because they are an abomination *to his heart* (cf. Prov. 8:7), and does certain things because *his heart* desires to do them (cf. Ezra 7:10). In other words, the legalist does something because he *has to*, but the *tsaddiq* does something because he *wants* to. The legalist omits doing something because he is not *allowed* to do that, but the *tsaddiq* omits doing something because he does not *want to*.

This does not mean that the *tsaddiq* has nothing to do with the law (anymore); on the contrary, he finds his *delight* in the law because it requires of him, or prohibits him, the very things that he loves to do, or not to do (Ps. 1:2; 19:8; 119:16, 47, 70, 77, 92, 143, 174; Rom. 7:22). For the legalist, the law is a yoke (Acts 15:10), which goes against his nature; it is to him a "law of slavery." He will be all the prouder when he still observes the law so properly (Luke 18:11–12). For the *tsaddiq*, the law is a "law of freedom" (James 1:25; 2:12) because it does not require from him anything else than what he, that is, his new nature, desires.

Chapter 3
New Perspectives on Paul

Zechariah . . . and . . . Elizabeth . . .
  they were both righteous before God,
walking blamelessly
  in all the commandments and statutes of
the LORD.
Luke 1:5-6

For it is not the hearers of the Torah
  who are righteous before God,
but the doers of the Torah
  who will be justified.
Romans 2:13

What good is it, my brothers, if someone says he has faith
  but does not have works?
Can that faith save him? . . .
  faith by itself, if it does not have works, is dead . . .
Do you want to be shown, you foolish person,
  that faith apart from works is useless?
Was not Abraham our father justified by works
  when he offered up his son Isaac on the

> altar?
> You see that faith was active along with his works,
> > and faith was completed by his works . . .
>
> You see that a person is justified by works
> > and not by faith alone.
> >
> > James 2:14-24

Summary: *In order to properly understand Paul's view of contemporaneous Judaism, we first have to properly understand this Judaism ourselves. In this respect, much has changed, especially through Ed Sanders' work of 1977. Others, such as James Dunn and N. T. Wright, have also contributed to the "New Perspective(s) on Paul" (NPP). "Covenantal nomism" is the new key phrase (although rather little attention is paid to the role of the sacrifices, as well as to the views of present-day orthodox Jews). Paul's main problem with Judaism was not just its legalistic and ethnocentric aspects – although they were there – but the fact that it believed it was able to continue as it was even after Christ had come and had accomplished his sacrificial work. Many* **tsaddiqim** *did recognize Christ and found in him the fulfillment of their deepest convictions. Understandably, conflicts have broken out between advocates of NPP and traditional Reformed scholars, partly based on misunderstandings and confessionalism. The chapter ends with a summary of a number of exegetical and theological issues brought up by NPP. I suggest that in several respects middle roads between NPP and the traditional view will have to be sought.*

3.1 Paul and Judaism
3.1.1 A Proper View of Judaism

IN THE PREVIOUS CHAPTER, we have seen how Paul dealt with the negative aspects of *nomos* (law, Torah), namely, in the sense of legalism or ethnocentrism. Legalism is the attitude of people who believe they can accomplish their own salvation in their own strength. Ethnocentrism is the attitude of people who arrogantly boast in Israel as God's covenantal people, and require the circumcision of repenting Gentile males as a means to join God's chosen people, and thus share their blessings. This legalistic and/or ethnocentric polity as such is sometimes briefly called *nomos* by Paul (§2.9.1; cf. Rom. 2:12, 17, 23; 3:19, 31; 4:14–15; 5:20; 6:14; etc.). In this sense – *nomos* as "legalism" – *nomos* is the "ministry of death" and the "ministry of condemnation" (2 Cor. 3:7, 9), a polity that "brings wrath" (Rom. 4:15), and brings people "under a curse" (Gal. 3:10), because no one can observe the Torah in his own strength. In *this* sense, the believer can say that he has been "released from the law" (Rom. 7:2, 6; 8:2), has "died to the law" (7:4; Gal. 2:19), that is, released from and died to *legalism*. Such a person is no longer part of a polity in which people are expected to accomplish the Torah in their own strength, with an unregenerate heart and without the power of the Holy Spirit.

In the twentieth century, the important question arose as to whether such a (man-made) polity *has ever existed*. Theologians began seeking the identity of the enemy Paul was actually fighting when he was describing such a polity of Judaist legalism and/or ethnocentrism. In his day, who were the people who really believed that one could earn salvation by accomplishing, in one's own strength, the works of the Torah? Was this, among the Jews in the days of Jesus and the apostles, indeed the general attitude toward the Torah? Or does the New Testament not at all suggest that this was the overall picture of first-century Judaism?

A second question has arisen as well. It is amazing that both Martin Luther and John Calvin as well as other Reformers not only saw New Testament Judaism as a legalist polity of works-righteousness, but also viewed it as identical with the Roman Catholic way of salvation in their own time.[1] For centuries, this identification was an essential element in

---

1. See Thielman (1994, 18–24) for a summary of the Reformers' views. See for the traditional view about Paul's and Luther's views, respectively, of the legalism of their days, e.g., Berkouwer (1954, 70–72). See also extensively, Carson *et al.* (2001; 2004).

Protestant theology. This view betrayed not only a strong hostility toward Roman Catholic thought, but also a certain measure of anti-Judaism. In summary, the two questions are: (a) Was first-century Judaism in general a system of legalism and ethnocentrism? (b) Was sixteenth-century official Roman Catholicism a similar system of at least legalism, a polity of works-righteousness, accomplished in one's own strength? At least the latter is suggested in the Belgic Confession (Art. 22): "Therefore, for any to assert that Christ is not sufficient, but that something more is required besides Him, would be too gross a blasphemy; for hence it would follow that Christ was but half a Savior. Therefore, we justly say with Paul, that we 'are justified by faith' alone, or 'by faith apart from works'" The great question is which Roman Catholic authority would have indeed published such a statement that one can be saved only by Christ plus good works!

For the moment, we limit ourselves to the first question: Was first-century Judaism in general a system of legalism and ethnocentrism? Two works have strongly enhanced this negative attitude toward Judaism. The one was written by Ferdinand Weber.[2] Through a very unilateral selection of quotations from rabbinical writings of the post-New Testament time, Weber tried to establish the exaggerated picture of Judaism as a strictly legalist polity of works-righteousness. In the same period, Emil Schürer gave an equally dark view of Judaism, in which he denied the presence of virtually any godliness in Israel.[3] These and other works supported the picture of Judaism as this had been given earlier by the Reformers, and darkened it further. At first glance, it seemed to be supported by Paul's own allegedly negative view of Judaism.

3.1.2 The Picture Changes

At the beginning of the twentieth century, the picture changed

---

2. Weber (1880/1897).
3. Schürer (1885–1891).

dramatically. The first protest came from the Jewish theologian Claude de Montefiore who, in an article around the turn of the century, and later in a complete book, strongly refuted Weber's view.[4] He emphasized that rabbinic literature, including the Talmud, contains almost every conceivable opinion. As a consequence, one could "prove" from these writings anything one wishes. Instead, we should ask: What is the *usual* opinion, the *dominant* view of the Jewish religious leaders? Weber was describing a caricature, claimed Montefiore; the Torah was, and is, not at all a legalistic burden for godly Jews but rather a blessing and a joy. The rabbis themselves emphasized time and again that for a true observance of the Torah good intentions are just as important as good actions, and that every trespass of the Torah, if followed by sincere repentance, would be blotted out by God's forgiving mercy. Similar protests against Weber and Schürer were expressed by a non-Jewish scholar, specialized in rabbinic Judaism, George Foot Moore.[5]

At the time, the effect of the writings by Montefiore and Moore was not very large. The first to change the picture was the Swedish Lutheran theologian Krister Stendahl.[6] He published an article questioning the traditional Lutheran view of Paul's doctrine, and argued that it was more based on certain prejudicial standpoints than on a careful exegesis of Paul's letters. Far more influential was the book published by Ed Sanders, half a century after Montefiore and Moore, entitled *Paul and Palestinian Judaism*.[7] He supported the views of Montefiore and Moore, but did this from the perspective of New Testament scholarship. He compared Paul's view of Judaism with the picture of Judaism emerging from contemporaneous Jewish literature.

Sanders called this picture *covenantal nomism*, that is, the

---

4. Montefiore (1900/01, 1914).
5. Moore (1921, 1927–30).
6. Stendahl (1963; also see 1976).
7. Sanders (1977; see also 1983, 1985, 1990, 1992).

view that the covenant requires the right response of people, namely, their obedience to its commandments, while also supplying the means for atoning trespasses.[8] In other words, real Judaism, despite its diversity, is a *religion of grace*, first, in the sense that entering into the covenant is a matter of God's *electing* grace, and second, because remaining in the covenant is indeed a matter not only of obedience but also of God's *atoning* grace, which provides forgiveness after failure and repentance. This distinction between "entering" and "remaining" also has consequences for the doctrine of justification.[9]

Along broad lines, this "covenantal nomism" is the very thing I have described in the two previous volumes in this series. Three basic elements that I myself have strongly underscored include: (a) the positive view of the Mosaic Torah and of Torah observance, (b) the view of Judaism as a polity primarily of redemption and grace, not of works of the law, and (c) the difference between the Old and the New Covenants as being only relative.

Rarely in the history of New Testament scholarship has one single book brought about as dramatic a change as Sanders' book. Many New Testament scholars were inclined to accept Sanders' dramatic conclusion: Judaism is not a legalistic religion at all, but a religion of grace![10] Obviously, this had consequences not only for New Testament scholarship but also for the practical relationship between (religious) Jews and Christians.

3.2 Meaning of the Sacrifice
3.2.1 No Covenantal Nomism without Propitiation

I should add a few points here, however. First, Sanders was in fact not at all the first to point out these things to us. Jewish authors had done so before, but Christians had paid little attention to them. Too often, Christians felt that, since Jews

---

8. Sanders (1977, 75).
9. Cf. Wright (1997, chapter 7: Justification and the Church).
10. Thielman (1994, 31).

have a "veil over their hearts" (2 Cor. 3:15), why listen to them anyway? In §3.4 I will return to this point.

Second, the description of Judaism just given is not complete. Remaining in the covenant is indeed a matter of obedience. But it is also a matter of God's *atoning* grace, which provides forgiveness after failure and repentance, but we should add: *without exception this takes place on the basis of the sin offering*. It has been like this from the very beginning, even long before the Torah was given. Since Genesis 2:17 ("in the day that you eat of it you shall surely die") we know that "the wages of sin is death" (Rom. 6:23). Therefore, sin cannot be blotted out other than through death: the death of a sacrifice, that is, of an innocent substitute. In the Mosaic Torah, this sacrificial ministry occupies a significant place; it is the main subject of the book of Leviticus.

Many centuries after the Torah was given, godly Jews in the New Testament were fully conscious of the necessity of the animal sacrifice. Joseph and Mary brought a burnt offering and a sin offering for the newly born Jesus with a view to the mother's cleansing (Luke 2:24; cf. Lev. 12:6–8). Jesus told the ten lepers to bring a burnt offering and a sin offering for their cleansing (Luke 5:14; cf. Lev. 14:19). Even after Easter, Peter and John went to the temple at the ninth hour, that is, the "hour of prayer," that is, the hour at which the evening burnt offering was brought (Acts 3:1). Similarly, after Easter, Paul brought a burnt offering and a sin offering for the purification of some friends (Acts 21:26; cf. Num. 6:14, 16).

Of special interest are the words of the tax collector in Jesus' parable: "God, be merciful to me, a sinner" (Luke 18:13). Literally this is, "God, be propitious (Greek, *hilasthēti*) to me, a sinner," that is, show mercy to me on account of a propitiatory sacrifice (a sin offering) (cf. JUB: "reconcile me"; YLT: "be propitious to me"). We find the same root word in Hebrews 2:17, where it is said that Christ became "a merciful and faithful high priest in things relating to God, to make propitiation (Greek, *hilaskesthai*) for the sins of the people," namely through presenting himself as the true sin offering. Jesus made the tax collector not just ask for forgiveness and redemption, but he made him express this deep Old Testament truth: "I have given it [i.e., the blood] for you on the altar to make atonement for your souls, for it is the blood that makes atonement by the life" (Lev. 17:11). In the New Testament version: "[W]ithout the shedding of blood there is no forgiveness of sins" (Heb. 9:22).

In other words, God forgives not only because he is gracious and merciful, but because he has a holy *foundation* for his forgiveness: the propitiatory sacrifice. God's grace and mercy are not sufficient; propitiation is needed.[11] *With* a propitiatory sacrifice God is not only gracious and merciful when he forgives the sin of those who come and plead on the basis of this sacrifice, but also *righteous* (Rom. 3:26; 1 John 1:9). He is righteous when he forgives because he has received true satisfaction. This is the ongoing teaching of both the Old and New Testaments. We cannot truly speak of "covenantal nomism" without taking into account the necessity and the availability of the sacrifice.

New Testament Judaism was fully aware of the significance and necessity of the sin offering. Paul and the other apostles had not the slightest reason to blame the Jews of their day on this point. However, the situation drastically changed during the catastrophe of AD 70: the temple was destroyed, and the sacrificial ministry became impossible. Judaism had to come to terms with this new situation, which, incidentally, has lasted until this very day. It needed at least to point to possible substitutes for the sacrifices, even if temporary (until the time of the Third Temple).

3.2.2 *Tefillot*

Indeed, the rabbis considered the sacrifices to have been replaced after AD 70 by three other things. These are mentioned,

---
11. See extensively, Ouweneel (2009).

among other places, in the prayer *Unetanneh Tokef* in the Rosh haShanah and the Yom Kippur liturgy: prayer, repentance, and charity are needed to "annul the severe decree."[12] In a different order:

(a) *Teshuvah*, "return," here in the sense of repentance and conversion connected with fasting. However, this is not new at all; it was always a vital element of the sin offerings in general, and of Yom Kippur (Atonement Day) in particular (Lev. 16:29, 31 NKJV: "afflict your souls"). No forgiveness without repentance and confession (e.g., Prov. 28:13; 1 John 1:9). As such, it cannot be a substitute for the sacrifices since it always was a necessary concomitant element of the sacrificial ministry.

(b) *Tsedaqah*, "righteousness," here in the sense of charity. However, good works, no matter how valuable in themselves, can never replace sacrifices, either. The principle of charity as a means of atonement is that the person *himself* makes up for his bad works by good works. This is unbiblical. The principle of sacrifice is that an *innocent substitute* makes up for the person's bad works precisely because the offerer *cannot* himself make up for his own bad works.

(c) *Tefillah* (plural: *tefillot*, or anglicized *tefillahs*), "prayers," here in the sense of fixed prayer recitations. This is the most important of the three as replacement for the sacrifices after these had stopped. In the tract Berakoth, Rabbi Joshua ben Levi says: "The *Tefillahs* were instituted to replace the daily sacrifices,"[13] a statement that was not denied by other rabbis. According to tradition, these prayers had been instituted by the "Men of the Great Synagogue," a legendary Synod in the sixth to the fourth century BC. Of the three traditional prayer services, the first two correspond to the morning and evening burnt offerings (cf. Exod. 29:36–46). The second of these is called *Minha*, and is named after the flour offering accompanying the burnt offering (Lev. 2). The significance

---
12. Cf. Schmelzer (1993).
13. Talmud: Berakoth 26b (Soncino-ed. p. 160).

of these three *Tefillot* was greatly enhanced by the legendary suggestion that each of them had been instituted by the three patriarchs: Abraham instituted the first prayer because "early in the morning" he was at the place where he had "stood" before the Lord (Gen. 19:27), Isaac instituted the second because he "prayed" "toward evening" (24:63 JUB), and Jacob instituted the third prayer after "the sun had set" (Gen. 28:11, "came to" = prayed).[14]

Hosea 14:2 (NKJV) speaks of the "sacrifices of our lips," showing that the Old Testament already knew the figurative sense of sacrifices (bloody animal offerings), namely, the utterances of believers' lips: prayers and praise (cf. Heb. 13:15). Similarly, in places like Psalm 50:23, "to offer praise" (NKJV; Heb., *zebach todah*) is literally "to bring a sacrifice of praise" (cf. ESV, NIV), which, however, is meant here in a figurative sense (cf. vv. 8-9). Another link is Isaiah 56:7: the new temple will be a place for "burnt offerings and sacrifices," but will be called a "house of prayer." However, none of these passages ever intended to diminish the value of the animal sacrifices, or to suggest that prayers could form a substitute for sacrifices.

Of course, passages such as 1 Samuel 15:22 ("Has the Lord as great delight in burnt offerings and sacrifices, as in obeying the voice of the Lord? Behold, to obey is better than sacrifice, and to listen than the fat of rams") and Hosea 6:6 ("For I desire steadfast love and not sacrifice, the knowledge of God rather than burnt offerings") cannot be used to suggest that the bloody sacrifices were not that important after all. The fact that *hesed* is more desirable than sacrifices, does not mean that sacrifices are not important. It is quite obvious that such passages criticize a sacrificial ministry that is conducted with an evil attitude; they do not criticize the sacrificial ministry as such (cf. Isa. 1:11; 66:3; Jer. 6:20; Amos 5:22). This would be impossible: the sacrificial ministry was given by God himself.

Therefore, as soon as the temple and the sacrificial minis-

---

14. Ibid.

try will be restored, no orthodox Jew will ever claim that sacrifices are no longer necessary because we now have *teshuvah*, *tsedaqah*, and *tefillah*. These are quite important in themselves, but when it comes to the significance of sacrifices, they are only a temporary compensation.

3.2.3 Conclusion

The conclusion I want to draw at this point is that it seems inevitable to me that, if we speak of "covenantal nomism," we must also speak of the bloody sacrifice. No Bible student can get around the conclusion that blood shedding is the indispensable foundation for the grace with which God grants forgiveness for trespasses committed under the covenants. "[W]ithout the shedding of blood there is no forgiveness of sins" (Heb. 9:22). This principle remains permanently valid and known, not only by those who have been saved by the blood of Christ, but also with respect to Second Temple Judaism.[15] We cannot speak of justification without always realizing that we have been "justified by (Greek, *en*, 'in [the power of]') his blood" (Rom. 5:9). There can be no justification without the shedding of blood; this was true from the time of Adam, and it will remain true until the last day.

We find this neatly summarized in Romans 3:24–25: it is said that believers

(a) "are justified *by his grace* [Greek, *chariti*, a common dative] as a gift,

(b) through [*dia*, by means of] the redemption that is in Christ Jesus,

(c) whom God put forward as a propitiation [*hilastērion*; cf. §3.2.1] by [*en*, in the power of] his blood,

(d) to be received by [*dia*, by means of] faith(fulness, confidence)."

Notice the triad here: God's grace (a) and human faith

---

15. I prefer the term Second Temple Judaism to first-century Judaism, in order to maintain the distinction between pre-AD 70 and post-AD 70 Judaism.

(d) are not sufficient. A third element is needed (b, c): the sacrifice, which is here the true sacrifice of Christ. There is the divine motive (grace, mercy), there is the formal foundation for forgiveness (the blood of Christ), there is the indispensable human side (faith[fulness], confidence in God), and there is the result (the redemption that is in Christ Jesus, plus walking in the Torah of Christ, mentioned, e.g., in Rom. 8:4; 13:8-10).

This corresponds one-hundred percent with "covenantal nomism." Judaism was thoroughly familiar with all these elements: the divine motive (grace, mercy), the formal foundation for forgiveness (the blood of the prescribed sacrifice), the indispensable human responsibility (faith[fulness], confidence in God), and the result (the redemption from sin, [re-]entrance in the covenantal relationship with God, walking again in the Torah of Moses, looking forward to the Messianic Kingdom).

In summary, both Judaism and Christianity are unequivocally polities characterized by:

(a) *sovereign grace* on the side of God,

(b) *blood*, viz., that of an appropriate sacrifice prescribed by God,

(c) *faith* on the side of humanity (confiding in God, entrusting oneself to him),

(d) *forgiveness* on the side of God,

(e) the *Torah* as given by God and observed by humans.

So the question becomes: What then is the fundamental *difference* between Judaism and Christianity, according to the apostles, especially Paul?

3.3 Judaism Lacks Christ
3.3.1 The Shadows and the Reality

In no way should we ever imagine that it was Paul's intention to belittle Judaism as such. How could this ever be? In its essence—I am not speaking of what some hypocrites made of it—Judaism was nothing but the polity that God himself had given to his people at Mount Sinai. Not Judaism as such is a polity of works-holiness (works-righteousness), but Jewish legalism and ethnocentrism are. So why, then, could Paul not go along with God-given Judaism? Because since the coming of Christ, it was simply *outdated*. Everything in Judaism pointed forward to the Messiah. This is why the book of Hebrews tells us that the Old Covenant was not "faultless" (Heb. 8:7), and that it was "becoming obsolete and growing old," and therefore "ready to vanish away" (v. 13). That is, it was perfect in itself — because it was God-given — but it lacked Christ. As soon as Christ had come, this polity had become obsolete. Please notice: what had become obsolete was not the Mosaic Torah as such, but only the polity within which it functioned.

As I have argued elsewhere,[16] the great difference between the Old and New Covenants is not that the Torah has been abolished — it has not — but the difference is *Christ* and the *Holy Spirit*. The Old Covenant could not be anything other than what it was as long as Christ had not yet come, and as long as the Holy Spirit had not yet been poured out. In itself, this covenant was good; how could it be otherwise since God himself had given it? But it was incomplete: it did not include Christ.[17] Now that Christ has come, and the Holy Spirit has been poured out, the old polity has necessarily been done away with.

This is what Paul tries to make clear: it is both foolish and misleading to intermingle the old and the new polities. His objection against the old polity in the present era is that it lacks Christ. This means: there is nothing wrong with the polity of the Mosaic Torah — the Sinaitic or Old Covenant — as such. However, it lost its significance after Christ had come, who is the foundation, the essence, and the fulfillment of the Torah. This was and is not grasped by those who reject Christ, or the so-called "Judaizers," who wanted, and still want, to intermingle the new polity with the old polity. The Sinaitic

---

16. Ouweneel (2015b, §6.5.3).
17. Cf. Sanders (1977, 552).

covenant is still a source of divine knowledge for those who wish to study redemptive history, or wish to investigate the Torah's typological meaning. But it is no longer a proper way of serving God; this may become clearer in the following chapters.[18]

Please note here that this does not mean that God's grace has stopped with respect to Jews who continue within the framework of the Sinaitic covenant, while rejecting Christ. We should never lose sight of the important fact that a "veil" lies over the hearts of Jews who reject Jesus (2 Cor. 3:14-16). I will return to this point in §3.3.4.

3.3.2 The Bloody Sacrifice

The best way to illustrate the incompleteness of the Sinaitic covenant is what I mentioned in §3.2: the bloody sacrifice. The starting point for our thoughts is, of course, Hebrews 10:4, "For it is impossible for the blood of bulls and goats to take away sins." This does not mean that the Old Testament sacrifices were worthless—why then would God have given them?—but they had no propitiatory value *in themselves*. As far as this point is concerned, the blood of animal sacrifices *as such* could not atone for Israel's sins any more than their *tefillot*, their *teshuvah*, and their *tsedaqah*.

The value of the Old Testament sacrifices lay in their *anticipatory* character, as the book of Hebrews makes clear: "Consequently, when Christ came into the world, he said, 'Sacrifices and offerings you have not desired, but a body have you prepared for me; in burnt offerings and sin offerings you have taken no pleasure. Then I said, 'Behold, I have come to do your will, O God, as it is written of me in the scroll of the book.'" [Ps. 40:7-8] When he said above, 'You have neither desired nor taken pleasure in sacrifices and offerings and burnt offerings and sin offerings' (these are offered according to the Torah), then he added, 'Behold, I have come to do your will.' He does away with the first in order to establish the sec-

---
18. See also Ouweneel (2015b, chapter 6).

ond. And by that will we have been sanctified through the offering of the body of Jesus Christ once for all" (Heb. 10:5-10). In short: the thousands of Old Testament bloody sacrifices have all been fulfilled in, as well as replaced by, the one and only sacrifice of Christ. Their only value in God's eyes lay in their pointing forward to the cross. To phrase it in the following way: when God said, "[W]hen I see the blood, I will pass over you" (Ex. 12:13), what he in fact "saw" was the blood of Christ, the true Passover Lamb (cf. 1 Cor. 5:7).

Notice here the words of Peter: "[Y]ou were ransomed from the futile ways inherited from your forefathers, not with perishable things such as silver or gold, but with the precious blood of Christ, like that of a lamb without blemish or spot. He was foreknown before the foundation of the world but was made manifest in the last times for the sake of you" (1 Pet. 1:18-20). This is the divine order. First, the true Lamb was foreknown before creation. Second, from Sinai to Christ, the people had to work with "shadows": literal lambs, bulls, goats. Third, since the coming of Christ, the figures have made place for the spiritual reality (cf. Heb. 8:5; 10:1). The shadows were fine as long as the reality had not yet come; since the coming of Christ, the shadows became obsolete.

Colossians 2:16-17 expresses this in a neat figurative way: "Therefore let no one pass judgment on you in questions of food and drink, or with regard to a festival or a new moon or a Sabbath. These are a shadow of the things to come, but the substance [Greek, *soma*, lit. "body"] belongs to Christ." Already before a body appears around a corner, we may see its shadow. As long as we see the shadow, we may be fascinated by it. The shadow must not be despised; it is far better than nothing. It is a promise: a body is coming! However, as soon as the body appears, the shadows are forgotten. We now have the substance, the real thing.

3.3.3 The Greater Light

Ed Sanders was one of the most powerful authors in the

twentieth century to underscore the fact that Paul could never have asserted that there was anything wrong with the Mosaic Torah as such, and with living according to this Torah. It was God who had given this Torah. Nor could Paul ever have claimed that there was anything wrong with the sacrificial ministry as such. It was God who had given this sacrificial ministry. Upon closer investigation, it become clear that Paul did not work with some juxtaposition between faith and works (in spite of Rom. 3:27-28; 4:5; 9:32; Gal. 2:16; 3:2, 5), or between grace and merit as such (in spite of Rom. 4:4). Rather, he wished to emphasize that the Jew should not continue clinging to the shadows. The Mosaic Torah is no longer sufficient now that we have Jesus, who is the fulfillment of the Torah. The Sinaitic sacrificial ministry is no longer enough now that we have the one and only perfect sacrifice of Christ.

Consider, for instance, Galatians 2:16-19 ("we know that a person is not justified by works of the law but through faith in Jesus Christ, so we also have believed in Christ Jesus, in order to be justified by faith in Christ and not by works of the law. . . . For through the law I died to the law, so that I might live to God"), and 3:10-12 ("For all who rely on works of the law are under a curse; for it is written, 'Cursed be everyone who does not abide by all things written in the Book of the Law, and do them.' [Deut. 27:26] Now it is evident that no one is justified before God by the law, for 'The righteous shall live by faith.' [Hab. 2:4] But the law is not of faith, rather 'The one who does them shall live by them.' [Lev. 18:5]"). Paul's point is not so much that observance of the Torah as such is impossible (cf. Rom. 2:13), or that human efforts lead only and necessarily to carnal arrogance. His point is rather that, if it were possible to earn righteousness in one's own strength—that is, *not* by drawing from the divine "streams of water" (Ps. 1:3)—then Christ would have died in vain.

Paul never speaks of the previous—God-given!—polity in a derogatory way. Take, for example, 2 Corinthians 3:9-11: "For if there was glory in the ministry of condemnation, the ministry of righteousness must far exceed it in glory. Indeed, in this case, what once had glory has come to have no glory at all, because of the glory that surpasses it. For if what was being brought to an end came with glory, much more will what is permanent have glory." Here, Paul gladly recognized that the old ministry, although it was one of "condemnation," definitely possessed "glory" — it was simply surpassed by a ministry that was even more glorious, and that even far exceeded the old one in glory. It was not darkness as opposed to light, but light as opposed to a far greater light.

Also notice how Paul speaks of the previous polity in Philippians 3:4-9: "If anyone else thinks he has reason for confidence in the flesh, I have more: . . . as to righteousness under the Torah, blameless. But whatever gain I had, I counted as loss for the sake of Christ. . . . For his sake I have suffered the loss of all things and count them as rubbish, in order that I may gain Christ and be found in him, not having a righteousness of my own that comes from the law, but that which comes through faith in Christ, the righteousness from God that depends on faith." On the one hand, Paul shows here very clearly that a "Torah-righteousness" definitely does exist. As far as this righteousness was concerned, he could honestly say that, before his conversion, he had been blameless (cf. Acts 23:1, "Brothers, I have lived my life before God in all good conscience up to this day"; cf. 24:16). On the other hand, since he had met Christ, this type of righteousness had become to him loss and rubbish; he was not at all interested in it anymore.[19]

Paul was like the man with ordinary but decent clothes, who was offered royal garments. Such a man drops his old clothes, not because they are worthless — they are not at all — but because he receives something far better. It was a great privilege to have been circumcised on the eighth day, to be of the people of Israel, of the tribe of Benjamin, a Hebrew of

---

19. Sanders (1977, 482–85, 492–93, 505, 551; 1983, 17–27, 43–44, 137–41).

Hebrews; as to the Torah, a Pharisee; as to righteousness under the Torah, blameless (Phil. 3:5-6).[20] But it was all of little value in comparison to this one great thing: finding Christ.

In fact, Paul's problem with Judaism involved not so much the idea of a legalistic works-righteousness but rather that its inability to bring about true salvation, something possible through Christ alone. Sanders summarized his position in stating that what Paul had against Judaism was that it was not Christianity.[21] I myself would never state it this way; the situation did not require or need one "religion" to be replaced by another. I would rather say — and I trust this is what Sanders really wished to say — that there was nothing wrong with the polity of the Torah as such, but that, when Christ came, who was the fulfillment of the Torah, this polity became worthless to those who rejected Christ. Jesus Christ is the *telos* (end, goal, purpose, and then also: sense, content, fulfillment) of the Torah (Rom. 10:4; *not* the "end" in the sense of the abolishment of the Torah; Matt. 5:17). Now that Christ has come, any observance of the Mosaic Torah with a conscious denial of Christ has lost its purpose; such religious conduct has become an empty shell.

3.3.4 Three Groups

As a further attempt at clarification, I would like to make the following distinction between three groups of *tsaddiqim*:

(a) Those who lived in the time that Christ had not yet appeared in public. They were living proof of the fact that "the doers of the Torah are justified" (Rom. 2:13), and that it was indeed possible to be blameless when it came to the "righteousness that is from the law" (Phil. 3:9 NKJV; Greek, *tēn ek nomou*). Several times I have cited Zechariah and Elizabeth as striking examples (Luke 1:6). There can be no doubt that, along this road, they were "saved," or, in more Jewish

---

20. The only point that does not fit in here is: "as to zeal, a persecutor of the church."
21. Sanders (1977, 552).

language, would have a share in the Messianic Kingdom ("inherit everlasting life"). In light of Scripture as a whole, we hasten to add that this was not apart from, and in contrast with, (1) the grace and mercy of God, (2) the work of the Holy Spirit in their hearts, and (3) faith(fulness, confidence) on their part. But this should not take anything away from the fact that theirs was a righteousness entirely according to the requirements of the Torah. This is precisely what Jesus himself told the young ruler: "'[I]f you want to enter into life, keep the commandments.' He said to him, 'Which ones?' Jesus said, '"You shall not murder," "You shall not commit adultery," "You shall not steal," "You shall not bear false witness," "Honor your father and mother," and, "You shall love your neighbor as yourself"' (Matt. 19:17–19). Jesus gave the young man a correct answer, although it was not a complete answer (see under [b]).

(b) During the time that Christ appeared in public, many Jews were confronted with his person. As long as people still lived under (a), it was very hard to distinguish the hypocrites from the true *tsaddiqim*. But as soon as they met Jesus, their true nature became manifest: "[T]his is the judgment: the light has come into the world, and people loved the darkness rather than the light because their works were evil. For everyone who does wicked things hates the light and does not come to the light, lest his works should be exposed. But whoever does what is true comes to the light, so that it may be clearly seen that his works have been carried out in God" (John 3:19–21). I have already mentioned a number of such *tsaddiqim* in the Gospels, people who recognized Jesus and found the fulfillment of their righteousness in him (§2.3.3). In opposition to them stand the spiritual leaders of Israel who rejected Jesus and delivered him to the Gentile authorities. Jesus unmasked them as hypocrites, as pseudo-*tsaddiqim* (e.g., Matt. 6:2, 5, 16; 7:5; 15:7; 22:18; 23:13–29). It is hardly conceivable that any genuine *tsaddiq* who was intensely and consciously confronted with Jesus refused to accept him.

A possible exception might be Gamaliel, "a teacher of the law held in honor by all the people," who tried to keep a neutral stand toward Jesus and his followers (Acts 5:33-39). Gamaliel (Heb., *Gamli'el*), named *haZaqên*, "the Elder," was a grandson of the famous Rabbi Hillel. Gamaliel was the first *nasi* ("prince," here something close to "president") of the Great Sanhedrin of Jerusalem, the well-known "council" of Matthew 5:22, 26:59, and many times in Acts. Inevitably, stories arose about the alleged conversion of the sympathetic and non-hostile Gamaliel. Chrysostom suggested that Gamaliel must have eventually become a Jesus-believer,[22] Pseudo-Clement asserted that the man *was* a secret Jesus-believer,[23] and the ninth-century bishop Photius cited an earlier source claiming that Gamaliel had been secretly baptized by Peter and John.[24] Not too much historical value may be attached to such stories. But the central question behind them remains: Could there have been a real *tsaddiq* in Israel during Jesus' days who got to know Jesus well, and yet refused to accept him?

(c) What was true for the Jews in Jesus' day is not necessarily true for Jews in later centuries, especially after the Christian persecutions of the Jews had begun (fourth century). Peter told the Jews in Jerusalem: "I know that you acted in ignorance, as did also your rulers" (Acts 3:17). Paul says that, as long as he rejected and even persecuted Jesus, he "acted ignorantly in unbelief" (1 Tim. 1:13). If this was true for the Jews in Jesus' day and immediately after, how much more is it true for Jews in later ages, who had never met Jesus in the flesh. Apart from the New Testament, the only portrait of Christ that Jews in later ages received came from Christians — and that was often a very poor picture indeed. Things became far worse when, after the Roman Empire had become "Christian," Christians began to view themselves as the true

---

22. Homilies on Acts 14.1.
23. Recognitions 1.65.
24. *Codex 171*, p. 199.

Israel (supersessionism[25]), and began to persecute ethnic Israel.[26] In the present time, it would be hard to find a genuine Jewish *tsaddiq*, who has *really* been confronted with the Jesus of the New Testament—not just from hearsay—and has rejected him. (I have met orthodox Jews who have seen Jesus in a vision, and were converted to him.) In the end, however, this is a matter that we have to leave in God's hands. It is God himself who must remove the veil and open their eyes (cf. 2 Cor. 3:16).

3.4 Further Developments
3.4.1 Paul's Critics

The approach of Montefiore, Moore, Stendahl, Sanders, and others has elicited several kinds of responses. In the first place, some accepted Sanders' evaluation of first-century Judaism but went much further in their criticism of Paul's evaluation of it. Already Sanders himself was critical of Paul, which did not help to gain the support of orthodox Protestant theologians for his views. He found Paul occasionally incoherent, and he blamed him here and there for not having more understanding of Second Temple Judaism. Nevertheless, even traditional Protestants were tempted by him to see far more theological continuity between Second Temple Judaism and early Christian doctrine as especially Paul presented it. However, someone like Heikki Räisänen went much further in his criticism of Paul.[27] He even accused Paul of putting Judaism in a false light, and doubted if Paul could be called a profound theologian.[28] Other theologians have spoken of a certain development in Paul's thinking, and of contradictions to which this development allegedly led.[29]

It goes without saying that this type of criticism was shared by Jewish thinkers who were familiar with the New

---

25. See extensively, Ouweneel (2015b, §§4.5.3, 6.6.2, 7.5.2, 9.3.2).
26. See extensively, Ouweneel (2013b, chapter 8).
27. Räisänen (1983; 1986; 1992).
28. Räisänen (1983, 266–67); see the refutation by Van Spanje (1999).
29. See especially Hübner (1984).

Testament and believed that Paul gave a very unfair picture of contemporaneous Judaism. An example is the well-known Jewish scholar Hans-Joachim Schoeps.[30] He saw Paul's presentation as delusive and monstrous, and part of a broader Christian polemic—especially among Protestants—directed against the Torah. He blamed Paul and his followers for having suggested that Jews abuse the Torah as a means for becoming justified through works. Schoeps supposed that, during his experience on the road to Damascus, Paul lost an insight that as a scholar, he certainly had possessed earlier: *the Torah was never given to make the Jews righteous and acceptable before their Father in heaven*. The Torah was the expression of the holy will of the heavenly Father to those who already were his children (Deut. 14:1).

Most Christian theologians would reject such a representation of Paul because it does no justice to what he really wrote. But many would readily admit that earlier generations of theologians, especially during the Reformation, have contributed to such criticisms as that by Schoeps. The latter gave a fair picture of Second Temple Judaism, but failed to see that Paul would largely agree with him! Schoeps looked at Paul through the wrong "Christian" glasses.

3.4.2 Sanders' Allies

In the second place, there were those who did not want to go as far as Räisänen but by and large accepted the views of Sanders on Second Temple Judaism, and elaborated upon them. They have tried to give a more positive view of Paul's theology. James D. G. Dunn coined the term "New Perspective on Paul" (NPP),[31] and became one of the best-known representatives of it. The "Old Perspective on Paul" is the traditional Lutheran-Reformed view of Paul, today still defended by many Lutheran and Reformed theologians. The great

---

30. Schoeps (1963); see on this subject extensively, Schoeps (1961), especially chapter 6 on Paul's view of the Torah.
31. Dunn (1983).

difference between the two Perspectives was not at all based on a renewed exegesis of Paul's letters, but on a new view of contemporaneous Judaism. When the identity of Paul's actual enemy became clearer, this also threw much light on what Paul was arguing in opposition to this enemy. To state the matter this way: as long as Protestants thought that Paul was dealing with question A, they thought that he was presenting answer B. Now that they began to think that Paul was instead dealing with question P, they began to realize that the answer he gave was not at all B but Q.

For the rest, the phrase "New Perspective on Paul" should rather be replaced by the phrase "New Perspectives on Paul" because there is not much unity in the movement, as we will see. The main things that unite the NPP theologians is the new view of Second Temple Judaism as well as the conviction that the traditional Lutheran-Reformed view of Paul cannot be maintained for a number of rather different reasons. We will be dealing extensively with these matters.

As explained in the first volume of this series, Dunn believed that Paul was combatting not so much Jewish legalism but rather Jewish-nationalistic ethnocentrism. This is the view that Second Temple Judaism associated the fact that Israel was "under the Torah" with the fact that Israel was God's chosen covenant people, so that male Gentiles who desired to share in God's covenant promises necessarily had to join Israel through circumcision.[32] As a consequence, Dunn developed quite a different view on justification by faith.[33] In opposition to the allegation that God had limited his saving grace to one single nation, Paul preached that this grace was extended to all those who wished to receive it, simply on account of faith in Christ. It does not matter anymore whether one stands under the Sinaitic Torah, that is, whether one is a Jew or a Gentile. The only thing that matters is one's faithful surrender to Christ. If Paul does set faith in opposition to the

---

32. Dunn (1990; 1996; and especially 1998).
33. Dunn in Dunn and Suggate (1993, 28).

Torah at all, then it is in this sense: a Gentile *without* the Torah but *with* Christ is better off than the Jew *with* the Torah but *without* Christ. This may irritate Jews such as Hans-Joachim Schoeps—but at any rate one cannot derive from this that Paul had a negative view of the Mosaic Torah as such.

Another theologian in this category is Nicholas Thomas ("Tom") Wright, who has been quite prolific on the subject, especially on a more popular level.[34] At the same time, Wright is a striking example of the wide variety among the NPP scholars. In 2003 he distanced himself from both Sanders and Dunn, and added "that there are probably almost as many 'New Perspective' positions as there are writers espousing it – and that I disagree with most of them."[35] Sanders, Dunn, and Wright have been called the three "leading exponents" of the NPP, who at the same time represent what could be almost called three different schools within the movement.

3.4.3 Pinchas Lapide

The discussion about what Second Temple Judaism actually taught, how it functioned in practice, and whether the apostle Paul gave a fair picture of it, continues to this day. One of the most substantial contributions to this controversy came from Donald A. Carson, Peter T. O'Brien and Mark A. Seifrid, who heavily criticize Sanders' notion of "covenantal nomism."[36] Amazingly, until now this has been mainly a Christian discussion. What Jewish Bible scholars of recent centuries have to say about Second Temple Judaism, and even about Paul's view of it, has played a minor role. Not only liberal Jews, such as Claude Montefiore, have had their say, but also orthodox Jewish authors. I learned about what is now called "covenantal nomism" not first from Sanders, Dunn or Wright, but from Pinchas Lapide (1922–1997), and related scholars.

Lapide and others, such as Hans-Joachim Schoeps (1909–

---

34. Wright (1991; 1997; 2002; 2005; 2009; 2013; 2014)
35. http://ntwrightpage.com/Wright_New_Perspectives.htm
36. Carson *et al.* (2001).

1980) mentioned earlier,[37] David Flusser (1917–2000),[38] and Géza Vermes (1924–2013, for a while a Roman Catholic priest, who afterward returned to Judaism),[39] but also Messianic Jews such as David H. Stern (b. 1935),[40] deserve much more attention in the NPP debate.[41] One reason why this has happened so little is that much of this literature was originally written in German, and Anglo-Saxons happen to know less German than Germans know English. As a consequence, one often gets the impression that only Anglo-Saxons (Sanders, Dunn, Wright, etc.) have contributed to the discussion.

Lapide belonged to those religious Jews who in the twentieth century acquired a great knowledge of the New Testament and Christianity as well as of Second Temple Judaism. Of Viennese origin, Lapide was an Israeli, who from the seventies worked as a professor of religious studies and New Testament in Frankfurt am Main (Germany). He wrote more than thirty-five books (translated into twelve languages), among which are a number of books on Jesus and the New Testament.[42] I mention here especially his book *Mit einem Juden die Bibel lesen* ("Reading the Bible with a Jew"), which introduced me to "covenantal nomism," without at that time knowing the term.[43] Together with Christian theologian Peter Stuhlmacher, he wrote the book *Paulus: Rabbi und Apostel*,[44] which in 1984 appeared in English.

Let me give an idea of what Lapide wrote in his 1982 book, from the chapter that in English would be entitled: "The Joy of

---

37. Especially Schoeps (1961; 1963).
38. Flusser (1988; 1998).
39. Vermes (1983; 1993; 2003; 2010).
40. Stern (1997; 1999; 1996).
41. Of these four authors, only Flusser and Vermes are mentioned in Carson *et al.* (2001); Schoeps is mentioned once in Carson *et al.* (2004), and in none of the others.
42. Lapide (1979; 1980; 1988).
43. Lapide (1982).
44. Lapide and Stuhlmacher (1981).

the Law."⁴⁵ Interestingly, he connects with a lecture by Karl Barth, called *Evangelium und Gesetz* ("Gospel and Law").⁴⁶ Barth reversed the traditional Lutheran order (law and gospel), and pointed out how dangerous it is to break up law and gospel, this world and the world beyond, church and state, politics and religion, and divide them over two neatly separated realms ("kingdoms"). Barth argued that the Torah is the revealed will of God, and even the necessary form of the gospel, whose content is pure grace. The law does not precede the gospel but is contained within the gospel, just as the two tablets of stone were contained in the ark of the covenant. For instance, what does the first commandment ("You shall have no other gods before me") involve other than the gospel of the love of God? There is no contrast between God's law and God's divine grace and love; on the contrary, the two are inseparably interwoven.

3.4.4 Lapide, Bonhoeffer, Luther

Lapide goes on to quote Barth's pupil, Dietrich Bonhoeffer, who wrote on the second Sunday of Advent 1943 in a Nazi camp: "Only when one accepts the law of God as binding for oneself may one perhaps sometimes speak of grace."⁴⁷ Lapide comments that, if Bonhoeffer had lived longer — he was murdered in 1945, 39 years old — he would have discovered how believing Jews view this. Bonhoeffer discovered the Jewish writings for the first time when he was in prison. He would have learned from them that law and grace, gospel and Torah, are simply two aspects of one and the same love of God, says Lapide: "Jews faithful to the Torah have never seen them except as an unbreakable unity." Without the joyful message of the Exodus there would have been no Sinai with the divine commandments. And without Sinai there would have been no active life in faith. For the Jew, love and law are never in

---

45. Hebrew: *Simhat Torah*; the term refers to a festival day observed immediately after *Sukkot*.
46. Barth (1935).
47. Bonhoeffer (2009, 213).

conflict. On the contrary, they are a harmonious continuity, for it is out of love that the Torah was given, and out of love that the Torah is obeyed.

What the Torah means to the Jew, says Lapide, is not a frenetic striving for (self)justification but a life lived believingly and joyfully for and with God. This comes to light even in the daily liturgy of the synagogue ministry. One of the central blessings concerns the revelation of the Torah; the name of this blessing is not "revelation" or "law," but *Ahava*, "love." Giving the Torah was love, obeying the Torah is love.

Lapide blames Martin Luther for having suggested that the Torah was ever a way of salvation, a way of self-justification, and that today the way of salvation is the way of grace in *opposition* to the "yoke" of the law (cf. Acts 15:10). Lapide ripostes that *no rabbi ever suggested that the Torah is a way of salvation leading to heaven.* (I would say that the rabbis did not talk much about "going to heaven" anyway, so let us put it this way: no rabbi ever suggested that the Torah is a way of salvation leading to the Messianic Kingdom.) On the contrary. No world record in the domain of Torah observance can take away anything from God's sovereign, loving grace, says Lapide. The Torah is not about self-justification but about the connection between freedom from bondage and voluntary obedience. Only that person is free who voluntarily submits to the divine commandments. The rebel is not free but a slave of his sinful instincts. Thus, for Jews Sinai with its Torah is first and foremost the great song of the "freedom of a Jew," according to Lapide. Though not a Christian himself, he nonetheless calls all believing Jews in fact disciples of that Jew John, who in good rabbinic fashion wrote: "Whoever says 'I know him' but does not keep his commandments is a liar, and the truth is not in him" (1 John 2:4).

This does not mean that Lapide is free from all misunderstandings himself. For instance, he suggests that Paul wanted to reduce the entire Torah to the commandment of Leviticus

19:18, "You shall love your neighbor as yourself." Apparently, Lapide was thinking of these Pauline statements: "Owe no one anything, except to love each other, for the one who loves another has fulfilled the law. For the commandments, 'You shall not commit adultery, You shall not murder, You shall not steal, You shall not covet,' and any other commandment, are summed up in this word: 'You shall love your neighbor as yourself.' Love does no wrong to a neighbor; therefore love is the fulfilling of the law" (Rom. 13:8-10), and: "For the whole law is fulfilled in one word: 'You shall love your neighbor as yourself'" (Gal. 5:15). However, Paul certainly did know of the plural "commandments": "For neither circumcision counts for anything nor uncircumcision, but keeping the commandments of God" (1 Cor. 7:19).

Lapide points to German Christian theologian Jürgen Moltmann, who wrote: "[O]bedience to the will of God according to the Torah—that is to say, living commitment to the service of righteousness—is also part of the special call of the Jews. Obedience to the Torah cannot be legalistically deprived of its legitimacy, for the Torah is the prefiguration and beginning of the divine rule on earth."[48] This, says Lapide, is not a matter of merits, of achievements or self-righteousness but first and foremost a matter of love—a love that does express itself in acts pleasing to God (cf. Matt. 7:21). Love and righteousness go hand in hand; they are correlative. The Jew knows that love without righteousness leads to anarchy, and righteousness without love leads to tyranny. The God of Israel does not desire any "cheap grace" (Bonhoeffer), nor superhuman justice, but *tsedaqah*—this peculiar notion in which benevolence (love, favor, mercy) and righteousness are bound together.

3.5 The Wright–Piper Conflict
3.5.1 The Position of Piper
New Testament scholars who did accept Sanders' view of Sec-

---
48. Moltmann (1993, 147).

ond Temple Judaism tried to develop a position somewhere between those of Sanders and Dunn, on the one hand, and the traditional view on the other.[49] Among them were Stephen Westerholm, Thomas Schreiner, and Frank Thielman. Some of them were afraid that, due to Sanders and especially to people like Räisänen, the traditional view would be discredited to such an extent that Luther, Calvin, and the entire Protestant tradition, threatened to be pilloried as a retribution for what they had done to Judaism.[50]

Just like Dunn, these theologians are convinced that the Mosaic Torah cannot be separated from the Sinaitic covenant, which was rooted in God's electing grace. This was the grace that God had shown in delivering Israel from Egypt (Exod. 20:2; Deut. 5:6), as well as the grace that God continued bestowing upon them to cover the sins they committed under the Torah, as long as they had a repentant heart—a grace based on a bloody sacrifice. The covenant was not rooted in God's requirement to observe the Torah—even though Torah observance was important for the *maintenance* of the covenant—but in God's unconditional love (Deut. 7:6-8).[51] The Sinaitic covenant was a "closed system" of divine love and grace: first, the grace of God's election; second, the grace of God's redemption; third, the grace of God's care; and fourth, the grace of God's forgiveness after sin and repentance.

One of the theologians standing even more on the traditional side and critical of certain NPP views was John Piper, who took issue with N. T. Wright.[52] According to Piper (and the traditional view), "justification is the moment or the event

---

49. Westerholm (1988; 2003); Schreiner (1993); Thielman (1994); cf. also the contributions by Davies (1984, 91–122: "Paul and the Law: Reflections on Pitfalls in Interpretation"); Moo (1987); Gaston (1987); Klinghardt (1988); Snodgrass (1988); Liebers (1989); Martin (1989); Swidler *et al.* (1990); Segal (1990); Winger (1992); Wenham (1995); Finsterbusch (1996); Das (2001); and VanLandingham (2006).
50. Thielman (1994, 46).
51. See extensively, the second volume in this series.
52. Piper (2007).

when you put your faith in Jesus Christ and at that moment God is no longer against you—he's for you, and he counts you as acceptable, forgiven, righteous, obedient because of your union with Christ. You are perfectly acceptable to God and he is totally on your side. At that moment you are declared and constituted just, even though you're ungodly. Romans 4:4 [read: 5] talks about the justification of the ungodly, and Romans 3:28 says that 'we hold that one is justified by faith apart from works of the law.' . . . It's the moment and means by which we pass from being under the enmity of God to being under the favor of God, from being utterly unrighteous and damnable to being counted righteous in Christ by God so that he's our father and he's totally for us. There's what's at stake—How do you move from being on the wrong side of God to the right side of God? Paul said, 'We were by nature children of wrath.' [Eph. 2:3] We Christians—even we elect Christians—were by nature children of wrath. And now we're not under wrath anymore. Something happened."[53]

3.5.2 The Position of Wright

Piper placed this in opposition to several statements by N. T. Wright: "'Justification' in the first century was not about how someone might establish a relationship with God. It was about God's eschatological definition, both future and present, of who was, in fact, a member of his people. . . . [Justification] was not so much about 'getting in', or indeed about 'staying in', as about 'how you could tell who was in.'"[54] "Justification is not how someone becomes a Christian. It is the declaration that they have become a Christian."[55] Please note where the actual problem lies. It is not at all about the question whether there has been a moment in the life of the Christian when he "was converted," has "come to faith," has "passed from death to life," was "raised with Christ," was "reconciled with God,"

---

53. http://www.desiringgod.org/interviews/interview-with-john-piper-about-the-future-of-justification-a-response-to-n-t-wright.
54. Wright (1997, 119).
55. Ibid., 125.

etc. *The question is whether Scripture ever calls this moment, among other things, "justification."* In other words, is justification one of the many terms for this transitional moment, *or* is it rather a description of the new situation that has originated?

Now what is this question other than the question we dealt with in §1.3.2: the distinction between an "analytic" and a "synthetic" view of justification? We saw that analytic justification means that God, so to speak, "analyzes" Man, and then finds *in* him sufficient good because he himself had made Man righteous: justification is *declaring* the renewed person righteous, that is, the person who first had been renewed by God (comparable to the view of Wright). And this declaration is not an instantaneous thing, but a continual one: the saved person is continually shown to be righteous by his righteous way of life. In opposition to this, the "synthetic" approach puts all the emphasis on the fact that, at one specific moment, God justifies the *ungodly* (Rom. 4:5). Therefore, justification is thought to be, not a *declaring* the person righteous, but instantaneously *making* him righteous through a "synthesis" between the sinner and the righteousness of Christ (comparable to the view of Piper). In the former case, allegedly the emphasis lies on the justified person, in the latter case on Christ. In the former case, justification is allegedly an ongoing process; in the latter case, justification is an instantaneous event. We saw that some theologians called the former view more Lutheran — or even Roman Catholic — and the latter view more Reformed.

In my view, the entire distinction is basically a false one, since the New Testament teaches both that the ungodly is *made* righteous (Rom. 4:5, "synthetic") and that the believer united with Christ in his resurrection is *declared* to be righteous (cf. Rom. 6:7, "analytic"). There is nothing wrong with an "analytic" (Wrightian) approach as long as this definitely does not involve some righteousness that a person has in himself by nature, but only the righteousness that he has in union with Christ in his death and resurrection. There is nothing wrong with a "synthetic" (Piperian) approach either as long as justice is done to Romans 6:7, "For one who has died has been set free [or, justified] from sin": it is the one who has died and has been risen with Christ who in this condition is declared to be free of sin. Notice the perfect form *dedikaiōtai*: the person living in and through the risen Christ is judicially free from the power of sin as a consequence of something that happened to him in the past.

The Wright–Piper conflict is a typical example of what often happens in theology — or in academic discussions in general — namely, that there is truth in both positions. The same Paul who wrote Romans 4:5 also wrote Romans 6:7. I am afraid that Piper is too keen on defending the traditional view, thus missing the elements of truth in the newer view (which is not so new at all). Justification is both analytic and synthetic, both a process and instantaneous.

3.5.3 Salvation

There is another theological issue in the Wright–Piper conflict that I must mention here. John Piper blamed N. T. Wright for having made statements like these: "My proposal has been that 'the gospel' is not, for Paul, a message about 'how one gets saved.'"[56] "Paul's gospel to the pagans was not . . . a doctrine about how to get saved."[57] "'The gospel' is not an account of how people get saved. It is . . . the proclamation of the lordship of Jesus Christ."[58] The answer to such statements is not at all emphasizing how important it is to get saved, as Piper does. That is missing the point. Both Wright and Piper know that it is very important to get saved, otherwise one is eternally lost: "Whoever believes and is baptized will be saved, but whoever does not believe will be condemned" (Mark 16:16). "God did not send his Son into the world to condemn the world, but in order that the world might be saved through

---

56. Ibid., 60.
57. Ibid., 90.
58. Ibid., 133.

him" (John 3:17). "And there is salvation in no one else, for there is no other name under heaven given among men by which we must be saved" (Acts 4:12). "Then he brought them out and said, 'Sirs, what must I do to be saved?' And they said, 'Believe in the Lord Jesus, and you will be saved, you and your household'" (16:30-31). Wright knows and accepts these passages just as Piper knows and accepts them.

If I understand Wright correctly, he is making a point that I myself made several times in the previous volume in this series.[59] Salvation through Christ is of key importance, but it is not the pivotal point in the New Testament message. Salvation is not the primary *purpose* of the gospel, but rather the (indispensable) *means* to achieve the purpose of the gospel, which is the Kingdom of God in Christ. Reformed theologians declare God's forgiveness of sins, his redemptive grace for poor sinners, and getting them to heaven, as the core of "the" (biblical) gospel. However, as I argued in the previous volume, the redemption of sinners is never an aim in itself, but always only a means to an aim. That aim is not some place in heaven but the Kingdom of God on earth. Federalism even goes so far as to claim that all covenants are just varieties of the *one* "covenant of grace," which is specifically God's redemptive grace for sinners. In reality, *none* of the covenants is about God's redemptive grace as such, as I have endeavored to show.

When it comes to the Great Commission, Reformed theology puts too much emphasis on the gospel of "repentance and forgiveness of sins" (Luke 24:47), and too little emphasis on the "gospel of the Kingdom" (Matt. 4:23; 9:35; 24:14; cf. 28:18-19). Reformed theology is a theology of election and covenant; historically, it has hardly been Kingdom theology (except in the very broad sense of the Kingdom as God's universal, providential rule). I personally find the Kingdom a more central and comprehensive biblical notion than the

---

59. E.g., Ouweneel (2015b, §§9.1.2, 9.3.2).

covenant. It is more precise to say that the New Covenant is a *Kingdom* covenant than a form of the covenant of *grace*.[60]

To be sure, it is a tremendous thing that, from Adam until today, millions of people have been saved for eternity by surrendering themselves in faith to God (since Jesus, this includes faith in Jesus), by repenting and confessing their sins, and by receiving forgiveness of sins on account of a vicarious sacrifice (since Jesus, we know that this can only be *his own* sacrifice). All these people were in the mind of God from eternity; they were the objects of an election and predestination from before the foundation of the world. This is all wonderful. *But only to a limited extent does this involve the pivotal center of the New Testament message.* This may sound shocking in Reformed ears (including Piper's). To them, "the" covenant is everything, and redemption is everything, so the two must belong closely together. I have tried to show, however, that the main purpose of the covenants was not the eternal salvation of souls — no matter how precious this is in itself — but *the establishment of the Messianic Kingdom on earth.*

Of course, everything is related with everything. What would the Kingdom be without the eternal redemption of its subjects? But we should not confuse things. The thrust of the covenants is not the gospel of God's grace for poor sinners, but the *gospel of the Kingdom*. The reason federalists have difficulty seeing this is because of the enormous preponderance, since the church father Augustine, of the subject of God's redemptive grace for sinners. Individual redemption of sins and going to heaven are seen as God's ultimate *goal* instead of a *means* to a goal. However, in Scripture, the real goal is a collective one: the "kingdom of our Lord and of his Christ" (cf. Rev. 11:15).

3.6 Three Groups of Jews
3.6.1 Legalists

The problem signaled by Paul with respect to contempora-

---

60. Ibid., §§9.1.4 and 9.2.

neous Judaism did not lie in covenantal nomism as such, but in the way in which it was viewed by many Second Temple Jews. Both their literature and the New Testament point to (a) Jews who had replaced covenantal nomism with a legalistic polity of redemption through Torah observance as such, as well as to (b) Jews who entirely embraced what is called today "covenantal nomism." Let us look at these two groups, and additionally at a third group.[61]

As far as the first group is concerned, an apocryphal passage to be mentioned here is Sirach 15:15–17, "If you want to, you can keep the Lord's commands. You can decide whether you will be loyal to him or not. He has placed fire and water before you; reach out and take whichever you want. You have a choice between life and death; you will get whichever you choose."[62] Another example is Psalms of Solomon 14:1–2, "Faithful is the Lord to them that love Him in truth, to them that endure His chastening, to them that walk in the righteousness of His commandments, in the law which He commanded us that we might live."[63] Such passages do not exhibit any legalistic arrogance, or legalistic fear of God's judgment. Yet, especially the former passage does contain the idea that salvation depends, at least to a certain extent, on one's willingness to do good and to avoid evil, and to practice this.

In the New Testament, this is clearer still. In opposition to Ed Sanders, Heikki Räisänen and others, I maintain that there cannot be any doubt that in New Testament times there were legalistic Jews who confided in their own works-righteousness. I think of the Pharisee in Jesus' parable. Jesus "told this parable to some who trusted in themselves that they were righteous, and treated others with contempt" (Luke 18:9). Je-

---

61. Cf. Thielman (1994, 65–68); see also the extensive research by Carson *et al.* (2001; 2004).
62. Cf. Carson *et al.* (2001, 216–217).
63. http://wesley.nnu.edu/sermons-essays-books/noncanonical-literature/noncanonical-literature-ot-pseudepigrapha/the-psalms-of-solomon/; cf. Carson *et al.* (2001, 38, 40, 46).

sus' woes to the scribes (Torah-scholars) and the Pharisees were intended to expose their hypocrisy (Matt. 23:1-36; Luke 11:37-52). Besides hypocrisy, there was also real self-deception in their conviction "that they were righteous" and highly surpassed the tax collectors, the sinners, and the prostitutes (Matt. 9:10-17; 11:19; 21:28-32; Luke 7:36-50; 15:1-2; 19:7).

Paul's double presentation of the Torah (§3.1.1) fully agrees with this. On the one hand, the Torah is the guideline for those who wish to serve God under his gracious covenant (see [b] and cf. Rom. 2:13; 8:4; 13:8-10; 1 Cor. 9:20-21; Gal. 5:14; 6:2; Eph. 6:2-3). On the other hand, Paul strongly rejects any polity that presents the Torah as a way to obtain works-righteousness, and thus to earn salvation (legalism), or as a polity of Jewish arrogance (ethnocentrism) (Rom. 2:17-27; 3:19-31; 4:13-15; 6:14-15; 7:1-8:4; 9:30-32; 10:4; 1 Cor. 15:56; Gal. 2:16-19; 3:1-5:4, 18; Phil. 3:6, 9; 1 Tim. 1:7-10). It cannot be reasonably doubted that Jews forwarding such a polity really existed.

3.6.2 The Faithful

Of course, Judaism knew that "all our righteous deeds are like a polluted garment" (Isa. 64:6), as is also clearly expressed in the Jewish penitential litany *Avinu Malkeinu*. It was written by the famous Rabbi Aqiva (second century),[64] and is prayed at certain Jewish festivals. It says among other things: "Our Father, our King, have mercy on us and answer us, for lacking among us are good deeds. Do with us with [or, let there be among us] justice and steadfast love, and deliver us." Many upright Jews were, and are, conscious of the fact that divine salvation can be rooted only in the love and mercy of God, who demands obedience to the Torah, but also supplies the means for restoration after his people have broken the Torah.

The apocryphal books contain some beautiful examples of prayers of repentance and signs of faith in God's grace: "The Lord our God is righteous, but we are still covered with shame

---

64. Cf. Talmud: Ta'anith 25b.

... because we have sinned against the Lord our God and have disobeyed him. We did not listen to him or live according to his commandments. From the day the Lord brought our ancestors out of Egypt until the present day, we have continued to be unfaithful to him, and we have not hesitated to disobey him. . . . We refused to obey the word of the Lord our God which he spoke to us through the prophets. Instead, we all did as we pleased and went on our own evil way. We turned to other gods and did things the Lord hates. . . . We sinned against the Lord our God and refused to obey him. . . . The Lord our God is always righteous, but we and our ancestors are still burdened with our guilt. Even though the Lord punished us as he had threatened, we still did not turn to him and pray that we would abandon our evil thoughts" (Baruch 1:15–3:8).[65] Another example is the well-known Prayer of Manasseh (vv. 8–13; cf. 2 Chron. 33:12–13), which was written down by a godly Jew, probably shortly before AD 70.[66]

In opposition to the traditional view of Second Temple Judaism, it cannot reasonably be doubted that what we call "covenantal nomism" today was known and practiced in New Testament times. Earlier I mentioned several faithful Jews who observed the Torah but were conscious of the fact that their salvation depended on God's merciful forgiveness and deliverance (compare again Luke 1:6 with vv. 68–71). As far as the priests, the scribes (Torah scholars), and the Pharisees were concerned, definitely not all of them were hypocrites. Some of them assumed a positive attitude toward Jesus, and some even converted to him; consider the scribe in Mark 12:28–34; the friendly Pharisees in Luke 13:31, Acts 15:5 and 23:9; the wise Gamaliel (Acts 5:34–39); and as to the priests: "a great many of the priests became obedient to the faith" (6:7). The tax collector's prayer: "God, be merciful to me, a sinner!" (Luke 18:13) is as authentic an utterance of contem-

---

65. Cf. Carson *et al.* (2001, 8–9, 17).
66. See, e.g., http://beggarsallreformation.blogspot.nl/2011/06/luther-added-books-to-his-bible.html; cf. Carson *et al.* (2001, 157, 376).

poraneous Judaism as the legalistic arrogance of the Pharisee (vv. 11–12).

3.6.3 A Third Group

There may have been a third group posited by Sanders that did not necessarily boast in the Torah, but simply kept following the road of works-righteousness instead of accepting the true and only gospel of salvation: "Israel who pursued a law that would lead to righteousness did not succeed in reaching that law. Why? Because they did not pursue it by faith, but as if it were based on works.... Brothers, my heart's desire and prayer to God for them is that they may be saved. For I bear them witness that they have a zeal for God, but not according to knowledge. For, being ignorant of the righteousness of God, and seeking to establish their own, they did not submit to God's righteousness. For Christ is the end [goal, purpose, content, fulfillment] of the law for righteousness to everyone who believes" (Rom. 9:31–10:4).

Such Jews may have pursued this road in an earnest and humble way. However, by refusing the salvation in Christ they had to manage with their own works of legalistic righteousness. The point was not only that such works were insufficient. This was something that Jews who understood what Sanders called "covenantal nomism" ought to know; they did know that the true *tsaddiq* lives only by grace. Their real difficulty was that they had stumbled over Jesus: "They have stumbled over the stumbling stone, as it is written, 'Behold, I am laying in Zion a stone of stumbling, and a rock of offense [Ps. 118:22; Isa. 8:14]; and whoever believes in him will not be put to shame' [28:16]" (Rom. 9:32–33).

Chris VanLandingham has argued that mainstream Judaism in Paul's day indeed represented a religion that pleaded for good works as a way to God's favor, and that Paul in fact was not at all against this, but quite the contrary. His point was, however, that such a life of good works was possible only for those who, through Christ, had received forgiveness of sins.[67] In his works, N. T. Wright thought along the same lines. He argued that a person *is* justified by works, not in an (alleged) Judaist or Roman Catholic sense, but in the sense of James 2:14-26: "You see that a person is justified by works and not by faith alone" (v. 24). For Wright, this means that the actual justification—being declared righteous—takes place only at the end: the courtroom, of which the doctrine of forensic justification loves to speak, is only the "judgment seat of God (or, Christ)" (Rom. 14:10; 2 Cor. 5:10). John Piper has tried to refute this view on the basis of the traditional standpoint,[68] with an appeal to Pauline passages speaking of justification as the present possession of the believer (e.g., Rom. 3:24, 28; 10:10; 1 Cor. 6:11). Again, there is clear truth in both positions.

3.7 Again: The Two Polities
3.7.1 "Closed Systems"

Paul recognized the existence of the group described in §3.6.2: those Jews who were fully conscious of the import of "covenantal nomism," and precisely for this reason had come to faith in Jesus. He said himself, "We ourselves are Jews by birth and not Gentile sinners; yet we know that a person is not justified by works of the Torah but through faith in Jesus Christ, so we also have believed in Christ Jesus, in order to be justified by faith in Christ and not by works of the Torah, because by works of the Torah no one will be justified" (Gal. 2:15-16).

Justification by faith is not just a matter standing on its own. It is part of the new polity that has been introduced in the person and through the work of Christ. This new polity was called the New Covenant, involving the forgiveness of trespasses committed under the Torah as well as writing God's Torah in the hearts of his people. One day this New Covenant will be formally established with the house of Israel and the house of Judah. But the blessings of this New Cov-

---

67. VanLandingham (2006).
68. Piper (2007).

enant have been introduced already now in that the central figure of this covenant has entered into the world, and his blood has secured for all believers an "eternal redemption" (Heb. 9:12).[69]

I have extensively argued that the Old and the New Covenants have much more in common than many theologians seem to have been aware of. Both polities are "closed systems" of divine grace. They start with God's *electing* grace, they continue with God's *redemptive* grace. They subsequently place the redeemed on the footing of obedience to the Mosaic and the Messianic Torah, respectively, which, in fact, is grace, too: the gift of such a wonderful Torah is an act of the grace of God ("And what great nation is there, that has statutes and rules so righteous as all this law that I set before you today?" Deut. 4:8). Last but not least, each of the two covenants completes its respective polity with God's *atoning* grace, through which the failures in the people's disobedience are dealt with by animal sacrifices and by the sacrificial death of Christ, respectively. Both covenants are thoroughly Messianic in this sense that the Old Covenant pointed forward to the Messiah, and the New Covenant offers the fulfillment in the Messiah. All of this has been extensively dealt with in the two previous volumes in this series.

3.7.2 Torah and Christ

Perhaps this deep coherence of the two covenants comes to light nowhere more clearly than in Deuteronomy 30:11-14, to which Paul refers in Romans 10:5-8, where he says, "For Moses writes about the righteousness that is based on the Torah, that the person who does the commandments shall live by them. But the righteousness based on faith says, 'Do not say in your heart, "Who will ascend into heaven?"' (that is, to bring Christ down) 'or "Who will descend into the abyss?"' (that is, to bring Christ up from the dead). But what does it say? 'The word is near you, in your mouth and in your heart.'"

---

69. See Ouweneel (2015b, chapter 9).

The "But" at the beginning of verse 6, in ESV and many other translations, is quite interesting. It betrays the long tradition that creates a contrast between the old and the new polities. Upon closer look, it seems to me (and others) far more convincing to assume that Paul does not speak here in terms of contrast but of similarity. Thus, we should rather translate the Greek word (*de*, not *alla*) as "And," "Moreover," "Furthermore," or "All the stronger," "implying that what follows continues the thought already begun."[70] The reason is that exactly what Moses says concerning the righteousness that is by the Torah is said by Paul about the righteousness that is by faith. Again, there is no contrast here, but a clear similarity. Just as the Israelite should not say, "Who will ascend to heaven for us and bring it to us, that we may hear it and do it?" (Deut. 30:12), the Jesus-believer should not say that either. The Israelite does not have to ascend to heaven to bring the Torah down, because the Torah already descended on Mount Sinai, and was now in the heart of every faithful Israelite. The Jesus-believer does not have to ascend to heaven to bring the Messiah down, because the Messiah already descended into this world, and is now in the heart of every faithful believer.

There is no opposition here, but a strict parallelism, similar to the one Paul brings out in 2 Corinthians 3:2-3. The Old and the New Covenants can speak with one voice here. Of course, there *is* a contrast between Torah and gospel, but this should not be exaggerated: Paul makes the gospel speak in the language of the Torah.[71] The Torah is not abolished but absorbed by the gospel, under the influence of the Holy Spirit. We do not have to descend into the abyss in order to arrive at the core of the gospel because Christ has already been brought up from the abyss (death and the tomb). He is the Eternal Torah who now lives in the hearts of his people.[72]

In the summary of Frank Thielmann: the difference be-

---

70. Stern (1999, 397–400).
71. Thielman (1994, 243).
72. See extensively, Ouweneel (2015a).

tween Paul's view and that of common Judaism did not lie in the way each of them viewed the balance between God's grace and human responsibility.[73] In this sense, there was great similarity. No, the difference lay in the position of each in redemptive history. The Old Covenant had a strong anticipatory element in it: it looked forward to the restoration of Israel, and the establishment of the New Covenant. It realized its great lack: Israel waited for the coming of Messiah. Paul did not quarrel with the Old Covenant as such — he simply announced that its anticipation and expectation had now been fulfilled.

Judaism was not a wrong religion. How could this ever be, given the fact that God himself had given this ministry to his people. But it was a religion with a hole in its heart,[74] a hole that could be filled only by the Messiah. All of Judaism was intensely anticipatory; its entire identity lay in the expected and coming Messiah. All the more tragic, then, that when he indeed appeared, the majority of the Jews rejected him because he did not correspond with the specific form that their expectation had gradually acquired. What sense did Judaism continue to have after it rejected him who was its very goal, purpose, meaning, and fulfillment? It was like a bride who, after waiting for her bridegroom, when he arrives rejects him because she does not recognize him.

Jesus and the apostles never turned against the Jewish religion of their day because it would ostensibly be — or have become — a false religion. Rather, Jesus said about Jerusalem: "Would that you, even you, had known on this day the things that make for peace! But now they are hidden from your eyes" (Luke 19:42). Since those days, there is a veil over Israel: "[T]heir minds were hardened. For to this day, when they read the old covenant, that same veil remains unlifted, because only through Christ is it taken away. Yes, to this day

---

73. Thielman (1994, 245).
74. The metaphor reminds us of Blaise Pascal, who in his *Pensées* (chapter XXII) speaks of "a God who fills the soul and heart that He possesses."

whenever Moses is read a veil lies over their hearts" (2 Cor. 3:14-15). However, this is just as certain as the fact that, when Israel one day will turn to the Lord, this veil shall be taken away (v. 16 Darby).

3.8 NPP Issues
3.8.1 Linguistic Issues

For the traditional Lutheran-Reformed view of justification, many things were self-evident and undisputed that have now come to be questioned by NPP scholars. Here is a summary of some of the most important or interesting exegetical issues.

(a) Does the expression "God's righteousness" especially in Romans 1:17 and 3:21 refer to righteousness as an attribute of God's essence, or to a human righteousness according to God's criteria? The traditional view prefers the latter, many modern expositors prefer the former (see extensively chapter 1). This leads to other questions: How does God's righteousness relate to God's love and faithfulness? How can God at all be righteous when he declares ungodly people righteous (cf. Rom. 3:26; 1 John 1:9)?

(b) What does the expression *pistis Christou* mean, which Paul uses several times (Rom. 3:22, 26; Gal. 2:16, 20; 3:22; Phil. 3:9; cf. James 2:1; Rev. 14:12)? In other words, is *Christou* here an objective genitive, that is, does Paul refer to *our* faith in Christ (traditional view)? Or is it a subjective genitive: the "faith(fulness) of Christ" *to God* (e.g., NET and CEB in the passages mentioned; also the notes in ERV and EXB; cf. also Rom. 3:3 *pistin tou theou*, "faithfulness of God"; 4:16 "faith of Abraham"; 2 Tim. 2:18 "faith of some")? Or is it perhaps an adjectival genitive: *our* faith(fulness) to God like that which Christ on earth possessed toward God? Today, expositors differ greatly on this matter, which comes to light in the various modern Bible translations as well. I do accept the traditional view but leave this matter for what it is because it does not have great consequences for our view of God's righteousness and of justification (see further in §5.2.3).

(c) In the traditional view, the Greek word *charis* ("grace") was usually taken in the sense that the entire matter of our redemption was left to God's initiative, and any human activity was excluded. Today, people doubt that such a contrast is really involved in the term *charis* as such. The word does not necessarily stand in opposition to human *effort* but rather to human *merit*.[75] The point is not so much that people *cannot* do anything for their own salvation; this may in itself be true, but is a matter distinct from that of divine grace. The point is rather that people do not *deserve* anything from God, especially after their fall into sin.

Moreover, in the ancient world, *charis* always referred to a favor granted with the expectation of something in return, like a loan that has to be repaid.[76] Likewise, it is thought, God sent us his grace in the person of Jesus Christ *not* just because it was in his heart to grant us his blessings but because he wished to teach people how they could properly serve God. "We love because he first loved us" (1 John 4:19). The "grace of God has appeared," says Paul, *not only* "bringing salvation for all people," *but also* "training us to renounce ungodliness and worldly passions, and to live self-controlled, upright, and godly lives in the present age" (Titus 2:11-12). God's grace waits for a response — *not* as if, after all, we do have to contribute to our own salvation (because we cannot), but as a fruit that God himself works in and through us: "Therefore, my beloved, . . . work out your own salvation with fear and trembling, for it is God who works in you, both to will and to work for his good pleasure" (Phil. 2:12-13).

(d) Traditionalists like to point to a passage such as Ephesians 2:8 ("by grace you have been saved through faith. And this is not your own doing; it is the gift of God") to show that

---

75. Cf. Heidelberg Catechism, Q&A 21: ". . . These are gifts of sheer grace, granted solely by Christ's merit." Q&A 60: ". . . without any merit of my own, out of sheer grace." Q&A 63: "This reward is not earned; it is a gift of grace."
76. DeSilva (2000, 117).

Paul understood by "faith" that phenomenon through which a person instantaneously moves from the state of not-having-been-saved to the state of having-been-saved. To a certain extent, this may be correct. However, that does not change the fact that the Greek word *pistis* not only means "faith" but also "faithfulness," a firm commitment in an interpersonal relationship, in the case of humans even with the connotation of "surrender, submission."

In a situation where A has *pistis* toward B, B standing on a higher social level than A, *pistis*, "faithfulness," even borders on "obedience." To a large extent, saying that a slave is faithful to his master is identical to saying that the slave is obedient to his master. In other words, the Christian faith cannot be separated from surrender, submission, following Jesus, discipleship, devotion, consecration. In no way may faith ever be reduced to intellectually assenting to certain dogmas. In simple terms, true faith is not only embracing Jesus as Savior but also submitting to Jesus as Lord (see more extensively chapters 5 and 6).

3.8.2 Theological Issues (1)

(a) If we say that a person is justified by faith alone, what exactly do we mean by the word "alone"? The obvious traditional answer is: faith without works; think of the famous Reformed adagia *sola gratia* ("by grace alone") and *sola fide* ("by faith alone").[77] Today we ask: But can such a faith exist? What about James 2? In Galatians, Paul very sharply opposes the view that anyone can be justified by works; yet in this epistle faith is apparently "faith *working* [!] through love" (5:6), that is, faith producing *works* of love. Moreover, he admonishes: "Bear one another's burdens, and so fulfill the Torah of Christ" (6:2). So he pleads for "works of the Torah" after all! With him, it is not faith *versus* works, but faith in Christ with

---

77. Cf. Heidelberg Catechism, Q&A 60: "Q. How are you righteous before God? A. Only by true faith in Jesus Christ; . . . ." Q&A 61: "Q. Why do you say that you are righteous by faith only?"

the necessary works accompanying and evidencing faith, as opposed to, on the one hand, an empty faith (a faith without the necessary works accompanying and evidencing faith), and on the other hand, works without faith in Christ as their proper source and motivation.

(b) In line with the previous point, the question has arisen whether we can speak of a chronological order, as the traditional view has suggested: first, there is the faith by which a person is justified; subsequently there are the works that result from this faith (often linked with "sanctification"). Can faith and works indeed be distinguished, or even separated in this way? What evidence exists at all that, as the traditional view suggests, justification indeed occurs at a certain point in time: before that moment, the person was ungodly, and then there is the moment of conversion and regeneration, the moment of faith by which the person is henceforth righteous? God is the one who justifies the ungodly (Rom. 4:5), but does this mean that people turn in one moment of faith from ungodly into *tsaddiqim*? What is the biblical evidence for this?

N. T. Wright has argued several times that there is no evidence for this. Yet, I would like to point to Luke 18:14 ("this man went down to his house justified," the cardinal point being that before his confession he was *not* yet justified). See further Romans 3:24 (if the unredeemed can become a redeemed in the moment of faith, then the parallelism suggests that the unrighteous becomes a righteous in that same moment); 4:5 (justifying the ungodly suggests that at a certain moment the ungodly turns into a *tsaddiq*); 5:9 (we *have* been justified, and we *will* be saved); 1 Corinthians 6:11 ("washed," "sanctified," and "justified" apparently refer to the same moment of conversion).

(c) Following these questions, others arise: What is the relationship between being declared righteous and leading a righteous life? What is the relationship between analytic and synthetic justification? Is justification a declaration of *being* righteous, or is it a being *made* righteous? Is there a basic difference between saying, on the one hand, that God graciously enables the individual to believe, which first leads to salvation and second to good works (traditional view), and saying, on the other hand, that God graciously enables the individual to believe *and do good works*, which lead to salvation (NPP)?

(d) What exactly is Paul's objection to "works of the law"? Or is the traditional view false, and does Paul *in principle* have no objection at all? Does the expression "works of the law" necessarily involve a kind a righteousness that people try to obtain in their own strength? Both the traditional and the NPP views maintain that no person can obtain justification in his own strength, apart from divine regeneration and the power of the Holy Spirit. However, whereas NPP scholars maintain that God in the end does demand works-righteousness, traditionalists would object to such an idea. In other words, in the end, before the judgment seat of God, what is the decisive question? Is the person judged according to the works he has done, meeting the standards of the Torah or not (see for this many passages mentioned in §2.2.1)? Or will the only question that matters be whether the person "is not his own," but belongs, "body and soul, in life and in death," to his "faithful Savior, Jesus Christ"?[78] Or is this a false contrast?

(e) Is it true, as NPP suggests, that for Paul, justification is not so much about our relationship with God as it is about our relationship to our brothers and sisters in the church, that is, the unity of Jewish Christians and Gentile Christians in the church? Is it true that, thus, justification is more about who is part of the covenant community, and what are its boundary markers, than about how a person stands before God? The minimum that I wish to say at this point is that no one can seriously deny that justification is about a person's standing before God. First, "the tax collector, standing far off, would not even lift up his eyes to heaven, but beat his breast, say-

---

78. Cf. ibid., Q&A 1.

ing, 'God, be merciful to me, a sinner!' I tell you, this man went down to his house justified" (Luke 18:13-14). His relationships to other people were not involved at all; the only thing that mattered was his standing before God. Second, in Abraham's example (Gen. 15:6; Rom. 4:1-12), his horizontal relationships were not involved at all. It was all a matter of his confidence in God. But it is exactly Abraham who is *the* model of justification, both in Romans 4 and in James 2 (see further Rom. 4:25; 5:1, 9; 8:33).

3.8.3 Theological Issues (2)

(f) In line with this, is it correct, as especially Wright has argued many times, that justification is more about identifying someone as a member of the covenantal family of God's people, than about identifying his position before God? Does justification belong to ecclesiology rather than to soteriology? Of course, there is some truth in this. If the totality of all *tsaddiqim* coincides with the people of God, then the question who is a true *tsaddiq* is also a question who is a member of God's people, and who is not. Yet, it is not either-or. There seems clearly to be reactionary theology here. I already quoted Luke 18; let me now add 1 Corinthians 6:9-11, "Or do you not know that the unrighteous will not inherit the Kingdom of God? Do not be deceived: neither the sexually immoral, nor idolaters, nor adulterers, nor men who practice homosexuality, nor thieves, nor the greedy, nor drunkards, nor revilers, nor swindlers will inherit the Kingdom of God. And such were some of you. But you were washed, you were sanctified, you were justified in the name of the Lord Jesus Christ and by the Spirit of our God."

The context here is as soteriological as one could wish. The same holds for Titus 3:3-7, "For we ourselves were once foolish, disobedient, led astray, slaves to various passions and pleasures, passing our days in malice and envy, hated by others and hating one another. But when the goodness and loving kindness of God our Savior appeared, he saved us, not because of works done by us in righteousness, but according to his own mercy, by the washing of regeneration and renewal of the Holy Spirit, whom he poured out on us richly through Jesus Christ our Savior, so that being justified by his grace we might become heirs according to the hope of eternal life."

(g) Does justification consist of the imputation of the righteousness of Christ? If yes, what exactly does this mean? Are we speaking of the righteousness that Christ acquired on the cross for our justification and salvation, or are we speaking of the righteousness that Christ acquired during his life on earth by fulfilling the Mosaic Torah—a righteousness that, as it is alleged, subsequently is "imputed" to us, transferred to our spiritual account? (See extensively the next chapter.) In this context, what does it mean that Christ is the believers' righteousness (1 Cor. 1:30)? Or what does it mean that the believers have become God's righteousness in Christ (2 Cor. 5:21)?

It is amazing to see how vehemently the adherents of the traditional view respond especially to critical questions concerning the imputation doctrine. There is no doubt that the righteousness that the believers possess in Christ was acquired for them by Christ on the cross. However, for the traditionalists it seems quite difficult to see that this is something very different from some alleged "imputation of the righteousness of Christ," especially if this "righteousness" turns out to involve not (only) what Christ did on the cross but (also) his obedient fulfillment of the Torah during his life. The simple truth is that such an idea appears nowhere in Scripture, as we will see. This idea of the imputation of Christ's law-fulfillment to the believer is an invention of early Protestantism, and has acquired such an enormous power, also through confessional documents, that most Reformed leaders do not seem capable anymore of tolerating any serious question concerning this view. On the contrary, where such an imputation is denied—because it is not in Scripture—Reformed leaders respond as if the heart of the gospel is being attacked. This is a mystery to me.

Here are two examples. In answer to N. T. Wright, John Piper says, "To say that the imputation of God's righteousness across the courtroom onto the defendant in union with Jesus Christ is nonsense [as does Wright] is devastating."[79] Please note, it is not devastating for the gospel—how can anything that is not in the Bible, and is even contrary to Scripture (see chapter 4), be devastating for the gospel? No, it is devastating only for the Reformed doctrine of justification. The notion of imputation is its Achilles heel.

Another example: J. Ligon Duncan assures us that you are "preaching Paul correctly when you speak of justification as 'an act of God's free grace, wherein he pardoneth all our sins, and accepteth us as righteous in his sight, only for the righteousness of Christ imputed to us, and received by faith alone.'"[80] The quotation is from the Westminster Shorter Catechism Q&A 33. In discussing this matter, one Presbyterian church's website explains: "Imputation is God's act of reckoning righteousness or guilt to a person's credit or debit. It is as if we had obeyed the law and had satisfied justice."[81] This is a double error: nowhere in Scripture is justification seen as "reckoning righteousness to a person's credit," and nowhere in Scripture do we find the thought that Christ fulfilled the Torah as our substitute. But the Westminster Standards say so! That is supposed to be decisive; therefore, for J. Ligon Duncan, too, to doubt these notions is to doubt the gospel itself.

Undoubtedly, NPP scholars have made their own mistakes. But many Reformed theologians hardly gave them a fair trial. For some NPP critics, the mere fact that NPP deviated from the Westminster Standards was sufficient to condemn them. We have encountered the same problem with re-

---

79. http://www.desiringgod.org/interviews/interview-with-john-piper-about-the-future-of-justification-a-response-to-n-t-wright
80. http://www.ligonier.org/learn/articles/attractions-new-perspectives-paul/
81. http://www.cambridgepres.org.uk/cat/cat33.html.

spect to the covenant.[82] Once a matter has been stated in the Westminster Standards a fair discussion is no longer possible. This is not academic theology at work; this is confessionalism.

---

82. See Ouweneel (2015b, §§4.2, 4.3).

Chapter 4
The Imputation Doctrine

[Y]ou are in Christ Jesus, who became to us
  wisdom from God,
  righteousness
  and sanctification
  and redemption.
                                    1 Corinthians 1:30

For our sake he made him to be sin
  who knew no sin,
so that in him we might become
  the righteousness of God.
                                    2 Corinthians 5:21

Summary: *This chapter entails an attempt to refute the ancient Reformed idea (already found with Calvin) that the righteousness of Christ, that is, his Torah obedience, has been imputed to (i.e., transferred to the account of) the believers, and that this is the essence of biblical justification. First, it is a wrong rendering of the Greek verb* **logizomai**. *Second, the theory is based on a wrong idea of Christ's vicarious obedience. Third, it involves a mistaken idea of Christ's Torah obedience: the latter does not alleviate our guilt, but aggravate it. Fourth, even if this obedience could be "imputed" to us, it would not really be of any help to us. Fifth, the New Testament does* *not link our justification with Jesus' life on earth but with his death and resurrection. Not his obedience is credited to us, but his status as the risen and glorified Christ. Today, more and more Reformed theologians seem to begin to grasp the New Testament evidence.*

4.1 Introduction
4.1.1 Confessional Testimonies

IN THIS CHAPTER, I deal especially with two related misunderstandings that are common to the Reformed doctrine of justification. The first misunderstanding has to do with the term "imputation" ("imputed righteousness"), and the second one with the term "righteousness of Christ." The two phrases meet with one another in the fundamental misunderstanding that some "righteousness of Christ," taken to be his observance of the Mosaic Torah, would be "imputed" to believers(-to-be).

The Heidelberg Catechism has this to say: God "grants and imputes to me the perfect satisfaction, righteousness, and holiness of Christ, as if I had never committed nor had any sins, and had myself accomplished all the obedience which Christ has fulfilled for me; . . ." (Q&A 60).

The Belgic Confession says (Art. 22 and 23) "Jesus Christ, imputing to us all His merits, and so many holy works which He has done for us and in our stead, is our righteousness. . . . David and Paul teach us, declaring this to be the blessedness of man that 'God imputes righteousness to him apart from works.'"

The Westminster Confession tells us (XI.1): "Those whom God effectually calleth, He also freely justifieth . . . by imputing the obedience and satisfaction of Christ unto them." And further (XI.3): "Christ . . . in as much as . . . His obedience and satisfaction [are] accepted in their stead. . . ."

The Westminster Larger Catechism says (Q&A 70–71): "Justification is an act of God's free grace unto sinners, in which he pardoneth all their sins, accepteth and accounteth their persons righteous in his sight . . . for the perfect obedience and full satisfaction of Christ, by God imputed to them, and received by faith alone ... inasmuch as God accepteth the satisfaction from a surety ... and did provide this surety, his own only Son, imputing his righteousness to them" (cf. also Q&A 77).

Finally, the Second Helvetic Confession (XII) says: "Christ is the perfecting of the Law, and our fulfilling of it; who as He took away the curse of the Law, when He was made a curse for us so He communicates unto us by faith His fulfilling thereof, and His righteousness and obedience are imputed unto us." Further (XV): "God, therefore, is merciful unto our sins, for Christ alone, that suffered and rose again, and does not impute them unto us. But He imputes the righteousness of Christ unto us for our own: so that now we are not only cleansed from sin, and purged, and holy, but also endued with the righteousness of Christ; yes, and acquitted from sin, death, and condemnation (2 Cor. 5:19–21); finally, we are righteous and heirs of eternal life."

In summary, besides many good and biblical things, these Reformed confessions and catechisms tell us this about justification: God grants, or credits, or imparts, or imputes to me the righteousness of Christ, that is, (among other things) the obedience of Christ, that is, Christ's perfect fulfillment of the Torah. In other words, Christ accomplished for us, and in our stead, what we could not accomplish ourselves: the obedience to or fulfillment of the Torah. This obedience of Christ is imputed (granted, credited, imparted, conveyed, transferred) to the believer so that God views him as if he had fulfilled the Torah himself. Generally speaking, righteousness is identical with the fulfillment of the Torah. Justification is making righteous, that is, bringing someone in a state as if this person had himself fulfilled the Torah. Since he could not do this, due to his sinfulness, Christ did this in his stead. Christ's fulfillment of the Torah is imputed to the sinner so that God can now view him as righteous.[1]

---

1. See for this imputation doctrine already *Luther's Works* XXV (Lectures on Romans) 35, 36.2, and Calvin, *Institutes* 3.11.2 and 3.11.12.

4.1.2 "Counting as Righteousness"

The starting point for our discussion of the imputation doctrine is Genesis 15:6, where we read: Abraham "believed the Lord, and he [i.e., the LORD] counted it to him [i.e., to Abram] as righteousness." As I said in §2.5.2, the expression "he counted it to him as righteousness" is not immediately transparent, and is therefore rendered in many different ways: "He accounted it to him for righteousness" (NKJV; cf. GNV), "he credited it to him as righteousness" (CJB, NIV, MEV; cf. WEB), "He reckoned it to him as righteousness" (RSV, NASB). Much more freely is "God considered him righteous on account of his faith" (TLB), which I consider to be a fair rendering of the verse. One might say that it is faith that is counted as righteousness, as some translations suggest (cf. Paul in Rom. 4:5); this is not wrong as long as faith is not taken as a kind of meritorious act. Perhaps it will cause less misunderstanding if we say that the believer is counted as righteous on account of his faith.

Paul deals with this verse in Romans 4. As we saw, in Romans 3:25, Paul speaks of justification on account of the *death* of Christ (his blood; cf. 5:9). In Romans 4:25, he speaks of justification on account of the *resurrection* of Christ. This implies a distinction in the nature of the believer's faith as well. In Romans 3:22 and 26 it is faith *in Christ*, on account of which God acquits a person of his sins in a righteous way. In Romans 4:24-25 it is faith *in God*, "who raised from the dead Jesus our Lord, who was delivered up for our trespasses and raised for our justification," so that we, "since we have been justified by faith, have peace with God through our Lord Jesus Christ" (5:1).[2] The believer trusts in Christ, who through his propitiatory death made the believer's justification possible, and he trusts in God, who gave his Son unto death and resurrection in order to make the believer's justification possible.

Abraham is here Paul's example: he justified, so to speak,

---

2. See Han (1995, 231–39) on Rom. 4:25.

God (declared God to be righteous) in *his* words and works (cf. Luke 7:29; Rom. 3:4–5), and therefore God justified *him* (declared *him* righteous). He put all his confidence in God and his promises, and on account of this faith God recognized him as a *tsaddiq*. As Paul explains, Abraham believed that God was mighty to produce life from a condition of death, and on account of this faithful confidence in and submission to God and his promises he was declared to be righteous.[3] What Abraham did here in view of what God was *going* to do in and through the "son of promise" typologically represents what the believers of the present dispensation are doing in view of what God *has* done in and through the Son of promise (cf. §2.5.3). God has produced life from a condition of death in that he raised Christ, who had died for our sins, in view of our justification. And he did this not only by forgiving us our sins, but first and foremost by uniting us with the risen Christ in his new position. The person who believes that God has done this for him will receive his share in this. God sees him just as righteous as the dead and risen Christ.

4.1.3 Acquittal

Whereas Romans 3 deals with what *Jesus* has accomplished for us, Romans 4 deals with what *God* in Jesus has accomplished for us. Whereas Romans 3 deals with the *grace* of God, on account of the blood of Christ, Romans 4 deals with the *strength* of God toward us. The Torah required strength of humanity, but humanity does not possess this strength: "For while we were still weak, at the right time Christ died for the ungodly" (Rom. 5:6). However, God raised Jesus from the dead in order to unite these weak persons with Jesus in his resurrection. The *blood* of Christ constituted the foundation; it is on this basis that we can be cleansed from our sins. The *resurrection* of Christ puts us in a clean place and in a position before God that is perfectly new. It is about what we now have and are: through his blood we *have* the forgiveness of

---

3. Coates (1926, 68–69).

our sins, through his resurrection we *are* what the risen and glorified Christ is: righteous before God.

God acquits the believer of sins. This is not only in the sense that God has forgiven him his sins, because this would actually not be an acquittal. A genuine acquittal means being exculpated because the legal and convincing evidence of the indicted crime has not been delivered. In this sense the sinner is *not* acquitted; on the contrary, the convicting evidence *has* been delivered: "Now we know that whatever the Torah says it speaks to those who are under the Torah [i.e., the Jews], so that every mouth [i.e., not only Gentile but also Jewish mouths] may be stopped, and the whole world may be held accountable to God. For by works of the law no human being will be justified in his sight, since through the Torah comes knowledge of sin" (Rom. 3:19-20).

Every human being is found guilty—yet, there is acquittal. How can this be? God acquits the believer of sins in the sense that, since the latter's conversion and regeneration, God views this person as a "new man" in an altogether new position. This is the believer united with a risen Christ, so that this person has nothing to do anymore with his former sinful state: "For one who has died has been set free from sin. Now if we have died with Christ, we believe that we will also live with him. We know that Christ, being raised from the dead, will never die again; death no longer has dominion over him. For the death he died he died to sin, once for all, but the life he lives he lives to God. So you also must consider yourselves dead to sin and alive to God in Christ Jesus" (Rom. 6:7-11).

Who shall bring any charge against the risen Jesus? Unthinkable. But precisely there, in the risen Jesus, we find the measure and character of our own justification. Is such a justification not worthy of God? He does not overlook sin, he does not pass over any trespasses; they are blotted out by the blood of Christ. But even more than that: in the risen Christ, God has presented to us the true character of our righteousness.

The righteousness we possess is more than mere forgiveness; our righteousness is of the same character as that of the risen Christ.[4]

"We were buried therefore with him by baptism into death, in order that, just as Christ was raised from the dead by the glory of the Father, we too might walk in newness of life" (Rom. 6:4). It was with glory, and with infinite satisfaction, that the Father raised the Son, in order that he would be the object of the Father's pleasure entirely beyond the reach of sin and death—and this all happened in view of *our* walking in newness of life.[5] No one will ever understand the New Testament doctrine of justification unless one begins to grasp the union of the believer with the risen and glorified Christ.

This is the view that differs essentially from that of the imputation doctrine, as we will see. In this doctrine, the measure and character of our justification is not the *glory* of the *risen* Christ but the *obedience* of the *humbled* Christ on earth. Of course, there is a measure of understanding concerning what Jesus did in his death and resurrection. But when it comes to the character of the righteousness that the believer possesses before God, the Reformed doctrine does not primarily look at the risen and glorified Christ, but to what he did during his life as an obedient Jew under the Mosaic Torah. The two approaches are miles apart. This is what we now have to consider.

4.2   Imputation?
4.2.1   "Counting as Righteousness"

In Genesis 15:6, the verb "to count" is Hebrew *h-sh-b*, as we find it, for instance, in 2 Samuel 19:19 (NKJV), "Do not let my lord impute iniquity to me" (ESV: "Let not my lord hold me guilty"), or in Psalm 32:2 (NKJV), "Blessed [is] the man to whom the Lord does not impute iniquity" (ESV: "Blessed is the man against whom the Lord counts no iniquity"). Already

---
4. Ibid., 71.
5. Ibid., 106.

in these verses, we see immediately that "imputing" does *not* mean "transferring" iniquity from one account to another, but "counting": "imputing iniquity" to someone means holding him guilty, counting him as guilty. This is the regular meaning of *h-sh-b*, for instance: "he thought she was a prostitute" (Gen. 38:15, lit.: he counted [viewed] her as a prostitute); "Eli took her to be [i.e., counted (viewed) her as] a drunken woman" (1 Sam. 1:15); "Why do you . . . count me as an enemy?" (Job 13:24; cf. 33:10); "[they] count me as a stranger" (19:15).

This fully explains Genesis 15:6: God counted Abraham as righteous, held him to be righteous, viewed him as righteous on account of his faith. One might say: God *imputed* righteousness to him, as long as this is not taken to mean "transferred" (imparted, conveyed) righteousness from one account to another, as the imputation doctrine wrongly understands it. Imputing iniquity or righteousness *never* means transferring iniquity or righteousness; it means "counting as evil (guilty)" and "counting as righteous," respectively, on account of someone's bad behavior, or of someone's faith and/or good behavior, respectively.

To put it in the words of N. T. Wright: If we use the language of the law court, it makes no sense whatever to say that the judge imputes, imparts, bequeaths, conveys, or otherwise transfers his righteousness to either the plaintiff or the defendant. Righteousness is not an object, a substance, or a gas that can be passed across the courtroom. If and when God does act to vindicate his people, his people will then, metaphorically speaking, have the status of "righteousness." But the righteousness they have will not be God's own righteousness. Such a way of putting it would make no sense at all.[6]

John Piper responded to this: "To say that the imputation of God's righteousness across the courtroom onto the defendant in union with Jesus Christ is nonsense is devastating."[7]

---

6. Wright (1997, 98–99).
7. http://www.desiringgod.org/interviews/interview-with-john-piper-about-the-future-of-justification-a-response-to-n-t-wright.

But devastating for what? It is indeed devastating for the classical Reformed doctrine of justification. But it is *not* devastating for the Pauline doctrine of justification, because Paul *nowhere* teaches that God transferred (imputed, imparted, bequeathed, conveyed) some righteousness of Christ to believers. We have been justified (declared righteous) in Christ, we have become God's righteousness in Christ, Christ has become our righteousness—but that is something essentially different from a righteousness transferred from Christ to us, especially if this righteousness is thought to be Christ's Torah obedience. People may quote the Westminster Standards for that, but they cannot quote Paul or any other apostle for that.

Let us look at this matter more closely. The Greek term used in the translation of Genesis 15:6 in Romans 4 is *logizomai*: "For what does the Scripture say? 'Abraham believed God, and it was counted [*elogisthē*] to him as righteousness.' Now to the one who works, his wages are not counted [*logizetai*] as a gift but as his due. And to the one who does not work but believes in him who justifies the ungodly, his faith is counted [*logizetai*] as righteousness, just as David also speaks of the blessing of the one to whom God counts [*logizetai*] righteousness apart from works: 'Blessed are those whose lawless deeds are forgiven, and whose sins are covered; blessed is the man against whom the Lord will not count [*logizētai*] his sin'" (vv. 3-8). Let us now investigate how these terms *h-sh-b* and *logizomai* have given rise to several misunderstandings in the Reformed doctrine of justification.

As a starting point for my considerations, it seems to me undeniable that what in Romans 4:3 and at other places is called "counting someone's faith as righteousness" is exactly the same as "counting someone as righteous on account of faith," or "counting righteousness to someone on account of faith" (vv. 6, 10-11, 23), and this is identical with what is called elsewhere in Romans "justifying someone by faith." Likewise, "attaining righteousness" (Rom. 9:30; cf. 10:3-6, 10; 1 Cor. 1:30; Phil. 3:9) is the very same as "being justified."

Linguistically, there is no difference of opinion on this matter anymore.[8]

In Romans 4, the verb "to count" is linked with "righteousness" in two ways: *logizomai eis dikaiosynē* (vv. 3, 5, 9–10, 22; Gal. 3:6; cf. James 2:23), that is, "counting as [lit., for, to] righteousness," and *logizomai dikaiosynēn* (vv. 6, 11), that is, "counting righteousness" (to someone). I repeat, the two expressions mean exactly the same thing. A small difference appears in verse 4, because here it is not a question of "righteousness" but of "wages": "his wages are not counted as a gift but as his due," that is, to credit someone's wages, recording them as assets.

4.2.2 Imputing Righteousness

The expressions "counting against someone his sin" (v. 8; 5:13) and "counting righteousness" to someone (vv. 6, 11; cf. 23–24) constitute each other's counterpart. The former means: declaring someone to be sinful (if so desired: recording someone's sin as asset) in order to punish him on account of this. Parallel with this, the latter means: declaring someone to be righteous (if so desired: recording someone's righteousness as asset) in order to acquit him on account of this. *Logizomai* means "to count," and hence also "to appreciate, to estimate," for instance, Greek *eis outhen*, "as [lit., for, to] nothing" ("the temple of the great goddess Artemis may be counted as nothing," Acts 19:27), *eis sperma*, "as offspring" ("the children of the promise are counted as offspring," Rom. 9:8). *Eis dikaiosynēn* thus means: count "for righteousness," namely, someone's faith. In other words, on account of a person's faith, he is viewed as a righteous one.

Now the essential point in our discussion is that in the New Testament *logizomai never* means transferring the righteousness of Christ from Christ's account to the believer's ac-

---

8. See extensively, Kittel *et al.* (1967, 4:284–92); Brown (1992, 3:822–26); cf. Ridderbos (1959, 92–93); Murray (1968, 1:134–35); Moo (1996, 262, incl. n35).

count. At Romans 5:18 ("one act of righteousness leads to justification"), the Annotation in the *Statenvertaling* (the Dutch equivalent of the King James Version) points to Philemon 1:18 ("If he has wronged you at all, or owes you anything, charge that to my account"). However, this is incorrect, since in the latter verse we do not find *logizomai* but *ellogeō*.

It is incredible to see how widely this mistake has spread even in our own time. Karl Barth speaks of "a divine accounting or crediting (3:28) in favor of Man."[9] Bruce Demarest says that believers are justified in that God credits righteousness on their account.[10] David Kasali, too, translates *logizomai* as "to credit" and explains this as that which happens in a financial transaction: pay a certain amount on someone's account.[11] Johan Heyns speaks of "crediting the acquittal,"[12] which even linguistically seems unacceptable to me. Many more examples from relatively recent authors could be mentioned.

Rudy Budiman has rightly emphasized the established fact that *logizomai* never involves a granting (conveying, imparting, transferring, consigning) of a righteousness, as it were, from one account to another.[13] On the contrary, it always involves a declaration that someone *possesses* righteousness, which is the same as: *is* righteous, namely, on account of faith. This is also clear from the parallel with verse 8: "[B]lessed is the man against whom the Lord will not count (*logizētai*) his sin" (cf. Ps. 32:2, "Blessed is the man against whom the Lord counts [*h-sh-b*] no iniquity"). Counting sin against someone means: declaring that someone is sinful, guilty, and *not*: granting (conveying, imparting, transferring, consigning) sin to someone, or even: transferring someone else's sin to

---

9. Barth (1933, ad loc.).
10. Demarest (1997, 371).
11. D. M. Kasali in Adeyemo (2006, 1358).
12. Heyns (1988, 312).
13. Budiman (1971, 118–19); cf. the title of Van Genderen (1988): *Gerechtigheid als geschenk* ("Righteousness As a Gift").

this person, as it were, booking an entry from that person to this person. Everyone understands that, and as far as I know no one has ever given this interpretation. But if this is so, why is it so difficult to see that it is exactly the same with counting righteousness to someone? This is declaring that this person is righteous, *not* granting someone else's righteousness to this person, or transferring the righteousness of that other person to this person, as it were booking an entry from that other person to this person.

4.2.3 Iustitia Aliena

The incorrect interpretation of (*h-sh-b* and) *logizomai* has led to the notion of the *iustitia aliena*, "alien righteousness." On a website we are told concerning this notion by an anonymous author (italics added): "*Iustitia aliena* is a Latin phrase meaning 'alien righteousness.' This was and continues to be the heartbeat of the Reformation—the basis of the Christian's justification before God. The reason that we are, as Luther said, *simul iustus et peccator* (righteous and simultaneously sinner) before God is because of this *iustitia aliena* credited to the Christian's account by grace alone through faith alone in Christ alone. Without the active obedience of Christ imputed to us, God would not be both 'just and the justifier of the one who has faith in Jesus' (Rom. 3:26). Thus, God declares the sinner who has faith in Christ righteous, not based on the sinner's own righteousness, but based solely on the righteousness of Christ."[14]

Notice what happens here. With deep conviction I am claiming that the idea of an "alien righteousness" is a mistake, whereas the anonymous writer tells us that it is the "heartbeat of the Reformation"! Let me hasten to add that, of course, I do believe that Jesus has obtained my righteousness through his death on the cross and his resurrection (Rom. 3 and 4). That is not the issue. I do believe that Christ has become "righteousness" to me (1 Cor. 1:30), and that in him I have become "the

---

14. https://iustitiaaliena.wordpress.com.

righteousness of God" (2 Cor. 5:21). What I do *not* believe is that the personal righteousness of Christ, exhibited in his observance of the Torah, has been transferred from his account to mine; in the words of the anonymous author: an alien righteousness "credited to the Christian's account . . . the active obedience of Christ imputed to us." I do not believe this for two reasons: first, the New Testament never tells me this, and second, in my view, the New Testament *could* not possibly tell me such a thing.

This is an unpleasant situation: I am implicitly told that I deny the "heartbeat of the Reformation." To my delight, I will be able at a later stage to mention some Reformed authors who have problems with this *iustitia aliena* as well.

To begin with, the notion of the *iustitia aliena* has been defended by many Reformed authors.[15] Writing on Romans 3:1, Karl Barth also used the term *iustitia aliena*,[16] though not in the first print of the second edition of his *Römerbrief* ("Epistle to the Romans"). In his hand copy of the second print he added this in handwriting, and since the third print it has been included in the text.[17]

An incorrect starting point, once chosen, subsequently leads to all kinds of superfluous, time wasting discussions. A striking example is the question whether imputation implies that the believer now really possesses righteousness (Augustine), or whether it remains an alien righteousness, that is, outside the believer, so that God only deals with him "as if" he possesses this righteousness (Luther).[18] In banking terms: has this righteousness become an asset registered in the believer's account, or does it remain an asset in Christ's account for the benefit of the believer? The discussion surrounding this ques-

---

15. To mention only a few more recent theologians: Hoek (1988, 74); Van Genderen and Velema (2008, 611); Spykman (1992, 494); Demarest (1997, 359); White (2001, chapter 7); Piper (2007, chapter 8).
16. Barth (1933, ad loc.).
17. C. van der Kooi in ibid., 537n175.
18. See McGrath (2010, 457–59).

tion has sometimes flared up heatedly.[19] This is deplorable, because the entire discussion is unnecessary and mistaken, as one can recognize as soon as the idea of "counting" in the sense of "granting (crediting, imparting, conveying, transferring)" has been surrendered. No righteousness was "given" to Abraham, no righteousness was transferred from God's account to his account, whatever this may mean. No, because of his confidence in God he was "counted" (viewed, marked) as righteous. It is this Abraham whom Paul uses as a model, because today the person placing his trust in God is likewise "counted" (viewed, considered, marked) as righteous in Christ.

R. C. Sproul has focused the discussion on the question whether the believer's righteousness is inherent to him, or has been credited (transferred) to him from Christ. In line with the Reformers, Sproul resolutely chooses the latter, and even makes this the core of the allegedly biblical doctrine of justification.[20] I myself resolutely choose the former. Scripture does not know anything of a transference or crediting of Christ's righteousness to the believer. However, it does know — and in my view *this* is the core of the matter — a righteousness that is indeed inherent to the believer, that is, inherent to his new position in the risen and glorified Christ. I emphasize that this righteousness is *not* inherent as if the believer could ever have such a righteousness on account of anything that he possesses by nature. But it definitely is inherent to the *new* man, "created after the likeness of God in true righteousness and holiness" (Eph. 4:24). And even more clearly: in Christ we have *become* the "righteousness of God" (2 Cor. 5:21). In Christ the believer *is* righteous(ness); it is inherent to what he now is in Christ.

4.3 More About *Logizomai*
4.3.1 No Transference

In order to explain further the meaning of *logizomai*, let us look

---

19. Berkouwer (1954, 85–88).
20. Sproul (1995, chapter 5, especially 99–103).

at Romans 2:26, "So, if a man who is uncircumcised keeps the precepts of the law, will not his uncircumcision be regarded [or, counted] as circumcision?" That is, will this person, though uncircumcised, not be counted as (viewed as, held to be, considered to be) circumcised? Here again, *logizomai* does *not* mean some kind of granting (conveying, imparting) circumcision, and even less does it mean transferring someone else's circumcision to that person's account. That would be absurd. However, Reformed traditionalists refuse to see that transferring someone else's righteousness to another person's account is equally absurd. At any rate, such a view follows neither from the meaning of *logizomai*, nor from any direct New Testament statement. *Logizomai* means *always*: counting (viewing) a person as this or that, holding him to be this or that, *never* transferring anything to that person.

Why is it so difficult to see this? In fact, today we should not need to have any discussion on these linguistic aspects anymore, in light of the modern Bible translations of Romans 4:5 (NKJV "his faith is accounted for righteousness"): "Then he [i.e., God] accepts their faith, and that makes them right with him" (ERV); "it is this faith that God takes into account in order to put them right with himself" (GNT). "God declares sinners to be good in his sight if they have faith in Christ" (TLB); "that trusting-him-to-do-it is what gets you set right with God, *by* God" (MSG). "God accepts their faith, and that makes them right with him" (NCV); "that man is made right with God because of his trust in God" (NLV). Likewise, Romans 9:30 (NKJV "have attained to righteousness") becomes: "were made right with God" (ERV; cf. NCV, NLV); "were put right with him" (GNT).

In summary, Romans 4:5 or 9:30 is not dealing with the "righteousness of God" or the "righteousness of Christ" (whatever this may be; see §4.5), but with the "righteousness by [on account of] faith" (4:11). The first type of righteousness is usually the righteousness of God himself, which he demonstrates when declaring someone righteous (3:26). What the second one might be, I will try to explain later in this chapter. The third one is the believer's *own* righteousness after God has declared him to be righteous on account of faith. It is Christ who, through his propitiatory death and resurrection, has made the believer's righteousness possible. But that is something essentially different from some practical righteousness (Torah observance) of *Christ himself* that allegedly would have been transferred to the believer's account. The latter is the righteousness that Christ possesses himself, comparable with the righteousness *of* God, that is, the one that God himself possesses, and that must be distinguished from the righteousness *[stemming] from* (Greek, *ek*) God, which the believer possesses (Phil. 3:9).

The believers *owes* his righteousness to God's grace and to the redemptive work of Christ — but this is something essentially different from the claim that the believer himself would have received the righteousness of God or Christ. Of course, if a person who is thoroughly sinful by nature is declared righteous, that is, is counted (viewed, marked) as righteous, this is always *from* God. By himself Man can never attain any form of righteousness; it is the work of the Holy Spirit. However, this in no way implies that the personal righteousness of *God* or of *Christ* himself has been transferred to his account. The New Testament nowhere makes such a statement, and it does not follow from the words *h-sh-b* and *logizomai*. Apparently, we must conclude that it is a Reformational invention.

4.3.2 Again: Imputation

We have to occupy ourselves at length with the term *logizomai* because the Reformed doctrine of justification has attached such far-reaching consequences to it. As a starting point for our further investigation, I take the Annotation of the Dutch *Statenvertaling* on Romans 4:5 (freely rendered): God is said to account someone's sin to this person if he wants this sin to be blotted out by punishment. God is said to *not* account this sin to this person if he forgives it and cancels the earned penalty

(Rom. 4:8). Likewise, he accounts faith to righteousness in the sense that God grants, credits, imparts, and accounts to believers the righteousness of Christ, who is accepted in faith by them, and even grants, imparts and credits this righteousness graciously to them as if it were their own righteousness.

In my view, there is minimal logic in this argument. We would be dealing with a valid analogy only if it were based on a consistent argument: accounting sin to someone implies viewing him as a sinner on account of this sin, and accounting righteousness to someone implies viewing him as a righteous one on account of his faith. The idea of transferring some righteousness from elsewhere is just as absurd as transferring some sin from elsewhere. Sinners *themselves* are sinful, that is, they are *counted* (viewed, marked) as sinful. Likewise, believers *themselves* are righteous, that is, they are counted (viewed, marked) as righteous, not because of anything they are or have of themselves but because they are in Christ, as having died and been raised with him.

Let me point here to a certain ambiguity that is present in the word "impute" as such, and that may be viewed as a major cause of the entire problem. In Leviticus 17:4 we read: "[B]loodguilt shall be imputed to that man." It would be absurd to assume that "imputation" means here that some guilt is transferred from someone else's account to this man's account. No, here "imputing" means the same as "counting": the man is "counted" as guilty. "Imputing iniquity" to someone (NKJV in 2 Sam. 19:19; Ps. 32:2; Rom. 4:6, 8; 5:13; 2 Cor. 5:19) means counting this person as unrighteous. Likewise, "imputing righteousness" to someone (Rom. 4:11, 23–24 NKJV) means counting this person as righteous. *Never in the New Testament does* logizomai *mean some transference from one account to another*. Nonetheless, the idea of Christ's righteousness being "imputed" to the believers—transferred from his account to theirs—is called the "imputational" doctrine of justification. Inadvertently—I assume—the word "impute" is being used here in an essentially different way than it is used in the New Testament, especially in the (N)KJV, where the verb occurs more than in other translations.

The imputation doctrine must be right because the word "imputation" is in the Bible, it is argued. Why do so few Reformed theologians see that they use the term in an essentially different way than the Bible does? The imputation doctrine must be right, it is argued, because it was Christ, and no one else, who has obtained the righteousness of believers through his death and resurrection. This is perfectly correct. But why do so few Reformed theologians see that this is something essentially different from the notion that Christ's *own righteousness* — not only the righteousness obtained on the cross but his righteousness as a perfect Torah observant Jew — would have been transferred to the believer's account? Time and again we will have to ask this question.

Reformed theologian Jan van Genderen rightly wrote: "The word 'impute' does occur in the Bible, but a doctrine of the imputation of the righteousness of Christ can only be found in Reformed theology and in the Reformed confession."[21] This is an honest and correct rendering of the situation — to which I have to add that in this theology and confession, the meaning of "imputation" in no way corresponds with the biblical meaning of "imputation."

Anglican theologian Leon Morris underscored that Paul never explicitly says that the righteousness *of Christ* is imputed to believers, and he even doubted whether Paul had this in mind when he dealt with justification. Nevertheless, Morris believes that it might be an implication of Paul's doctrine of the union of the believer with Christ[22] — which I seriously doubt. Believers are counted as righteous because God views them as united with the risen Christ. But that is something very different from some transference of Christ's righteousness to the believers' account. As C. Anderson Scott put it, we must conclude that the righteousness that is involved in

---
21. Van Genderen (1988, 67).
22. Morris (1955, 257).

justification is neither credited nor apportioned—it is an attributed *status*.[23] This hits the nail on the head.

4.3.3 The Obedience of Christ

The idea of the imputation of the righteousness of Christ is both linguistically incorrect and theologically totally foreign to the New Testament. Nonetheless, this idea was introduced into Reformed theology at an early stage. As I quoted in §4.1.1, the Heidelberg Catechism (Q&A 60) says (less than half a century after the outset of the Reformation) that "God . . . grants and credits to me the perfect satisfaction, righteousness, and holiness of Christ," and refers to "the obedience which Christ has fulfilled for me" (i.e., in my stead). This matter of the "obedience of Christ" plays a vital role in the Reformed imputation doctrine, and is based on Romans 5:19, "For as by the one man's [i.e., Adam's] disobedience the many were made sinners, so by the one man's [i.e., Christ's] obedience the many will be made righteous." The meaning of this phrase will be dealt with extensively in §4.5.3.

The word "obedience" re-occurs in the Westminster Confession (XI.1): ". . . imputing the obedience and satisfaction of Christ unto" believers, and (XI.3): "[Christ's] obedience and satisfaction [are] accepted in their stead." It occurs again in the Westminster Larger Catechism (Q&A 70): ". . . the perfect obedience and full satisfaction of Christ, by God imputed to them, and received by faith alone" (also cf. Q&A 77). Allegedly, this "obedience" is Christ's observing the Torah, as it is said in the Second Helvetic Confession (XII): "Christ is the perfecting of the Law and our fulfilling of it. . . . [S]o He communicates unto us by faith His fulfilling thereof, and His righteousness and obedience are imputed unto us."

The questions that must be raised here are: What precisely *is* this "righteousness of Christ"? What does it mean that God allegedly imparts to the believer this righteousness of Christ, and that Christ has allegedly accomplished a certain obedi-

---

23. Anderson Scott (1927, 97).

ence for the believer (in his stead)? Where do we read that God does this, and that Christ has done this, respectively? At any rate, not in the various Bible passages to which the confessions and catechism refer.

In the Belgic Confession (Art. 22), we find the same thoughts in a less outspoken form: "Jesus Christ, imputing to us all His merits, and so many holy works which He has done for us and in our stead, is our righteousness." If we understand by this that the merit of Christ's work on the cross is imparted to those who believe, I do not see any problem, although we have to admit that the expression "all his merits, and so many holy works which He has done for us and in our stead" seems to be much wider than Christ's work on the cross (see below). But the real difficulty lies in the Heidelberg Catechism (Q&A 60) and in the Annotation on Romans 4:5: What does the righteousness of Christ entail, and what does it mean that God credits this to us?

4.3.4 Woelderink and Berkouwer

It is striking that a Reformed theologian such as Gerrit C. Berkouwer in his significant study on justification hardly touches upon this question. In an uncritical way, he accepts the Reformed tradition on this point without submitting it to closer scrutiny,[24] which is quite amazing for such an astute dogmatician. He objects to those who assert that Romans 4 "does *not* deal with the imputation of Christ's righteousness but with the subjective righteousness of faith"[25] — whereas the latter is the very subject of Romans 4, as Reformed theologians Harm Jan Jager and Jan Gerrit Woelderink have argued.[26] Thus, Woelderink rightly opposed these words of Herman Bavinck: "The phrase 'to reckon faith as righteousness' is an abbreviated way of saying that God in faith imputes his righteousness, — the righteousness granted in Christ — to persons and

---

24. Zook in Berkouwer (1954, 41–42).
25. Berkouwer (1949a, 85; omitted from the English edition).
26. Jager (1939); Woelderink (1941); cf. Van Genderen (1988, 68).

The Imputation Doctrine

on that basis acquits them."[27] Woelderink called this a magical playing (*goochelen*) with words, which was quite harsh. However, Berkouwer did nothing but support Bavinck without offering the Scriptural underpinning that Bavinck failed to offer as well.

I cannot explain this in any other way than by the power of a paradigm, in this case the "justification by imputation" paradigm. This is a power so strong that no adherent takes the trouble anymore to supply us with any evidence. If "everybody" believes a certain thing, why prove the truth of it? In such a situation, independent Reformed thinkers such as Woelderink are seen as being simply a pain in the neck.

A little later, Berkouwer said: "When Jager and Woelderink combat the traditional [read, Reformed] exegesis, they can do so only by removing from the word 'imputation' its weighty force, and by leveling it down in the direction of the divine ascertaining, namely, of the subjectively present righteousness of faith."[28] But I repeat, this is exactly what *logizomai* means, as I have shown from all the biblical examples. No theological prejudice can ever change this undeniable linguistic fact. The "weighty force" in the word "imputation" exists only in Berkouwer's bias, *not* in the root-meaning of *logizomai*. Therefore, that other Reformed theologian, Woelderink, was perfectly correct when he said: "The meaning of these words that faith is counted to him as righteousness is therefore none other than that God recognizes the believer as righteous before him. . . ."[29]

That which does not fit our theology cannot be removed from the text through linguistic emendation, nor are we allowed to read into the text that which does fit our theology. Woelderink saw in this an unfortunate result of the battle against Remonstrantism (Arminianism), and he might be right

---

27. Woelderink (1941, 210); cf. Bavinck (2008, 4:212).
28. Berkouwer (1949a, 87; omitted from the English edition).
29. Woelderink (1941, 208).

in this:[30] the words "he counted it to him as righteousness" have been "botched up exegetically in an awful way, and in various manners people wanted to read the impartation and imputation of Christ's righteousness into these words, whereas they cannot mean anything else than that God has counted faith as righteousness." He even called it "a rather coarse deviation from the doctrine of Scripture when some of our divines in the eighteenth century taught that the justification of the believer consists in the fact that God imparts and imputes the righteousness of Christ to the one who believes."[31]

I can only wholeheartedly agree with these words, no matter how sharply some theologians may have responded to Woelderink. To put it even more strongly: I am glad that it was precisely Reformed theologians who put their finger on this ancient error, so that it is not always outsiders who point out mistakes in the Reformed tradition. I have great respect for all those theologians who have the courage to expose in *their own* tradition errors that have been handed down throughout the ages. To this end, one needs an open mind as well as spiritual courage. Good examples are some other recent discussions: the one between Robert H. Gundry, who is opposed to the classical imputation idea, and Donald A. Carson, who is an adherent of it,[32] as well as the one between N. T. Wright, who is opposed to the classical imputation idea,[33] and John S. Piper, who is an adherent of it.[34]

4.4 Bestowed Righteousness
4.4.1 Righteousness of God in Christ

The fact that the word *logizomai*, "to (ac)count," has been misunderstood so often, namely, in the sense of an "imputation" (transference) or "impartation," raises the question whether we can speak at all of a "granted" (imparted, given,

---

30. Ibid., 209.
31. Ibid.
32. In Husbands and Treier (2004).
33. Wright (1997; 2002; 2009).
34. Piper (2007).

conveyed) righteousness. Of course, many have spoken like this. Thus, Johan Heyns wrote: "God justifies Man by imparting to him the righteousness of Christ in the form of faith in Christ."[35] Herman Bavinck even wrote: "[B]elievers do indeed obtain the righteousness of Christ by infusion."[36] Others have claimed that God imparts to the believers his own righteousness.

Can we indeed say this? God's righteousness is manifested in the fact that he declares the person righteous who has faith in Jesus (Rom. 3:21-26). But this is not the same as granting his own righteousness to such a person. Scripture never says anything like it, and this is certainly striking. It never speaks of a "granting" ("imparting") God's or Christ's righteousness to believers. However, it is not sufficient to establish this fact. What matters is the question whether such an expression is in the spirit of Scripture. In my view, this is the case in a certain limited sense and to a certain limited extent — as long as one does not connect this with the root meaning of *logizomai*.

Let us look first at 2 Corinthians 5:21: "For our sake he made him to be sin who knew no sin, so that in him we might become the righteousness of God." Since the Epistle of Mathetes to Diognetus (second century) this has been referred to as the "holy" or "sweet exchange" (Greek: *glykeia antallagē*; Latin: *sacrum* or *admirabile commercium*) or "joyful exchange" (German, *fröhlicher Wechsel*, Latin, *beatum commercium*, so Luther): the righteous Christ became sin for sinners, so that sinners could become the righteousness of God.[37] This is what the Epistle said (9:5): "O the sweet exchange, O the inscrutable creation, O the unexpected benefits; that the iniquity of many should be concealed in One Righteous Man, and the righteousness of One should justify many that are iniquitous!"[38] Also compare the similar idea in 2 Corinthians 8:9,

---

35. Heyns (1988, 313).
36. Bavinck (2008, 4:249).
37. See, e.g., Luther's *Commentary on Galatians*, on Gal. 3:13.
38. Cf. Ouweneel (2009, §§7.2.3, 9.1.2, 9.3.4) on this "sweet exchange."

"For you know the grace of our Lord Jesus Christ, that though he was rich, yet for your sake he became poor, so that you by his poverty might become rich."

Having *become* "righteousness of God" is the same as saying that God has *made* us "righteousness of God." Here, "righteousness of God" certainly does *not* mean the same as what it means, as I see it, in Romans 1:17; 3:21–22 (see §§1.6 and 1.7), namely God's own being righteous (cf. 3:25–26). In 2 Corinthians 5:21, Paul deals with *our* having become (or been made, or been declared) righteous in the sense of Philippians 3:9, ". . . having a righteousness . . . which comes through faith in Christ, the righteousness from God." This is about "having" (Greek, *echōn*) righteousness, which is substantially the same as having been justified, or being righteous.[39] However, what we "have" we do not "have" by and from ourselves; in this sense one can certainly say that we have "received" it. This righteousness is *ek theou*, "from (or, out of) God" (Phil. 3:9), and we possess it *en autoi*, "in him," that is, Christ (2 Cor. 5:21).

4.4.2 Christ Our Righteousness

In this context, 1 Corinthians 1:30 is of interest: "And because of him [or, from him, out of him, i.e., of God; Greek, *ex autou*] you are in Christ Jesus, who became to us wisdom from God, righteousness and sanctification and redemption." This is a new way of expressing the same old truth: Christ *is* our righteousness, represents our righteousness, is the foundation for our righteousness, is the embodiment of our righteousness.

The verse reminds us of an Old Testament formulation: "[T]his is the name by which he [i.e., the Branch, i.e., the Messiah] will be called: 'The Lord is our righteousness'" (Jer. 23:6; cf. 33:16, where the same name is applied to Jerusalem). In God's eyes, we are what the Son of God is: righteous.[40] The "new man" has been "created after the likeness of God in

---

39. Hughes (1962, 214); Harris (1976, 354–55).
40. Bernard (1979, 73).

true righteousness and holiness" (Eph. 4:24). In principle, the "new man," that is the person that has been made one with the risen and glorified Christ, is just as righteous as God himself or Christ himself is.

We see that the expression "righteousness of God" can mean two very different things. On the one hand, it means God's own righteousness, his own being righteous. This has certainly to do with justification because God is righteous in justifying the penitent sinner who comes pleading on the blood of Christ (Rom. 3:26; cf. 1 John 1:9, the righteousness of the forgiving God). On the other hand, the "righteousness of God" refers to the righteousness of the believing person, a righteousness that is "from" ("out of") God (Phil. 3:9), and is possessed "in" Christ. This righteousness characterizes the new man to such an extent that it can be said of him that he *is* "righteousness of God" (2 Cor. 5:21) and "created in true righteousness" (Eph. 4:24). We might express this by saying that the justified person has become a monument to God's own righteousness.

However, Scripture never describes this as a transference of God's, or Christ's, own intrinsic or practical righteousness to the believer (the imputation doctrine). The believer is counted as righteous in Christ, he is not credited with a righteousness from somewhere else, namely, the Torah obedience of Christ.

4.4.3 "Clothed" with Righteousness

There is a practical illustration in Scripture that underscores the fact that, as such, it is not wrong to say that God has granted (imparted) righteousness to the believer: "I will greatly rejoice in the Lord; my soul shall exult in my God, for he has clothed me with the garments of salvation; he has covered me with the robe of righteousness" (Isa. 61:10). We find a similar thought in Psalm 132:9 and 16: "Let your priests be clothed with righteousness, and let your saints shout for joy. . . . Her priests I will clothe with salvation, and her saints will shout for joy." A practical application of this is found in the high priest Joshua: "And the angel said to those who were standing before him, 'Remove the filthy garments from him.' And to him he said, 'Behold, I have taken your iniquity away from you, and I will clothe you with pure vestments.' And I said, 'Let them put a clean turban on his head.' So they put a clean turban on his head and clothed him with garments. And the angel of the Lord was standing by" (Zech. 3:4-5).

In this context, Alister McGrath refers to Martin Luther, who said that the believer is "clothed" with the righteousness of Christ, in the broad sense of Ezekiel 16:8, "When I passed by you again and saw you, behold, you were at the age for love, and I spread the corner of my garment over you and covered your nakedness; I made my vow to you and entered into a covenant with you, declares the Lord God, and you became mine."[41] The passages mentioned before this one are clearer because they refer explicitly to "righteousness" and "iniquity" ("unrighteousness"). The believer is "clothed" with righteousness; this is the same as saying that he has been justified (declared/made righteous); this is the same as saying that he *is* righteousness, namely, righteousness from God and in Christ.

Somewhat excessive is the description by Lewis Sperry Chafer: "[D]ivine justification is . . . a divine decree which declares the believer to be eternally clothed with the righteousness of God."[42] This is followed by the amazing statement: "[I]t has no relation to the resurrection of Christ, but is based only upon His death" — this in spite of Paul's statement: ". . . Jesus our Lord, who was delivered up for our trespasses and *raised for our justification*" (Rom. 4:24-25).

Similarly excessive is the statement by John R. Rice: "Jesus took off the seamless robe of righteousness so we could wear it . . . Let God count us righteous for Jesus' sake even as He counted Jesus as a sinner and let Jesus die on the cross! God

---

41. McGrath (2010, 458).
42. Chafer (1983, 2:278).

would clothe us with the garments of salvation and the robe of righteousness, even as He covered Adam's and Eve's nakedness with garments of skins from innocent animals."[43] Jesus took off his own righteousness, and was counted by God as a sinner? Do we need any stronger language than Paul already used in 2 Corinthians 5:21: God "made him to be sin"?

The idea of being "clothed" with righteousness does not imply, as Rome has sometimes alleged against the Reformation, that this would only be a covering cloth of Christ's righteousness, whereas "underneath" everything would remain what it was.[44] There seems to be some basis for this reproach because Luther argued that the believer is *simul iustus et peccator*, that is, simultaneously righteous (in hope, or *de iure*) and sinner (*de facto*). That is, inwardly we remain sinners, but in God's eyes we are righteous.[45] Here we come across the disturbing "as if" again (see above): *are* the believers really righteous, or *are* they really still sinners, but righteous "only" (a) in the verdict (acquittal) of God, and (b) in an anticipatory sense: looking forward to what they will be in the heavenly bliss (as Karl Barth, too, continually argues in his *Römerbrief*)?

I would like to ask the counter-question here: Does 2 Corinthians 5:21 — we *are* righteousness of God in Christ — leave any room for an "as if"? Paul even says: "God shows his love for us in that while we *were* still sinners, Christ died for us" (Rom. 5:8). What a stark difference! On the one hand, we have Luther's (and the Reformed) view: we *are* still sinners but at the same time righteous *before God*. On the other hand, we have the Pauline view: we *were* sinners, but *now* we are, as a matter of principle, righteous (*tsaddiqim*), even though we still have the "flesh" (the sinful nature) in us.

The sinner, that is, the "old man," is not simply the person who still has the sinful nature in him, but the person who is *dominated* by it (Rom. 6:12; cf. as a contrast vv. 18, 22; 8:2:

---

43. Rice (2000, 29).
44. Berkouwer (1952, 28).
45. Ibid., 71–73; McGrath (2010, 458–59).

"[set] free from [the power of] sin"). The righteous person, that is, the "new man," is one who still has the sinful nature within him, but who is no longer *dominated* by sin but by righteousness. This is the force of what 1 John says: "No one who abides in him keeps on sinning; no one who keeps on sinning has either seen him or known him. . . . No one born of God makes a practice of sinning, for God's seed abides in him, and he cannot keep on sinning because he has been born of God" (3:6, 9). "We know that everyone who has been born of God does not keep on sinning, but he who was born of God protects him, and the evil one does not touch him" (5:18). Applied to justification: "If you know that he is righteous, you may be sure that everyone who practices righteousness has been born of him" (2:29). "Whoever practices righteousness is righteous, as he is righteous . . . whoever does not practice righteousness is not of God" (3:7, 10).

4.5 Righteousness of the Law?
4.5.1 Evangelical and Reformed

From where does the expression "the righteousness of Christ," which figures so strongly in the Reformed doctrine of justification, come? What is its content and import? This is what we will now have to investigate more closely. The claim that justification involves the "imputation of the righteousness of Christ" is engrained so deeply in the Reformed tradition that later authors hardly seemed, and seem, to take the trouble to explain to us what exactly they understand by the "righteousness of Christ." Here we encounter the power of a dogma: once it has been (a) defended by influential religious leaders, (b) set forth in confessional documents, (c) and generally accepted within a certain tradition, later generations expend hardly any effort to investigate its legitimacy. This was the case, for instance, for Louis Berkhof and Gerrit Berkouwer, but I suppose that it has happened to most theologians at one time or another. Yet, just as the Reformers questioned the Roman Catholic doctrine of justification, there can be no objection if we question the Reformational doctrine of justification.

If those who hold the imputation doctrine do take the trouble of explaining what exactly they believe, they come up with biblical explanations such as: we are justified by faith, on account of the death of Christ; our righteousness was obtained by Christ on the cross. I wholeheartedly embrace this view. However, that is something very different from the personal righteousness *of Christ* being imputed (transferred) to us, especially if this righteousness is linked not only with Christ's death but also with his life of obedience under the Torah.

Incidentally, it is not only Reformed authors but also, for example, Pentecostals such as Guy P. Duffield and Nathaniel M. Van Cleave who tell us, without any further supporting argumentation, that the righteousness of Jesus Christ is imputed to all those who believe in him, and they call this the basis of our justification and redemption.[46] Later they tell us that the imputation of the perfect righteousness of Christ is like this righteousness being put in our account.[47] Apparently, such Evangelicals have adopted these ideas uncritically from the Reformed tradition. It does not even occur to them to scrutinize such a powerful dogma in the light of Scripture.

Herman Bavinck frequently referred to the "righteousness of Christ," giving us only once—as far as I can assess—a hint as to what he understands by this (without this time mentioning the expression): "For when God justifies the ungodly, he does it on the basis of a righteousness that he himself has effected in Christ. By Christ's sacrifice, against all hostile powers, he has acquired the right to acquit the ungodly, ..."[48] Elsewhere, he claims that the "imputed righteousness of Christ" would be his active obedience, that is, his observance of the Torah, although he warns against "too sharp a distinc-

---

46. Duffield and Van Cleave (1996, 180).
47. Ibid., 234–35; see further 237–38.
48. Bavinck (2008, 4:214); cf. 223–24.

tion between Christ's passive and his active obedience."[49] We encounter here the important expressions "active" and "passive obedience" of Christ, which we will have to investigate below (§4.7.1).

Reformed theologian Willem H. Velema points in the same direction: "In Paul's epistles, to justify someone always means *to declare him righteous by imputing to him the righteousness obtained through Christ's sacrifice.*"[50] The truth is that Paul's letters *never* speak of justification this way, but it is positive that Velema at least takes the trouble to describe the "righteousness of Christ": it is the righteousness that Christ has obtained for us through his sacrifice. Unfortunately, he detracts from this himself by speaking elsewhere of "atonement ... in Christ's vicarious sacrifice in obedience to the law."[51]

Reformed theologian Jan van Genderen, too, connects justification with Christ's sacrificial death: "Righteousness is not to be taken here as an attribute or condition, but as imputed righteousness. The condemnation of Christ was our acquittal, and by his wounds we have been healed [Isa. 53:5; 1 Pet. 2:24]."[52] And thus, Reformed writer Aart Moerkerken rightly describes the "righteousness of Christ" as "the righteousness that Christ has obtained through his death."[53]

Even if we might stumble over the formulations being used, at any rate these are more biblical answers than what we find with Martin Luther and John Calvin. The reason is that the latter, unfortunately, do not speak (only) of the *death* of Christ, but (first and foremost) of the *life* of Christ, his living obediently under the Mosaic Torah. Both argued more or less as follows: I need a righteousness that perfectly satisfies the requirements of God's law—this cannot mean anything else than the Mosaic Torah—and with which I can stand be-

---

49. Ibid., 224.
50. Van Genderen and Velema (2008, 610; cf. 616-18).
51. Ibid., 637.
52. Van Genderen (1988, 71).
53. Moerkerken (2004, 246).

fore the judgment seat of God. Such a righteousness is the righteousness of Christ because he has perfectly fulfilled the Mosaic Torah for me, in my stead. I need not only forgiveness of my trespasses of the Torah, but I need a perfect obedience to the Mosaic Torah as well. I do not have this; however, the active righteousness of Christ is imputed to me. *That* is my justification.

Now my point is not so much what exactly Luther and Calvin have written, although many theologians are constantly fighting over this matter. My point is not to attack or, for that matter, to defend Luther and Calvin. Rather, I am seeking to examine what their followers, Lutherans and Calvinists, have to say about the imputation of Christ's active righteousness (his observance of the Mosaic Torah) to the believer, as it comes to light especially in their confessional documents.

4.5.2 Calvin and Calvinists

As a good starting point, then, let us begin with John Calvin. In his *Institutes of the Christian Religion*, he writes (3.14.12) about "the free goodness with which the Father embraces us in Christ when he clothes us with the *innocence* of Christ, and accepts it as ours, so that in consideration of it he regards us as holy, pure, and innocent. For the righteousness of Christ (as it alone is perfect, so it alone can stand the scrutiny of God) must be sisted for us, and as a surety represent us judicially. Provided with this righteousness, we constantly obtain the remission of sins through faith. Our imperfection and impurity, covered with this purity, are not imputed but are as it were buried, so as not to come under judgment" (italics added).[54] And elsewhere (3.17.10): "Therefore, as we ourselves when ingrafted into Christ appear righteous before God, because our iniquities are covered with his *innocence*" (italics added).[55]

We are stunned: the righteousness of Christ is his *inno-*

---

54. http://www.biblestudytools.com/history/calvin-institutes-christianity/book3/chapter-14.html.
55. Idem, chapter-17.html.

cence? It is not so much his blood shed for us but rather his innocence that as a "surety" represents us judicially? It is not so much the vicariously dying Jesus but rather the sinless Jesus who is my advocate before the judgment seat of God? Where do we find this in Scripture? Naturally, we need a high priest who is "holy, innocent, unstained" (Heb. 7:26) — but the first thing we learn about him is that he became "a merciful and faithful high priest in the service of God, to make propitiation for the sins of the people. For because he himself has suffered when tempted, he is able to help those who are being tempted" (2:17-18).

Of course, there are many places in the *Institutes* where Calvin speaks of the significance of Jesus' blood and redemptive work. But in the passages just quoted, *this* turns out to be our justification: once we were guilty, but now we are clothed with the innocence of Christ. However, this is not what we find in Scripture: according to the New Testament we need someone to pay for our sins (Matt. 26:28; Acts 2:38; 5:31; 10:43; 13:38; 26:18; 1 Cor. 15:3; Gal. 1:4; Col. 1:14; Heb. 1:3; 2:17; 10:12; 1 Pet. 2:24; 3:18; 1 John 2:2; 4:10; Rev. 1:5), not someone whose innocence is imputed to us.

We find similar thoughts in Calvin's commentary on Romans: "First, the question respecting our justification is to be referred, not to the judgment of men, but to the judgment of God, before whom nothing is counted righteousness, but perfect and absolute *obedience to the law*; which appears clear from its promises and threatenings: if no one is found who has attained to such a perfect measure of holiness, it follows that all are in themselves destitute of righteousness. Secondly, it is necessary that Christ should come to our aid; who, being alone just, can render us just by *transferring to us his own righteousness*. You now see how the righteousness of faith is the righteousness of Christ" (italics added).[56]

Now, in connection with the "obedience of Christ," Cal-

---

56. http://www.ccel.org/ccel/calvin/calcom38.txt on Rom. 3:22.

vin does rightly say "that Christ, in satisfying the Father, has provided a righteousness for us."[57] But *when* did Christ satisfy the Father? Through his obedient life under the Torah, or through his propitiatory death? Indeed, there are the passages where Calvin does not refer to Christ's propitiatory death at all but only to the personal righteousness of Christ: his being righteous during his life on earth; or even simply his innocence (sinlessness, guiltlessness, perfection). Moreover, *this* would allegedly be the righteousness that is "transferred" (Calvin's term) to us. And *this* in essence would be what Paul calls "justification."

Louis Berkhof, too, tells us that Christ's observance of the Mosaic Torah was necessary for our justification. He does not take the trouble to base this on any scriptural evidence but simply sees it as a consequence of the Reformed doctrine of the covenant.[58] This is a striking example of how self-evident a certain unbiblical idea can become within a certain tradition. This situation is rooted in the (mistaken) argument that a (supposedly) logical conclusion from a (supposedly) biblical doctrine is just as biblical as that doctrine itself.[59]

In the old Reformed Form for the Celebration of the Lord's Supper we find the same argument: Christ has "fulfilled all obedience and righteousness of the divine law for us, in particular [but apparently not exclusively, WJO] when the weight of our sins and of the wrath of God pressed out of him the bloody sweat in the Garden," etc. Here it is said unequivocally that Christ fulfilled the law of God (that is, the Mosaic Law) *for us*; this cannot mean anything else than "as our substitute."

Even the simplest believer may rightly wonder where we

---

57. Idem on Rom. 5:19.
58. Berkhof (1949, 380–81).
59. Cf. Westminster Confession of Faith (I.6): "The whole counsel of God concerning all things necessary for his own glory and man's salvation, faith, and life, is either expressly stated in Scripture or by good and necessary inference may be deduced from Scripture: . . . ."

find in Scripture that Christ's observance of the Mosaic Torah is imputed to the believer. We have to ask some very serious questions here.

(a) What have I, as a Gentile believer, to do with the Mosaic Torah? I was never under it, I *am* not under it, or under a part of it; see extensively the first volume in this series on this vital point. Therefore I do not need at all a righteousness that corresponds with the Mosaic Torah. At best we might say that I need a righteousness that corresponds with the Eternal Torah of God — see again the first volume — but such a distinction is never made in Reformed theology.

To be more specific: Why would I need at all someone who fulfilled the Sabbath laws for me, in my stead? Why do I need someone who fulfilled the *kashrut* (food laws) for me? Why do I need someone who fulfilled the festival laws for me? Why do I need someone who fulfilled the circumcision law for me? Why do I need someone who fulfilled the sacrificial laws for me? Fulfilling the law is fulfilling the law; we cannot just pick out some of the "moral" parts of it, such as the Ten Commandments, because, as I argued in the first volume, the Bible does not make this kind of distinction. Did people who asserted and assert that Christ fulfilled the law in our stead really think this through?

(b) Where do we read that God imputes to me the righteousness (innocence, Torah obedience) of Christ? Paul tells us that God "imputes righteousness" to believers (Rom. 4:6, 11, 23-24 NKJV), but as we have seen, this unequivocally means that believers are "counted as" righteous, and never that some righteousness from outside was credited to their account. But even if we would have to believe that some righteousness is transferred to believers from outside, a righteousness coming from God, on what basis are we required to assume that this is the innocence (Torah obedience) of Christ?

(c) Where do we read at all about the righteousness of Christ? Hardly ever. Christ has become righteousness to us

(1 Cor. 1:30), but that is not the same. 2 Peter 1:1 does indeed speak of "the righteousness of our God and Savior Jesus Christ," but here the point is what this righteousness does for us. There is no reference to any righteousness, to say nothing of Christ's observance of the Torah during his life on earth, that is transferred to us.

4.5.3 Imputed Obedience?

Of course, the critical questions I am raising here do not as such constitute sufficient refutation of the imputation doctrine. I am not even too much concerned if certain expressions do not occur in Scripture (famous examples are "trinity" and "substitution"). However, we are dealing here not with certain expressions that do not occur, but with full-fledged theological arguments, for whose basis I can find no trace in Scripture, and which are not in the spirit of Scripture either, as I intend to show. Take the very starting point of both Luther and Calvin: I need a righteousness that perfectly satisfies the requirements of God's highest moral standards, and with which I can stand before the judgment seat of God. I completely agree. How does a person get this righteousness? The believer has it through being united, by faith, with the dead and risen Christ (Rom. 4:24–5:1; 6:6–7). The righteousness of the risen Christ is the believer's righteousness.

No, say the Reformers, that will not do. A righteousness that perfectly satisfies the requirements of God's law—viz., the Mosaic Torah—can be the righteousness only of someone who has perfectly *obeyed* the Torah. We could not do that, so Christ did it for us; and the righteousness he thus obtained has been imputed (transferred) to us. Where do we read this in the Bible? Nowhere. Not a trace. As a faithful Jew, Christ perfectly obeyed the Mosaic Torah. But first, the Bible never suggests that he did this as the believers' substitute. Second, the Bible *could* not have suggested this because Gentile believers never *were* under the Mosaic Torah. Third, the Bible never says that this practical Torah obedience of Christ has been transferred to believers, so that God sees them now as if they themselves had fulfilled the Mosaic Torah. Believers are not justified by the *life* of the Torah obedient Christ, but by his *death* and *resurrection* only. Or, to put it this way: not by the life of the humble Jesus living on earth, but by the life of the risen and glorified Christ.

I can find only two Pauline statements that seem to give some support to the Reformed paradigm. The first statement is this: "And because of him you are in Christ Jesus, who became to us wisdom from God, righteousness and sanctification and redemption" (1 Cor. 1:30). Christ has become righteousness to us, for indeed, the righteousness that we possess is based on who he is and what he did for us on the cross (the verse links justification with redemption). Secondly, Paul does indeed speak of the obedience of Christ: "For as by the one man's disobedience the many were made sinners, so by the one man's obedience the many will be made righteous" (Rom. 5:19). But does this obedience of Christ refer to his observance of and obedience to the Mosaic Torah? Yes, says Herman Bavinck: "For Christ has not only restored us to the state of Adam as it was before the fall but also fulfilled the law for us and acquired eternal life for us."[60] Therefore, he describes our justification as the "imputation of Christ's obedience as a whole," that is, active and passive, with reference to Romans 5:19.

I cannot agree with any of these statements. First, Christ brings us to a state that is far beyond the state Adam occupied before the fall.[61] Second, Scripture does *not* teach that Christ observed the law "for us," as our substitute (on the contrary, his observance of the Torah only *increased* our own guilt, as we will see). Third, Scripture does *not* teach that Christ's personal righteousness—the practical righteousness of his Torah observance—was imputed (credited, transferred) to us; Christ is our righteousness through our having been united

---

60. Bavinck (2008, 4:223).
61. See Ouweneel (2015b, chapters 7 and 9).

with him in his death and resurrection, which is a completely different matter.

Reformed theologian and revivalist Jonathan Edwards (1703-1758) extensively described the righteousness of Christ. In his view, this is the righteousness through which Christ merited heaven for himself and for all those who believe in him.[62] To this belonged primarily his fulfillment of the divine commandments he had to obey as Mediator, but also his observance of all divine laws under which he had been placed as a Man, and especially as a Jew.[63] All of Christ's Torah observance contributed to our salvation. Please note, this does not only mean that his Torah observance was a condition for being able to accomplish the work of redemption; no Christian can doubt this. No, it means that Christ's Torah observance *was part of this work of redemption itself.* Every scriptural proof for this thesis was lacking with Edwards, apparently because he believed the matter to be self-evident.

4.5.4 More Recent Views

With reference to the obedience of the One Man referred to in Romans 5:19, Karl Barth spoke of "what in the life and death of the one Jesus is to be viewed and appreciated as an act of obedience."[64] He thus connected this obedience not only with the sacrificial death of Christ, but also with his entire life that preceded this death.

Reformed theologian John Piper wrote that Christ lived and died in order to fulfill for us the righteous requirements of the law[65] — but neither Colossians 2:13-14, to which he refers, nor any other Bible passage says anything relating to a vicarious law-observance. He also wrote that Christ suffered and died to fulfill the obedience that became our righteousness[66] — but neither Romans 5:19, 2 Corinthians 5:21, Philippi-

---

62. Edwards (2003, 217).
63. Ibid., 214–17.
64. Barth (1933, ad loc.).
65. Piper (2004, 37).
66. Ibid., 46.

ans 2:8 and 3:9, to which he refers, nor his own argumentation supplies us with any evidence for this thesis. However, he does get a little closer to the truth than the previous authors by connecting the obedience of Christ (more) explicitly with Christ's death.

Bruce Demarest, too, tells us that God does not impute righteousness to us because of Christ's perfect observance of the law.[67] He claims that, according to Paul, sinners are justified on account of the satisfaction of God's moral law by Jesus Christ, and even adds that the basis for justification is first and foremost *Christ's virtuous life*.[68] Again, where does Paul suggest such a thing even in the remotest sense? Jesus' virtuous life does not save us, but rather condemns us; his perfection throws all the more light on our own guilt and sinfulness.

However, we do find more biblical approaches. Reformed theologian Herman Ridderbos wrote about Romans 5:18: "With this one act of righteousness, which stands over against Adam's fall, is meant the obedience (cf. v. 19) with which Christ gave himself unto death, as the highest and finishing act of his self-surrender."[69] That is, *not* so much Christ's observance of the law, but rather his sacrificial death. In my view, this is the scriptural approach.

So we do find Reformed theologians who connect the obedience of Christ with his propitiatory work. Thus, John Murray applied the obedience mentioned in Romans 5:19 to "the work of Christ on behalf of believers," and saw "in the cross of Christ and the shedding of his blood" the "climactic expression" of this obedience, although he adds: "obedience comprehends the totality of the Father's will as fulfilled by Christ."[70] In a general sense, of course, this is perfectly true. The point, however, is what precisely Paul means with the

---

67. Demarest (1997, 362); so also Sproul (1995, 103–05) without any Scriptural evidence.
68. Demarest (1997, 368–69), with reference to Packer (1984, 596).
69. Ridderbos (1959, 121); cf. Berkouwer (1965, 316–19).
70. Murray (1968, 1:205).

term "obedience" in Romans 5:19. Paul refers to the *one act* of disobedience by Adam, and as a contrast must refer to the *one act* of obedience by Christ, which can refer only to his self-surrender on the cross.

James Denney presented both views: some expositors (Johann C. K. von Hofmann, Gotthard V. Lechler) see obedience as referring to the "whole life and work of Jesus conceived as the carrying out of the Father's will" (cf. Phil. 2:8), but Denney himself preferred to limit obedience to "Christ's death as the one great act of obedience on which the possibility of justification depended" (cf. 3:25; 5:9).[71]

Similarly, Douglas J. Moo wrote: "Paul may be thinking of the 'active obedience' of Christ, his lifelong commitment to 'do his Father's will' and so fulfill the demands of the law [with reference to Frederick L. Godet and Richard N. Longenecker]. But Paul's focus seems rather to be on Jesus' death as the ultimate act of obedience. This is suggested by the parallel with Adam's (one) act of disobedience, Phil. 2:8 — Jesus 'became obedient unto death, even the death of the cross' — and the consistent connection Paul makes between justification and Jesus' death" (with reference to Heinrich A.W. Meyer and James D.G. Dunn).[72] I may add here a word from John's Gospel: "For this reason the Father loves me, because I lay down my life that I may take it up again. No one takes it from me, but I lay it down of my own accord. I have authority to lay it down, and I have authority to take it up again. This *charge* I have received from my Father" (10:17–18). It was the Father's command that Jesus would lay down his life; thus, this self-surrender was an act of obedience.

Other expositors, too, see Christ's obedience limited to his death as the one great act of obedience that made our justification possible (cf. Rom. 3:25; 5:9). Thus, William Vine said that in Romans 5:18, *dikaiōma* refers to what Christ has accom-

---

71. Denney (1979, 630).
72. Moo (1996, 344).

plished in his death.[73] Vine sees the evidence for this in verses 8-10: "God shows his love for us in that while we were still sinners, Christ *died* for us. Since, therefore, we have now been justified *by his blood*, much more shall we be saved by him from the wrath of God. For if while we were enemies we were reconciled to God by the *death* of his Son, much more, now that we are reconciled, shall we be saved by his life." He added the important argument that nowhere else in Paul's writings is it said that we have been justified on account of the (personal, practical) righteousness of Christ displayed during his life on earth. Justification is always linked with Christ's righteous work on the cross. We are justified "through the redemption that is in Christ Jesus, whom God put forward as a propitiation by his blood" (Rom. 3:24-25). God "raised from the dead Jesus our Lord, who was delivered up for our trespasses and raised for our justification" (4:24-25).

Reformed theologian Norman Shepherd continues to use the confusing imputation language, which has created so much havoc. But at least he links the righteousness of Christ not with Jesus' Torah observance but with his death and resurrection: "What does Paul mean by justification in Romans 3:28? First, justification is the forgiveness of sins so that we are accepted by God as righteous and receive the gift of eternal life. Second, justification is the forgiveness of sins grounded upon the imputation of the righteousness of Christ. Third, the righteousness of Christ imputed for our justification is his death and resurrection for us and in our place."[74] And again: "That righteousness [of Jesus Christ] is his propitiatory sacrifice offered on the cross in obedience to the will of the Father in heaven."[75]

Now listen to how Elam, Van Kooten, and Bergquist respond to Shepherd: "Shepherd eventually denied the imputation of the active obedience of Christ, which is foundational

---

73. Vine (1985, 1:427).
74. Shepherd (2009, 33).
75. Ibid., 34.

to the Reformed doctrine of justification. Shepherd rejected . . . the need for and reality of the imputed merits of Christ's active obedience for believers. . . . The imputation of the full obedience of Christ (both active and passive) is the ground of the believer's righteous standing before God. . . . In our view . . . [Shepherd's] denial of the imputation of the active obedience of Christ in justification, places him beyond the pale of the Westminster Standards, as well as other Reformed creeds and confessions."[76]

This apparently is the issue. Elam, Van Kooten, and Bergquist make not the slightest effort to prove from Scripture that justification consists of the imputation of the active obedience of Christ. They *could* not prove this, because it is simply nowhere in the Bible. But that does not seem to be their (main) concern. Shepherd contradicts the Westminster Standards, and that is enough to condemn him. Shepherd has denied what is "foundational to the Reformed doctrine of justification," which is seen, of course, as being identical with the biblical doctrine of justification. But if someone denies the foundations of the biblical doctrine of justification, can such a person be saved? Do Elam, Van Kooten, and Bergquist realize what is the ultimate outcome of their reasoning? Can *anyone* who denies the Westminster view of justification be *justified*?

4.6 Evaluation
4.6.1 Obedience Beyond the Torah

Of course, the question concerning the obedience of Christ is related to the question whether only Christ's work on the cross *or* Jesus' entire life had propitiatory, vicarious significance. In Appendix I, I provide extensive arguments why I believe the former to be the correct answer. In the previous section, I referred to Dunn, Lechler, Meyer, Moo, Murray, Ridderbos, Shepherd, Vine, and von Hofmann, who all believe(d) that Romans 5:19 refers, at least primarily, to Christ's propitiatory work, and not to his Torah observance. Frederick

---
76. Elam *et al.* (2014, 25–26).

W. Grant even saw a link with the Old Testament burnt offering: the "one man's obedience" reminds us of the "pleasing aroma" of Christ's offering (cf. Exod. 29:18, 25, 41; Lev. 1:9, 13, 17). Being in Christ does not mean only that our sins have been removed, nor simply that our "old man" has been put aside, but that we have been accepted before God in all the preciousness of Christ's obedience, that is, his death as the perfect burnt offering.[77]

It is striking that Bruce Demarest argues extensively and correctly that Christ has indeed perfectly observed the law, that he was personally perfectly righteous, and that he has perfectly accomplished the will of the Father.[78] This is all undeniably true. However, he completely fails to answer the question that is really at stake: where is the scriptural evidence that Christ's perfect Torah observance *as such had vicarious and propitiatory significance*, in other words, *that it formed part of the actual work of atonement?* Apparently, Demarest fails to see the essential difference between the condition for a thing and that thing itself. Jesus' perfect life — as a Jew, as a Man — was a condition for his propitiatory work; but that does not mean it was *part* of that propitiatory work.

To use sacrificial language again: each burnt offering (representing Christ's atoning death) was unthinkable without a grain offering (representing Christ's perfect life; see, e.g., Exod. 29:40–41); this grain offering was also a "pleasing aroma" to the Lord (Lev. 1:2, 9, 12). However, as such the grain offering had *no* atoning value, unlike the burnt offering (Lev. 1:4), because atonement was only through the shedding of blood (17:11; Heb. 9:22).

Jesus' obedient life is indeed of eminent importance; without it, our reconciliation and justification would not have been possible. However, what "righteousness of the law" — shorter: what *law* — required that Jesus would give his life for sinners, and that he would bear the curse of the law for them?

---

77. Grant (1901, 223).
78. Demarest (1997, 368–69).

Does the Bible not rather tell us that he learned obedience through what he *suffered* (Heb. 5:8)? He became "obedient to the point of death, even death on a cross" (Phil. 2:8). What link is there between *this* obedience and the Mosaic Torah? Does the Torah make a righteous person suffer? However, it was *this* suffering, it was the shedding of his blood, his surrender into death, which became the foundation for our justification. What does this have to do with (observing) the Mosaic Torah?

Would it at all be possible to say that "he fulfilled the commandments of the Torah, even to the point of the death of the cross"? Christ's obedience (Rom. 5:19) is put in very opposition to the Mosaic Torah; it forms a contrast with it: "by the one man's obedience the many will be made righteous. Now the Torah came in to increase the trespass, but where sin increased, grace abounded all the more" (vv. 19-20). As Son, Jesus obeyed the command of the *Father*, namely, to surrender his life unto death (John 10:18), and to give eternal life to people on account of his death (12:50; cf. 14:31; 15:10). These and similar commandments infinitely surpassed his observing the Mosaic Torah as a faithful Jew. The *Father* commanded the Son to lay down his human life (John 10:18)—the Mosaic Torah does not demand this of any Jew, and even less from the sinless Son.

4.6.2 "Why Then the Torah?"

"Why then the Torah?"[79] It was "added," says Galatians 3:19, namely, added to cast all the more light on the condition of the first Adam and his offspring, and this only in Israel, because only Israel was placed under the Mosaic Torah (". . . to increase the *trespass* [of the law]," Rom. 5:20). But the whole argument in Romans 5 is that righteousness is not only for those who are under the Torah but also for all those who had not been under the Mosaic Torah, and had nevertheless sinned (vv. 13-14). Righteousness is preached everywhere "where sin [not just trespass] increased" (v. 20). The whole purpose

---

79. For a more extensive treatment, see again Ouweneel (2015a).

of the apostle is to leave the polity of the Mosaic Torah aside: "But now the righteousness of God has been manifested apart from the law" (*chōris nomou*, without the article: apart from any principle of law) (3:21).

The point that Paul is making here is as follows: Gentiles were never under the Mosaic Torah, and it was never required of them to fulfill that Torah, or exhibit a righteousness that would be in accordance with *that* Torah. The most one could say is that the genuine righteousness of any person must be in accordance with the Eternal Torah of God.[80] But what do Gentile believers have to do with the Mosaic Torah? They never broke that Torah because they were never under it. Therefore, again I ask: Why would Gentile believers need someone who, in their stead, would perfectly fulfill the Mosaic Torah for them? We just read it: In the present polity, God has manifested his righteousness *entirely apart from the Mosaic Torah*, even *apart from any principle of law*. My justification has nothing to do with the Mosaic Torah whatsoever; it does *not* consist in the obedience of someone who fulfilled that Torah for me, because I was never under it, and I did not need anyone to fulfill it for me.

Romans 10:5-8 (NKJV) distinguishes between the "righteousness which is [out] of [Greek, *ek*] the law" and the "righteousness which is [out] of faith." "[T]he law is not [out] of [Greek, *ek*] faith" (Gal. 3:12). Paul's point is not about the one who accomplishes the righteousness of the law, either the sinner himself or Christ who did it in his stead. The point is rather that righteousness is "[out] of faith," not "[out] of the law" at all; it is entirely beyond the sphere of the Torah. Paul does say in Romans 3:21 that "the Law and the Prophets" (read, the Tanakh) bear witness to the righteousness of God. However, the manifestation of this righteousness is entirely apart from the Mosaic Torah, even apart from any principle of law. Natural Man cannot keep the Torah, but — other than the Jew — he

---

80. Ibid.

never *was* under the Mosaic Torah anyway. "[W]e know that whatever the law says it speaks to those who are under the law" (v. 19), that is, to Israel, and to no one else. "For all who have sinned without the law [i.e., Gentiles] will also perish without the law, and all who have sinned under the law [i.e., Jews] will be judged by the law. . . . Gentiles do not have the law" (2:12, 14).

What does natural man, who is destined to perdition, need? Someone who observed the Mosaic Torah "for him" (whatever this may mean), under which he had not even been placed? What natural man needs is:

(a) a person who has borne in his stead the penalty for his sins (which, as Paul underscores, goes further than "trespasses" of the Torah);

(b) a person with whom redeemed people can be associated, both in his death and in his resurrection; and

(c) a person who in this position, and in the power of the Holy Spirit, can learn to live the life of the *tsaddiq*.

This is what justification is according to the New Testament, especially in the writings of the apostle Paul.

4.6.3 The Use of Someone Else's Good life

Compare it with a criminal who has killed and robbed. What does he need? Someone else, who "in his stead" (whatever this may mean), has led a *good* life, according to the laws of the land, without killing and robbing? What use is it to assert that, in some way or another, that good life can be "imputed" to the criminal? What does this help him? The good acts of that other person can at best put him to shame by proving to him that a good life, without killing and robbing, *is* possible, so that he has no excuse. But in no way can the good life of another person be of any value to him. It is not only unscriptural but also absurd to assert that the good life of one—whoever he is—can be of benefit to another. What the criminal really needs is someone who in his stead bears the consequences of his evil deeds, *and* gives him the strength and the guidance to henceforth lead a better life.

In Scripture it is precisely the same. Not the Torah observance of someone else, even if this is Christ, can benefit the sinner; at least, the Bible does not say anything in this direction. It is a scholastic, inferentialist invention. To put it even more strongly, Christ's faithful Torah observance does not at all alleviate the distress of the sinner. On the contrary, it worsens his distress: Jesus has shown that God did not require the impossible but that a person can definitely observe the Torah, if only he fulfills the conditions (see again Appendix I). No, what the sinner needs is:

(a) *Christ*, who vicariously bore the penalty for his sins on the cross: "He himself bore our sins in his body on the tree, that we might die to sin and live to righteousness" (1 Pet. 2:24);

(b) *God*, who not only forgives the sinner's sins on account of Christ's work ("In him we have redemption through his blood, the forgiveness of our trespasses," Eph. 1:7), but also completely renews the sinner in that he counts him as having died and risen with Christ: ("[Faith] will be counted [as righteousness] to us who believe in him who raised from the dead Jesus our Lord, who was delivered up for our trespasses and raised for our justification" (Rom. 4:24–25); and

(c) the *Holy Spirit* who henceforth gives him the strength to live the life of a *tsaddiq*, that is, to live according to the Messianic Torah: ". . . in order that the righteous requirement of the law might be fulfilled in us, who walk not according to the flesh but according to the Spirit" (Rom. 8:4).

4.7 The Place of the Torah
4.7.1 Active and Passive Righteousness

Let us now try to develop further what we have found so far. Reformed theology makes a distinction between the active and the passive righteousness (or obedience) of Christ. The active righteousness of Christ is thought to refer to his active fulfillment of the will of God. This included both his obedience to the Mosaic Torah and his obedience to fulfill God's will on the cross. Christ's passive righteousness involved his work of undergoing the penalty for our sins. In order to better understand the difference between the two, it is vitally important to first answer the question whether Christ underwent the penalty for our sins, on the cross *or* during his entire life, including the cross. In Appendix I, I strongly defend the former position. However, Reformed theology generally defends the latter position.

If people at all feel the need of distinguishing between some active and some passive obedience of Christ, those who defend the former position, as I do, will refer Christ's active obedience to his sinless (Torah observing) life. They will refer his passive obedience mainly to his work on the cross. Of course, during his life Jesus also suffered under the hands of wicked humans, but these were not *vicarious* sufferings. However, Reformed theologians defending the latter position will tell us that both the active and the passive righteousness (obedience) of Christ refer to his entire life, including the cross. Christ was actively righteous by obeying God's commandments, both during his life and on the cross. And Christ was passively righteous by undergoing the sufferings involved in the penalty for our sins, both during his life and on the cross.[81]

I leave this matter to be discussed further in Appendix I; it is sufficient at this stage to understand the Reformed distinction between the active and the passive obedience of Christ. Reformed theology in general asserts that *both* the active and the passive righteousness of Christ were necessary for our salvation in the sense that *both* have been imputed to us, that is, reckoned to our account. We not only need Christ dying for our sins, we allegedly also need to have his active obedience to the Mosaic Torah imputed to us.

---

81. See, e.g., Berkhof (1949, 379–80) and Murray (1955, 20–22).

My answer to this is that we find the former extensively in the New Testament, and the latter nowhere. Jesus was "obedient to death" (Phil. 2:8), and thereby saved all those who believe in him and his work. But it is absurd to claim that Jesus was *Torah-obedient to death*, for the simple reason that Torah-obedience never leads to death but always to life (Rom. 10:5; Gal. 3:11–12). Death is the wages of *sin* (Rom. 6:23), not the wages of Torah-obedience. Apparently, Reformed theology distinguishes too little between matters that in the New Testament are so clearly distinguished.

(a) Jesus' perfect Torah-obedience was not unto death but unto life; in no way did it contribute to our salvation but only to our guilt. The more obedient he was, the more guilty were we shown to be. There is not the slightest hint in the Bible that Jesus' Torah observance contributed to our justification. I repeat: it is nothing but scholastic inferentialism.

(b) Jesus' obedience to the will of the Father—namely, that he would bear our sins—was entirely outside the scope of the Torah. It was not unto life but unto (his) death, and was the only thing that could bring about our salvation (Rom. 5:10): "[W]e were reconciled to God by the *death* of his Son," and by his death (and resurrection) *alone*; and "now that we are reconciled, *shall* we be saved by his life" (future tense); not his life on earth but the life of the risen and glorified Man at God's right hand (cf. 4:24–25).

4.7.2 The Righteousness That Comes From the Law

If the Torah-obedience of Christ would indeed be imputed (transferred) to us, then the righteousness that believers receive would be a "righteousness from [Greek, *ek*] the law" (Rom. 10:5) after all. But Paul tells us that, since he had met Christ, he was not even *interested* in any "righteousness from [Greek, *ek*] the law" (Phil. 3:9). In these two passages, the "righteousness from [or, on account of] the law" is contrasted with the "righteousness from [or, on account of] faith" (Rom. 10:6) and the "righteousness from God on account of [Greek, *epi*] faith" (Phil. 3:9), which is virtually the same. Whether Paul himself, through his Torah-faithful life before his conversion, had built up such a "righteousness [coming] from the law" (cf. v. 6), or whether it would have been the "righteousness [coming] from the law" that Christ allegedly would have built up for him, this *type* of righteousness simply did not appeal to him anymore. He wanted another *type* of righteousness: not the one based on a faithful, Torah observant life—his own or Christ's—but one based on the death and resurrection of Christ.

Moreover, a "righteousness [coming] from the law" involves only what we ourselves should have done: "Do this, and you will live" (cf. Luke 10:28). But this will not do, for at least two reasons. First, as we saw, God never placed Gentiles under the Mosaic Torah, so he never expected from them a "righteousness [coming] from the law." Second, if *Christ's* "righteousness [coming] from the law" was imputed to us, we would be entitled to nothing but what the Mosaic Torah promises to its observers: a long life in the promised land (Exod. 20:12), or at best, life in the Messianic kingdom (cf. Matt. 19:16, 29; 25:46). Such a "righteousness [coming] from the law" can as such never entitle me to union with the risen Christ (Rom. 4:25; 6:7-8), to the glory of God (3:23-24; 5:1-2; cf. 8:30), and to eternal life (2:7; 5:21; 6:22-23), not even eternal life in the Johannine sense: communion with the Father and the Son (John 17:3; 1 John 1:1-4).[82]

God first tried humanity *without* any (explicit) law (from Adam to Moses), and humans became lawless ones. Then God tried humans *under* the law (Israel since Mount Sinai), and they became trespassers of the law. Humans never had any righteousness of themselves, neither without the law, nor under the law. Then God did something new: he manifested *his own* righteousness, *apart from any principle of law* (Rom. 3:21). What did this entail? This: that Christ did not earn a

---

82. See extensively, Ouweneel (2015b, especially chapters 7 and 9).

human Torah righteousness for us — by his life or his death, or by both — but that God in him, that is, in his sacrificial death, radically condemned the "old man," and placed the "new man" in the sphere of his own righteousness (cf. 2 Cor. 5:21; Eph. 4:24), that is, in Christ, the heavenly Man, who is (entails, constitutes) now our righteousness (1 Cor. 1:30). The "old man" does not have an external righteousness imputed to him that he himself could not produce because, strictly speaking, this would still be a refurbishing of the "old man." On the contrary, God has radically condemned the "old man" on the cross, and in the death and resurrection of Christ replaced him by the "new man."

This "new man" does not need some Torah observance imputed to him because this "new man" is in and of Christ, and as such does not exist any longer in terms of the polity of the Mosaic Torah: believers "have died to the law through the [dead and risen] body of Christ, so that you may belong to another, to him who has been raised from the dead, in order that we may bear fruit for God" (Rom. 7:4). The point is not that by God's intervention, the "new man" now does satisfy the requirements of the Mosaic Torah — under which the Gentile was never placed — but that, through the death and resurrection of Christ, he is *beyond the reach* of the Mosaic Torah. The fact that through the Holy Spirit, in this "new man" the same high, and even much higher moral principles are realized than were ever contained in the Mosaic Torah (cf. Rom. 8:4; 13:8, 10) is an altogether different matter. *Our* Torah is not the Mosaic Torah anyway, not even the Ten Commandments, but ours is the "Torah of Christ" (1 Cor. 9:21; Gal. 6:2; cf. Rom. 8:4; 13:8-10; James 1:25; 2:8, 12; see extensively the first volume in this series).

So what is now the righteousness of the believer? Did God refurbish the "old man" by imputing to him the righteousness of Christ, namely the Torah observance in which the "old man" had failed? Did God not rather condemn the "old man" totally, did he not bring him into the death of Christ, and put a "new man" in his stead, who is alive in Christ before God? Did God make up for our failures in the flesh by imputing to us the righteous acts of Christ, *or* did he altogether put an end to Man in the flesh? Did God refurbish the "old man" by blotting out his sins, or did he bring the "old man" into the judgment of the cross? Did God make sure that the believer, through "imputation," would possess the righteousness of the Mosaic Torah after all, or did he, in Christ, place him beyond death in the realm of resurrection, *beyond the very righteousness of the Mosaic Torah*, or the righteousness of any principle of law?

4.8 Christ's Torah Observance
4.8.1 The First and the Last Adam

As I briefly suggested above, we cannot say, of course, that Christ's life, including his perfect Torah obedience, had nothing to do at all with our righteousness. Rather, it is essential that the very person "who knew no sin" was made to be sin for us, so that in him we might become the righteousness of God (2 Cor. 5:21). As Louis Berkhof rightly put it:[83] "[I]f Christ had not rendered active obedience [i.e., his perfect Torah observance], the human nature of Christ itself would have fallen short of the just demands of God, and He would not have been able to atone for others." The pleasing aroma of his perfect burnt offering on the cross was inconceivable without the pleasing aroma of the grain offering represented by his perfect life (Lev. 1 and 2).[84] He showed to God the righteousness of a perfect Man, and he showed to Man the righteousness of God.

At the same time we have to establish that in *these* qualities there could be no single connection between Christ and humanity. If the "grain of wheat" does not fall into the earth *and die*, "it remains alone" (John 12:24) — if it were otherwise, why would Jesus have had to die? If Christ's Torah observance is

---
83. Berkhof (1949, 380).
84. See Ouweneel (2009, §4.4).

imputed to us, why did he have to bear our sins? In that case wouldn't he have vicariously supplied that in which we had failed? Why die for our failures? Wouldn't our failures have been fixed by his accomplishing for us what *we* should have accomplished?

Yes—but they would not have been propitiated. "[I]f righteousness were through [Greek, *dia*] the law, then Christ died for no purpose" (Gal. 2:21). But if Christ fulfilled the Torah for us, in our stead, then righteousness *is* "through the law," and Christ has died for no purpose. However, humans in the first Adam (as such) *are* not justified at all, but only humans in the last Adam. And believers are in the last Adam, and thus free of the entire old Torah polity, which required obedience from humans (formally only from Jews) and condemned us (them) (Rom. 6:14; 7:4, 6; 10:4; Gal. 2:19).

However, if this is true—and it is true—then we do not at all need someone who fulfilled the Mosaic Torah for us, in our stead. As a matter of principle, the Mosaic Torah furnishes a *human* righteousness for the *first* Adam (Rom. 2:13), but this has no significance for us anymore because we are in the last Adam. What we need, and have now, is not a *human* righteousness in the *first* Adam but *God's* righteousness in the *last* Adam. I do not need the Torah observance of Christ because, first, I never *was* under the Mosaic Torah, and second, because such a Torah observance would not contribute to my salvation anyway. I am not saved through the earthly life of Christ (see again Appendix I), but through his death and resurrection.

I repeat, the Mosaic Torah does not bring us some Torah righteousness in Christ after all, but it does the reverse: it proves the total hopelessness of the first Adam. The Torah could do only one thing to sinners: kill them. But we underwent this death in Christ—we were "crucified with him" (Rom. 6:6)—and now we are in him, the last Adam, "apart from the Torah," beyond its reach. The Torah is righteous and holy (Rom. 7:12), but it does not *make* righteous; it only brings to light *un*righteousness, and as such it is not for the righteous but for the unrighteous (1 Tim. 1:8–10). Christ was born under that Torah (Gal. 4:4) in order to save those who were under it. He did this not by observing the Torah—although that Torah observance necessarily made him fit for accomplishing the work of redemption—but by becoming a curse for them, in their stead, and by redeeming them from the curse of the Torah (Gal. 3:13).

The sacrificial death of Christ decides everything—but this death was entirely outside the realm of the Torah because the Torah does not require the death of the righteous. As we saw, in Romans 5, where the first and the last Adam are put in juxtaposition, Paul refers to this death of Christ and to the Torah in verses 13-14 and 20. The two family heads are put there in juxtaposition in order, through death, to replace the "first man" by the "Second Man." The obedience of Christ to which Paul refers is not his Torah observance—although he perfectly obeyed the Torah—but stands in opposition to the Torah (vv. 19–20).

4.8.2 Conclusion

Is it truly the case that the righteousness that we one day must possess before God's judgment seat is nothing less than a Torah righteousness, namely, the active Torah observance of Christ that allegedly has been imputed to us (in addition to his payment for our failures on the cross)? Is the pleasure that God takes in the "new man" not infinitely *more* than that? If we have been made "accepted in the Beloved" (Eph. 1:6 NKJV), is that Beloved not infinitely more than a Man who perfectly fulfilled the Mosaic Torah? Is this Beloved not the Son who has perfectly glorified the Father on earth, having accomplished the work that the Father gave him to do (John 17:4)? I can imagine a Jew fulfilling the Mosaic Torah. But the Son coming into this world to keep the commandments of his *Father* and to abide in his love (15:10)—did he in this way do nothing more than fulfill the Mosaic Torah? But what about the commandment of the Father to lay down his life that he might take it up again (10:17-18) — where do we find this commandment in the Mosaic Torah? And the commandment to testify of eternal life and secure it for believers (12:49-50) — was this a Mosaic commandment? *What, if anything, do the Father's commandments to the Son have to do with the Mosaic Torah?*

No, Scripture never tells us that the Torah observance of Christ has been imputed (transferred) to us, but that Christ is our righteousness — and what a Christ this is! He is the One who in his life and his death perfectly glorified the Father; the One who glorified a holy and righteous God on the cross, at the very place where the judgment for sin came upon him. This is the Christ who was raised by the glory of the Father (Rom. 6:4), and to whom the Father showed his righteousness by glorifying him in the Father's house (John 16:10, 14; cf. 13:1, 32; 14:2; 17:1, 5). We may look to all that glory, and realize: that Christ is our righteousness, is our life (Col. 3:4).

The reality is not that his Torah observance replaced our failures, but that he *died* for our failures. He did not fulfill the Torah for us, but bore the curse of the Torah for us. Through his perfect life he did not perfect our "old man"; on the contrary, his perfect life involved one enormous *judgment* on the "old man." However, through his death and resurrection, we have been clothed with the "new man"; for our "old man" has been crucified with him (Rom. 6:6), and now we are in the last Adam. We are in him, the risen and glorified Lord, and *he* is our life. Not the humble, Torah-obedient Man on earth is my life, but the dead and risen Christ at the right hand of God is my life (Col. 3:1-4).

For God, the question is not whether he sees at all some Torah righteousness in us — in whatever form — but whether Christ is formed in us (Gal. 4:19; cf. v. 21). For God, there is only one Man: Christ. Not the Christ who merely fulfilled the Torah — although he did this perfectly — but the Christ who glorified God at the very place of judgment. Christ, the Son of Man seated at the right hand of God (Luke 22:69; Eph. 1:20; etc.), the Son of the Father who is in the bosom of the Father (John 1:18), is everything for the heart of God. But God be praised, we are united to this person, and he is our life; *in him* we have been made acceptable before God. We have died to sin (Rom. 6:10-11), and died to the Torah (7:4, 6), and "the life I now live in the flesh I live by faith in the Son of God, who loved me and gave himself for me. I do not nullify the grace of God, for if righteousness were through the Torah, then Christ died for no purpose" (Gal. 2:20-21).

Chapter 5
Justification in the New Testament

For there is no distinction:
for all have sinned
   and fall short of the glory of God,
and are justified by his grace as a gift,
   through the redemption that is in Christ Jesus,
whom God put forward as a propitiation by his blood,
   to be received by faith.
                              Romans 3:22–25

Do you want to be shown, you foolish person,
   that faith apart from works is useless?
Was not Abraham our father justified by works
   when he offered up his son Isaac on the altar?
You see that faith was active along with his works,
   and faith was completed by his works;
and the Scripture was fulfilled that says,
   "Abraham believed God,
and it was counted to him as righteousness" –

> *and he was called a friend of God.*
> *You see that a person is justified by works*
> *and not by faith alone.*
> James 2:20–24

Summary: *Justification is a work of the triune God. The Bible teaches us both the wrong means (e.g., works in one's own strength) and the right means of justification: God's grace, Christ's blood, and the believer's faith (heart confidence in God). The purpose of justification is life; justification implies that death has intervened. The difference between "dying for sin" and "dying to sin" is explained, as well as the fact that the distinction between "making righteous" and "declaring righteous" is a false one: both are true for the believer. To a certain extent, another distinction is false as well: that between "justification by faith" and "justification by works." It should rather be "justification by faith resulting in works" versus "justification by works without faith." Such faith-works have individual, but also societal and eschatological aspects. Reformed theology speaks of justification as followed by sanctification; this should be: positional justification* **and** *sanctification are followed by practical sanctification* **and** *justification. Paul's examples of Abraham and Habakkuk show that he even hardly thinks of instantaneous justification in Romans and Galatians; he rather seems to deal with the question: "How can a person become, and learn to live as, a* **tsaddiq***?" Finally, the chapter deals with the relationship between justification and peace, with the help of two typological examples: Esther and Mephibosheth.*

5.1 Means of Justification
5.1.1 Wrong Means

THE WORK OF JUSTIFICATION is a sovereign work of redemption in which all three persons of the Godhead are involved.

(a) *God the Father:* "If God is for us, who can be against us? He who did not spare his own Son but gave him up for us all, how will he not also with him graciously give us all things? Who shall bring any charge against God's elect? It is God who justifies. Who is to condemn?" (Rom. 8:31–34). We "believe in him who raised from the dead Jesus our Lord, who was delivered up for our trespasses and raised for our justification" (4:24-25). "Christ was raised from the dead by the glory of the Father" (6:4).

(b) *The Man Jesus*, who is *God the Son:* "[W]e know that a person is not justified by works of the law but through faith in Jesus Christ, so we also have believed in Christ Jesus, in order to be justified by faith in Christ and not by works of the law, because by works of the law no one will be justified . . . [we] endeavor to be justified in Christ" (Gal. 2:16-17).

(c) *God the Spirit:* "But you were washed, you were sanctified, you were justified in the name of the Lord Jesus Christ and by the Spirit of our God" (1 Cor. 6:11). "To those who are elect exiles of the Dispersion . . . according to the foreknowledge of God the Father, in the sanctification of the Spirit, for obedience to Jesus Christ and for sprinkling with his blood" (1 Pet. 1:1-2).

It is entirely God — the triune God — who is the subject of justification. It is true: the *believer* believes; he believes in God who justifies him, and even in justification by faith as such. Herein is the believer subject, and justification is object. However, materially it is the God who justifies who is the subject, and the believer who is justified is the object.[1]

There are at least five means concerning which the Bible says that through them justification is *not* brought about.[2]

(a) *Physical descent:* the Jew must be justified just as the Gentile because both are sinners. It is to Jews that Paul says, "[B]y him everyone who believes is freed from everything from which you could not be freed by the law of Moses" (Acts 13:39), and to the (Jewish and Gentile) Romans: "For I am not ashamed of the gospel, for it is the power of God for salvation to everyone who believes, to the Jew first and also to the Greek" (Rom. 1:16). "What then? Are we Jews any better off?

---
1. Berkhof (1979, 438).
2. Coates (n.d.-b, 32–33).

No, not at all. For we have already charged that all, both Jews and Greeks, are under sin . . . for all have sinned and fall short of the glory of God, and are justified by his grace as a gift, through the redemption that is in Christ Jesus . . . Or is God the God of Jews only? Is he not the God of Gentiles also? Yes, of Gentiles also, since God is one—who will justify the circumcised by faith and the uncircumcised through faith" (3:9, 23-24, 29-30; cf. 2 Cor. 11:22; Phil. 3:5). Along the same lines, Jesus tells Nicodemus, "You [plural! Jews! Torah-scholars!] must be born again" (John 3:7).

(b) *Torah observance:* "[I]f righteousness were through the law, then Christ died for no purpose" (Gal. 2:21); " . . . freed from everything from which you could not be freed by the law of Moses" (Acts 13:39). "For by works of the law no human being will be justified in his sight . . . For we hold that one is justified by faith apart from works of the law" (Rom. 3:20, 28). "[W]e know that a person is not justified by works of the law but through faith in Jesus Christ, so we also have believed in Christ Jesus, in order to be justified by faith in Christ and not by works of the law, because by works of the law no one will be justified" (Gal. 2:16; cf. 3:11; 5:4).

(c) *Performance of good works*, of whatever nature, as such: "But when the goodness and loving kindness of God our Savior appeared, he saved us, not because of works done by us in righteousness, but according to his own mercy, by the washing of regeneration and renewal of the Holy Spirit" (Titus 3:4-5). "For if Abraham was justified by works, he has something to boast about, but not before God. . . . David also speaks of the blessing of the one to whom God counts righteousness apart from works" (4:2, 6; cf. 3:27; 9:11). "For by grace you have been saved through faith. And this is not your own doing; it is the gift of God, not a result of works, so that no one may boast" (Eph. 2:8-9). "God, who saved us and called us to a holy calling, not because of our works but because of his own purpose and grace, which he gave us in Christ Jesus before the ages began" (2 Tim. 1:9). Incidentally, it is never said that we are not justified because of *good* works; the term "good [Greek, *kalos* or *agathos*] works" is reserved for believers (Matt. 5:16; Acts 9:36; Eph. 2:10; 1 Tim. 2:10; 5:10, 25; 6:18; Titus 2:7, 14; 3:8, 14; Heb. 10:24; 1 Pet. 2:12).

(d) *Rites*, especially circumcision: "Is this blessing then only for the circumcised, or also for the uncircumcised? For we say that faith was counted to Abraham as righteousness. How then was it counted to him? Was it before or after he had been circumcised? It was not after, but before he was circumcised" (Rom. 4:9–10). "For in Christ Jesus neither circumcision nor uncircumcision counts for anything, but only faith working through love" (Gal. 5:6). Baptism and the Lord's Supper as such cannot transfer saving grace, either.

(e) *Godliness* as such; in order to be justified one should not think oneself to be righteous: "I came not to call the righteous, but sinners" (Matt. 9:13). It is not the "righteous" who are justified, but the ungodly (Rom. 4:5). It is not the "(self-)righteous" Pharisee who is justified, but the penitent tax collector (Luke 18:9–14).

5.1.2 The Grace of God

There are three means through which justification *is* brought about: God's grace, Christ's blood, and the believer's faith. In the notion of *grace* we have to do with the attitude of *God* who has made justification possible, and makes it available to sinners. The *blood* is the actual means of cleansing that *Christ* has furnished on the cross. *Faith* is the confident receptivity that is needed on behalf of *Man*.

In order to call something a "means" in justification we have to pay attention to the various cases or prepositions, which can hardly be rendered accurately in English:

* "by grace" (Greek, *chariti*, a simple dative; Rom. 3:24);

* "according to grace" (*kata charin*, Rom. 4:4, 16 NKJV);

* "by his blood" (*en tōi autou haimati*, lit., "in [the power of]," Rom. 3:25; 5:9);

* "by faith" (*pistei*, a simple dative; Rom. 3:28);
* "by faith" (*ek pisteōs*, lit. "from/out of faith," Rom. 1:17; 3:30; 9:32; 14:23; Gal. 3:12; James 2:24);
* "through faith" (*dia [tēs] pisteōs*, Rom. 3:22, 25, 31);
* "[that depends] on faith" (*epi tēi pistei*, Phil. 3:9).

The objective means (on the side of God) are the grace of God and the blood of Christ. The subjective means (on the side of Man) is faith.

We enter into the broad topic of faith more closely in the next two chapters (but also see §5.2). Let us now look at the first two means.

First, the justification of the ungodly is rooted in the sovereign, unmerited *grace* of God: "[A]ll have sinned and fall short of the glory of God, and are justified by his grace as a gift, through the redemption that is in Christ Jesus" (Rom. 3:23–24; cf. Gal. 5:4); we are "justified by his grace" (Titus 3:7).

In Romans 4:4 Paul says, "Now to the one who works, his wages are not counted as a gift but as his due." If a person could be justified (declared righteous) on account of his own works of the law, then there would be no question of grace, because in that case this person would have earned this justification all by himself. But God is the one who justifies the *ungodly* (v. 5). This is the person who has a natural tendency to hate God and his neighbor (Heidelberg Catechism, Q&A 5). This is the person who cannot contribute anything to his redemption, and even has no interest in this, and even less a longing for this. "[M]an is but a slave to sin, and 'can receive nothing, except it has been given him from heaven'" (Belgic Confession, Art. 14; cf. Ps. 19:11). The fact that such a person is nonetheless going to become a *tsaddiq* is nothing but the work of God's grace.

Don Carson has written that God's *mercy* consists in that you do *not* get what you deserve, and God's *grace* consists in that you get what you do *not* deserve.[3] Such a distinction is

---
3. Carson (1982, 27).

rather artificial, but at any rate both aspects are found in justification. It is God's *mercy* that he justifies the ungodly, and does not impute to him his iniquities. It is God's *grace* that he justifies the ungodly in Christ, and grants him all the blessings involved in this. God's *mercy* is concerned with *miserable* Man (cf. Latin, *misericordia*, "mercy," and *miseria*, "misery"), and God's *grace* is concerned with *rightless* Man.

In Romans 5:15-17, Paul uses both the word *charis* ("grace") and the word *charisma* ("free gift," lit. "portion of grace"), in addition to the words *dōrea* and *dōrēma* ("gift"), in ESV also rendered "free gift": "But the free gift [one word: *charisma*] is not like the trespass [of Adam]. For if many died through one man's [i.e., Adam's] trespass, much more have the grace [*charis*] of God and the free gift [one word: *dōrea*] by the grace [*charis*] of that one man Jesus Christ abounded for many. And the free gift [one word: *dōrēma*] is not like the result of that one man's [i.e., Adam's] sin. For the judgment following one trespass [of Adam] brought condemnation, but the free gift [one word: *charisma*] following many trespasses brought justification. For if, because of one man's [i.e., Adam's] trespass, death reigned through that one man [Adam], much more will those who receive the abundance of grace (*charis*) and the free gift [one word: *dōrea*] of righteousness reign in life through the one man Jesus Christ." The trespass is guilt and brings death; justification is grace and brings life (see §5.3).

5.1.3 The Blood of Christ

Second, justification is founded upon Christ's *blood*, that is, his work of redemption: ". . . Christ Jesus, whom God put forward as a propitiation [Greek, *hilastērion*, NIV: "sacrifice of atonement"] by [Greek, *en*, in the power of] his blood, to be received by [one word: *dia*] faith" (3:24-25). The comma here is quite important; it is not "faith in his blood," as GNV has it, but the blood of Christ is here the foundation for our justification. Most translations rightly connect "blood" not with "faith" but with "propitiation": "God gave Jesus as a way to forgive people's sins through their faith in him. God can forgive them because the blood sacrifice of Jesus pays for their sins" (ERV).

Another interesting passage with intriguing prepositions is this one: "Jesus our Lord, who was delivered up for [*dia* + accus.] our trespasses and raised for [*dia* + accus.] our justification" (Rom. 4:24–25). The interesting aspect is that the Greek preposition *dia*, as well as the English rendering "for," seem to have here two slightly different meanings: Jesus was delivered up because of our sins, and raised for the purpose of our justification (or, if we look for identical rendering: Jesus was delivered up "in view of" our sins, viz., to blot them out, and raised "in view of" our justification, viz., in order to make it possible).

"Since, therefore, we have now been justified by [Greek, *en*, in the power of] his blood, much more shall we be saved by [*dia* + genit.] him from the wrath of God" (5:9). God needs a holy and righteous *foundation* for the justification of the ungodly; he can never bypass and overlook sins (cf. Hab. 1:13). Declaring the ungodly righteous can never be done at the expense of God's own righteousness. It must be crystal clear to all that God is not only benevolent and tolerant in justifying the ungodly, but that he is *righteous* in doing so: "If we confess our sins, he is faithful and just [or, righteous] to forgive us our sins and to cleanse us from all unrighteousness" (1 John 1:9). "God gave Jesus to show that he always does what is right and fair. He was right in the past when he was patient and did not punish people for their sins. And in our own time he still does what is right. God worked all this out in a way that allows him to judge people fairly and still make right any person who has faith in Jesus" (Rom. 3:25–26 ERV).

William E. Vine has rightly emphasized that we should not read here "and yet": God is just, "and yet" he justifies the ungodly. This would sound as if justification in some way conflicts, or seems to conflict, with God's righteousness,

Justification in the New Testament

whereas in reality it is the reverse: justification is a necessary *consequence* of God's righteousness.[4] It is not: God is righteous, *and yet* he forgives/justifies.[5] Strictly speaking it is not even: God is righteous *in that* he forgives/justifies.[6] But: God is righteous, and *therefore* he forgives/justifies. He would not be just if he would not forgive/justify, because he owes this to the redemptive work of Christ. That is, in the very maintenance of his own righteousness God found the basis for our justification in Christ's work of atonement. Not only "found": he supplied this basis himself: he "did not spare his own Son but gave him up for us all" (Rom. 8:32).

Through this propitiatory sacrifice, the believer knows that his sins have been blotted out, and that he has been united with Christ in his death and resurrection (Rom. 6:5-11). It is *this* person, no matter how ungodly (evil, wicked) by nature, who can be declared righteous by God without any reservation, on account of faith (Rom. 4:5).

5.2 Faith
5.2.1 "Out of Faith"

In the next two chapters we will enter more deeply into the phenomenon of faith. Here, I wish simply to mention a few aspects that are directly related to justification.

In view of justification, *faith* is needed on behalf of Man: "It was to show his righteousness at the present time, so that he might be just and the justifier of the one who has faith [*ek pisteōs*, lit. who is out of faith] in Jesus. . . . For we hold that one is justified by faith [*pistei*, without a preposition] apart from works of the law. . . . God is one—who will justify the circumcised by faith [*ek pisteōs*, out of faith] and the uncircumcised through faith [*dia tēs pisteōs*]" (Rom. 3:26, 28, 30). "Therefore, since we have been justified by faith [*ek pisteōs*],

---
4. Vine (1985, 1:407).
5. Cf. Cranfield (1975, ad loc.); Moo (1996, 242): God is "just *even in* justifying."
6. Thus, e.g., Käsemann (1996, ad loc.).

we have peace with God through our Lord Jesus Christ" (5:1). "What shall we say, then? That Gentiles who did not pursue righteousness have attained it, that is, a righteousness that is by faith [*ek pisteōs*]" (9:30). "[W]e know that a person is not justified by works of the law but through faith [*dia pisteōs*] in Jesus Christ, so we also have believed in Christ Jesus, in order to be justified by faith [*ek pisteōs*] in Christ" (Gal. 2:16). "And the Scripture, foreseeing that God would justify the Gentiles by faith [*ek pisteōs*] . . ." (3:8). "So then, the law was our guardian until Christ came, in order that we might be justified by faith [*ek pisteōs*]" (v. 24).

It is not easy to render *ek pisteōs* properly in English (it is much easier in German [*aus Glauben*] and Dutch [*uit geloof*]). If we put the phrase "justified by faith" alongside the phrase "justified by God," we immediately see the difficulty. In Greek, the former "by" is usually *ek*, but the latter "by" would be *hypo* (cf. *hypo [tou] theou*, "by God," in the same epistle: 13:1, "instituted by God"; 15:15, "given by God"). The latter phrase could be reversed as follows: "God justifies"; but can we likewise say that "faith justifies"? That is more doubtful; as is said in the Belgic Confession (Art. 22): "However, to speak more clearly, we do not mean that faith itself justifies us, for it is only an instrument with which we embrace Christ our righteousness. But Jesus Christ, imputing to us all His merits, and so many holy works which He has done for us and in our stead, is our righteousness. And faith is an instrument that keeps us in communion with Him in all His benefits, ..."

The phrase *ek pisteōs* does not mean that faith is the basis of our justification because that basis can be only the redemptive work of Christ. Faith is the means or the instrument through which we share in justification. "Through" faith might be a more accurate rendering, but the problem is that Paul also uses the phrase *dia [tēs] pisteōs*, where the translation "through" ("by means of") is more obvious. Perhaps the phrase *ek pisteōs* suggests that justification is for those who live, love, think, feel, want, and act out of faith.

In the words of Gerrit Berkouwer: "It is not faith as a work with a creative causality or mediation or worthiness, through which this faith in some way or another would now—instead of the works of the law—have become the *ground* of justification."[7] Not faith but Christ is the basis of justification.[8] Protestant theologians never weary, and rightly so, of assuring us that faith should in no way be viewed as a good work, which as such would be the "ground" for justification. Thus, for instance, the Heidelberg Catechism (Q&A 61): "Q. Why do you say that you are righteous by faith only? A. Not that I am acceptable to God on account of the worthiness of my faith, but because only the satisfaction, righteousness, and holiness of Christ is my righteousness before God; and I can receive the same and make it my own in no other way than by faith only."

In opposition to this, however, we place two other arguments. First, the Greek phrase *ek pisteōs* stands in juxtaposition with the phrase *ex ergōn nomou*, lit. "out of works of the law" (Rom. 3:20), which certainly can be read as "on the basis of works of the law." In this sense, it cannot be all that wrong to speak of justification "on the basis of" faith.

Second, we may maintain that faith as such is never a basis of justification, while at the same time speaking of a "justifying faith." At any rate, the Canons of Dort, which strongly reject the Arminian view of faith, do speak of a "justifying faith" (II.8): "For this was the sovereign counsel and most gracious will and purpose of God the Father that the quickening and saving efficacy of the most precious death of' His Son should extend to all the elect, for bestowing upon them alone the gift of justifying faith, thereby to bring them infallibly to salvation; . . . ." The Canons are not taking a risk in using the expression "justifying faith," as if the idea could arise that something of humanity itself is the basis of justification, because they speak of this faith as being "granted" by God.

---

7. Berkouwer (1949a, 79; omitted from the English edition).
8. Van Genderen and Velema (2008, 609).

However this may be, any view of justification will always have to account for two undeniable facts: on the one hand, faith cannot be the actual *basis* of justification; on the other hand, it is an indispensable *condition* of justification: without faith no justification occurs. One could also put it as follows: on the one hand, faith is always a *person's* faith: it is this person who believes. On the other hand, faith is God's gift: "For by grace you have been saved through faith. And this is not your own doing; it is the gift of God" (Eph. 2:8)[9] (cf. the expression "saving faith," comparable to "justifying faith," discussed in the next chapter).

5.2.2 Prepositions

It is worthwhile to pay some more attention to the various prepositions that Paul uses when speaking of faith, because they are quite enlightening (cf. §5.1.2):

* *Ek pisteōs eis pistin:* "For in it [i.e., the gospel] the righteousness of God is revealed *from faith to faith*" (Rom. 1:17 NKJV). What does the latter phrase mean? "From faith in the law to faith in the gospel"?[10] Or, "from one phase of faith to the other" (cf. GNV note: "from faith which increaseth daily"; Phillips: "a process begun and continued by their faith")?[11] Or does it simply mean that everything is of faith, from the beginning to the end (cf. the construction in 2 Cor. 2:16 "from death to death ... from life to life"; 3:18 "from glory to glory," and see ERV: "God's way of making people right begins and ends with faith"; GNV: "it is through faith from beginning to end")?[12] Or does it mean the same as in 3:22 (see below):

---

9. The construction of Eph. 2:8 is not entirely clear, though: *touto* ("this") may refer back to *pisteōs* ("faith") (Bruce [1984, 289])—but *touto* is neutral and *pistis* is feminine—or to the "being saved" (Salmond [1979, 289]), or to the entire preceding sentence (Grosheide [1960, 40]; Wood [1978, 37]).
10. Augustinus (*De Spiritu et littera* 11.18), who also proposed: "from the faith of the preacher to the faith of the hearer."
11. Calvin (1973, 28).
12. Dodd (1932, ad loc.); Van Leeuwen and Jacobs (1952, 36); Ridderbos (1959, 35, 39; 1966, 185); Denney (1979, 591); Moo (1996, 76).

"to all who believe"?¹³ Or does it mean: "from the Faithful to the faithful," as a Jewish tradition says: the Torah came "from Faithful to faithful, from Righteous to righteous," that is, from God to Moses?¹⁴ Or does it mean: justification is received by faith, and also has faith, not works, as its goal?¹⁵ See further: "The good news tells how God accepts everyone who has faith, but only those who have faith (or, and faith is all that matters)" (CEV); "through faith for faith" (RSV).

* *Dia [tēs] pisteōs:* "through faith" (Rom. 3:22, 25, 31): faith is the means employed by the person through which God's righteousness is of benefit to him.

* *Eis pantas [kai epi pantas] tous pisteuontas:* the Received Text has the longer version, as we find it in (N)KJV: ". . . the righteousness of God, through faith in Jesus Christ, to all and on all who believe" (Rom. 3:22). The variant reading might mean that justification is offered to all but only becomes the portion of all those who believe (cf. §5.9.2).¹⁶ The reading "to all who believe" is more probably right. This might seem to be a superfluous addition after *dia [tēs] pisteōs*, unless one places the accent here on "all": justification comes to *all* who believe because "there is no difference" (v. 22).¹⁷

* *Pistei* (without a preposition): "by faith" (3:28): a simple instrumental dative: faith is the means through which a person is justified. It is the same with *chariti* (Rom. 3:24; Titus 3:7), another common dative: grace is the divine basis on which a person can be justified, this taking place *en tōi haimati autou*, "in (the power of) his blood" (Rom. 5:9; cf. 3:25).

* *Ek pisteōs . . . dia tēs pisteōs:* lit. "out of faith . . . through faith": "God . . . who will justify the circumcised by faith and

---

13. Philippi (1878, ad loc.); Murray (1968, 1:31–32); Vine (1985, 1:374).
14. Gen.R. 1.11; so Shulam (1998, 43); cf. Barth (1933, 41–42: from the faithfulness (of God) to the faith (of humans); cf. CEB: "from faithfulness to faith."
15. Zahn (1925, ad loc.); Schlatter (1962, ad loc.).
16. Kelly (*Bible Treasury* 6.376).
17. Murray (1968, 1:31–32, 111–12); Moo (1996, 225–26); cf. Ridderbos (1959, 84).

the uncircumcised through faith" (3:30). If it is true that God justifies both Jews and Gentiles through the same means, namely, through faith, why does Paul make a distinction here? Should we not look too deeply for an explanation (he seems to alternate between *ek* and *dia*)?[18] Or does the difference between the two lie especially in the article ("out of faith . . . through *the* faith"), which we might view as possessive here: "justify the circumcised by faith and the uncircumcised through *their* faith" (cf. ERV, GNT),[19] or deictic: "through *that* faith" that *they* possess, or "*that* faith that also the circumcised possess" (NIV: "through that same faith")?[20]

* *Epi tēi pistei:* "the righteousness from God that *depends on faith*" (Phil. 3:9; NIV: "on the basis of faith"): justification finds its origin (*ek*), the means for its realization (*dia*) and its basis (*epi*) in faith: justification is built upon faith.

As I said, in no way may faith be viewed here as a kind of good work in the sense of a merit or achievement.[21] Such a view would eviscerate Paul's entire argument: we are not justified by works, not even the work of faith. In the variety of prepositions (*ek, dia* + genit., *eis, epi*) there is one preposition conspicuously absent, namely *dia* + accusative, "because of." We are not justified "because of" our faith, as if this faith would be a merit on our behalf; it is a gift of God (Eph. 2:8):[22] "The *of* [*ek*] and *through* [*dia* + genit.] *faith* direct us to the objectivity of God's grace in Christ, which, of and through faith, is recognized and received as wholly divine grace."[23] That is, God does not justify us *because of* our faith but *because of* his own grace, which is embraced by faith.

---

18. Ridderbos (1959, 89); Murray (1968, 1:124); Denney (1979, 614); Moo (1996, 252).
19. Kelly (*Bible Treasury* 6.377).
20. Grant (1901, 207); Van Leeuwen and Jacobs (1952, 85).
21. Berkouwer (1954, 79–80).
22. See note 9.
23. Berkouwer (1954, 80).

5.2.3 Faith and Justification

Let me mention here three other special characteristics of faith in connection with justification (about faith more generally, see chapters 6 and 7):

(a) *Faith is supra-rational*. Faith is never exclusively the rational acceptance of certain truths, such as: I am a sinner—a righteous God should condemn me—Jesus died for my sins. No, there is no genuine faith without genuine repentance and genuine confession of sins. God would not be righteous if he would justify an unrepentant sinner. The only thing that separates a person from evil is repentance. Justification cleanses him in a judicial respect, but repentance cleanses him in a moral respect:[24] "[H]e who confesses and forsakes [his transgressions] will obtain mercy" (Prov. 28:13). "If we confess our sins, he is faithful and just to forgive us our sins and to cleanse us from all unrighteousness" (1 John 1:9).

We could also express the same truth as follows: there is no faith through which *humans* are justified if this faith, so to speak, does not justify *God* first: "Against you, you only, have I sinned and done what is evil in your sight, so that you may be justified in your words and blameless in your judgment" (Ps. 51:4). This word is quoted in Romans 3:4-5, "Let God be true though every one were a liar, as it is written, 'That you may be justified in your words, and prevail when you are judged' ... our unrighteousness serves to show the righteousness of God." People will begin having "wisdom in the secret heart" (Ps. 51:6) only when they begin "justifying" God in his judgment on natural humanity.[25] David first had to experience a deep fall before, in Psalm 51, he came to the point of seeing (again) that God was "justified" in everything he had said about humanity. There are things that we do not learn from a book but only through—sometimes hard—experience.

(b) *Faith is focused on Christ*. The fact that justifying faith

---
24. Coates (1926, 33–34).
25. Ibid., 49.

does not involve only embracing certain dogmas is evident from the fact that we are dealing here with *pistis Iēsou Christou*, the "faith of Jesus Christ," which means, according to the traditional view (which I accept), the faith of which Jesus is the object: "faith *in* Jesus" (Rom. 3:22, 26; Gal. 2:16, 20; 3:22; Phil. 3:9; James 2:1; Rev. 14:12; see §3.8.1). A good example is Galatians 2:20, "[T]he life I now live in the flesh I live by faith in the Son of God." It makes more sense to think here of living by our faith in Christ than to believe that the faith(fulness) of Christ himself is meant. It is the same in James 2:1, where believers are "holding" (Greek, *echete*, "have") the faith in Jesus; what sense does it make to believe that believers are "having" the faith(fulness) of Christ himself? It is the same in Revelation 14:12, where the text speaks of "those who keep the commandments of God and their faith in Jesus"; in what sense could we be "keeping" the faith(fulness) of Christ himself?

There cannot be any doubt that *pistis Christou* can mean "faith *in* Christ'; it seems most obvious to accept this rendering also in the passages speaking of justification. See, for example, Romans 3:22-26: there can be little doubt that "faith" in verse 25 is the faith of believers. But then it is obvious that in verses 22 and 26 "faith" (in Christ) is also the faith of believers. Where "faith" is not followed by a genitive, there can be little doubt that the faith of believers is meant. Now look at Philippians 3:9 (NKJV): ". . . not having my own righteousness, which [is] from the law, but that which [is] through faith in Christ [Greek, *dia pisteōs Christou*], the righteousness which is from God by faith [*epi tēi pistei*]." If the latter "faith" is that of believers, then the former is too: it is the faith *of* believers, and the faith *in* Christ.

Now my point is that "faith in Christ" is never only faith in a set of truths, but faith in him who *is* the Truth (John 14:6; cf. Eph. 4:21). There is a personal object of faith; not only a finished work to rest upon but a person dear to the heart. The more conscious we are that we fall short of the glory of God (Rom. 3:23), the more thankful we will be that we believe in

One who did not fall short, but in whom shines the glory of God in the way of grace.[26]

(c) *Faith bears fruit.* There is no genuine faith that does not come to expression in the fruit of the Spirit: "love, joy, peace, patience, kindness, goodness, faithfulness, gentleness, self-control" (Gal. 5:22-23) and in good works (see §5.4). How could we be justified by faith if there would not be a very practical hungering and thirsting for righteousness (Matt. 5:6)? There is not just "faith" but the "obedience of faith," not only when coming to faith (Rom. 1:5), but also the obedience of a faithful life: "Do you not know that if you present yourselves to anyone as obedient slaves, you are slaves of the one whom you obey, either of sin, which leads to death, or of obedience, which leads to righteousness?" (6:16). It is a matter of "faith working through love" (Gal. 5:6), that is, faith that expresses itself in works in observing the "Torah of Christ" (6:2) (see §§5.4.2 and 5.5.2). It is a matter of faith doing the "work of faith by his power" (2 Thess. 1:11; cf. 1 Thess. 1:3), fighting "the good fight of the faith" (1 Tim. 6:12), knowing the "testing of your faith" (James 1:3) and the "tested genuineness of your faith" (1 Pet. 1:7), a faith that is "completed" by works (James 2:22), a faith that "overcomes the world" (1 John 5:4-5), etc.

In simple terms: no one can say that he has been justified (declared righteous) by faith if he—albeit in much weakness—does not *live* as a righteous person. You cannot have been *made* righteous if you do not produce the *fruit* of righteousness (cf. Phil. 1:11; Heb. 12:11; cf. James 3:17-18). This will be dealt with in the next sections.

5.3   Life as the Goal of Justification
5.3.1   "Righteousness of Life"

We have seen that it is the *ungodly* who is said to be justified by God (Rom. 4:5). The goal of justification is that the ungodly is redeemed of his ungodliness, his wickedness, and cleansed

---
26. Ibid., 56–57.

of all his iniquities. This is the negative aspect of justification. The positive aspect is *life*: "For if, because of one man's [i.e., Adam's] trespass, *death* reigned through that one man, much more will those who receive the abundance of grace and the free gift of righteousness reign in *life* through the one man Jesus Christ. Therefore, as one trespass led to condemnation for all men, so one act of righteousness leads to justification and *life* [lit., justification of life] for all men . . . so that, as sin reigned in death, grace also might reign through righteousness leading to eternal *life* through Jesus Christ our Lord" (Rom. 5:17–18, 21).

The phrase "justification of life" (Greek, *dikaiōsin zōēs*, v. 18) has been rendered in several ways: "justification and life" (NIV, ESV); "sets all people free and gives them life" (GNT; cf. CEV); "the righteous requirements necessary for life" (CEB); "it makes all people right with God. And that brings them true life" (ERV; cf. TLB). These are fair renderings, better than those that suggest that justification as such consists of life.[27] The idea is that justification *results in* life; compare verse 21: "righteousness leading to eternal life."[28]

James Denney wrote: "When God justifies the sinner, he [i.e., the latter] enters into and inherits life."[29] And Douglas Moo: "Paul, in this paragraph, uses justification to describe the status of the believer in this age, while 'life' is confined to the eschatological future."[30] However, this is probably too one-sided: also in the "present age" there is the justified person's true life in Christ. Both meanings of "life" can be found in Romans: Paul speaks of it as a present possession (6:2, 4, 11, 13; 8:2, 6, 10, 12–13) and as an eschatological notion (2:7; 5:10, 17, 21; 6:8, 22–23). The latter is the extension and expansion of the former.

---

27. So, e.g., Lightfoot (1895, ad loc.), who reads here a genitive of apposition.
28. Cf. Sanday and Headlam (1950, ad loc.); Murray (1968, 1:202, 209); Cranfield (1975, ad loc.); Vine (1985, 1:428); Moo (1996, 341n126).
29. Denney (1979, 630).
30. Moo (1996, 341n126).

The believer's justification is characterized by the life of the risen Christ; this life constitutes both the cause and the character of their new position. Christ was "raised for our justification" (4:25). Through his death and resurrection, Christ has arrived at a position beyond the reach of the problem of sin: "Christ, having been offered once to bear the sins of many, will appear a second time, not to deal with sin but to save those who are eagerly waiting for him" (Heb. 9:28). And believers, too, as united with Christ in his death and resurrection, are beyond the reach of the problem of sin: "as he is so also are we in this world" (1 John 4:17), that is, as he is *now*, as the risen and glorified Christ. This has tremendous practical consequences. Our acceptance, our standing in the grace (favor, benevolence) of God (Rom. 5:2), cannot be separated from a godly life as dead to sin and alive to God in Christ Jesus (6:11), resting in the perfection of what he is to God. Our justification leads to a *life* in righteousness, a life characterized by the practical righteousness of the risen Christ.

With this, we finally touch upon the full bearing of a conscious possession and enjoyment of righteousness and of peace with God. Our justification is rooted in the death and blood shedding of Christ (Rom. 5:6–11), but we will never fully grasp and appreciate it if we do not see in what way his life as the risen Lord is involved in this: his resurrection life as *dedikaiōtai apo tēs hamartias* (lit., "justified from sin"; a perfect tense, which can be rendered as: "[set] free from sin" through an event in the past: Christ's death and resurrection). The successive chapters in Romans place the accents a little differently:

(a) In *Romans 4*, Christ's resurrection is related to our justification (v. 25).

(b) In *Romans 5*, Christ's resurrection is related to our salvation (v. 10), and again to our justification (v. 21).

(c) In *Romans 6*, Christ's resurrection is related to our life as people who have died to sin, and are now alive to God in

Christ Jesus (vv. 4–11).

(d) In *Romans 7*, Christ's resurrection is related to our new condition as people who have died to the law, and are now bearing fruit for God (v. 4).

(e) In *Romans 8*, Christ's resurrection is related to our own bodily resurrection (v. 11), and to his intercession for us (v. 34).

5.3.2 Dying for Sin, Dying to Sin

It may seem to be a dull subject, but prepositions are important, as we have already seen (§§5.1.2 and 5.2.2)! In Romans 8:3, we read: "By sending his own Son in the likeness of sinful flesh and for sin [Greek, *peri hamartias*], he condemned sin in the flesh." So also: "Where there is forgiveness of these, there is no longer any offering for sin [*peri hamartias*]" (Heb. 10:18). "For the bodies of those animals whose blood is brought into the holy places by the high priest as a sacrifice for sin [*peri hamartias*] are burned outside the camp" (Heb. 13:11). This "dying *for* sin" is very different from "dying *to* sin": "For the death he died he died to sin [*tēi hamartiai*], once for all, but the life he lives he lives to God [*tōi theōi*]. So you also must consider yourselves dead to sin [*tēi hamartiai*] and alive to God in Christ Jesus" (Rom. 6:10).

The difference is conspicuous. The former is *propitiation*: Jesus undergoing the divine judgment on sin. "Dying for sin" is dying as an *offering* for sin; that is what the Old Testament calls the "sin offering." The latter is *justification*: Jesus who through his death and resurrection has nothing to do with the problem of sin anymore, and in this position unites us with himself: "There is therefore now no condemnation for those who are in Christ Jesus. For the law of the Spirit of life has set you free in Christ Jesus from the law of sin and death" (Rom. 8:1-2). Being "dead to sin" means being beyond the reach of sin and death; these are powers that forever have been dealt with.

In the former case, Christ is the subject, and the believer

is merely the object: Christ died for sin, that is, he died for the sinner, as his substitute: "For while we were still weak, at the right time Christ died for the ungodly. . . . God shows his love for us in that while we were still sinners, Christ died for us" (Rom. 5:6, 8). In the latter case, both Christ and the believer are the subjects: the believer has died to sin together with Christ: "We know that our old self was crucified with him in order that the body of sin might be brought to nothing, so that we would no longer be enslaved to sin" (Rom. 6:6; cf. Gal. 2:20; 5:24; 1 Pet. 4:1-2).

Wickedness, iniquities, eventually leads a person to eternal death. Justification—redemption from iniquities, through which the ungodly becomes a righteous person—leads to eternal life: "But now that you have been set free from sin and have become slaves of God, the fruit you get leads to sanctification and its end, *eternal life*. For the wages of sin is death, but the free gift of God is *eternal life* in Christ Jesus our Lord" (Rom. 6:22-23). "But if Christ is in you, although the body is dead because of sin, the Spirit is *life* because of righteousness" (8:10). God has saved us "so that being justified by his grace we might become heirs according to the hope of *eternal life*" (Titus 3:7).[31]

If, as in Anselm of Canterbury's forensic doctrine of justification, one emphasizes too strongly and unilaterally the *judicial* aspect of justification[32]—that is, God's acquittal and rehabilitation of the person who by faith is in Christ—other aspects are easily lost. I think of the *moral* aspect: the element of *forgiveness* that is present in justification, of becoming a *tsaddiq*, a "righteous person," whose justification is evident from his words and acts (see §5.6). I also think of the *biotic* analogy: wickedness leads to death, justification to life. Let us enter a little more deeply into this matter.

---

31. See further Ouweneel (2010a, §§4.1 and 4.2).
32. Van Genderen and Velema (2008, 608) contend against the idea of any one-sidedness here (cf. 627-29).

5.3.3 Justification Leads to Life

God views us as united with the once dead but now risen Lord. The "justification of life" is justification due to, and in connection with, the resurrection life of Christ. I already pointed to Romans 6:7, "For one who has died has been set free [or, has been justified] from sin." This verse has often, and rightly, been taken as a general statement in the following sense: the evildoer who has died has fulfilled the requirement of justice and is no longer punishable.[33] As I said before, the Greek perfect tense *dedikaiōtai* refers to something in the past of which the results have effects in the present. Thus, some Dutch translations say: "For one who has died is judicially free from sin," that is, is judicially beyond the reach of sin and its consequences. As Jan Gerrit Woelderink put it: in the resurrection, "the Surety of God has been declared righteous, discharged from all further legal proceedings, and the entrance into eternal glory has been disclosed to him. But what is valid for him, is valid for all God's Church. In the resurrection of Christ, all his own receive the discharge from the righteously deserved judgment and the title to eternal life."[34]

The person who has died with Christ and was raised with him is both set free from sin and beyond the reach of eternal judgment, and has been clothed with the perfection of Christ. A righteous God can do nothing else than declare such a person to be righteous. To put it even more strongly, such a person is, just as Christ, beyond the reach of death. Therefore, the text continues: "Now if we have died with Christ, we believe that we will also *live* with him. We know that Christ, being raised from the dead, will never die again [cf. John 11:25–26]; death no longer has dominion over him. For the death he died he died to sin, once for all, but the life he lives he lives to God.

---

33. Ridderbos (1959, 130); Murray (1968, 1:222); Denney (1979, 633); Vine (1985, 1:433); Moo (1996, 377); cf. the Talmud tract Shabbat 151b: "Once man dies he is free from [all] obligations . . . once a man is dead he is free from religious duties."
34. Woelderink (1941, 193).

So you also must consider yourselves dead to sin and alive to God in Christ Jesus" (Rom. 6:8–11).

This relationship between justification and life is of even greater importance than I have indicated so far. The sins of the sinner are only the symptoms of a deeper power within him.[35] The word "sin" is not just the singular of "sins" but it is also the biblical word for the evil power in the sinner, which is the corrupt source from which the sins (the evil acts) proceed (cf. Rom. 3:9; 5:12–13, 21; 6:1–2, 6–7, 10–23; 7:8–9, 11, 13–14, 17, 20, 23, 25; 8:2–3, 10). The sinner's sins can be forgiven, but this is insufficient. The problem of *sin*, the evil nature in him, must be tackled. This evil nature cannot be forgiven; the activity of this nature can be ended only by death, that is, through the righteous death sentence of God. However, humans cannot undergo this judgment without being lost forever.

God's solution for this major problem—one that is larger even than the problem of *sins*—is that Christ has undergone the death sentence for all those who believe in him. Or even stronger than this, the believer may know that in Christ he *himself* has undergone the death sentence, namely, on the cross (Rom. 6:6, "crucified with him"). The "natural person" (1 Cor. 2:14) who comes to faith finds his end in the death of Christ because, in this death, God has executed the judgment on sin, the evil power that makes the natural person a sinner.

Not only this: Christ was "raised from the dead by the glory of the Father," so that now we can walk in "newness of life," as is illustrated in baptism (Rom. 6:3–4). His resurrection is the proof that his redemptive work is truly finished. Jesus has nothing to do with the problem of sin anymore, which means that it has been completely solved (v. 7). As Herman Bavinck put it: "For Christ, therefore, his resurrection constituted a divine endorsement of the work he had accomplished, a proof that he was the Son of God (Rom. 1:4), that our sins had been expiated by him (1 Cor. 15:17), . . ."[36] And *this* means

---
35. Moo (1996, 377) on Rom. 6:7: "set free from [the power of] sin."
36. Bavinck (2008, 4: 217).

that he who has died with Christ has nothing to do with the problem of sin anymore, either: the sinful "flesh" (the "old nature") does still dwell in him, but he himself, that is, his earlier personality (the "old man"), has died to sin (see §9.5.2 for the important distinction between the "old man" and the "old nature"): "Let not sin therefore reign in your mortal body, to make you obey its passions. Do not present your members to sin as instruments for unrighteousness, but present yourselves to God as those who have been brought from death to life, and your members to God as instruments for righteousness. For sin will have no dominion over you, since you are not under law but under grace" (Rom. 6:12–14).

As we saw, Hebrews 9:28 expresses the same thought: "[S]o Christ, having been offered once to bear the sins of many, will appear a second time, not to deal with sin [Greek, *chōris hamartias*, lit. "apart from sin"] but to save those who are eagerly waiting for him." That is, he will appear a second time, but this time without having anything more to do with the problem of sin.

5.3.4 Making or Declaring Righteous?

In summary, we may conclude that it is biblical to say that God *makes* the ungodly righteous (Rom. 4:5), but that it is equally biblical to say that God *declares* the sinner righteous, namely, the person who is no longer counted as a sinner because by faith he has been united with a dead and risen Christ. The "old man" was thoroughly unrighteous—but this "old man" no longer exists because he has found his end in the death of Christ on the cross. In its stead, a "new man" has arrived, who is connected with Christ in his resurrection. The life and the nature of this "new man" have a name: it is the risen Christ himself. The "new man" is the person who, "according to God" (Greek, *kata theon*), was created in true righteousness and holiness (Eph. 4:24 NKJV). Therefore, God can testify of this person, in justice and truth, that he is righteous and holy.

Incidentally, *kata theon* has been interpreted as "according to the *will* of God" (several Dutch translations), but it is more likely that "after the *likeness* of God" is meant (ESV, cf. GNT, NASB, RSV, WEB), or "according to God's image" (CEB, cf. GNV note, NET), or "to be like God" (CEV, ERV, NLT). In this way, the verse clearly seems to be connected with Genesis 1:26-27, "Then God said, 'Let us make man in our image, after our likeness. . . .' So God created man in his own image, in the image of God he created him; male and female he created them."

Coming back to the notion of "God's righteousness" (chapter 1), let me ask two rhetorical questions here.

(a) Is God not righteous when he *makes* righteous every person who believes in Christ by forgiving this person his sins? Is not this the reason, that Christ has given his blood precisely for blotting out the sins of all those who would believe in him? Would it not be unrighteous of God if he would not justify the person who comes pleading on the blood of Christ?

(b) Is God not righteous if he *declares* righteous every person who believes in him? Is not this the reason, that precisely for such persons God has raised Christ from the dead, in order that such persons would be united with Christ, not only in his death but also in his resurrection? Would it not be unrighteous of God if he would not justify the person who has been united with the risen and glorified Christ?

I add to the previous thoughts the significant fact that plays a central role in all these chapters, namely, that all the blessings mentioned are through Christ. None of these blessings can be viewed apart from each other, and even less apart from Christ. Whatever blessing from God we may imagine, whatever life we have received, these things cannot be separated from Christ because of our union with him as the risen and glorified one. In Romans 5, we are told no fewer than seven times that all is "through him" ("through" being here Greek, *dia* + genitive, indicating the means by which something occurs or becomes possible):[37]

(1) *Peace* (v. 1): "Therefore, since we have been justified by faith, we have peace with God *through* our Lord Jesus Christ." Here, Christ is the means through which believers have received peace (undisturbed rest and harmony with God).

(2) *Access* (v. 2): "*Through* him we have also obtained access by faith [Greek, *tēi pistei*, a common dative] into this grace in which we stand, and we rejoice in hope of the glory of God." Here, Christ is the means through which believers have obtained access into the grace of God.

(3) *Salvation* (v. 9): "Since, therefore, we have now been justified by [Greek, *en*, "in (the power of)"] his blood, much more shall we be saved by [or, *through*] him from the wrath of God." Here, Christ is the means through which believers not only *have* been justified, but *shall* also be saved in eternity.

(4) *Rejoicing* (v. 11a): "More than that, we also rejoice in God *through* our Lord Jesus Christ." Here, Christ is the means through which believers have all reason to rejoice in God.

(5) *Reconciliation* (v. 11b): ". . . Jesus Christ, *through* whom we have now received reconciliation." Here, Christ is the means through which believers have been reconciled with God.

(6) *Reigning* (v. 17): ". . . much more will those who receive the abundance of grace and the free gift of righteousness reign in life *through* the one man Jesus Christ." Here, Christ is the means through which believers learn to know the true life that is the consequence of justification.

(7) *Eternal life* (v. 21): ". . . so that, as sin reigned in (Greek, *en*, in [the power of]) death, grace also might reign through righteousness leading to eternal life *through* Jesus Christ our Lord." Here, Christ is the means through which believers will ultimately even attain eternal life.

---

37. Cf. Coates (n.d.-b, 63).

5.4 Righteousness by Works
5.4.1 The Confessions and Catechisms

The person justified and made alive in Christ will naturally also produce the *fruits* of that new life. As we read in the Belgic Confession (Art. 24): "Therefore, it is so far from being true that this justifying faith makes men remiss in a pious and holy life, that on the contrary without it they would never do anything out of love to God, but only out of self-love or fear of damnation. Therefore it is impossible that this holy faith be unfruitful in man; for we do not speak of a vain faith, but of such a faith which is called in Scripture a 'faith working through love,' which excites man to the practice of those works which God has commanded in His Word. These works, as they proceed from the good root of faith, are good and acceptable in the sight God, forasmuch as they are all sanctified by His grace. Nevertheless they are of no account towards our justification, for it is by faith in Christ that we are justified, even before we do good works; otherwise they could not be good works, any more than the fruit of a tree can be good before the tree itself is good."

In the Heidelberg Catechism we read (Q&A 86): "Q. Since, then, we are redeemed from our misery by grace through Christ, without any merit of ours, why must we do good works? A. Because Christ, having redeemed us by His blood, also renews us by His Holy Spirit after His own image, that with our whole life we show ourselves thankful to God for His blessing, and that He be glorified through us; then also, that we ourselves may be assured of our faith by the fruits thereof; and by our godly walk win also others to Christ."

The Westminster Confession of Faith tells us (XI.2): "Faith, thus receiving and resting on Christ and His righteousness, is the alone instrument of justification: yet it is not alone in the person justified, but is ever accompanied with all other saving graces, and is no dead faith, but worketh by love." And a bit later (XVI.2-3, 6): "These good works, done in obedience to God's commandments, are the fruits and evidences of a true and lively faith: and by them believers manifest their thankfulness, strengthen their assurance, edify their brethren, adorn the profession of the Gospel, stop the mouths of the adversaries, and glorify God, whose workmanship they are, created in Christ Jesus thereunto, that, having their fruit unto holiness, they may have the end, eternal life. Their ability to do good works is not at all of themselves, but wholly from the Spirit of Christ. And that they may be enabled thereunto, beside the graces they have already received, there is required an actual influence of the same Holy Spirit, to work in them to will, and to do, of His good pleasure: yet are they not hereupon to grow negligent, as if they were not bound to perform any duty unless upon a special motion of the Spirit; but they ought to be diligent in stirring up the grace of God that is in them. . . . [T]he persons of believers being accepted through Christ, their good works also are accepted in Him; not as though they were in this life wholly unblameable and unreproveable in God's sight; but that He, looking upon them in His Son, is pleased to accept and reward that which is sincere, although accompanied with many weaknesses and imperfections."

In all these passages the main message is this: just as works do not play any role in the actual justification, so too good works are the necessary *results* of justification. No one can be justified by works—but no one can say he *has been* justified if the resulting good works are lacking. This is precisely the message of James 2:17–26, "[F]aith by itself, if it does not have works, is dead. . . . Show me your faith apart from your works, and I will show you my faith by my works. . . . You see that a person is justified by works and not by faith alone. . . . For as the body apart from the spirit is dead, so also faith apart from works is dead."

5.4.2 Fruit-Bearing

Perhaps, "fruit" is a more appropriate word than "works."

Justification in the New Testament

Of course, Paul does write about the "good works" of the believers, for example: "For we are his workmanship, created in Christ Jesus for good works, which God prepared beforehand, that we should walk in them" (Eph. 2:10); ". . . our great God and Savior Jesus Christ, who gave himself for us to redeem us from all lawlessness and to purify for himself a people for his own possession who are zealous for good works" (Titus 2:13-14). However, in Galatians 5, Paul places the "*works* of the flesh" (v. 19) in opposition to the "*fruit* of the Spirit": "love, joy, peace, patience, kindness, goodness, faithfulness, gentleness, self-control" (v. 22-23). Paul thus implies that not only the acts ("good works") are important but also the root of these works, the moral attitude behind them.

This is why fruit-bearing is such an important subject in the New Testament. To begin with Jesus: "I am the true vine, and my Father is the vinedresser. Every branch in me that does not bear fruit he takes away, and every branch that does bear fruit he prunes, that it may bear more fruit. . . . As the branch cannot bear fruit by itself, unless it abides in the vine, neither can you, unless you abide in me. I am the vine; you are the branches. Whoever abides in me and I in him, he it is that bears much fruit, for apart from me you can do nothing. . . . By this my Father is glorified, that you bear much fruit and so prove to be my disciples" (John 15:1-8). And Paul says, "But now that you have been set free from sin and have become slaves of God, the fruit you get leads to sanctification and its end, eternal life" (Rom. 6:22).

In connection with justification, the expression "fruit of righteousness" is of special interest: ". . . filled with the fruit of righteousness that comes through Jesus Christ, to the glory and praise of God" (Phil. 1:11). "For the moment all discipline seems painful rather than pleasant, but later it yields the peaceful fruit of righteousness to those who have been trained by it" (Heb. 12:11). "Now the fruit of righteousness is sown in peace by those who make peace" (James 3:18 NKJV). Also compare this statement: "For you were once darkness, but now [you are] light in the Lord. Walk as children of light (for the fruit of the Spirit[38] [is] in all goodness, righteousness, and truth)" (Eph. 5:8–9 NKJV). In other words, having been justified (declared righteousness) necessarily produces the "fruit of righteousness" in the practical lives of the righteous.

What James calls the "fruit of righteousness" (3:18) is more or less what he earlier calls "works" by which one is "justified" (proven to be righteous): "Was not Abraham our father justified by works when he offered up his son Isaac on the altar? You see that faith was active along with his works, and faith was completed by his works; and the Scripture was fulfilled that says, 'Abraham believed God, and it was counted to him as righteousness' [Gen. 15:6]—and he was called a friend of God [2 Chron. 20:17; Isa. 41:8]. You see that a person is justified by works and not by faith alone. And in the same way was not also Rahab the prostitute justified by works when she received the messengers and sent them out by another way? For as the body apart from the spirit is dead, so also faith apart from works is dead" (James 2:21-26).[39]

By the way, these two examples also show that good works must be measured by God's standards, not human standards. Abraham was prepared to kill his son, and Rahab was betraying her own country. According to the laws of our modern nations, both would be guilty of very serious crimes. But in God's eyes, these were good works, which proved that Abraham and Rahab were true *tsaddiqim*.

For James, these works are even "works of the law," namely, the "law of [Christian] freedom" (1:25; 2:12), or, the "royal law" (2:8), that is, the law of the Kingdom of God. This is what Paul calls the "law of Christ": ". . . not being outside the law of God but under the law of Christ" (1 Cor. 9:21). "Bear one another's burdens, and so fulfill the law of Christ" (Gal. 6:2). Also compare Romans 8:4, ". . . in order that the righ-

---

38. So the Textus Receptus; modern text editions have "fruit of light."
39. On James 2 in relation to Paul's doctrine of justification, see Berkouwer (1954, 129–39).

teous requirement of the law might be fulfilled in us, who walk not according to the flesh but according to the Spirit," and 13:8–10, "Owe no one anything, except to love each other, for the one who loves another has fulfilled the law. For the commandments, 'You shall not commit adultery, You shall not murder, You shall not steal, You shall not covet,' and any other commandment, are summed up in this word: 'You shall love your neighbor as yourself.' [Lev. 19:18] Love does no wrong to a neighbor; therefore love is the fulfilling of the law." In the eyes of the world, Abraham may have been a child abuser, and Rahab a quisling—but both were driven by love for the one and true God.

5.4.3 Justification by Works: Societal Aspects

At this point, let us look again at the distinction between "justified by faith" and "justified by works (of the law)" (see earlier in chapter 2). We should not create here a false juxtaposition, because in essence the cleft does not exist between *these* two. The real conflict is between a (spiritually) *dead* person who works in his own strength, and a *living* (born again, believing) person who works in God's strength (cf. Rom. 8:4, the law fulfilled in the power of the Spirit). In terms of Psalm 1:3 and Jeremiah 17:6–8, it is the difference between the "tree planted by the streams of water, that yields its fruit in its season," and the "shrub in the desert . . . in the parched places of the wilderness, in an uninhabited salt land."

A person may have faith; but whether this is a genuine or a false faith will become evident from the works of faith, the "fruit in its season." This is why we speak of *positional* justification, which is a one-time matter, on account of faith: a person *changes* from an ungodly into a righteous one. But in addition, we speak of *practical* justification: the believer should *turn out* to be a righteous person; his righteousness should manifest itself in his practical life of faith. As Martin Buber explained: the word *tsaddiq* is usually translated as "righteous one," but actually it means the person proven to be righteous, the person found to be good (see further in §5.5).⁴⁰

This practical righteousness is of great personal, but also societal and eschatological importance. As far as the *societal* importance is concerned, this is dealt with in Romans 13, where, in spite of the reality of Emperor Nero's régime, the ideal government is presented: "Therefore whoever resists the authorities resists what God has appointed. . . . Would you have no fear of the one who is in authority? Then do what is good, and you will receive his approval, for he is God's servant for your good. But if you do wrong, be afraid, for he does not bear the sword in vain. For he is the servant of God, an avenger who carries out God's wrath on the wrongdoer. Therefore one must be in subjection, not only to avoid God's wrath but also for the sake of conscience" (vv. 2-5).

Martin Luther adduced this passage to oppose the rebellious farmers during the German Peasants' War (1524-25). Why did he not rather emphasize the fact that good authorities should have been good to these farmers? What would have happened if Luther had better understood James 2, that is, justification by works, or, justification by faith *working in love* (Gal. 5:6)?⁴¹ What does justification by faith mean if this faith does not produce fruit, not only individual, but also societal fruit, including mercy for the oppressed? James even says, "Religion that is pure and undefiled before God, the Father, is this: to visit orphans and widows in their affliction, and to keep oneself unstained from the world" (1:27). Luther consciously chose the protection of the authorities that were benevolent to him. In this way, he turned against the farmers instead of turning against the authorities that oppressed them.

The one-sidedness of Luther's doctrine of justification came to light in a painful way in his conflict with Thomas Müntzer (ca. 1489-1525), who at first was a Lutheran pastor.

---

40. Buber (2006, 23).
41. Luther called the book of James scornfully an "epistle of straw" (Luther's Preface to the New Testament, 1522, in Luther [1943, 443-44]).

Luther blamed him for drawing radical societal conclusions from Luther's own Reformation.[42] We have learned to view Müntzer mainly through Lutheran glasses, but this should not close our eyes to the positive sides of his "evangelical-radical" attitude. He rejected infant baptism and the clergy, believed in the present-day significance of prophecy, and had a strong eschatological tendency. Whatever one may think of this, in 1524 Müntzer pleaded for divine righteousness, and became one of the leaders of the Peasants' War that was so strongly condemned by Luther. If the latter had better understood "justification by works," as well as the societal (in addition to the individual) significance of justification, he might have cooperated in bringing the social abuses in Germany to an end sooner.

5.4.4 Justification by Works: Eschatological Aspects

As far as the *eschatological* aspects of justification by works are concerned, we notice that Romans 5–8 is followed by chapters 9–11, where Paul deals with what could be called the ultimate justification of Israel. Originally, "Israel who pursued a law that would lead to righteousness [lit., a law of righteousness] did not succeed in reaching that law" (9:30–10:3). But then we hear: "[A] partial hardening has come upon Israel, until the fullness of the Gentiles has come in. And in this way all Israel will be saved, as it is written, 'The Deliverer will come from Zion, he will banish ungodliness from Jacob'; 'and this will be my covenant with them when I take away their sins' [Isa. 27:9; 59:20]" (Rom. 11:25-27).

Isaiah says, "In the LORD all the offspring of Israel shall be justified and shall glory" (45:25). We should not read into this the Pauline doctrine of justification; rather, the idea seems to be that God has put his people within their rights (cf. ERV: "will help the people of Israel live right," note: "find justice"). John N. Oswalt says on this verse: the LORD "is the one who

---

42. Cf. among others Hinrichs (1952); Ebert (1990); Friesen (1990); Goertz (1993).

has vindicated them" (cf. NET: "All the descendants of Israel will be vindicated by the Lord").[43] In fact, this is an altogether new aspect of justification: declaring someone to be righteous over against those who have accused this person, thereby vindicating this person, doing justice to him, putting him within his rights (cf. §1.8.2).

Isaiah 60:21 says, "Your people shall all be righteous; they shall possess the land forever, the branch of my planting, the work of my hands, that I might be glorified." This is clearly practical righteousness again, just as it is elsewhere in Isaiah: 1:26, "And I will restore your judges as at the first, and your counselors as at the beginning. Afterward you shall be called the city of righteousness, the faithful city"; 9:7, "Of the increase of his government and of peace there will be no end, on the throne of David and over his kingdom, to establish it and to uphold it with justice and with righteousness from this time forth and forevermore"; 26:2, "Open the gates, that the righteous nation that keeps faith may enter in"; 28:17, "I will make justice the line, and righteousness the plumb line"; 32:1, 16–17, "Behold, a king will reign in righteousness, and princes will rule in justice. . . . Then justice will dwell in the wilderness, and righteousness abide in the fruitful field. And the effect of righteousness will be peace, and the result of righteousness, quietness and trust forever"; and 33:5, "The Lord is exalted, for he dwells on high; he will fill Zion with justice and righteousness".

This is the proper candidate for membership in the Messianic Kingdom: "He who walks righteously and speaks uprightly, who despises the gain of oppressions, who shakes his hands, lest they hold a bribe, who stops his ears from hearing of bloodshed and shuts his eyes from looking on evil, he will dwell on the heights; his place of defense will be the fortresses of rocks; his bread will be given him; his water will be sure. Your eyes will behold the king [i.e., Messiah] in his beauty;

---

43. Oswalt (1998, 225).

they will see a land that stretches afar. . . . And no inhabitant will say, 'I am sick'; the people who dwell there will be forgiven their iniquity" (Isa. 33:15-17, 24).

John Oswalt gives a beautiful summary of righteousness in Isaiah when dealing with 60:21: "Here then is a synthesis of chs. 1-39 and 40-55. Chs. 1-39 call for lived-out righteousness, and threaten punishment as the alternative. Chs. 40-55 offer redemption from that punishment solely on the basis of the righteousness of God. Finally, chs. 56-66 again call for lived-out righteousness, but show that such living is possible only through the gracious righteousness of God. In short, if it is true that we still look for the perfection of the Kingdom of God, we are expected to know a taste of its reality as we allow the power of the arm of the Lord to make us a righteous people for his name's sake."[44]

5.5 Practical Righteousness in the New Testament
5.5.1 Living Righteously

When speaking of justification by faith, Paul refers primarily — but not exclusively — to *positional* justification (being *made* righteous). When speaking of justification by faith, James refers primarily to *practical* justification (*living out* righteousness). Paul deals with *iustitiae imputationem apud Dei tribunal* ("imputation of righteousness before the judgment seat of God"). James deals with *demonstrationem iustitiae ab effectis, idque apud homines* ("demonstration of righteousness from the results, namely, toward people").[45] When Paul adduces Abraham as evidence for his doctrine, he refers to his faith mentioned in Genesis 15:6. When James adduces Abraham as evidence for his doctrine, he refers to the *fruit* of his faith mentioned in Genesis 22.[46]

As I said, fruit goes deeper than works (cf. Gal. 5:19-22). Thus, the joy and peace of faith are not works but fruits

---
44. Ibid., 559.
45. Calvin, Commentary on James (ad loc.).
46. Berkouwer (1954, 135–36, 138–39).

(v. 22). Someone may say that he has faith in God's redemptive grace. But if this does not fill his heart with joy, if he does not experience the peace of God, it is evident that such faith does not mean much to him. The knowledge of the love and grace of God leads a person to submit to God; it breaks the power of sin, and fills his heart with heavenly joy and peace.[47] Compare these Pauline statements: "Not that we lord it over your faith, but we work with you for your joy, for you stand firm in your faith" (cf. 2 Cor. 1:24). "Convinced of this, I know that I will remain and continue with you all, for your progress and joy in the faith" (Phil. 1:25). "So flee youthful passions and pursue righteousness, faith, love, and peace, along with those who call on the Lord from a pure heart" (2 Tim. 2:22).

The New Testament often speaks of this practical righteousness, also in the context of the Kingdom of God, so that in fact it is as central a notion as *tsedaqah* in the Old Testament. I mention only a few passages: "Blessed are those who hunger and thirst for righteousness, for they shall be satisfied.... Blessed are those who are persecuted for righteousness' sake, for theirs is the kingdom of heaven. . . . For I tell you, unless your righteousness exceeds that of the scribes [i.e., Torah scholars] and Pharisees, you will never enter the kingdom of heaven" (Matt. 5:6, 10, 20). "Exceeds" here does not refer only to a quantitative but also to a qualitative difference, as we see in 23:1–33, where in verse 23 we read that the righteousness of the Torah scholars did involve tithing "mint and dill and cumin," but neglected "the weightier matters of the Torah: justice and mercy and faithfulness" (Luke 11:42: "justice and the love of God"); or in verse 24 we read about "straining out a gnat and swallowing a camel" (see §2.8.2). The Kingdom of God is not about all kinds of tertiary issues, but about *righteousness and peace and joy in the Holy Spirit* (Rom. 14:17): "[S]eek first the kingdom of God and his righteousness" (Matt. 6:33).

In Romans, we are *made* righteous in order to *live* righ-

---

47. Coates (n.d.-b, 13).

teously. We have not been justified only to be set free from the fear of God's judgment, or set free in order to simply continue our ways in the "present evil age" (Gal. 1:4). We have been set free for a totally new order of things, a new world, where everything is a pleasure to the heart of God.[48] This world is characterized by the grace of God, by the hope of the glory of God, by the love of God poured into our hearts through the Holy Spirit (5:1-5). It is a world of salvation and reconciliation (vv. 9-11). It is a world of resurrection life, "eternal life" (vv. 18-21; 6:22-23). It is a world that we inwardly have entered through faith, and outwardly through baptism: "Do you not know that all of us who have been baptized into Christ Jesus were baptized into his death? We were buried therefore with him by baptism into death, in order that, just as Christ was raised from the dead by the glory of the Father, we too might walk in newness of life" (6:3-4). It is a world characterized by the risen Christ (4:25; 6:6-7). He who died *for* our sins is now dead *to* sin, and we are dead to sin as well, and alive through and for him (6:9-14).

5.5.2 Slaves of Righteousness

Paul strongly emphasizes this practical righteousness because, to him, being justified (made/declared righteous) cannot but lead to a righteous life: "Do not present your members to sin as instruments for unrighteousness, but present yourselves to God as those who have been brought from death to life, and your members to God as instruments for *righteousness* . . . having been set free from sin, [you] have become *slaves of righteousness*. I am speaking in human terms, because of your natural limitations. For just as you once presented your members as slaves to impurity and to lawlessness leading to more lawlessness, so now present your members as *slaves to righteousness* leading to sanctification" (Rom. 6:13). Being a slave of righteousness is essentially the same as being a slave of God or of Christ (Rom. 1:1; 1 Cor. 4:1; 2 Cor. 11:23;

---

48. Coates (1926, 72).

Gal. 1:10; Phil. 1:1; Titus 1:1; James 1:1; 2 Peter 1:1; Jude 1:1), that is, being under the law of Christ (1 Cor. 9:21; Gal. 6:2).

"[I]t is my prayer that your love may abound more and more, with knowledge and all discernment, so that you may approve what is excellent, and so be pure and blameless for the day of Christ, filled with the *fruit of righteousness* that comes through Jesus Christ, to the glory and praise of God" (Phil. 1:9-11). "He who supplies seed to the sower and bread for food will supply and multiply your seed for sowing and increase the harvest of your righteousness" (2 Cor. 9:10). "But as for you, O man of God, flee these things. Pursue *righteousness*, godliness, faith, love, steadfastness, gentleness" (1 Tim. 6:11; cf. Isa. 51:1). "So flee youthful passions and pursue *righteousness*, faith, love, and peace, along with those who call on the Lord from a pure heart" (2 Tim. 2:22). "All Scripture is breathed out by God and profitable for teaching, for reproof, for correction, and for training in *righteousness*, that the man of God may be complete, equipped for every good work" (2 Tim. 3:16-17).

We find similar admonitions in other New Testament writings: "[E]veryone who lives on milk is unskilled in the *word of righteousness*, since he is a child. But solid food is for the mature, for those who have their powers of discernment trained by constant practice to distinguish good from evil" (Heb. 5:13-14). Peter says that Jesus died "that we might die to sin and live to *righteousness*" (1 Pet. 2:24). For the apostates, "it would have been better for them never to have known the *way of righteousness* than after knowing it to turn back from the holy commandment delivered to them" (2 Pet. 2:21). And John speaks of "everyone who practices *righteousness*," and thus proves to have been born of God (1 John 2:29): "Whoever practices *righteousness* is righteous, as he is righteous. . . . By this it is evident who are the children of God, and who are the children of the devil: whoever does not practice *righteousness* is not of God, nor is the one who does not love his brother" (3:7, 10; see further Matt. 5:6, 10; 6:1; Acts 10:35; Rom. 5:21;

2 Cor. 6:7; Eph. 5:9; 6:14; Heb. 11:33; James 1:20; 1 Pet. 3:14; Rev. 19:8; 22:11).

5.6 Practical Versus Positional Righteousness
5.6.1 Instantaneous Justification?

From the passages mentioned it is evident that positional and practical justification should be distinguished but never separated. Those who view Romans too strongly from a forensic point of view, according to the criteria of Roman law, will emphasize too unilaterally the *positional* justification, that is, the judicial "moment" of the acquittal and rehabilitation of the ungodly. In the Reformed tradition, what allegedly *follows* upon this "moment" of justification is distinguished from justification as sanctification (see chapters 8 and 9): "These works, as they proceed from the good root of faith, are good and acceptable in the sight God, forasmuch as they are all sanctified by His grace. Nevertheless they are of no account towards our justification, for it is by faith in Christ that we are justified, even before we do good works" (Belgic Confession, Art. 24; cf. §5.4.1). This is clear language: *first* justification, which is by faith alone, *then* sanctification, in which this faith produces good works.

The Westminster Confession of Faith says (chapter XIII): "They, who are effectually called, and regenerated [and, one may add, justified. WJO], having a new heart, and a new spirit created in them, are further sanctified, really and personally . . . and [are] more and more quickened and strengthened in all saving graces, to the practice of true holiness, without which no man shall see the Lord. This sanctification is throughout, in the whole man; . . . and so, the saints grow in grace, perfecting holiness in the fear of God." Here the same message: first *instantaneous* justification, then the *process* of sanctification. In no sense, the good works must be connected to the "moment" of justification; they are part of the *subsequent* process of sanctification.

I am not aware of any Reformed distinction between positional and practical justification, as well as between positional and practical sanctification, although this distinction is so important. Coming to faith leads to both positional justification *and positional sanctification* (see chapter 8). Living after having come to faith involves both practical justification and practical sanctification. The entire Reformed picture of (positional) justification first, and then (practical) sanctification, is mistaken. In 1 Corinthians 6:11 the order is even reversed: "But you were washed, you *were sanctified*, you were justified in the name of the Lord Jesus Christ and by the Spirit of our God." Here, sanctification is clearly linked with the moment of being regenerated ("washed") and being justified; in other words, Paul speaks here of *positional* sanctification. It is not first justification, and then sanctification, but it is first positional justification and positional sanctification, and then practical justification and practical sanctification.

The consequences of this different approach are evident: when we make the distinction as I just described it, we shall be much more open to an *Old Testament* approach—say, a *Jewish* approach—toward the epistle of Romans. Traditionally, Christian theology summarizes the content of Romans as follows: "How can I, a sinner, receive acquittal and rehabilitation in God's courtroom?" From a Jewish point of view, the central question of Romans would rather be formulated as follows: "How can I, a sinner, become a *tsaddiq*?" In this case, the emphasis is not at all placed on the *moment* of acquittal, as happens in traditional theology, but rather on the *life* and *walk* of the *tsaddiq* into which the repentant sinner wishes to enter. In such a view, positional and practical justification form a continuum, just like positional and practical sanctification.

One could even say that, if this continuum is well understood, the distinction between positional and practical may be strongly relativized. "How do I become a saint?" is then the same as: "How do I learn to live as a saint?" To use a common parallel: one answer to the question "What is it to be a father?" is this: it entails having fathered one or more children. The better answer is: it entails not only having fathered children, but raising them: be a father to them. And to return to biblical examples: both Abraham and Habakkuk illustrate this point in an excellent way.

5.6.2 Abraham and Habakkuk Again

Look at the way Paul deals with the example of Abraham. Apparently, in his view, Abraham's justification did not in the least entail the idea that there was a moment in Abraham's life that he turned from an ungodly person into a *tsaddiq*. Abraham was a *tsaddiq* from the moment—and probably long before—he was called by God. What Genesis 15:6 indicates is not the moment of Abraham's justification—and even less of his regeneration—but the way in which his being righteous was evidenced by his confidence in God. Viewed in this light, Paul is not at all describing to us some moment of justification but rather deals with the question: What is a genuine *tsaddiq*? His answer is: a *tsaddiq* is someone who lives out of confidence in God, in the power of the Holy Spirit, and as such produces good works.

This makes understandable also how he handles Habakkuk 2:4, "[T]he righteous shall live by his faith." This verse does not describe a moment of justification either, but explains to us the secret of the true *tsaddiq*: his practical confidence in God even under the most difficult circumstances. This is the way the verse is quoted in Hebrews 10:38; no expositor has ever thought here of some moment of justification. In Romans 1:17 ("For in it [i.e., in the gospel] the righteousness of God is revealed from faith for faith, as it is written, 'The righteous shall live by faith'") and Galatians 3:11 ("Now it is evident that no one is justified before God by the law, for 'The righteous shall live by faith'"), it was traditionally considered to be different. However, even in these verses there is no reason to assume that Paul refers here to some moment of justification when the ungodly instantaneously turns into a *tsaddiq*. Rather, fully in line with the context of Habakkuk 2, Paul tells us that the true *tsaddiq* is recognized first and foremost by his confidence in God.[49] In other words, Paul is not so much concerned here with positional justification but rather with practical justification.

The fact that Paul speaks of salvation in Romans 1:16 does not necessarily change this picture. Many Protestants are familiar with questions like: "When and how were you saved?" They thus refer to a moment of salvation, just as many think of a moment of justification. Now, I am not denying that when a person is radically converted, such a person has turned in a moment from being dead to being alive, from unclean to clean, and therefore also from lost to saved, from ungodly to righteous, from wicked to holy. Examples of instantaneous salvation in the book of Acts are the three thousand Jews on the Day of Pentecost (2:37-41), the converted Samaritans (8:4-17), the Ethiopian eunuch (8:26-39), Saul of Tarsus (9:1-19), Cornelius and his people (10:44-48), Lydia (16:14-15), and the Philippian jailer (16:27-34).

The point is not whether there is, or can be, a moment of salvation and justification. The point is rather whether Paul's emphasis in Romans (and Galatians) is on the occurrence of such a moment. Romans is, among other things, about salvation (1:16), but not necessarily as an instantaneous thing. On the contrary, it is true that "we *were* saved" (8:24), but it is equally true that "we *shall* be saved" (by Christ from the wrath of God, by the life of the risen Christ; 5:9-10), and: "[S]alvation is nearer to us now than when we first believed" (13:11). Likewise, Paul does not emphasize the moment of justification, but the way we can recognize the true *tsaddiq*, namely, by his confidence in God and in Christ, and by the works that are a result of this faith.

5.6.3 Fulfilling the Law

I find it strange that Herman Ridderbos views the Jewish notion of righteousness as more forensic, and the Hellenist no-

---
49. Cf. Y. Dembele in Adeyemo (2006, 1065).

tion as more ethical.[50] In my view, righteousness in the New Testament is both forensic and ethical. At any rate, with positional and practical righteousness we are dealing with essentially one and the same forensic as well as ethical righteousness. This has been strongly underscored by the Messianic rabbi Joseph Shulam.[51] Instead of asking the more negative forensic question: How can a person escape from the verdict of the righteous Judge?, we may summarize his study with the question: How can an ungodly person become a *tsaddiq*, a godly person, who lives in the spirit of the Torah, or even more strongly, who lives as being conformed to the image of *the* Righteous One?

In my view, this is indeed a fairer approach to the way Paul deals with justification in Romans. The same Paul who so sharply rejects the Torah as a means to earn eternal bliss by one's own strength, also writes: God "condemned sin in the flesh, in order that the righteous requirement of the law [Greek, *to dikaiōma tou nomou*] might be fulfilled in us, who walk not according to the flesh but according to the Spirit" (8:3-4). The person who is "filled" with the Spirit (Greek, *plēroō* in Eph. 5:18) is able to "fulfill" (again *plēroō* in Rom. 8:4) the (Messianic) Torah.[52] Likewise, Romans 13:8-10 says, "Owe no one anything, except to love each other, for the one who loves another has fulfilled [*peplērōken*] the law. For the commandments, 'You shall not commit adultery, You shall not murder, You shall not steal, You shall not covet,' and any other commandment, are summed up in this word: 'You shall love your neighbor as yourself.' Love does no wrong to a neighbor; therefore love is the fulfilling [*plērōma*] of the law."

The Torah is *life*: "You shall . . . keep my statutes and my rules; if a person does them, he shall *live* by them: I am the Lord" (Lev. 18:5; cf. Neh. 9:29; Ezek. 20:11; Rom. 10:5; Gal. 3:12). "And now, O Israel, listen to the statutes and the rules

---

50. Ridderbos (1975, 164).
51. Shulam (1998).
52. Ibid., 278.

that I am teaching you, and do them, that you may *live*" (Deut. 4:1). "And the Lord your God will circumcise your heart and the heart of your offspring, so that you will love the Lord your God with all your heart and with all your soul, that you may *live*" (30:6). "See, I have set before you today *life* and good, death and evil. If you obey the commandments of the Lord your God that I command you today, by loving the Lord your God, by walking in his ways, and by keeping his commandments and his statutes and his rules, then you shall *live*. . . . I call heaven and earth to witness against you today, that I have set before you *life* and death, blessing and curse. Therefore choose *life*, that you and your offspring may *live*, loving the Lord your God, obeying his voice and holding fast to him, for he is your *life* and length of days" (30:15-16, 19-20). "For it is no empty word for you, but your very *life*" (32:37). "If you would enter [eternal] *life*, keep the commandments" (Matt. 19:17).

Here "life" has one of the two meanings of this word: "life" is either the life principle within us — both in the natural sense (biotic life) and in the spiritual sense (cf. Rom. 8:10; 2 Cor. 4:10-12; 1 John 3:15) — or it is the life we lead. In Galatians 2:20, we have both meanings in juxtaposition: "It is no longer I who live, but Christ who lives in me [first meaning]. And the life I now live in the flesh I live by faith in the Son of God [second meaning], who loved me and gave himself for me." It is important so see that in connection with justification, "life" has *both* meanings. We have seen that the justified person is characterized by the life of the risen Christ that is in him. And we have seen that the justified person leads a life characterized by the works of the Messianic Torah, performed in the power of the Holy Spirit. Through the life that is in him, the justified person leads the life of a true *tsaddiq*.

5.6.4 The One Commandment

We must repeatedly emphasize that the commandments mentioned in the previous section are never an appeal to show the ungodly how he can *attain* life, but to show God's *redeemed* people how they can go the *way of life*, the *way of righteousness*, and can avoid the curses.[53]

Rabbi Simlai (ca. AD 250) taught that the Mosaic commandments in the Tanakh are summarized as follows.[54]

(a) By David in *eleven* commandments: walk blamelessly, do what is right, speak truth, do not slander, do no evil to your neighbor, do not take up a reproach against your friend, despise a vile person, honor those who fear the Lord, keep your oaths, do not put out your money at interest, do not take a bribe against the innocent (Ps. 15:2–5). Notice the question with which this Psalm opens: "O LORD, who shall sojourn in your tent? Who shall dwell on your holy hill?"

(b) By Isaiah in *six* commandments: walk righteously, speak uprightly, despise the gain of oppressions, do not accept bribes, stop your ears from hearing of bloodshed, shut your eyes from looking on evil (Isa. 33:15–16). Notice the preceding words: "The LORD is exalted, for he dwells on high; he will fill Zion with justice and righteousness. . . . 'Who among us can dwell with the consuming fire? Who among us can dwell with everlasting burnings?'" (vv. 5, 14).

(c) By Micah in *three* commandments: do justice, love kindness, walk humbly with your God (Micah 6:8).

(d) Again by Isaiah in *two* commandments: keep justice (Heb., *mishpat*), do righteousness (*tsedaqah*) (Isa. 56:1).

(e) And finally by Amos in *one* commandment: "Seek me and *live*" (Amos 5:4; cf. v. 6: "Seek the Lord and live"; v. 14: "Seek good, and not evil, that you may live"). Rabbi Nachman ben Isaac (about AD 350) replaced Amos 5:4 by Habakkuk 2:4, "the righteous shall live by his faith." This point is very special: *life* as a commandment; more specifically: living in faith is commanded. When Jesus summarizes the law, his

---

53. See again extensively, Ouweneel (2015a).
54. Makkot 23b; cf. Cranfield (1975, 1:101); Strack and Billerbeck (1922, 3:542–45); Shulam (1998, 44). Of course, such a number is relativized; from Ezek. 18:5–9 one could easily derive fifteen commandments.

emphasis is on *love*: "Teacher, which is the great commandment in the Law?" And Jesus answered, "'You shall love the Lord your God with all your heart and with all your soul and with all your mind.' This is the great and first commandment. And a second is like it: 'You shall love your neighbor as yourself.' On these two commandments depend all the Law and the Prophets" (Matt. 22:36-40; cf. Deut. 5:10; 7:9; 11:11, 13; Josh. 22:5; Neh. 1:5; Dan. 9:4; John 14:15, 21; 15:10; Rom. 13:9; 1 John 5:2-3; 2 John 1:6).

Simlai's emphasis is on *life*, which is no different from Moses' emphasis in Deuteronomy (sometimes in connection with love: ". . . you will *love* the LORD your God with all your heart and with all your soul, that you may *live*"; 30:6). As God said when he found Israel as a newborn babe: "Live!" (Ezek. 16:6). Thus, the Torah is presented many times to the people with the goal: "that you may live" (Deut. 4:1; 5:33; 8:1; 11:9; 16:20; 22:7; 30:6; cf. Ezek. 18:32). As Paul says to Timothy: "Take hold of the eternal *life* to which you were called," and of believers: ". . . so that they may take hold of that which is truly *life*" (1 Tim. 6:12, 19). The Torah is a "way" or "path of life" (cf. Ps. 16:11; Prov. 2:19; 5:6; 6:23; 15:24; Jer. 21:8; Acts 2:28). Therefore, Jesus, who is the true, eternal Torah, could say, "I am the *way* and the truth and *life*" (John 14:6).[55]

5.7 Peace with God
5.7.1 Forms of Peace

We have seen that not only have our sins been blotted out by the blood of Christ, but morally speaking *we are now as he is*. He was righteousness and became sin, we were sin and became the righteousness of God (2 Cor. 5:21). John explains that what was true in Christ is now also true in us (1 John 2:8); as he is so also are we in this world (4:17). We have been united with Christ in his new position as the one who has been dead, who was raised and glorified: "For if we have been united with him in a death like his, we shall certainly be united with

---

55. See again extensively, Ouweneel (2015a).

him in a resurrection like his" (Rom. 6:5). "[T]hose whom he foreknew he also predestined to be conformed to the image of his Son, in order that he might be the firstborn among many brothers. And those whom he predestined he also called, and those whom he called he also justified, and those whom he justified he also glorified" (8:29-30). God "worked in Christ when he raised him from the dead and seated him at his right hand in the heavenly places. . . . And you were dead in the trespasses and sins. . . . But God, being rich in mercy, because of the great love with which he loved us, even when we were dead in our trespasses, made us alive together with Christ— by grace you have been saved—and raised us up with him and seated us with him in the heavenly places in Christ Jesus" (Eph. 1:20-2:6).

We enjoy the fruits of Christ's death, but we are also associated with him who did not remain in death, but was raised and glorified at God's right hand. Romans 3 speaks of our justification on account of the *death* of Christ; in this chapter, justification is hardly anything more than forgiveness of sins. But Romans 4-8 links our justification with the *resurrection* of Christ. In a perfectly righteous way, we have been brought in a new position, as associated with the risen Lord, and in this position, God openly recognizes us as being righteous.

Romans 5 sheds some additional light on this matter. The resurrection of Christ (4:25) supplies us with a certain ground for assurance and confidence, so that, through faith in God who raised Christ, we have peace with[56] God. We not only have forgiveness of sins, but we have a new *position*, so that we "stand" in his favor, and rejoice in the hope that one day we will be with Christ in the glory (v. 2 NKJV). We who are now united with him in his resurrection will one day be united with him in his glorification with God (cf. 8:30).

Peace with God is a great thing, especially if we think of the riches contained in the Hebrew equivalent *shalōm*: whole-

---

56. Greek *pros* + accus.: here referring to a friendly relationship (cf. *en* in Mark 9:50; *meta* in Rom. 12:18 and Heb. 12:14); cf. §7.9 and Moo (1996, 299).

ness, harmony, health, rest, blessing, and bliss.

(a) Peace with regard to all that we *formerly* have done, for all this has been put aside in the death of Christ, as we, in the confidence of faith, know from the fact that God raised him from the dead (5:1).

(b) Peace with regard to all that we are *now*, for we are enjoying the present favor of God, to which we have received access by faith (v. 2a).

(c) Peace with regard to all that we will receive in the *future*, because, in the joyful confidence of faith, we live in the happy expectation of the glory of God (v. 2b).

(d) Peace especially with regard to *God himself*. Notice the important difference between Romans 3 and 5: in chapter 3 we find God as the frightening Judge, but believers cling to Christ in order to escape from the judgment of a righteous God. But in chapter 5 we are perfectly at ease with God because we have realized that it was God himself who gave his Son for our forgiveness and justification (4:24-25): God shows his love for us in that, "while we were still sinners, Christ died for us" (5:8). Therefore, "we also rejoice in God through our Lord Jesus Christ, through whom we have now received reconciliation" (v. 11). "If God is for us, who can be against us? He who did not spare his own Son but gave him up for us all, how will he not also with him graciously give us all things? Who shall bring any charge against God's elect? It is God who justifies. Who is to condemn?" (8:31-34).

Being at ease with God, then, we even say "Abba" to him, which is the intimate, familiar way of addressing a father: "[Y]ou have received the Spirit of adoption as sons, by whom we cry, 'Abba! Father!'" (8:15). "And because you are sons, God has sent the Spirit of his Son into our hearts, crying, 'Abba! Father!'" (Gal. 4:6;[57] cf. Mark 14:36).

---

57. See on this Luther, *Comm. on Galatians* (ad loc.); cf. Moo (1996, 503).

5.7.2 Peace Rooted in Righteousness

We cannot have true peace with God if we have not first been aware of his righteousness. Disquieted souls may find comfort in the fact that God so loved the world that he gave his only Son (John 3:16), and that, when they believe in God, they do not come into judgment, but have passed from death to life (5:24). But that is insufficient for having true peace with God because such believers may always be uncertain as to the question whether, in spite of his love, God might find some other reason to condemn them. It is only the *righteousness* of God that offers a sure foundation for peace.[58] This is why the gospel is not in the first place about the love of God—in spite of what many evangelists tell us today—but about the righteousness of God (Rom. 1:16-17). In this regard, it is remarkable that in the book of Acts *the word "love" does not even occur*, but the words "righteous/just" and "righteousness/justice" do occur a number of times: Christ is the Righteous One (3:14; 7:52; 22:14), and Paul speaks of righteousness in connection with the future judgment of the world (17:31; 24:15, 25; cf. 13:10).

In preaching the gospel, we present the *love* of God because it is God's love that breaks the sinner down in leading him to repentance and self-judgment. But the "full gospel"[59] includes the presentation of the *righteousness* of God because this supplies the sinner with a foundation on which he can stand. That is, he learns to see that God is not only loving (merciful, gracious) when he justifies him, but that he is *righteous* in doing so: "It was to show his righteousness at the present time, so that he might be just [or, righteous] and the justifier of [i.e., the one who declares righteous] the one who has faith in Jesus" (Rom. 3:26). In other words, realizing God's *love* for us is a tremendous blessing, but it does not procure us a foundation for genuine peace with God. We will learn

---

58. Coates (1926, 53).
59. It is interesting to see how various Christian movements have claimed this term for *their* version of the gospel; cf. Rom. 15:18–19 (NKJV).

to know this peace only when we begin to see that it is God's *righteousness* (Christ) who intervened for us.[60]

It is not only Christ who accomplished a work for us, it is the righteous God himself who acted in favor of us. It was God who gave up his own Son (Rom. 8:32), and it was God who proved that the work of Christ had given him perfect satisfaction by raising him from the dead. As a consequence, God could righteously unite us with the risen Christ in the latter's new position beyond death (4:25; 6:4-11).

Peace with God means that there is an unclouded sky between God and the soul. The Judge himself has become our Redeemer. Believers who have this peace are like Noah, who looked up to a clear sky after all the waters of judgment had disappeared from the earth (Gen. 8:1-13). Or they are like Israel, when the people saw their enemies lying dead on the seashore, and could praise the Lord as their strength, their song, and their salvation (Exod. 14:30-15:18).[61] Or, I may add, they are like the army of Israel, when it saw the head of Goliath in the hands of David (1 Sam. 17:50-54). Or they are like the Roman soldiers, when they saw how the earth shook, and the rocks were split, and exclaimed: "Truly this was the Son of God" (Matt. 27:51-54).

Love involves God's affection, his inclination, his feelings toward us. By contrast, righteousness involves objective judicial *facts*, which constitute the foundation for our peace with God. It is great to know that "God is love" (1 John 4:8, 16), but it is equally great to know that "the Lord our God is righteous in all the works that he has done" (Dan. 9:14). God's love touches me in the deepest corners of my soul; God's righteousness gives me solid ground under my feet. If God would be only love, there might always be a "but": "To be sure, God is love but . . ." (he cannot but punish us after all, etc.). If God is righteous, and has dealt with us righteously, no power in the world can challenge our new position.

---

60. Coates (1926, 53).
61. Ibid., 75.

Incidentally, it is difficult to say which is greater: in Romans 8 we see especially what we are in Christ *for God*, but in Romans 5:1–11 we see what God in his grace is *for us*. It is tremendous to see what *we* have become in Christ (Rom. 8), but perhaps it is even greater to see what *God* has done for us in Christ (Rom. 5): he has poured his love into our hearts through the Holy Spirit who has been given to us (v. 5). He shows his love for us in that, while we were still sinners, Christ died for us (v. 8). He justified us (declared us righteous) on account of Christ's blood (v. 9). He has reconciled us to himself by the death of his Son (v. 10–11). He will save us from the wrath of God by the life of Christ (v. 9–10). No wonder that we not only rejoice in hope of the glory of God (v. 2), and rejoice in our sufferings (v. 3), but above all rejoice in God through our Lord Jesus Christ (v. 11).

5.8 Typology
5.8.1 Esther

Let me illustrate with some biblical examples what we have found. In this way, I am defending the good use of typology (not to be confused with allegoresis), as I have done in several volumes of my dogmatic series.[62]

How great is the God who, like Ahasuerus, has held out to us his favor with a golden scepter, as it were.[63] Esther had been worried about this: "All the king's servants and the people of the king's provinces know that if any man or woman goes to the king inside the inner court without being called, there is but one law—to be put to death, except the one to whom the king holds out the golden scepter so that he may live. But as for me, I have not been called to come in to the king these thirty days" (4:11). According to the rules of the law, there was no hope for Esther (nor for God's people, for that matter); she was totally dependent on the king's grace.

Nevertheless, Mordecai had encouraged her to continue,

---
62. See Ouweneel (2007a; 2007b; 2009; 2010a; 2010b).
63. For the typology, see Ouweneel (n.d., ad loc.).

and, so to speak, to cast herself into the arms of grace. Esther had answered: "Go, gather all the Jews to be found in Susa, and hold a fast on my behalf, and do not eat or drink for three days, night or day. I and my young women will also fast as you do. Then I will go to the king, though it is against the law, and if I perish, I perish" (v. 16). Indeed, Esther received grace from the king, but there was also righteousness involved: the moment the king stretched out his scepter, the person involved was *entitled* to be blessed by the king.

The (deuterocanonical) Greek version of the book of Esther contains a moving prayer by Esther (4:14-15, 17-18, 23, 25, 30 CEB): "My Lord, you alone are our king. Help me! I have no one to help me but you, and I am in great danger now . . . we have sinned before you, and you have delivered us into the power of our enemies because we worshipped their gods. You are just, Lord. . . . Remember us, Lord, and reveal yourself in the time of our distress. Give me courage, king of the gods and ruler of every authority. . . . Deliver us by your actions, and help me, I who am alone and have no one except you, Lord. . . . All-powerful God, listen to the voice of those who despair, and deliver us from the hands of those who do wrong, and deliver me from my fear!"

How many have not gone to God with this same attitude, namely, in great fear and concern about the question whether he would be willing to accept them. Others have believed in Christ to escape from God's condemnation because they knew that Christ was for them. But they were uncertain about the question whether *God* was for them too. Adherents of what I call the "placation" theory (see Appendix II) can be sure about the love of Christ—but they may be unsure about the question whether *God* is benevolent toward them. Has his wrath toward the sinner really been satisfied? Christ may have intervened between God and us, just as a mother does when a furious father wants to attack one of the children. But can the sinner be convinced that *God* is favorable toward him? Will not a furious God try to condemn him after all? "It is a fearful thing to fall into the hands of the living God" (Heb. 10:31) — with this statement many a regenerated person has been tormented in his righteous soul. *Christ* is on our side — he gave his life for us — but what about *God*? How can he love us, given the fact that by nature we are such great sinners? How can he spare us given the fact that he is "of purer eyes than to see evil and cannot look at wrong" (Hab. 1:13)?

This is the mighty testimony of Romans 8: *God himself* "is for us, who can be against us? He who did not spare his own Son but gave him up for us all, how will he not also with him graciously give us all things? Who shall bring any charge against God's elect? It is God who justifies. Who is to condemn?" (vv. 31–34) There is no need for anyone to intervene between Ahasuerus and Esther. As soon as the king noticed his favorite queen, his heart was full of affection and benevolence. It was he himself who held out to her the golden scepter. No outside power needed to move him to do so, or would even be *able* to move him. The grace that he bestowed upon Esther proceeded entirely from himself.

5.8.2 Mephibosheth

To mention another Old Testament example: Mephibosheth was a grandson of King Saul, and thus belonged to a family hostile to David (2 Sam. 9:1-3). Moreover, he was crippled in his feet (vv. 3, 13), whereas David's soul hated the lame and the blind (5:8). Apparently Mephibosheth could expect nothing from David; on the contrary, he had every reason to fear him. Nobody took it into his head to plead for him with David. No, the initiative for his acceptance had to proceed entirely from David himself. The king said, "Is there still anyone left of the house of Saul, that I may show him kindness for Jonathan's sake? . . . Is there not still someone of the house of Saul, that I may show the kindness [Heb., *ḥēsed*] of God to him?" (9:1, 3).

When Mephibosheth came to David, he "fell on his face and paid homage" (v. 6), as is the fitting attitude of the sinner when coming to God. As David showered his favors on him — held out, so to say, the golden scepter to him — Mephibosheth said, "What is your servant, that you should show regard for a dead dog such as I?" (v. 8). This is an equally fitting answer for a sinner who is privileged to experience God's benevolence. "So Mephibosheth ate at David's table, like one of the king's sons.... So Mephibosheth lived in Jerusalem, for he ate always at the king's table. Now he was lame in both his feet" (vv. 11, 13). As he reclined at the king's table, his crippled feet were behind him; but before him were the benevolent eyes of David. In them he read that David's favor went so far as to count him among the king's own sons.

During a later crisis in David's life, Mephibosheth's faithfulness came to light: "He had neither taken care of his feet nor trimmed his beard nor washed his clothes, from the day the king departed until the day he came back in safety" (2 Sam. 19:24). His heart had accompanied David. His life was so attached to David that he had no interest in anything that happened wherever David was absent. The death sentence rested upon him and his house ("all my father's house were but men doomed to death before my lord the king," v. 28), but with David he had found life.[64]

Mephibosheth's story is full of the king's grace, favor and benevolence. But there is also an element of righteousness in it. Years before, Mephibosheth's father, Jonathan, had asked of David: "[D]o not cut off your steadfast love [Heb., *hēsed*] from my house forever" (1 Sam. 20:15), and made David swear by his love for him (v. 17). Therefore, the later story tells us: "[T]he king spared Mephibosheth, the son of Saul's son Jonathan, because of the oath of the Lord that was between them, between David and Jonathan the son of Saul" (2 Sam. 21:7). This implies that David not only was *merciful* toward Mephibosheth but also showed *righteousness* to him. What he did to

---

64. Coates (n.d.-b, 67–68); this apart from the question who was right: Mephibosheth or his servant Ziba, who had accused him of infidelity; cf. Youngblood (1992, 1036–37).

Jonathan's son he owed to the oath he had sworn to Jonathan. It is similar with the repentant sinner who comes to God. He may be impressed by the love and mercy of God, and very rightly so. But it will greatly strengthen his assurance of faith if he realizes that God is also *righteous* in justifying him (Rom. 8:26; cf. 1 John 1:9). What God does to the sinner is something he owes to Christ and his redemptive work.

5.9 Sins and Sin
5.9.1 Effects of One Sin

In Romans 3 and 4, Paul speaks of "sins," sinful acts (3:25; 4:7). Where we find the word "sin," it is—except in 3:9—the singular of "sins," not "sin" as an evil power (3:20; 4:8). In Romans 5:1, too, "peace" is especially the joyful consciousness and assurance of the perfect blotting out of the sins before a holy and righteous God through the blood of Christ and our union with a risen Christ. However, this new position can be truly understood only if we see not only what happened to our *sins*, but also how the problem of *sin*, viewed as an evil power in us, has been solved (see §5.3.3).

This question is dealt with in Romans 5:12 and following.[65] Through one man (Adam) sin came into the world, and through sin also death, and so death spread to all men (all of Adam's descendants): not only because Adam sinned but because all gave evidence of the sinful nature they had inherited from Adam by sinning just like him.[66]

In this passage, it is no longer a question of our sinful acts, but of the fact that, as a consequence of the one sin of our family's head, we are all sinners by nature. People do not just sin—they are under the *power* of sin. In other words, people are not sinners because they sin, but they sin because they are sinners. Even the regenerated person, who does not yet know

---

65. Interestingly, this is also what John the Baptist meant: "Behold, the Lamb of God, who takes away the sin [sing.] of the world!" (John 1:29). However, for centuries the Roman Catholic mass has rendered this: *qui tollis peccata mundi*, plural (Vulgate: *qui tollis peccatum mundi*).
66. See extensively, Ouweneel (2008a, 189–94).

the power of the Holy Spirit (Rom. 8) says in Romans 7: "It was sin, producing death in me through what is good, in order that sin might be shown to be sin. . . . I am of the flesh, sold under sin. . . . So now it is no longer I who do it, but sin that dwells within me. For I know that nothing good dwells in me, that is, in my flesh. . . . Now if I do what I do not want, it is no longer I who do it, but sin that dwells within me. . . . I see in my members another law waging war against the law of my mind and making me captive to the law of sin that dwells in my members. . . . So then, I myself serve the law of God with my mind, but with my flesh I serve the law of sin" (vv. 13-25).

Concomitantly, Christ is not primarily viewed in Romans 5:12-21 as the one who bore our sins, but especially as the head of a new family. Paul does not deal here with the sinful acts of individuals, but with the sinful condition they occupy because of the head under whom they are born. Thus, in this passage two human families with their respective heads are placed in opposition: Adam with his physical family caught in sin, and Christ with his spiritual family freed from sin. Adam and his trespass are placed in opposition to Christ and God's grace (vv. 13-17). Through Adam, sin came into the world, and through sin, death reigned in the world, also during the time that the Mosaic Torah had not yet been given (vv. 12-14). Even those who had not, like Adam, trespassed some explicit commandment, fell under death because they too, even without an explicit law, were sinners because of their sinful nature.

However, God's grace surpassed the seriousness of Adam's transgression. Indeed, through Adam's trespass "the many" (Greek, *hoi polloi*, not just "many"), that is, Adam's family, have died. However, much more have the grace of God and the free gift by grace, which is also through one man, Jesus Christ, abounded for "the many," that is, Christ's family (v. 15). And indeed, on the basis of one trespass, God's judgment led to condemnation; but God's grace led from many trespasses to justification (v. 16).

Justification in the New Testament

Two legal bases stand here in opposition: over against the righteous legal basis for the condemnation—a righteous Judge must condemn the sinner—we find the righteous legal basis for justification (*dikaiōma*; see §1.4.2). And indeed, through the trespass of the one man, Adam, death has reigned through that one man. But much more will those who receive the abundance of grace and of the free gift of righteousness (*dikaiosynē*) reign in life through the one man, Jesus Christ (v. 17). God's gift (*dōrea*) in grace (v. 15), his *charisma* (vv. 15-16), the abundance of grace (v. 17), is a righteous gift as well. God gives, not only out of grace but also out of righteousness.

5.9.2 Romans 5:18

In verse 18, the apostle picks up the point of verse 12 again: through one sin, death spread to all men. He compares this now with the consequences of Christ's redemptive work. Just as one man dragged all humanity down in his fall, likewise the work of One Man had significance for all humanity. The text implies that, although the Mosaic Torah was limited to one nation, God's gift of grace could not be limited to that one nation, Israel. The reason is that sin and its consequences involved all humanity, not just Israel. Should the grace of God not equal this? Each human is a sinner, whether he is under the Torah or without Torah; this is why the gospel comes to all humanity. Therefore, as the effects of one trespass leads to condemnation for all humanity, likewise one "act of righteousness" (*dikaiōma*) concerns all humanity in bringing "justification of life" (*dikaiōsis zōēs*) to all who believe (v. 18).

We have to read carefully here, because the words "led" and "leads" (ESV) have been added; there is no verb in the original: "Therefore, as through one trespass [it is] for all men for condemnation, so also through one righteous act[67] [it is] for all men for justification of life." The translations (including ESV) often seem to imply some form of universalism ("in

---

67. Or "through the trespass of one . . . through the righteous act [one word: *dikaiōma*] of One."

the end all people will be saved"), which many translators of course do not wish to suggest. NKJV gives less basis for such a suggestion: "even so through one Man's righteous act [the free gift came] to all men, resulting in justification of life," without suggesting that all indeed *receive* it (cf. GNV, NET). ERV is far worse: "Christ did something so good that it makes all people right with God"; so GNT: "the one righteous act sets all people free and gives them life," and WEB: "through one act of righteousness, all men were justified to life." Safer is CEB: "So now the righteous requirements necessary for life are met for everyone through the righteous act of one person." Other translations remain on the safe side by introducing "us": "But because of the good thing that Christ has done, God accepts us and gives us the gift of life" (CEV).

We may add that "all" does not always mean "each distinct human (or thing)," as is clear from Romans 12:17-18, 14:2, and 16:19.[68] But even apart from this, the text should be clear: the results of Christ's redemptive work are for all men, without saying that all in effect receive a share in these results. In other words, through Christ's work each person can be justified, without saying that in the end each person *will* be justified.

The terminology in Romans 5:18 is very important. *Dikaiōma* is the "righteous act," the act that answers to the justice of God (§1.4.2). In my view, this is here *not* so much the act of justification (as in v. 16), as many have suggested.[69] Rather, the text says that the *dikaiōma* of One may bring justification to all. The *dikaiōma* must be *Christ's* "act of righteousness," namely, his sacrificial death. This is supported by the parallelism with "obedience" in verse 19.[70]

---

68. Moo (1996, 344).
69. Godet (1998, ad loc.), Shedd (1999, ad loc.); further Meyer (1876, ad loc.); Sanday and Headlam (1902, ad loc.); Calvin (1973, 117).
70. Philippi (1878, ad loc.); Lightfoot (1895, ad loc.); Haldane (1958, ad loc.); Ridderbos (1959, 121); Kittel *et al.* (1964, 2:221); Murray (1968, 1:200); Hodge (1972, ad loc.); Denney (1979, 630); Vine (1985, 1:427); Moo (1996, 341n127).

5.9.3 Romans 5:19

In both halves of verse 18, the reference is to "all men," without any restriction. The consequences of Adam's act and Christ's act, respectively, extend to all men. However, in verse 19, Paul deals again with the two human families, just as in verse 15; these are "the many" of Adam and "the many" of Christ. Verse 18 implies that the work of Christ is *sufficient* for all men, that is, all may receive the "justification of life" if only they believe. Verse 19 implies that the work of Christ is *effective* only for those who indeed are his own by faith: "the many" who form his spiritual family. Verse 18 shows that Adam's act was sufficient to bring death to all people, while Christ's act was sufficient to bring life to all people. Verse 19 shows that Adam's disobedient act made sinners of all those who belong to *his* family ("the many"), while Christ's obedient act constituted as *tsaddiqim* all those who belong to *his* family ("the many"). In effect this means that some *remain* in the family of Adam, while others by faith *move* from the family of Adam to the family of Christ.

I find it amazing that the difference between *eis pantas* ("to all," twice in v. 18) and *hoi polloi* ("the many," twice in v. 19) is not brought out more clearly in the translations. NIV, NASB, and ESV give a literal rendering, others (NKJV, RSV, ERV, GNV, CEB, CEV, TLB, NET, NLT, WEB) have only "many" (without the article). GNT does not make any distinction between "all" and "many": "And just as all people were made sinners as the result of the disobedience of one man, in the same way they will all be put right with God as the result of the obedience of the one man." In this way, the distinction between verses 18 and 19 is entirely lost.

In verse 18 we find the *extent* of Christ's redemptive work, in verse 19 the factual *result*. The work of Christ is sufficient for all, and is offered to all. But it has practical effect only for "the many," the family of all those who belong to Christ by faith. The extent of Christ's work includes all, not just many;

the effect of his work is found with "the many," not with all.

The difference between the two verses is related to that between two other terms from traditional atonement theology: *satisfaction*, that is, atonement provides to *God*, and *substitution*, that is, what atonement provides for *the people*.[71] The two principles are illustrated in an excellent way by the two goats of *Yom Kippur* (the Day of Atonement; Lev. 16). Satisfaction must be paid to God's honor and God's justice. This is shown in the first goat, the "goat for the Lord" (vv. 8-10), or the "goat for the sin offering" (v. 15). Its blood is brought inside the veil, and is sprinkled upon the ark, as a confirmation and coronation of a perfectly borne judgment upon sin. It is also sprinkled in front of the ark, to indicate that the way for humanity to approach God has been cleansed and sanctified again by the blood of the sin offering. On the basis of Christ's perfect sin offering, God's redemption can be offered to *all* people because the satisfaction that Christ has brought to God is perfect and complete, sufficient for all.

The second goat, the "live goat" (v. 20), bears all the iniquities of the people "to a remote area . . . in the wilderness" (v. 21). This goat has significance for the true people of God, the believers, who know by faith that Christ has borne all their iniquities to the land of death. This is the truth of *substitution*. Scripture never teaches that Christ bore the sins of all individual people; he tasted death "for everyone" (Heb. 2:9, the *sufficiency* of Christ's work) but he "bore *our* sins," the sins of the believers (1 Pet. 2:24, the *efficacy* of Christ's work).

The truth of satisfaction implies that the gospel is for all; this is illustrated in Romans 5:18. The truth of substitution implies that Christ has taken away the sins of those who believe in him; this is illustrated in Romans 5:19. God's honor has been violated; this is why the first goat was needed. The sins of believers must be taken away; this is why the second goat was needed. Christ has accomplished both through his one

---

71. See extensively, Ouweneel (2009, §5.2).

and only work on the cross. We could also put it this way: the first goat illustrates how Christ solved the problem of *sin* (the power of sin, the sinful nature). The second goat illustrates how he solved the problem of our *sins* (sinful acts). In Romans 5:18 we may see a reminder of the first goat, in verse 19 a reminder of the second goat. Both aspects of Christ's work were needed for our salvation and justification.

Chapter 6
Saving Faith

And the people believed;
  and when they heard
that the Lord had visited the people of Israel
  and that he had seen their affliction,
they bowed their heads
  and worshiped.
                              Exodus 4:31

Israel saw the great power
  that the Lord used against the Egyptians,
so the people feared the Lord,
  and they believed in the Lord
  and in his servant Moses.
         Exodus 14:31 (cf. Ps. 106:12)

"Hear me,
  Judah and inhabitants of Jerusalem!
Believe in the Lord your God,
  and you will be established;
believe his prophets,
  and you will succeed."
                          2 Chron. 20:20

Oh! Had I not believed

> that I shall look upon the goodness of the Lord
> in the land of the living!
>
> Psalm 27:13 (note)

Summary: *If believers have been justified by faith, what then is faith? How does it relate to divine grace, and how does it relate to human responsibility? What are the levels of faith ("believing that . . .," "believing in . . .," "entrusting oneself to . . .")? What are the forms of faith (immanent and transcendent faith, true faith and false faith, the faith **that** we believe and the faith **by which** we believe)? What do we actually have to believe? The gospel of God's grace for poor sinners, or (also) the gospel of the Kingdom of God? Is true Christian faith only accepting Jesus as Savior, or does it necessarily also include accepting Jesus as Lord? In this connection, we enter into the heated "lordship salvation" controversy. In certain respects, this discussion is strikingly similar to the Luther–Rome debate, again with deplorable misunderstandings on both sides. Another important issue is the perseverance of the believer, a subject in which once again the grace of God is often played off against the responsibility of Man. Lastly, we deal with the assurance of faith, and the true and false grounds for it. We deal briefly with nine common objections against this assurance of salvation.*

6.1   What Is Faith?
6.1.1   Introduction

THE WORD "FAITH" (Heb., *ēmunah*, Greek, *pistis*, Latin, *fides*) is a key term in the biblical doctrine of salvation.[1] As we saw in the previous chapter, this is already the case in the Old Testament: Abram "believed[2] the Lord, and he counted it to him as righteousness" (Gen. 15:6), and "the righteous shall live by

---

1. See Kittel *et al.* (1968, 6.174–228); Brown (1992, 1:593–606); Pop (1999, 191–220).
2. The English words "faith" and "believe" have very different etymological origins but have the same meaning (cf. Greek, *pistis* and *pisteuō*; German, *Glaube* and *glauben*). Interestingly, in Latin there is a difference, too: *fides* and *credere*; likewise in the Romanic languages.

his faith" (Hab. 2:4). Believing the prophets is believing God's words (Exod. 19:9; 2 Chron. 20:20), and this leads to believing God himself (Exod. 4:31; Ps. 106:12; Isa. 43:10; Jonah 3:5), and even believing *in* God (Exod. 14:31; Ps. 78:22), and to count on his goodness (Ps. 27:13). Sometimes, no object is mentioned, while it is yet clear that God is meant (Ps. 116:10; Isa. 7:9).

The well-known "Whoever believes will not be in haste" (Isa. 28:16) has sometimes been beautifully rendered: "Anyone who trusts in that rock [cf. v. 16a] will not be disappointed" (ERV; cf. CEV); "the one who relies on it will never be stricken with panic" (NIV; cf. NET), and even: "A trusting life won't topple" (MSG). This phrase refers back to verse 16a: "Behold, I am the one who has laid as a foundation in Zion a stone, a tested stone, a precious cornerstone, of a sure foundation." In the New Testament, this verse, together with Psalm 18:22 ("The stone that the builders rejected has become the cornerstone"), is applied to Christ several times (Matt. 21:42; Rom. 9:33; 10:11; 1 Pet. 2:4, 6; cf. Eph. 2:20.) The Messianic message, then, is this: anyone who believes in this foundation, this precious cornerstone, is saved, that is, safe. Here believing is: finding one's safety and security in some place or person.

Jesus emphasized this same principle: he says to the sinful woman, "Your faith [in me, or, in God] has saved you" (Luke 7:50); and to Nicodemus, God "so loved the world, that he gave his only Son, that whoever believes in him should not perish but have eternal life" (John 3:16). "Believe in the Lord Jesus, and you will be saved," says Paul to the Philippian jailer (Acts 16:31). Time and again, faith is the intended, and indeed occurring, response of people to the gospel (Acts 2:44; 4:4; 6:7; 8:12-13; 9:42; 10:43-44; 11:17, 21; 13:12, 39, 48; 14:1, 22-23, 27; 15:5, 9, 11; 16:34; 17:12, 34; 18:8; 19:2, 4, 18; 20:21; 21:20; 22:19; 24:24; 26:18, 27). A person is saved by faith in the "gospel of your salvation" (Eph. 1:13; cf. 1 Cor. 15:1-2), that is, faith in Christ the Savior (Luke 2:11; John 4:22; Acts 5:31; 13:23; 2 Tim. 1:10; Titus 1:4; 2:13; 2 Pet. 1:1, 11; 2:20; 3:2; 1 John 4:14).

The letters of the apostles describe the phenomenon of faith extensively; some examples: Paul speaks of "the righteousness of God through *faith* in Jesus Christ for all who *believe* . . . Christ Jesus, whom God put forward as a propitiation by his blood, to be received by *faith* . . . so that he might be just and the justifier of the one who has *faith* in Jesus" (Rom. 3:22-26). Similarly, Peter speaks of "the outcome of your *faith*, the salvation of your souls" (1 Pet. 1:9). And John says, "[T]hese [signs] are written so that you may *believe* that Jesus is the Christ, the Son of God, and that by *believing* you may have life in his name" (John 20:31). "Everyone who believes that Jesus is the Christ has been born of God" (1 John 5:1).

In such verses, the tension between the divine side of salvation — the divine work of regeneration in a person — and the human side — the repentance and conversion of that person — are clearly encountered.[3] On the one hand, faith is a matter of obedience: "[A] great many of the priests became obedient to the faith" (Acts 6:7). See the parallelism in John 3:36, "Whoever *believes* in the Son has eternal life; whoever does not *obey* the Son shall not see life, but the wrath of God remains on him." Paul says that God "commands all people everywhere to repent" (Acts 17:30), and speaks of the "obedience of faith [Greek, *hypakoē pisteōs*] . . . among all the nations" (Rom. 1:5; cf. 16:26). I take *hypakoē pisteōs* to mean "obedience expressing itself (or, leading to) faith" (obedience at conversion); others take it to mean the obedience that is the result of faith (the walk of faith) (see §6.6.1).[4]

On the other hand, faith is also a gift of God: "[I]t has been granted to you that for the sake of Christ you should . . . believe in him" (Phil. 1:29). "For by grace you have been saved through faith. And this is not your own doing; it is the gift of God" (Eph. 2:8).[5] *Humans* are responsible, even obliged, to

---

3. Cf. Van Genderen and Velema (2008, 596-97); Ouweneel (2010a, chapters 2 and 3).
4. See Moo (1996, 51–53).
5. See chapter 5n9 above.

believe—but it is equally true that it is *God* who grants them this faith. No less true, nor more true, but equally true. Jesus includes both truths in one sentence, first the latter, then the former: "All that the Father gives me will come to me, and whoever comes to me I will never cast out" (John 6:37). And Paul emphasizes first the former, then the latter: "I press on to *make* it my own, because Christ Jesus has *made* me his own" (Phil. 3:12). It is true that faith arises in a person's heart because he is obedient to the gospel, and it is equally true that he is obedient to the gospel because he has received the divine gift of faith.

God's work and a human being's work cannot be squeezed into one scheme: faith is one hundred percent a matter of human responsibility, and one hundred percent a matter of God's sovereign grace.[6] It appears that neither Francis Gomarus (who emphasized the former), nor his colleague, Jacob Arminius (who underscored the latter), seems to have sufficiently realized this balanced harmony (1604–1609, University of Leyden in the Netherlands). Nowhere do we see this more clearly than in this lovely paradox of Paul: "Therefore, my beloved, as you have always obeyed, so now, not only as in my presence but much more in my absence, work out your own salvation with fear and trembling, for it is God who works [Greek, *energōn*] in you, both to will and to work [*energein*] for his good pleasure" (Phil. 2:12-13). That is, live as if your salvation totally depends on you, and at the same time realize that it is entirely God's work in you, for he grants both the will and the energy to this end. In other words, live as if Arminius was right, but realize that Gomarus was right, too.

6.1.2 Terminology

The root meaning of the Greek noun *pistis* is "faithfulness" or "confidence," and that of the adjective *pistos* is "faithful." Many times, these words are used for human faithfulness (Matt. 23:23; 25:21, 23; Luke 16:10-12; 19:17; Acts 16:15;

---

6. See extensively, Ouweneel (2008b).

1 Cor. 4:2, 17; 7:25; Gal. 5:22; Phil. 2:20; Col. 1:7; 2 Thess. 3:2; 1 Tim. 1:12; 3:11; Titus 2:10; Heb. 3:5; 11:11; 3 John 1:5; Rev. 2:10), but also for divine faithfulness; for instance, "the Lord is faithful" (2 Thess. 3:3). About the faithfulness of God, or of the Lord, Paul has this to say, "What if some were unfaithful (*ēpistēsan*)? Does their faithlessness (*apistia*) nullify the faithfulness (*pistin*) of God?" (Rom. 3:3). In other translations, the connection between *ēpistēsan*, *apistia*, and *pistin* is lost, so that the sense is obscured. It is the same in 2 Timothy 2:13, "[I]f we are faithless, he remains faithful." Likewise, Hebrews 2:17 speaks of Christ as "a merciful and faithful high priest," and 3:2, "Jesus . . . who was faithful to him who appointed him."

It is remarkable that, in his *Römerbrief* (his commentary on Romans), Karl Barth refers the term *pistis* several times to God ("faithfulness"), whereas other expositors and translators refer the term to the believer ("faith"). He does so, for instance, in Romans 1:17 (Greek, *ek pisteōs*, "from faithfulness"), in 3:22 (*pistis Iēsou*, God's faithfulness that manifests itself in Jesus), and further in 3:25, 27–28 and 30.[7] Barth sees a close link between this divine *pistis* and that of humans, even to the extent that claiming that the phrases "by God's faithfulness" and "by human faith" amount to the same thing: God's righteousness is manifested where God's faithfulness and human faith meet each other.[8] In other words,[9] faith is God's faithfulness as always hidden behind and beyond all human approval, attitude, and achievement toward God. Commenting on Romans 3:27 ("By what kind of law? By a law of works? No, but by the law of faith"), Barth suggests that the law to which Paul refers is "*the law of the faithfulness of God*," which is basically the same as the "law of [human] faith," because it is only God's faithfulness that makes human faith possible and supports it; there is no human faith without God's faithful-

---

7. Barth (1968, ad loc.).
8. Barth (1933, 41).
9. Ibid., 110; italics original.

ness.[10] In my view, making such a link between God's faithfulness and human faith is clarifying, but this does not mean that the two terms should be confused in both translation and exposition. Therefore, most expositors and translators prefer the rendering of "faith," that is, human faith, in Romans 1:17 and 3:22-30.

Etymologically, we may add to "faith" and "faithfulness" the notion of "truth." Hebrew *ēmet* means "certainty, constancy, trustworthiness, faithfulness," but also "truth," not in any modern (epistemo)logical sense but in the sense of "truthfulness," which is close to "trustworthiness." Sometimes, (N)KJV has "truth" where more modern translations have "faithfulness" (e.g., Gen. 24:27; 1 Kings 3:6; Ps. 25:10). The same ambivalence is also found in the Germanic languages. English "true" is etymologically related to German *treu* and Dutch *trouw*, which both mean "faithful." All three words are related to Scandinavian *tro*, which means "to believe." The terms "faith" and "faithfulness" come from Latin *fides*, which, just as Greek *pistis*, means both "faith" and "faithfulness" or "trust" (a word that itself is related to "true").

The three terms, "faithfulness" ("trust"), "faith" and "truth," are connected by questions such as: What is true (real, genuine, certain)? What is trustworthy (reliable, from Latin, *religare*, "to fasten," and then "to fall back on")? To what can we give credence (from Latin, *credere*, "to believe"), what is worth our confidence (also from Latin, *fides*)? At the deepest level this means: what is so truthful and trustworthy that we can submit to it, even surrender to it, even *entrust* ourselves to it? This is the subject of the next sections.

6.2 Levels of Faith
6.2.1 Believing That . . .

One conclusion of the preceding section is that the root-idea in all "faith" (Greek, *pistis*) and "believing" (*pisteuō*) is "trust, confidence." If Philip Melanchton distinguishes within faith

---

10. Barth (1968, ad loc.).

between Latin, *notitia* ('knowledge"), *assensus* ("assent"), and *fiducia* ("trust, confidence"),[11] the third element is etymologically certainly the primary meaning. Compare the Heidelberg Catechism (Q&A 21): "True faith is not only a sure knowledge, . . . but also a hearty trust, ..."

This trust is found in each of the various stages of faith, varying from believing what someone says to fully *entrusting* oneself to another person. The lowest level is believing someone, believing that what he says is correct, believing that something is true, especially in a rational sense. Moses passed God's words on to the people, and Aaron performed miraculous signs, and then it is said, "And the people believed" (Exod. 4:31; MSG: "And the people trusted and listened believingly that God was concerned with what was going on with the Israelites"). That is, they thought Moses' words to be trustworthy, words that, in their view, referred to how the situation really, truly, in truth, was.

Afterward the LORD said to Moses, "And the LORD said to Moses, 'Behold, I am coming to you in a thick cloud, that the people may hear when I speak with you, and may also believe you [NIV: put their trust in you] forever'" (Exod. 19:9). That is, they will always have confidence that what you say is true. Likewise, King Jehoshaphat said to the people, "Have faith in the LORD your God and you will be upheld; have faith in his prophets and you will be successful" (CEB: "Trust the LORD your God, and you will stand firm; trust his prophets and succeed!") (2 Chron. 20:20). That is, have confidence that what the prophets say is true: "Then they believed his words" (CEB: "So our ancestors trusted God's words") (Ps. 106:12).

Let me add some New Testament examples. Zechariah did not believe the angel's words (Luke 1:20), whereas the official with the sick son "believed the word that Jesus spoke to him" (John 4:50). That is, the one did not believe, and the other did believe, that the spoken words referred to how the situation

---

11. Quoted in Van Genderen and Velema (2008, 593).

really, truly was. Jesus told his disciples: "Then if anyone says to you, 'Look, here is the Christ!' or 'There he is!' do not believe it. . . . So, if they say to you, . . . 'Look, he is in the inner rooms,' do not believe it" (Matt. 24:23, 26); that is, it is not true what those people assert. The disciples did not believe what the women told them about the risen Lord (Mark 16:11, 13-14). Of the Jews in Rome it is said, "And some were convinced by what he said, but others disbelieved" (Acts 28:24), that is, some were convinced that Paul spoke the truth, others did not (cf. Luke 8:13; 24:11; John 2:23; 4:21; 7:31; 9:18; 17:8; Acts 8:12-13).

"Believing *that* . . ." is certainly important for salvation: ". . . the word of faith that we proclaim . . . if you confess with your mouth that Jesus is Lord and believe in your heart *that* God raised him from the dead, you will be saved. For with the heart one believes and is justified, and with the mouth one confesses and is saved" (Rom. 10:8-10). At the same time, "believing *that* . . ." is not sufficient. In true faith, the "believing that . . ." is embedded in the faith and confidence *in* the God who did this for us.[12] It is not only believing *that* God has done certain things, but also believing *in* the God who has done them. This is not just believing that God exists—although that is part of it—but loving, thankful confidence.[13] In other words, "believing *that* . . ." is true faith if, and only if, it is connected with "believing *in* . . ." (see next section).

The Bible gives us a clear example of a "believing that . . ." which is *not* embedded in a "believing in . . .": "You believe that God is one; you do well. Even the demons believe—and shudder!" (James 2:19). Demons, and some unregenerate people as well, do believe in the factual truth of what we find, for example, in the Apostles' Creed. They believe that God is the Creator of the world, that Jesus was conceived by the Spirit, died, and rose again—but they have no personal relationship with this God or this Jesus. They could not genuinely

---
12. Wright (2006, 207).
13. Ibid.

say, "Jesus died and rose again *for me*" (cf. Gal. 2:20; Rom. 5:8; 1 Thess. 5:10). They believe "in" the forgiveness of sins in the sense that they do believe *that* God forgives sin—but they cannot say that *their* sins have been forgiven.

6.2.2 Believing In = Trusting Someone

The next level is "believing (in) someone," that is, trust someone, not only (sometimes) his words, but *himself*. It is not just the words that matter here, but the person who speaks them—the person whom one considers to be trustworthy, in whom one places one's confidence. This may still have an everyday meaning, namely, that this person means something, or does something, for me, without this having any eternal value. Thus, there were people who believed in Jesus because of the miracles he did (a so-called "miraculous faith").

Here is a negative example: "Now when he was in Jerusalem at the Passover Feast, many believed [Greek, *episteusan*] in his name when they saw the signs that he was doing. But Jesus on his part did not entrust [*episteuen*] himself to them, because he knew all people and needed no one to bear witness about man, for he himself knew what was in man" (John 2:23-25). Please notice how one and the same verb (*pisteuō*) seems to be rendered here rather differently. One might say that many people put their confidence in Jesus, but Jesus did not put his confidence in *them*. Further notice that the text speaks of a faith that does orient itself to Jesus, yet apparently does not have any value for eternity.

Several very positive examples are found in the two chapters concerning Jesus' Kingdom signs (Matt. 8-9), following the Sermon on the Mount, which is the constitution of the Kingdom, so to speak (Matt. 5-7). First the Roman centurion: ""[W]ith no one in Israel have I found such faith. . . . Go; let it be done for you as you have believed" (8:10, 13). Then concerning the four friends of the paralytic: "And when Jesus saw their faith, he said to the paralytic, 'Take heart, my son; your sins are forgiven'" (9:2). Then to the woman with the discharge: "Take heart, daughter; your faith has made you well" (v. 22). Then the two blind men: "When he entered the house, the blind men came to him, and Jesus said to them, 'Do you believe that I am able to do this?' They said to him, 'Yes, Lord.' Then he touched their eyes, saying, 'According to your faith be it done to you'" (vv. 28-29; see further 15:28; 17:21; 21:21; Mark 2:5; 4:40; 5:34, 36; 9:23-24; 10:52; 11:22; Luke 5:20; 7:9, 50; 8:25, 48, 50; 17:5-6, 19; John 4:48). Although in all these cases we are dealing with faith in relation to miracles, we cannot escape from the impression that this is a faith that has value for eternity. The reason is that the people involved do not just believe what Jesus says but they surrender to him, they entrust themselves to him with all their problems, sins, and diseases.

Even higher than this is "believing in someone" in the sense of "trusting someone," namely, that this person means something to me, or does something for me, in some existential-transcendent sense. This is always a faith that has existential and eternal value; it is *saving* faith. Here is a negative example: "[T]he devil comes and takes away the word from their hearts, so that they may not believe and be saved" (Luke 8:12; cf. John 7:5, 48; 12:37-38). Here are some positive examples: John the Baptist "came as a witness, to bear witness about the light, that all might believe through him" (John 1:7; cf. 4:41, 53; 11:27; 20:8, 29). "[B]y him [i.e., Jesus] everyone who believes is freed from everything from which you could not be freed by the law of Moses" (Acts 13:39; cf. 3:16; 4:4; 6:7; 14:9, 27; 15:7, 9, 11; 17:12, 34). "[W]e believe that we will be saved through the grace of the Lord Jesus" (15:11). "Believe in the Lord Jesus, and you will be saved" (16:31). Also compare in the Old Testament: "[T]hey did not believe in God and did not trust his saving power" (Ps. 78:22).

The difference between this kind of faith and the previous one could be described as the difference between a transcendent faith and an immanent faith: one with eternal value, and one with only temporal value. There is an overlap between the two kinds where the borderline cannot be sharply drawn. That is, *we* cannot clearly see to what category a certain faith belongs. But "the Lord knows those who are his" (2 Tim. 2:19; cf. John 10:14).

6.2.3 Entrusting Oneself to Someone

The highest level is "believing *in* . . ." in the sense of not only putting one's confidence in someone, but surrendering to that person, *entrusting* oneself to that person. In the Greek New Testament, this "in" is expressed through a common dative (e.g., 1 John 3:23), or through the prepositions *en* (e.g., John 3:15) or *eis* (e.g., 1 John 5:13) or *epi* (e.g., Acts 16:31), and sometimes through a substantive followed by a genitive, as with *pistis Christou*, "faith *in* Christ" (see §5.2.3). This is faith in the full transcendent-religious sense of the word. Often in the previous case (§6.2.2), but at any rate in the present case, we are dealing with *saving* faith, an expression that we find, for instance, in the Canons of Dort (I.15; V.7; Dutch: *zaligmakend*[14] *geloof*). The Canons also contain the expression "justifying faith," and we saw (§5.2.1) that such expressions are not entirely correct because it is not faith that saves or justifies, but *God* who justifies on account of faith.

However, seen from the viewpoint of human responsibility, it is perfectly clear why Jesus can say to the sinful woman, "Your *faith* has saved you" (Luke 7:50). In other passages, Jesus says to diseased people who are healed, "Your *faith* has made you well" (Matt. 9:22; Mark 10:52; Luke 17:19), but this is the same verbal construction; literally, "[Y]our faith has saved you." So it is always God who saves, on account of faith from the human side, but apparently this is identical to saying that it is this faith that saves the person concerned. What believers receive is according to the measure of God's sovereign grace — but it is also according to the measure of their faith (cf.

---

14. The term is not entirely correct: *zaligmakend* is something like "bliss-making," and "bliss" (cf. Greek, *makarios*, "blissful") is not a good rendering of *sōtēria*, "salvation."

Saving Faith

Matt. 8:13; 9:29; 15:28; see further chapter 7).

The matter as such is clear enough: it is faith on account of which one is saved: "Whoever *believes* and is baptized will be *saved*" (Mark 16:16). "But we *believe* that we will be *saved* through the grace of the Lord Jesus" (Acts 15:11). "*Believe* in the Lord Jesus, and you will be *saved*" (16:31). "[T]he gospel . . . is the power of God for *salvation* to everyone who *believes*" (Rom. 1:16). "[I]f you confess with your mouth that Jesus is Lord and *believe* in your heart that God raised him from the dead, you will be *saved*. For with the heart one *believes* and is justified [lit., believes unto righteousness], and with the mouth one confesses and is *saved* [lit., confesses unto salvation]" (10:9-10). "[I]t pleased God through the folly of what we preach to *save* those who *believe*" (1 Cor. 1:21). "I would remind you, brothers, of the gospel I preached to you, . . . by which you are being *saved*, . . . unless you *believed* in vain" (15:1-2). "In him you also, when you heard the word of truth, the gospel of your *salvation*, and *believed* in him, were sealed with the promised Holy Spirit" (Eph. 1:13). "For by grace you have been *saved* through *faith*" (2:8); ". . . the sacred writings, which are able to make you wise for *salvation* through *faith* in Christ Jesus" (2 Tim. 3:15); ". . . obtaining the outcome of your *faith*, the *salvation* of your souls" (1 Pet. 1:9).

Sometimes, the word *pisteuō* is indeed translated as "to entrust," for instance: "If then you have not been faithful in the unrighteous wealth, who will entrust to you the true riches?" (Luke 16:11). "[T]he Jews were entrusted with the oracles of God" (Rom. 3:2). "I am still entrusted with a stewardship" (1 Cor. 9:17). "I had been entrusted with the gospel to the uncircumcised, just as Peter had been entrusted with the gospel to the circumcised" (Gal. 2:7; cf. 1 Thess. 2:4; 1 Tim. 1:11; 2 Tim. 2:2; Titus 1:3). In these passages, the text speaks of "entrusting" a certain task to certain people. In John 2:24 it is an "entrusting" oneself to people (though in the negative): "Jesus on his part did not entrust himself to them, because he knew all people." Often, *pisteuō* has this very meaning: "to believe" in the sense of "to entrust" oneself to someone. This is the backdrop of Paul's word: "I know whom I have believed" (2 Tim. 1:12). One believes not only what God or Christ says — for instance about people and about himself — but one also believes *him*, even deeper: *in him*, even deeper: one entrusts oneself to him for everything in this life, and for everything in eternity.

Faith is commitment; faith is submission; faith is surrender. In this sense, the word occurs many times in the New Testament epistles (relevant passages will be quoted in the rest of this chapter and the next). This faith rises far beyond the mere acceptance of certain dogmas *concerning* God and Christ. Yet, we still encounter traditional Christians who really believe that if someone believes everything that is said in, say, the Nicene Creed, then that person is a true believer. Already the Reformers distinguished between a "historical faith" (an intellectual acceptance of dogmas) and a "saving faith," sprouting from a regenerated heart. Sometimes, dogmaticians speak of a *fides humana* ("human faith") and a *fides divina* ("divine faith") to express the difference.[15] One could also speak of a "dead faith" (cf. James 2:17) and a "living faith."

Faith is not only believing certain statements about Christ, but also *surrender to* Christ. As Emil Brunner put it: faith is "the soul's self-abandonment to God, dropping the drawbridge, on which the divine Conqueror enters from the Beyond into the immanent world, and draws the glory to himself."[16] It is putting your own life and world behind you, beyond a point of no return. It is the total surrender to someone who has totally surrendered himself for us: ". . . Jesus Christ, who gave himself for our sins" (Gal. 1:3-4); ". . . the Son of God, who loved me and gave himself for me" (2:20). "Christ loved us and gave himself up for us, a fragrant offering and sacrifice to God" (Eph. 5:2). ". . . Jesus Christ, who gave himself for us to redeem us" (Titus 2:13-14). *This* faith is the condition for our salvation (see the passages quoted above) and for eternal life

---

15. See, e.g., Luther in *Luther's Works*, Vol. 29, passim.
16. Brunner (1923, 101).

Saving Faith

(John 3:16; etc.), as well as the power through which the person who *has been* saved, and *has* eternal life, lives his everyday life (see next chapter): "my righteous one shall live by faith" (Heb. 10:38; cf. Hab. 2:4).

This will be explicated later. For now, let me mention just one example, namely, the remarkable fact that Christ is not only *object* of our faith, but also *example* of faith He is "the founder and perfecter of our faith" (Heb. 12:2). He is not only the One who, along the way of faith, leads the believers to perfection (cf. 11:40), but who, here on earth, brought the life of faith itself to a perfect summit. He lived here as "Jesus," the humble Man on earth,[17] in perfect confidence toward his God and Father. Thus, through his own perfection, he attained the perfect goal of the way of faith, and entered into glory by his own merit. And now, not only through his example but also by his power, he leads believers into that glory (2:10).[18]

6.3 Forms of Faith
6.3.1 Immanent and Transcendent Faith

The term "faith" has several different meanings in the New Testament, meanings that must be carefully distinguished theologically. I already mentioned the difference between immanent (non-saving) and transcendent faith, to which belongs saving faith, but also — I must add — all kinds of apostate faiths. The latter are often equally a matter of the heart's deepest convictions — in this case, an unregenerate heart — as saving faith. There is transcendent-religious *true* faith and transcendent-religious *false* faith. Let us look a little more closely at these three forms: strictly immanent faith (which is always false), transcendent true faith, and transcendent false faith.

In fact, the matter is even more complicated. *Every* human has some form of faith, in the broadest sense of the term. This is an ultimate commitment to some Ultimate Ground for all

---
17. Cf. all the passages in Heb. that mention only the name Jesus (especially 2:9; 3:1; 4:14; 5:7; 6:20; 10:10; 13:12).
18. Ouweneel (1982, 2:74).

of one's certainties and convictions. If we define "religion" in a philosophical way, namely, as an ultimate commitment, then we may even say that every human is religious in the broad sense, because every (thinking) human has some basic (i.e., heart) convictions as to the meaning (or non-meaning) of the world and of his own life, and has some basic values and norms. The point is now that we must distinguish between two forms of religiosity.[19]

(a) There is a form in which someone's religious beliefs (mainly) proceed from such an ultimate commitment, such that the two are in harmony with each other. This form is sometimes called "intrinsic religiosity." In this case, someone's beliefs are rooted in his *transcendent faith*, whether the true faith of the Scriptures or some false (pagan, apostate) religion. The deeply convinced Muslim, living out of the true convictions of his heart of hearts, is characterized by "intrinsic religiosity" (that is, his heart and his beliefs match), though a false (apostate) one (turned away from the God of the Bible).

(b) There is a form in which the heart is under the influence of some different ultimate commitment, which does not agree with one's religious beliefs. This form is sometimes called "extrinsic religiosity." In this case, we are usually dealing only with some *immanent faith*. This may, for instance, be the person who outwardly adheres to a number of Christian beliefs without his heart being in agreement with them. With his heart he serves another "god" (cf. Phil. 3:19). He is not necessarily a hypocrite; he may simply be a stranger to his own heart (cf. Jer. 17:9). He may really have certain Christian convictions; he might even be prepared to fight for them; but his heart is "somewhere else." His heart does not serve the God (or god) of his beliefs, but some other god (often none other than his own self-interest).

The three important elements in these two descriptions are: first, the factual condition of the heart, which basically

---

19. See some of the pioneers who have explored this field: Adorno *et al.* (1950); Glock (1965); Dittes (1969); Rokeach (1969); Allen and Spilka (1973).

is: regenerate or unregenerate; second, someone's confessed religion, one's beliefs, and the way one practices them; and third, the (close or vague) relationship between these two. The sincere Muslim and the nominal Christian both have an unregenerate heart—but at least the former is serious about his beliefs, while the latter is not. The *biblical* believer is characterized by intrinsic religiosity, that is, a transcendent faith as well as beliefs that correspond with it, and that proceed from a regenerate heart, in the power of the Holy Spirit. The *nominal* "believer" is characterized by extrinsic religiosity, that is, on the one hand, a transcendent (apostate) faith, and on the other hand, Christian beliefs that do not correspond with it, and that proceed from an unregenerate heart.

6.3.2 More on Intrinsic and Extrinsic Religiosity

Extrinsic religiosity is outward religiosity, a matter of social status and self-interest, often rooted in someone's psychical need for security, such as the safety of "the group" (the family, the denomination, the local church). In intrinsic religiosity, it is not so much someone's own needs that are central, but certain ethical-religious values (biblical or non-biblical). Such a person is much less dominated by (the values of) "the group," and far more by his heart's own religious values and convictions. With some care, we might say: the God (or god!) whom he serves in his actions is also the true God (or god!) of his heart.

Applied to Christians this means the following. The intrinsically religious Christian is to some extent (because the sinful nature is still present in him) dominated by a Christian-religious ethos, whereas the extrinsically religious Christian is partly or entirely dominated by some apostate-religious ethos. In biblical terms this means that the latter has either an unregenerate heart (that is, he is a nominal Christian), or a regenerate heart that is strongly dominated by the flesh, i.e., the sinful nature (cf., e.g., John 6:63; Rom. 8:4–14; Gal. 5:16–22; 1 Pet. 1:22–2:1). The intrinsically religious Christian lives out of his *transcendent* relationship with the God of the Bible, with Jesus Christ. The extrinsically religious Christian, however, is mainly *immanently* oriented: he is dominated by intellectual, societal, and psychical interests. To put it a bit more bluntly: the intrinsically religious Christian serves God and his fellow humans (even though in weakness), the extrinsically religious Christian serves mainly himself.

If we maintain the useful distinction between (transcendent) *faith*, either biblical or apostate, and (immanent) *beliefs* (biblical or apostate), we can distinguish four categories of religious people (in the broad sense of the term):

(a) Those who have an *apostatic* faith and *apostate* beliefs. In this category, we find both extrinsic religiosity (the most deplorable group) and intrinsic religiosity (think of serious and sincere Muslims, Hindus, and Buddhists).

(b) Those who have a *biblical* faith and *apostate* beliefs. These may be serious, sincere Christians who are caught in many fundamental heresies. We cannot judge the hearts of such persons, but we cannot exclude the possibility that there are truly regenerate Christians in this category. In this respect, we expect more intrinsically than extrinsically religious persons in this group.

(c) Those who have an *apostate* faith and *biblical* beliefs. These are nominal Christians, that is, people with unregenerate hearts who profess to have accepted certain Christian beliefs. Often, they are part of local churches, but they have no personal relationship with God the Father, and with his Son, Jesus Christ. They do not know the power of the Holy Spirit. In this respect, we expect far more extrinsically than intrinsically religious persons in this category.

(d) Those who have a *biblical* faith and *biblical* beliefs. These are true Christians, people with regenerate hearts, whose (immanent) beliefs are in basic harmony with their (transcendent) faith (the true faith of his heart). In this respect, we expect far more intrinsically than extrinsically religious persons in this category.

6.3.3 *Fides Qua* and *Fides Quae*

In its immanent meaning, the term "faith" may sometimes refer to the truth of faith, that which is believed, *depositum fidei*, the "deposit of faith," the totality of Christian beliefs, what we describe as the "Christian faith" or "Christian religion," or "Christianity." Consider for example: "[A] great many of the priests became obedient to the faith" (Acts 6:7); "stand firm in the faith" (1 Cor. 16:13; cf. 1 Pet. 5:9); "[e]xamine yourselves, to see whether you are in the faith" (2 Cor. 13:5); "[h]e who used to persecute us is now preaching the faith he once tried to destroy" (Gal. 1:23; cf. 3:23, 25); "striving side by side for the faith of the gospel" (Phil. 1:27); "established in the faith" (Col. 2:7); "[n]ow the Spirit expressly says that in later times some will depart from the faith" (1 Tim. 4:1; cf. v. 6; 1:19b; 5:8); and "some have wandered away from the faith" (6:10; cf. v. 21).

In all these cases, "faith" means that which is believed, as distinct from "faith" in the sense of the act of believing. Traditionally, the former is described with the Latin phrase *fides quae creditur*, "the faith that is believed," and the latter as *fides qua creditur*, "the faith by which one believes." In the sentence, "I wholeheartedly believe the truth of the Christian faith," we have to do successively with *fides qua creditur* ("believe") and *fides quae creditur* ("faith"), that is, the act of believing, and what is believed. "Faith" is not only "confidence" in God, "entrusting" oneself to God, but also knowing *what* is believed: the "content" of faith, someone's beliefs.

The *fides quae creditur* without the *fides qua creditur* is what we have described above as biblical beliefs that are embraced—for instance, because one's church, or one's parents, had embraced them—without a changed (regenerate) heart. As we have seen, this is sometimes referred to as a "historical faith."[20] However, this does not mean that the *fides quae*

---

20. See Kersten (1983, 2:397–98).

creditur would be something inferior because, allegedly, "it is the heart that really matters." On the contrary, "the churches were strengthened in the *faith*" (Acts 16:5). This does not mean only that their confidence was strengthened, but also that they were further rooted in the *fides quae creditur*, that which is believed. This is even clearer in Jude 1:3, "I found it necessary to write appealing to you to contend for the faith that was once for all delivered to the saints" (Jude 3; cf. v. 20). This is the biblical truth, that which is called the "Christian faith," the totality of Christian beliefs.

Please notice especially 1 Timothy 1:18–20, "This charge I entrust to you, Timothy, . . . that . . . you may wage the good warfare, holding *faith* and a good conscience. By rejecting this, some have made shipwreck of their *faith*, among whom are Hymenaeus and Alexander, whom I have handed over to Satan that they may learn not to blaspheme." In the latter case (*pistis* with the article), Paul clearly refers to the *fides quae creditur*, the "Christian faith." One could say that the persons concerned had "swerved from the truth" (2 Tim. 2:18; cf. 3:8; 4:7; 1 Tim. 5:8; 6:21). In the former case, however (*pistis* without the article[21]), I presume it is *fides qua creditur* that is meant.[22] The lesson of this verse, then, is this: if you reject your *fides qua creditur*, you risk losing your *fides quae creditur* as well. In other words, give up faith and a good conscience, and you will probably end up in heresy. Already John Chrysostom had this to say on this subject: "When a life is [morally] corrupt, it engenders a [heretical] doctrine congenial to it."[23]

The *fides qua* and the *fides quae* must always be kept together as closely as possible. A *fides quae* without *fides qua*—beliefs without (transcendent) faith—is nothing but a dry, indifferent doctrinal system without any spiritual content and reality.

---

21. The article is often lacking when *pistis* has this meaning; see, e.g., Matt. 17:20; Mark 4:30; Luke 17:5; Acts 14:9; 20:20; 1 Cor. 12:9; 13:13; Gal. 5:6, 22; 1 Tim. 6:11; 2 Tim. 2:22; Titus 1:1, 4; Heb. 11:1, 3; and 2 Pet. 1:1.
22. So, e.g., Bouma (1937, 52); Vine (1985, 3:234–35).
23. Quoted in White (1979, 101).

Conversely, a *fides qua* with a minimum of *fides quae* — an act of faith without (much) faith content (beliefs) — is the faith of "children, tossed to and fro by the waves and carried about by every wind of doctrine, by human cunning, by craftiness in deceitful schemes" (Eph. 4:14).[24]

In the *fides qua creditur*, we may distinguish between, on the one hand, the *fides* by which we "*come* to faith," the *fides* linked with conversion and regeneration, and on the other hand, the *fides* by which we live our life of faith, from our regeneration until the end of our earthly existence. We could speak here of a *positional* faith, which determines once for all our position (or *state*) before God, and a *practical* faith, the faith by which we lead our daily lives, that is, our (spiritual) *standing* (condition). In certain hyper-Calvinist circles, the terms "state" and "standing" (Dutch: *staat* and *stand*) are quite common. Practical faith (our "standing") is the subject of the next chapter.

6.4 "Jesus Is Lord"
6.4.1 The Gospel of the Kingdom

In the New Testament, it is very clear that true, saving faith involves embracing Jesus not only as Redeemer but also as Lord. This is "the word of faith that we proclaim; because, if you *confess with your mouth that Jesus is Lord* and believe in your heart that God raised him from the dead, you will be saved. For with the heart one believes and is justified, and *with the mouth one confesses and is saved*" (Rom. 10:8–10). Of course, such a verbal confession must go hand in hand with deeds, that is, with the concrete recognition of Jesus' lordship by submitting to his commandments, by following and serving him consistently. Therefore, in this passage it is not only the heart's faith but also the mouth's confession that is a condition for salvation. Compare Heidelberg Catechism Q&A 34: "Q. Why do you call Him 'our Lord'? A. Because not with silver or gold, but with His precious blood, He has redeemed

---
24. Cf. Heyns (1988, 308).

and purchased us, body and soul, from sin and from all the power of the devil, to be His own."

The calling to faith is also a calling to obedience because the Jesus who is our Redeemer is the legitimate Lord and Master of the universe. This is why Paul can speak of the "obedience of faith," if taken to mean the obedience that is the result of faith (Rom. 1:5; 16:26).[25] Coming to faith implies that from now on the believer will be an obedient follower of Jesus; without this resulting obedience, there cannot have been any genuine faith in the first place: "But thanks be to God, that you who were once slaves of sin have become obedient from the heart to the standard of teaching to which you were committed" (6:17; cf. 15:18; 16:19). Please notice, here again, that *pistis* can also mean "faithfulness, loyalty." The message of the gospel is the good news that Jesus is the only true "emperor," who rules the world under his own sign of love that gives itself away.[26] People are invited to become "faithful" (loyal) to this mighty ruler.

Indeed, the emperor of Rome was venerated as (Greek) *kyrios kai theos*, or (Latin) *dominus et deus* ("Lord and God"; cf. Acts 12:22; 25:26). In opposition to this, Peter testifies about Jesus "that God has made him both Lord and Christ [i.e., Messiah, Anointed One]" (Acts 2:36), and "he is Lord of all" (10:36; cf. Eph. 1:20-23; Phil. 2:9-11; Col. 2:15; 1 Pet. 3:21-22). Already Thomas uttered the tremendous confession that the risen Jesus, and no one else, was *kyrios kai theos* (John 20:28). Or, more precisely, *ho kyrios mou kai ho theos mou,* "*my* Lord and *my* God." There can be no true faith without this very personal recognition of Jesus as "my" Lord (cf. Luke 1:43; John 20:13; Phil. 3:8) and "my" God (cf. Rom. 1:8; 1 Cor. 1:4; 2 Cor. 12:21; Phil. 1:3; 4:19; Philemon 1:4).

Therefore, Paul says, "For if we live, we live to the Lord, and if we die, we die to the Lord. So then, whether we live or whether we die, we are the Lord's. For to this end Christ died

---

25. Wright (2007, 180).
26. Ibid.

and lived again, that he might be Lord both of the dead and of the living" (Rom. 14:8-9). And elsewhere: "[H]e died for all, that those who live might no longer live for themselves but for him who for their sake died and was raised" (2 Cor. 5:15). Peter says, "[I]n your hearts honor Christ the Lord[27] as holy" (NIV "in your hearts revere Christ as Lord") (1 Pet. 3:15). The Holy Spirit works the confession of Jesus' Lordship in believers' hearts: "[N]o one can confess 'Jesus is Lord,' without being guided by the Holy Spirit" (1 Cor. 12:3). Conversely, we can equally say, No one can be guided by the Holy Spirit without confessing Jesus as Lord.

6.4.2 Spiritual Growth

No one, except spiritual babies, can come to truly know Jesus as Savior if one is not prepared to accept him as Lord.[28] "Babies" is not meant here in any derogatory sense; it is quite conceivable that the baby in Christ knows him only as Savior, and as yet is hardly conscious of his Lordship (think of literal children who love Jesus). Sometimes they are not able to say much more than what the blind man said after he had just been healed: "One thing I do know, that though I was blind, now I see" (John 9:25). However, in his spiritual growth the believer must also arrive at a true surrender to Jesus as Lord. No one can expect to *receive* everything from Jesus who is not prepared to *give* everything to him: one's heart, one's life. Paul's conversion started with the question: "What shall I do, Lord?" (Acts 22:10); he became an "imitator" (follower) of Christ the Lord (1 Cor. 11:1; 1 Thess. 1:6; cf. 1 Pet. 2:21; Rev. 14:4). Therefore it is sometimes said: *Becoming* a Christian costs you nothing, *being* a Christian costs you everything. This is expressed in the term "discipleship" (Luke 14:26-27, 33),[29] and also in James 2, where true faith proves itself through works of *obedience* (vv. 20-24). Notice the time sequence in

---
27. Cf. Textus Receptus: "[S]anctify the Lord God in your hearts" (see, e.g., GNV and NKJV).
28. Stott (1959, 37); Boice (1986, 10, 21).
29. MacArthur (1988, 21, 30); see extensively, Ouweneel (2011, chapter 11).

John 10:27-28 (NKJV), "My sheep hear My voice, and I know them, *and they follow Me*. And I give them eternal life."

In this connection, it is important to pay attention to one of the special biblical descriptions of the gospel, namely, as the "gospel of the kingdom" (Greek, *euangelion tēs basileias [tou theou]*, Matt. 4:23; 9:35; 24:14; Mark 1:14; also cf. *euangelizō tēn basileian tou theou*, "evangelizing [preaching the good news of] the Kingdom of God," Luke 4:43; 8:1; 16:16). In the widest sense of the word, the Kingdom of God is the dominion of Christ over heaven and earth, and in the present redemptive epoch very concretely in the hearts and lives of Christians.[30] We have been transferred to the Kingdom of the Son of the Father's love (Col. 1:13). The Kingdom is the sphere of operation of the Holy Spirit (Matt. 12:28; Rom. 14:17; cf. 1 Cor. 4:20). In the book of Acts, preaching the Kingdom takes a central place: ". . . you among whom I have gone about proclaiming the kingdom" (20:25; cf. 1:3, 6; 8:12; 14:22; 19:8; 28:23, 31). When Paul was taken captive in Thessalonica, he was not accused of preaching forgiveness—nobody would have bothered—but the complaint was that these men "are all acting against the decrees of Caesar, saying that there is another king, Jesus" (17:7).

There is not only the message of salvation for poor sinners, but also that of the dominion of Christ over all who accept this salvation. Conversion, regeneration, and faith bring a person not only in connection with the Savior, and with the Father's heart, but also under the authority of the Lord, who is the Master of the universe. The dispensationalist view, which limits the gospel of the Kingdom to the preaching of Jesus and to that of believing Jews during the Great Tribulation,[31] totally misses the mark. Not only the future "remnant of Israel" (taken in whatever sense) but also the church has everything to do with the Kingdom of God (see, e.g., Matt. 12:28; Acts 1:3; 19:8; 20:25; Rom. 14:17–18; 1 Cor. 4:20; Col. 1:13; 1 Thess. 2:12; 2 Thess. 1:5), and thus also with the good news about the Kingdom.[32] Everything the New Testament epistles discuss in

---

30. See extensively, Ouweneel (2011, §§13.3, 13.4).
31. See, e.g., Gaebelein (1910, 2:189–92).
32. See more extensively, Ouweneel (2012a, §9.2).

terms of the Lordship of Christ involves presenting us with Kingdom truth, even where the word "Kingdom" is missing.

6.5 A Fierce Debate
6.5.1 Charles C. Ryrie

The biblical data mentioned in §6.4.1 have been flatly denied by some theologians as being conditions for salvation.[33] Thus, Charles C. Ryrie argued that the message of faith alone and the message of commitment of life cannot both be the gospel, and that therefore one of the two is a false gospel. He who preaches the latter comes under the curse of distorting the gospel and of preaching a different gospel (Gal. 1:6-9).[34] Apparently, Ryrie takes the *sola fide* ("by faith alone") so literally that one is not allowed to say that faith is no true faith without surrender to Christ the Lord. This extreme viewpoint claims that the Lordship of Christ in Romans 10:9 would only involve his deity. However, Acts 2:36 says that God *made* him both Lord and Christ [i.e., Messiah]; God exalted him in order that every tongue would confess that Jesus is Lord (Phil. 2:9-11). Thomas confessed him as "my Lord and my God," thus distinguishing between Jesus' Lordship and Jesus' divinity. Jesus died and rose again in order that he would be *Lord* (Rom. 14:9, *kyrieusēi*). Through his death and resurrection, Jesus has become both our Savior and our Lord (1 Cor. 8:6; Eph. 4:5).

Ryrie fell a victim to at least two snares that were dealt with in the previous chapters. First, the Reformation may have launched the slogan of *sola fide*, but this *sola* is nowhere in the Bible. We have seen that the New Testament picture is not simply justification by faith *or* justification by works, but more precisely justification by faith resulting in works *or* justification by works without faith. *No one is justified by faith without works.* It is either a "faith working in love" (Gal. 5:6), or a "dead faith" (James 2:17, 26), which is not a saving faith

---
33. See the summary by Demarest (1997, 265-70).
34. Ryrie (1969, 170).

at all. A vital aspect of these works is the spiritual attitude behind them: surrendering to the Lordship of Christ is the true motivation for good works.

Second, we have seen that it is quite unilateral to link justification too strongly to a certain *moment* when the godly turns into a righteous person. The message is not so much: How can I reach that important "moment," but rather: How can I learn to live as a *tsaddiq*? Of course, that presupposes the "moment" of conversion, regeneration, coming to faith (although often even these are extended processes), but it emphasizes far more the entering into the *life* of the righteous, a life of righteous deeds, words, and thoughts, as imitators of Christ. Reformational theology has created a lot of confusion by its distinction between justification (meaning *positional* justification) and subsequent sanctification (meaning *practical* sanctification), instead of recognizing that positional justification *and* sanctification are followed by practical sanctification *and* justification. One is not saved simply by positional justification, but by a *justification* in which the positional and the practical aspects are inseparable.

6.5.2 Zane C. Hodges

Zane Hodges is another example of remarkable one-sidedness. Hodges argued that faith is the *inner conviction* that what God says to us in the gospel is true, and adds that only this is "saving faith."[35] In §6.2 we have seen that faith is not only putting one's confidence in certain statements, but also surrender — entrusting oneself — to the One making these statements. This entrusting, or true surrendering, is precisely what Hodges denies by appealing to the story of the Samaritan woman (John 4:1-30): she only had to receive the living water, and did not have to surrender. Hodges even argues that repentance, as a condition for salvation, would be a corruption of justification

---

35. Hodges (1989, 31); directed especially against MacArthur (see his 1994, orig.: 1988). The debate became known as the "lordship (salvation) controversy."

Saving Faith

by faith alone, and the requirement of accepting Jesus as Lord would be a return to the principle of the law.[36]

These are amazing views, to say the least. First, what can we prove by one New Testament story? Let me mention just a few other stories: "Jesus in pity touched their eyes, and immediately they recovered their sight *and followed him*" (Matt. 20:34). The healed leper "fell on his face at Jesus' feet, giving him thanks" (Luke 17:16). The first question of the converted Saul was: "What shall I do, Lord?" (Acts 22:10). He says of certain co-workers: "[T]hey *gave themselves* first to the Lord and then by the will of God to us" (2 Cor. 8:5). What is Hodges' argument? Is "giving oneself to the Lord" a voluntary option only *after* actual justification? And if you refuse to follow this option, is that okay with the Lord? It does not affect your justification?

Second, if repentance, as a condition for salvation, would be a corruption of the justification by faith alone, then what is *faith*? Just believing acceptance of certain truths? Just "drinking from the living water"? What does this involve? Is there no repentance reverberating in the words of that same Samaritan woman, "Come, see a man who told me *all that I ever did*" (John 4:29)? Do not verses that speak of repentance see this as a condition for forgiveness? "Whoever conceals his transgressions will not prosper, but he who confesses and forsakes them will obtain mercy" (Prov. 28:13). "And if he has committed sins, he will be forgiven. Therefore, confess your sins to one another and pray for one another" (James 5:15–16). "If we confess our sins, he is faithful and just to forgive us our sins" (1 John 1:9). Moreover, why did John the Baptist, Jesus and the apostles constantly call for repentance (Greek, *metanoia*; Matt. 3:2; 4:17; Mark 6:12; Luke 5:32; 13:3, 5; Acts 2:38; 3:19; 5:31; 8:22; 11:18; 17:30; 26:20)? Sometimes, this was in direct connection with faith: "The time is fulfilled, and the kingdom of God is at hand; repent and believe in the gospel" (Mark

---

36. Hodges (1989, 18).

1:15); "... testifying both to Jews and to Greeks of repentance toward God and of faith in our Lord Jesus Christ" (Acts 20:21); "... a foundation of repentance from dead works and of faith toward God" (Heb. 6:1).

Third, the idea that the requirement of accepting Jesus as Lord would be a return to the principle of the law betrays a serious misunderstanding with respect to the law.[37] Paul says, "Bear one another's burdens, and so fulfill the law of Christ" (Gal. 6:2; cf. 1 Cor. 9:21). "If you love me, you will keep my commandments" (John 14:15; cf. v. 21; 13:34; 15:10-17; 1 John 2:3-8; 3:22-24; 5:2-3); "... in order that the righteous requirement of the law might be fulfilled in us, who walk not according to the flesh but according to the Spirit" (Rom. 8:4). "Love does no wrong to a neighbor; therefore love is the fulfilling of the law" (13:[8-]10). These New Testament statements imply that the principle of the law definitely does have a place in Christian life. It is even a commandment to fulfill the "law of Christ." Would it be acceptable to God if someone would argue: Sorry, I have believed, and that is enough—I refuse to accept any commandments because I have done away with the principle of the law?

Fourth, Hodges makes a correct distinction between coming to faith and coming to spiritual maturity. But that is not the point at all. We, his opponents, do not confuse the two. We even agree that "simple faith" is enough to be eternally saved. But even the "simplest" faith is far more than just the acceptance of certain teachings. It is very simple to say, "I believe that Jesus died for my sins." But either this is an empty statement—a statement of the intellect or of the emotions—and thus without fruit, or it is a fruit-bearing faith. It is unbiblical and senseless to look at faith *per se*, disregarding the fruits, because it is these very fruits that prove whether this faith is genuine or not.

---

37. See extensively, Ouweneel (2015a).

6.5.3 Other Views

Part of the discussion centered around the rendering of Colossians 2:6, "[Y]ou received/accepted Christ Jesus *the* Lord . . ." (most older translations), or "*as* Lord . . ." (many newer translations: CJB, CEV, ERV, GNT, NET, NI[R]V, NLT). It is pointless to argue that the word "as" (Greek, *hōs*) is not in the original, because such an "as" construction is perfectly grammatical. Compare 2 Corinthians 4:5, "we preach Christ Jesus (others, Jesus Christ) *the* Lord," or "*as* Lord" (e.g., ASV, CEB, DLNT, ESV, HCSB, ISV, NABRE, NASB, [N]RSV, WEB). A third example is 1 Peter 3:15, "[S]anctify the Lord Christ[38] in your hearts" (DRA), where many translations have "Christ *as* Lord" (e.g., ASV, CJB, GNT, ISV, LEB, NASB, NET, NIV, NLT, RSV).

It is obvious that, since the rise of the "lordship salvation" controversy, the adherents of Ryrie and Hodges began to dislike such renderings, especially "accepting Christ as Lord." However, even if one does not like the translation "as," the sense is clear: believers are people who have accepted Christ Jesus the *Lord*, that is, in *that* quality: not just the Jesus who died and rose for them but Jesus the *Lord*.

As to the word "alone" — saved/justified by faith alone (*sola fide*) — I have no difficulty basically accepting the expression. In fact, the discussion does not involve this point at all, but rather involves the question what biblical faith truly is. According to Ryrie and Hodges, faith as such excludes, for instance, repentance and surrender. In their view, it is nice if such things are there as well, but they are no *condition* for salvation or justification. In opposition to this, others have rightly argued that, indeed, we are saved "by faith alone," but this faith is no genuine, biblical faith if it does not entail repentance, confession of sins, surrender to Christ, submission to his dominion. Ryrie and Hodges argue that it is a false gospel to suggest that we are saved by faith *plus* something.

---

38. See note 27.

Others have rightly argued that we are saved by faith alone, but repentance and surrender are essential aspects of faith as such, of the true *fides qua creditur*.

The debate has been fierce because others have used equally strong words to defend their view in opposition to Ryrie and Hodges. Just as Ryrie called the message of faith plus surrender a false gospel, Aiden W. Tozer called the view that repentance and surrender are not necessary a pure "heresy," even in the title of his book.[39] Various authors have called Ryrie and Hodges "modern antinomian extremists" and teachers of a "lawless grace."[40] In this way, the one party accused the other one of legalism, and the other party accused the first one of antinomianism. James Packer spoke of faith-alone-ism, and pointed out the illogical element in it: how can anyone seriously believe that a person needs only to believe in Jesus as the One who bore our sins if this person does not at the same time sincerely wish to break with sin, and to this end wants to place his life under the Lordship of Christ?[41]

This seems to me perfectly correct. He who shouts: "Faith is enough!" may be reminded of James 2:19, "Even the demons believe—and tremble!" Faith is perfected by, or completed in (Greek, *eteleiōthē*), the works of obedience and service that flow from it (v. 22). Indeed, justification is by faith alone—but there is no genuine faith without repentance and confession, surrender to the dominion of Christ, imitation of Christ, and obedience to him. Romans 10:9 is very clear: "If you openly say, 'Jesus is Lord' and believe in your heart that God raised him from death, you will be saved" (ERV). This is not just some outward confession: "But in your hearts revere Christ as Lord" (1 Pet. 3:15 NIV). We are justified by faith alone—but faith is no faith if it does not work through love (Gal. 5:6).

---

39. Tozer (1991).
40. Various authors in Horton (1992).
41. Packer (1970, 89).

6.6 Obedience of Faith
6.6.1 A Continuum

We have seen (§6.1.1) that there are two explanations of the Greek expression *hypakoē pisteōs* ("obedience of faith," Rom. 1:5; 16:26): either it means: "obedience expressing itself in (or, leading to) faith" (obedience at conversion), or it refers to the obedience that is the result of faith (the walk of faith).[42] In fact, the two meanings are not too far apart because they form a continuum, just as positional and practical justification, as well as positional and practical sanctification, both form an inseparable continuum (see the next three chapters).

At any rate, it is clear from Scripture that the act of conversion and coming to faith is called "obedience": ". . . the Holy Spirit, whom God has given to those who obey him" (Acts 5:32); "a great many of the priests became obedient to the faith" (6:7). Believers are those who "obey the truth" (Rom. 2:8; cf. Gal. 5:7). "Do you not know that if you present yourselves to anyone as obedient slaves, you are slaves of the one whom you obey, either of sin, which leads to death, or of obedience, which leads to righteousness? But thanks be to God, that you who were once slaves of sin have become obedient from the heart to the standard of teaching to which you were committed" (Rom. 6:16–17). People "have not all obeyed the gospel" (10:16); ". . . what Christ has accomplished through me to bring the Gentiles to obedience" (15:18).

"We . . . take every thought captive to obey Christ" (2 Cor. 10:5). "Therefore, my beloved, as you have always obeyed, so now . . . work out your own salvation with fear and trembling" (Phil. 2:12). There are "those who do not obey the gospel of our Lord Jesus" (2 Thess. 1:8; cf. 1 Pet. 4:17); ". . . the sanctification of the Spirit, for obedience to Jesus Christ" (1 Pet. 1:2). Unbelief is the same as disobedience to the gospel: "[W]hoever does not obey the Son shall not see life, but the wrath of God remains on him" (John 3:36); ". . . the spirit that

---
42. See Moo (1996, 51–53).

is now at work in the sons of disobedience" (Eph. 2:2; cf. Titus 3:3); "... those who formerly received the good news failed to enter because of disobedience" (Heb. 4:6).

I spoke of a continuum of coming to faith and living by faith; both can be referred to as events of obedience. It is in the *nature* of faith to obey; we have seen that a faith that accepts Jesus without wishing to entrust oneself, or submit, to him *is* no faith at all in the biblical sense. Faith is not just placing one's confidence in the Jesus who died, but in him who has been seated "far above all rule and authority and power and dominion, and above every name that is named" (Eph. 1:21). "[Y]ou have been filled in him, who is the head of all rule and authority" (Col. 2:10).

6.6.2 Faith Is the Beginning

This very discussion took place already during the age of the Reformation. The Council of Trent declared at its sixth session (1547) (Canon 12): "If anyone says that justifying faith is nothing else than confidence in divine mercy, which remits sins for Christ's sake, or that it is this confidence alone that justifies us, let him be anathema."[43] The text refers to chapter IX of the same session, where we read: "But though it is necessary to believe that sins neither are remitted nor ever have been remitted except gratuitously by divine mercy for Christ's sake, yet it must not be said that sins are forgiven or have been forgiven to anyone who boasts of his confidence and certainty of the remission of his sins, *resting on that alone*" (italics added).

According to Alister McGrath, the Council feared that people might think that they could be justified in the sense intended here, that is, by faith "alone," without the need of obedience or inner renewal.[44] Listening to people such as Ryrie and Hodges, we would have to acknowledge that the Council's fear was fully justified. However, it is not a fair picture of what Martin Luther intended, who understood very

---

43. http://www.ewtn.com/library/councils/trent6.htm.
44. McGrath (2010, 460–61).

Saving Faith

well that a non-fruit-bearing faith is no true faith. He may have said nasty things about the book of James (an "epistle of straw") but that does not mean that the matter was entirely lost on him.

Presumably, Luther would have agreed without much reservation with the following statement by the Council of Trent (chapter VIII): "[W]hen the Apostle says that man is justified by faith and freely [Rom. 3:24; 5:1], these words are to be understood in that sense in which the uninterrupted unanimity of the Catholic Church has held and expressed them, namely, that we are therefore said to be justified by faith, because faith is the *beginning* of human salvation, the foundation and root of all justification, without which it is impossible to please God [Heb. 11:6] and to come to the fellowship of His sons [cf. 1 Cor. 1:9; 1 John 1:3]; and we are therefore said to be justified gratuitously, because none of those things that precede justification, whether faith or works, merit the grace of justification. For, if by grace, it is not now by works, otherwise, as the Apostle says, grace is no more grace [Rom. 11:6]" (italics added).[45]

Please notice the word "beginning" in this quotation: a justification by faith without being connected with a true consciousness of sins and repentance, and without the fruits of that faith, that is, without practical righteousness and holiness, without an inner renewal toward Christ (2 Cor. 3:18; Gal. 4:19; Eph. 4:13; Col. 1:9-11; 2:19; 1 John 2:13-14), *is* no justification. In our terminology: positional justification cannot be viewed *per se*, as existing apart from practical justification: *it is only in practical justification that we can establish that positional justification has taken place at all.*

As John the Baptist said, "Every tree ... that does not bear good fruit is cut down and thrown into the fire" (Matt. 3:10). And Jesus: "So, every healthy tree bears good fruit, but the diseased tree bears bad fruit. A healthy tree cannot bear bad

---

45. See note 39.

fruit, nor can a diseased tree bear good fruit. Every tree that does not bear good fruit is cut down and thrown into the fire" (7:17-19); "the tree is known by its fruit" (12:33). No one can boast in positional justification alone; it is only when we see the fruit that we know the tree is alive; it is only when we see good fruit that we know the tree is healthy.

6.6.3 Misunderstandings

The Rome–Reformation conflict seems to me to be a classical example of a theological misunderstanding rooted in disagreement on an important theological term: "faith."[46] The conflict has never died. Whereas Catholics and Lutherans came to a certain agreement on the matter (see §1.2.3), it is now Protestants fighting among themselves. Interestingly, the Rome–Reformation conflict described in §6.6.2 is quite similar to the MacArthur–Hodges conflict described in §6.5.2, in which I am definitely more on the side of the Reformed MacArthur than on that of the dispensationalist Hodges.

Luther accused Rome of requiring a justification by faith *plus* (works), while Rome blamed Luther (without mentioning him) for claiming a justification by a meager faith without repentance and obedience. In §§1.2.2 and 1.2.3, I have described how apparently only by the end of the twentieth century, Lutheran and Roman Catholic theologians began to see that they basically agreed on the matter. On the one hand, followers of the Reformation are beginning to see everywhere more clearly — except for authors such as Ryrie and Hodges — that faith is more than just the acceptance of Jesus and his redemptive work. And followers of Rome should recognize everywhere — as Trent in fact already did — that justification is by grace alone (*sola gratia*). Listen to Trent again: "For, if by grace, it is not now by works, otherwise, as the Apostle says, grace is no more grace."

Of course, it is easy to blame both Rome and the Reformation for their deep mutual misunderstandings. This *is* a

---

46. Cf. McGrath (2010, 462).

difficult matter, on which even Protestant theologians today do not agree, as we saw, accusing each other of heresies. Likewise, the readers in Paul's day had difficulty understanding him. They thought that his doctrine of justification by faith implied a license to keep sinning: "And why not do evil that good may come?—as some people slanderously charge us with saying" (Rom. 3:8). "What shall we say then? Are we to continue in sin that grace may abound? By no means! How can we who died to sin still live in it? . . . What then? Are we to sin because we are not under law but under grace? By no means!" (6:1, 15; cf. James 2:14–26; 2 Pet. 3:16).[47]

It is even conceivable, though speculative, that the entire matter of justification by faith belonged to the things in Paul's letters that Peter found "hard to understand."[48] However, Peter felt no need to defend those who had difficulty understanding Paul and therefore distorted his teaching. On the contrary, Peter spoke of the "ignorant and unstable" who twisted Paul's doctrine "to their own destruction, as they do the other Scriptures" (2 Pet. 3:16). We do not get very far with our "sympathy" for all the misunderstandings that Paul's teachings have caused. Therefore, it is wise to underscore the dangers in the views of Ryrie and Hodges because they also "twist" Paul's doctrine. They are preaching the "cheap grace" (*billige Gnade*) against which Dietrich Bonhoeffer has warned so intensely.[49]

We do believe that we are justified "by faith alone," but this is always a "faith working through love" (Gal. 5:6), a faith producing the fruit of the Spirit (v. 22) and manifesting itself in fulfilling the law of Christ (6:2; Rom. 8:4; 13:8–10; 1 Cor. 9:21). The same apostle who says, "For by grace you have been saved through faith. And this is not your own doing; it is the gift of God, not a result of works, so that no one may boast," adds immediately after: "For we are his work-

---

47. See Berkhof (1979, 435).
48. See Blum (1981, 288).
49. Bonhoeffer (1966, chapter 1).

manship, created in Christ Jesus for good works, which God prepared beforehand, that we should walk in them" (Eph. 2:8-10). Of course, I realize that many will respond: We are justified by faith *alone*, and *then* there are the works that result from it. I reply to this with what I see as the biblical view: such a separation is contrary to the thrust of Scripture. We should learn to bring the two closer together: we are justified by a works-producing-faith. The issue is not so much: justified by faith and not by works, but more precisely: justified by a works-producing-faith, and not by works without faith.

6.7 Perseverance
6.7.1 Perseverance according to the Creeds

Traditionally, Reformed theology adds to the series of (1) "calling," (2) "conversion," (3) "regeneration," (4) "faith," (5) "justification," and (6) "sanctification," a seventh point: "perseverance" (in modern translations: "endurance" or "steadfastness").[50] See, for instance: "[W]hatever was written in former days was written for our instruction, that through endurance and through the encouragement of the Scriptures we might have hope. May the God of endurance and encouragement grant you to live in such harmony with one another, in accord with Christ Jesus" (Rom. 15:4-5). "May you be strengthened with all power, according to his glorious might, for all endurance and patience with joy" (Col. 1:11). "Therefore we ourselves boast about you in the churches of God for your steadfastness and faith in all your persecutions and in the afflictions that you are enduring" (2 Thess. 1:4). "You ... have followed my teaching, my conduct, my aim in life, my faith, my patience, my love, my steadfastness" (2 Tim. 3:10; cf. Titus 2:2; see further Rev. 1:9; 2:2, 19; 13:10; 14:12). *The* great example of endurance is Christ (2 Thess. 3:5; cf. Rev. 3:10).

The matter is especially referred to in the Canons of Dort

---

50. Bavinck (2008, 4:266–70); Berkhof (1949, 545–49); Berkouwer (1958); Heyns (1988, §2.2.2); Spykman (1992, 500–504); Van Genderen and Velema (2008, §43); Demarest (1997, chapter 11).

(chapter I, rejection of errors 1): Holy Scripture testifies "that God will not only save those who will believe, but that He has also from eternity chosen certain particular persons to whom, above others, He will grant, in time, both faith in Christ and perseverance; . . . ." Subsequently (rejection of errors 5), the Canons reject the error "that therefore faith, the obedience of faith, holiness, godliness, and perseverance are not fruits of the unchangeable election unto glory [as the Canons maintain], but are conditions which, being required beforehand, were foreseen as being met by those who will be fully elected, ..."

Of course, this is quite a unilateral picture. Perseverance is one hundred percent a matter of God's electing and preserving grace. But it is also one hundred percent a matter of human responsibility; otherwise the following apostolic admonitions would be incomprehensible: "Pursue righteousness, godliness, faith, love, steadfastness, gentleness" (1 Tim. 6:11). "[M]ake every effort to supplement your faith with virtue, and virtue with knowledge, and knowledge with self-control, and self-control with steadfastness, and steadfastness with godliness, and godliness with brotherly affection, and brotherly affection with love" (2 Pet. 1:5-7). The Lord said, "[T]he one who endures to the end will be saved" (Matt. 10:22; 24:13). The Canons would rather say: "The one who will be saved will certainly endure." This is not wrong, but unilateral; it leaves out our responsibility: "By your endurance you will gain your lives" (Luke 21:19).

6.7.2 Unilaterality

The Westminster Confession of Faith has a whole chapter (XVII) dealing with the "Perseverance of the Saints": "They, whom God hath accepted in His Beloved, effectually called, and sanctified by His Spirit, can neither totally nor finally fall away from the state of grace, but shall certainly persevere therein to the end, and be eternally saved. This perseverance of the saints depends not upon their own free will, but upon the immutability of the decree of election, flowing from the free and unchangeable love of God the Father; upon the efficacy of the merit and intercession of Jesus Christ, the abiding of the Spirit, and of the seed of God within them, and the nature of the covenant of grace: from all which arises also the certainty and infallibility thereof. Nevertheless, they may, through the temptations of Satan and of the world, the prevalency of corruption remaining in them, and the neglect of the means of their preservation, fall into grievous sins; and, for a time, continue therein: whereby they incur God's displeasure, and grieve His Holy Spirit, come to be deprived of some measure of their graces and comforts, have their hearts hardened, and their consciences wounded; hurt and scandalize others, and bring temporal judgments upon themselves."

We find the same one-sidedness here, leaving out human responsibility. Again, I see this as a consequence of the Arminian trauma, which caused every emphasis on human responsibility to be *a priori* suspect. Notice again Philippians 2:12–13, where the force of verse 12 is not spoilt by verse 13: "[W]ork out your own salvation with fear and trembling, for it is God who works in you, both to will and to work for his good pleasure." A unilateral emphasis on God's sovereign grace may lead to a *false* assurance of faith, just as a unilateral emphasis on human responsibility may wrongly affect our faith assurance, for instance, by leaning entirely upon Hebrews 6:5–6 ("For it is impossible, in the case of those who have once been enlightened, who have tasted the heavenly gift, and have shared in the Holy Spirit, . . . and then have fallen away, to restore them again to repentance") or Hebrews 10:26–27 ("For if we go on sinning deliberately after receiving the knowledge of the truth, there no longer remains a sacrifice for sins, but a fearful expectation of judgment, and a fury of fire that will consume the adversaries").

Let me mention here a striking example of the Arminian trauma, in connection with the very subject of justification. It concerns the Scottish-Dutch theologian Alexander Comrie

(1706–1774), "undoubtedly one of the most able Reformed theologians of the eighteenth century."⁵¹ When it comes to the relationship between faith and justification, Wilhelmus à Brakel (1635–1711), another well-known Reformed theologian, had defended the rather obvious viewpoint that justification follows upon faith. If a person is justified on account of his faith, this faith logically precedes justification. The gift becomes the possession of the beggar only if and when the person factually accepts it. Comrie, however, suffering from what I call the Arminian trauma, saw in Brakel's view the danger of a refined Arminianism, and argued that justification must necessarily *precede* faith. He even concluded that, first, the elect have been justified from eternity through the imputation to them of the righteousness of Christ before the foundation of the world. Second, Comrie postulated an unconscious justification at the point of regeneration, when the sinner receives the *habitus fidei* ("habit [Dutch, *hebbelijkheid*] of faith") and is incorporated into Christ. Third, there is a conscious justification by a purely receiving ("passive") faith in the "court of conscience" (Dutch, *vierschaar der consciëntie*).⁵²

For this complex model there is not a sliver of evidence in the Bible. Scripture does not know of a justification from eternity, nor of a justification that precedes faith. There is only one justification, namely, on account of the faith that the repentant sinner has in God and in the redemptive work of Christ. Yet, Comrie's theory is still accepted by thousands of Reformed Christians in the Netherlands and North America, although it was already refuted by a third Reformed theologian of the time, Theodorus van der Groe (1705–1784).⁵³ Comrie's model is not only a sad consequence of the Arminian trauma, but also of the re-introduction of Aristotelian and Thomistic concepts into the Reformed faith. The fear of ascribing too inde-

---

51. See Ouweneel (2015b, §5.3.3).
52. For the history of this discussion, see Harinck (2007, 118–48, and the summary: 170–75).
53. Ibid., 148–68, and the summary: 175–77.

pendent of a role to faith is a consequence of a unilateral emphasis on predestination.[54] The perspicuity of the gospel has been replaced here by scholastic speculation. In opposition to Comrie and his followers, we maintain that it is quite possible to defend that justification is by faith without at all becoming an Arminian.

6.7.3 "If Indeed"

A unilateral emphasis of God's sovereign grace involves belittling the force of the *if indeed* in, for instance, Colossians 1:22-23 ("he has now reconciled in his body of flesh by his death, in order to present you holy and blameless and above reproach before him, *if indeed* you continue in the faith, stable and steadfast, not shifting from the hope of the gospel that you heard"), or Hebrews 3:6 and 14 ("Christ is faithful over God's house as a son. And we are his house *if indeed* we hold fast our confidence and our boasting in our hope. . . . For we have come to share in Christ, *if indeed* we hold our original confidence firm to the end"). Seen from God's viewpoint, it is perfectly true that if we have been reborn, God will make sure that we will endure until the end. Seen from the human viewpoint, it is equally true that, if and only if we endure until the end, will we be saved. In no way may the two viewpoints be played off against each other.

Of course, the same problem arises with the doctrine of election (a subject that I cannot enter into here; it would demand a separate volume).[55] There is no doubt that Arminius was wrong in limiting predestination to foreknowledge; Paul clearly makes the distinction in Romans 8:29, "For those whom he foreknew he also predestined to be conformed to the image of his Son." Foreknowledge is passive, predestination is rooted in God's active and sovereign grace. However, such a statement may never be played off against human responsibility. "And when the Gentiles heard this, they began

---

54. See Wisse (2003).
55. See extensively, Ouweneel (2008b).

rejoicing and glorifying the word of the Lord, and *as many as were appointed to eternal life* believed" (Acts 13:48) — that is the divine side of election. But five verses later we read, "Now at Iconium they entered together into the Jewish synagogue and spoke *in such a way* that a great number of both Jews and Greeks believed" (14:1) — that is the human responsibility of both the speaker and the listener. God "commands all people everywhere to repent" (17:30) — that is human responsibility.

We have to live with this paradoxical two-sidedness, which cannot be fit into a logical scheme. The authors of the Canons of Dort were already conscious of this paradox. They strongly underscored that election is a work of God's sovereign grace, but they also emphasized that if people refuse to convert, it is their own fault that they will perish (II.6): "And, whereas many who are called by the gospel do not repent nor believe in Christ, but perish in unbelief, this is not owing to any defect or insufficiency in the sacrifice offered by Christ upon the cross, but is wholly to be imputed to themselves." Of course, strictly logically this does not hang together: some are saved by God's mercy, others are lost by their own fault. But we have to live with this because we fully maintain this paradoxical two-sidedness: one hundred percent God's sovereign grace, one hundred percent human responsibility. This is the nature of perseverance. Evangelical theologians who place all the emphasis on human responsibility are mistaken. Reformed theologians who place all the emphasis on God's sovereign grace are equally mistaken.

6.8 Assurance of Faith[56]
6.8.1 Certitude

This tradition of adding perseverance to the enumerated list (§6.7.1) began already with Augustine, who spoke even of the

---

56. See more extensively and practically, Ouweneel (2008c); see further, e.g., Bavinck (1980); Graafland (1961); Erskine (2010; orig.: 1730); Van 't Spijker (1993).

gift of perseverance.[57] In fact, perseverance is nothing but the extension of rebirth, faith, positional justification, and sanctification in the practical life of faith, to which belongs matters such as spiritual growth, spiritual warfare, discipleship, and practical justification and sanctification (see next chapters).

At this point I refer to one peculiar aspect of perseverance, in Latin called *certitudo fidei*, "certitude (assurance) of faith." In ancient theology, this was carefully distinguished from *securitas*, "self-assurance," which is rooted in pride, whereas true assurance of faith is rooted in humility.[58] The Council of Trent earnestly warned against this "vain confidence" (VI.9): "But, although it is necessary to believe that sins neither are remitted, nor ever were remitted save gratuitously by the mercy of God for Christ's sake; yet is it not to be said, that sins are forgiven, or have been forgiven, to any one who *boasts of his confidence and certainty* of the remission of his sins, and rests on that alone; seeing that it may exist, yea does in our day exist, amongst heretics and schismatics [read, Protestants]; and with great vehemence is this *vain confidence*, and one alien from all godliness, preached up in opposition to the Catholic Church" (italics added).

There are two extremes to be avoided here: on the one hand, the lack of possible certainty that the Council preached, and on the other hand the proud conceit against which it rightly warns. The assurance of salvation is not rooted in our own arrogance but in God's merciful promises.

In Reformed circles, the matter of faith assurance is often viewed against the backdrop of what is called the "appropriation (Dutch, *toe-eigening*) of salvation." The question involved in this matter is whether one may appropriate salvation simply by believing and, as a consequence, may assert that one possesses it, and if so, on what grounds one may do this. This question played a great role in discussions between, on the one hand, the Christian Reformed Churches in the Nether-

---

57. *De dono perseverantiae*, "On the Gift of Perseverance."
58. Van Genderen and Velema (2008, 626).

Saving Faith

lands and, on the other hand, the Reformed Churches Liberated (in North America paralleled by the Free Reformed Churches and Canadian Reformed Churches) and the Netherlands Reformed Churches. The book by Willem Van 't Spijker shows how this question has been needlessly complicated by restricting the biblical statements with statements of earlier theologians, with statements from the liturgical Forms (for baptism, the Lord's Supper, etc.) and the confessional writings, and with covenant-theological views.[59] The complaint of Johan Blaauwendraad, from the Netherlands Reformed Congregations—"It has become complicated" [60]—fits into this context as well.

6.8.2 Underestimating Grace

The deepest underlying problem in the entire matter of faith assurance is an underestimation of the riches of God's grace (cf. Eph. 1:7; 2:7; 3:8). Doubters do not know whether they have repented profoundly enough, or whether they have enough faith, or whether they have the right kind of faith. They are far too occupied with themselves—spiritual navel-gazing—and see far too inadequately that God's actions are not based on our (measure of) repentance, or (measure of) faith, but *on his own being*, and on the value of Christ and his work. Those who look at the depth of their repentance, or at the quantity or quality of their faith, are surreptitiously inventing human conditions again. On God's side, the whole matter is complete, and in no way dependent on the measure of our repentance or faith. God comes to a person, not on account of the latter's having fulfilled certain (often complicated) conditions but on account of the fullness of his (God's) grace and the all-sufficiency of Christ's work.[61]

The objection will be raised that faith *is* the condition for receiving this grace of God. Without faith we will not receive

---

59. Van 't Spijker (1993).
60. Blaauwendraad (1997).
61. Cf. Coates (n.d.-b, 10–11).

God's grace. In itself, this is right, but we have to be careful here with the word "condition." Conditional grace is in fact no grace at all. The sinner's faith adds nothing to the gospel as such, just as the windows of our houses add nothing to the light of the sun that is streaming in.[62] The sun shines for everyone; our windows let the light come into our rooms, so that we enjoy it and are warmed by it. Likewise, the sun of God's grace shines for everyone; faith is the window that lets the light and warmth of grace come into the sinner's soul.

To use another example: if someone is drowning, and we throw a lifeline to him, and he grabs it, this person will be saved. Technically speaking, we might say that his grabbing the line is a "condition" for his salvation. But such speaking does not do justice to the situation. The drowning man is not presented with two options: grabbing the line, or not. He *has* no option but to grab the line if he does not wish to die. If he grabs it, this is no merit, it is no achievement, it is not a laudable act—it is a matter of life and death. And it is certainly not a matter of navel-gazing: Is the line really for me? Am I allowed to grab it? Am I in the right mental condition for it? Do I deserve that line? Do I know how to properly grab it? What will people say if I grab it "just like that"? No, stop puzzling—*grab it*. The line is *pure grace*—enjoy it!

There is yet another point to be mentioned here. Those who claim to have (assurance of) faith but, because of their indifference, hardly know the joy of faith, do not underestimate the grace of God—they *despise* it. Those, however, who do not know the assurance of faith but do yearn for it, often have a deep sense of God's grace—so deep that they suffer under the opposite problem: the burning question whether such riches of grace could really be for them. Such persons must learn to disregard their feelings entirely, and even (the quality or quantity of) their faith, and learn to look to God and to Christ alone.[63]

---

62. Ibid., 12.
63. Ibid., 13–14.

"See to it that no one fails to obtain the grace of God" (Heb. 12:15; NKJV: ". . . looking carefully lest anyone fall short of the grace of God"). Do you earnestly *desire* to receive God's grace? Then listen: "[L]et the one who is thirsty come; let the one who *desires* take the water of life without price" (Rev. 22:17) — a reference to Isaiah 55:1, "Come, everyone who thirsts, come to the waters; and he who has no money, come, buy and eat! Come, buy wine and milk without money and without price."

6.9 Knowledge of Faith
6.9.1 Believing Is Knowing

Biblical believing is different than what people mean in everyday parlance ("you should not 'believe' but know for sure"). It is a certain assurance: "[F]aith is the assurance of things hoped for, the conviction of things not seen" (Heb. 11:1). The former part of this verse represents the horizontal dimension: God's promises whose fulfillment lies before us (cf. vv. 9-16); the latter part represents the vertical dimension of faith: looking up to God (cf. v. 27).

Faith is all the more certain because, so to say, God has placed the seal of the Holy Spirit on it (Eph. 1:13): "The Spirit himself bears witness with our spirit that we are children of God" (Rom. 8:16). The Heidelberg Catechism combines the two elements of knowing and trusting (Q&A 21): "True faith is not only a sure knowledge, whereby I hold for truth all that God has revealed to us in His Word, but also a hearty trust, which the Holy Ghost works in me by the Gospel, that not only to others, but to me also, forgiveness of sins, everlasting righteousness, and salvation are freely given by God, merely of grace, only for the sake of Christ's merits."

Strikingly, according to Reformed writer Aart Moerkerken, this "wholehearted trust" does *not* mean "the assurance of faith."[64] However, what does Q&A 21, entirely in the spirit of Scripture, mean other than that faith leans on the

---
64. Moerkerken (2004, 109–110).

sure promises of God's Word and *in them* seeks and finds its assurance? See, for instance: "Believe in the Lord Jesus, and you will be saved" (Acts 16:35). "[I]f you confess with your mouth that Jesus is Lord and believe in your heart that God raised him from the dead, you will be saved" (Rom. 10:9). The basis for our certainty is not faith as such, but the promises of God.[65] As the Canons of Dort put it (V.10): "This assurance, however, is not produced by any peculiar revelation contrary to or independent of the Word of God, but springs from faith in God's promises, which He has most abundantly revealed in His Word for our comfort; from the testimony of the Holy Spirit, witnessing with our spirit that we are children and heirs of God (Rom. 8:16); and lastly, from a serious and holy desire to preserve a good conscience and to perform good works."

Time and again, this is the message: if we do A (repent, believe, confess, come to God), God on his behalf guarantees that he will do B (accept, assure, regenerate, justify, sanctify). This is the *objective* feature of faith assurance: it does not lie in our feelings, our mood of the moment, but in the solid, immovable promises of God. He who does A may surely know that God will do B: "[E]veryone who calls upon the name of the Lord *shall be saved*" (Joel 2:32; Acts 2:21; Rom. 10:13). "Come to me, all who labor and are heavy laden, and *I will give you rest*" (Matt. 11:28). "[W]hoever hears my word and believes him who sent me *has eternal life*. He does not come into judgment, but has passed from death to life" (John 5:24). "My sheep hear my voice, and I know them, and they follow me. *I give them eternal life*, and they will never perish, and no one will snatch them out of my hand" (10:27-28). Confess your sins, and *God will surely forgive* you your sins and cleanse you from all unrighteousness (1 John 1:9). All these passages supply us with an absolute guarantee without any further conditions. You only have to stretch out your hand, and God will fill it (cf. Ps. 104:28).

---

65. Van Genderen and Velema (2008, 670).

The *subjective* feature we find in the Canons of Dort (I.12): "The elect in due time, though in various degrees and in different measures, attain the assurance of this their eternal and unchangeable election, . . . by observing in themselves with a spiritual joy and holy pleasure the infallible fruits of election pointed out in the Word of God—such as, a true faith in Christ, filial fear, a godly sorrow for sin, a hungering and thirsting after righteousness, etc." (cf. 2 Cor. 13:5).

The advantage of the objective feature of faith assurance is that the latter lies entirely in God's promises, and not in anything that one observes in or with oneself. People find the assurance in God's Word, not in their inward parts. The advantage of the subjective feature is that by it they can measure the reality that, since they confessed their sins and accepted Jesus in faith, something has really changed in them. The alleged disadvantage of the objective feature is that some people would love to have more than "just" a promise. They would like to see some renewal within themselves before they would dare to be assured of God's promise. The alleged disadvantage of the subjective feature is that some would rather concentrate on their own fruits, observing their ups and downs within themselves, and then conclude from the downs that presumably they are not really saved after all. Such Christians must always and repeatedly be pointed back to God's unchangeable promises.[66]

6.9.2 Five Objections

Many Reformed Christians, especially those who suffer under a one-sided preaching of predestination (hyper-Calvinists), often doubt their salvation. They wrestle with questions like the following.[67]

(1) *How can I know whether I have been elected?*

Reply: Paul knew that the Thessalonian believers had been

---
66. Cf. Berkhof (1979, 471–76).
67. Cf. Ouweneel (2008b, especially chapters 10–14); also see Ouweneel (2008c).

elected on account of their acceptance of the gospel: "For we know, brothers loved by God, that he has chosen you, because our gospel came to you not only in word, but also in power and in the Holy Spirit and with full conviction . . . you became imitators of us and of the Lord, for you received the word in much affliction, with the joy of the Holy Spirit" (1 Thess. 1:4-6). No one can know whether he has been elected as long as he has not accepted the gospel. To put it even more strongly: every claim that someone had first received the assurance of his election before he converted is nothing but (self-)deceit. It is first conversion and faith, then the assurance of salvation. Therefore, in Scripture, election—or eternal reprobation for that matter—is never preached as a threat to unbelievers, but only as a consolation to believers.

(2) *How can I know whether the gospel is for me too?*

Reply: the gospel is for *all* people: "For God so love the *world* . . ." (John 3:16); "one act of righteousness leads to justification and life for *all men*" (Rom. 5:18); "God our Savior, who desires *all people* to be saved and to come to the knowledge of the truth" (1 Tim. 2:3-4); "the grace of God has appeared, bringing salvation for *all people*" (Titus 2:11). The Lord is "not wishing that any should perish, but that *all* should reach repentance" (2 Pet. 3:9).[68] Let no one try to convince us otherwise: God *means* it when he desires all people to be saved, and does not wish that any should perish. There is no one to whom the gospel is offered without God *meaning* it, there is no one who allegedly is ineligible for it, there is no one who needs to be scared because of some alleged decree of reprobation. The gospel is for everyone: it needs only to be accepted. Only hyper-Calvinists—those who preach a unilateral doctrine of predestination—have difficulty with this.

(3) *Can one receive Christ "just like that"?*

Reply: Scripture mentions no impediment: "[T]o *all* who did receive him, who believed in his name, he gave the right

---

68. Cf. Ouweneel (2008b, chapter 13).

to become children of God" (John 1:12); "as you received Christ Jesus the Lord, so walk in him" (Col. 2:6); "you became imitators of us and of the Lord, for you received the word in much affliction, with the joy of the Holy Spirit" (1 Thess. 1:6; cf. 2:13). To put it even more strongly: you not only *may* receive Christ, you *must* receive Christ; this is an act of obedience, as we saw earlier (John 3:36; Acts 6:7; Rom. 1:5). We *must* be born again, says Jesus (John 3:7), and we *must* be saved, says Peter, namely through Jesus (Acts 4:12). God commands all people everywhere to repent (17:30). Those who do not come to Christ cannot appeal to whatever doctrine of reprobation or appropriation; they are guilty because they are disobedient to the gospel.

(4) *Is my repentance profound enough?*

Reply: Who will ever dare to claim that he has sufficiently regretted his sins? And where does Scripture make salvation depend on the depth of our repentance? Even the slightest repentance suffices to set God into motion (1 Kings 21:27-29). "If you, O Lord, should mark iniquities, O Lord, who could stand? But with you there is forgiveness, that you may be feared" (Ps. 130:3-4). For the psalm writer, this was enough. 1 John 1:9 does not speak of the depth of our contrition but of the necessity of confessing our sins. Of course, such confession must be genuine, and this presupposes a certain measure of contrition. But forgiveness is never rooted in the depth of our contrition and repentance, but in the depth of God's mercy.

(5) *Is my faith great enough?*

Reply: Probably not; who would ever say of himself that his faith is great enough? The disciples with their "little faith" (Matt. 6:30; 8:26; 14:31; 16:8; 17:20; cf. the contrast with 15:28) were nevertheless true believers (see §7.1). They prayed, "Increase our faith!" (Luke 17:5-6), and sometimes we pray this too. However, this has more to do with our daily walk of faith than with our eternal salvation.

6.9.3 Four Other Objections

(6) *Do I have true faith, or is mine only a faith "for a while" (Luke 8:13), or only a "historical faith" (a belief in dogmas without a regenerate heart), or a "miraculous faith" (John 2:23–25)?*

Reply: In the parable of the sower, true faith is the faith that produces fruit (Matt. 13:8, 23) (cf. the Canons of Dort as quoted in §6.9.1). It is even better if the believer does not look at all to himself and his fruits, but only to Christ: "And the Lord said to Moses, 'Make a fiery serpent and set it on a pole, and everyone who is bitten, when he sees it, shall live.' So Moses made a bronze serpent and set it on a pole. And if a serpent bit anyone, he would look at the bronze serpent and live" (Num. 21:8–9).

Sometimes it is preached to indecisive souls: "'Son of man, dig in the wall.' So I dug in the wall, and behold, there was an entrance. And he said to me, 'Go in, and see the vile abominations that they are committing here.' Then he said to me, 'Son of man, have you seen what the elders of the house of Israel are doing in the dark . . .? You will see still greater abominations that they commit'" (Ezek. 8:8–9, 12–13). In other words, Do not imagine too quickly that you have faith; first dig deeper, and you will find even more abominations; only when you will have reached the bottom will we start talking about conversion.

Such preaching is not only mistaken—it is cruel. Such preachers demand a sea of contrition before they allow the poor sinner a teacup of grace, whereas in the Bible it is the other way round. Ezekiel 8 does not speak at all to poor, unsure souls, but to the prophet who had to judge the spiritual condition of Israel. In a similar way, unsure believers can be discouraged by certain preachers with Matthew 7:22–23, "On that day many will say to me, 'Lord, Lord, did we not prophesy in your name, and cast out demons in your name, and do many mighty works in your name?' And then will I declare to them, 'I never knew you; depart from me, you workers of lawlessness'" — as if indecisive believers could ever be called "workers of lawlessness." "But woe to you, scribes and Pharisees, hypocrites! For you shut the kingdom of heaven in people's faces. For you neither enter yourselves nor allow those who would enter to go in" (Matt. 23:13-14).

(7) *I do pray for forgiveness, but I do not feel anything.*

Reply: You cannot feel whether someone has forgiven you; you can only take him at his word. You may feel that his words are sincere, but it is his words that are decisive, not your feelings. Our assurance is not rooted in what we feel, experience, and argue, but in what we believe; it is a matter of trust in God and his Word. He has said that he forgives our sins when we confess them (1 John 1:9). Either you believe this, or you don't. A person does not know that he has been forgiven by feeling good, rather he will feel good when he believes that he has been forgiven. The only thing that one has to do is confess one's sins. Whether, in reply to this, God forgives us, we will know by believing God's promises, not by feeling. The joy of salvation (cf. Ps. 51:12) is not a condition for, but a result of, salvation. Faith is not rooted in feeling, but feeling in faith.

(8) *But I still commit so many sins . . .*

Reply: That is a pity, for it is not necessary: "[S]in will have no dominion over you, since you are not under law but under grace" (Rom. 6:14); the "righteous requirement of the law" is "fulfilled in us, who walk not according to the flesh but according to the Spirit" (8:4). "My little children, I am writing these things to you so *that you may not sin*. But if anyone does sin, we have an advocate with the Father, Jesus Christ the righteous" (1 John 2:1). Unfortunately, you may still sin — but this does not alter your regeneration. A bad child is a child of his parents just as much as a good child. This does not take away the Christian's responsibility to live a holy life, but learning to deal with the sinful nature in the power of the Holy Spirit is quite a developmental process (see next chapters). Babies in

Christ do not have to be ashamed that they still make (many) babylike errors; they would have to be ashamed only if, after ten years, they were still behaving like babies (1 Cor. 3:1-3; Heb. 5:12-14).

(9) *How do I know whether I will endure to the end?*

Reply: If this would depend on your own strength and faithfulness, this would indeed remain an open question. In fact, without taking away anything from your own responsibility, in the end this depends on the faithfulness of God, on his promises and his Spirit (see next chapter).

Some people seem to think that it is very humble of them to openly doubt their own salvation, but in fact there is an element of pride in this. True humility is recognizing that everything is of God, and nothing of ourselves. The "best robe" has been put on you (Luke 15:22), so who are you to keep speaking of your "polluted garment" (Isa. 64:6)? The Father has qualified you to share in the inheritance of the saints in light (Col. 1:12), so why do you keep talking about your lack of quality? Your sins have been cast into the depths of the sea (Micah 7:19), so how dare you bring them above the surface time and again? That is not humility but unbelief, if not arrogance. True humility is not that you talk bad about yourself all the time, but that you stop talking about yourself, and start talking about God and his grace, Christ and his glory. That will make you a happier person.

Chapter 7
Practical Faith

"But if God so clothes the grass of the field,
. . .
will he not much more clothe you,
O you of little faith? . . .
But seek first the kingdom of God and his righteousness,
and all these things will be added to you."
Matthew 6:30–33

The apostles said to the Lord,
"Increase our faith!"
And the Lord said, "If you had faith like a grain of mustard seed,
you could say to this mulberry tree,
'Be uprooted and planted in the sea,'
and it would obey you."
Luke 17:5–6

She said, "Yes, Lord, yet even the dogs eat the crumbs that fall from their masters' table."
Then Jesus answered her, "O woman, great is your faith!
Be it done for you as you desire."

> *And her daughter was healed instantly.*
> Matthew 15:27-28

Summary: *Positional justification is attained by means of saving faith, practical justification is maintained by practical everyday confidence. Such faith can be little, growing, or great; the New Testament supplies us with examples of all three levels. The chapter further deals with overcoming faith, discouraged faith, susceptible faith, the power of unbelief, miracle-working faith, creative faith (understanding things that were not explicitly revealed to it, or finding inventive ways to the Lord), immanent and transcendent-existential doubt of faith (and how to handle it), and conditions of faith. Can faith bring about things with God? That is, can God change his mind, or has he determined all events from eternity? If yes, what then is the use of a great faith and of the prayer of faith? What is the perseverance of Christians, and how does it relate to the question whether Christians can fall away from their faith? If the latter can happen, how is assurance of faith possible? What are the theological and the pastoral aspects of this important question?*

7.1 Little Faith[1]
7.1.1 Introduction

THE PREVIOUS CHAPTER and this one seem to deal with two different subjects: saving faith, linked with positional justification, and practical faith, linked with practical justification. Just as we will never understand positional justification without understanding what saving faith is, we will never understand practical justification if we do not understand what practical faith is. Take the two examples of James 2: Abraham was justified in the *practical* sense by doing a great *work* of faith: offering up his son Isaac (v. 21). And Rahab was justified in the *practical* sense by also doing a great *work* of faith: receiving the messengers of Israel, and sending them out by another way (v. 25). We are *positionally* justified by faith resulting in works, and we are *practically* justified by works of faith.

---
1. See on this chapter Ouweneel (2004b, chapter 10).

Practical Faith

The two kinds of faith are clearly distinct, though inseparably connected. One might put it this way: saving faith takes us to heaven, practical faith takes us through this world. The first great question of life that every human has to answer is: Satan's kingdom or God's Kingdom (Matt. 12:25-28)? After this question has been resolved through regeneration, faith, and justification, the second question arises: do we wish to live for the present world (2 Tim. 4:10), or for the world to come (Heb. 2:5)? Or, viewed from a different perspective: we have faith to become part of the Messianic Kingdom that is to come—but do we also have (enough) faith to get through this world on our way to the Kingdom? We have faith to enter into the promised land, but do we also have faith to get through the wilderness? We trust God as far as our eternal destination is concerned. Do we also (sufficiently) trust him as far as our daily circumstances and our course through this world are concerned?

The point is that these are not two different "faiths"—it is the one faith that takes us to the world to come *and* that takes us through the present world, although we do distinguish between saving grace and practical faith. By the way, we realize that, in the New Testament, salvation is sometimes viewed as a present possession (Eph. 2:5, 8), but more often it is presented as a future reality: "Since, therefore, we have now been justified by his blood, much more *shall* we be saved by him from the wrath of God. For if while we were enemies we were reconciled to God by the death of his Son, much more, now that we are reconciled, *shall* we be saved by his life" (Rom. 5:9-10). "[S]alvation is nearer to us now than when we first believed" (13:11). "For God has not destined us for wrath, but to obtain salvation through our Lord Jesus Christ" (1 Thess. 5:9). "Therefore I endure everything for the sake of the elect, that they also may obtain the salvation that is in Christ Jesus with eternal glory" (2 Tim. 2:10). The believers are those "who by God's power are being guarded through faith for a salvation ready to be revealed in the last time" (1 Pet. 1:3-5). This is the "salvation" linked with the Messianic Kingdom: "Now the salvation and the power and the kingdom of our God and the authority of his Christ have come" (Rev. 12:10).

In this sense, practical faith is just as much saving faith in that it is the faith that carries us through all circumstances of life until we reach the goal of our lives, the Kingdom of God, which is also called "salvation." Positional and practical justification form an unbreakable continuum. If we do not observe practical faith in a person's life, we are not allowed to conclude that there ever was something like positional justification or saving faith in the person. The believer puts his trust in God for his eternal destiny as well as for his daily circumstances, for Canaan and for the wilderness; in essence, it is one and the same faith. Sometimes the two aspects of faith can hardly be distinguished, as for instance, in Luke 22:32, where Jesus says to Peter: "I have prayed for you that your faith may not fail."

The two must not be separated but definitely must be distinguished. Take, for example, "I believed, even when I spoke: 'I am greatly afflicted'" (Ps. 116:10), or, "Immediately the father of the child cried out and said, 'I believe; help my unbelief!'" (Mark 9:24), or, "Have faith in God. Truly, I say to you, whoever says to this mountain, 'Be taken up and thrown into the sea,' and does not doubt in his heart, but believes that what he says will come to pass, it will be done for him. Therefore I tell you, whatever you ask in prayer, believe that you have received it, and it will be yours" (11:22-24). These are instances of practical faith, not of saving faith.

7.1.2 "Size" of Faith?

Gerrit C. Berkouwer nowhere acknowledges any difference between the two kinds of faith,[2] whereas, in my view, Scripture does so clearly. For example, whether saving faith is weak or strong does not in fact make any difference when it comes to entering into God's Kingdom. With practical faith

---
2. Berkouwer (1954, chapter 7).

this is very different: those who have a great faith stand differently—better—in life than those with little faith. Let us take a closer look.

The Greek terms *oligopistia* ("little faith," only in Matthew 17:20) and *oligopistos* ("one of little faith," four times in Matthew) never have anything to do with saving faith, but always with practical, everyday confidence in God. If a lack of faith assurance is a lack of confidence in the former sense (saving faith), then little faith is a lack of confidence in the latter sense (practical faith). Richard T. France says: "In [Matthew] 17:20 we shall see that *oligopistia* means having faith less than a mustard seed, in effect no faith at all. 'Faith,' in Matthew, means the confidence that God can and will act on his people's behalf; without that, however much a person may 'believe' intellectually, they are for practical purposes 'faithless.'"[3] Here, the heart of the matter is clearly indicated: in Matthew, faith is practical confidence that God will never fail his people.

However, in my view, it goes too far to identify little faith with no faith at all, as France does: "Faith is not a measurable commodity but a relationship, and what achieves results through prayer is not a superior 'quantity' of faith but the unlimited power of God on which faith, any faith, can draw."[4] Indeed, faith is a relationship, but it is definitely quantifiable: one can have much or little confidence in God. What would be the use of speaking of "little faith" and "great faith," and of an "increase" of faith (Luke 17:5), if faith were not quantifiable in any way? Paul can speak of a person's "great confidence [Greek, *pepoithēsis*] in you" (2 Cor. 8:22), also of "great confidence [*parrēsia*] in the faith that is in Christ Jesus" (1 Tim. 3:13). Elsewhere, France does make a distinction: he calls *oligopistia* a "less absolute term" than *apistia* ("unbelief").[5] Of course; I would even say that having little faith is infinitely different

---

3. France (2007, 270).
4. Ibid., 662-61.; cf. also 264n6, 336, 566n6.
5. Ibid., 550.

from unbelief. Compare the distinction in John 15 between "no fruit" (implied in v. 6), which leads to eternal perdition, and "little fruit," which should become "more fruit" (v. 2) and eventually "much fruit," for the glory of the Father (vv. 5 and 8). There is a tremendous difference between "little life" and "no life," "little fruit" and "no fruit," "little faith" and "no faith." It is the difference between life and death.

There is one event in which Jesus seems to make hardly any distinction between "no faith" ("O faithless and twisted generation . . .") and "little faith" (Matt. 17:17 and 20). But this is only true if in verse 17 the disciples are thought to be included in Jesus' rebuke. Some expositors have flatly denied this, such as John Gill: Jesus' words are "a way of speaking, which is never used of the disciples, and indeed could not be properly said of them; for though they often appeared to be men of little faith, yet not faithless; nor were they so rebellious, stubborn, and perverse, as here represented, though there was a great deal of perverseness in them."[6] But the Pulpit Commentary says, "He seems to include in this denunciation all who were present—the father, scribes, people, apostles, especially the nine. Want of faith appertained to all."[7] Donald A. Carson even believes that "the disciples' unbelief is central to Jesus' exasperation."[8] Richard T. France seems to include the disciples as well.[9]

7.1.3 Five Cases

These are the five cases of "little faith" (*oligopistia*) in Matthew.

(a) *Worry:* "But if God so clothes the grass of the field, which today is alive and tomorrow is thrown into the oven, will he not much more clothe you, *O you of little faith*? Therefore do not be anxious, saying, 'What shall we eat?' or 'What shall we drink?' or 'What shall we wear?' For the Gentiles

---

6. http://biblehub.com/matthew/17-17.htm.
7. Ibid.
8. Carson (1984, 391).
9. France (2007, 660).

seek after all these things, and your heavenly Father knows that you need them all" (Matt. 6:30-32; cf. Luke 12:28-31). The apostles have picked up this theme as well: "[D]o not be anxious about anything, but in everything by prayer and supplication with thanksgiving let your requests be made known to God" (Phil. 4:6); ". . . casting all your anxieties on him, because he cares for you" (1 Pet. 5:7). It belongs to spiritual maturity that, even under the most difficult circumstances, the believer trusts God for his daily needs: flood and clothing: "[I]f we have food and clothing, with these we will be content" (1 Tim. 6:8; cf. Matt. 16:8-9). "Who among us can dwell with the consuming fire? . . . He who walks righteously and speaks uprightly . . . his bread will be given him; his water will be sure" (Isa. 33:14-16). A theologian from a poor country wrote about this:[10] "Instead of worrying, we must learn to focus on serving the Lord wholeheartedly, doing our best and leaving the rest to him ([Mat.] 6:33)."

(b) *Fear:* "And behold, there arose a great storm on the sea, so that the boat was being swamped by the waves; but he was asleep. And they went and woke him, saying, 'Save us, Lord; we are perishing.' And he said to them, 'Why are you afraid [Greek, *deilos*], O you of little faith?' Then he rose and rebuked the winds and the sea, and there was a great calm" (Matt. 8:24-26). The spiritually mature Christian entrusts himself with confidence to God, even in the greatest distress: "God gave us a spirit not of fear [*deilia*] but of power and love and self-control" (2 Tim. 1:7, which here refers especially to the fear of witnessing). Fear is not only a sign of little faith but even more so of unbelief; it is striking to read: "But as for the cowardly [*deilos*], the faithless [*apistos*], . . . their portion will be in the lake that burns with fire and sulfur, which is the second death" (Rev. 21:8). Here, the cowardly are the opposite of the conquerors (v. 7; cf. 12:11; 15:2). Even a little faith may be enough to overcome; the cowardly have no faith at all.

---

10. J. Kapolyo in Adeyemo (2006, 1123).

(c) *Doubt:* "Peter got out of the boat and walked on the water and came to Jesus. But when he saw the wind, he was afraid, and beginning to sink he cried out, 'Lord, save me.' Jesus immediately reached out his hand and took hold of him, saying to him, 'O you of little faith, why did you doubt?'" (Matt. 14:29-31). The spiritually mature dares to leave the safety of the boat, and to undertake great works of faith together with the Lord — walking on water — without doubting and being concerned about circumstances: "[T]he one who doubts is like a wave of the sea that is driven and tossed by the wind. For that person must not suppose that he will receive anything from the Lord; he is a double-minded man, unstable in all his ways" (James 1:6-8). For more about doubt, see §7.6.

(d) *Pettiness:* "When the disciples reached the other side, they had forgotten to bring any bread. Jesus said to them, 'Watch and beware of the leaven of the Pharisees and Sadducees.' And they began discussing it among themselves, saying, 'We brought no bread.' But Jesus, aware of this, said, '*O you of little faith*, why are you discussing among yourselves the fact that you have no bread?'" (Matt. 16:5-8). The accusation of having little faith refers here to the disciples' narrow-minded perspective: always occupied with bread, and not with the Kingdom of God:[11] "But seek first the kingdom of God and his righteousness, and all these things will be added to you. Therefore do not be anxious about tomorrow, for tomorrow will be anxious for itself. Sufficient for the day is its own trouble" (6:33-34).

(e) *Weakness:* "Then the disciples came to Jesus privately and said, 'Why could we not cast it out?' He said to them, 'Because of your *little faith*. For truly, I say to you, if you have faith like a grain of mustard seed, you will say to this mountain, "Move from here to there," and it will move, and nothing will be impossible for you'" (17:19-20; cf. 21:21; Mark

---

11. Bruce (1979, 221).

11:23; Luke 17:6; 1 Cor. 13:2). Jesus does not necessarily suggest that the disciples' faith was even smaller than a mustard seed, but points out what even a limited faith can bring about, just as a mustard seed can grow out to become a tree (cf. Luke 13:19).[12] Some would identify this faith as *fides miraculorum:* faith as susceptibility to miracles (also called "miraculous faith"; see §§7.2-7.4). In this case, this miraculous faith has a positive meaning (cf. §6.2.2). A striking example is the following: "When he entered the house, the blind men came to him, and Jesus said to them, 'Do you believe that I am able to do this?' They said to him, 'Yes, Lord.' Then he touched their eyes, saying, 'According to your faith be it done to you.' And their eyes were opened" (Matt. 9:28-30).

7.2 Growing Faith
7.2.1 Practical Exercises

In Luke 17:5, we find something similar to Matthew 17:19-20: "The apostles said to the Lord, 'Increase our faith!'" In Greek this is *prosthes hēmin pistin,* "Increase to us [our] faith" (GNT, "Make our faith greater"; ERV and MSG, "Give us more faith!"). The Lord answered (v. 6), "If you had faith like a grain of mustard seed, you could say to this mulberry tree, 'Be uprooted and planted in the sea,' and it would obey you." I link this passage with the references in Matthew just given: those who have *little* faith can ask for *more* faith. The disciples do so here, and indirectly Jesus seems to answer their question in a positive way. He makes clear to them that the disciples need a faith as vital and powerful as a mustard seed, which ineluctably grows into a stout tree.[13]

A faith of this size (a quantitative term) or nature (a qualitative term) can bring about great miracles. In the power of this faith, the believer can conquer *this* mountain or *this* mulberry tree—not *every* mountain or tree, but this special one,

---

12. Ibid., 233.
13. *Contra* P. J. Isaak in Adeyemo (2006, 1237), who wants to conclude from Jesus' reply that faith is *not* a quantity that can be measured.

which stands directly in the believer's way. For a mature faith *nothing is impossible*, as Jesus implicitly indicates (Matt. 17:20). That is, to be sure, all things are possible *with God* (Mark 10:27) but in practice, this does not imply that all things are possible *with believers*. This is the case only with those who have a great faith (see §7.3).[14]

The disciples' faith was mixed with doubt and worry, and as a consequence it had little strength. However, this does not imply that our Christian life depends only upon the size of our faith. Believers should not look to their little faith, or to the size of their faith in general, but to Jesus. The father of the boy with the unclean spirit said to Jesus, "I believe; help my unbelief" (Mark 9:24). The little faith of the father did not have to be ratcheted up before the miracle could take place.[15] The father, and the disciples as well, needed only to look to Jesus. As he said to Jairus, "Do not fear, only believe" (5:36), he said to the boy's father, "All things are possible for one who believes" (9:23).

Incidentally, Jairus provides us a good example of a growing faith. This man had sufficient faith for Jesus to come to his house and heal his sick daughter but, at the outset, he did not have enough faith for Jesus to raise his daughter from the dead. This is why he hurried Jesus as much as he could. The people around Jairus had the same limited faith: "While he [i.e., Jesus] was still speaking, there came from the ruler's house some who said [to Jairus], 'Your daughter is dead. Why trouble the Teacher any further?'" (5:35). They really thought it was too late now: the sick daughter had become a dead daughter, and was now beyond the reach of Jesus' power. When Jesus replied, "Do not fear, only believe," he was trying to convince Jairus that even in this greater distress he should place his confidence in him (Jesus), even if he would now need a greater faith than he had before.

It was a bit similar with the official in Capernaum (John

---

14. Ouweneel (2004a, 172–73).
15. Cf. Kraan (1974, 394).

4:46–53). At the outset, he had faith enough for Jesus to come to his house and heal his sick son. However, Jesus refused. Instead, he tested the man's faith by a simple word: "Go; your son will live" (v. 50). What would the official do now? Would he be disappointed that Jesus did not want to come with him? No, his faith began to grow: "The man believed the word that Jesus spoke to him and went on his way." He had come to the insight that Jesus' pure word of power, in spite of the distance, would be sufficient to heal his son.

7.2.2 The Measure of Faith

We can pray that the Lord will increase our faith, but sometimes the Lord is doing this already by the circumstances through which we have to go. It is part of every Christian's spiritual growth that God helps us to develop a greater faith. The two fathers described in the previous section had to learn to have greater expectations of the Lord than they had possessed so far.

Consider the story in Matthew 9:27–30: "And as Jesus passed on from there, two blind men followed him, crying aloud, 'Have mercy on us, Son of David.' When he entered the house, the blind men came to him, and Jesus said to them, 'Do you believe that I am able to do this?' They said to him, 'Yes, Lord.' Then he touched their eyes, saying, 'According to your faith be it done to you.' And their eyes were opened." Please notice that the two men did not explicitly ask for healing; they simply entrusted themselves to the mercy of the Lord. It is not certain, then, whether, at the outset of the event, they had sufficient faith to be healed. In our day we would say that the blind men would already have accepted it as a wonderful token of God's mercy if they had received a guide dog or the financial means to learn Braille. But the Lord challenged their faith; in my words: "Do you have faith enough to be *healed*?" *Then* the men say, "Yes, Lord." And notice the Lord's reply: "According to your faith — which can be read as: According to the *measure* of your faith — be it done to you."

This element of a "measure" of faith is clearer in Romans 12:3, where Paul exhorts the believers "to think with sober judgment, each according to the measure of faith [Greek, *metron pisteōs*, GNT: amount of faith] that God has assigned." And a little further (v. 6): "Having gifts that differ according to the grace given to us, let us use them: if prophecy, in proportion to our faith [*kata tēn analogian tēs pisteōs*]." The word "proportion" (cf. NKJV, NASB) suggests "measure" or "amount" here, as in verse 3. Others prefer a translation that is not so much quantitative but rather qualitative: "Whoever has the gift of prophecy should use that gift in a way that fits the kind of faith they have" (v. 6 ERV). As August Tholuck wrote: "Faith in an unseen Christ brings man into connection with a world unseen, in which he moves without distinctly apprehending it; and in proportion as he learns to look with faith to that world, the more is the measure of his spiritual powers elevated."[16]

Here again, "measure" can also be viewed from a more qualitative standpoint. The man that was born blind did have faith to carry out the strange task that Jesus gave him (vv. 6-7, "he spit on the ground and made mud with the saliva . . . anointed the man's eyes with the mud and said to him, 'Go, wash in the pool of Siloam'"). However, he did not yet believe *in Jesus*, simply because he did not yet know him. When Jesus asked him: "Do you believe in the Son of Man?" the man said, "And who is he, sir, that I may believe in him?" Jesus replied, "You have seen him, and it is he who is speaking to you." He said, "Lord, I believe," and he worshiped him (vv. 35-38). The man's faith grew from a "believing *that*" into a "believing *in*." First, his faith involved a miracle, afterward his faith involved the miracle-doer.

7.2.3 Faith and Hyper-Calvinism

Just as a growing faith can receive more from the Lord than before, a dwindling faith, or the absence of faith, can hinder

---

16. Tholuck (2008, ad loc.).

us receiving from him (cf. Mark 6:5). In a hyper-Calvinist view, in which God's sovereignty is taken to mean that no action on Man's behalf can ever influence what God does, this is incomprehensible. The hyper-Calvinist could never have written: "[T]he prayer of faith will save the one who is sick" (James 5:15),[17] because, allegedly, prayers cannot heal a person, only God can do that. Moreover, faith allegedly does not add anything to God's sovereign will either to heal a person or not to heal him. However, Scripture speaks otherwise. It is not said that *God* can move mountains—of course he can (Ps. 104:8)—but that *faith* can do that: ". . . if I have a faith that can move mountains" (1 Cor. 13:2 NIV; cf. Matt. 17:20; 21:21). In a freer rendering: "I may have faith so great that I can move mountains" (ERV); "I may have all the faith needed to move mountains" (GNT). The hyper-Calvinist could never say, "Your *faith* has saved you" (Luke 7:50; thus also literally in Mark 5:34; 10:52; Luke 17:19), because, he would insist that only God can save.

Faith asks great things of God, a growing faith asks even greater things of God, a great faith asks the greatest things of God. "You do not have, because you do not ask," says James 4:2, whereas the hyper-Calvinist would say, "You do not have because God sovereignly decided not to give to you." Jesus says: "Ask, and it will be given to you" (Matt. 7:7; Luke 11:9). Of course, we have to "ask according to his will" (1 John 5:14). But this does not change the fact that Scripture makes a direct connection between our asking in faith and God's answering in response. The hyper-Calvinist, however, would argue that everything God wishes to give us was decided before the foundation of the world; our asking does not add anything to this fact.

Perhaps the most impressive example in Scripture is Ezekiel 22: "The people of the land have practiced extortion and committed robbery. . . . And I sought for a man among them

---

17. See on this passage extensively, Ouweneel (2004a, chapter 10).

who should build up the wall and stand in the breach before me for the land, that I should not destroy it, but I found none. Therefore I have poured out my indignation upon them" (vv. 29-31). Here it is said in clear language: according to his righteousness, God had to judge the nation; but in his love, he wanted to show them his mercy. However, there was no one who asked for it, there was no intercessor, so that God, humanly speaking, had no other choice than to punish his people. There was no one who had the *courage of faith* to expect the miracle of God's mercy at this solemn moment. God loves to grant his blessings in answer to *prayers*.

Doubt is the greatest enemy of the faith that is called upon to grow. Therefore, Jesus said, "Have faith in God. Truly, I say to you, whoever says to this mountain, 'Be taken up and thrown into the sea,' and *does not doubt in his heart*, but believes that what he says will come to pass, it will be done for him. Therefore I tell you, whatever you ask in prayer, believe that you have [already] received it, and it will be yours" (Mark 11:22-24). Faith is complete confidence in God; doubt is a faltering confidence in God. The more one's faith is mingled with doubt the more it will diminish. Conversely, a growing faith is a faith from which doubt is more and more expelled. Let the believer "ask in faith, with no doubting, for the one who doubts is like a wave of the sea that is driven and tossed by the wind. *For that person must not suppose that he will receive anything from the Lord*" (James 1:6-7). Again, in spite of hyper-Calvinist claims, there is a direct link here between believers' faith and what the Lord will give them.

Jude 20 speaks of "building yourselves up in your most holy faith." Gerrit C. Berkouwer seemed to interpret this, too, as a form of a growing faith.[18] However, presumably we should think here of the meaning that faith has in verse 3: "I found it necessary to write appealing to you to contend for the faith that was once for all delivered to the saints." This faith

---

18. Berkouwer (1954, 188).

Practical Faith

is the Christian *depositum fidei*, the truth of faith, for which believers have to contend, and which also forms the foundation for their building themselves up (cf. v. 20 DRA: "building yourselves upon your most holy faith").

7.3   A Great Faith[19]
7.3.1   The Blind and the Centurion

We have seen that Scripture speaks of *little* faith, of a *growing faith*, and of a *great faith*. A lovely example is that of Bartimaeus: "[A]s he was leaving Jericho . . ., Bartimaeus, a blind beggar, . . . was sitting by the roadside. And when he heard that it was Jesus of Nazareth, he began to cry out and say, 'Jesus, Son of David, have mercy on me!' . . . And Jesus stopped and said, 'Call him.' And they called the blind man, saying to him, 'Take heart. Get up; he is calling you.' And throwing off his cloak, he sprang up and came to Jesus. And Jesus said to him, "What do you want me to do for you?" And the blind man said to him, 'Rabbi, let me recover my sight.' And Jesus said to him, 'Go your way; your faith has made you well.' And immediately he recovered his sight and followed him on the way" (Mark 10:46–52). The beautiful little element in this story is that, when Bartimaeus was called by Jesus, he threw off his beggar's cloak, apparently *because he was convinced he would not need it any further*. In this case, too, Jesus tells the healed man (literally), "Your faith has saved [*sesōken*] you."

Jesus speaks explicitly in several places about a great faith: "When he had entered Capernaum, a centurion came forward to him, appealing to him, 'Lord, my servant is lying paralyzed at home, suffering terribly.' And he said to him, 'I will come and heal him.' But the centurion replied, 'Lord, I am not worthy to have you come under my roof, but only say the word, and my servant will be healed. For I too am a man under authority, with soldiers under me. And I say to one, "Go," and he goes, and to another, "Come," and he comes, and to my servant, "Do this," and he does it.' When Jesus heard this, he

---

19. Ouweneel (2004a, 173–75).

marveled and said to those who followed him, "Truly, I tell you, with no one in Israel have I found such faith.' . . . And to the centurion Jesus said, 'Go; let it be done for you as you have believed'" (Matt. 8:5-13; cf. Luke 7:2-9). In Greek the phrase "such faith" is *tosautē pistis*, which means "such great faith," as many translations have it (ASV, DRA, GNV, LEB, MEV, [N]KJV, NASB, NCV, NIV, WEB, etc.).

The special thing about the centurion's faith was his confidence in Jesus' *power word*, the word that is invested with divine *authority*; "authority" (Greek, *exousia*) is the word that the centurion used himself. One word spoken with formal and moral authority ("Go," "Come," "Do this") can work miracles (cf. Ps. 107:20, "He sent out his word and healed them"). Likewise, the centurion expected that one word by Jesus, spoken with his authority, would be sufficient for healing his servant. To speak the one word is not a kind of magic; it is not uttering the right formula at the right moment. This is apparently what Simon the Magician (!) believed; he asked for the power (*exousia*, authority) to grant the Holy Spirit to someone (Acts 8:19). But it is not a trick that you can teach someone. It is divine authority such as Jesus gave to his disciples to cast out demons and heal diseases (Matt. 10:1). It is the power we find implied in Mark 9:23, "All things are possible (Greek, *dynata*) for one who believes" (cf. 10:27; 14:36). The root word here is *dynamis* ("power, strength"): the power of faith.

Richard T. France has pointed out that Greek *pistis* ("faith") in Matthew always (except in 23:23, where it means "faithfulness") has the meaning of "the practical faith which expects a miracle [from Jesus], and in several cases, as here in v. 13 [of Matt. 8], such 'faith' is explicitly cited as the reason for a miraculous healing (9:2, 22, 29; 15:28). The remarkable 'faith' of this centurion, then, is to be understood not in the Pauline sense of a soteriological commitment, but as the practical conviction that Jesus has the authority to heal."[20] And, as I would

---

20. France (2007, 315).

add in a wider sense: has the power to intervene for his own in a supernatural way. I do see a soteriological link, though: here the centurion was not so much positionally justified by faith, but he was certainly practically justified by his faith.

7.3.2 The Apostle and the Canaanite Woman

The centurion's faith was *great* because he believed that very *little* from Jesus was needed to perform a *great* miracle. Just one word was enough because everything depended, not on the amount of words that had to be spoken but on the amount of power that resided in this one word by Jesus. This was the anointing that was upon Jesus: "God anointed Jesus of Nazareth with the Holy Spirit and with power.[21] He went about doing good and healing all who were oppressed by the devil, for God was with him" (Acts 10:38). This same anointing has been granted to believers (2 Cor. 1:21-22; 1 John 2:20, 27). Thus, words of faith are identical with words spoken in the power of the Spirit; as the apostle Paul says, "[M]y speech and my message were not in plausible words of wisdom, but in demonstration of the Spirit and of power [Greek, *dynamis*],[22] so that your faith might not rest in the wisdom of men but in the power [*dynamis*] of God" (1 Cor. 2:4-5). "For the kingdom of God does not consist in talk but in power [*dynamis*]" (4:20). "Our gospel came to you not only in word, but also in power [*dynamis*] and in the Holy Spirit[23] and with full conviction" (1 Thess. 1:5). In all these passages, ordinary words are distinguished from words spoken in the power of the Spirit.

Matthew tells us in his Gospel of two Gentiles whose faith was called "great" by Jesus. In addition to the centurion of chapter 8, there was the Canaanite woman of chapter 15: she "came out and was crying, 'Have mercy on me, O Lord, Son of David; my daughter is severely oppressed by a demon.'

---

21. A *hendiadys*: "with the power of the Holy Spirit." This is a literary figure expressing a complex idea by conjoining two words with "and": "looking with eyes and greed" means "looking with greedy eyes."
22. Again a *hendiadys*: "of the power of the Holy Spirit."
23. Again a *hendiadys*: "in the power of the Holy Spirit."

But he did not answer her a word. And his disciples came and begged him, saying, 'Send her away, for she is crying out after us.' He answered, 'I was sent only to the lost sheep of the house of Israel.' But she came and knelt before him, saying, 'Lord, help me.' And he answered, 'It is not right to take the children's bread and throw it to the dogs.' She said, 'Yes, Lord, yet even the dogs eat the crumbs that fall from their masters' table.' Then Jesus answered her, 'O woman, great [Greek, *megalē*[24]] is your faith! Be it done for you as you desire.' And her daughter was healed instantly" (vv. 22–28).

Apparently, Jesus tested her faith by first remaining silent, and then telling her that his mission concerned only Israel, and that it would not be right to take the bread destined for the children (i.e., Israel) and throw it to the dogs (i.e., the Gentiles). Now notice her answer: just a few crumbs are enough to heal my daughter! Here we see why Jesus called her faith great. Just as the centurion's faith was *great* because he believed that *just one word* from Jesus was needed to perform a *great* miracle, likewise the woman's faith was *great* because she believed that *just a few crumbs* from Jesus were needed to perform a *great* miracle. A great faith is a faith that has a great view of Jesus. The greater the picture that faith has of him, the more faith realizes that even the smallest act of Jesus—one word, one "crumb"—can do tremendously much.

Of course, it is no coincidence that both the centurion and the woman were non-Jewish. It is part of Matthew's goal to explain (a) that Jesus is the Messiah of Israel, (b) why the majority of Israel had not believed in him, and (c) why the Gentiles today have such a great place in the Kingdom of God. The answer is: because of their faith. In opposition to Israel's unbelief (13:58; cf. 17:17, "faithless"), he describes the faith of certain Gentiles. After having mentioned the centurion's faith, Matthew noted the following words by Jesus, "I tell you, many will come from east and west and recline at table

---

24. The Greek word *megalē* is stronger than *tosautēn* ("so great") in 8:10; see France (2007, 595–96).

Practical Faith

with Abraham, Isaac, and Jacob in the kingdom of heaven, while the sons of the kingdom will be thrown into the outer darkness. In that place there will be weeping and gnashing of teeth" (8:11-12). The "sons of the kingdom" are here the Israelites, to whom the Kingdom belongs on account of God's promises, but which they forfeit due to their unbelief. In Matthew 13:38, the "sons of the kingdom" has become a term used for *Gentiles* ("the field is the world"!) who by contrast do accept the gospel of the Kingdom and receive a place in it.

7.3.3 Faith That Overcomes

A great faith is associated with spiritual maturity. It is the faith that removes mountains (1 Cor. 13:2). As John writes: "For everyone who has been born of God overcomes the world. And this is the victory that has overcome the world — our faith. Who is it that overcomes the world except the one who believes that Jesus is the Son of God?" (1 John 5:4-5). One might think that it is not so much the size of faith that matters here, but the kind of faith: one must believe that Jesus is the Son of God. This seems to be more a reference to saving faith than to practical faith. However, overcoming the world is not just a positional matter — it is very practical (cf. Rom. 8:35-37, ". . . in all these things we are more than conquerors through him who loved us . . .").

As John Gill wrote: faith "overcometh the world; the god of the world, Satan; the lusts which are in the world; false prophets gone forth into the world; and the wicked men of the world, who by temptations, snares, evil doctrines, threatenings, promises, and ill examples, would avert regenerate ones from observing the commands of God; but such are more than conquerors over all these, through Christ that has loved them: and this is the victory that overcometh the world, even our faith . . . great things, heroic actions, and wonderful victories, are ascribed to faith; see Hebrews 11:33; which must not be understood of the grace itself, as separately considered, but of Christ the object of it, as supported, strengthened, assisted, and animated by him: and then it does wonders, when it is enabled to hold Christ, its shield, in its hand, against every enemy that opposes."[25]

The blessing that the Roman centurion and the Canaanite woman received (see previous sections) was, so to speak, proportional to their faith: "Go; let it be done for you *as you have believed*" (8:13). "O woman, great is your faith! Be it done for you *as you desire*" (15:28). They both received what they had asked for, not according to the measure of the grace that the Lord wished to grant them sovereignly—although, of course, it was not apart from this sovereign grace either—but according to the measure of their faith. The Lord gave them according to the degree of what they were able to receive—and that degree was high.

Faith is concerned not only with what God *can* do.[26] Even the smallest faith is convinced that God can do great things. Even many non-Christians will easily admit that, if there is a God, he must be able to do mighty wonders. Such a faith is no great thing. Moreover, it is often a theoretical faith because, in the case of a desired intervention of God, many Christians think in their hearts: God *can* do it, but I do not believe at all that he *will* do it. These are two aspects of faith: what *can* God do, and what does he *want* to do? The father of the boy with the unclean spirit was wondering about the first question: "[I]f you can do anything, have compassion on us and help us," to which Jesus replies with some indignation, "'If you can'! All things are possible for one who believes." The father cried out: "I believe; help my unbelief!" (Mark 9:22-24) This is the first step of faith: the conviction that the Lord *can* do a miracle. Little faith is needed for this.

However, the leper brought up a more difficult issue; he said, "If you *will*, you can make me clean." Moved with pity, Jesus stretched out his hand and touched him and said to him, "I will; be clean" (1:40-41). "I will" is here "I am willing," "I

---

25. http://biblehub.com/1_john/5-4.htm.
26. Cf. Ouweneel (2004a, 265).

Practical Faith

want to" (cf., e.g., ERV, GNT, NASB, NIV, NKJV). Faith with *insight*, with a firm conviction, worked by the Holy Spirit in the heart, that God *wants* to do a certain thing, is the faith that he *will* do this wondrous thing here and now. One of the most impressive examples in the Bible is Elijah on Mount Carmel, who is *confident* that, after the false priests have prayed to their god, the God of Israel will listen to him and send down fire from heaven on Elijah's altar (1 Kings 18:20-40). Hebrews 11 gives us many more examples of such practical faith, such as Noah building the ark, Abram going to a land he did not know, Abraham offering his son, Moses choosing the side of Israel, Moses leading Israel out of Egypt. In each of these cases, it is hardly a matter of *saving* (*justifying*) faith and much more a matter of *practical* faith: not the faith taking us to heaven, but the faith taking us through the world.

John says, "[T]his is the confidence that we have toward him, that if we ask anything according to his will he hears us. And if we know that he hears us in whatever we ask, we know that we have the requests that we have asked of him" (1 John 5:14-15; MSG: "[H]ow bold and free we then become in his presence, freely asking according to his will, sure that he's listening. And if we're confident that he's listening, we know that what we've asked for is as good as ours"). It is not just a question of faith in God's *power*, but factually *opening* ourselves to that sovereign power in our own lives, like those who "through faith conquered kingdoms, enforced justice, obtained promises, stopped the mouths of lions, quenched the power of fire, escaped the edge of the sword, were made strong out of weakness, became mighty in war, put foreign armies to flight. Women received back their dead by resurrection. Some were tortured, refusing to accept release, so that they might rise again to a better life. Others suffered mocking and flogging, and even chains and imprisonment. They were stoned, they were sawn in two, they were killed with the sword. They went about in skins of sheep and goats, destitute, afflicted, mistreated — of whom the world was not worthy — wandering about in deserts and mountains, and in dens and caves of the earth" (Heb. 11:33-38).

7.3.4 Discouraged Faith[27]

The practical confidence of many believers is so limited that they do not dare, or wish, to reckon with God's wondrous intervention. A striking example is presented by the invalid in John 5:1-18. Presumably, the sin of this man, about which Jesus hints in verse 14 ("See, you are well! Sin no more, that nothing worse may happen to you"), and the consequences of it, had led to a certain measure of bitterness and disappointment (v. 7). Just like many who suffer with a chronic illness he was full of unbelief, reinforced by years of failing attempts to get healed in the miraculous bath water (vv. 3-4 KJV). So when Jesus addressed him, it was with the knowledge that the man "had already been there a long time" (v. 6).

Jesus asked the man whether he wanted to be healed. To a certain extent, this could also imply the question whether he was prepared to turn away from his bitterness in order to be healed of his physical problem as well.[28] This was a difficult question for the invalid because it implied an appeal to his own responsibility. This is why the man tried to shift the blame for his unbelief to others: "Sir, I have no one to put me into the pool when the water is stirred up, and while I am going another steps down before me" (v. 7). This seems to imply that the invalid thought that God could do nothing for him because other people failed to help him. In his comment on this reply, John Calvin wrote: "This ill man does what almost all of us do. He limits God's help to his own ideas, and does not dare to promise himself more than he can imagine in his mind."[29]

The invalid sang a lament of self-pity and unbelief. Therefore, the first thing that Jesus told him was: "Get up, take up

---

27. Ibid., 266–67.
28. Wimber and Springer (1986, 85).
29. Comm. on John (ad loc.).

your bed, and walk" (v. 8). In this way, the man was deflected from his reproaches toward others, and cast back upon his own responsibility. *He* had to do something: he had to *believe* in Jesus' power, and *obey* Jesus' command. Objectively speaking, he was healed by the power of Jesus, subjectively speaking he was healed by his own obedience of faith. That is, he might have replied: "I *cannot* get up, you should know that! I have not been lying here all these years for nothing." Instead, he *got up*.

Today, it is not any different. Time and again, we hear about believers whose circumstances do not improve, even after having consulted counselors and therapists. One cause might be that they—unconsciously—do not wish to break with the identity that they have derived from the bitterness in their soul. After thirty-eight years, the man's disability had become the major part of his identity. However, through the Lord's grace, his bitterness was overcome, and he found healing; perhaps we may say, first for his soul, and then also for his body. This grace is still available for all those who stretch out for it.

7.4 The Strength of Faith
7.4.1 Receptivity

The practical faith of everyday Christian life is the complete confidence in God and his promises, and consequently, completely entrusting oneself to him: "Therefore let those who suffer according to God's will entrust (Greek, *paratithesthōsan*) their souls to a faithful Creator while doing good" (1 Pet. 4:19). It is, for instance, the inner faith conviction given by God that, if he opens a door for a certain work of faith, he is able and willing to do, and shall do, this work in a given situation at a given time. He does so through the person who has received this faith to this end, and who completely entrusts himself to God in this respect: "What then shall we say to these things? If God is for us, who can be against us?" (Rom. 8:31). "[A] wide door for effective work has opened to me, and there are many adversaries" (1 Cor. 16:9), that is, in spite of the many adversaries God has opened a wide door. "Behold, I have set before you an open door, which no one is able to shut" (Rev. 3:8). It is the unflinching and unassailable faith of women such as Rahab, Deborah, Jael, Abigail, and Hulda, and of men such as Abraham, Moses, David, Elijah, and Jeremiah.

I apologize for giving some more New Testament examples of healing; it is simply a fact that the role of practical faith comes to light in a special way in the healing stories. I already quoted James' word: "[T]he prayer of *faith* will save the one who is sick" (5:15). After the healing of the paralytic at the Beautiful Gate, Peter said: "And his [i.e., Jesus'] name—by *faith* in his name—has made this man strong whom you see and know, and the *faith* that is through Jesus has given the man this perfect health in the presence of you all" (Acts 3:16). In all such cases, faith could be described as the susceptibility for God's power manifesting itself in the believers' lives.

Faith within the *sick* person is no necessary condition for the healing at all, in spite of what is asserted by certain Pentecostal and charismatic faith healers: if the person is not healed, they blame *him* for his alleged unbelief. This is both unbiblical and unfair. In the New Testament, the diseased are never rebuked for their lack of faith, but those who pray for them are (Mark 9:19). Today, too, if there is anyone to be blamed at all it is rather the healing minister than the sick person. James 5 and Acts 3 do not speak of the sick person's faith, but of that of the healing ministers. Not only the lame man of Acts 3, but also the invalid of John 5 and Naaman in 2 Kings 5:10-14, prove that faith on the part of the sick person is not an absolute condition.

This does not change the fact, however, that faith on the part of the sick helps a great deal. Jesus said to the woman with the discharge of blood: "Take heart, daughter; your *faith* has made you well" (Matt. 9:22); to Bartimaeus: "Go your way; your *faith* has made you well" (Mark 10:52); and to the leper: "Rise and go your way; your *faith* has made you well" (Luke 17:19). "Now at Lystra there was a man sitting who could not use his feet. He was crippled from birth and had never walked. He listened to Paul speaking. And Paul, looking intently at him and seeing that he had *faith* to be made well, said in a loud voice, 'Stand upright on your feet.' And he sprang up and began walking" (Acts 14:8-10).

7.4.2 The Power of Unbelief

In such a situation as just mentioned, there is *always* faith to which God can respond, if it is not faith within the healing minister or within the sick person, then at least within the parents, the friends, or the companions of the sick, such as the centurion asking for his servant (Matt. 8:10, 13), the four friends of the paralytic ("When Jesus saw *their* faith . . .," 9:2), the Canaanite woman asking for her daughter (15:21-28), father Jairus (Mark 5:36), the companions of the deaf man (Mark 7:32), the father in Mark 9:23-24, and the father in John 4:46-54. In all these cases the faith of the accompanists was sufficient to set God's power in motion for their friend or child.

Absence of faith means that the people involved have closed themselves to the power of God. In Matthew 13:58 we read: "And he [i.e., Jesus] did not do many mighty works there, because of their unbelief." Mark 6:5-6 puts it even more strongly: "And he *could* do no mighty work there, except that he laid his hands on a few sick people and healed them. And he marveled because of their unbelief."[30] Of course, this inability ("he could not") did not reside in Jesus' own being—he healed some sick after all—but in the lack of receptivity on the part of his audience. It is like someone who wishes to pour out oil, but there are no vessels available (anymore) to contain it (cf. 2 Kings 4:6). It is like a radio station that broadcasts spoken words, but there are no radio receivers around, so that the message gets lost.

It seems that Jesus in some cases drove out the curious,

---

30. Matthew seems to avoid the "*could* not" (France (2007, 550).

or took the sick apart from the curious, in order to eliminate these unbelieving spoilers: "And when he had entered, he said to them, 'Why are you making a commotion and weeping? The child is not dead but sleeping.' And they laughed at him. But *he put them all outside* and took the child's father and mother and those who were with him and went in where the child was" (Mark 5:39-40). "And they brought to him a man who was deaf and had a speech impediment, and they begged him to lay his hand on him. And *taking him aside from the crowd privately*, he put his fingers into his ears, and after spitting touched his tongue," etc. (7:32-33). "And he took the blind man by the hand and *led him out of the village*, and when he had spit on his eyes and laid his hands on him, he asked him, 'Do you see anything?'" etc. (8:23).

Jesus brought the sick who were to be healed outside the negative, opposing sphere of the doubters and the critics. We find what seems to be a general rule: the more there is faith present in the situation, the more we will see God's intervening power; the more there is unbelief present in the situation, the less we will see God's intervening power. This seems to be the purport of Jesus' question in Luke 18:8, "[W]hen the Son of Man comes, will he find faith [lit., *the* faith, perhaps *this* faith] on earth?" This is not saving faith, but the practical faith of the widow just described. It is the faith that God "will . . . give justice to his elect, who cry to him day and night" (v. 7). This is the faith that the Lord is looking for: faith that continual prayer will move the heart of God: "Pray without ceasing" (1 Thess. 5:17); "be constant in prayer" (Rom. 12:12). "Continue steadfastly in prayer, being watchful in it with thanksgiving" (Col. 4:2).

7.4.3 Faith Essential, But Not Sufficient

Faith — with the healing minister, or with the accompanists, or with the sick themselves — is a *necessary* condition, but it is not a sufficient condition. Not every "word of faith" brings about the intended miracle.

(a) If the disease is caused by a *mistaken lifestyle*, people do not need a miracle, they need a substantial change in their way of living.

(b) If the disease is caused by a *sinful life* — which is often *not* the case (John 9:2-3), but sometimes it is (cf. Ps. 32:1-5; Matt. 9:2; John 5:14) — the sins have to be repented and confessed (James 5:15-16).

(c) If the disease is caused by *demonic bonds* (Luke 13:10-17; cf. the "dumb and deaf spirits" in 11:14; Matt. 9:32-33; Mark 9:25), the demons have to be cast out (cf. Acts 10:38; 19:12). In such a case, the sick person does not primarily need healing but deliverance.

(d) Sometimes it is not God's time for the miracle: Elijah had to pray seven times before God sent the rain he had promised (1 Kings 18:1, 41-45). Jesus presumably passed the lame man at the Beautiful Gate at the temple many times, but apparently only in Acts 3 had the divine time of the man's healing arrived.

(e) Sometimes a disease is simply God's means of calling his dear child home: "Now when Elisha had fallen sick with the illness of which he was to die . . ." (2 Kings 13:14).

No doubt the apostle Paul had enough faith in God's healing and restoring power. Yet, the "thorn in the flesh" was not taken away from him: "[T]o keep me from becoming conceited because of the surpassing greatness of the revelations, a thorn was given me in the flesh, a messenger of Satan to harass me, to keep me from becoming conceited. Three times I pleaded with the Lord about this, that it should leave me. But he said to me, 'My grace is sufficient for you, for my power is made perfect in weakness.' Therefore I will boast all the more gladly of my weaknesses, so that the power of Christ may rest upon me. For the sake of Christ, then, I am content with weaknesses, insults, hardships, persecutions, and calamities. For when I am weak, then I am strong" (2 Cor. 12:7-10). It is definitely not certain if this thorn was a disease, or some other trouble,[31] but this does not affect the general principle. In spite of his prayers, and in spite of whatever words of faith his friends may have proclaimed over him, the thorn did not disappear. Sometimes we lack the faith to receive miracles — but sometimes there is faith enough, yet God has decided otherwise.

Jesus was the greatest example of faith in God who ever lived; he is even "the founder and perfecter of *our* faith" (Heb. 12:2). He did what Philippians 4:6 asks of *us*: "[D]o not be anxious about anything, but in everything by prayer and supplication with thanksgiving let your requests be made known to God." He did so in Gethsemane, where he prayed: "Abba, Father, all things are possible for you. Remove this cup from me. Yet not what I will, but what you will" (Mark 14:36). Jesus fulfilled the principle of 1 John 5:14 by asking according to the Father's will. It was not his faith that failed, nor the boldness with which he approached the Father. The only impediment was that God wanted him to go a different way than he had asked for. Mark's Gospel begins with the leper who asked: "If you will . . .," and Jesus answered: "I will . . ." (Mark 1:40-41). Toward the end of the Gospel it is Jesus himself who asks as it were: "If you will . . .," and God's answer was No.

7.5 The Creativity of Faith
7.5.1 Abraham

One of the fascinating aspects of a great practical confidence in God is its creativity or originality. Faith *sees* and *does* things that do not belong to the normal patterns. As to "seeing," by faith Abraham saw things of which we do not read that they had ever been explicitly revealed to him: "Your father Abraham rejoiced that he would see my day. He saw it and was glad" (John 8:56). This is a remarkable statement, although it is not very clear to what time the expression "my day" refers. Leon Morris thinks of the day of the incarnation of the Word.[32]

---

31. See Ouweneel (2004a, §6.4); cf. Barnett (1997, 566–70).
32. Morris (1971, 471).

Practical Faith

William Barclay reminded us of unnamed Jewish sources that point to God's promise: "I will bless those who bless you, and him who dishonors you I will curse, and in you all the families of the earth shall be blessed" (Gen. 12:3). He believed that Abraham rejoiced in the fact that the Messiah would be born of his seed (cf. 17:6, "kings shall come from you").[33] Other rabbis, he tells us, thought of the vision of Genesis 15, and believed that at that occasion Abraham foresaw the future of his people, and thus the Messiah as well. Some even thought that he entered into all the days of the future because of Genesis 24:1 (Heb., *ba bayyamim*, lit. "he went in[to] the days").[34] Others again believed to find the joy of Abraham in his laughter (he "fell on his face and laughed," Gen. 17:17).[35] Merrill Tenney supposed that Abraham saw something of the Messiah himself in Isaac's miraculous birth, in the latter's firm confidence in his father, his preparedness to become the sacrifice required by God, and his redemption from a certain death.[36]

Another example of Abraham's "seeing" in faith is Hebrews 11:9-10: "By faith he went to live in the land of promise, as in a foreign land. . . . For he was looking forward to the city that has foundations, whose designer and builder is God." This is the "city of the living God, the heavenly Jerusalem" (12:22), the "city that is to come" (13:14), the heavenly center of the "world to come" (2:5) in the "age to come" (6:5), the center of the "kingdom that cannot be shaken" (12:28).[37] The "God of glory" had revealed himself to Abraham (Acts 7:2); the heavenly glory of this God made him see that there was more than (the promise of) an earthly people and an earthly land. Therefore, his faith faced a "heavenly country" (11:16) with a heavenly city.

---

33. Barclay (1975, ad loc.).
34. Strack and Billerbeck (1922, 2:525–26).
35. Jubilees 16:19; cf. the name Isaac, Heb., *Yits-haq*, derived from *ts-h-q*, "to laugh."
36. Tenney (1981, 98–99); cf. Bouma (1927, 128); Gaebelein (1980, ad loc.).
37. Ouweneel (1982, 2:56–57, 86–87, 101–02).

Just to be clear: this does not imply that Abraham learned to esteem heaven more important than the earth, as if he rejoiced in "going to heaven" one day. Of such a "going to heaven" the Old Testament believer knew nothing, not even in Psalm 73:24 ("afterward you will receive me to glory"; cf. GNT, "at the end you will receive me with honor," i.e., in the Messianic kingdom; cf. Vulgate: *cum gloria suscepisti me*). Abraham was looking forward to the *Kingdom of God*, as this would be embodied in the "city of God," the *civitas Dei*, to speak with Augustine.

7.5.2 Peter and Others

A very different example of the creative "acting" of a great faith is that of Peter walking on the sea. He said, "Lord, if it is you, command me to come to you on the water." Jesus answered: "Come." So Peter got out of the boat and walked on the water and came to Jesus (Matt. 14:28–29). It was Peter's faith that took the initiative. Just as one word sufficed for the centurion (8:8), and one crumb for the Canaanite woman (15:27), likewise one word (Greek, *elthe*, "Come") sufficed for Peter. Just as his sinking was an act of "little faith" (v. 31), his walking on the water was an act of great faith. It was a faith that had the courage to deviate from the customary pathways, and dared to abandon the relative safety of the boat. It is the faith that not only performs its common duties, not only fulfills what is expected of it, but rises above the ordinary. It is a pity that we are usually more occupied with Peter's sinking than with his walking, more with the failure of faith than with the activity thereof. Who knows a painting or drawing that depicts Peter as walking on the water? The ones I know all depict him as sinking.

A comparable initiative of faith was that of the woman with the discharge of blood. She "had suffered much under many physicians, and had spent all that she had, and was no better but rather grew worse. She had heard the reports about Jesus and came up behind him in the crowd and touched his garment. For she said, 'If I touch even his garments, I will be made well'" (Mark 5:26-28). This woman, too, left the common pathways. Because of her discharge, which was probably of a menstrual nature, she was ritually "unclean," and was not allowed to touch any person (Lev. 15:25-33; Num. 5:1-4).[38] Nonetheless she pressed herself through the crowd in order to touch the fringe of his garment (Matt. 9:20), probably referring to the tassels on the corners of the garment (cf. Num. 15:38; also see Mark 3:10; 6:56). In this way, according to the strict interpretation of the Torah, the woman transmitted her ritual uncleanness to Jesus. However, Jesus did not reproach her in any way, but said: "Daughter, your *faith* has made you well [lit., has saved you]; go in peace, and be healed of your disease" (Mark 5:34).

Incidentally, it is amazing that, through physical contact, Jesus identified with all three unclean groups mentioned in Numbers 5:1 that ought *not* to be touched: a leper (Mark 1:41), someone with a discharge (5:27), and a dead person (v. 41). He touched the leper and the dead body, but the woman touched *him*. Rather than Jesus becoming unclean as a consequence, the three persons instead were cleansed, healed, and raised, respectively. In this way, the Torah was not disobeyed, but Jesus rose above the Torah by reversing its principle: he who ought to have become unclean through the touch, in reality cleansed (healed, raised) the unclean (sick, dead) ones.

Jesus spoke the words, "Your faith has saved you; go in peace," also to another woman who took a remarkable faith initiative: the "sinful woman" of Luke 7:37-50. She had the nerve to gain complete access into the Pharisee's house in order to show Jesus her love and to receive forgiveness. It was not just Jesus who saved her, although from the divine side this was certainly true. But from the viewpoint of human responsibility it was her *faith* that had saved her. She received her forgiveness by the *grace* of God, through the *blood* that

---

38. Cf. the Talmud tracts Niddah and Zabim, and further 11Qtemple 48:14-17.

Jesus would one day pour out also for her, and on account of her *faith* (see these three elements in Rom. 3:24–26).

The four friends, too, who let a paralytic down through the roof in order to get him near Jesus, thus demonstrated a peculiar initiative of faith. The text says that Jesus saw the *faith*, not so much of the paralytic but of the four friends (Luke 5:20). The French say, *L'Amour rend inventif*, "Love makes inventive." We may add: faith makes inventive, too. The same was true for the blind beggar who kept shouting in order to catch Jesus' attention. Jesus said to him, "Recover your sight; your *faith* has made you well [lit., has saved you]" (18:42).

Finally, I mention Zacchaeus (even though his story does not contain the word "faith"): "He was a chief tax collector and was rich. And he was seeking to see who Jesus was, but on account of the crowd he could not, because he was small in stature. So he ran on ahead and climbed up into a sycamore tree to see him, for he was about to pass that way. And when Jesus came to the place, he looked up and said to him, 'Zacchaeus, hurry and come down, for I must stay at your house today'" (Luke 19:2–5). Presumably the man was also driven by guilt (cf. v. 8). But that does not change the fact that he took a remarkable initiative to come into contact with Jesus. And if he was "saved" (vv. 9–10), this can only have been on account of his faith.

7.5.3 The Human Aspect

Reformed theologians rightly emphasize that it is *God* who does the wondrous work, just as it is *God* who sent the disease in the first place. The Heidelberg Catechism (Q&A 27) tells us that "rain and drought, fruitful and barren years, meat and drink, health and sickness, riches and poverty, indeed, all things come not by chance, but by His fatherly hand." Of course, this picture has to be nuanced. Often, it is *humans* who bring upon themselves or others bad harvests (cf. Prov. 20:4; 24:30–31), disease (e.g., through an unhealthy life style or contagion), and poverty. Moreover, diseases and other catastrophes are sometimes explicitly brought about by Satan (Job 1:9-19; 2:6-7; Luke 13:10-17; Matt. 13:39; 2 Cor. 12:7; 1 Thess. 2:18). It is true that this always occurs because God allows it — but such things being allowed is not the same as such things actively coming to us "by God's fatherly hand."

Yet, Job was right, too: "The LORD gave, and *the LORD* [not Satan!] has taken away; blessed be the name of the LORD" (1:21); and to his wife: "Shall we receive good from God, and shall we not receive evil [that is, from God]?" (2:10; GNT: "When God sends us something good, we welcome it. How can we complain when he sends us trouble?"). The believer accepts good and bad things from God's hands, even though he knows about the role of humans and demons. He does so in the confidence "that for those who love God all things work together for good, for those who are called according to his purpose" (Rom. 8:28). "My times [my life, my fortune, my future] are in your hand" (Ps. 31:15).

Likewise, the believer always accepts healing from God's hands, whether the healing occurred "spontaneously," or through medical doctors (cf. Matt. 9:12, those who are sick need a physician; also cf. Col. 4:14), or through the healing ministry (Mark 16:17-18; 1 Cor. 12:9, 28-30; James 5:14-16). However, just as we have to nuance the picture of only *God* sending sickness, so too we have to nuance the picture of only *God* healing sickness. It is God who heals, but Jesus literally says that *faith* can heal as well (Mark 5:34; 10:52; Luke 17:19). Jesus did not tell his apostles, and later the seventy-two: "Pray for the sick, and if it pleases God he will heal some of them." Instead, he said: "Heal the sick" (Matt. 10:8; Luke 10:9). *They* had to heal the sick, albeit in the power of God. Sick persons sometimes are healed, not only because at that moment it is God's sovereign will that this happens but also because those who minister to the sick take their responsibility and exercise their faith. Sick persons sometimes are *not* healed, not only because at that moment it is not God's sovereign will that this happens, but also because those who minister to the sick do not assume their responsibility and are led by unbelief. Even Jesus could hardly perform any miracles if there was so much disbelief around him (Mark 6:5).

7.6 Doubt of Faith[39]
7.6.1 Two Kinds of Doubt

In my view, when speaking of the doubt of faith, we have to distinguish between doubt that has more to do with our immanent-functional life, and transcendent-existential doubt. For instance, Bruce Demarest speaks of (a) intellectual ("cognitive"), "affective" doubt (emotional scars) and (b) "spiritual" doubt.[40]

(a) Doubt in our immanent-functional life means, for instance, that intellectual or emotional doubt can easily arise in someone: Do I see this matter correctly? Do I have the proper view of that subject? Does it feel good? Did I make the right decision? The Holy Spirit told Peter about Cornelius' messengers: "Arise therefore, go down and go with them, doubting nothing; for I have sent them" (NKJV; cf. ERV: "Go with these men without wondering if it's all right, because I sent them"). Another example: even the most ardent believer can suddenly become sensitive to atheistic arguments: what if "they" are right? But such a doubt will pass as soon as the person concerned becomes conscious again of his own arguments. Such an intellectual doubt touches the *fides quae creditur*; this is very different from existential doubt, which concerns the *fides qua creditur*, that is, which involves the *heart*.

I do recognize, though, that the two forms of doubt can sometimes hardly be distinguished. Thus, people wrestling with their assurance of faith, often suffer from an intermingling of the two forms of doubt. Primarily, we are dealing here with — in my view mistaken — biblical arguments, but these clearly overlap with existential doubt. Also people who

---

39. Cf. extensively, Rietkerk (2000).
40. Demarest (1997, 273–75); cf. Wiersinga (1952, 78–79) on "objective" and "subjective" doubt.

suffer from great distress may start doubting God: Does he see me at all? Does he care about me? Here again, theological and existential questions are intermingled.

(b) Genuinely existential doubt of faith dilutes God's power in the believer's life, or even takes it away. See again Mark 11:23, "[W]hoever says to this mountain, 'Be taken up and thrown into the sea,' and *does not doubt in his heart*, but believes that what he says will come to pass, it will be done for him." Or James 1:6-8, "But let him ask in faith, with no *doubting*, for the one who *doubts* is like a wave of the sea that is driven and tossed by the wind. For that person must not suppose that he will receive anything from the Lord; he is a double-minded man, unstable in all his ways." In Matthew 17:16-20 the faith of the disciples was intermingled with doubt and worry, and that meant an impediment. Moreover, instead of doing their job they were arguing with the Torah scholars (Mark 9:14). It is no wonder that they did not manage to cast out the evil spirit, and Jesus ascribed this to their "little faith" (in Matt. 17:17 even called "faithlessness").

Please note that the doubt that we are referring to here is not doubting one's own ability. Such a doubt can be very wholesome (perhaps this is what Paul means in Phil. 2:12, "work out your own salvation *with fear and trembling*," viz., doubting your own abilities but not doubting God's power; see v. 13). James 1:6-8 is not even referring to believing persons fighting their own doubts, but instead of someone who is "double-minded" (Greek, *dipsychos*, lit. someone with "two souls"), that is, someone who has fundamental doubt toward God.[41] One could almost say that he behaves like a person with a believing and an unbelieving soul.

7.6.2 Support from Others

The Christian who, in his practical walk, experiences doubt of faith can be strongly supported by other believers, who in a certain sense and under certain circumstance can have faith

---
41. Paul (1997, 113); Ouweneel (2009, §14.3.3).

"for" him, in his stead. I already referred to parents, friends, and other accompanists who took certain people to Jesus to be healed. Without this faith, they would not have taken the trouble to bring the sick person into contact with Jesus or his servants. Sometimes, Jesus appealed to the faith of *these* people, and not to the faith of the sick persons for whom they asked help. As we have seen, especially parents have a great responsibility to *believe* on behalf of their young children, who need the power of the Lord to intervene for them. Jesus told Jairus with regard to his dead daughter: "Do not fear, only believe" (Mark 5:36). And to the father of the boy with the unclean spirit he said: "All things are possible for one who believes" (9:23).

To take an Old Testament example: after Elisha had given Naaman the order to wash himself in the Jordan, the man was angry and went away. He had believed the words of his wife's servant (vv. 2-4), but strangely enough, he did not believe the words of the prophet: "Behold, I thought that he would surely come out to me and stand and call upon the name of the Lord his God, and wave his hand over the place and cure the leper. Are not Abana and Pharpar, the rivers of Damascus, better than all the waters of Israel? Could I not wash in them and be clean?" (2 Kings 5:11-12). So he turned and went away in a rage. But his servants came near and said to him, "My father, it is a great word the prophet has spoken to you; will you not do it? Has he actually said to you, 'Wash, and be clean'?"

What if these servants had never spoken to their master? They had more faith than he had! On account of *their* faith, not his own, Naaman "dipped himself seven times in the Jordan, according to the word of the man of God, and his flesh was restored like the flesh of a little child, and he was clean" (v. 14). What if the four friends had not had the faith to take their invalid friend to Jesus (Matt. 9:1-8)? What if some other friends had not taken their deaf friend to Jesus (Mark 7:31-37)?

Noah's faith was enough for his entire family to be saved

in the ark. Abraham's faith was enough to lead his entire family to the promised land, and Moses' faith was enough to lead the entire nation of Israel through the Red Sea. David's faith was enough to defeat Goliath and save all Israel. Supernatural miracles were not involved in all these cases. Saving a family in a boat or leading them to another country is not necessarily supernatural. The dry pathway through the Red Sea certainly was supernatural, but David's victory was not necessarily so. But seen from the divine side, all these cases were examples of God's gracious intervention. What was decisive was not the possible supernatural miracle, but the faith of certain persons in the God who can, and loves to, intervene for his people.

Practical faith is *more* than receptivity to divine miracles. For instance, faith is needed to walk a troublesome path that God is pointing out to us, or to accept that a route that *God* takes is the best one for you and your nation. This is the profound meaning of faith that we find in Habakkuk 2:4, "[T]he righteous shall live by his faith." It is of great interest to see how the book of Hebrews quotes this verse (10:38), and then practically applies it to many examples of Old Testament believers in their various challenging circumstances.

It is an undeniable fact, though, that most biblical examples of concrete, practical confidence of faith do involve miracles. Just look at the examples of Hebrews 11:33-35: conquering kingdoms (see the book of Joshua), stopping the mouths of lions (see Dan. 6), quenching the power of fire (cf. Dan. 3), putting foreign armies to flight (e.g., Judg. 7), women receiving back their dead by resurrection (1 Kings 17:17-24; 2 Kings 4:18-37), etcetera. It is the faith that moves mountains (Mark 11:23; 1 Cor. 13:2). It is the faith that expects *mira*cles from God that we can ad*mire*, and *wonders* about which we can *wonder*.

Faith is also the ability through which we can recognize the *sign* character of many wonders. I am not referring to the sensational "faith" of John 4:48 ("Unless you see signs and wonders you will not believe"). I am not referring to the unbelief for which not even the greatest miracles are convincing: "[H]ow long will they not believe in me, in spite of all the signs that I have done among them?" (Num. 14:11); "despite his wonders, they did not believe" (Ps. 78:32). "If they do not hear Moses and the Prophets, neither will they be convinced if someone should rise from the dead" (Luke 16:31). What I am referring to is the faith of those who, by the Spirit of God, were able to recognize God's signs and develop a true faith: "This, the first of his signs, Jesus did at Cana in Galilee, and manifested his glory. And his disciples believed in him" (John 2:11).

7.6.3 Conditions of Faith

The prayer of faith never brings forth automatic effects; it is bound to conditions.

(a) Praying *in Jesus' name:* "Whatever you ask in my name, this I will do, that the Father may be glorified in the Son. If you ask me anything in my name, I will do it" (John 14:13-14): "... so that whatever you ask the Father in my name, he may give it to you" (15:16; cf. 16:23) — of course as long as it furthers not primarily one's own interests but the interests of that name.[42] In prayer in the Lord's name, the believer, in communion with the Lord, has assured himself that in his stead the Son would pray the same thing. This demands a confident and intimate relationship with him, a learning to listen to his voice. Jesus himself says, "[A]sk whatever you wish, and it will be done for you" (John 15:7). But we do have to pay attention to the conditions mentioned here: "If you abide in me, and my words abide in you. . . . I appointed you that you should go and bear fruit and that your fruit should abide, so that whatever you ask the Father in my name, he may give it to you" (vv. 7 and 16).

(b) Praying *according to his will:* "And this is the confidence that we have toward him, that if we ask anything according to his will he hears us. And if we know that he hears us in

---

42. S. Ngewa in Adeyemo (2006, 1284).

Practical Faith

whatever we ask, we know that we have the requests that we have asked of him" (1 John 5:14-15). But here again, we have to give heed to the conditions: praying "according to his will," and: "[I]f our heart does not condemn us, we have confidence before God; and whatever we ask we receive from him, because we keep his commandments and do what pleases him" (3:21-22). We do not need faith only, but also a pure conscience, and the conviction that we are walking in the way of the Lord, pleasing to him. This is the wisdom of Psalm 66:18, "If I had cherished iniquity in my heart, the Lord would not have listened."

Where we ourselves have no words anymore, the Spirit knows how to pray *in* us "according to the will of God": "For we do not know what to pray for as we ought, but the Spirit himself intercedes for us with groanings too deep for words. And he who searches hearts knows what is the mind of the Spirit, because the Spirit intercedes for the saints according to the will of God" (Rom. 8:26-27).

Praying according to God's will implies that we can learn to speak the prayer of faith only if, in fellowship with the Lord, we have learned to know his will. Paul prayed three times to the Lord that the "thorn" in his flesh be taken way, but it turned out not to be the *will* of the Lord (2 Cor. 12:7-9). Praying according to God's will does not involve telling the Lord about our needs, and then simply leaving them to his will. First, this is not necessary—the Lord already knows our needs—and second, this is not *praying* (ardently beseeching) with all your heart.

Such fervent praying, for instance, is this: "And Moses cried to the Lord, 'O God, please heal her—please'" (Num. 12:13). "Then Hezekiah turned his face to the wall and prayed to the Lord, and said, 'Please, O Lord, remember how I have walked before you in faithfulness and with a whole heart, and have done what is good in your sight.' And Hezekiah wept bitterly. Then the word of the Lord came to Isaiah: 'Go and say to Hezekiah, Thus says the Lord, the God of David your father: I have heard your prayer; I have seen your tears'" (Isa. 38:2-5). "Then you will call upon me and come and pray to me, and I will hear you. You will seek me and find me, when you seek me with all your heart" (Jer. 29:12-13; cf. such prayers in Matt. 8:5-10; 15:22-28; Mark 5:22-23; John 4:47-49).

Such prayers are meant in James 5:16b: "The prayer of a righteous person has great power as it is working," or, "The effective [Greek, *energoumene*, full of energy] prayer of a righteous person has great power [*poly ischyei*]" (cf. CEB: "The prayer of the righteous person is powerful in what it can achieve"; NIV: ". . . is powerful and effective"). We have seen that it is one-sided to say that only God can do wonders; *faith* can do them too (though only in the power of God). We can now add that the prayer of a *tsaddiq* can do the same (I repeat: only in the power of God). The Lord always desires to bless us, but he desires even more to give us such blessings explicitly in answer to our prayers: "And Jesus said to him, 'What do you want me to do for you?' And the blind man said to him, 'Rabbi, let me recover my sight'" (Mark 10:51). Isaiah 65:24 does say, "Before they call I will answer; while they are yet speaking I will hear." But this does not mean that calling on him is of no avail anymore. It means only that God can even anticipate our supplications.

7.6.4 Can God Change His Mind?

Scripture contains quite a few examples of prayers through which God is persuaded to do something different from what he had announced beforehand.[43] I just mentioned the example of Hezekiah, who was told that he was going to die, but who received fifteen more years after his fervent prayer. God told Abraham that he would destroy Sodom, but at the prayer of Abraham God promised that he would not do this if

---

43. For this notion the Dutch uses the unique expression *(zich laten) verbidden*, which occurs eight times in the Statenvertaling (the Dutch equivalent of the King James Version); see extensively, Ouweneel (2008b, chapter 8).

Practical Faith

there would be found ten righteous persons in the city (Gen. 18:23–32). The LORD told Moses that he was going to destroy the nation, but after Moses' fervent prayer he "relented from the disaster that he had spoken of bringing on his people" (Exod. 32:14). During the pestilence, David cried to the LORD, and "the LORD relented from the calamity and said to the angel who was working destruction among the people. . . . So the LORD responded to the plea for the land, and the plague was averted from Israel" (2 Sam. 24:16, 25). God said of the prophet Micah: "Did he not fear the LORD and entreat the favor of the LORD, and did not the LORD relent of the disaster that he had pronounced against them?" (Jer. 26:19). God had announced that he would overthrow Nineveh in forty days, but after the inhabitants had repented and cried out to him, he "relented of the disaster that he had said he would do to them, and he did not do it" (Jonah 3:10).

On a strictly Reformed standpoint, according to which all things that ever occur have been decreed by God before the foundation of the world, it is simply inconceivable that God would ever change his mind.[44] The Reformed writer Terry L. Johnson told us that Reformed people pray because prayer can change us, and it can change the world.[45] Not for a moment does it ever occur to him that prayer might also change the mind of *God*. Apparently, to him this would be unthinkable. However, we would have to distort the biblical stories just mentioned in a serious way in order to adapt them to this Reformed view. God tells us he will do a certain thing, God's servants fervently entreat him, God listens to them, and averts the announced evil. The Reformed theologian tells us that what God did was in his mind all the time after all. But this is not what the texts tell us. These texts suggest very strongly that time and again God changed his mind. If God's answer to prayer had been in his mind from eternity, then,

---

44. Cf. Brother Andrew and Susan DeVore Williams (2012, book title: *And God Changed His Mind . . . Because His People Dared To Ask*).
45. Johnson (2000, 134–48).

first, the answer is not an "answer" at all, and, second, the text gives a false picture of what God had in mind before people began to beseech him.[46]

Reformed theologians may say such things in order to save their model, but they do not have the biblical texts on their side. The Bible says that God *added* fifteen years to Hezekiah's life (Isa. 38:5). No, says (hyper-)Calvinism, God "added" nothing; those fifteen years were in his mind from eternity. The Bible says that God forgave the people *according to the prayer of Moses* (Num. 14:20). No, says (hyper-)Calvinism, God would have forgiven them anyway, because this was in his mind from eternity. The Bible says that God sent an angel to Jerusalem *to destroy it*, but at the moment that this would happen David cried to the Lord, God relented, and the destruction stopped (1 Chron. 21:14-17). No, says (hyper-)Calvinism, it was in God's mind from eternity to save the city at this point.

(Hyper-)Calvinist R. C. Sproul even goes so far as to call all those who deny that God has *determined* all events from eternity "atheists."[47] His idea that God's sovereignty necessarily implies that he determined all events beforehand has been refuted in the second volume of this series (Appendix III). At this point, it is enough to maintain that the "prayer of a righteous person has great power as it is working" (James 5:16). Instead, (hyper-)Calvinists believe that prayers do not effectuate anything; they themselves are just part of God's eternal decree. The Bible says: Prayer B leads to effect C. (Hyper-)Calvinism says: Prayer B and (seeming) "effect" C are both effects of counsel A.

What use would the many biblical references about the *effectuality* of practical faith be if, as (hyper-)Calvinism claims, all these effects are pseudo-effects in that both the prayers and their alleged effects had been decreed by God from eternity? Where do we find this in Scripture? (Hyper-)Calvinistic

---

46. Cf. Boyd (2000, 7).
47. Sproul (1986, 25-26).

Practical Faith

determinism is but a product of an overheated scholastic rationalism concerning God's sovereignty, in direct opposition to the clear statements of Scripture: God announces that he will do A, faith's fervent prayer intervenes, God relents, and decides not to do A but rather B, as faith has asked.[48]

7.7 Once Saved, Always Saved?
7.7.1 Remonstrantism and Dort[49]

In §6.7 I mentioned perseverance, which is often viewed as the finishing touch of God's work *in* us, and which has everything to do with practical faith. In the Reformed tradition, this perseverance or endurance occupies an important place. It is radically opposed to the doctrine of the (alleged) apostasy of the saints, the doctrine that true believers can fall away from the faith and go to perdition. Indirectly, this Reformed doctrine reverberates in many answers in the Heidelberg Catechism and in various articles of the Belgic Confession,[50] and very directly in the Canons of Dort, as a reply to the Remonstrants,[51] who doubted the perseverance of all the saints, that is, did not want to exclude the possibility of the apostasy of some of them.[52]

In 1610, the Remonstrants stated the following (Article V): "That those who are incorporated into Christ by a true faith, and have thereby become partakers of his life-giving Spirit, have thereby full power to strive against Satan, sin, the world, and their own flesh, and to win the victory, it being well understood that it is ever through the assisting grace of the Holy

---

48. See extensively, Ouweneel (2008, chapters 3–5 and 8).
49. Non-Reformed readers must know that the word "Dort" (or "Dordt") is short for "Dordrecht," the Dutch city where in 1618–1619 the (national and international) Synod of Dordrecht (or Dor[d]t) was held (the Dutch adjective to Dordrecht is "Dordts," and the inhabitant of Dordrecht is a "Dordtenaar"). The Canons of Dor[d]t were issued by the Synod of Dord[rech]t.
50. Berkouwer (1958, 19–31).
51. I leave aside here the question if, and in how far, Remonstrantism is the same as Arminianism; cf. http://johnmarkhicks.com/wp-content/uploads/sites/10/2010/03/jmh-diss-rev.pdf
52. Berkouwer (1958, 25–31).

Ghost [Phil. 1:19]; and that Jesus Christ assists them through his Spirit in all temptations, extends to them his hand, and if only they are ready for the conflict, and desire his help, and are not inactive, keeps them from falling, so that they, by no craft or power of Satan, can be misled, nor plucked out of Christ's hands, according to the word of Christ, John x. 28: 'Neither shall any man pluck them out of my hand.' But whether they are capable, through negligence, of forsaking again the first beginnings of their life in Christ, of again returning to this present evil world [2 Tim. 4:10], of turning away from the holy doctrine which was delivered them [cf. Jude 1:3], of losing a good conscience [1 Tim. 1:19], of becoming devoid of grace [Heb. 12:15], that must be more particularly determined out of the Holy Scriptures before they can teach it with the full persuasion of their minds [Rom. 14:5]."[53]

It is striking to see how carefully the Remonstrants express themselves. They do not *teach* the apostasy of saints but wish to leave that possibility open; they simply ask for further theological investigation. But apparently, the Counter-Remonstrants did not need that. Not only the Counter-Remonstrance of 1611 (especially Article 6), but the entire chapter V in the Canons of Dort (1618–1619) is devoted to the perseverance of the saints, in close coherence with the doctrine of predestination. I only quote here V.6-7: "[6] For God ... does not take the Holy Spirit from his own completely, even when they fall grievously. Neither does God let them fall down so far that they forfeit the grace of adoption and the state of justification, or commit the sin which leads to death (the sin against the Holy Spirit), and plunge themselves, entirely forsaken by God, into eternal ruin. [7] For, in the first place, God preserves in those saints when they fall the imperishable seed from which they have been born again, lest it perish or be dislodged. Secondly, by his Word and Spirit God certainly and effectively renews them to repentance. . . ." Articles 12 and 13 add that this assurance must be an incentive to godliness, and

---

53. http://en.wikipedia.org/wiki/Five_Articles_of_Remonstrance.

no inducement to carelessness.

7.7.2 Perseverance

The entire argument concerning perseverance is rooted in the preservation by God, who does not forsake the work of his hands (cf. Ps. 138:8). This one-sided emphasis on God's sovereign work could be expected from the Counter-Remonstrants, just like the one-sided emphasis on human responsibility could be expected from the Remonstrants.[54]

To be sure, the true believer may reckon with God's preservation, and besides many other things God is also the "God of endurance" (Rom. 15:5; or "of perseverance," MEV; Greek, *hypomonē*). However, in general, Scripture connects the term "perseverance" or "endurance" rather with human responsibility, and thus with the practical confidence of faith. It is *we* who have to persevere or endure. For instance, in the parable of the sower we hear: "As for that [seed] in the good soil, they are those who, hearing the word, hold it fast in an honest and good heart, and bear fruit with patience [*hypomonē*]" (Luke 8:15).

There are many of such passages that connect perseverance (endurance, patience, steadfastness, *hypomonē*) with our responsibility: "By your *endurance* you will gain your lives" (Luke 21:19). God "will render to each one according to his works: to those who by *patience* in well-doing seek for glory and honor and immortality, he will give eternal life" (Rom. 2:6-7). "For you have need of *endurance*, so that when you have done the will of God you may receive what is promised" (Heb. 10:36). "[L]et us . . . lay aside every weight, and sin which clings so closely, and let us run with *endurance* the race that is set before us" (12:1). "And let *steadfastness* have its full effect, that you may be perfect and complete, lacking in nothing" (James 1:4). "Behold, we consider those blessed who *remained steadfast* [*hypomeinantas*]" (5:11; see further Acts 1:14; 2:42; Rom. 5:3-4; 8:25; 15:5; 2 Cor. 12:12; Eph. 6:18; Col. 1:11;

---

54. Cf. Ouweneel (2008b, chapters 10–14).

1 Thess. 1:3; 2 Thess. 1:4; 3:5; 1 Tim. 6:11; 2 Tim. 3:10; Titus 2:2).

Perseverance is something that God does not do for believers but that they must do themselves, though, of course, by the power of the Holy Spirit. See especially Luke 21:19 just quoted: "You will be saved by being faithful to me" (CEV). "You will save yourselves by continuing strong in your faith through all these things" (ERV). "By your endurance you will gain your lives" (NASB). Endurance is *our* work, though, I repeat, it is not possible without the preserving power of God. Yet, it is primarily *our* responsibility. Therefore, I view it as unwise to couple the question of the (non-)apostasy of saints to the term "perseverance," as Reformed tradition has done, because many confessing Christians did *not* "endure to the end" (Matt. 24:13). When it comes to the Christians' responsibility one may wonder how many will safely reach the finish at all: "[T]he righteous is scarcely saved" (1 Pet. 4:18).

7.7.3 God's Preservation: Exegetical

In opposition to the believer's responsibility we find the divine side: assurance of faith (or, assurance of salvation) can be *assurance* only if it does not depend simply on our perseverance but on the preserving hand of God. Here again, the New Testament is perfectly balanced by underscoring both sides. People have a natural tendency to one-sidedness. Those who emphasize "once saved always saved" emphasize the divine side; those who reject "once saved always saved" accentuate the human side. Both have an arsenal of Bible passages at their disposal, as we will see. But both make the same mistake of selective Bible reading.

In fact, the situation is even more complicated. In the former theory we may distinguish between a classic-Calvinistic (federalist) and a moderate Calvinistic view, and in the latter theory we may distinguish between a "Reformed"-Arminian[55] and a Wesleyan-Arminian view. At least, these are the

---

55. Jacob Arminius always continued to consider himself to be thoroughly Reformed; cf. De Boer (2010).

Practical Faith

four views that have been defended by Michael S. Horton, Norman L. Geisler, Stephen M. Ashby, and J. Steven Harper, respectively, in a comparative study on eternal security.[56] Nevertheless, basically there are only two views: truly regenerate Christians cannot fall away, or they can (and sometimes do).

The *first* view, which is defended by Calvinists but also by certain Evangelicals such as Joseph Prince of Singapore,[57] likes to refer to passages such as John 5:24, "[W]hoever hears my word and believes him who sent me has eternal life. He *does not come into judgment*, but has passed from death to life"; 6:39, "And this is the will of him who sent me, that I should *lose nothing* of all that he has given me, but raise it up on the last day"; and 10:28–29, "I give them [i.e., my sheep] eternal life, and they will *never perish*, and no one will snatch them out of my hand. My Father, who has given them to me, is greater than all, and no one is able to snatch them out of the Father's hand."

Jesus' intercession is the guarantee for the believers' eternal salvation:[58] "I do not ask that you take them out of the world, but that you keep them from the evil one. . . . Father, *I desire* [lit., I *will* or *want*] that they also, whom you have given me, may be with me where I am, to see my glory that you have given me because you loved me before the foundation of the world" (17:15, 24); "I have prayed for you that your faith may not fail" (Luke 22:32). "Therefore he is able to save *completely* those who come to God through him, because he always lives to intercede for them" (Heb. 7:25 NIV).[59]

Paul says, "I am sure of this, that he who began a good work in you will bring it to *completion* at the day of Jesus Christ" (Phil. 1:6). "Who shall separate us from the love of Christ? Shall tribulation, or distress, or persecution, or fam-

---

56. Pinson (2002).
57. See Prince (2008).
58. See Berkouwer (1958, 131–41).
59. Also see ibid., 83–84 for an appeal to many Old Testament passages.

ine, or nakedness, or danger, or sword? . . . For I am sure that neither death nor life, nor angels nor rulers, nor things present nor things to come, nor powers, nor height nor depth, nor anything else in all creation, will be able to separate us from the love of God in Christ Jesus our Lord" (Rom. 8:35, 38–39). Regeneration has as its aim "an inheritance that is imperishable, undefiled, and unfading, kept in heaven for you, who by God's power are being *guarded* through faith for a salvation ready to be revealed in the last time" (1 Pet. 1:4–5). Our eternal destiny is entirely in God's hand: "[T]he God of all grace, who has called you to his eternal glory in Christ, will himself restore, confirm, strengthen, and establish you" (5:10).

7.7.4 God's Preservation: Theological

In addition to exegetical arguments, theological arguments have been adduced as well: the doctrine of the possible apostasy of true saints is allegedly in conflict with that of predestination and of the covenant: "'For the mountains may depart and the hills be removed, but my steadfast love shall not depart from you, and my covenant of peace shall not be removed,' says the Lord, who has compassion on you" (Isa. 54:10). "God's purpose of election" will "continue, not because of works but because of him who calls" (Rom. 9:11). "For the gifts and the calling of God are irrevocable" (11:29).

An important set of arguments has to do with regeneration and the "new man." It is argued that it is inconceivable that a person who is born again—renewed down to the roots, one might say—and has the Holy Spirit dwelling in him—who is "to be with you forever"! (John 14:16)—could perish after all. The new, divine life in the believer cannot possibly end in eternal death. The "old man" does not exist anymore; he has been nailed to the cross once and for all, and put aside (Rom. 6:6). Instead, a "new man" has come into existence (Eph. 2:15; 4:23–24; Col. 3:9–11). This "new man" can never perish because he is nothing less than Christ himself as he is displayed in his saints. And this "new man" can in no way be converted back into the "old man." It is the non-regenerates and those invested with the "old man" who come to be lost — never the regenerates and those invested with the "new man."

In short, the view that the regenerate person can never perish clearly seems to have a firm foundation. The discussion is not about the question whether people who *confess* to be Christians can perish. There is no doubt about this, for there are indeed false confessors: "Not everyone who says to me, 'Lord, Lord,' will enter the kingdom of heaven, but the one who does the will of my Father who is in heaven" (Matt. 7:21; cf. Luke 6:46). "[F]rom among your own selves will arise men speaking twisted things, to draw away the disciples after them" (Acts 20:30). "[P]eople will be lovers of self, lovers of money, . . . lovers of pleasure rather than lovers of God, *having the appearance of godliness*, but denying its power" (2 Tim. 3:1–5). "[T]here will be false teachers among you, who will secretly bring in destructive heresies" (2 Pet. 2:1). "[N]ow many antichrists have come . . . They went out from us, but they were not of us" (1 John 2:18–19; cf. Rev. 2:20–23; 3:15–17).

I repeat, theologians generally agree that those who confess to be Christians can fall away and lose their faith. That is not the issue. The real question is whether people who not only confess to be Christians but genuinely *are* (regenerate, sanctified, justified) Christians, invested with the "new man," can perish after all. Yes, is the reply of those whom we are going to scrutinize in the next sections.

7.8 Once Saved, *Not* Always Saved?
7.8.1 Biblical Arguments

The *second* view — true believers can fall away from their faith and perish — is defended by Roman Catholics, Lutherans, Arminians,[60] and many Evangelicals.[61] The striking thing is that they can point to at least as many Bible passages as the

---
60. See on these three movements Berkouwer (1958, chapter 3).
61. See Pawson (1996, especially chapter 3); also cf. Duffield and Van Cleave (1996, 271–77).

first party. It begins already in the Old Testament; we read of young King Saul: "'Then the Spirit of the Lord will rush upon you, and you will prophesy with them and be turned into another man.' . . . When he turned his back to leave Samuel, God gave him another heart" (1 Sam. 10:6, 9). That is strong language! In the light of the New Testament, hardly anyone would hesitate to say that Saul was born again (cf. Ezek. 18:31; 36:26; cf. Eph. 1:18). Yet, we read afterward: "[T]he Spirit of the Lord departed from Saul, and a harmful spirit from the Lord tormented him" (1 Sam. 16:14). After this, Saul slipped away into darkness ever further, and finally Samuel told him: "[T]he Lord has turned from you and become your enemy" (28:16). A few hours later, Saul took his own life (31:4).

The apostle Paul, too, uses strong language. In 1 Corinthians 5:11, he speaks of someone "who bears the name of brother," thus avoiding the question whether he is a real brother or not. But elsewhere he explicitly does speak of a "brother": "[I]f your *brother* is grieved by what you eat, you are no longer walking in love. By what you eat, do not destroy the *one for whom Christ died*" (Rom. 14:15); "by your knowledge this weak person is destroyed, *the brother for whom Christ died*" (1 Cor. 8:11).[62] There is no doubt that here "destroying" is to be taken as MSG renders the former verse: "These, remember, are persons for whom Christ died. Would you risk sending them to hell over an item in their diet?" Apparently, Paul sees this as a possibility even for himself: "I discipline my body and keep it under control, lest after preaching to others I myself should be disqualified" (1 Cor. 9:27, assuming that "disqualified" really means being lost forever).

The New Testament mentions a number of "if's" (Greek, *ei mē, ei ge, ean,* or *eanper*) that seem to relativize the assurance of faith, starting with Jesus himself: "If [*ean*] anyone does not abide in me he is thrown away like a branch and

---

62. The (Reformed) Annotation in the Dutch Statenvertaling weakens this: he *would* perish if he were not preserved by God's power and Christ's intercession. But this is reading one's own theology into the text.

Practical Faith

withers; and the branches are gathered, thrown into the fire, and burned" (John 15:6; cf. vv. 7, 10, 14). Paul speaks of "the gospel . . . by which you are being saved, if [*ei*] you hold fast to the word I preached to you—unless you believed in vain" (1 Cor. 15:1-2). "For in this tent we groan, longing to put on our heavenly dwelling, if indeed [*ei ge*] by putting it on we may not be found naked [i.e., unsaved]⁶³" (2 Cor. 5:2-3); ". . . in order to present you holy and blameless and above reproach before him, if indeed (*ei ge*) you continue in the faith, stable and steadfast, not shifting from the hope of the gospel" (Col. 1:22-23). "Christ is faithful over God's house as a son. And we are his house if indeed (*ean* or *eanper*) we hold fast our confidence and our boasting in our hope. . . . For we have come to share in Christ, if indeed [*eanper*] we hold our original confidence firm to the end" (Heb. 3:6, 14). "If [*ean*] what you heard from the beginning abides in you, then you too will abide in the Son and in the Father" (1 John 2:24; cf. v. 3; 4:20). In all these cases, through the expression "if (indeed)," salvation is made dependent on the believers' faithfulness, their endurance, their authenticity: you are saved *if indeed* you endure to the end.

Much emphasis has always been placed on Hebrews 6:4-6 as proof for the idea that apostasy of true believers is possible: "For it is impossible, in the case of those who have once been enlightened, who have tasted the heavenly gift, and have shared in the Holy Spirit, and have tasted the goodness of the word of God and the powers of the age to come, and then have *fallen away* [Greek, *parapesontas*], to restore them again to repentance, since they are crucifying once again the Son of God to their own harm and holding him up to contempt."⁶⁴ And chapter 10:26-29: "For if we go on sinning deliberately after receiving the knowledge of the truth, there no longer remains a sacrifice for sins, but a fearful expectation of judg-

---

63. The text is capable of multiple interpretations; cf. Barnett (1997, 262–63); I follow Ellis here (1957, 220–21); Grosheide (1959, 144–45).
64. See Ouweneel (1982, 1:77–79); cf. Berkouwer (1958, 116–20).

ment, and a fury of fire that will consume the adversaries. . . . How much worse punishment, do you think, will be deserved by the one who has trampled underfoot the Son of God, and has profaned the blood of the covenant by which he was sanctified, and has outraged the Spirit of grace?"[65]

7.8.2 Perseverance and Apostasy

In this context, let us look at some passages on perseverance (endurance, steadfastness) again: "Therefore do not throw away your confidence, which has a great reward. For you have need of endurance, so that when you have done the will of God you may receive what is promised" (Heb. 10:35-36). And Jesus said, "[Y]ou will be hated by all for my name's sake. But the one who endures to the end will be saved" (Matt. 10:22; cf. 24:13). In both passages, the apparent implication is: the one who does *not* endure to the end will *not* be saved. Here lies the full emphasis on the side of human responsibility: "[W]ork out *your own* salvation with fear and trembling" (even though the text continues with: ". . . for it is God who works in you, both to will and to work for his good pleasure") (Phil. 2:12-13). "But you, beloved, building *yourselves* up in your most holy faith and praying in the Holy Spirit, keep *yourselves* in the love of God" (Jude 20-21).

Many have wondered: What is the sense of all these biblical warnings if true believers *cannot* fall away anyway? Gerrit C. Berkouwer does believe in the perseverance of the saints, yet takes the admonitions to not fall away very seriously.[66] Natural branches "were broken off because of their unbelief, but you stand fast through faith. So do not become proud, but fear. For if God did not spare the natural branches, neither will he spare you. Note then the kindness and the severity of God: severity toward those who have fallen, but God's kindness to you, *provided* [Greek, *ean*] you continue in his kindness. Otherwise you too will be cut off" (Rom. 11:20-22). "There-

---

65. See Ouweneel (1982, 2:43-44); cf. Berkouwer (1958, 120-21).
66. Berkouwer (1958, chapter 4 on perseverance and admonition).

fore let anyone who thinks that he stands take heed lest he fall" (1 Cor. 10:12). "Examine yourselves, to see whether you are in the faith. Test yourselves. Or do you not realize this about yourselves, that Jesus Christ is in you? — unless indeed you fail to meet the test" (2 Cor. 13:5). "Brothers, if anyone is caught in any transgression, you who are spiritual should restore him in a spirit of gentleness. Keep watch on yourself, lest you too be tempted" (Gal. 6:1).[67]

"Take care, *brothers*, lest there be in any of you an evil, unbelieving heart, leading you to fall away from the living God. But exhort one another every day, as long as it is called 'today,' [Ps. 95:7] that none of you may be hardened by the deceitfulness of sin" (Heb. 3:12-13). Apparently, *brothers* can fall away![68] "Therefore, while the promise of entering his rest still stands, let us fear lest any of you should seem to have failed to reach it. . . . Let us therefore strive to enter that rest, so that no one may fall by the same sort of disobedience" (4:1, 11). "See that you do not refuse him who is speaking. For if they did not escape when they refused him who warned them on earth, much less will we escape if we reject him who warns from heaven" (12:25).

"Be sober-minded; be watchful. Your adversary the devil prowls around like a roaring lion, seeking someone to devour" (1 Pet. 5:8). "For if, after [some] have escaped the defilements of the world through the knowledge of our Lord and Savior Jesus Christ, they are again entangled in them and overcome, the last state has become worse for them than the first. For it would have been better for them never to have known the way of righteousness than after knowing it to turn back from the holy commandment delivered to them" (2 Pet. 2:20-21).

When speaking of falling away from faith, the New Testament contains not only warnings but also genuine proph-

---
67. Cf. ibid., chapter 6 on perseverance and temptation.
68. Even the Annotation of the Dutch Statenvertaling supposes that in a "brother" (!) there can be a heart "that, being seemingly a Christian, yet is unbelieving."

ecies. What in 2 Peter 3:17 is only a threat ("You therefore, beloved, ... take care that you are not carried away with the error of lawless people and lose [Greek, *ekpesēte*] your own stability") is in 1 Timothy 4:1 a prediction: "Now the Spirit expressly says that in later times some will depart [*apostēsontai*, related to *apostasia*] from the faith by devoting themselves to deceitful spirits and teachings of demons." Before the day of the Lord there will be first the apostasy (*apostasia*), that is, the "general apostasy from the purity of the gospel" (Annotation, Dutch Statenvertaling), connected with the rise of the Antichrist (2 Thess. 2:3), that is, at the very heart of Christianity. Already in the New Testament we hear about specific Christian apostates: Hymenaeus, Alexander and Philetus (1 Tim. 1:20; 2 Tim. 2:17), Demas (2 Tim. 4:10), the antichrists who left (1 John 2:18-19), and perhaps Ananias and Sapphira (Acts 5:1-11; see §7.9.3).

7.9 Evaluation
7.9.1 Reconciliation Possible?

I suppose there are few examples in theology in which two views are so diametrically opposed to each other, and both have so much Scriptural evidence on their sides. Several have spoken of an "antinomy, a diametrical opposition."[69] Reconciliation of the two viewpoints seems to be totally excluded *a priori*, for it is black or white: true regenerates can perish after all, or they cannot perish. An intermediate viewpoint is impossible. Or is this only seemingly the case? Howard Marshall has argued that there is truth in both viewpoints, and that therefore a middle road must certainly be possible.[70] And Adrio König looks for a kind of "pastoral compromise": encourage the doubting believers with Jesus' promises (John 10:28-29), and warn backsliding believers that they can be saved only if they endure to the end (Matt. 24:13).[71]

---

69. Berkouwer (1958, 96).
70. Marshall (1969).
71. König (2006, 475).

Practical Faith

It is not difficult to imagine how both parties have tried to disprove the Scriptural evidence of the opponents. Thus, those who teach the possibility of true believers falling away can reject the arguments of their opponents by arguing that the passages quoted present us with only the firm promises of God, which people on their part may reject. And those who deny the possibility of true believers falling away can wave aside the arguments of their opponents by arguing that human responsibility can never annihilate God's eternal counsel and irrevocable promises.

One of the striking examples in which Scripture's paradoxical speaking comes to light is the term "keeping" or "guarding." On the one hand, it is God who keeps his own safely to the end: "Holy Father, keep [Greek, *tēreō*] them in your name. . . . I do not ask that you take them out of the world, but that you keep [*tēreō*] them from the evil one" (John 17:11, 15). "And the peace of God, which surpasses all understanding, will guard [*phroureō*] your hearts and your minds in Christ Jesus" (Phil. 4:7). "[M]ay your whole spirit and soul and body be kept [*tēreō*] blameless at the coming of our Lord Jesus Christ" (1 Thess. 5:23). "But the Lord is faithful. He will establish you and guard [*phylassō*] you against the evil one" (2 Thess. 3:3). On the other hand, we hear: "[K]eep [*tēreō*] *yourself* pure" (1 Tim. 5:22). "Religion that is pure and undefiled before God, the Father, is this: to visit orphans and widows in their affliction, and to keep [*tēreō*] *oneself* unstained from the world" (James 1:27). "[H]e who has been born of God keeps [*tēreō*] *himself*" (1 John 5:18 NKJV),[72] and: "But you, beloved, building yourselves up in your most holy faith and praying in the Holy Spirit, keep [*tēreō*] *yourselves* in the love of God" (Jude 1:20–21).[73]

---

72. Cf., however, NIV: "the One who was born of God keeps them safe"; cf. Ouweneel (2007b, 286–87).
73. See Berkouwer (1958,103–106).

7.9.2 The Two Sides

It is with this matter as with the gracious, sovereign election by God and the conversion and faith resulting from human responsibility.[74] These two sides seem to be logically contradictory, but they would be so only if the terms involved were conceptualized. Instead, we have to do here with "boundary concepts" or "ideas."[75] It is exactly the same, on the one hand, with the firm promises and preservation by God, so that the believer has no reason to worry about his salvation. The promises of the Father, the intercession by the Son, and the power of the Holy Spirit are the common guarantee for the believer's salvation. On the other hand, the Christian who consciously chooses to follow God-dishonoring pathways has every reason to be concerned about his salvation. There is no falling away of the saints (holy Christians), but there is definitely a falling away of *un*holy Christians.

The two sides may never be confused. Confessing Christians who enter into wicked ways may never hide themselves behind the *first* (non-apostasy) view, as if, thanks to God's grace, nothing could happen to them. In certain hyper-Calvinist circles, this is referred to as "sewing pillows to the armholes" (Ezek.13:18 KJV; cf. ESV: ". . . women who sew magic bands upon all wrists").[76] I remember the example of a mother who, when told that her daughter was a prostitute and a drug addict, nonetheless praised the Lord because her daughter had made a decision for the Lord when she was seven; the mother was convinced that they would see each other in heaven again. I do not wish to hurt any mother's feelings, but this mother had not the slightest ground for her conviction: if the daughter had chosen this pathway in full freedom, and would not repent, she would perish.

Conversely, Christians who sincerely confess their sins

---

74. Ouweneel (2008b, chapters 10–14).
75. Ibid., §§1.4–1.5; also see Ouweneel (2014a; 2014b).
76. See, for instance, William Huntington (c. 1800), in *The Arminian Skeleton* (http://www.williamhuntington.net/Works/Volume07/07004.htm).

Practical Faith

before God and put their confidence in his promises, should not be confused by the *second* (apostasy) view, as if they, because of the shortcomings they still find in themselves, could still perish. From a pastoral point of view, this is of the greatest importance. To those who choose a way of backsliding we must definitely witness that such a *way* ends in eternal destruction. Whether they will repent in time (human side), or whether God will bring them back from this road in time (divine side), is another matter. However, to the sincere but wavering souls we must say that they should not be diverted by their shortcomings but should look to Christ and to the firm promises of God. The former Christians (the trespassers) look *too little* at themselves and at their sins, and hide behind a false appeal to God's promises. The latter (wavering) Christians look *too much* at themselves, and hide behind their sins instead of hiding behind the blood of Christ.

7.9.3 Theological Versus Pastoral

Perhaps I can summarize the matter as follows: *theologically* I feel more at home with the *first* (non-apostasy) view, *pastorally* more with the *second* (apostasy) view. As to the first view: a person in whom the new, divine life, and the Holy Spirit dwells cannot perish. I repeat (see §7.7.3): it is inconceivable that a person who is truly born again could perish after all. The "new man" can never perish because he is nothing less than Christ himself as he is displayed in his saints. And this "new man" can in no way be changed back into the "old man." Renewed people cannot go to hell; the new life of regeneration can never perish. He who has eternal life will one day definitely enter into eternal life.

Think of Hebrews 6:4-6 again: there is *nothing* in this passage that can be limited to reborn Christians only. These people have been "enlightened," as is true for every person who has come under the sound of the gospel. They have "tasted" the heavenly gift but not necessarily "eaten." And having "shared" (Greek, *metochous*) in the Holy Spirit does not necessarily mean anything more than that they ware participants in the "domain" (family, church) where the Holy Spirit worked.[77] I am not aware of any Bible passage in which it is said that reborn people, those who have received eternal life, those who have been invested with the "new man," etc., could still perish. In all the passages mentioned it is possible to think of false confessors.

Pastorally, however, I feel more at home with the *second* (apostasy) view, for the evildoer may never be lulled to sleep through a wrong appeal to God's promises. To the wavering Christian we say: Look to Christ, he will preserve and save you. To the evildoing Christian we say: Look at your wickedness and repent, return to the Lord, otherwise you will perish. It does not matter what kind of "fantastic Christian" he may have been before his fall. God is the only One "who knows the hearts of all" (Acts 1:24; cf. 15:8; John 2:24-25; Jer. 17:9). We hear someone's confession and see his behavior, but only God knows if someone is genuinely regenerate; we may misjudge someone's fruits completely.

Some biblical examples: Ananias and Sapphira had been admitted to the congregation but we cannot know for sure whether they were born again. In Acts 5:1 they are simply called "a man with his wife," whereas usually in Acts we find a more faith-related description of Christians who are newly presented, such as "son of encouragement" (4:36), "disciple" (9:10; 16:1), "devout man who feared God" (10:2; cf. 22:12), "evangelist" (21:8). Even Simon the Magician believed and was baptized (8:13), yet Peter says to him later on: "May your silver perish with you! . . . your heart is not right before God. Repent, therefore, of this wickedness of yours. . . . For I see that you are in the gall of bitterness and in the bond of iniquity" (vv. 20-23).

When a so-called "fantastic Christian" enters upon a road

---

77. *Contra* T. Kassa in Adeyemo (2006, 1497): "They have *tasted* and experienced God's heavenly gift fully through sharing in the Holy Spirit's baptism."

of wickedness and iniquity, we are never allowed to say that he will be all right. If he is really born again, God will certainly put him right—but it would be the greatest foolishness to tell him that when he is still on that evil road. What we do have to say is that the *road* on which he is walking leads to hell. We cannot look into his heart, but we do know where the *road* on which he is will end. Whether God will bring him back from this road is another matter; at this moment this is not the concern of either the pastor or the evildoer. The only thing we do is earnestly warn him about the *way* he is going.

This is a matter of "rightly dividing the word of truth" (2 Tim. 2:15 NKJV). The Word of God must be handled as the "sword of the Spirit" (Eph. 6:17), not as a "sword of the flesh." It is pure flesh if we batter wavering souls with New Testament warning passages, or if Christian evildoers are lulled to sleep with comforting passages. With the Bible in our hand we can deliver devastating blows if Scripture is made subservient to the flesh. It is like the "Thus says the Lord" of the false prophets (1 Kgs 22:11; Jer. 28:2), who "smear with whitewash" (Ezek. 13:10-15; 22:28). It is like the sweet honey that does not belong to the grain offering (Lev. 2:11).

Of the true believers it is said that "while we *were* still sinners, Christ died for us" (Rom. 5:8). Believers can still sin but they are no longer sinners, that is, people who are in the *power* of sin (cf. "set free from sin," 6:7, 18, 22; 8:2). However, just the same, James 5:19-20 says: "My *brothers*, if anyone *among you* wanders from the truth and someone brings him back, let him know that whoever brings back a *sinner* from his wandering will save his soul from death and will cover a multitude of sins." No believer is *too good* that he cannot become an evildoer, erring on wicked roads. And no believer is *too bad* that he cannot put his confidence in the firm promises of God.

Chapter 8
Positional Sanctification

But you were washed,
you were sanctified,
you were justified
in the name of the Lord Jesus Christ
and by the Spirit of our God.
                    1 Corinthians 6:11

To those who are elect exiles . . .
according to the foreknowledge of God the
Father,
in the sanctification of the Spirit,
for obedience to Jesus Christ
and for sprinkling with his blood.
                    1 Peter 1:1–2

[W]e have been sanctified
through the offering of the body of Jesus
Christ
once for all.
                    Hebrews 10:14

Summary: *Closely linked with justification is sanctification; positional justification and sanctification are followed by practical justification and sanctification. "Holiness" is a description of God's* *being, as well as of things and persons that God has declared to be holy because they have been separated from evil and consecrated to God, and are reflections of his righteousness and holiness. Reformed theology formally recognizes only positional justification and practical sanctification; it hardly ever refers to practical justification and positional sanctification. Moreover, this theology emphasizes the individual more than the collective aspects of justification and sanctification.*

There are three phases in justification and sanctification: (a) the moment of conversion, (b) spiritual maturation ("perfection"), and (c) eschatological completion. There is also an outward sanctification, like that of children in a Christian family, or nominal Christians in churches. In Hebrews, sanctification is discussed especially in view of the priestly ministry. The chapter briefly discusses the liberal, the sacramental, the perfectionist, the Pentecostal, the Reformed, and the (or an) Evangelical view. Great emphasis is placed on the nature of God's holiness, both in judgment and in redemption, because the believers' holiness is a reflection of it.

Finally, the biblical view of sanctification is compared with the Reformed view of Romans 7 as a description of the normal Christian condition. It is argued that the "I" in verse 7-16 is definitely born again, but has not (yet) learned to live by the power of the Holy Spirit. Saying that this is the normal Christian life is just as mistaken as the other extreme: the view that the believer can, here on earth, get rid of the sinful nature (perfectionism). In spiritual growth, the Christian knows his sin more and more (loathing his old self) and knows ever more profoundly the grace of God.

8.1 Sanctification and Justification
8.1.1 Terminology: Old Testament

WHY DO I INCLUDE two chapters on sanctification in a book on justification? Because of the Reformed model that places justification first, followed by sanctification. I argued why this is a mistake. What is first is not justification, but *positional* justification *along with positional sanctification* followed by *practical* sanctification *along with practical justification*. I even believe that positional justification cannot be understood properly without taking into account positional sanctification, and that practical sanctification cannot be understood properly without taking into account practical justification.

Let me first point out the well-known riches of the English language, which are sometimes a bit overdone. We saw this with the Romanic terms "just," "justice," and "justify/justification," which correspond with the Germanic terms "righteous," "righteousness" and "making/declaring righteous." Similarly, the Romanic terms "saint" or "sacred," "sanctity" and "sanctify/sanctification/consecration" correspond with the Germanic terms "holy," "holiness" and "hallow" or "making/declaring holy." This correspondence is something we constantly have to keep in mind. Even if fine distinctions may have developed in the English language between "justice" and "righteousness," or between "sanctity" and "holiness," they have no theological significance: Hebrew *qadosh* and Greek *hagios* both mean "holy" as well as "saint," these two terms being identical.[1]

In the Old Testament, the root *q-d-sh* primarily refers to the cultic. This root is presumably related to *q-d*, "to cut," and hence means "to separate, set apart." It pertains to that which is separated from the secular (cf. Ezek. 42:20), withheld from profane use, and set apart for, or consecrated to, God. "Holy" (or "sacred") places, with "holy/sacred" objects (utensils), are places that have been particularly consecrated to God, or places where God's holiness dwells, or becomes manifest, such as the burning bush (Exod. 3:2–6), the tabernacle (29:44–45; etc.), Gilgal (Josh. 5:15), the "holy temple" (1 Kings 8:27–30; 1 Chron. 29:3; Ps. 5:7; 79:1; 138:2; Isa. 64:11), Zion the "holy mountain/hill" (Ps. 2:6; 43:3; Isa. 11:9; 27:13; 56:7; Dan. 9:16), Jerusalem the "holy city" (Neh. 11:1, 18; Isa. 48:2; 52:1; Dan. 9:24; cf. Matt. 4:5; 27:53; Rev. 11:2; 21:2, 10; 22:19).

On the high priest's turban it was written: "Holy to the

---

1. Kittel *et al.* (1964, 1:90); Brown (1992, 3:877–87); Von Rad (2001, 205–207).

Lord" (Exod. 28:36), and in the Messianic Kingdom this phrase will even be written on the bells of the horses (Zech. 14:20). It means, "Set apart/Dedicated/Consecrated/Sacred to the Lord" (cf. CJB, CEV, GNT, TLB, NABRE), so that even in the smallest details his holiness (glory, majesty, luster) will become manifest.

"Holy" is also that which belongs to God, or that in which his holiness becomes visible: his "holy" word (Ps. 105:42 NASB), the "Holy" Scriptures (Rom. 1:2; 2 Tim. 3:15). The same holds for the "Holy" Spirit (from Ps. 51:11 and Isa. 63:10-11 to Jude 20), which is the Spirit who makes *us* holy too (cf. Gal. 5:16, 18; 1 Thess. 4:7-8; 2 Thess. 2:13; 1 Pet. 1:2). Also institutions that express the glory of God, such as the covenant (Dan. 11:28, 30) and the Shabbat (Gen. 2:3; Exod. 20:22; Deut. 5:12), are called holy.[2] And of course, as God is holy, that which expresses his being, that is, his name, is holy too (Lev. 20:3; 22:2; 1 Chron. 16:10, 35; Ps. 33:21; 103:1; Ezek. 36:20-23).

One reason, though a negative one, why God is called "holy" is that he is exalted above all that is secular or profane (Isa. 5:16; 6:3; Hos. 11:9). Where God is manifested, or presented, or praised in his holiness, he is "hallowed" or "sanctified" (Num. 20:12-13; Isa. 5:16; Ezek. 20:41; 28:22, 25; 36:23; 38:16; 39:27; cf. Matt. 6:9; Luke 11:2). In such phrases, "hallow" or "sanctify" means "*proclaim* as holy." Twenty-nine times Isaiah calls God the "Holy One of Israel," in relation to both judgment and redemption.

Herman Bavinck referred to Hermann Cremer,[3] who emphasized that holiness is not primarily a relationship established from below upward, that is, from humanity toward God, but from above downward. That is, holiness is primarily an attribute of God, and subsequently in a derived sense also

---

2. Strikingly, *q-d-sh* can also be used for that which is consecrated to the false gods, and is therefore actually very *un*holy. Thus, *qadēsh* (fem.: *qedēshah*) is the sacred temple prostitute (both in Deut. 23:18).
3. Bavinck (2004, 2:219); Cremer (1917).

of creatures displaying (something of) God's holiness. No creature is ever holy in itself, nor can it ever hallow (sanctify) itself. All holiness and all sanctification proceed from God. He can hallow (sanctify) things or persons, that is, separate them from the profane and consecrate them to himself, but he alone is holy in himself. It is this very attribute that in every revelation of God brings people under the impression of his deity. If God swears by his holiness (Amos 4:2) this is the same as swearing by himself (6:8). This holiness manifests itself in redemption, consolation, faithfulness, but also in punishment and chastisement.[4]

8.1.2 Terminology: New Testament

In the New Testament, the use of the Greek *hagios* largely corresponds with that of the Hebrew *qadosh* in the Old Testament, although here the ceremonial to some extent makes room for ethical aspects.[5] God is the "holy Father" (John 17:11), the "Sovereign Lord holy and true" (Rev. 6:10). In 1 Peter 1:15–16 God is called holy in reference to Leviticus 19:2. The description *hagios* is also used for Christ (Mark 1:24; Luke 1:35; 4:34; John 6:69; Acts 3:14; 4:27, 30; 1 John 2:20; Rev. 3:7), and especially for the Holy Spirit (from Matt. 1:18 to Jude 1:20).[6]

The word *hagios* is related to *hagnos* (cf. *hazo*, "to venerate"), "pure" (2 Cor. 11:2; Phil. 4:8; 1 Tim. 5:22; Titus 2:5; James 3:17; 1 Pet. 3:2; 1 John 3:3). This element of purity is present in the one dimension of *hagios*, namely, being separated from sin. But at least as important is the positive dimension of *hagios*, which, if used other than for God or for Christ, means "consecrated/dedicated to God/Christ." The term *hagios* may sometimes refer to some outward holiness (1 Cor. 7:14; Heb. 9:1–25; see §8.4), but in general it refers to inward holiness. As we will see, when the term "holiness" is used for people, it means basically "godlikeness": "You shall be holy, for I am holy"

---

4. See extensively, Bavinck (2004, 2:220–21).
5. Demarest (1997, 407).
6. See Ouweneel (2007a, 244–45).

(1 Pet. 1:16, a quotation from Lev. 11:44–45; 19:2; 20:26; cf. 21:8). This will all be further explained below.

Derived from *hagios* are the following three nouns plus one verb:

(a) *Hagiasmos*, in ESV rendered "sanctification" (Rom. 6:19, 22; 1 Cor. 1:30; 1 Thess. 4:3; 2 Thess. 2:13; 1 Pet. 1:2) or "holiness" (1 Thess. 4:4, 7; 1 Tim. 2:15; Heb. 12:14). The term indicates the state of holiness ("separation from sin and consecration to God"), or the act leading to this state ("sanctification").

(b) *Hagiōsynē*, rendered "holiness," that is, the holy character of Christ (Rom. 1:4) and believers (2 Cor. 7:1; 1 Thess. 3:13).

(c) *Hagiotēs*, rendered "holiness," that is, the nature of God (Heb. 12:10) (in some of the manuscripts also in 2 Cor. 1:12).

(d) *Hagiazō*, rendered "to hallow" (God's name: Matt. 6:9; Luke 11:2), or "to consecrate" (of Christ: John 10:36; 17:19), or "to sanctify," either goods (Matt. 23:17, 19; 1 Tim. 4:5), or Israelites (Heb. 9:13), or believers (John 17:17, 19; Acts 20:32; 26:18; 1 Cor. 1:2; 6:11; Eph. 5:26; 1 Thess. 5:23; Heb. 2:11; 10:10, 14; 13:12), or confessors falling away (Heb. 10:29), or the unbelieving spouse of a believer (1 Cor. 7:14), or the "offering of the Gentiles" (Rom. 15:16), or "to set apart as holy" (2 Tim. 2:21), or "honor as holy" (1 Pet. 3:15). In most cases, it is "to make" something holy or sacred that was not thus before; sometimes it is "to treat" as holy (that is, something that was already holy before; e.g., Matt. 6:9; 1 Pet. 3:15). In Revelation 22:11 ("Let . . . the holy still be holy"), the sense of the verb is either "to continue to be holy" (cf. ERV), or "to become holier" (cf. TLB).

Much more clearly than in the Old Testament, in the New Testament the God who is *hagios* ("holy") is the God of *hagiasmos* ("sanctification"), that is, the God who separates people from the domain of all that conflicts with his being, and consecrates them to himself.

In addition to this, God is *hosios*, usually rendered "holy,"

Positional Sanctification

but in Acts 13:34 it is a rendering of the Hebrew *hasid* in Isaiah 55:3. The Septuagint has *hosios* here; in this ancient Greek version of the Tanakh, *hosios* is the rendering of *hasid*, never of *qadosh*. It has connotations such as "pious," "pure," and "righteous" (Rev. 5:4; 16:5; cf. Heb. 7:26), but—if used for God—also "gracious, merciful, benevolent, faithful," referring to covenant loyalty. The related *hosiotēs* is rendered "holiness" (Luke 1:75; Eph. 4:24), but with connotations of "holy attitude, piety, devotion."

There is yet a third New Testament term: *hieros*, "holy" in the sense of "sacred, consecrated," especially in connection with the temple ministry. *Ta hiera ergazomenoi* is "ministering the holy things" (1 Cor. 9:13 NKJV; ESV: "employed in the temple service"). *To hieron* means "temple" in the wide sense (Matt. 12:5-6; Acts 19:27; etc.), to be distinguished from *naos*, the actual temple house (Matt. 23:16-17; 26:61; etc.). Also compare *archiereus* and *hiereus*, "high priest" and "priest," and *hierothytos*, "offered in sacrifice [to idols]" (1 Cor. 10:28), *hierateia* (Luke 1:9; Heb. 7:25) and *hierateuma* (1 Pet. 2:5, 9), "priesthood, priestly ministry, priestly office," and *hierateuō*, "to serve as priest," and still other related words (*hieroprepēs, hierosyleō/hierosylos, hierourgeō, hierosynē*).

8.1.3 Reformed Sources

The Heidelberg Catechism seems to be conscious of what I am calling positional sanctification, as in Q&A 36: Christ "is our Mediator, and with His innocence and perfect holiness covers, in the sight of God, my sin, wherein I was conceived." And Q&A 60: ". . . without any merit of mine, of mere grace, grants and imputes to me the perfect satisfaction, righteousness, and holiness of Christ, as if I had never committed nor had any sins, ..." Apart from the imputation doctrine (see chapter 4), at least justification and sanctification are linked here in reference to the state of the believer that he has received by faith. In Q&A 70, this is followed by what I am calling practical sanctification: To be washed with Christ's Spirit means "... to be renewed by the Holy Spirit and sanctified to be members of Christ, so that we may more and more die unto sin and lead holy and unblameable lives." Here on earth, however, this process of sanctification has only limited success (Q&A 114): "... even the holiest men, while in this life, have only a small beginning of such obedience, yet so that with earnest purpose they begin to live not only according to some, but according to all the Commandments of God."

In the Belgic Confession, the justification of sinners (Article 23) and the sanctification of sinners (Article 24) are distinguished according to the common Reformed view: justification is treated from the strictly positional viewpoint, and sanctification from the strictly practical viewpoint. The title of Article 24 speaks of "Man's Sanctification and Good Works," but this turns out to refer to the good works that the justified person is deemed to produce: "Therefore, it is so far from being true that this justifying faith ... makes men remiss in a pious and *holy* life, that on the contrary without it they would never do anything out of love to God, ... Therefore it is impossible that this *holy* faith be unfruitful in man; for we do not speak of a vain faith, but of such a faith which is called in Scripture a 'faith working through love,' [Gal. 5:6] which excites man to the practice of those works which God has commanded in His Word. These works, as they proceed from the good root of faith, are good and acceptable in the sight God, forasmuch as they are all *sanctified* [i.e., made *or* declared holy] by His grace. Nevertheless they are of no account towards our justification, for it is by faith in Christ that we are justified, even before we do good works; otherwise they could not be good works, any more than the fruit of a tree can be good before the tree itself is good" (italics added).

In the Westminster Confession of Faith we find the same typically Reformed distinction: chapter XI is on (positional) justification and chapter XIII on (practical) sanctification: "[I] They, who are once effectually called, and regenerated, having a new heart, and a new spirit created in them, are further *sanctified*, really and personally, through the virtue of Christ's death and resurrection, by His Word and Spirit dwelling in them: the dominion of the whole body of sin is destroyed, and the several lusts thereof are more and more weakened and mortified; and they more and more quickened and strengthened in all saving graces, to the practice of true *holiness*, without which no man shall see the Lord. [II] This *sanctification* is throughout, in the whole man; yet imperfect in this life, there abiding still some remnants of corruption in every part; whence arises a continual and irreconcilable war, the flesh lusting against the Spirit, and the Spirit against the flesh. [III] In which war, although the remaining corruption, for a time, may much prevail; yet, through the continual supply of strength from the *sanctifying* Spirit of Christ, the regenerate part does overcome; and so, the saints grow in grace, perfecting *holiness* in the fear of God."

There are many excellent things in these descriptions. Yet, they are all rooted in the same misunderstanding: first there is (positional) justification, then there is (practical) sanctification—without discerning what is *positional* sanctification and *practical* justification. This is also the picture presented by the Reformed writer Lambertus (or Lambrecht) Mysteras (1676–1740), who in his day was one of the most widely read Reformed authors. He wrote: "Justification precedes, and sanctification follows. In justification, the guilt and punishment of the sins are taken away; in sanctification the defilement of the sins is taken away more and more. Justification is perfect ... Sanctification is in the life of God's children on earth imperfect."[7]

To quote also a twentieth-century example, Louis Berkhof wrote: "The Reformers ... made a clear distinction between justification and sanctification, regarding the former as a legal act of divine grace, affecting the judicial status of man, and the latter, as a moral or re-creative work, changing the inner

---

7. www.iclnet.org/pub/resources/text/nederlandse/myseras-ov04.html.

nature of man . . . Justification is at once followed by sanctification, since God sends out the Spirit of His Son into the hearts of His own as soon as they are justified, and that Spirit is the Spirit of sanctification . . . by which He delivers us more and more from the power of sin and enables us to do good works."[8] My basic objections here are: (a) Berkhof describes justification too much from a judicial point of view (I have dealt with that earlier), (b) he does not distinguish *positional* sanctification, and (c) he emphasizes the "more and more" (I have mentioned this expression now six times in this chapter), which suggests that, on average, more mature Christians are "holier" than more immature Christians. Sanctification is identified here too strongly with spiritual growth alone. All these points will be dealt with in this and the following chapters.

8.1.4 Collective Aspects

This is a good moment to underscore a point that often seems to receive too little attention in Reformed theology. Redemption, salvation, atonement, calling, conversion, regeneration, faith, justification, and sanctification have an obvious individual side. But they have a collective aspect as well, which has often been neglected. "God first visited the Gentiles, to take from them a *people* for his name" (Acts 15:14). Christ "gave himself for us . . . to purify for himself a *people* for his own possession who are zealous for good works" (Titus 2:14). And more specifically in connection with sanctification: "Christ loved the church and gave himself up for her, that he might *sanctify* her, having cleansed her by the washing of water with the word, so that he might present the church to himself in splendor, without spot or wrinkle or any such thing, that she might be *holy* and without blemish" (Eph. 5:25–27).

God desired not only individual saints (holy ones) but also a holy *people*, as he had expected Israel to be in the time of the Old Testament (Exod. 19:6; Deut. 7:6; 14:2, 21; 26:19;

---

8. Berkhof (1949, 530).

28:9; Isa. 63:18). The New Testament people of God are an "offering" from all Gentile nations, "acceptable, *sanctified* by the Holy Spirit" (Rom. 15:16). "I will make my dwelling among them and walk among them, and I will be their God, and they shall be *my people* [Exod. 29:45; Lev. 26:11; Ezek. 37:27]. Therefore 'go out from their midst, and be separate from them, says the Lord, and touch no unclean thing; then I will welcome you, and I will be a father to you, and you shall be sons and daughters to me, says the Lord Almighty' [Jer. 31:1]" (2 Cor. 6:16–18). "[Y]ou are a chosen race, a royal priesthood, a *holy nation*, a *people* for his own possession, that you may proclaim the excellencies of him who called you out of darkness into his marvelous light. Once you were not a people, but now you are *God's people*; once you had not received mercy, but now you have received mercy" (1 Pet. 2:9–10).

The call to holiness (sanctification) is a collective one, coming to the saints as *people* of God: "Come out of her [i.e., the great Babylon], *my people*, lest you take part in her sins, lest you share in her plagues" (Rev. 18:4). And on the new earth: "Behold, the dwelling place of God is with man. He will dwell with them, and they will be *his people*, and God himself will be with them as their God. He will wipe away every tear from their eyes, and death shall be no more, neither shall there be mourning, nor crying, nor pain anymore, for the former things have passed away" (Rev. 21:3–4).

The expression "new man" is often applied in an individual way, for instance, by rendering it as the "new self" (ESV, NIV, and others). But in fact, it rather possesses a collective nature; it is never said that believers have become "new men." Believers from Israel and those from the Gentiles have been forged into "one new man" (Eph. 2:15). They have been collectively clothed with the "new man," who has been created after the image of God in true righteousness *and holiness* (Eph. 4:24; Col. 3:10). In this "new man" there is no distinction anymore between Jews, Greeks, barbarians and Scythians, slaves and free persons, men and women (Gal. 3:28). The "new man" implies that "Christ is all, and in all" (Col. 3:11), that is, in all of these people he is everything (cf. 1 Cor. 12:6; 15:28; Eph. 1:23; also see 1 Cor. 9:22; 10:33). This can be interpreted as meaning that, in a sense, Christ himself is this "new man" — not in person (for he was not "created," cf. Eph. 4:24) but as he is being displayed in believers. It requires *all* the believing Jews and Gentiles, *all* the believing slaves and free people, and *all* the believing men and women, in order to collectively display this one picture of Christ. This is one reason why the Ecclesia of God is so much more than the sum of all the individual believers.

8.2 Salvation as Spiritual Maturity
8.2.1 Stages of Salvation

There is another introductory subject to be mentioned here. In the traditional Reformed view, there is the one moment of justification, which is sufficient for one's eternal salvation. It is like a judicial acquittal in court: "You are free!" Life afterward is important; this is why traditional Reformed theology pays a lot of attention to sanctification, in which one's salvation is worked out, so to speak. People may make great progress in their sanctification, or very little, but thank God, that does not affect their eternal salvation; that was decided at the moment they were justified by faith.

I do not believe that such a view does full justice to the New Testament picture. Take one simple example: "Strive for peace with everyone, and for the holiness *without which no one will see the Lord*" (Heb. 12:14). In other words, if you do not strive, or do not strive enough, for holiness, you cannot be saved! How does this fit into the traditional Reformed model? Even if we assume that the text refers to nominal Christians, who after a while fall away from their Christian confession, this does not solve the difficulty. The text does not say that such people did not have genuine faith, that they were not regenerated, or the like; no, it suggests that people can perish because their sanctification has been ineffective. This is why I not only distinguish between positional and practical justification as well as positional and practical sanctification, but also see a clear continuum between the positional and the practical.

We have seen this earlier: to be sure, we are not justified by works but by faith—but I hasten to add that this is a faith resulting in works, a "faith working in love" (Gal. 5:6). Without these good works resulting from faith no one can be said to have been truly "justified by faith" because such "faith" is not biblical faith; this is the great message of James 2 (cf. Eph. 2:8–10). In other words, there is no positional justification without the practical justification resulting from it. Conversely, there is no practical sanctification without the positional sanctification in which it is rooted. It is bad doctrine to suggest that, in principle, one could be saved once and for all, in one moment, whereas that person's practical justification and sanctification could be a big failure.

Let me illustrate this with the comprehensive term "salvation." The Greek term *sōtēria* has at least the following three meanings:

(a) At the moment a person is born again and justified, he *is* saved for eternity; he "does not come into judgment, but has passed from death to life" (John 5:24). "God . . . made us alive together with Christ—by grace you have been saved—and raised us up with him and seated us with him in the heavenly places in Christ Jesus . . . For by grace you have been saved through faith" (Eph. 2:4–8). "But when the goodness and loving kindness of God our Savior appeared, he saved us . . . by the washing of regeneration and renewal of the Holy Spirit" (Titus 3:4–5).

(b) At the same time, it is true that, in most cases, the believer still has to complete a shorter or longer journey upon this earth. "Salvation," then, in the full sense of the word, is reached only when we reach the end of this journey, or more precisely, the resurrection of the body, and thus God's "eternal kingdom" (2 Pet. 1:11): "[W]e wait eagerly for adoption as sons, the redemption of our bodies. For in this hope we *were* saved. Now hope that is seen is not hope. For who hopes for what he sees? But if we hope for what we do not see, we wait for it with patience" (Rom. 8:23–25); this is both achieved and expected salvation. "[W]e await a Savior (Greek, *sōtēr*, the One bringing salvation), the Lord Jesus Christ, who will transform our lowly body to be like his glorious body" (Phil. 3:20–21). As their "helmet," Christians wear "the hope of salvation. For God has not destined us for wrath, but to obtain salvation through our Lord Jesus Christ" (1 Thess. 5:8–9).

As surely as the believer *has been* saved, just as surely must a lot of effort be expended before he *will be* saved. All divine aids must be employed, for it is good to remember that, humanly speaking, "it is hard for the righteous to be saved," (1 Pet. 4:18 NIV).[9] Paul understood the believer's responsibility in this respect, but also emphasized God's indispensable help: "[W]ork out your own salvation with fear and trembling, for it is God who works in you, both to will and to work for his good pleasure" (Phil. 2:12–13).

(c) There is a third meaning, which, in my view, involves salvation as a fruit of sanctification, or of spiritual growth: "Like newborn infants, long for the pure spiritual milk,[10] that by it you may grow up into salvation" (1 Pet. 2:2). "[R]eceive with meekness the implanted word, which is able to save your souls" (James 1:21). According to Donald W. Burdick, James is calling "for a full and intelligent appropriation of the truth as the Christian grows in spiritual understanding."[11] Paul rejoices in everything that "shall turn to my salvation through your prayer, and the supply of the Spirit of Jesus Christ" (Phil. 1:19 KJV), which seems to refer more to his earthly walk than

---

9. Davids (1990, 172) refers to Prov. 11:31 (LXX); Mark 13:19–20; Luke 13:23–24.
10. Greek, *logikon gala*, i.e. perhaps, "milk of the Word" (cf. 1 Pet. 1:23–25); thus NKJV, NASB, and others; see Davids (1990, 83).
11. Burdick (1981, 175).

to the end thereof. Homer Kent thinks here of "the unfolding of his [i.e., Paul's] Christian life and his ultimate hope of standing unashamed both before human judges and before his Lord."[12] Others think here only of the release from prison that Paul was hoping for.[13]

8.2.2 Parallels

At any rate, soteriology (the doctrine of salvation) cannot avoid paying attention to, first, the salvational road that leads from the initial touch of the Spirit to regeneration, second, from regeneration to spiritual maturity, and third, to the Kingdom of God.[14]

For the three stages in salvation just mentioned in §8.2.1, there are various parallels in the New Testament. First, we think of eternal life:[15] as surely as it is true that (a) believers *have* eternal life (not just the "admission ticket" to eternal life, but the thing itself; John 3:15-16, 36; 5:24, 39; 6:27, 40, 47; etc.), it is just as surely true that (b) they will one day *inherit* eternal life (Matt. 19:29; Luke 10:25; 18:18). To this, we may add that (c) here on earth there is already a "taking hold" — both anticipation and practical realization — of eternal life as part of spiritual maturation (1 Tim. 6:12). Just as with the term "salvation," there is a *past* meaning (believers received eternal life when they came to faith), a *present* meaning (taking hold of eternal life), and a *future* meaning (inheriting eternal life).

Another striking example is the New Testament notion of "perfect" (Greek, *teleios*; the verb "to perfect" is *teleioō*),[16] where we find the same three meanings. First, the regenerate person has received a perfect conscience (Heb. 9:9; 10:1-2, 14; cf. 7:11; Matt. 19:21; 1 John 2:5), that is, a conscience that is no longer plagued by any (consciousness of) guilt. The believer is immediately "qualified . . . to share in the inheritance of

---

12. Kent (1978, 114).
13. E.g., Kennedy (1979, 426–27).
14. See earlier Ouweneel (1999; 2008c; 2010a).
15. See more extensively, Ouweneel (2010a, §§4.1 and 4.2).
16. Kittel *et al.* (1972, 8.67–78); Brown (1992, 2:59–65).

the saints in light" (Col. 1:12). Second, we learn of the perfection that the believer reaches at the end of his earthly journey in the sense of being without the sinful nature, without the weaknesses of the mortal body, clothed with the perfection of Christ himself (cf. Phil. 3:12; Heb. 11:40; 12:23). But third, one is perfect not in the sense of being sinless but of being spiritually mature and complete, having reached the goal of spiritual growth. Translators often have to choose here between the terms "perfect" and "mature" (cf. ESV: "perfect" in Matt. 5:48; Gal. 3:3; 1 John 4:17–18; "mature" in 1 Cor. 2:6; Eph. 4:13; Phil. 3:15; Col. 1:28; 4:12; Heb. 5:14; "completed" in James 2:22).

Several other examples could be mentioned: we have seen that there is not only saving faith, but also practical faith, the life of confidence toward God. In this case, however, it is no use speaking of a future meaning of faith if we interpret 2 Corinthians 5:7 in such a way that one day faith will make room for sight. There is a one-time conversion, but Reformed theology has often spoken of "daily conversion" as well. There is the one-time "adoption as sons" (Rom. 8:15, 23; Gal. 4:5; Eph. 1:5), but there is also a practical learning to live as sons of God: "For all who are *led* by the Spirit of God [not just have the Spirit of God dwelling in them] are sons of God" (Rom. 8:14). There is the one-time regeneration, which is the reception of a "new nature" ("That which is born of the flesh is flesh, and that which is born of the Spirit is spirit," John 3:6). But one cannot be called regenerate without showing the fruits of this new nature. There is the one-time quickening (God "made us alive together with Christ," Eph. 2:1, 5; Col. 2:13). But one cannot be called spiritually alive without the signs of this new life. Here again, we may also distinguish a future aspect in that one day God "will also give life to your mortal bodies through his Spirit who dwells in you" (Rom. 8:11).

We find the same three aspects in justification. We were justified in the *past* when we came to faith in Christ. We are being justified *at present* through the works that flow from our faith in the power of the Holy Spirit, and we will be justified in the *future* when we will be perfectly righteous also in the practical sense, without all the sins and weaknesses of the flesh. It is exactly the same with sanctification. We distinguish between a positional sanctification that we received in the *past* through regeneration and faith in Christ, and the practical sanctification *at present*, as part of our spiritual maturation, and the perfect holiness we will possess in the *future*, when there will be nothing unholy in us anymore. It is as saints (holy ones) that we will be manifested with Christ (Zech. 14:5; 1 Thess. 3:13; 2 Thess. 1:10; Jude 1:14; in some of these passages angels may be meant or included, cf. Matt. 25:31; 2 Thess. 1:7; Rev. 14:10).

The aim of the rest of this chapter is to explore sanctification as a present possession, and in the next chapter we will deal with sanctification as an ongoing process. Elsewhere I have discussed sanctification, salvation, eternal life, and perfection in their eschatological sense.[17] In other publications I have linked sanctification with related topics, such as the imitation of Christ (discipleship) and what the Eastern Orthodox tradition calls *theosis*.[18]

8.3   Holiness as a Present Possession
8.3.1   The Reformed View

When Reformed theology states that justification is first, and is then followed by sanctification, there is truth in this statement but also inaccuracy. The *truth* is that the moment of conversion (regeneration, faith, redemption, reconciliation) must be distinguished from, and precedes, the life of faith. This is the life in which this conversion must be worked out in terms of spiritual fruits, good works, spiritual growth, discipleship, dedication, consecration, *theosis*. First there is regeneration (reception of a new nature), then the fruits of this new nature. First there is birth, then the life of a newborn person.

---

17. Ouweneel (2012a).
18. Ouweneel (2010a, chapters 13 and 14; 2015b, §9.7).

As it is said in the Canons of Dort (III/IV.11): God "infuses new qualities into the will, which, though heretofore dead, He quickens; from being evil, disobedient, and refractory, He renders it good, obedient, and pliable; actuates and strengthens it, that like a good tree, it may bring forth the fruits of good actions." First there is faith, then the works that are the fruit thereof. First there is redemption, then the redeemed life. First there is justification (declaring someone righteous), then the righteous life (practical justification).

The *inaccuracy* that I referred to is that not only is there first positional justification (declaring someone righteous), then the righteous life (practical justification), but likewise there is first positional sanctification (declaring someone holy), then the holy life (practical sanctification). This emphasis reverberates often throughout the present study: it is *not* first justification, then sanctification. Rather, it is first positional justification and sanctification, then practical justification and sanctification. At the moment of conversion, the person is declared by God to be both righteous and holy, and this is worked out in a life of righteousness and holiness. At a certain moment, the person *becomes* righteous and holy as far as his position before God is concerned, by faith in Christ and his redemptive work. Afterward, the believer *turns out* to be righteous and holy through righteous and holy works. That which is positionally true before God, must also become practically true. And as I emphasized earlier, without the clear signs of this practical justification and sanctification no one is entitled to identify the person as positionally justified and sanctified.

Of course, Reformed theology is not void of any insight regarding this positional sanctification. For instance, positional and practical sanctification are sometimes distinguished as *passive* and *active* sanctification.[19] In §8.1.2, I referred to the Heidelberg Catechism, which at least does mention that "God

---

19. Kersten (1983, 2:425–26).

... grants and imputes to me the perfect satisfaction, righteousness, and *holiness* of Christ" (Q&A 60). But for the rest, the Catechism exhibits the same inaccuracy by dealing with justification in what I call its *positional* sense in Lord's Days 11–19 (about "God the Son and Our Redemption"), and again in Lord's Days 23–24 (about righteousness), whereas sanctification is dealt with in what I call its *practical* sense in Lord's Days 20–22 (about "God the Holy Spirit and Our Sanctification"). Implicitly, sanctification is also touched upon in Q&A 56: ". . . the sinful nature with which I have to struggle all my life long."

Reformed writer Aart Moerkerken says of this: "[T]here can never be forgiveness of guilt without sanctification, without the renewal of life, without the struggle against sin."[20] Of course, in itself this is correct; but again, sanctification is viewed here as that which practically *follows upon* forgiveness of guilt, *not* positionally as that which is *involved in* this forgiveness.

As we have seen (§8.1.2), in the Belgic Confession the same inaccuracy is found: first (positional) justification, then (practical) sanctification. It speaks of "justifying faith" and "a pious and holy life" (Article 24): "Therefore, it is so far from being true that this justifying faith makes men remiss in a pious and holy life, that on the contrary without it they would never do anything out of love to God, but only out of self-love or fear of damnation." Here sanctification is doing good works that flow forth from justifying faith.

8.3.2 *"You Were Sanctified"*

In Scripture, holiness is both a status that is *granted* to a person (positional sanctification) and a dynamic work to which the person is *called* (practical sanctification). Thus, sanctification is not only an *ontic* (positional) but also an *ethical* (practical) reality.[21] The two may be distinguished as the indicative of

---

20. Moerkerken (2004, 305).
21. Heyns (1988, 319–20).

sanctification ("you are holy") and the imperative of sanctification ("be holy").[22]

Positional (passive, ontic, indicative) sanctification is clearly taught at many places. After having described several kinds of wicked people, Paul says to the Corinthian believers: "And such were some of you. But you were washed, you were sanctified, you were justified in the name of the Lord Jesus Christ and by the Spirit of our God" (1 Cor. 6:11; both "in" and "by" are here Greek, *en*, "in [the power of]"). This is why Karl Barth can view justification and sanctification as two sides of the same matter: Scripture refers to acts through which God declares the renewed sinner to be both righteous and holy.[23] This declaration is then followed by the practical realization; as to justification, "*Pursue* [Greek, *diōke*] righteousness" (1 Tim. 6:11; 2 Tim. 2:22), and as to sanctification, "*Strive* [*diōkete*] . . . for the holiness without which no one will see the Lord" (Heb. 12:14). As Reformed theologian Johan Verkuyl expressed it: "In Christ we are holy, but the Holy Spirit works this mystery out in us."[24]

1 Corinthians 6:11, just quoted, mentions sanctification even before justification. Gerrit C. Berkouwer may speak of "biblicism" if someone emphasizes this order,[25] but in this case this objection seems out of place. The redemptive order given here is not a *chronological* order, for washing, justification, and sanctification all occur at the same moment. But in my view there is certainly a *logical* order: first the washing away of sins by the blood of Christ in the power of the Holy Spirit is referred to (conversion, regeneration). This is logically followed by the fact that the washed (cleansed) person is set apart for (consecrated to) God by making this person one with a dead and risen Christ. From this it follows logically that the person who is thus cleansed and sanctified is

---

22. Demarest (1997, 407).
23. See the presentation by McConnachie (1931).
24. Verkuyl (1992, 314).
25. Berkouwer (1954, 32); cf. also Bavinck (2008, 4:208).

declared to be righteous by God. We have the same order in Luke 1:74-75 ("... that we, being delivered from the hand of our enemies, might serve him without fear, in holiness [*hosiotēs*] and righteousness before him all our days"; but note the opposite order in Eph. 4:24, "righteousness and holiness [*hosiotēs*]").

Here we find one of the most important characteristics of sanctification: *positional* sanctification involves a person being set apart for God, in Christ, once and for all, being consecrated to God in separation from evil. This happens at the moment of regeneration and faith, when all the results of the redemptive work of Christ are imputed to the converted person. It is this moment when it becomes true what Paul says: "And because of him [or, from him, i.e., God; Greek, *ex autou*] you are in Christ Jesus, who became to us wisdom from God, righteousness and sanctification [or, holiness; Greek, *hagiasmos*] and redemption" (1 Cor. 1:30). That is, the saved sinner possesses all these blessings in Christ, who for him personifies both justification and sanctification (or, righteousness and holiness). In this sense, I suppose 2 Corinthians 5:21 could have said just as well: "For our sake he made him to be sin who knew no sin, so that in him we might become the holiness of God."

8.3.3 "Once For All"

The positional aspect of sanctification is clearly indicated in the "once for all" of Hebrews 10:10, "And by that will we *have been* sanctified [Greek, *hēgiasmenoi esmen*, lit., we are the sanctified ones] through the offering of the body of Jesus Christ *once for all*." But in verse 14 we read, "For by a single offering he has perfected for all time those who are being sanctified [Greek, *hagiazomenous*]." Just as in 2:11 ("those who are sanctified," Greek, *hagiazomenoi*), this "being sanctified" does not indicate some process, but it is a kind of timeless present tense, indicating the character of the believers (cf. Acts 20:32; 26:18). They are people who are (being) sanctified by the blood of Christ (cf. 13:12, "So Jesus also suffered outside the gate in order to sanctify the people through his own blood").[26] This is similar to the "being saved" in 1 Corinthians 1:18 ("to us who are being saved it [i.e., the gospel] is the power of God") and in 2 Corinthians 2:15 ("For we are the aroma of Christ to God among those who are being saved and among those who are perishing"), although here the future aspect seems to be included as well (cf. 1 Cor. 3:15; 5:5).

In a similar way, Peter addresses believers: they are "elect . . . according to the foreknowledge of God the Father, in [Greek, *en*, in virtue of] the sanctification of the Spirit, for obedience to Jesus Christ and for sprinkling with his blood" (1 Pet. 1:1-2). On account of this positional sanctification, *all* believers can be addressed at all times as "saints (holy ones)" (Rom. 1:7; 2 Cor. 1:1; Eph. 1:1; Phil. 1:1), or "sanctified" (1 Cor. 1:2), or "holy brothers" (Col. 1:2, "saints and faithful brothers" *or* "holy and faithful brothers"; Heb. 3:1) just as this occurs at the start of several New Testament letters, but also elsewhere. I simply mention Matthew 27:52 ("saints who had fallen asleep"), and cases in which "saints" is the equivalent of "believers" or "Christians" (Acts 9:13, 32, 41; 26:18; Rom. 8:27; 12:13; 15:25-26, 31; 16:2, 15; 1 Cor. 14:34; 16:1, 15; 2 Cor. 8:4; 9:1, 12; 13:13; Eph. 1:15; 2:19; 3:8, 18; 4:12; 5:3; 6:18; Phil. 4:22; Col. 1:4, 26; 1 Tim. 5:10; Philemon 1:5, 7; Heb. 6:10; 13:24; 1 Pet. 3:5 ["holy women"]; Jude 1:3; Rev. 5:8; 8:3-4; 11:18; 18:20; 19:8; 20:9).

In 1 Corinthians 6, the word "saint" in verses 1-2 is equivalent to "brother" in verses 5-8. In Ephesians 1:18, Colossians 1:12 and 2 Thessalonians 1:10 "saint" is especially what the believers will be in the coming glory. In Colossians 3:12 ("holy and beloved"), one could also read: "saints and beloved ones." In some places, some expositors are inclined to understand "saints" as angels, as in 1 Thessalonians 3:13 (". . . the coming of our Lord Jesus with all his saints").[27] In

---

26. Ouweneel (1982, 2:33–34).
27. Apart perhaps from Psalm 89:5 ("the assembly of the holy ones"), it is questionable whether there is any passage in the Bible where "saints" (or "holy

the book of Revelation the "saints" are sometimes especially the martyrs: the beast "was allowed to make war on the saints and to conquer them" (13:7; cf. v. 10). "Here is a call for the endurance of the saints, those who keep the commandments of God and their faith in Jesus" (14:12); "they [i.e., the enemies] have shed the blood of saints and prophets" (16:6). "I saw the woman [i.e., the great Babylon], drunk with the blood of the saints, the blood of the martyrs of Jesus" (17:6; cf. 18:24).

8.4 Outward Sanctification
8.4.1 "Set Apart"

A person sanctified by God is a person separated from sin and set apart to God. Because of this fundamental aspect of sanctification of being a setting apart, the term can also be used in a purely outward sense. When speaking of inward sanctification, we emphasize that we share God's own holiness (Heb. 12:10; see further in §8.6). Outward sanctification involves a being set apart without any reference to the inward condition of the persons involved.

A well-known example is this: "[T]he unbelieving husband is made holy [or, sanctified, Greek, *hēgiastai*] because of his wife, and the unbelieving wife is made holy [or, sanctified, Greek, *hēgiastai*] because of her husband. Otherwise your children would be unclean, but as it is, they are holy [Greek, *hagia*]" (1 Cor. 7:14). The Christian family is a sacred place, where God's Word is read and heard, and where the Holy Spirit is working. The child growing up in such a family finds him- or herself in an atmosphere different from that of the child growing up in the world, far from God and his commandments. However, this being set apart does not mean that the child is also inwardly sanctified, that is, shares God's holiness. This is the case only when the boy or girl is born again.

Another example of outward sanctification is found in Hebrews 10:29, where we hear of people who were "sanctified"

---

ones") unequivocally means "angels."

by "the blood of the covenant," but afterward have "trampled underfoot the Son of God." They had been "sanctified" by entering into the domain of Christianity, and in this sense had even begun to "share in the Holy Spirit" (cf. 6:4), that is, to be under the blessed influence of the Spirit. But apparently, they had never *inwardly* "shared in the Spirit" through regeneration and faith (cf. §7.7). In the same sense, Israel is called a holy nation, although only a part of the Israelites can be considered to have been truly born again: "[Y]ou shall be to me a kingdom of priests and a holy nation" (Exod. 19:21). "You shall be consecrated to me" (22:31), literally "be men of holiness to me." "Yes, he loved his people, all his holy ones were in his hand" (Deut. 33:3). "Your holy people held possession for a little while" (Isa. 63:18; cf. 62:12; Dan. 12:7).

In Romans 11:7 we read: "Israel failed to obtain what it was seeking. The elect [Greek, *hē eklogē*] obtained it, but the rest were hardened." *All* Israel is a "chosen people" (Deut. 4:37; 7:6-7; 14:2) in the outward sense, but on the inside there is an "elect part" consisting of those truly regenerates, who will be saved forever. Israel is a holy nation in the outward sense, but only part of it is holy on the inside.

Likewise, the church is a "holy nation" (1 Pet. 2:9-10; cf. Titus 2:14), although not all so-called Christians—seen outwardly, from the viewpoint of human responsibility (cf. 1 Pet. 4:17; Rev. 2 and 3)—inwardly share God's holiness. Of course, outward holiness *may* be linked with inward holiness, but unfortunately this is not always the case.

8.4.2 The Believers' Consecration

Because of the meaning "setting apart," sanctification can also have the meaning of "consecration, dedication." Thus we hear: "Consecrate [Hebrew, *qaddesh*, sanctify] to me all the firstborn" of Israel (Exod. 13:2). We find the same for the officials, there being a connection between the two because the firstborn were later replaced by the Levites (Num. 3:11-13, 40-51; 8:16-18). Moses "poured some of the anointing oil on Aaron's head and anointed him to consecrate [sanctify] him" (Lev. 8:12); "the man whom the Lord chooses shall be the holy one" (Num. 16:7). Compare in the New Testament: "[Y]ou yourselves like living stones are being built up as a spiritual house, to be a holy priesthood, to offer spiritual sacrifices acceptable to God through Jesus Christ. . . . [Y]ou are a chosen race, a royal priesthood, a holy nation, a people for his own possession, that you may proclaim the excellencies of him who called you out of darkness into his marvelous light" (1 Pet. 2:5, 9). Likewise, the prophet is a "holy man" (2 Kings 4:9; Mark 6:20).

In the book of Hebrews, sanctification seems to have especially this meaning: consecration to the worship ministry in the heavenly sanctuary (cf. 9:13-14).[28] This is already the case in 2:11, "For he who sanctifies and those who are sanctified all have one source [lit. are all of one {source?}, Greek, *ex henos*]," that is, they are of one piece, or they are from the same origin, the same root. Those who spiritually, and by the Spirit, may enter into the heavenly sanctuary (10:19-22), and may bring to God "sacrifices of praise" (13:15), have been sanctified or consecrated to this ministry, just like the priests in Leviticus 8:12 (also cf. Heb. 10:10, 14). Christ is the true high priest, and the believers form the house, the consecrated family, of this high priest (3:1-6, 14), comparable to the "house of Aaron" (Lev. 16:6, 11; 1 Chron. 12:27; Ps. 115:12; 118:3). Just as the high priest was sanctified (consecrated) for his office, so too the priests.

In Hebrews 9:24 ("Christ has entered, not into holy places made with hands, which are copies of the true things, but into heaven itself, now to appear in the presence of God on our behalf"), believers are implicitly assured of a place in the heavenly sanctuary because Christ is there as their representative. This is confirmed in Hebrews 10, where the believers have no "consciousness of sins" anymore (v.2), and where

---

28. See extensively, Ouweneel (1982, 1:41–42; 2:18, 31).

they are now consecrated in order to enter into the sanctuary themselves: "Therefore, brothers, since we have confidence to enter the holy places by the blood of Jesus, by the new and living way that he opened for us through the curtain, that is, through his flesh, and since we have a great priest over the house of God, let us draw near with a true heart in full assurance of faith, with our hearts sprinkled clean from an evil conscience and our bodies washed with pure water" (vv. 19-22).

Please notice how the author uses here the terminology of the consecration of Aaron and his sons: the sprinkling with blood (Exod. 29:21; Lev. 8:30) and the washing with water (Exod. 29:4; Lev. 8:6). Perhaps this is one of the most fascinating aspects of New Testament positional sanctification: it is consecration for priestly ministry in the heavenly sanctuary by the power of the Holy Spirit: "Through him [i.e., Jesus] . . . let us continually offer up a sacrifice of praise to God, that is, the fruit of lips that acknowledge his name" (Heb. 13:15; cf. Hos. 14:2, "we will pay with bulls the vows [Septuagint and Syriac: the fruit] of our lips").

8.4.3 Jesus' Consecration

There is a close relationship between the priestly office of believers and that of Jesus. They and he are of the same lump, or of the same root (Heb. 2:11), and Jesus is a "minister in the holy places [or, the sanctuary]" (8:1-2) in order that believers could minister in the holy places as well (9:24; 10:19-22; cf. 13:15). This corresponds with the close connection between Aaron and his sons in Exodus 29 and Leviticus 8, although Aaron is the high priest,[29] and his sons are only priests. By the way, believers are never called "priests" in Hebrews — perhaps to place all the emphasis on Jesus, the (high) priest.

Through the connection between Jesus and believers, we can understand the term "sanctified" (or "consecrated," Greek, *hēgiasen*) of John 10:36, where Jesus says of himself that he had been consecrated (many translations: "hallowed"

---

29. In Hebrew, *kohen gadol*, literally "great priest" (cf. Heb. 10:21).

or "sanctified") by the Father, that is, consecrated to his earthly ministry. When it comes to the holiness and sanctification of Jesus, we have to distinguish between at least five aspects, on which we cannot dwell right now:

(a) As the eternal Son of the Father, Jesus was and is holy as the Father and the Spirit are holy.

(b) When the Son was born as the human Jesus, he was a holy human; literally, "that holy matter" that was born of Mary (Luke 1:35 KJV).[30]

(c) Also as human, Jesus was in his person the "Holy One": "[W]e have believed, and have come to know, that you are the Holy One of God," as Peter confessed him (John 6:69; cf. Acts 2:27; 13:35). Even the demons sometimes refer to him as such (Mark 1:24; Luke 4:34). Peter also referred to him as "the Holy and Righteous One" (Acts 3:14). When John says, "But you have been anointed by the Holy One" (1 John 2:20), he is not referring to the Holy Spirit but to Christ: believers have been anointed *with* the Holy Spirit, but their anointing comes from him who is the Holy One. Thus, he calls him elsewhere "the holy one, the true one" (Rev. 3:7). In Revelation 16:5, however, the "Holy God" is (the triune) God.

(d) As I said, John 10:36 refers to the ministry of Christ: he was sanctified or consecrated by the Father to this end. We understand that there is quite a difference between the eternal holiness of Jesus in his person and the holiness of his temporary office on earth.

(e) There are also offices of Jesus that were and are being continued after his work on earth: "[F]or their [i.e., the disciples'] sake I consecrate [or, sanctify, Greek, *hagiazō*] myself, that they also may be sanctified [or, consecrated, *hēgiasmenoi*] in truth" (John 17:19), which (as the note in ESV indicates) in both cases means consecrated/sanctified for holy service.

---

30. Understandably but erroneously, NKJV changed this into "that Holy One"; Luke did not write *ho hagios* (masculine) but *to hagion* (neuter).

8.5 Models of Sanctification
8.5.1 Erroneous Models

In the history of theology, believers' sanctification has been viewed from many different angles.[31] I observe the following principal models.

(a) *Liberal view*. In this view, the problem of sin plays a minor role, while human nature and its achievements are highly esteemed. In both respects, this view is far removed from what I consider to be the biblical picture. In several passages, a direct link is made between God's holiness and human sins, as for instance: "You are not able to serve the LORD, for he is a holy God. He is a jealous God; he will not forgive your transgressions or your sins" (Josh. 24:19). "Ah, sinful nation, a people laden with iniquity, offspring of evildoers, children who deal corruptly! They have forsaken the LORD, they have despised the Holy One of Israel" (Isa. 1:4). "Since we have these promises, beloved, let us cleanse ourselves from every defilement of body and spirit, bringing holiness to completion in the fear of God" (2 Cor. 7:1). "Now may the God of peace himself sanctify you completely, and may your whole spirit and soul and body be kept blameless at the coming of our Lord Jesus Christ" (1 Thess. 5:23). I see liberation theology along the same lines, since it offers a secularized picture of sanctification. Of course, this does not mean that sanctification does not have important practical consequences for politics and society,[32] but it can never be reduced to that.

(b) *Sacramental view*. In the Roman Catholic view, sanctification has acquired a special form in canonization, that is, declaring certain deceased believers to be saints (for instance, since his canonization in 2014, the deceased pope John Paul II is now "saint John Paul II"). For the rest, sanctification is strongly linked with the use of the sacraments, especially baptism, confirmation, the Eucharist, confession, and the anointing of the sick, and further with works of love plus the

---

31. See extensively, Gundry (1987); Demarest (1997, 386–405).
32. See §5.4.3 and, e.g., Van Genderen and Velema (2008, 662-65).

merits of Mary and the saints (canonized believers to whom Catholics believe they can pray).[33] Of course, Roman Catholic theology knows of holiness in the sense of moral perfection, but the strong emphasis on its sacramental aspects strikes the Protestant as being not very much in accord with the spirit of the New Testament.

(c) *Perfectionist view*. In this view, sanctification means that the believer can reach a state of sinlessness already here on earth; this is sometimes called "entire sanctification."[34] Especially the name of John Wesley,[35] but also the names of various holiness movements (the Church of the Nazarene, the Salvation Army, the Quakers, various Methodist Churches, early Pentecostal movements) are forever linked with this view. In the next chapter, we will analyze this view further.

(d) *Pentecostal view*. John Wesley introduced the term *second blessing*, which was adopted by Pentecostal theologians and specifically applied by them to the baptism of the Holy Spirit. Elsewhere I have discussed as well as critiqued this view.[36] Ultimately, this would mean that persons who have never spoken in tongues, and therefore have never received the baptism of the Holy Spirit, would never have attained true sanctification. In reality, many men and women of God who, as far as we know, never spoke in tongues are for us the very examples of a holy and dedicated life.

8.5.2 Again: The Reformed Model

As we have seen, Reformed theology in general views sanctification as follows.

(a) Sanctification is something practical that follows upon (positional) justification. In my view, it is more Scriptural to

---

33. A good introduction can be found in Van der Meer (1941).
34. See the essay by the Wesleyan Adam Clarke, *Entire Sanctification*, Amazon Digital Services or https://shuttie27.files.wordpress.com/2012/01/clarke_entiresanct.pdf.
35. See Wesley (2013) (cf. http://wesley.nnu.edu/john-wesley/a-plain-account-of-christian-perfection/).
36. Ouweneel (2007a, §8.4).

say that practical sanctification *as well as practical justification* follow upon positional justification *as well as positional sanctification*. I do not see how one could possibly understand practical sanctification without having first grasped positional sanctification.

(b) In line with Augustine, sanctification is principally a struggle against sin (the exegesis of Rom. 7:14–26 plays an essential role here; see §8.7). In the present and the following chapters, I am seeking to show that sanctification has a far more positive goal: sharing in God's holiness, which involves not just separation from evil, but involves, or overlaps with, God's loftiness, glory, magnificence, splendor, luster, sheen, brilliance, beauty, grandeur, greatness, majesty, radiance, shine, effulgence.

(c) Sanctification is something that, just like justification, is essentially rooted in faith, and as such is linked more with divine sovereign grace than with human responsibility. See the link between the "word of God's grace" and sanctification in Acts 20:32, and between the "Spirit of grace" and sanctification in Hebrews 10:29. We have been called with a "holy calling" because of God's "purpose and grace" (2 Tim. 1:9). Of course, this is not to deny the aspect of human responsibility, as we have it presented very powerfully in 2 Corinthians 7:1 ("[L]et us cleanse ourselves from every defilement of body and spirit, bringing holiness to completion in the fear of God") and Hebrews 12:14 ("Strive ... for the holiness without which no one will see the Lord"; cf. ERV, "try to keep your lives free from sin" [cf. EXB, NCV], in which we recognize again a negative approach to sanctification; cf. [b]). See extensively the next chapter.

(d) Sanctification is a continuous, gradual process of increasing holiness. As said before, this would suggest that, on average, more mature Christians are holier—in the sense of sinning less—than more immature Christians. In the next section, I present a view that nuances this idea of a process.

When it comes to the notion of a process, we would rather think of terms such as spiritual growth (Eph. 4:15-16; 2 Thess. 1:3; 1 Pet. 2:2; 2 Pet. 3:18; cf. 1 Cor. 2:6; 14:20; Eph. 4:13; Phil. 3:15; Col. 1:28; 4:12; Heb. 5:14; 6:1), renewal (Rom. 12:2; 2 Cor. 4:16; Eph. 4:23; Col. 3:10; cf. Titus 3:5, which refers to positional renewal), and transformation (Rom. 12:2; 2 Cor. 3:18).

8.5.3 An Evangelical Model

The Evangelical doctrine of sanctification seeks to avoid two extremes. On the one hand, there is the "poor sinner" view of many traditional Protestants: believers remain "poor sinners" as long as they are still on this earth (cf. §8.7.1). It is expressed in the Heidelberg Catechism (Q&A 114) as follows: ". . . [E]ven the holiest men, while in this life, have only a small beginning of such obedience, ..." One could hardly imagine a greater discouragement to a striving for holiness than such a statement. This is a view very much at home in Romans 7:24, "Wretched man that I am! Who will deliver me from this body of death?" But this view hardly knows how to deal with Romans 6:18, "having been *set free from sin*, [you] have become slaves of righteousness," verse 22, "now that you have been *set free from sin* and have become slaves of God, the fruit you get leads to sanctification and its end, eternal life," and 8:2, "the law of the Spirit of life has *set you free* in Christ Jesus *from the law of sin and death.*"

On the other hand, there is perfectionism, the doctrine of "entire sanctification," which involves freedom from willful sin, even from the sinful nature, even from the orientation to sin, and even from temptations, that is, being free from the possibility of sin. "The fruit of the Spirit is so perfected in the entirely sanctified, that 'works of the flesh' are no longer possible because of the perfection in love."[37] This erroneous doctrine will be dealt with in the next chapter.

Influential Evangelical writers (John N. Darby, Robert

---

37. Chris Bounds, http://cbounds.blogspot.nl/2006/05/what-is-entire-sanctification.html.

P. Smith, Frederick B. Meyer, Handley C. G. Moule, Andrew Murray, William Graham Scroggie) have emphasized that sanctification is not so much a process but rather an instantaneous act of determinate surrender and consecration to Christ.[38] In this sense, there is a very close link between positional and practical sanctification. The New Testament distinction between the non-consecrated Christian (living by the flesh) and the consecrated Christian (living by the Spirit) plays an important role in this (see next chapter).[39] Just like practical justification, practical sanctification is a matter of both God's sovereign grace and human responsibility, in the indispensable power of the Holy Spirit. The *gift* of the Spirit as such is an act of God's grace; the extent to which we allow the Spirit to work in our lives is a matter of our own responsibility.

I see the Reformed view of sanctification as largely a passive one of resignation and acquiescence ("even the holiest among us have only a minimum of holiness"). I see the perfectionist view of sanctification as being largely an active one with an apparent lack of self-knowledge, if not a measure of hybris and self-inflation. To the former group John says, "My little children, I am writing these things to you so that you may not sin" (1 John 2:1). To the latter group he says, "If we say we have no sin, we deceive ourselves, and the truth is not in us" (1:8). For the rest, I refer the reader to the next chapter.

8.6   The Holiness of God
8.6.1   Holiness as Luster, Majesty, Glory

In the New Testament, it is obvious that sanctification, in some way or another, is a reflection of God's own holiness,[40] for God says: "You shall be holy, for I am holy" (1 Pet. 1:16). This

---

38. Two nineteenth-century books that have exerted a great influence in this regard are Boardman (1858) and Ryle (1877).
39. Cf. Demarest (1997, 415–16), who does not agree with a sharp distinction between the two.
40. On God's holiness, cf. Trevethan (1995); Willis (2002); Ouweneel (2009, §3.4).

is a quotation from Lev. 11:44–45, "I am the LORD your God. Consecrate yourselves therefore, and be holy, for I am holy. You shall not defile yourselves with any swarming thing that crawls on the ground. For I am the LORD who brought you up out of the land of Egypt to be your God. You shall therefore be holy, for I am holy" (cf. 19:2). "You shall be holy to me, for I the Lord am holy and have separated you from the peoples, that you should be mine" (20:26; cf. 21:8; also see Exod. 19:6). Compare Numbers 15:40, "So you shall remember and do all my commandments, and be holy to your God" (also see Deut. 23:14).

Reformed theologian Arie Noordtzij even called this phrase, "You shall be holy, for I am holy," "the core of the entire Old Testament divine revelation, which never ceases to place all emphasis on the Lord's holiness (i.e., the uniqueness of His nature over against all other gods) and on this basis to demand of Israel that it manifest in its own life a reflection of this uniqueness."[41] A bit later he argued that God wishes to see the spotless purity of his Being reflected in a holy nation.[42] This touches the core of the matter: the norm for the holiness of God's people is the holiness of God himself. If God appeals to us to be holy just as he is holy, we will first have to investigate the nature of his own holiness in order to understand the norm that he is presenting to us.

In the first place, God's holiness seems to be an attribute of God to which we, humble creatures, cannot even come close. To put it more strongly, the word "attribute" is too weak. God's holiness involves the *being* of God, insofar as it is at all meaningful to maintain the scholastic distinction between God's "attributes" and God's "being." I have argued elsewhere that, in my view, this is not the case: every so-called attribute expresses at the same time God's being.[43] God *is* holiness, just as he is spirit (John 4:24), light (1 John 1:5), and love

---

41. Noordtzij (1982, 129–30).
42. Ibid., 192.
43. See Ouweneel (2007b, 293–96; 2010a, §14.2.2; 2013a, chapters 3–5).

(4:8, 16).

God's holiness has the sense of loftiness, glory, magnificence, splendor, luster, sheen, brilliance, beauty, grandeur, greatness, majesty, radiance, shine, effulgence. This is what the seraphim expressed when they said, "Holy, holy, holy is the LORD of hosts; the whole earth is full of his glory!" (Isa. 6:3). It is far too one-sided to describe holiness as separation from evil. Thus, the Westminster Confession of Faith understands by being "sanctified" (XIII.1): "the dominion of the whole body of sin is destroyed, and the several lusts thereof are more and more weakened and mortified," etc. (see §8.1.2). Separation from evil is a negative aspect; it is not the positive aspect that the seraphim want to express. God is holy from all eternity. He was holy long before humanity's fall, that is, long before it was meaningful to use the expression "separation from evil" at all. What the seraphim say is that God is lofty, glorious, magnificent, resplendent, brilliant, beautiful, grand, majestic, radiant, great, splendid, shining, effulgent. In this way, they tell *who God is*, entirely apart from the problem of sin.

Only after the fall did it become meaningful to make a comparison: God is majestic, just as sin is mean. He is beautiful, just as sin is base. He is resplendent, just as sin is repulsive. He is glorious, just as sin is gloomy. He is lofty, just as sin is low.

God's holiness finds its counterpart in the believer's holiness—he is a "saint"—but also in related notions that describe the believer's attitude toward God, such as piety (Acts 3:12) or godliness (2 Cor. 1:12; 7:9–11; 1 Tim. 2:2, 10; 3:14, 16; 4:7–8; 5:4; 6:3, 5–6, 11; 2 Tim. 3:5, 12; Titus 1:1; 2:12; 2 Pet. 1:3, 6–7; 2:9; 3:11). The Greek *eusebeia* is derived from the verb *sebō*, "to venerate." We find it in the expression *sebomenos*, "devout" (Acts 13:50; 17:4, 17), or *sebomenos ton theon*, "worshiper of God" (16:14; 18:7; cf. John 9:31, *theōsebēs*, "God-worshipping"). This veneration of God is not very different from the fear of God (Acts 10:2, 22; 13:16, 26). The Greek word for "to fear" is *phobeō*, "to be afraid, to fear," and hence "to respect, to venerate." This is very often said of humans toward God. The believer does not have to be afraid of God; yet, Jesus tells his disciples: "[D]o not fear [*mē phobeisthe*] those who kill the body but cannot kill the soul. Rather fear [*phobeisthe*] him who can destroy both soul and body in hell" (Matt. 10:28).

Klaus Berger has pointed out that in this passage, the fear of our adversaries is directly compared to the fear of God, but also that this passage begins and ends with: "Fear not" (vv. 26 and 31).[44] There is a healthy fear of the holiness of God, but only in case one is living in sin: "Since we have these promises, beloved, let us cleanse ourselves from every defilement of body and spirit, *bringing holiness to completion in the fear of God*" (2 Cor. 7:1). "Perfecting holiness" (NKJV, NIV, NASB, etc.) is something one does out of love for God, but also out of fear of *God's* holiness. True consciousness of God's grace and forgiveness does not make the believer careless but rather God-fearing: "But with you there is forgiveness, [in order] *that* you may be feared" (Ps. 130:4). To those who do confess Christ it is said: "It is a fearful thing to fall into the hands of the living God" (Heb. 10:31), and: "[O]ur God is a consuming fire" (12:29; cf. Deut. 4:24; 9:3).

8.6.2 Holiness in Judgment and Redemption

God's holiness may frighten the sinner, and at the same time encourage the pious person. Indeed, since the fall God manifests his holiness in various ways. He may demonstrate it in judgment, as in the case of Aaron's sons whom he killed: "Among those who are near me I will be sanctified," that is, I will show my holiness (cf. GW, HCSB, NOG, NLT), namely, in judgment, even toward those who are near me (Lev. 10:3). "For you alone are holy. All nations will come and worship you, for your righteous acts [lit. righteousnesses] have been revealed" (Rev. 15:4). "Just [or, Righteous] are you, O Holy

---

44. Berger (2004, 113).

One, who is and who was, for you brought these judgments" (16:5).

This manifestation of God's holiness in judgment is also the first thing that many Christians think of when God's holiness is referred to: his wrath toward sin. However, remarkably enough, God's holiness comes to light to a similar extent in creation and redemption. We find both elements together in Exodus 15:11 (after Israel's miraculous passage through the Red Sea, which brought judgment upon the Egyptians and redemption to the Israelites): "Who is like you, O LORD, among the gods? Who is like you, majestic in holiness, awesome in glorious deeds, doing wonders?"

There is a phrase that we often hear but which is doubtful: "God is full of love, but also holy" (or, "God is holy, but also merciful"). Or, in the version of the Heidelberg Catechism (Q&A 11): "God is indeed merciful, but He is likewise just; . . . ." We understand the good intentions of such a statement; yet, the phrase may suggest a false contrast between God's love (grace, mercy) and God's holiness. Such a suggestion overlooks the fact that both love and holiness are expressions of God's very being, between which there can be no conflict. In his holiness, God is and remains always full of love and mercy. In his mercy, God is and remains always perfectly holy. God cannot deny himself, that is, he always remains faithful to his own being (cf. 2 Tim. 2:13). Therefore, his holiness can never hide behind his mercy, and his mercy never hide behind his holiness.[45]

Some examples may illustrate this. God tells Israel: "Fear not, you worm Jacob, you men of Israel! I am the one who helps you . . .; your Redeemer is the *Holy One* of Israel . . . you shall rejoice in the LORD; in the *Holy One* of Israel you shall glory . . . that they may see and know, may consider and understand together, that the hand of the LORD has done this, the *Holy One* of Israel has created it" (Isa. 41:14, 16, 20). God

---

45. Cf. how Trevethan (1995) considers God's goodness as belonging to his holiness.

Positional Sanctification

is called here "the Holy [God] of Israel," though not as the judging God but as the One bringing redemption. In the salvation that God brings about his holiness comes to light just the same as in his judgments. Likewise, notice the logical connection in Hosea 11:9, "I will not execute my burning anger; I will not again destroy Ephraim; for I am God and not a man, the *Holy One* in your midst, and I will not come in wrath." In brief: I am holy, *therefore* I will not judge you.

8.6.3 "Sanctifying" God

We just read in Leviticus 10:3 that God 'sanctified" himself (Heb., ēqqadēsh). Of course, this does not mean that God *made* himself holy (although this is the literal meaning of Latin *sanctificare* [*facere sanctus*], from which "sanctify" was derived). It means that God *showed* himself to be holy. Likewise, when God's name is "hallowed" (which is a rendering of the same Greek term as "sanctified"; Matt. 6:9; Luke 11:2), this does not mean that his name is *made* holy but that it is *declared* to be holy. That is, the holiness of his name is manifested by people honoring that name through their worship and their walk. In the same vein, we can say that people "glorify" God when his glory is manifested through their worship and their walk. Likewise, we have seen that people can "justify" God (e.g., Luke 7:29), not by *making* him just (righteous) but by *declaring* him to be just; or, his righteousness comes to light in their worship and their walk. Likewise, God is great (Latin, *magnus*, Greek, *megas*), yet people can "magnify" him (Greek, *megalynō*, e.g., Luke 1:46; Acts 10:46; Phil. 1:20).

In all theses cases, people do not add anything to God's righteousness, holiness, glory, or greatness, but they do declare (show, manifest) that God *is* righteous, holy, glorious, and great. They do this by worshiping him, and in their worship they extol his righteousness, holiness, glory, and greatness, or in their walk they extol these wonderful characteristics of God's being. In the believers' walking righteously and holy, God's own righteousness and holiness are glorified.

Compare, for instance, the hallowing of God's name with Ezekiel 36:23 (NKJV): "I will sanctify My great name, which has been profaned among the nations, which you have profaned in their midst; and the nations shall know that I [am] the LORD . . . when I am hallowed in you before their eyes." In this verse, it is God himself who sanctifies (ESV: vindicates the holiness of) his name; in the Lord's Prayer it is God's people who vindicate the holiness of his name. As Reformed theologian Willem Aalders put it: "'Hallowed be your name' means that God may be acknowledged for what he is . . . thus, not made holy, but considered to be holy."[46] Likewise, sanctifying Christ as Lord in our hearts (1 Pet. 3:15 ASV; cf. Isa. 8:12-13) means honoring him as holy (ESV; cf. CEB, CJB, ERV), giving him the place in our hearts and lives that he deserves, submitting to him, honoring him through our worship, our walk, our ministry.

Actually, the difference between humans sanctifying God, and God sanctifying humans, is perhaps smaller than it may seem. It is the same here as with justification. If in justification the emphasis is laid less on *making* someone righteous, and more on *declaring* someone to be righteous, there is little difference between a person declaring God to be righteous, and God declaring the person who, through faith, has been identified with the crucified and risen Christ to be righteous. In both cases, someone is declared (shown, manifested) to be something he already is. The major difference is that God has always been righteous, long before we declared him to be so, whereas the person who is declared to be righteous has been *made* righteous by God transforming this ungodly person into a *tsaddiq* (Rom. 4:5).

Likewise, there is little difference between a person declaring God to be holy, and God declaring the person who, through faith, has been identified with the crucified and risen Christ to be holy. The major difference is that God has been

---

46. Aalders (1931, 17).

holy from eternity (cf. Isa. 6:3), long before any seraph or cherub or human declared him to be so. In contrast to this, the person who is declared to be holy has been *made* holy by God transforming the unholy person into a saint: sanctified by the Spirit and belief in the truth (2 Thess. 2:13), for obedience to Jesus Christ (1 Pet. 1:2).

8.6.4 Holiness in the Theological Tradition

It is striking that God's grace was not always viewed by many theologians as an actual virtue of God, and even more striking is this with respect to God's holiness.[47] Peter Lombard and Thomas Aquinas did not mention holiness as a divine attribute. Protestant theologians often reckoned God's holiness to God's perfection, his righteousness, his goodness, his veracity, his wisdom, his sovereignty, or his majesty, etcetera, or saw it as a purely relational notion, not as an essential quality of God.[48]

A passage such as Isaiah 6:3 shows how difficult it is to maintain such a view. The seraphim praise God as the Thrice Holy (the well-known *Trisagion*), and this returns in the song of the four living creatures in Revelation 4:8, "Holy, holy, holy, is the Lord God Almighty, who was and is and is to come!" Since theologians do reckon God's love to his being—God *is* love—it is important to emphasize God's holiness precisely in connection with his love, because the two are inseparable.[49]

In 1917, the German theologian Rudolf Otto, who specialized in religious studies, published his famous work on the divinely holy as *mysterium tremendum et fascinans*, the "dreadful and fascinating mystery."[50] This work has inspired many other thinkers. For instance, Karl Barth placed the Holy *One* (Latin, *Sanctus*) over against "the holy" (*sanctum*, neuter) in general as viewed by Otto.[51] Following Rudolf Otto, other

---
47. Bavinck (2004, 2:216–17).
48. Diestel (1859).
49. Brunner (1949, 188–93).
50. Otto (1958).
51. Barth (1956, 2/1:360–61; see extensively, 358–68).

German theologians such as Emil Brunner and Paul Althaus used Isaiah 6:3 and other passages to argue that God's holiness is not just one of God's many attributes, let alone that it would be only an ethical attribute.[52] In this regard they stand in opposition to the overwhelming majority of Roman Catholic and Protestant systematic theologians. Brunner and Althaus view holiness as a reference to God's essential *being*, which, as Althaus feels, holds for God's glory and God's bliss as well. Thus, the Spirit is the *Holy* Spirit, not because holiness is one out of many attributes but because this term expresses God's essence. The holy is that which is lofty, inscrutable, majestic, mysterious, inaccessible, and this in a much wider sense than morally inaccessible.

In my view, Althaus and Brunner touch the core of the matter here much better than many other systematic theologians. At the same time, one may wonder whether this is not simply a problem with *all* so-called "attributes."[53] Is love ("God is love," 1 John 4:8, 16), is light ("God is light," 1:5), is spirituality ("God is spirit," John 4:24) just one attribute out of many? God *is* altogether love, altogether light, altogether spirit, and likewise he also *is* altogether holiness, bliss, glory, majesty, etc. Yet, although God's love, spirituality, righteousness, and holiness are never in conflict with each other, they are not synonyms either. Because of this very embarrassment we keep speaking of distinct attributes. This is supported by the fact that Scripture places holiness alongside other divine attributes: "holy and awesome is his name" (Ps. 111:9); "Holy Father . . . righteous Father" (John 17:11, 25), "the Holy and Righteous One" (Acts 3:14), "Sovereign Lord, holy and true" (Rev. 6:10).

Also compare other such juxtapositions: "pure and holy" (Exod. 30:35), "high and holy" (Isa. 57:15), "holy and beautiful" (Isa. 63:15; 64:11), "righteous and holy" (Mark 6:20), "holy and sure" (Acts 13:34), "holy and righteous and good"

---

52. Brunner (1949, 157–74); Althaus (1952, 289–92).
53. Cf. Ouweneel (2007b, 293–96; 2013a, chapter 3).

(Rom. 7:12), "holy and acceptable" (12:1), "holy and blameless" (Eph. 1:4; Col. 1:22; cf. Eph. 5:27), "holy and beloved" (Col. 3:12), "holy and righteous and blameless" (1 Thess. 2:10), "blessed and holy" (Rev. 20:6).

8.7 "Wretched Man That I Am!"
8.7.1 Three Exegeses

In the discussions involving sanctification, Romans 7:14-26 has always played a role, especially verse 24: "Wretched man that I am! Who will deliver me from this body of death?" Is this "I" the apostle Paul himself, or some imaginary "I"? If the latter, is it an unregenerate or a regenerate person who speaks here? And if the latter, does he speak here as representing the Christian's normal condition, or an abnormal one?

It is striking that someone like Reformed theologian Gerrit C. Berkouwer only sees two possibilities here, whereas I just enumerated three.[54] In his view, the passage speaks either of the not-yet-Christian, or of the Christian's normal condition. In contrast to this, I am convinced that Paul speaks of a regenerate person, but in an abnormal condition, not intended by God. Together with the Greek church fathers and the early Augustine,[55] and with Pietists like August Hermann Francke and Johannes Bengel, and the Methodist John Wesley, Paul Althaus was convinced that the first exegesis (the protagonist is an unregenerate person) is the correct one; so too Werner Kümmel, Herman Ridderbos, and Douglas Moo.[56] One argument for this view seems to be verses 7-14, especially verses 10 ("The very commandment that promised life proved to be death to me") and 14b ("I am of the flesh, sold under sin"). However, Anders Nygren has offered an extensive and con-

---

54. Berkouwer (1952, 55–63); cf. Spykman (1992, 499–500). It is also striking that in regard to Rom. 7:14–26, Karl Barth (1933, 257–70) does not even enter into this kind of preliminary question.
55. Cf. Van der Zwaag (2008, 169–71).
56. Althaus (1938); Kümmel (1929); Ridderbos (1959, 154; cf. 162–71); Moo (1996, 445–49).

vincing refutation of this view.[57]

Just like the later Augustine and almost all Reformers, Berkouwer adheres to the second exegesis (the person in Rom. 7 is regenerate).[58] A well-known defender of this exegesis was Hermann F. Kohlbrugge in his highly reputed "comma sermon" (on the comma in v. 14b, "I am carnal, sold under sin").[59] Martin Luther saw in this passage the main ground for his adage *simul iustus et peccator* ("simultaneously just and sinner"). Douglas J. Moo summarized: "The interpretation of vv. 14–25 in terms of 'normal' Christian experience was typical of Lutheran and Reformed theology right into the twentieth century and is still widespread."[60]

In my view, both interpretations commit the same error: Berkouwer cannot understand—rightly so—how Romans 7 could speak of a not-yet-Christian, and *thus* the passage must refer to the common condition of the Christian. Althaus cannot understand—rightly so—how Romans 7 could speak of the normal condition of the Christian, and *thus* the passage must refer to a not-yet-Christian. Apparently, neither of them sees the third obvious possibility: the passage refers to a regenerate Christian, but in an abnormal condition. In a rather denigrating way, Douglas J. Moo called this a "compromise view, better represented in popular than in scholarly literature."[61] Amazingly, he refused to pay any further attention to this view.

The entire subject is of great importance for any doctrine of sanctification because, if Romans 7:14–26 would indeed be describing the normal condition of the believer, then we can understand many passages in the Heidelberg Catechism. The Catechism clearly says that the Lord ". . . He has redeemed and purchased us . . . from sin" (Q&A 34, in line with Rom.

---

57. Nygren (1978, 284–303).
58. See note 53.
59. Kohlbrugge (2009).
60. Moo (1996, 444).
61. Ibid., 447.

6:7, 18, 22), and that "true repentance or conversion" involves "the dying of the old man, and the making alive of the new" (88). But it also speaks of ". . . the sinful nature with which I have to struggle all my life long; . . ." (56); ". . . even our best works in this life are all imperfect and defiled with sin" (62); ". . . even the holiest men, while in this life, have only a small beginning of such obedience, . . ." (114). This definitely smacks more of the gloomy mood of Romans 7 than of the joyous atmosphere of Romans 8.

Q&A 70 describes that ". . . so that we may more and more die unto sin and lead holy and unblameable lives" (*not:* since the moment we came to faith we *are* dead to sin, as Rom. 6:11 indicates). This "more and more" (progressive sanctification) is also found in Q&A 76: ". . . to be so united more and more to His sacred body by the Holy Spirit, . . ." (*not:* since the moment we came to faith we *are* fully united to Christ); and 81: true believers ". . . desire more and more to strengthen their faith and to amend their life. . . ."; and 89: "Q. What is the dying of the old man? A. Heartfelt sorrow for sin, causing us to hate and turn from it always more and more." Even the experienced believers still identify as "miserable sinners " (126). Believers long to "be renewed more and more after the image of God, until we attain the goal of perfection after this life" (115). ". . . [S]o govern us by Thy Word and Spirit, that we submit ourselves to Thee always more and more; . . ." (123). For a more extensive discussion of progressive sanctification, see the next chapter.

8.7.2 A Third Possibility

Berkouwer and others are right insofar as several statements in Romans 7 cannot possibly be applied to unregenerate persons: "I do not do what I want, but I do the very thing I hate. Now if I do what I do not want, I agree with the law, that it is good. So now it is no longer I who do [evil], but sin that dwells within me. . . . For I delight in the law of God, in my inner being" (vv. 15–17, 22). The text is about a person who loves what is good, and hates what is evil, who has learned to make a distinction between his "I" (ego)[62] and his sinful nature, and who delights in God's law.[63] This can be the language only of the regenerate person.[64]

Althaus and others are right insofar the Christian in his normal condition lives by the power of the Holy Spirit, and thus is no longer dominated by sin (cf. Rom. 6:12, 14, 18, 22); Christ lives and rules in him.[65] The language of such a person, at least as far as his sinful nature is concerned that is still in him, is not: "Wretched man that I am" (v. 24), but rather: "[I]n all these things we are more than conquerors through him who loved us" (Rom. 8:37; actually, this is already expressed in 7:25, "Thanks be to God through Jesus Christ our Lord!"). In his normal spiritual condition, the believers goes "from strength to strength" (cf. Ps. 84:7), not from defeat to defeat, as he does in Romans 7. Even though in this chapter Paul speaks in the first person, what he describes here does not at all correspond to the usual way he speaks in his letters about the normal Christian life.[66]

Both viewpoints have had many reputed adherents, in addition to those I have already mentioned. Great thinkers have confronted each other in this matter: Augustine and Pelagius, Luther and the humanists (Erasmus), the Jansenists and the Jesuits. Relatively few theologians arrived at the idea of the third exegesis: Romans 7:14-16 is about regenerate believers (here the Reformational tradition was right), but not about

---

62. Notice how the "I" is linked here with the new nature, whereas in Gal. 2:20 it is linked with the old nature: "It is no longer I who live, but Christ who lives in me."
63. Cf. Greijdanus (1933, 346).
64. Also cf. the transition from vv. 7–13 to the present tense in vv. 14–26; so Murray (1968, 1:256; also see his further comments: 256–73); see further Bavinck (2006, 3:81–82); Greijdanus (1933, 330–41); Van Leeuwen and Jacobs (1952, 154–59); Barth (1956, 4/1:588); Cranfield (1975, ad loc.); Harrison (1976, 84); Moo (1996, 446–47).
65. Althaus (1938, 70–72); cf. Moo (1996, 445–46).
66. Cf. Nee (1997).

the normal Christian life (here Althaus and many others were right). These theologians realized that Romans 7 is *not* about the conflict between the flesh and the Spirit, as in Galatians 5:14–16 (". . . the desires of the flesh are against the Spirit, and the desires of the Spirit are against the flesh, for these are opposed to each other"), simply because mention of the Spirit is entirely absent in this passage (it does occur earlier in Rom. 7:6, in a different context).[67] It is not the conflict between the flesh and the Spirit here, but between the flesh (the sinful nature) and the reborn "I," *which does not (yet) know and experience the power of the Holy Spirit*. This is the abnormal element in Christian life as it is depicted here. The passage is about a regenerate soul, which has experienced that rebirth does grant a new nature and new life, but must yet experience the accompanying spiritual strength. This strength has to come from elsewhere: from the Holy Spirit. Such a person is like a newborn baby: he does have life, but no strength.

8.7.3   A Pre-Stage?

If we prefer to see here in Romans 7 an abnormal condition of a regenerate person, we are faced again with two possibilities. First, the situation of verses 17–26 could be a "pre-stage" of the "release" (being-set-free) of Romans 8:2 ("the law of the Spirit of life has set you free in Christ Jesus from the law of sin and death") and what follows. The second interpretation sees in this passage a hypothetical situation, which Paul describes for purely doctrinal reasons, *not* for biographical reasons.

The difficulty of the first interpretation is that the text nowhere suggests anything a kind of "pre-stage." In itself, it is certainly possible to distinguish a phase after rebirth in which the reborn person does not yet possess the assurance of salvation, that is, has not yet truly embraced the gospel of their salvation. In other words, the person is born again (he has sincerely confessed his sins, and does believe that Jesus is the only way of salvation) but does not yet possess that faith on

---

67. See, e.g., Althaus (1938, 104–05); *contra* Harrison (1976, 84).

which God can put the seal of the Holy Spirit (Eph. 1:13; cf. 2 Cor. 1:22). I believe that Saul of Tarsus was in this condition between the moment that he was converted (on the road to Damascus) and the moment that he received the assurance of salvation as well as the Holy Spirit (Acts 9:10, 17). In fact, the converted Jews in Acts 2, the converted Samaritans in Acts 8, and Cornelius in Acts 10, all were converted some time before they actually received the Holy Spirit.

To be sure, those who today accept with their hearts the gospel of their salvation, are sealed with the Holy Spirit immediately. However, in principle it is still possible that, especially under defective preaching, there are those who are born again without having acquired the assurance of salvation, so that there is not yet that saving faith on which God can put his seal. In the end, such persons will definitely be saved; but they may spend decades in a kind of Romans 7 condition, especially if they are told repeatedly that this is the "normal" condition for a Christian.[68]

One of the best-known Reformed theologians in the Netherlands in the eighteenth century was Alexander Comrie (of Scottish descent). He made of this abnormal condition a *rule*: every elect person receives first the justification that belongs to the moment of regeneration, and afterward the justification by faith in the "court of conscience" (Dutch: *vierschaar der consciëntie*). The first justification is unconscious, the second one is conscious.[69] In my terminology: only at the moment of the second justification does the believer receive the assurance of salvation—although even afterward he may go through many temptations—and the sealing with the Holy Spirit.

Even if we grant the possibility of a pre-stage (in which the person is reborn but has not been sealed with the Holy Spirit), this does not mean that Romans 7 necessarily is about such a pre-stage. It is equally possible that the person in Romans 7 does possess the assurance of salvation, and thus has

---

68. On this topic, see Ouweneel (2007a, 213–15).
69. See Harinck (2007, 118–48, and the summary: 170–75).

definitely received the Holy Spirit—but has never learned to live by the power of the Holy Spirit. Such a person will never make much progress with his sanctification, because he has no real idea of the true energy source.

This does not mean that the Heidelberg Catechism has no valuable things to say about the power of the Spirit in sanctification. It does tell us that ". . . we are born again by the Spirit of God" (Q&A 8), and that "by His Holy Spirit, [Christ] also assures me of eternal life, and makes me heartily willing and ready from now on to live unto Him" (Q&A 1). It tells us in general terms that the Holy Spirit is for our sanctification (24); ". . . by [the Spirit's] power we seek those things which are above, where Christ sits at the right hand of God, and not things on earth" (49), and "by His Holy Spirit He pours out heavenly gifts upon us, His members (Eph. 4:10-12); then, that by His power He defends and preserves us against all enemies" (51). "Christ, having redeemed us by His blood, also renews us by His Holy Spirit after His own image, that with our whole life we show ourselves thankful to God for His blessing" (86); "all the days of my life I rest from my evil works, allow the Lord to work in me by His Spirit, and thus begin in this life the everlasting sabbath" (103). We are encouraged that "without ceasing we diligently ask God for the grace of the Holy Spirit, that we be renewed more and more after the image of God, . . ." (115). "[B]e pleased to preserve and strengthen us by the power of Thy Holy Spirit, that we may make firm stand against them and not be overcome in this spiritual warfare, until finally complete victory is ours." (127).

8.8 A Hypothetical Situation
8.8.1 A Rhetorical Aid

As I said, the second interpretation sees in Romans 7:14-26 a hypothetical situation, which Paul, in spite of speaking in the first person, describes for purely doctrinal, *not* for biographical reasons. In my view, this is by far the best approach to the passage (see below). Romans 7 describes the situation that arises when a person is born again but does not live by the power of the Holy Spirit but tries to serve God in his own strength. Please notice carefully that neither Christ nor the Spirit is mentioned in verses 7–24, and also how often we find here the words "I," "me," and "my."[70] The message, then, would be that a life of sanctification is not possible in one's own strength, not even for the regenerate person, but only by having Christ before one's eyes, in the power of the Holy Spirit, as becomes clear afterward in Romans 8.

At any rate, today we understand better that speaking in the first person does not prove that Paul is literally speaking about himself here, whether in his regenerate or in his earlier unregenerate state. In antiquity, the first person pronoun was used now and then as a rhetorical aid to express something that is applicable to others. Paul had done so earlier in this epistle: "But if our unrighteousness serves to show the righteousness of God, what shall we say? That God is unrighteous to inflict wrath on us? (I speak in a human way.) By no means! For then how could God judge the world? But if through my lie God's truth abounds to his glory, why am I still being condemned as a sinner?" (Rom. 3:5–7). And elsewhere: "[W]hy should my liberty be determined by someone else's conscience? If I partake with thankfulness, why am I denounced because of that for which I give thanks?" (1 Cor. 10:29–30).[71] We know this type of rhetoric also from the book of Ecclesiastes: the author places himself in a certain hypothetical situation—viewing things only as they look "under the sun"—in order to communicate a certain message.

Once again, the "I" of Romans 7 is the regenerate person who in his own strength tries to be good and holy, and every time is repelled by the strength of indwelling sin.[72] These are

---

70. If we include the occurrences of "I" concealed in the verbal forms, then I count about fifty (!) occurrences of "I," "me," and "my" in this short passage.
71. See Kümmel (1929, 128–31); Harrison (1976, 83).
72. Griffith Thomas (1946, 191).

not the experiences of the person described in Romans 6:17–19: "But thanks be to God, that you who were once slaves of sin have become obedient from the heart to the standard of teaching to which you were committed, and, having been set free from sin, have become slaves of righteousness . . . so now present your members as slaves to righteousness leading to sanctification." And in 7:4–6: you "have died to the law through the body of Christ, so that you may belong to another, to him who has been raised from the dead, in order that we may bear fruit for God. For while we were living in the flesh, our sinful passions, aroused by the law, were at work in our members to bear fruit for death. But now we are released from the law, having died to that which held us captive, so that we serve in the new way of the Spirit and not in the old way of the written code." Or in 8:1–2: "There is therefore now no condemnation for those who are in Christ Jesus. For the law of the Spirit of life has set you free in Christ Jesus from the law of sin and death." Living out these three passages is like living on a different planet, compared to 7:7–26.

8.8.2 Some Testimonies

Already Philip Doddridge (eighteenth century) wrote[73] that, to suppose that Paul was writing all the words of Romans 7:7–26 with respect to himself, that is, to the established Christian he really was when writing this epistle, is not only alien to, but in conflict with, the entire flow of his argument and with other passages in Romans. In my view this is the correct approach, which we also find with, for instance, William Manson.[74] He spoke of an unreal, in the sense of non-historical, hypothetical situation that is evoked for us in Romans 7. It does not correspond with any actual phase in either the Jewish-Christian or the Pauline-Christian existence, for in none of these situations can we imagine that the darkness of the soul is not illuminated by a ray of heavenly grace. Paul has set the

---

73. Quoted in W. Kelly (*Bible Treasury* 7.326).
74. Manson (1967, 159).

scene for an investigation that is prescribed by a purely argumentative necessity: *What is living under the law according to the logic of its nature?*

Everett Harrison followed the same line of thinking.[75] He called the experience described in Romans 7 not entirely autobiographic, but a presentation of what would be the situation of someone who was confronted with the requirements of the law and the power of sin in his life, and would try to solve his problem independently of the strength of Christ and the authority of the Spirit. Similarly, William Kelly wrote that it is clear that the described condition is not that of the deliverance: the being set free as we find it in Romans 6:7, 18, 22 and 8:2.[76] Kelly saw in it not the normal condition of a Christian, but one of transition: the "I" has been renewed by the work of regeneration, but is bound to experience that, in itself, it is powerless.

To put it in this brief form: the ungodly person is neither *willing* nor *able* to serve God. The person of Romans 8 is both *willing* and *able* to serve God (through the power of the Holy Spirit). The person of Romans 7 is *willing* to serve God, but *unable* (because he tries to do it in his own strength, and does not yet know the power of the Holy Spirit). Please note: the problem of the person in Romans 7 is not necessarily that he does not (yet) possess the assurance of his salvation. That is not the issue at all. The issue is that he does not know where to find the power for his sanctification, and this makes him desperate.

8.8.3 Five "Laws"

In this context, it is important to pay attention to the word "law" in verse 21 ("I find it to be a *law* that when I want to do right, evil lies close at hand") and verse 23 ("I see in my members another law waging war against the law of my mind and making me captive to the *law* of sin that dwells in my mem-

---
75. Harrison (1976, 84).
76. Kelly (*Bible Treasury* 7.326–27).

bers"). The "*law* of sin" in the believer's members is something different from the sinful nature that is still in him.[77] Here on earth, the believer will never get rid of this sinful nature—but he definitely can be delivered from the "*law* of sin," that is, the compulsiveness, dominance, power of sin: "[T]he law of the Spirit of life *has* set you free in Christ Jesus from the law of sin and death" (8:2, italics added; cf. 6:7, 18, 22).

Altogether I see in Romans 7:14–8:4 no less than five different meanings of the Greek word *nomos* ("law").

(a) The law (Torah) of Moses (7:14, 16, 22, 26; 8:3–4).

(b) The law (rule, principle, like a law of nature) of sin, that is, the principle that the person in the flesh cannot but sin because he does not have the power to act otherwise (7:23, 26; 8:2).

(c) The law (rule, principle) of the (renewed) mind, that is, the principle that the new nature of the regenerate person is characterized by the desire (tendency, impulse) to do good and serve God (7:23).

(d) The law (rule, principle) of the Spirit of life, that is, the Spirit as characterized by the life that the believer has in Christ Jesus (8:2).

(e) The law (rule, principle) that the person oscillates back and forth between the law of his renewed mind and the law of sin (7:21, "I find it to be a law that when I want to do right, evil lies close at hand"—unless this "law" is the same as [b]).

Romans 7:14–26 describes the regenerate person who rejoices in God's Torah (a) because of his new nature (c), but has not yet been set free of the *law* of sin (b), and is therefore tossed to and fro (e) between (b) and (c). Romans 8, by contrast, describes the regenerate person in whom the principle of the Spirit (d) has put aside the principle of sin (b), so that in the power of this Spirit the principle of the new nature (c) can come to fruition. The "oscillation law" (e) is no longer operative. The believer rejoices in the Torah (a) but now also

---

77. Grant (1901, 242–43).

has the power to keep it (v. 4, "the righteous requirement of the law" is in principle "fulfilled in us, who walk . . . according to the Spirit").

Please note that this does not mean that the believer could not fall into sin anymore. "[W]e all stumble in many ways" (James 3:2). "If we say we have no sin, we deceive ourselves" (1 John 1:8). But the believer who has been set free in the sense of Romans 8:2 is no longer under the *power* of sin; the *law* of sin is no longer reigning in his life. The difference is this. The person of Romans 7 is still in the *power* of sin, and therefore basically cannot but sin. The person of Romans 8 *can* still sin — and unfortunately he is sometimes foolish enough to sin — but through the power of the Holy Spirit his sinning is no longer *inevitable*. The wild apple tree cannot but produce inferior apples; the cultivated tree produces superior apples, although once in a while there may be a bad apple among the good ones.

The hypothetical believer of Romans 7 is still under the law of sin. He thinks he has the power to combat the operations of his sinful nature, but time and again he discovers that he does not have that power. Formally he is not, but factually he is still a "slave of sin" (cf. Rom. 6:16-22). The sinful nature remains in the believer as long as he lives; but Paul had written: "Let not sin therefore reign in your mortal body, to make you obey its passions. Do not present your members to sin as instruments for unrighteousness, but present yourselves to God as those who have been brought from death to life, and your members to God as instruments for righteousness. For sin will have no dominion over you, since you are not under law but under grace" (vv. 12-14). Notice here the following aspects.

(a) The fact that Paul has to write these things to believers indicates that it is still possible for a regenerate person to be in the power of sin; this is the case with the person whom Paul describes in Romans 7.

(b) At the same time Paul's words demonstrate that there is no *necessity* for the regenerate to remain in the power of sin. Paul encourages him to live a life in which he is no longer *dominated* by sin. In chapter 8 he shows that this is possible only through the Holy Spirit. Not even the indwelling of the Spirit as such is enough; the believer has to actively *submit* to the Spirit: he has to *walk* or *live* according to the Spirit (v. 4–5), has to *set the mind* on the Spirit (v. 6), has to *put to death* the deeds of the body by the Spirit (v. 13), has to be *led* by the Spirit (v. 14).

(c) There is a refined distinction in the forms of the Greek verbs in 6:13. The first verb "present" (*paristanete*) is a continual activity (present tense), that is, "let it never happen" (that you present your members to sin as instruments for unrighteousness). But the second "present" (*parastēsate*) is a one-time event (aorist tense): "present . . . your members *once and for all* to God as instruments for righteousness." It is the same in verse 19: "[P]resent your members *once and for all* as slaves to righteousness leading to sanctification." This is important because it shows that Paul does not view Christian life as one of trial and error: falling down and standing up again, falling down and standing up again, and perhaps, in the process, become holier (think of the mentioned "more and more'" in the Heidelberg Catechism). No, *once and for all*, through the power of the Holy Spirit, you present yourself to God as committed to righteousness; this is your sanctification. You may fail in this once in a while, but that does not alter the fundamental attitude of life that you possess from now on: you are committed to holiness, not in your own strength but in that of the Holy Spirit.

8.9 Humbling Oneself
8.9.1 Poor Sinners or Perfect Christians?

The reason why some people apparently wish to view Romans 7:14–26 as a description of normal Christian life is that the experiences depicted in it are *their own* experiences instead of having learned to live by the power of, and being filled with, the Holy Spirit. So, for instance, Terry Johnson, who referred to pastor and professor John Duncan (nineteenth century). Duncan told his hearers that as long as they would be in his church, they would never get out of Romans 7. If you thought you could, said Johnson, you are a perfectionist.[78] Apparently, Duncan and Johnson can see only two possibilities: the poor-sinner faith (although you are reborn, you always remain a wretched sinner here on earth) or perfectionism (you can get rid of the sinful nature already here on earth). You either remain under the "law of sin" all your life — you are never "set free" of this law — or you lose the capacity to sin. There is nothing in between. In the next chapter I hope to show why I whole-heartedly reject both extremes as totally unscriptural, and even perilous.

It is incredible that apparently so few theologians ever think of a third possibility: you can be set free from the "law of sin" — through the power of the Holy Spirit sin is no longer *inevitable* — but here on earth you never lose the flesh, that is, the inclination to sin. In opposition to the poor-sinner view, I maintain that believers can be set free of (the power of) sin because this is what Paul says. In opposition to perfectionism, I maintain that believers on earth always retain the capacity to sin because this is what Paul says too. In opposition to the poor-sinner view, I maintain that believers can definitely lead a truly holy life — not in their own strength, but through the power of the Spirit. In opposition to perfectionism, I maintain that even the most mature Christian can still fall into sin — and sometimes does.[79]

The Heidelberg Catechism rightly tells us that the Torah must be preached so that "without ceasing we diligently ask God for the grace of the Holy Spirit, that we be renewed more and more after the image of God, until we attain the goal of perfection after this life" (Q&A 115). And Gerrit C. Berkouw-

---

78. Johnson (2000, 99).
79. See extensively, Ouweneel (2007a, especially chapters 4, 8–9, and 11–12).

er says: "This renewal of human life in gratitude and love has always been considered the work of the Holy Spirit."[80]

Of course, the fact that sanctification is the work of the Holy Spirit does not exclude the Christian's responsibility. On the contrary, *he* is the one who has to "strive for holiness" (Heb. 12:14). It is not the Spirit who does this for him, but it is *he* who does this in the power of the Spirit. It is *he* who receives the command to grow (become mature; 1 Pet. 2:2; 2 Pet. 3:18), to present his members as slaves to righteousness leading to sanctification (Rom. 6:19; cf. v. 13), to be transformed by the renewal of his mind (Rom. 12:2), to put off his old self, to be renewed in the spirit of his mind, and to put on the new self, created after the likeness of God in true righteousness and holiness (Eph. 3:22-24), etc. This responsibility involves not only the believers' acts and words, but even his thoughts (cf. Rom. 2:15-16, 29).[81]

Either there is hardly any spiritual growth, and believers do in fact remain "poor sinners," though saved by grace; in their view, their experiences just confirm the truth of Romans 7. *Or* there is a measure of outward growth, transformation, renewal, but not in the power of the Holy Spirit; the result is a holiness resting on works, a self-conceited boasting, as Paul describes at many places: "[D]o not be arrogant toward the branches" (Rom. 11:18). "What do you have that you did not receive? If then you received it, why do you boast as if you did not receive it?" (1 Cor. 4:7). "Your boasting is not good. Do you not know that a little leaven leavens the whole lump?" (5:6; cf. 1:29-31; 3:21). "'Let the one who boasts, boast in the Lord.' For it is not the one who commends himself who is approved, but the one whom the Lord commends" (2 Cor. 10:17-18; cf. Gal. 6:13; Eph. 2:9). "Do nothing from selfish ambition or conceit, but in humility count others more significant than yourselves" (Phil. 2:3). Paul speaks of the person who is "puffed up without reason by his sensuous mind" (Col. 2:18),

---

80. Berkouwer (1952, 78).
81. Cf. Coates (1926, 42–45).

and those who have "an appearance of wisdom in promoting self-made religion and asceticism and severity to the body, but they are of no value in stopping the indulgence of the flesh" (v. 23).

All these things are nothing but the spirit of Phariseeism.[82] They are the opposite of a truly spiritual maturation, whereby, through the Holy Spirit, the believer develops not less, but rather more consciousness of sinfulness, and thus, a growing humility. One who is forgiven much, loves much (cf. Luke 7:47). "For everyone who exalts himself will be humbled, and he who humbles himself will be exalted" (14:11; 18:14). "Humble yourselves before the Lord, and he will exalt you" (James 4:10). "Humble yourselves, therefore, under the mighty hand of God so that at the proper time he may exalt you" (1 Pet. 5:6).

8.9.2 Loathing Oneself

The Heidelberg Catechism (Q&A 115) points to the importance of preaching the Torah, so that "as long as we live we may learn more and more to know our sinful nature" — however, I hasten to add, without the despondency of Romans 7:24, "Wretched man that I am! Who will deliver me from this body of death?" It *is* possible to know the misery of one's own sinful nature more and more without falling into despondency because the believer is aware of his deliverance in Christ. Precisely on account of the assurance of salvation, the profoundest knowledge of sin and the deepest humbling of oneself are possible in a proper way. Notice here the order of Ezekiel 36, where the context is eschatological, but is applicable to New Testament Christians as well:

(a) *Regeneration:* "I will sprinkle clean water on you, and you shall be clean from all your uncleannesses, and from all your idols I will cleanse you. And I will give you a new heart, and a new spirit I will put within you. And I will remove the heart of stone from your flesh and give you a heart of flesh"

---

82. See extensively, Berkouwer (1952, chapter 6).

(vv. 25-26).

(b) *Indwelling of the Spirit:* "And I will put my Spirit within you, and cause you to walk in my statutes and be careful to obey my rule" (v. 27).

(c) *Loathing oneself:* "Then you will remember your evil ways, and your deeds that were not good, and you will loathe yourselves for your iniquities and your abominations" (v. 31; cf. 6:9; 20:43).

In the hyper-Calvinist view, there must be a lot of "loathing oneself" (c) before there can be any assurance of salvation [(a) and (b)]; a lot of Romans 7 before there can be Romans 8, and in a sense one never moves past Romans 7 here on earth. But God shows the prophet Ezekiel that it is the other way around: no believer will ever get to a really profound knowledge of his sinful nature (a "loathing oneself") as long as he does not have the assurance of salvation and is led by the Holy Spirit.[83] The person in Romans 7 is humbled but not built up (except at the end: "Thanks be to God through Jesus Christ our Lord!" v. 25). The person in Romans 8 is built up by the Spirit, and thus arrives at true self-knowledge. He is aware of the "deeds of the body" (i.e., here, the flesh; the sinful deeds), but nails them to the cross of Christ (v. 13): "[T]hose who belong to Christ Jesus have crucified the flesh with its passions and desires" (Gal. 5:24). Please note, the person of Romans 8 has not become negligent or indifferent with respect to the problem of sin; on the contrary, he knows what to do with the passions and desires of the sinful nature: he brings them under the death of Christ.

The New Testament does not know of any Christians doubting their salvation.[84] Some who do doubt may imagine they are quite humble; they feel too sinful or too small to accept such a salvation. But in fact, it has little to do with humility, and a lot with a lack of faith and proper spiritual

---

83. Cornelis Harinck (2001) describes the hyper-Calvinist position, but in a moderate and considerate way.
84. See Darby (n.d.-a, XXVIII, especially in sections on Rom. 7).

understanding. If God promises me that he will forgive me when I confess my sins (1 John 1:9), and I still doubt his forgiveness, I am not humble but unbelieving. There may even be an amount of egocentrism in it. What does the regenerate person in Romans 7 speak about? Himself. There is hardly a word about Christ and the Holy Spirit here. What kind of Christian is that? True humility is not talking about your sinfulness all the time, but not talking about yourself at all, only about Christ.

Scripture contains many such calls for humility: "Seek the Lord, all you humble of the land, who do his just commands; seek righteousness; seek humility" (Zeph. 2:3). Jesus says: "Take my yoke upon you, and learn from me, for I am gentle and lowly in heart" (Matt. 11:29). Paul speaks of "serving the Lord with all humility" (Acts 20:19): "I ... urge you to walk in a manner worthy of the calling to which you have been called, with all humility and gentleness, with patience, bearing with one another in love" (Eph. 4:1-2). "Put on then, as God's chosen ones, holy and beloved, compassionate hearts, kindness, humility, meekness, and patience" (Col. 3:12). "Live in harmony with one another. Do not be haughty, but associate with the lowly" (Rom. 12:16; cf. James 4:6; 1 Pet. 3:8; 5:5).

8.9.3 Living in Grace

Consciousness of sin and humility are linked with an increasing sense of divine grace.[85] Spiritual growth is precisely this: growing "in the grace and knowledge of our Lord and Savior Jesus Christ" (2 Pet. 3:18); "as sin reigned in death, grace also" will "reign through righteousness leading to eternal life through Jesus Christ our Lord" (Rom. 5:21). Justification is "by his grace," on account of faith, and it is the same with sanctification; compare 12:3, "For by the grace given to me I say to everyone among you ... to think with sober judgment, each according to the measure of faith that God has assigned." Our walk is "by the grace of God" (2 Cor. 1:12). Every minis-

---

85. See extensively, Yancey (1998).

Positional Sanctification

try is by grace: "According to the grace of God given to me, like a skilled master builder I laid a foundation" (1 Cor. 3:10). God, who "called me by his grace, was pleased to reveal his Son to [lit., in] me, in order that I might preach him among the Gentiles" (Gal. 1:15; cf. 2:9). "Of this gospel I was made a minister according to the gift of God's grace, which was given me by the working of his power. To me, though I am the very least of all the saints, this grace was given, to preach to the Gentiles the unsearchable riches of Christ" (Eph. 3:7-8; cf. 4:7; Acts 14:26; 15:40; Rom. 15:15; 15:10; 4:7).

The word "gift" in many passages (Rom. 1:11; 12:6-8; 1 Cor. 1:4-5, 7; 7:7; 12:4, 8-10, 28-31; 1 Tim. 4:14; 2 Tim. 1:6; 1 Pet. 4:10) is the Greek word *charisma*, derived from *charis*, "grace"; all the gifts of the Spirit are gifts of God's grace. Everything we ourselves may give to another is divine grace (2 Cor. 8:1, 6-7, 19; 9:8), every support in our life of faith is grace (Acts 4:33; 11:23; 13:43; 18:27; 20:32; 2 Cor. 12:9; 2 Tim. 2:1; 1 Pet. 2:19-20). Sanctification never involves a gradual emancipation with respect to Christ, but rather the reverse: learning more and more to live by his grace. There is a growing up "into salvation–if indeed you have tasted that the Lord is good" (1 Pet. 2:2-3). "For the grace of God has appeared, bringing salvation for all people, training us to renounce ungodliness and worldly passions, and to live self-controlled, upright, and godly lives in the present age, waiting for our blessed hope, the appearing of the glory of our great God and Savior Jesus Christ, who gave himself for us to redeem us from all lawlessness and to purify for himself a people for his own possession who are zealous for good works" (Titus 2:11-14).

Living by grace is never living a passive life. Hendrikus Berkhof refers here to "the spiritually carefree and lethargic person who likes to benefit from a cheap grace,[86] and thereby considers himself exempt from the struggle of the faith."[87]

---

86. The term is from Bonhoeffer (1937, chapter 1).
87. Berkhof (1979, 454).

Repeatedly, Paul calls us to action: "[E]arnestly desire the higher gifts" (1 Cor. 12:31; cf. 14:1, 12, 39). "Pursue love, and earnestly desire the spiritual gifts, especially that you may prophesy" (14:1); "strive to excel in building up the church" (v. 12); "earnestly desire to prophesy" (v. 39); "always seek to do good to one another and to everyone" (1 Thess. 5:15). "Not that I have already obtained this or am already perfect, but I press on to make it my own, because Christ Jesus has made me his own . . . I press on toward the goal for the prize of the upward call of God in Christ Jesus" (Phil. 3:12, 14). "But as for you, O man of God, flee these things. Pursue righteousness, godliness, faith, love, steadfastness, gentleness" (1 Tim. 6:11). "So flee youthful passions and pursue righteousness, faith, love, and peace" (2 Tim. 2:22). "Strive for peace with everyone, and for the holiness" (Heb. 12:14). "[W]ork out your own salvation"; to be sure, you do this "with fear and trembling" when thinking of your own incapacity; yet: be active (Phil. 2:12).

True humility is in balance here with a certain healthy self-confidence, which is entirely rooted in grace: "O Lord, my heart is not lifted up; my eyes are not raised too high; I do not occupy myself with things too great and too marvelous for me. But I have calmed and quieted my soul, like a weaned child with its mother; like a weaned child is my soul within me" (Ps. 131:1–2).

Chapter 9
Practical Sanctification

Since we have these promises,
 beloved,
let us cleanse ourselves
 from every defilement of body and spirit,
bringing holiness to completion
 in the fear of God.
                            2 Corinthians 7:1

Strive for peace with everyone,
 and for the holiness
without which no one
 will see the Lord.
                            Hebrews 12:14

As obedient children, do not be conformed
 to the passions of your former ignorance,
but as he who called you is holy,
 you also be holy in all your conduct,
since it is written,
 "You shall be holy,
 for I am holy."
                            1 Peter 1:14–16

Summary: *Practical sanctification is positive (taking part in God's* *holiness) rather than negative (subduing sin). It is the appeal to be practically what we are positionally. We strive for this, but in the power of the Holy Spirit. The norm is the Torah; this is elucidated with the help of Old and New Testament examples. Practical sanctification is renewal, or metamorphosis, or what Eastern Christians call* **theosis.** *Practical sanctification is "in Christ," an expression that Paul deals with differently than John. The relationship between practical sanctification and spiritual growth is discussed; does it involve a "dying away" of the "old self"? What must we understand by this? What are the differences between the "fathers," the "young men" and the "babies" in Christ? What does this mean in view of sanctification?*

In the second part of the chapter, the "poor-sinner" view is contrasted with perfectionism; both are refuted. Do we remain "poor sinners" all our earthly days? What does the New Testament say about this? How does this view affect our ideas about spiritual warfare and about divine discipline? And what is perfectionism in its various forms? What are its positive and negative features? How does it deal with the many New Testament appeals to believers not to sin? What standards of sin does it use? I finally conclude that (a) believers do not need to sin anymore, but (b) they nevertheless sometimes do (even the "fathers" in Christ).

9.1 "Be Holy!"
9.1.1 Negative and Positive

IN THE PREVIOUS CHAPTER, I entered rather extensively into the subject of the holiness of God because the practical sanctification of believers in essence is nothing but displaying, or learning to display, God's own holiness in their lives. As Willem Aalders says: "The word [sanctification] seeks its relationship to that which is holy, that is, to him who is holy, to God."[1] Practical sanctification is the continually renewed and increasing consecration to God and turning away from evil, and in that order. In the past, too much emphasis has been put on that aspect of sanctification that has to do with "subduing" or

---

1. Aalders (1931, 19; cf. 26).

"suppressing" sin. So, for instance, Willem H. Velema writes: "This sanctification targets especially *the stain and power of sin, which are eliminated through sanctification.* ... We can characterize sanctification as aversion to sin and resistance to it. This is a key aspect of sanctification."[2] And Donald G. Bloesch describes the life of sanctification as one of increasing battle against sin, death and devil.[3]

Such an approach is not only theologically one-sided, but pastorally it has repeatedly given rise to disappointment because many believers regularly faced the reality of the sinful nature that was still in them. The emphasis should rather be on being filled with the Holy Spirit[4] with the purpose of exhibiting the image of *God* in our Christian walk in the power of that Spirit. In the description of Louis Berkhof: sanctification is *"that gracious and continuous operation of the Holy Spirit, by which He delivers the justified sinner from the pollution of sin, renews his whole nature in the image of God, and enables him to perform good works."*[5] And in the description of Johan A. Heyns: sanctification is "the renewal of Man as image of God in the relatedness of faith to God's grace by the way of an obedient following of Christ."[6]

The goal of sanctification is not primarily negative but positive: "You shall be holy, for I am holy" (Lev. 11:44–45; 19:2; 21:8; cf. 1 Pet. 1:16). Or even: You shall be holy *as* I am holy. This sanctification is an ongoing development, closely corresponding with what the Eastern Orthodox tradition calls the *theosis:*[7] "deification" not in the sense of believers becoming, or having to become, God, but rather in the sense of exhibiting the image of God in their lives. It is not *positional* justification and sanctification that constitute God's final purpose for us,

---

2. Van Genderen and Velema (2008, 646).
3. Bloesch (1997, 182).
4. See Ouweneel (2007a, chapter 11; 2010a, §14.3.1).
5. Berkhof (1949, 532).
6. Heyns (1988, 319).
7. See extensively, Ouweneel (2010a, chapter 14).

but *practical* justification and sanctification, which entail *theosis*. The former leads to the one "new man," in which believing Jews and Gentiles have been united, and which has been "created after the likeness of God in true righteousness and holiness," that is, "Christ all and in all" (Eph. 2:15; 4:24; Col. 3:10). The latter debouches in the "new creation," in which righteousness and holiness will dwell (cf. 2 Pet. 3:13), and in which God will be "all in all" (1 Cor. 15:28).

Practical sanctification is an ongoing development, in which the justified and sanctified person effectively *turns out* to be righteous, or a saint. That is, divine holiness manifests itself practically in his life, which is governed by a dedicated heart. In view of this, Jesus prayed: "Sanctify them in the truth.... And for their sake I consecrate [or, sanctify] myself, that they also may be sanctified in truth" (John 17:17, 19). In my view, this does *not* mean: be sanctified *by* practicing truth, as Leon Morris suggests,[8] nor does it mean to be sanctified *in order to* practice truth, but be sanctified by virtue of "the truth," that is, the "word of truth" (2 Cor. 6:7; Eph. 1:13; Col. 1:5; 2 Tim. 2:15; James 1:18), that is, *Holy* Scripture. At least, this holds for verse 17; in verse 19 it is literally "in truth" (without the Greek article), which here does not necessarily mean anything more than "in reality," that is, in people's practical experience (cf. Col. 1:6; 1 John 1:1).[9]

What the text is saying is that Jesus will truly separate himself and consecrate himself before the Father for the benefit of his followers, in order that they too would be separated and consecrated. In my view, this does not mean that Jesus would consecrate himself for them by means of his sacrificial death, as several expositors assume,[10] but rather by means of taking his place with the Father as their representative and

---

8. Morris (1971, 730).
9. Vine (1985, 1:341).
10. Contra Morris (1971, 731–32, including note 52); Dods (1979, 844); Tenney (1981, 165).

intercessor.[11]

9.1.2 Be What You Are

The apostle Paul addresses the believers as "those . . . called to be saints" (Rom. 1:7, or "called saints"), but nevertheless tells them: "[P]resent your members as slaves [Greek, *doula*, enslaved] to righteousness leading to sanctification . . . now that you have been set free from sin and have become slaves of God [*doulōthentes tōi theōi*, enslaved to God], the fruit you get leads to sanctification and its end, eternal life" (Rom. 6:19, 22). Likewise, he addresses his second letter to the Corinthians to "all the saints who are in the whole of Achaia" (1:1), but nevertheless appeals to them: "[B]eloved, let us cleanse ourselves from every defilement of body and spirit, bringing holiness to completion in the fear of God" (7:1). In both cases, Paul is saying, as it were: You *are* holy, so *live* holy.

Paul writes to the Thessalonian believers: "[T]his is the will of God, your sanctification [or, holiness]," which turns out to mean in this case: "that you abstain from sexual immorality; that each one of you know how to control his own body[12] in holiness and honor. . . . For God has not called us for impurity, but in holiness" (1 Thess. 4:3-4, 7). "[M]ay the God of peace himself sanctify you completely, and may your whole spirit and soul and body be kept blameless at the coming of our Lord Jesus Christ" (5:23). Also in the sentence, "God chose you as the firstfruits to be saved, through sanctification by the Spirit and belief in the truth" (2 Thess. 2:13), Paul speaks not only of positional but also of practical sanctification on our way to perfect salvation.

The book of Hebrews speaks several times of believers as "sanctified" (2:11; 10:10, 14; 13:12; cf. 3:1; 6:10; 13:24), and nevertheless says that God disciplines us "for our good, that we

---

11. Darby (*Collected Writings* 33, 285); Kelly (1898, 363); Stuart (n.d., 339).
12. Lit., "vessel" (Greek, *skeuos*), i.e., either "body" (Morris [1959, 123–24]; Bruce [1982, ad loc.] even thinks specifically of the male reproductive organ), or "wife" (Van Leeuwen [1953, 131]; Thomas [1978, 271–72]; Moffatt [1979, 34]). Vine (1985, 3:91) leaves the matter undecided.

[in a very practical way!] may share his holiness.... Strive for peace with everyone, and for the holiness without which no one will see the Lord" (12:10, 14). Here again, positional and practical sanctification merge.

We may summarize all this as follows: you *are* righteous and holy, now *be* righteous and holy; or, you can *become* holy because in principle you *are* holy already. Strive, pursue, do your utmost, in order to practically make true what you are as far as your position in Christ is concerned: "Not that I have already obtained this or am already perfect, but I press on to make it my own, because Christ Jesus has made me his own ... one thing I do: forgetting what lies behind and straining forward to what lies ahead, I press on toward the goal for the prize of the upward call of God in Christ Jesus" (Phil. 3:12-14; cf. 1 Cor. 14:1; 1 Thess. 5:15; 1 Tim. 6:11; 2 Tim. 2:22).

In short: *be what you are*, or at least, *become what you are*. Make it visible in the fruits sprouting from your position in Christ. It is the fruit of the Spirit in redeemed lives that manifests itself in practical holiness.[13] To be sure, holiness is not mentioned in Galatians 5:22-23; but "love, joy, peace, patience, kindness, goodness, faithfulness, gentleness, self-control" — this *is* practical holiness.

Karl Barth says: "You are requested to be, have and do *another* — you, precisely you! As *if* 'sanctification' would be a human possibility! As *if* sin would not dwell in your mortal body, with which you are inseparably and inseverably one. . . . The possibility that this requirement can be fulfilled, that God's will on earth can be done with and through humans, that is, the possibility that a sanctified human life as such becomes a historic and visible moment, . . . not only can this possibility not be disputed, but from the viewpoint of grace it must be seen as the ultimate and after all only possibility, of which the realization must be expected with almost stormy impatience, desire and zeal."[14]

---

13. Demarest (1997, 407).
14. Barth (2008, 201–202).

9.1.3 Striving for Holiness

Practical sanctification has to be taken very seriously. Just as the believer is not justified by a fruitless faith—a faith that does not produce good works (James 2:14-26)—no one will "see the Lord" without practical sanctification (Heb. 2:14). Positional justification without righteous fruits *is* no justification; Positional sanctification without holy fruits *is* no sanctification. Compare Matthew 5:8, "Blessed are the pure in heart, for they shall see God." Positional and practical sanctification are, each in themselves, nothing. Positional sanctification *is* no sanctification if there is no holy life sprouting from it. Conversely, practical sanctification *is* no sanctification if it is not rooted in a person's position being well established in the risen and glorified Lord. He who "accepts" Christ but remains fruitless, will in the end be empty-handed. "But now that you have been set free from sin and have become slaves of God, the fruit you get leads to sanctification [or, holiness]" (Rom. 6:22). *From* (positional) sanctification one moves *to* (practical) sanctification, by means of the fruits.

An appeal to a "once saved, always saved" (§7.7-7.9) is totally out of place here. No human will be in heaven—will see God—who in this life has not produced fruit, whether fruit to holiness (Rom. 6:11), fruit of righteousness (Phil. 1:11; Heb. 12:11), or fruit of the Spirit (Gal. 5:22-23). Faith without the necessarily resulting works is useless, dead (James 2:17, 20, 26). It is the same with sanctification. If there is no striving for (pursuing of) holiness (Heb. 12:14)—no matter how weak and deficient—what certainty do we have that such a person will nevertheless see the Lord? Parallel to this: if there is no striving for (pursuing of) righteousness (1 Tim. 6:11; 2 Tim. 2:22), what certainty do we have that such a person has been justified by God? If there is no striving for (pursuing of) love (1 Cor. 14:1), what certainty do we have that in such a person God's love has been poured out (Rom. 5:5)?

The criminal on the cross, who came to faith at the last moment, is no exception to the rule that a fruitless life is in fact dead (Luke 23:40-42). The man produced at least four fruits of true regeneration: (a) he acknowledged that he had deserved the death sentence; (b) he appealed to his fellow-criminal to fear God; (c) he confessed Jesus as the innocent One, and implicitly even as the Messiah (the One who would return as King in order to establish his Kingdom on earth); and (d) he entrusted himself to Jesus. In the words of Joel B. Green: "[T]he second criminal, this religious and social outsider, thus exercises astounding insight into the status and identity of Jesus. . . . This criminal, whose reliability as a hermeneut is ratified by Jesus' gracious response to him, is the first to recognize that Jesus' death is not a contradiction of his messiahship, his role as Savior; he is the first to recognize that Jesus' crucifixion is a precursor to his enthronement (cf. Acts 5:30-31), and thus he anticipates in his request Jesus' kingly rule."[15]

Both positional and practical justification and sanctification contain both a divine and a human aspect. It is by God's sovereign grace that we are justified and sanctified (positionally), *and* that we work out this justification and sanctification in our further Christian life (practically). But at the same time, it is our responsibility to repent and receive Christ and his work in faith (positionally) as well as to live subsequently in a righteous and holy way (practically).[16] It is perfectly true that this is possible only through God's grace and the power of the Holy Spirit. But it is also perfectly true that it is the believer's responsibility to continually connect his walk with the power source of the Spirit. There are things that *God* pours out on us richly (Titus 3:6), but the counterpart of this is that there are things that we have to *let* dwell in us richly (Col. 3:16). "*Be filled with the Spirit*" (Eph. 5:18) is passive—another person has to fill us—but at the same time it is a command coming to believers (cf. the "be baptized" in Acts 2:28; 22:16). Believers are personally responsible for not being filled with the Spirit,

---

15. Green (1997, 822-23).
16. Cf. Berkouwer (1952, 21-22); Van Genderen (1988, 97).

because it means they did not open up to this. If this filling *is* present, there will also be a striving for righteousness and holiness.

Abraham Kuyper knew the tension between *having been* sanctified and practical sanctification, but in my view he used a wrong example to underscore this.[17] He referred to John 13: "Here too there is on the one hand the absolute statement, 'You are clean' [v. 10], and yet *unreconciled* alongside this the *seemingly* entirely contradictory appeal: 'If I do not wash you, you have no share with me' [v. 8]." However, there is nothing that is unreconciled or contradictory here, as Jesus himself explains: on the one hand, there is (what I am calling) the *positional, one-time* "bathing" of the entire body (cf. 1 Cor. 6:11; Titus 3:5, the "washing [or, bath] of regeneration"). On the other hand, there is the *practical* washing of the feet, which are polluted by the world in our daily walk. Jesus considered Peter to be someone who apparently had "bathed" already, that is, was born again. For quite some time, Peter had a part *in* Jesus; therefore, the text does not say *meris en* (Acts 8:21) or *metechō* (1 Cor. 9:12; 10:17, 21), or something similar.[18] But Peter ought to have a part *with* Jesus (Greek, *meros met' emou*), that is, blessings in common with Jesus, fellowship with Jesus (so many translations). To this end, the believer needs every day to have his feet washed (daily conversion).[19]

9.2 The Norm for Holiness
9.2.1 The Messianic Torah

The apostle Peter makes clear that, "as he who called you is holy, you also be holy in all your conduct, since it is written, 'You shall be holy, for I am holy'" (1 Pet. 1:15–16). The norm and the example for our holiness, then, is God's own holiness. This norm is expressed in the Torah of Christ (1 Cor. 9:21; Gal. 6:2), but our holiness is never legalistic, never compulsive. It

---

17. Kuyper (1873, 198).
18. In John 13:8 the RSV has "part in me," which is quite mistaken.
19. See Ouweneel (2007b, 496–97; 2010a, §2.6.2).

is not a yoke (Acts 15:10). Legalism is even in basic contrast with true holiness (see chapter 2). No, the Torah of Christ is a Torah of liberty (James 1:25; 2:12). A law of liberty is a law that perfectly harmonizes with the impulses and inclinations of our new nature, in loving surrender and dedication. It is a law of *liberty* because it does not restrict the inclinations of the new nature but allows them free rein. Stated simply, liberty is being able to do, and to omit doing, what one desires. If there is a law that prescribes exactly what the new self in virtue of his new nature — I do not speak of the flesh — desires to do and to omit doing, that is a "law of liberty."

It is also a law of love (cf. Matt. 22:36-40; John 13:34; Rom. 13:8-10; the "royal law," that is the law of the Kingdom, in James 2:8). This is the law that presupposes that everything that believers think, say, and do has been inspired by the love that has been poured out into their hearts through the Holy Spirit who has been given to them (Rom. 5:5). As Jesus said himself, "If you love me, you will keep my commandments. . . . Whoever has my commandments and keeps them, he it is who loves me. . . . If anyone loves me, he will keep my word" (John 14:15, 21, 23). "If you keep my commandments, you will abide in my love" (15:10). "[T]his is the love of God, that we keep his commandments" (1 John 5:3); "this is love, that we walk according to his commandments" (2 John 1:6). "For you were called to freedom, brothers. Only do not use your freedom as an opportunity for the flesh, but through love serve one another. For the whole law is fulfilled in one word: 'You shall love your neighbor as yourself'" (Gal. 5:13-14).[20]

Bringing holiness to completion (2 Cor. 7:1), striving for holiness (Heb. 12:14) — this is all nothing but fulfilling God's commandments out of the deep motive of love, toward God and toward the neighbor, and in the power of the Holy Spirit. It is nothing but displaying God's own holiness in our lives,

---

20. *Contra* Brunner (1937), who separates law and love. For my view of the Torah, see the first volume in this series; also compare Berkouwer (1952, chapter 8); Strickland (1993).

not in our own strength, but in faithful orientation toward Christ as the source of power: "[A]part from me you can do nothing" (John 15:5).

No form of "redemptive deism" should creep in here whatsoever, as if conversion and justification would be of God, but sanctification of human origin.[21] Deism is the view that once God created the world he no longer cared about it. "Redemptive deism," then, is the view that God regenerates a person at rebirth, but from this moment on leaves him to himself, as if from now on he can manage to run his own (new) life. No, the person who before his rebirth was totally dependent on the grace God and the power of the Holy Spirit, remains so also afterward, during his entire Christian walk, and in a certain sense, forever.

9.2.2 Old Testament Holiness

On the one hand, sanctification is the increasing display of God's being in the believers. Also in cases where sanctification explicitly means dedication or consecration *to* God this is not necessarily in conflict with the notion of such a display. This is because God's holiness implies that he is perfectly faithful to his own being: everything in him is perfect light, perfect transparency, perfect purity, perfect harmony. God's holiness consists of the highest and most glorious that could ever exist in any being. Our sanctification is *both* the display—as far as it is given to finite creatures—of this light, this transparency, this purity, this harmony, *and* the dedication to precisely this highest and most glorious that could ever exist in any being.

On the other hand, such a lofty view of sanctification may never lead us to lose sight of the fact that sanctification also involves very common, concrete, practical consequences of this consecration to God. One of the most striking examples of this is the following Old Testament commandment: "You shall have a place outside the camp, and you shall go out to it. And you shall have a trowel with your tools, and when

---
21. Heyns (1988, 321).

you sit down outside, you shall dig a hole with it and turn back and cover up your excrement. Because the LORD your God walks in the midst of your camp, to deliver you and to give up your enemies before you, *therefore your camp must be holy*, so that he may not see anything indecent among you and turn away from you" (Deut. 23:12-14).

This relationship between holiness and everyday life is seen in several enumerations of ethical qualities: "O LORD, who shall sojourn in your tent [i.e., the temple]? Who shall dwell on your *holy* hill [i.e., Zion]? He who walks blamelessly and does what is right and speaks truth in his heart; who does not slander with his tongue and does no evil to his neighbor, nor takes up a reproach against his friend; in whose eyes a vile person is despised, but who honors those who fear the LORD; who swears to his own hurt and does not change; who does not put out his money at interest and does not take a bribe against the innocent. He who does these things shall never be moved" (Ps. 15:1-5). "Who shall ascend the hill of the LORD? And who shall stand in his *holy* place [i.e., the temple]? He who has clean hands and a pure heart, who does not lift up his soul to what is false and does not swear deceitfully" (Ps. 24:3-4).

Passages that are comparable, though not mentioning the word "holy," are these: "'Who among us can dwell with the consuming fire [i.e., God]? Who among us can dwell with everlasting burnings [i.e., can stand God's judgment]?' He who walks righteously and speaks uprightly, who despises the gain of oppressions, who shakes his hands, lest they hold a bribe, who stops his ears from hearing of bloodshed and shuts his eyes from looking on evil, he will dwell on the heights; his place of defense will be the fortresses of rocks; his bread will be given him; his water will be sure" (Isa. 33:14-15).

"If a man is righteous and does what is just and right— if he does not eat upon the mountains or lift up his eyes to the idols of the house of Israel, does not defile his neighbor's wife or approach a woman in her time of menstrual impurity, does not oppress anyone, but restores to the debtor his pledge, commits no robbery, gives his bread to the hungry and covers the naked with a garment, does not lend at interest or take any profit, withholds his hand from injustice, executes true justice between man and man, walks in my statutes, and keeps my rules by acting faithfully—he is righteous; he shall surely live" (Ezek. 18:5-9). "He has told you, O man, what is good; and what does the LORD require of you but to do justice, and to love kindness, and to walk humbly with your God?" (Micah 6:8).

9.2.3 New Testament Holiness

The New Testament, too, speaks in a very practical way of the commandments of God or Christ. We should never speak of sanctification in such a heavenly manner that we forget the down-to-earth commandments: Always give your gifts in secret (Matt. 6:3). Never drag a fellow-Christian before a judge (1 Cor. 6:1-8). Never take revenge yourself (Matt. 5:39; Rom. 12:19). Always be reasonable (Phil. 4:5). Always be kind (Gal. 5:22; Col. 3:12). Always be hospitable (Rom. 12:13; Heb. 13:2; 1 Pet. 4:9). Always be helpful (1 Thess. 5:14). Give your money away cheerfully (2 Cor. 9:7). Do not worry (Matt. 6:31; Phil. 4:6). Do not judge another Christian in matters of conscience (Rom. 14). Always be forgiving (Matt. 6:14; Eph. 4:32; Col. 3:13). It is this very kind of everyday rules that most Christians tend to forget most of the time.[22]

This is the core of the matter: sanctification is learning to display the being of God. But then it is unthinkable that we still practice what is mentioned in several negative enumerations in the New Testament: coveting, wickedness, deceit, sensuality and sexual immorality, envy, slander, pride, foolishness, orgies and drunkenness, quarreling and jealousy, idolatry, theft, greediness, reviling, swindling, sorcery, enmity, strife, fits of anger, rivalries, divisions, slander, obscene

---

22. Wright (2007, 193).

talk, disobedience, slaves of various passions and pleasures, malice, hatred (Mark 7:22; Rom. 3:13; 1 Cor. 6:9–10; Gal. 5:19–21, 26; Col. 3:5–8; Titus 3:2–3; cf. Eph. 4:17–5:6; 1 Thess. 4:3–7; 2 Tim. 3:1–5; 1 Pet. 2:1).[23] Or to add a few more vices: hypocrisy (Matt. 6:2, 5, 16; 7:5), telling half-truths (Eph. 4:25; Col. 3:9), bitterness (Eph. 4:31; Heb. 12:15), love of money (1 Tim. 6:9–10), an unforgiving attitude (Matt. 18:35).

Avoiding these vices should not be done in a spirit of legalism and Pharisaism, for such a spirit would be particularly *un*holy. True sanctification is always in a spirit of love: "Love is patient and kind; love does not envy or boast; it is not arrogant or rude. It does not insist on its own way; it is not irritable or resentful; it does not rejoice at wrongdoing, but rejoices with the truth. Love bears all things, believes all things, hopes all things, endures all things" (1 Cor. 13:4–7). This text may impress us even more if we substitute here the name of Christ for the word "love": "Christ is patient and kind; Christ does not envy or boast; Christ is not arrogant or rude, does not insist on his own way, is not irritable or resentful; Christ does not rejoice at wrongdoing, but rejoices with the truth. Christ bears all things, believes all things, hopes all things, endures all things." And subsequently for believers who have been practically sanctified, that is, transformed in the image of Christ: "Saints are patient and kind; saints do not envy or boast; saints are not arrogant or rude, do not insist on their own way, are not irritable or resentful; saints do not rejoice at wrongdoing, but rejoice with the truth. Saints bear all things, believe all things, hope all things, endure all things."[24]

9.3 Holiness and Renewal
9.3.1 *Theosis*

To many Christians, the idea that our sanctification involves the (ever increasing) display of God's own holiness seems

---
23. This is what the Germans call *Lasterlisten*, "lists of sins."
24. See Ouweneel (2007a, 325), where I substituted the Holy Spirit for "love," which is equally applicable.

to be quite far-fetched. Did we not describe God's holiness in terms of excellence, loftiness, glory, luster, brilliance, and majesty, which are proper to God's uniquely holy being? Can we ever claim that it is God's intention that this glory, luster, and brilliance are transferred to redeemed humans? Yet, as we saw, it is God himself who borrows the norm for our holiness from nothing less than his own holiness.

We touch here upon the subject of *theosis*, which I briefly dealt with in the second volume of this series. It is the Greek term for "deification," which does not mean "becoming God," but "becoming *like* God": becoming transformed according to the image of God. The Bible is clear about what this entails: "You . . . must be perfect, as your heavenly Father is perfect" (Matt. 5:48). "Be merciful, even as your Father is merciful" (Luke 6:36). "Therefore be imitators of God, as beloved children. And walk in love" (Eph. 5:1-2), for "God is love" (1 John 4:8, 16). God is light (1:5), and it is said of the believers: "[N]ow you are light in the Lord" (Eph. 5:8). Of the "new Jerusalem," that is, the bride of the Lamb (Rev. 21:9), it is said that she is "having the glory of God" (v. 11). Sanctification can never be about anything less than this.

From a somewhat different angle, Willem Aalders comes up with the same picture: "A person can live pleasantly in a comfortable existence, spend his days with eating and drinking, work and diversion, cosiness and friendship—and yet live below his station, his calling, which is perhaps that of a warrior, even a martyr, in the service of the ideal, whose beauty was once revealed to him. He has dismayed the holiness that would like to grant him grace."[25]

This becomes even clearer when we realize that God's holiness descended to us in the person of Jesus Christ, who, as I mentioned earlier, is called several times the Holy One as well as the image of God (2 Cor. 4:4; Col. 1:15; cf. Heb. 1:3). In him, we see the first, as well as the highest, representation of

---

25. Aalders (1931, 30–31).

God's holiness ever displayed in a human being. What is said of God can be said of Jesus: he is the norm and the example for our holiness. This is evident from many passages, where terms like "holiness" and "sanctification" do not occur but where the root-idea is clearly present. Almost every Pauline epistle has a reference to this: "[L]et us . . . put on the armor of light. Let us walk properly as in the daytime . . . put on the Lord Jesus Christ" (Rom. 13:12-14). Christ Jesus in his own person "became to us . . . righteousness and sanctification" (1 Cor. 1:30); "we have the mind of Christ" (2:16). This is always the goal: that "Christ is formed [molded, taking shape] in you" (Gal. 4:19; ERV: ". . . until people can look at you and see Christ"). This is the fruit of sanctification: "For to me to live is Christ" (Phil. 1:21; cf. 3:8, 10). "Have this mind among yourselves, which is yours in Christ Jesus" (2:5).

This total renewal according to the image of Christ is what Paul desires to bring about in others: ". . . until we all attain to the unity of the faith and of the knowledge of the Son of God, to mature manhood, to the measure of the stature of the fullness of Christ" (Eph. 4:13). "Him we proclaim, warning everyone and teaching everyone with all wisdom, that we may present everyone mature in Christ" (Col. 1:28). "For in him the whole fullness [Greek, *plērōma*] of deity dwells bodily, and you have been filled [*peplērōmenoi*, brought to{the same} fulness] in him" (2:9-10). "[G]row in the grace and knowledge of our Lord and Savior Jesus Christ" (2 Pet. 3:18).

9.3.2 Metamorphosis

"[W]e all, with unveiled face, beholding the glory of the Lord, are being transformed into the same image from one degree of glory to another. For this comes from the Lord who is the Spirit" (2 Cor. 3:18). This transformation (Greek, *metamorphōsis*[26]) is essentially the same as sanctification, spiritual maturation, renewal, or whatever term the New Testament uses in

---

26. Cf. the "metamorphosis" from caterpillar to butterfly, an analogy for spiritual growth (Ouweneel, 2008c, 305–08).

referring to this.

This word *metamorphōsis* is derived from *morphē*, "form" in the sense of "(inner) shape," not to be confused with the Greek word *schēma*, "appearance," or "outer shape." For the difference, see Philippians 2:6–8, where Paul describes Christ Jesus, "being in the form [*morphē*] of God . . . taking the form [*morphē*] of a bondservant . . . being found in appearance [*schēma*] as a man."[27] *Morphē* means that he became a Man, even a bondservant, in his inner being, just as he in his being was and remained God. However, he became Man not only in his inner being but also in his outer appearance; this is indicated by the word *schēma*.[28] Jesus was both outwardly and inwardly truly Man, just as in his being he was also the eternal God.[29] Here on earth, Christ was, as far as his *morphē* was concerned, both God and Man; but as far as his *schēma* was concerned, people saw only a Man. As the Belgic Confession (Article 19) says, "[T]he Godhead did not cease to be in Him, any more than it did when He was an infant, though it did not so clearly manifest itself for a while." Likewise, the Heidelberg Catechism (Q&A 35) says, "[T]he eternal Son of God, who is and continues true and eternal God, took upon Himself the very nature of man."

This distinction may help us to understand, for instance, *morphē* in Galatians 4:19, "Christ is formed [*morphōtē*] in you." If Christ "takes shape" in the believer, this does not mean that he only speaks and acts like Christ. If his is only an outer similarity to Christ, spiritual people will soon see through this. The significance of the verb used here (*morphoō*, "be formed"), which is derived from *morphē*, is that a person is also to be renewed inwardly. This is thus both an outward and an inward renewal, and in addition, both a positional and a practical renewal.

This exegesis is supported by Romans, where we twice

---
27. Unfortunately, ESV and others have "form" three times here.
28. Cf. Trench (1976, 261–67).
29. Ouweneel (2007b, 322–23).

encounter derivations from *morphē*: first, *symmorphos* (8:29, "to be conformed to the image of his Son"). *Morphē* means here that, according to God's predestination, believers are transformed into the image of God's Son, primarily inwardly, though, of course, this must be made visible in practical sanctification. If, in their spiritual growth, they outwardly become more and more like Christ, this is primarily caused by Christ being formed *within* them. Only if they are fundamentally changed in their "(inward) form," practical changes in their outward appearance will be genuine and sustainable.

The second reference in Romans is *syschēmatizomai*, "be conformed to" (12:2, "Do not be conformed to this world"; cf. 1 Pet. 1:14), namely, in one's outer appearance. Presumably, Paul wants to indicate here that for a true believer it is impossible to be worldly on the inside, in one's deepest being (cf., e.g., Gal. 4:9; 6:14; Col. 2:8, 20; Titus 2:12). Those who in their inner being are conformed to the world are apparently still non-regenerates. But unfortunately it is possible that believers in their inner being have been "conformed to Christ" — his "form" (*morphē*) is in them — whereas in their outer appearance (way of thinking and speaking, habits, goals, motives; *schēma*) they are still adapted to the world.

This is why Paul continues by saying, ". . . but be transformed [*metamorphousthe*] by the renewal of your mind." This means here as much as: let the form of Christ that is in you be worked out in your practical sanctification. Thus, in rebirth not only the inner being has been renewed, but let this renewal come to light practically in your thinking, feeling, and willing, and from there also in your appearance and your behavior. Otherwise, Christians would be ambiguous beings: their inner *morphē* like Christ, their outer *schēma* like the world. It is not sufficient if this *morphē* is present in them; from within, their outward appearance (*schēma*) is to be changed head to toe. This is meta-morph-osis. This practical sanctification turns them into mature Christians. They can say that Christ has been "formed" in them in a very practical way only if he has become the determinative factor for their basic attitude in life. This means concretely that in all things they have learned to seek the will of God, and have gained enough practical experience to discern the true will of God. Hence Romans 12:2b: ". . . that by testing you may discern what is the will of God, what is good and acceptable and perfect" (cf. the renewed attitude of Saul in Acts 22:10, "What shall I do, Lord?").

9.4 Union with Christ
9.4.1 In Christ (Paul's Teaching)

There is a special aspect of practical sanctification that must be mentioned here. It is believers' union with Christ. First and foremost, this is a matter of their *position* in Christ; once for all, believers have been united with the risen and glorified Lord at God's right hand. But this has also practical consequences, which throw a special light on sanctification. Even apart from this, union with Christ is the "heart of Paul's religion" (far more than justification; see §1.1), and more than any other concept it is the key that discloses the secrets of his soul.[30] Indeed, one of the most striking descriptions of salvation is that believers are in Christ; for Paul being a Christian is being in Christ (Rom. 16:7; Gal. 1:22; Phil. 1:1; 4:21; Col. 1:2; 1 Thess. 2:14). Believers are "sanctified in Christ Jesus, called to be saints" (1 Cor. 1:2); it is "from God" that they are "in Christ Jesus," who became to them "sanctification" (v. 30). Even the spiritual "infants" are described as being "in Christ" (3:1). Peter describes the believers as "called to his eternal glory in Christ" (1 Pet. 5:10; cf. v. 14).

Being in Christ does not mean the same everywhere in the New Testament. We will have to distinguish especially between the Pauline and the Johannine use of the expression. In *Paul's* thought, that which Christ has obtained through his work on the cross is entirely imputed to the believers. In him they have, as it were, personally undergone death, burial and resurrection: "For if we have been united with him in a death

---
30. Cf. Stewart (2002, 147).

like his, we shall certainly be united with him in a resurrection like his. We know that our old self [lit., old man] was crucified with him in order that the body of sin might be brought to nothing, so that we would no longer be enslaved to sin. For one who has died has been set free [lit., justified] from sin. Now if we have died with Christ, we believe that we will also live with him . . . you must consider yourselves dead to sin and alive to God *in Christ Jesus*" (Rom. 6:5-11).

"God, being rich in mercy, because of the great love with which he loved us, even when we were dead in our trespasses, made us alive together with Christ—by grace you have been saved—and raised us up with him and seated us with him in the heavenly places *in Christ Jesus*" (Eph. 2:4-6). "*In him* also you were circumcised with a circumcision made without hands, by putting off the body of the flesh, by the circumcision of Christ, having been buried with him in baptism, in which [or, *in whom*] you were also raised with him through faith in the powerful working of God, who raised him from the dead. And you, who were dead in your trespasses and the uncircumcision of your flesh, God made alive together with him, having forgiven us all our trespasses" (Col. 2:11-13; cf. Rom. 8:1-2, 9-11; 2 Cor. 5:17, 21; Gal. 2:4; Eph. 1:1-14; 2:7, 13).

In a typically Pauline way, this is all about believers' *position* and *walk* in Christ. This involves, for instance, that there is now no longer any condemnation for them (Rom. 8:1), that what he has acquired is now also *their* share (Eph. 2:5-6), that in him is their strength and their life (Gal. 2:20; Phil. 4:13; cf. 2 Cor. 12:9), that in him they have been enriched (1 Cor. 1:4-5) and favored (Eph. 1:6 HCSB), that they are dead to sin but alive in the risen Christ (Rom. 6:11), that they have their life in him (2 Tim. 1:1), that they "fall asleep" in him (1 Cor. 15:18; 1 Thess. 4:16), that one day they will be made alive in him (1 Cor. 15:22), but spiritually this *has* already taken place: in him they *are* already seated in the heavenly places (Eph. 2:5-6). As a counterpart, Paul emphasizes that Christ is in believers as their life (Col. 1:27; 3:4).

9.4.2 In Christ (John and Others)

In *John's* thought, being in Christ means that he is the spiritual "atmosphere" in which believers now live and breathe. Repeatedly, Jesus himself says, or John says, that believers are "abiding," or (must) "abide," in him: "Whoever feeds on my flesh and drinks my blood *abides in me*, and I in him" (John 6:56). "In that day you will know that I am in my Father, and *you in me*, and I in you" (14:20). "Every branch *in me* that does not bear fruit he takes away, and every branch that does bear fruit he prunes, that it may bear more fruit. . . . *Abide in me*, and I in you. As the branch cannot bear fruit by itself, unless it abides in the vine, neither can you, unless you *abide in me*. . . . Whoever *abides in me* and I in him, he it is that bears much fruit, for apart from me you can do nothing. If anyone does not *abide in me* he is thrown away like a branch and withers; and the branches are gathered, thrown into the fire, and burned. If you *abide in me*, and my words abide in you, ask whatever you wish, and it will be done for you" (15:2-7). "By this we may know that we are *in him*: whoever says he *abides in him* ought to walk in the same way in which he walked. . . . If what you heard from the beginning abides in you, then you too will *abide in the Son* and in the Father. . . . But as his anointing teaches you . . . *abide in him*. And now, little children, abide in him" (1 John 2:5-6, 24, 27-28). "No one who *abides in him* keeps on sinning" (3:6; cf. v. 24).

In all these cases it is not so much position but rather *relationship* and *fellowship* with Christ, and in him with each other (1 John 1:3-4). As a counterpart, John too emphasizes that Christ is, or abides, in believers (see John 6:56; 14:20; 15:3; 1 John 4:13 just quoted): ". . . that they may be one even as we are one, *I in them* and you in me. . . . I made known to them your name . . . that the love with which you have loved me may be in them, and *I in them*" (John 17:22-23, 26; cf. 14:23).

Being in Christ also means that the believers are identified with him in a very practical way. He tells some of his disciples: "The cup that I drink you will drink, and with the baptism with which I am baptized, you will be baptized" (Mark 10:39). "A servant is not greater than his master. If they persecuted me, they will also persecute you. If they kept my word, they will also keep yours" (John 15:20); ". . . that I may know him and the power of his resurrection, and may share his sufferings, becoming like him in his death, that by any means possible I may attain the resurrection from the dead" (Phil. 3:10-11).

The key word "abiding" also indicates how believers can conduct their lives in practical unity with Christ: they must abide (Greek, *menō*) in his word (John 8:31), continue (*prosmenō*) in the grace of God (Acts 13:43), continue (*emmenō*) in the faith (14:22), again: continue (*epimenō*) in the faith (Col. 1:23), continue (*epimenō*) in God's kindness (Rom. 11:22), "continue [*menō*] in what you have learned and have firmly believed" (2 Tim. 3:14), abide (*menō*) in the light (1 John 2:10), abide (*menō*) in the teaching of Christ (2 John 1:9).

As far as the Christian's formal *position* is concerned—a Pauline topic—one is in Christ, that is, in the glorified Man at God's right hand. Where he is seated, in principle the believer is also seated (Eph. 2:6). What Christ has received, he shares with his Body, that is, his church (1:20-23). God views believers as being in the Beloved (Eph. 1:6). What he is (as Man), they are; what he has (as Man), they have; where he abides (as Man), they abide. The position of believers in Christ always has to do with what Christ is *as Man*: he died as Man on the cross for them, he rose as Man, he is now seated at God's right hand as Man. But when it is a question of believers' *relationship* and *fellowship* with Christ—a Johannine topic—we rather think of Christ as the Father's Son; *that* Son has become our life (1 John 5:11-12), and in this way his Father has become our Father (John 20:17).

Strictly speaking, this fellowship is not union with Christ. Union with the Son would come too close to an ontic deification of the believers, as Neo-Platonists and some mystical theologians would have it.[31] The believers have been *made one* with the *Man* Christ Jesus; they are as one with him as a body is with the head, forever inseparably bound together. They have *fellowship* with the Father and the Son (1 John 1:3), due to the Son's life that is in them. The believers are in the Man Christ—that is union, position (Paul's line). They are in the Son—that is life, relationship, fellowship (John's line).

Of course, we must not make a separation here. How could there be union without life and fellowship, and how could there be fellowship without union? The two are inextricably connected, just as are the human nature and the divine nature of Christ.[32] But just as we distinguish between these two natures, so too we distinguish between, on the one hand, the believers' union with the Man Jesus Christ and, on the other hand, their fellowship with the divine persons: the Father and the Son in the power of the Spirit. The former has to do with the Body of Christ, the latter with the Family of God, two very different metaphors.[33]

9.4.3 What Union Is Not

As I said, union with Christ must not be understood in an *ontic* way: it does not imply that believers have entered into the Godhead. Within the Family of God, as children of God, they are certainly associated with *the* Son of God, but when it is a matter of union it is with the *Man* Christ Jesus. What he has become, and has acquired, through his work on the cross, he can share with his own. Jesus said first: "I glorified you on earth, having accomplished the work that you gave me to do. And now, Father, glorify me in your own presence with the glory that I had with you before the world existed" (John 17:4-5), and then he says, "The glory that you have given me I have given to them" (v. 22). Please note: the glory that Jesus

---

31. See Demarest (1997, 314–16).
32 Cf. Belgic Confession, Article 19.
33. See more extensively, Ouweneel (2015b, chapters 7 and 9).

received was basically the same glory that he had possessed as the eternal Son with the Father (v. 5). But he now received this same glory *as Man*, because as Man he had accomplished the work, and only as Man could he share this glory with his human followers. He can share the glory that he has obtained as Man — but he can never share with us the glory of his deity.

This union is not *mystical* either, as if believers have lost their individuality in a kind of merging into him, or as if they are no longer on earth. Thus, Ephesians 2:6 (*"in* Christ seated[34] in the heavenly places") is followed in a very practical way by the earthly communities in chapters 4:25-6:9, in which Christians still fully participate. To put it in stronger terms: practical sanctification comes to light here in the degree to which their *heavenly* position is manifested in these very *earthly* relationships: (a) the community of faith (4:25-5:20), (b) the community of the family (marriage and children; 5:21-6:4), and (c) the community of work (6:5-9).

Union with Christ is not *sacramental* either, as if it is brought about and maintained by baptism and the Lord's Supper, as Roman Catholics, high church Lutherans, and high church Anglicans want to have it. Nor is it in the New Testament ever explicitly *covenantal*, as Reformed theologians see it.[35] Nor is it only *psychical*, just as two friends or even husband and wife are one. This union is a *Spiritual* bond, that is, a *position* established by the Holy Spirit, and *practically* maintained by the Spirit. It cannot be severed from the bond of *life*: in him believers live, move, and have their being (cf. Acts 17:28), and he is the divine life in them (Col. 3:4; 1 John 5:11-13). Here, the metaphor of John 15:1-7 is helpful: the "juices of life" flow from him to us because we are in him. This is why our union with him has to be experienced, lived, and realized in our practical

---

34. Gr. *synekathisen*, not just "given us a place" (CEV), or "a position" (GW), or even "a seat" (ICB, NCV) (one may have a "seat" without being actually "seated" there).
35. Demarest (1997, 317–21).

sanctification.[36]

9.4.4 Living and Walking in Christ

Scripture refers many times to the practical meaning of being in Christ for believers' sanctification (even though this term is not always used):[37] their ways must be in Christ (1 Cor. 4:17). His servants are led in triumphal procession in Christ (2 Cor. 2:14). They are weak in him but will live with him by the power of God (13:4). They are taught "in him, as the truth is in Jesus" (Eph. 4:21). "And the peace of God . . . will guard your hearts and your minds in Christ Jesus" (Phil. 4:7). They are brought to spiritual maturity in Christ (Col. 1:28). They "walk in him, rooted and built up in him and established in the faith" (2:6-7); living "a godly life in Christ Jesus" (2 Tim. 3:12); refreshing their hearts in Christ (Philemon 1:20); ". . . your good behavior in Christ" (1 Pet. 3:16).

This is what practical sanctification is: living, breathing, walking, being taught and built up, coming to maturity in Christ. The primary goal of sanctification is not triumphing over sin, for that is a negative orientation. Such triumphing is not even *possible* without the positive orientation; it will rather be a continual failure. This positive orientation entails a being directed to, and filled with, Christ. The practical triumphing over sin will then be a necessary and blessed side-effect. Make triumphing over sin your goal, and you will fail; make Christ your goal, and you will triumph over sin. Our truest and most genuine self-judgment is not brought about by looking at one's wrong acts in the past, or even by the law, but by the soul coming into the presence of the perfections of Christ.[38] In other words, how do you come to know your misery? Answer: by looking away from your own sinfulness to the perfection of Christ.[39]

---

36. Cf. ibid., 323–26, 330–33.
37. Cf. the counterpart as well—"Christ in us": Rom. 8:10; 2 Cor. 13:5; Gal. 4:19; Eph. 3:17; Col. 1:27 (see earlier in §9.4).
38. Coates (1926, 43).
39. For a contrast, cf. Heidelberg Catechism (Q&A 3); Paul did not come to

9.5 Sanctification and Spiritual Growth
9.5.1 Process or Decision?

In Revelation 22:11 we read: "Let... the holy still be holy," or, "be still sanctified (DRA, JUB, YLT; Greek, *hagiasthētō*); this means, "continue to be holy" (GW, NIV, etc.), or "continue on in greater holiness" (TLB), or "be hallowed yet" (WYC). Does this refer to a process of becoming ever holier? Or does it rather mean that the saint must keep himself ever holier,[40] or also: must give ever greater evidence of his holiness? In other passages we must be equally careful not to read into them a practical sanctification in the sense of a continual process of ever becoming holier. Thus, Louis Berkhof says that the Christian "is in duty bound to strive for ever-increasing sanctification.... Sanctification is usually a lengthy process."[41] In my view, however, striving for holiness (Heb. 12:14) does not mean: striving to *become* holier and holier, but: striving for *being* holy all the time.

At this point I refer to Romans 6:13 again (cf. §8.8.3): "Do not present your members to sin as instruments for unrighteousness, but present yourselves to God as those who have been brought from death to life, and your members to God as instruments for righteousness." The first "Do not present" (Greek, *mēde paristanete*) is a continual present tense in the sense of "Let it never happen." The second verb, "present yourselves" (*parastēsate*, aorist), is a one-time fact in the sense of "let it happen here and now, once and for all."[42] Likewise in verse 19: "... present [*parastēsate*] your members as slaves to righteousness leading to sanctification." This is not: "become ever holier," but: "dedicate yourselves here and now, once and for all, to the Lord in practical righteousness and ho-

---

know his misery through the law (on the contrary: Phil. 3:6) but through his encounter with Christ.
40. Vgl. Bauer (1971, 17).
41. Berkhof (1949, 534).
42. Cf. here Berkhof (1979, 451–52) on Kohlbrugge, who wishes to read: "*have presented,*" etc., which presupposes the outdated view that the aorist always refers to an event in the past.

Practical Sanctification

liness." Naturally, this presupposes the prayer for the power of the Holy Spirit (Rom. 8:1-6; cf. Luke 11:13), and naturally one may fail in this dedication by committing new sins, and then one will have to confess these sins and renew one's dedication. However, being allowed to make a new start, even several new starts, is very different from gradually becoming holier and holier.

This dedication here and now, once and for all, instead of a process-like[43] sanctification is found over and over in the New Testament: "I appeal to you . . . to present [*parastēsai*, aorist] your bodies as a living sacrifice, holy and acceptable to God, which is your spiritual worship" (Rom. 12:1); ". . . how to be [not become] holy in body and spirit" (1 Cor. 7:34). "[L]et us cleanse ourselves from every defilement of body and spirit, bringing holiness to completion in the fear of God" (2 Cor. 7:1). "Bringing to completion" is one word: *epitelountes*, a present tense participle, that is, bringing to ever further completion. But "cleanse" is *katharisōmen* (aorist): "cleanse here and now, once and for all." "[I]f anyone cleanses himself from what is dishonorable, he will be a vessel for honorable use, set apart as holy, useful to the master of the house, ready for every good work" (2 Tim. 2:21). "Set apart as holy" is one word: *hēgiasmenon*, a perfect tense, that is: one time in the past set apart *from* what is dishonorable and *to* the Lord, an act of which the consequences still continue. "Since all these things are thus to be dissolved, what sort of people ought you to be in lives of holiness and godliness" (2 Pet. 3:11). You ought to *be* holy—not *become* holy.

I am a little reluctant to speak of sanctification as a process because it might so easily create the impression that younger believers by definition cannot yet have made much progress in their sanctification, whereas it may be expected of elderly believers that they are very holy. In practice, it is all too of-

---

43. See extensively, Berkouwer (1952, chapter 5), especially his reference to Kohlbrugge (103–04). Strikingly he speaks of "a simple, evolutionistic doctrine of sanctification" (117; cf. 112).

ten just the opposite. Young believers may be very spiritual, old believers may be strongly dominated by the flesh. It all depends on these two factors: the inner choice (decision, determination) to dedicate oneself to the Lord, and the practical consciousness of the fact that this can only be done in the power of the Holy Spirit. Nevertheless, I realize that the New Testament does use terms such as "grow(th)" (1 Cor. 3:6-7; Eph. 2:21; 4:13, 15-16; Col. 1:10; 2:19; 1 Pet. 2:2; 2 Pet. 3:18), and is aware of an increase in the life of faith: "We ought always to give thanks to God for you, brothers, as is right, because your faith is growing abundantly, and the love of every one of you for one another is increasing" (2 Thess. 1:3). We already saw that the New Testament speaks of perfection here on earth (§8.2.2), but this refers to spiritual maturation rather than to reaching a state of sinlessness (see §9.10).

9.5.2 Sanctification is Dying Away?

Especially in Reformed circles, sanctification is often described as the gradual "dying-away" of one's old self (Latin, *mortificatio*; cf. "mortify" in Rom. 8:13; Col. 3:5 KJV), and the gradual deployment of the new self. Thus for instance in the Heidelberg Catechism (Q&A 89): "What is the dying of the old man? Heartfelt sorrow for sin, causing us to hate and turn from it always more and more."[44] And in the Westminster Confession of Faith (XIII.1): "They, who are once effectually called, and regenerated, . . . are further sanctified . . .: the dominion of the whole body of sin is destroyed, and the several lusts thereof are more and more weakened and mortified; and they are more and more quickened and strengthened in all saving graces, to the practice of true holiness, without which no man shall see the Lord." Notice that the phrase "more and more" appears three times in these two quotations.

---

44. Cf. Moerkerken (2004, 465) on this: "[A]ll that the old self is, my passions, my darkened understanding, my foolish conscience, my wicked will, must die away." Also see, e.g., L. Berkhof (1949, 533); Wiersinga (1952, 86–87); Heyns (1988, 321–22); H. Berkhof (1979, 463–67); Van Genderen and Velema (2008, 660-62).

Practical Sanctification

Bruce Demarest speaks of "killing" ("mortifying") the old nature, which is thoroughly impossible.[45] This error is based on the confusion between the "old man" (Greek, *palaios anthrōpos*) and the "old nature" — an expression that does not occur in the New Testament but is often used as an equivalent for "the flesh" (*sarx*) in the sense of "sinful nature" or "sinful inclination." Paul makes clear that the "old man" *has* been crucified (*synestaurōthē*, aorist) with Christ, once and for all, "so that we would no longer be enslaved to sin" (Rom. 6:6). The "old man" is the unregenerate person who is dominated by the "old nature." The "new man" (Eph. 4:24; Col. 3:9) is the regenerate person who is dominated by new life from God and by the Holy Spirit, but who still possesses the sinful inclination as well. However, this person is no longer *dominated* by this "old nature" (sinful inclination) unless he himself allows this to happen. This is what (N)KJV calls the "carnal" person, the regenerate Christian who is still strongly governed by the "flesh" (the sinful inclination; see, e.g., Rom. 8:6-7; 1 Cor. 3:1-4).

On the one hand, we realize practically in our mind that the "old man" *is* dead: "[Y]ou must consider yourselves dead to sin and alive to God in Christ Jesus" (Rom. 6:11), once and for all. The "old man" died on the cross of Calvary, and can never return to life again. "[T]hose who belong to Christ Jesus have crucified [*estaurōsan*, aorist] the flesh with its passions and desires" (Gal. 5:24), once and for all, namely, when they were converted. On the other hand, the believer has to rigorously deal with the possible fruits of the flesh. Here both the present tense and the aorist can be used: "[I]f by the Spirit you put to death [*thanatoute*, present tense, that is, continually, or repeatedly] the deeds of the body [read, the acts of the flesh], you will live" (Rom. 8:13). "Put to death [*nekrōsate*, aorist] therefore what is earthly [read, what is of the flesh] in you: sexual immorality, impurity, passion, evil desire, and covet-

---

45. Demarest (1997, 409); also see Owen and Rushing (2004) for the viewpoint of the Puritan John Owen (seventeenth century) on *mortification*.

ousness, which is idolatry . . . you must put them all away [*apothesthe*, aorist]: anger, wrath, malice, slander, and obscene talk from your mouth" (Col. 3:5, 8), here and now. In none of these passages is there any reference to a gradual dying away.

The "old *man*" (the unregenerate person) is dead in Christ, but the "old *nature*" (the "flesh," the sinful inclination) of the regenerate person can still produce evil fruits, if the believer is not alert. The aorist in Colossians 3:5 indicates that the Christian must put the fruits of the flesh, when they occur, into the death of Christ here and now, right away. But this does not mean that such a conscious act of "putting to death" may not have to be repeated: the present tense in Romans 8:13 indicates that such a "putting to death" unfortunately may have to occur many times. But putting to death the shoots of the "old nature" is fundamentally different from a gradual dying away of the "old man."

9.5.3 Ephesians 4:21-24

There is only one passage that seems to leave some room for the idea of a gradual dying away of the old self: Ephesians 4:21-24, but this is a matter of translation.[46] The ESV reads: you "were taught in him, as the truth is in Jesus, to put off [*apothesthai*, aorist] your old self, which belongs to your former manner of life and is corrupt through deceitful desires, and to be renewed [*ananeousthai*, present] in the spirit of your minds, and to put on [*endysasthai*, aorist] the new self, created [*ktisthenta*, aorist] after the likeness of God in true righteousness and holiness." If we read the text this way it suggests an instantaneous action in the *past*, which apparently was completed at conversion (cf. NIV). If we follow the (N)KJV, the text presents to us an ongoing command in the *present* time: ". . . that you put off . . . the old man which grows corrupt according to the deceitful lusts, and be renewed in the spirit of

---

46. See, e.g., Grosheide (1960, 72–73); Schlatter (1963, 219–21); Wuest (1977, 109–12); Wood (1978, 62–63); Salmond (1979, 342); and Bruce (1984, 357–59).

your mind, and that you put on the new man."[47]

The fact that the aorist is used here cannot help us decide between the two alternatives because the aorist indicates the instantaneous character of an action but does not exclude the possibility that an action must be repeated. The essence of the aorist is that the action must be complete at every occasion.[48] In our passage, therefore, putting off and putting on are instantaneous actions, which in principle are performed once and for all, but after failure can be repeated. In light of the parallel passage, Colossians 3:9-10 ("you have put off [*apekdysamenoi*, aorist] the old self . . . and have put on [*endysamenoi*, aorist] the new self"), I highly prefer the ESV/NIV approach to Ephesians 4:21-24. That is, there was a time in the past that you, Ephesian believers, were taught (by the gospel) to put off your old self and put on the new self, there and then. Once and for all, you took the decision from then on to live no longer under the dominion of the flesh but (in the power of the Holy Spirit) under that of the new nature.

In my view, the (N)KJV is incorrect insofar as there cannot be a command to put off the old man here and now, all the time, or time and again. This presupposes a constant struggle against the "old man." No, the "old man" *is* dead; he died at the cross of Jesus. Believers are not requested to undergo death continually but to consider themselves as *already being* dead to sin (Rom. 6:11).[49] What we still do indeed put to death are the shoots of the flesh, as we have seen (Col. 3:5). This is not a "process" of continual, ever-progressing "mortification," but a rigorous instantaneous action every time we come across such a sprout. In summary: the "old man" *has* died (on the cross), the "old nature" *cannot* be killed (we carry

---

47. The Darby translation offers a third option: ". . . your having put off according to the former conversation the old man which corrupts itself according to the deceitful lusts; and being renewed in the spirit of your mind; and [your] having put on the new man," but this is based on the outdated view referred to in note 42.
48. Vine (1985, 2:565).
49. Duffield and Van Cleave (1996, 257).

it with us all our lives), but its sprouts *can* and *must* be killed.

This entire idea of dying away (mortification) stands under the strong influence of the centrality of the concepts of sin and struggling against sin that belong to classic Western theology. In its most extreme presentation, this gradual dying away—this gradual triumphing in this life-long battle—is a rare, hard, and barely achievable process. Remember again the Heidelberg Catechism (Q&A 114): "[E]ven the holiest men, while in this life, have only a small beginning of such obedience" to God's commandments. Here, the poor-sinner view ("here on earth we always remain poor sinners") can easily prevail. Here we must walk the narrow path between two extremes: on the one hand, the poor-sinner view that is still prevalent in many Reformed circles (especially hyper-Calvinism) (see §§9.8–9.9); on the other hand, perfectionism ("here on earth we can, and ought to, reach sinlessness"), which is found, for instance, in certain Methodist circles (see §9.10).

We could express this in terms of the tension that we find within the New Testament itself. On the one hand: "[W]e all stumble in many ways" (James 3:2) and on the other hand: "[B]e all the more diligent to confirm your calling and election, for if you practice these qualities you will never fall" (2 Pet. 1:10). On the one hand: "If we say we have no sin, we deceive ourselves" (1 John 1:8), and on the other hand: "Whoever abides in Him does not sin . . . he cannot sin, because he has been born of God" (3:6, 9, NKJV). That is, in principle the believer has all means at his disposal (new life, the support of the Father, the intercession of the Son, the power of the Holy Spirit) to not sin anymore; recall Jesus' own command: "Sin no more" (John 5:14; 8:11). But James 3:2 and 1 John 1:8 remind us of the reality: everyone of us has the guarantee that, if he would just stay close enough to the Lord, he will not sin. But no one of us has the guarantee that he will always, or even *can* always, stay close enough to the Lord. Reformed theologian Johan Verkuyl summarized it in a question: "How do we escape on the one hand from the compromise that acquiesces to sin and suspends the struggle of sanctification, and on the other hand from the radicalism that forgets that, until the day of our death, we will need forgiveness?"[50]

9.6 Three Stages of Growth
9.6.1 Fathers in Christ

In 1 John 2:12–27, the apostle John seems to describe three stages of spiritual growth. Not every expositor agrees that we are indeed dealing with three stages here; some believe that the metaphors of child, young man, and father simply describe various aspects of Christian life. Others believe that the text speaks only of two stages of growth, young men and fathers, and that here the term "children" is a general description of all believers, even though the text contains two Greek words for "children": *teknia* (vv. 1, 12, 28) and *paidia* (vv. 13c/14a, 18).[51] In addition, some Greek manuscripts have *graphō* ("I write"; cf. ESV, NKJV, etc.) in verse 13c ("I write to you children"; in some versions this is v. 14a), others have *egrapsa* ("I have written"; cf. ASV, NASB, etc.). This has consequences for the division of verses 12–14. It is either four times *graphō* (*teknia, pateres, neaniskoi, paidia,* in which the first *graphō* is a general introduction to three categories) and two times *egrapsa* (*pateres, neaniskoi,* plus the *paidia* in v. 18). Or it is three times *graphō* (*teknia, pateres, neaniskoi*) and three times *egrapsa* (*paidia, pateres, neaniskoi*). The former option suggests that *teknia* and *paidia* are different categories, and thus seems rather to plead for a division into three groups (*pateres, neaniskoi, paidia*). The latter option suggests that *teknia* and *paidia* refer to the same category, and thus seems rather to plead for a division into two groups (*pateres, neaniskoi*), *teknia* = *paidia* being a description of all believers; but it can also be reconciled with a three-groups interpretation (*teknia* = *paidia, pateres, neaniskoi*).

Without entering into the exegetical problems, I myself

---
50. Verkuyl (1992, 317).
51. Cf. the discussion by Marshall (1978, 134–38).

believe that John refers to three stages of growth (babies, half-grown, adults), and that when using *teknia* (ESV: "little children"; Darby: "children") he refers to all his addressees, and when using *paidia* (ESV: "children"; Darby: "little children") he refers to the "babies" or "infants" in Christ.

In order to explain these stages, John makes use of familiar images from daily life. He describes the highest stage of growth as that of fathers. Supposedly this indicates not only that these believers have attained a certain stage of maturity, but also that they have fathered other believers, and are taking care of them. Compare the example of Paul: "I became your father in Christ Jesus through the gospel" (1 Cor. 4:15; cf. 16:10); ". . . my little children, for whom I am again in the anguish of childbirth until Christ is formed in you" (Gal. 4:19). "For you know how, like a father with his children, we exhorted each one of you" (1 Thess. 2:11-12). "I appeal to you for my child, Onesimus, whose father I became in my imprisonment" (Philemon 1:10; cf. 1 Tim. 1:2, 18; 2 Tim. 1:2; Titus 1:4).

It is quite remarkable that John describes these fathers very briefly, and moreover twice in the same way: ". . . because you know him who is from the beginning" (1 John 2:13-14). This "him" is of course Christ, the Son of the Father (cf. 1:1-3). This knowing is not (only) intellectual knowing, but (especially) experiential knowing. This is the only thing that is said of the fathers—and with this, *everything* is said, for this is the great goal of spiritual growth, that Christ has become everything for believers: "For to me to live is Christ" (Phil. 1:21). What they have and are is Christ. The image of God's Son has become manifest in them (Rom. 8:29), Christ has been formed in them (Gal. 4:19), they have become mature in him (cf. Col. 1:28). They have arrived at "the knowledge of the Son of God, to mature manhood, to the measure of the stature of the fullness of Christ, so that we may no longer be children" (Eph. 4:13-14). They have grown "in the grace and knowledge of our Lord and Savior Jesus Christ" (2 Pet. 3:18).

Practical Sanctification

There is nothing more to be said about the fathers, for these things fully express their spiritual condition. The children have come to know the wonderful redemption in Christ and what it is to be children of God. The young men have come to know Christ as their helper in battle (not the battle against their sinful nature but against Satan and the world; cf. §9.8). The fathers have come to know *him* in person; there is nothing more or higher than that.

9.6.2 Young Men

About the young men, too, we are told twice more or less the same thing, but the second time with an expansion. First it is said in verse 13: "I am writing to you, young men, because you have overcome the evil one"; after this in verse 14: "I write to you, young men, because you are strong, and the word of God abides in you, and you have overcome the evil one." On the one hand, the young men are not yet fathers because they did not yet pass through such a development that Christ has become everything for them. On the other hand, they are no longer children because they have already acquired quite some experience in spiritual warfare. Every believer who has made some progress on the road of faith has inevitably come into touch with the evil one (Satan). This in itself does not make a young man out of the child. To this end, he should not only have encountered Satan but also have experienced how one can gain spiritual victories over him in the power of Christ. In this way, they have experienced that the Christ whom they have received in faith dwells in them, and in and through them gains the victory: "Little children [*teknia*, i.e., all believers], you are from God and have overcome them [i.e., the erring minds], for he [i.e., the Holy Spirit] who is in you is greater than he [i.e., the spirit of the Antichrist] who is in the world" (4:4).

In 1 John 2:13 it is only the young men's overcoming the evil one that is mentioned. But in verse 14 not only this fact but also their spiritual state is described: ". . . because you are strong, and the word of God abides in you." This term "abide" (Greek, *menō*) occurs often in 1 John; it is we "abiding in him" (i.e., God or Christ; 2:6, 24, 27-28; 3:24; 4:13, 15-16), or "in the light" (2:10), or, conversely, it is God's Word (2:14), "what you heard from the beginning" (2:24), the anointing (2:27), God's seed (3:9), God's love (3:17), or God himself (4:12, 16), abiding in believers (see further 2:17; 3:14-15). The young men have acquired so much experience that they *know* what—and who!—abides in them. They have discovered that thereby they are strong, and in this way can overcome the evil one. Just the same, they are not yet fathers for they are still wrapped up by this battle.

For the fathers, the battle in a certain sense is no *battle* anymore; they have grown beyond it: the evil one does not touch "them anymore" (5:18; ERV, ICB: "cannot hurt them"; CEV, GW, GNT, ISV, NIV: "cannot harm them"; TLB: "cannot get his hands on him"). For the young men, however, John has some new exhortations, which show that they have not yet attained full maturity: "Do not love the world or the things in the world. If anyone loves the world, the love of the Father is not in him. For all that is in the world—the desires of the flesh and the desires of the eyes and pride of life—is not from the Father but is from the world. And the world is passing away along with its desires, but whoever does the will of God abides forever" (2:15-17).

The suggestion that these verses are still addressed to the "young men" seems to be supported by the fact that in verse 18 there is again a word for the children (*paidia*)—in my view, this is the third group to which John refers. In verse 28 the reference is again to the *teknia*, that is, *all* believers.

It is good for the young men that they have obtained personal experiential knowledge of the battle against the evil one. However, in another respect they have *not* yet overcome, namely, in their battle against the world and all that it contains: "the desires of the flesh and the desires of the eyes and pride of life."[52] Christ can be everything for the believers, as he is this for the fathers, only if they—in the power of the Holy Spirit—have overcome both the evil one and the world. It does not mean they are perfect in the sense of sinless, but they are perfect in the sense of mature (see §8.2.2).

9.6.3 Five Characteristics

The first epistle of John offers us five features by which one can recognize true believers, in order to distinguish them from the deceivers (cf. 1 John 2:19, 26; 3:7; 4:1-6; 2 John 1:7). In principle, these characteristics are of course valid for all regenerate persons, but it is obvious that they will come to light most clearly in those who have made the greatest progress in their practical sanctification: the fathers in Christ. Therefore, I briefly mention these five features here because they form a certain standard for true practical sanctification.

1. *Fathers keep the commandments of God*, that is, *practice righteousness*: "And by this we know that we have come to know him, if we keep his commandments. . . . If you know that he is righteous, you may be sure that everyone who practices righteousness has been born of him" (2:3-6, 29; cf. 3:22; 5:3). This is not at all intended in any legalistic way here; on the contrary: they keep God's commandments out of genuine love for him or for Christ. Hence the desire to do his will, as this is expressed in these commandments. Of course, this also holds for the infants in Christ, but a certain amount of spiritual growth is needed to learn to distinguish God's will; as Paul says, "[B]e transformed by the renewal of your mind, that by testing you may discern what is the will of God" (Rom. 12:2); ". . . that you may stand mature and fully assured in all the will of God" (Col. 4:12); ". . . so as to live for the rest of the time in the flesh no longer for human passions but for the will of God" (1 Pet. 4:2).

2. *Fathers love their fellow-believers*: "We know that we have passed out of death into life, because we love the brothers.

---
52. Cf. Ouweneel (2008a, 176–77).

Whoever does not love abides in death" (3:14; cf. 2:9-11; 3:18-19). "Beloved, let us love one another, for love is from God, and whoever loves has been born of God and knows God. Anyone who does not love does not know God, because God is love. . . . If anyone says, 'I love God,' and hates his brother, he is a liar; for he who does not love his brother whom he has seen cannot love God whom he has not seen. And this commandment we have from him: whoever loves God must also love his brother" (4:7-8, 20-21; cf. 5:2). In fact, this is one of the divine commandments referred to under 1. above, but in 1 John it is especially emphasized. No wonder: the commandment of brotherly love—the "new commandment" of Christ (John 13:34; cf. 1 John 2:7-8; 4:21; 2 John 1:5-6)—is the essence and summary of all God's horizontal commandments (those regulating relationships between people; for the vertical relationship cf. John 14:15, 21; 15:10). It demands a certain amount of spiritual growth (practical sanctification) to distinguish this brotherly love from purely human, natural affection.

3. *Fathers possess God's Spirit*: "[B]y this we know that he abides in us, by the Spirit whom he has given us" (1 John 3:24). "By this we know that we abide in him and he in us, because he has given us of his Spirit" (4:13). Again, this holds for all believers, including the "babies" (cf. the "anointing" in 2:27 with 2 Cor. 1:21-22, "God . . . has anointed us, and who has also put his seal on us and given us his Spirit in our hearts"; cf. Acts 10:38; Eph. 1:13). However, the fathers are those who, by definition, are *filled* with the Spirit (cf. Eph. 5:18), who have the most experience with the Spirit, and in whom the Spirit is most evidently working. They are spiritual persons, that is, persons governed by the Spirit (1 Cor. 2:16), and these are the opposite of people of the flesh, infants (baby believers) in Christ (3:1-3).

4. *Fathers do not practice sin*: "No one who abides in him keeps on sinning; no one who keeps on sinning has either seen him or known him. . . . No one born of God makes a practice of sinning, for God's seed abides in him, and he cannot keep

on sinning because he has been born of God. By this it is evident who are the children of God, and who are the children of the devil: whoever does not practice righteousness is not of God, nor is the one who does not love his brother" (1 John 3:6, 9-10). "We know that everyone who has been born of God does not keep on sinning, but he who was born of God protects him, and the evil one does not touch him" (5:18). John's intention is not to say that fathers never fall, or even never *can* fall, into sin, because this would contradict 1:8, "If we say we have no sin, we deceive ourselves, and the truth is not in us." John's intention is rather to say that (a) the believer's new nature (called "God's seed" in 3:9) cannot sin, and that (b) sin is no longer the common practice of the believer, as this was the case before his conversion (see further §9.10). Again, it is obvious that the practical realization of such a life is the product of practical sanctification (spiritual growth).

5. *Fathers confess Jesus as the Christ, the Son of God come in the flesh*: "[E]very spirit that confesses that Jesus Christ has come in the flesh is from God. . . . Whoever confesses that Jesus is the Son of God, God abides in him, and he in God" (4:2, 15). "Everyone who believes that Jesus is the Christ has been born of God, and everyone who loves the Father loves whoever has been born of him. . . . Who is it that overcomes the world except the one who believes that Jesus is the Son of God?" (5:1, 5; cf. 2:23; 2 John 1:7). Again, in principle this is valid for the "babies" in Christ as well. However, the very fact that their attention had to be drawn to these truths, which the deceivers had denied, shows that they were still too little aware of the significance of this confession of faith. The phrase "has come in the flesh" implies Christ's pre-existence as the Son of God before his incarnation.[53] The fathers have come to understand how central the person of the eternal Son of God is for faith as well as for the believer's practical everyday walk.

---

53. See Ouweneel (2007b, chapter 7).

9.7 Poor Sinners or Rich Sons?
9.7.1 Reformed Testimony

The poor-sinner view ("Christians remain poor sinners as long as they are still on this earth") is strongly embedded in Reformed thinking. See for instance the Belgic Confession (Article 24): "[W]e can do no work but what is polluted by our flesh, and also punishable." Please note: not only defiled by our flesh but also worthy of punishment. The unregenerate (but agitated) person can say: "[A]ll our righteous deeds are like a polluted garment" (Isa. 64:6) — but could the regenerate and Spirit-filled believer say the same thing? Is he, then, still under judgment? The heavenly bride's very wedding gown consists of "the righteous deeds of the saints" (Rev. 19:8)! They cannot be that bad, if they will forever adorn the Ekklesia.

Even more outspoken is the viewpoint of the Heidelberg Catechism (Q&A 114): "[E]ven the holiest men, while in this life, have only a small beginning of such obedience [to God's commandments]." So this is the best that even the holiest among us may hope to attain? According to Q&A 126, believers even have to pray: "[B]e pleased, for the sake of Christ's blood, not to impute to us miserable sinners our manifold transgressions, nor the evil which always cleaves to us . . . ." Please note that the Catechism *always* presupposes that those whom it addresses are true believers (from Q&A 1 onward). Yet, when praying to God, these regenerate and justified believers are supposed to call themselves "miserable sinners," to whom evil "always [!] cleaves." *God* has declared them to be righteous and holy as to their position in Christ, but *they* must constantly declare before God that they are *un*righteous and *un*holy as to the practical realization of this position. Is this not strange? God declares us to be clean, and we answer: Yes, but in practice we are filthy?

Now listen to what Paul says: "God shows his love for us in that while we were still sinners, Christ died for us" (Rom.

5:8) — in other words, *at present, believers are not sinners anymore*, let alone "*poor* sinners." Paul says that believers have been set free from sin (Rom. 6:7, 18, 22; 8:2). We still have the flesh within us, but (a) as long as we are not governed by it we cannot be called "sinners," and (b), through his Holy Spirit, God gives us the strength to not live in sin anymore: "For if you live according to the flesh you will die, but if by the Spirit you put to death the deeds of the body, you will live" (8:13). God says, You *are* holy, so *live* in a holy way, but we answer, It does not work, because we are still continually *unholy*. Apparently, we know better than God; we offend him by denying the means he has given to us to live as holy persons.

Moreover, are we really such "poor" people? God has bestowed his "riches" on us (Rom. 10:12; cf. 11:12, 33; 2 Cor. 6:10); by Christ's "poverty" we have been made "rich" (2 Cor. 8:9; cf. Col. 2:2; Titus 3:6); we are "rich in faith" (James 2:5). So what biblical foundation supports the Catechism still calling believers "poor sinners"? Why would we wish to be wiser than God's Word? Don't worry; I am not a perfectionist (see below). But I am not an adherent to the poor-sinner view either. I know what Luther wanted to say when he called the believer *simul iustus et peccator* ("righteous and sinner simultaneously"), but I do not agree with it. I *am* righteous, I am not a sinner anymore, although I can and do still sin.

9.7.2 New Testament Testimony

None of the apostles ever said that we are still "poor sinners." On the contrary, Paul does not speak of "the evil that constantly clings to us," but says, "[W]e have *renounced* disgraceful, underhanded ways. We *refuse* to practice cunning or to tamper with God's word" (2 Cor. 4:2). "Brothers, do not be children in your thinking. Be infants in evil, but in your thinking be mature" (1 Cor. 14:20). "Let all bitterness and wrath and anger and clamor and slander be put away from you, along with all malice" (Eph. 4:31; cf. Col. 3:8; James 1:21; 1 Pet. 2:1). Don't say: These exhortations are to the point, but we cannot fulfill them as long as we are still on this earth. This is wrong. Paul says, "[T]hose who belong to Christ Jesus *have* crucified the flesh with its passions and desires" (Gal. 5:24). And John says, "My little children, I am writing these things to you so that you may not sin" (1 John 2:1a). This is the *rule*: Don't sin. This is the *exception*: ". . . But if *anyone* does sin, we have an advocate with the Father, Jesus Christ the righteous" (v. 1b).

To be sure, this is the John who says, "If we say we have no sin, we deceive ourselves, and the truth is not in us" (1:8); that is, the flesh is still in us. But he also says, "Everyone who makes a practice of sinning also practices lawlessness; sin is lawlessness. . . . No one who abides in him keeps on sinning; no one who keeps on sinning has either seen him or known him. Little children, let no one deceive you. Whoever practices righteousness is righteous, as he is righteous. Whoever makes a practice of sinning is of the devil. No one born of God makes a practice of sinning, for God's seed abides in him, and he cannot keep on sinning because he has been born of God" (1 John 3:4–9; cf. 5:18).

Notice what is said here. If the Catechism were right that we are still "poor sinners" and speaks of "the evil that constantly clings to us," then, strictly speaking, we are "lawless" and "of the devil," according to John. If you are "born of God," you are *no longer* a poor sinner to whom evil constantly clings. You still have the flesh in you, and if you are not alert—if you are not led by the Spirit—you can still fall into sin. Such falling into sin is *not* natural, *not* automatic, *not* the normal course of things. The New Testament views it as the exception that confirms the rule, and so should we.

The more we tell ourselves and our hearers that we are still "poor sinners," the more people will believe it, and the more they will live accordingly: they will see sinning as the natural, inevitable way of life, and are happy that they can refer to Romans 7 as proof for it. But Christians never have any excuse whatsoever for falling into sin. We do have the flesh within us, but we have been set free from its power. If we do yield to it, it is our own foolish mistake. Such speaking as we find in the Catechism may unfortunately correspond to certain people's practical experience—but it does not reflect New Testament teaching. We therefore notice that people who in fact do live as "poor sinners" always refer to Romans 7 in self-defense. They have no other Scriptural proof, and do not understand that they totally distort the meaning of this chapter, as we have seen.

9.7.3 False and True Piety

If we do believe that even the holiest among us always remain beginners, how would we ever dare to believe that there are not only "babies" but also "young men" and even "fathers" in Christ (1 John 2:12-17)? The characteristic of these fathers is not that they constantly speak about their sinfulness, their unworthiness, about the evil that constantly clings to them. If people do that, we ought to tell them that they must repent and receive Christ. No, the primary characteristic of the fathers is not that they constantly speak ill of themselves, but that they constantly speak well of Christ. This is true humility.[54] Behind a lot of speaking ill of oneself there is a measure of pride, hypocrisy, pretended piety. *Forget* yourself, and become full of Christ. If we would really be full of him and cling to him, evil could not possibly "constantly cling" to *us*. What I am saying here is not to belittle sin; on the contrary, speaking too much of one's own sinfulness and too little of Christ is an offense to him. To put it bluntly: to be occupied with sinfulness all the time is itself a sin. To be occupied with Christ all the time is holiness.

Those speaking ill of themselves, are still speaking of *themselves*; but the fathers speak of Christ. Therefore, the *curriculum vitae* of the fathers is so brief: "[Y]ou know him who is from the beginning" (1 John 2:13-14). It is the feature of the mature, experienced Christian: "Indeed, I count everything

---

54. Darby (n.d.-a, XII, 197).

as loss because of the surpassing worth of knowing Christ Jesus my Lord . . . in order that I may gain Christ . . . that I may know him" (Phil. 3:8-10). Not a deep consciousness of sin as such is a sign of godliness, but being full of Christ. It is precisely the fathers who know their deep dependency upon Christ; it is they who have grown up in "the grace and knowledge of our Lord and Savior Jesus Christ" (2 Pet. 3:18), and thus also in consciousness of sin, and thus in humility. Practical sanctification never implies a kind of emancipation with regard to Christ.[55] On the contrary, as Reformed theologian Johan Verkuyl said: "The process of [practical] sanctification does not consist in us becoming ever more pious, ever holier and better, in our own strength. The process of sanctification consists in us becoming ever more dependent on God's grace, on the work of the Holy Spirit."[56]

Theologians of the poor-sinner view can seldom be caught preaching on spiritual growth and spiritual maturation, because such notions do not fit within their thought horizon. In their view, practical sanctification involves people who on earth always remain "babies." Or *if* they preach on it, as I know from experience, they confuse spiritual maturation with the assurance of faith. That is a categorial mistake of eminent importance: coming to the assurance of faith is, if we stay with our metaphors, like the development of a fetus into a baby. To many of these poor doubters, of whom there are so many in hyper-Calvinism, one could apply this word: "[C]hildren have come to the point of birth, and there is no strength to bring them forth" (Isa. 37:3). Spiritual growth, however, is like the development of a baby into an adult. Not only the adults but also the babies have assurance of salvation; if they did not, they would still be in some embryonic state, spiritually speaking.

God's goal is not the assurance of faith — at best it is a first

---

55. Cf. Berkouwer (1952, chapter 5), with reference to H. F. Kohlbrugge, I. da Costa and K. Barth, and chapter 6, about sanctification and humility.
56. Verkuyl (1992, 314).

step—but being "presented mature in Christ" (Col. 1:28). God's goal is not an ever-deeper consciousness of sin—although such a consciousness is indispensable—but being transformed into the image of Christ (2 Cor. 3:18). Christ must be formed in the believer (Gal. 4:19). God's goal is not an ever-growing knowledge of ourselves, but attaining to the "knowledge of the Son of God, to mature manhood, to the measure of the stature of the fullness of Christ" (Eph. 4:13). Every failure in this respect that hides itself behind an exuberant consciousness of one's own unworthiness and false humility is a slap in the face of Christ's (objective) work of atonement *for* us and the Holy Spirit's (subjective) work *in* us.

Many Christians never seem to come much further than this statement: "Father, I have sinned against heaven and before you. I am no longer worthy to be called your son. Treat me as one of your hired servants." Apparently they have never heard the voice of the Father saying: "Bring quickly the best robe, and put it on him, and put a ring on his hand, and shoes on his feet. And bring the fattened calf and kill it, and let us eat and celebrate" (Luke 15:18-19, 22-23). Immature Christians often speak in terms of servitude; these are the Christians who never address God as "Father." Mature Christians know the Spirit of sonship: "[Y]ou did not receive the spirit of slavery to fall back into fear, but you have received the Spirit of adoption as sons, by whom we cry, 'Abba! Father!'" (Rom. 8:15).

9.8 Spiritual Warfare
9.8.1 Poor Sinners or Overcomers?

In connection with practical sanctification and spiritual growth, theologians often speak about "spiritual warfare (conflict, battle)." Gerrit Berkouwer devoted an entire chapter to the *militia Christiana* ("Christian warfare" or "military service"), which, unfortunately (but as might have been expected), turns out to be nothing but the battle against one's own sinful nature.[57] John Ryle taught us that a true Christian does have peace in his conscience, but struggle within, and thus knows both peace and war.[58] Likewise also the Heidelberg Catechism (Q&A 56), where the believer speaks of his "sinful nature with which I have to struggle all my life long." Hyper-Calvinist writer Aart Moerkerken explains: "God's children do not ever become such arrived, converted people. In themselves, they always remain worriers, who have to struggle against a sinful nature."[59] If one is a warrior, then only as a worrier.

Where in the New Testament—except of course in Romans 7:24, which is quoted over and over again—do we find this picture of the worrier? Compare Luke 12:29, ". . . nor be worried," and 1 Peter 5:7 (cf. Ps. 55:2), ". . . casting all your anxieties on him, because he cares for you." Why do we hear so often about these poor trudgers, and so little about Romans 8:37, "[W]e are more than conquerors [Greek, *hypernikōmen*; ERV, GNT: we have complete victory; GW, NASB: we overwhelmingly conquer; NET: we have complete victory] through him who loved us"? Why did none of the New Testament writers ever write something like this: "We move from one spiritual defeat to the other, for we do remain poor sinners until our death"? And the sons of Korah should rather have written: "Wretched are those whose strength is indeed in you but who experience this so little on earth. . . . They go from weakness to weakness," instead of: "Blessed are those whose strength is in you. . . . They go from strength to strength; each one appears before God in Zion" (Ps. 84:6, 8).

I have known hyper-Calvinists who knew the miserable outcry of Romans 7:24 by heart: "Wretched man that I am! Who will deliver me from this body of death?" But they did not know the words that followed immediately: "Thanks be to God through Jesus Christ our Lord!" (Rom. 7:24-25). We

---

57. Berkouwer (1952, chapter 3).
58. Ryle (2013, 21).
59. Moerkerken (2004, 305).

hear so often the "Wretched man that I am!" and so little the "Thanks be to God!"

Moreover, we have to realize that the explicit notion of struggling against sin does not occur anywhere in the New Testament, not even in Romans 7. Galatians 5:17 does not speak of the believer's struggle, but of the flesh's desires and the Spirit's desires within them being opposed to each other in a way as if the believer himself is not actively involved (". . . to keep you from doing the things you want to do"). The opposition between the Spirit and the flesh is not described here in terms of a struggle between the two, in which sometimes the one, and sometimes the other, prevails. On the contrary, the believer needs only to "walk by the Spirit," and he "will not gratify the desires of the flesh" (v.16).

The only applicable reference seems to be Hebrews 12:4, "In your struggle against sin you have not yet resisted to the point of shedding your blood." However, Hebrews emphasizes our position in Christ: the believers have "no longer any consciousness of sins" (10:2). Nowhere does the book suppose that they would keep sinning: "For if we go on sinning deliberately after receiving the knowledge of the truth, there no longer remains a sacrifice for sins" (cf. v. 26). The book rather speaks of our struggle against *sinners*, in the sense of persecutors, as the preceding verse in Hebrews 12 shows: "Consider him who endured from sinners such hostility against himself, so that you may not grow weary or fainthearted" (v. 3).[60] Here the phrase "struggle against sin" refers to wrestling with the problem of *sinners* around us, who threaten us.

9.8.2 Warfare in the New Testament

It is quite remarkable that a notion that plays such an important role in traditional Reformed thought is basically unknown in the New Testament. This is no wonder: you cannot fight against something that is dead. Martin Luther wrote in the margin of his Bible: "Remember, the saints also have evil

---

60. Ouweneel (1982, 2:77).

carnal desires—to which they *do not* give in."[61] This is a marvelous statement. On the one hand, he quietly confirms that the flesh is still present in the believer. On the other hand, he implies that it is self-evident that this flesh does not prevail in the believer's life in giving rise to concrete sins. I add that this can become practical reality only if the believer keeps Christ before him, and lives by the power of the Holy Spirit. Only in cases where this power of the Spirit is not known, or is not realized, can a situation arise as the one described in Romans 7:14-26 (see §8.7).

Sometimes, the adherents of the poor-sinner view refer to James 4:1, ". . . your passions are at war within you." However, this is not about *our* struggle against sin, but about the *passions'* struggle against righteousness,[62] or their struggle to find satisfaction.[63] It is, so to speak, our flesh struggling to have its way. We are not supposed to fight back, but to rebuke, subdue, and ignore it in the power of the Spirit. Likewise, 1 Peter 2:1 says, "Beloved, I urge you as sojourners and exiles to abstain from the passions of the flesh, which wage war against your soul," that is, against your life, your person. Again, this is not about *our* (alleged) struggle against sin, but the very opposite: the battle of our flesh against *us*. If we fight back, we pay tribute to it. Instead, we should assign it its proper place: the cross, the death of Christ. We count ourselves to be dead to sin. We do not fight against it, but we ignore it in the name of the Lord.

Our actual *Christian* warfare is on very different fronts:[64] against the evil powers (Heb. 12:4), against Satan and his followers (Eph. 6:12-20), against the world (John 16:33; 1 John 2:15-17; 5:4-5), against the antichrists (2:18-27), a warfare in the midst of persecution (2 Cor. 7:5; Heb. 10:32). This is mainly a defensive battle, but then not so much against sin within

---

61. WA Deutsche Bibel 7:47.
62. Adamson (1976, 166).
63. Burdick (1981, 192).
64. See extensively, Ouweneel (1998).

us, but against the evil powers outside us — though it is undeniably true that this struggle is thwarted by the fact that these powers find an ally within us: our sinful flesh.

The actual Christian warfare is first and foremost a positive, offensive battle: for the spreading of the gospel (Phil. 1:27, 30; 1 Thess. 2:2), for the spreading and maintenance of Christian truth (2 Cor. 10:3-5; Col. 1:29-2:1; Jude 1:3), in exercising one's own ministry (1 Tim. 1:18; 4:10), a striving in one's prayers (Rom. 15:30; Col. 4:2). This is fighting the good fight of faith (1 Tim. 6:12; 2 Tim. 4:7).

According to the atheist evolutionist Richard Dawkins, Augustine's doctrine of salvation entailed the unhealthy preoccupation of early Christian theologians with sin.[65] Reformed theologian Klaas van der Zwaag argued that Dawkins is mistaken;[66] but he too, in thinking about sanctification in the Augustinian sense, can hardly move beyond the question of sin.[67] It is indeed a fact that, since Augustine, Western Christianity considers the entire Christian doctrine of salvation strongly and one-sidedly from the vantage point of sin and grace. As a consequence, unfortunately, sanctification as well is viewed mainly as a matter of subduing sin in Christian life, and the struggle against it.

In the New Testament, I see a different picture, which in my view has been better preserved in Eastern Christianity: there, warfare is rather viewed as the battle against the powers outside us, and sanctification is rather being practically brought into conformity to the image of God and his Son, in the power of the Holy Spirit.[68]

9.9 Discipline
9.9.1 Education, Not Punishment

In Hebrews 12:10 we read that God "disciplines us for our

---

65. Dawkins (2006, 252).
66. Van der Zwaag (2008, 131; cf. 189–96).
67. Ibid., 149.
68. See further Ouweneel (2010a, §13.2).

good, that we may share his holiness."[69] Herein an important spiritual law becomes visible: there is no practical sanctification without discipline. The *positive* drive in all sanctification, or, as verse 1 says, the "race," is being focused upon Jesus, who preceded us in the glory: ". . . looking [Greek, *aphorōntes*] to Jesus, the founder and perfecter of our faith, who for the joy that was set before him endured the cross, despising the shame, and is seated at the right hand of the throne of God" (v. 2). This is the true motive for all practical sanctification: not being focused upon subduing sin but upon following, and becoming like, Jesus. The Greek verb *aphoreō* means "to look away (*apo*)" from all other things, having the eyes oriented toward one object only; in this case, this is Christ the forerunner (6:20).

The *negative* drive in all true sanctification is God's discipline (12:5–11), that is, the measures he employs to free us from "every weight, and sin which clings so closely" (v. 1).[70] The Greek word for "discipline" is *paideia*, and for "to discipline" is *paideuō* (from *pais*, "child"), which entails not so much the idea of punishment but rather that of education, instruction, exhortation (cf., e.g., Acts 7:22; 1 Cor. 11:32; Eph. 6:4; 2 Tim. 2:25; Titus 2:12; regarding the painful aspect of discipline, see Luke 23:16, 22; 2 Cor. 6:9; Rev. 3:19). I mention this emphasis on the educational aspect because especially adherents of the poor-sinner view easily grow weary or fainthearted under the Lord's discipline (cf. v. 3). They see therein the *wrath* of God, who allegedly is against them, and with bewilderment they wonder for what sins they are being beaten. They are scared and say: God is punishing me, instead of being glad and thankful, saying: God is educating (instructing, exhorting) me.

The book of Hebrews never supposes that Christians still (consciously) sin; if they do, this is considered to be rebellion and apostasy (10:26–31). In such cases, discipline does have

---
69. Ouweneel (1982, 2:70–80).
70. Coates (n.d.-b, 133–53).

the aspect of punishment (cf. 1 Cor. 5:5; 1 Tim. 1:20). But when it is a matter of believers' practical sanctification we are never dealing with the element of punishment. On the contrary, all mischief (persecution because of faith, but also weakness and disease, the loss of loved ones, financial setbacks, and other adversities, unfulfilled desires, unjust treatment, disappointment, lack of success, etc.) is for our good (Heb. 12:10), as an indispensable part of our practical sanctification: "[W]e know that for those who love God all things work together for good" (Rom. 8:28).

"Count it all joy, my brothers, when you meet trials of various kinds, for you know that the testing of your faith produces steadfastness. And let steadfastness have its full effect, that you may be perfect and complete, lacking in nothing" (James 1:2-4). "[Y]ou rejoice, though now for a little while, if necessary, you have been grieved by various trials, so that the tested genuineness of your faith—more precious than gold that perishes though it is tested by fire—may be found to result in praise and glory and honor at the revelation of Jesus Christ" (1 Pet. 1:6-7). "But rejoice insofar as you share Christ's sufferings, that you may also rejoice and be glad when his glory is revealed" (4:13).

Such trials are called "discipline" because indeed they do not entail some kind of punishment for concrete sins but they do presuppose the believer's sinful nature. Thus, the thorn in the flesh that Paul had was a form of discipline in the flesh, not as a punishment but as a precaution: to keep him "from becoming conceited because of the surpassing greatness of the revelations" (2 Cor. 12:7). Job's sufferings, too, were not a punishment for his sins—in spite of the deplorable insinuations by his friends—but a form of discipline to bring him closer to God; as Job said, "I had heard of you by the hearing of the ear, but now my eye sees you; therefore I despise myself, and repent in dust and ashes" (Job 42:5-6).

Of course, we are allowed to try to eliminate persecution, disease, financial trouble, and other adversities, unjust treatment, disappointment, lack of success, etc. There is no place here for some kind of dull resignation.[71] For instance, the New Testament itself refers the sick person to the physician (Matt. 9:12) or to the elders (James 5:14-16), teaches us to pray for the authorities, "that we may lead a peaceful and quiet life" (1 Tim. 2:1-2), and calls upon us to take care of the poor (Luke 3:11; Rom. 15:26; 2 Cor. 9:9; Gal. 2:10; James 2:3, 6, 15-16; 1 John 3:17). However, in all these adversities, the believers concerned have to ask themselves what God wants to *tell* them through them. For even if he did not (actively) send them, he certainly did (passively) allow them.

This is the way I read the Heidelberg Catechism (Q&A 27): "[H]erbs and grass, rain and drought, fruitful and barren years, meat and drink (Jer. 5:24), health and sickness, riches and poverty, indeed, all things come not by chance, but by His fatherly hand." Also notice Q&A 1: "without the will of my Father in heaven not a hair can fall from my head," referring to Matt. 10:29 (cf. Luke 21:18). Although our adversities may not always be directly *sent* by him, he is nonetheless always *involved* in them, they are always his *concern*.

9.9.2 Dealing with Discipline

Discipline helps us to become free, not only of "evil that constantly clings to us" but also of every "weight" (Heb. 12:1). The latter item entails things that in themselves are not sinful—they may be the good things of God's creation (cf. 1 Tim. 4:4)—but may obstruct our practical sanctification. To put it simply: worldly things belong to the category of sin, earthly things to the category of weight. Earthly things in themselves are not sinful, but setting one's mind on them *is* sinful: "If then you have been raised with Christ, seek the things that are above, where Christ is, seated at the right hand of God. Set your minds on things that are above, not on things that are on earth. For you have died, and your life is hidden with Christ

---

71. See extensively, Ouweneel (2004a, §3.3).

in God" (Col. 3:2; cf. Phil. 3:18-19). It is part of our practical sanctification not only to put off the worldly things but also many of the earthly things if they cause us to lose our focus, and entail a waste of time and energy (career, luxury, hobbies, vacations).

It strikes me that adherents of the poor-sinner view often choose either of two roads. Either they choose—because doing your best does not help very much anyway—a life that is both fatalistic and materialistic. Or I see them being much more serious about laying aside weights and sins than many joyous, but superficial Christians. This can be done in a legalistic way, but this is not necessarily the case. However, these are also believers who have all the more difficulty with God's discipline. This is because they often see God's punishing hand in it, whereas the goal of this discipline is precisely to help them to know the Father's love better.

The things that God allows in our lives and that are described as discipline in Hebrews 12:5-11, do not belong to the weights that must be laid aside. We *cannot* even lay these things aside for that matter, even if we would like to, for they come upon us. The question is rather how we *deal* with this discipline:

(a) We can regard it lightly (v. 5), that is, feel elevated above it in a Stoic way, as if these trials are of no concern to us.

(b) Especially sensitive, insecure souls can become weary (NKJV: discouraged; NIV: lose heart) under the trials, or even collapse under them, become disappointed in God, begin to feel even more insecure with respect to their own assurance of faith and the love of God.

(c) One could reject the discipline in a rebellious way, refusing to be subject to it (this is implied in v. 9), which might even lead to apostasy.

(d) We may be trained by it (v. 11), that is, draw the right lessons from it, so that we can correct our way and behavior in order to attain a higher level of practical sanctification. It is this that God intends with the discipline, which is not a proof of his sternness but of his love (v. 6). Therefore, as far as it is possible, we must not shirk this discipline, for this would imply spiritual loss. Weights can and must be laid aside; discipline cannot be laid aside, and we should not desire this either. It helps us to get rid of weights, and positively, it yields fruit: practical sanctification (v. 10) and righteousness (v. 11). Weights hinder our sanctification, discipline furthers it. This is what sanctification entails: learning as we run our race to experience and enjoy more and more the Father's love, and getting closer to the finish line: the glorified Christ at God's right hand (v. 2). Strive for holiness (v. 14), that is, press on "toward the goal for the prize of the upward call of God in Christ Jesus" (Phil. 3:14).

9.10 Perfectionism
9.10.1 No More Sinning?

By perfectionism we understand the theological doctrine that it is possible for believers to reach a state of sinlessness already here on earth by the power of the Holy Spirit.[72] In its more moderate form, this doctrine does not deny that, until the end of our days, the sinful flesh still dwells in us, but it does deny that this flesh is necessarily active. It is still there, but through the working of the Spirit the working of the flesh is perfectly subdued. In its more extreme form, perfectionism claims that the believer is even set free from the sinful nature. It underpins this idea with several quotations from 1 John: "the blood of Jesus his Son cleanses us from all sin" (1:7), in which "sin" is understood not only as the singular of "sins," but also as a reference to the sinful nature, the source of sins. "Whoever abides in Him does not sin. . . .Whoever has been born of God does not sin, for His seed remains in him; and he cannot sin, because he has been born of God" (3:6, 9 NKJV).

---

72. Regarding this, for a Reformed perspective, see Hoekema (1989, 216–20); De Groot (1952, 264–73); Wiersinga (1952, 112–17); Warfield (1958). Also see Darby (n.d.-a, III, 164–205) *contra* John Wesley.

"We know that whoever is born of God does not sin; but he who has been born of God keeps himself, and the wicked one does not touch him" (5:18 NKJV). "Does not sin . . . cannot sin" — that is certainly strong language.

Reformed theologian Willem H. Velema claimed that perfectionists want to live by their own strength, and not by faith, that they substitute their own efforts for God's work, belittle Christ, and weaken the desire for the consummation of all things.[73] However, this is all plucked out of thin air. These are not at all the defects involved in perfectionism. I wonder if Velema would level similar accusations at someone like bishop Polycarp (second century), who wrote of the "love of God and Christ and neighbor. . . . For if one be in this company he has fulfilled the command of righteousness, for *he who has love is far from all sin.*"[74] Perfect love casts out fear (1 John 4:18) — but one might add that it casts out sin as well. Love and sin cannot go together. Polycarp's argument is: where there is love there can be no sin, and where there is sin there can be no love.

Martin Luther claimed that here on earth, believers will never reach sinless perfection; otherwise they would no longer need faith and Christ.[75] But this, too, is an irrelevant argument. Why would it not be conceivable in principle that someone reaches sinless perfection, or something that comes close to this, precisely *because of* his continual dependence on (his faith in) Christ? One may think whatever one wishes of perfectionism, but at least we must say that in this doctrine it is always Christ who takes the central place, as well as the Holy Spirit, through whose power the believer's God-pleasing work is exclusively possible.

The Old Testament examples listed by Bruce Demarest[76] are not very convincing either, because the position of Old

---

73. Van Genderen and Velema (2008, 652-53).
74. The Epistle of Polycarp to the Philippians III.3; italics added.
75. Quoted in Plass (1959, 1317).
76. Demarest (1997, 416–18).

Testament believers was much less delineated: they did not know union with Christ, nor the filling of the Holy Spirit (except in some specific cases). Their position can hardly be used as an example for New Testament believers, except in certain respects, indicated by the New Testament itself, such as faith that was counted to them as righteousness (Rom. 4), and living by the power of faith (Heb. 11).

At face value, perfectionism seems to have strong arguments at its disposal. It emphasizes that we have become a new creation (2 Cor. 5:17; Gal. 6:15), have been invested with the new man (Eph. 4:24; Col. 3:10),[77] that we are no more slaves of sin (John 8:31–36), even have been set free from sin (Rom. 6:7, 12–23; 8:2), and have been cleansed from all sin (1 John 1:7). It takes Jesus' appeal seriously: "You . . . must be perfect, as your heavenly Father is perfect" (Matt. 5:48), and: "Sin no more" (John 5:14; 8:11); similarly with Paul's appeal: "Let not sin therefore reign in your mortal body, to make you obey its passions" (Rom. 6:12); and Peter's appeal: ". . . so as to live for the rest of the time in the flesh no longer for human passions but for the will of God" (1 Pet. 4:2), and: "Therefore, brothers, be all the more diligent to confirm your calling and election, for if you practice these qualities you will never fall" (2 Pet. 1:10); along with John's appeal: "My little children, I am writing these things to you so that you may not sin" (1 John 2:1), and: "Whoever abides in Him does not sin" (3:6 NKJV); and James' appeal: "[L]et steadfastness have its full effect, that you may be perfect and complete, lacking in nothing" (James 1:4). What meaning would all such appeals have if, as a matter of fact, they could not be obeyed?

Another strong point in perfectionism is that it takes seriously the power and the filling of the Holy Spirit: "[D]o not be foolish, but understand what the will of the Lord is . . . be filled with the Spirit" (Eph. 5:18). God "condemned sin in the flesh, in order that the righteous requirement of the law might

---

77. See extensively, Ouweneel (2010a, §3.2.3).

be fulfilled in us, who walk not according to the flesh but according to the Spirit. . . . For all who are led by the Spirit of God are sons of God" (Rom. 8:3-4, 14). "[W]alk by the Spirit, and you will not gratify the desires of the flesh" (Gal. 5:16). It can hardly be denied that this is a central element in New Testament teaching: *if we walk with Christ closely enough,* which is essentially the same as saying: *if we are dominated by the Holy Spirit, we will not sin.*

9.10.2 Two Sides

At this point, however, we must consider the fact that New Testament appeals like those I have just quoted always have two sides. Adherents of perfectionism argue that such commands would not have been given to us if it were impossible in principle to perform them. To me, this seems perfectly correct. However, opponents of perfectionism argue that such commands prove that believers still *need* such appeals. To me, this seems perfectly correct too. It is to *all* believers that the appeal comes: "[L]et anyone who thinks that he stands take heed lest he fall" (1 Cor. 10:12). "Brothers, if anyone is caught in any transgression, you who are spiritual should restore him in a spirit of gentleness. Keep watch on yourself, lest you too be tempted" (Gal. 6:1). Even spiritual Christians still have to keep watch over themselves (cf. 5:15; 1 Cor. 16:13; 1 Tim. 4:16; 1 Pet. 5:8; 2 John 1:8). "[E]xhort one another every day, . . . that none of you may be hardened by the deceitfulness of sin" (Heb. 3:13). "Let us therefore strive to enter that rest, so that no one may fall by the same sort of disobedience" (4:11). "Beloved, I urge you as sojourners and exiles to abstain from the passions of the flesh, which wage war against your soul" (1 Pet. 2:11). The phrase "your soul" is general; it is not only the soul of immature believers.

Apparently, believers continually run the risk that sin gets the upper hand again, that they are governed anew by their passions, that they walk again according to the flesh, that they fall into foolishness, etc. Therefore, they keep praying: "Forgive us our debts" (Matt. 6:12). There is not the slightest hint in the New Testament that for a certain class of people this kind of appeal is no longer necessary because they allegedly have reached a level that is beyond such exhortations. If John says, "My little children [Greek, *teknia*], I am writing these things to you so that you may not sin" (1 John 2:1), he addresses *all* his readers: not only the infants (*paidia*) and the young men, but also the fathers in Christ. For all three categories this word remains valid: "If we say we have no sin, we deceive ourselves, and the truth is not in us" (1:8). As long as the sinful nature is still in them, even in the fathers—and this is the case until the end of their earthly days—it remains necessary to warn them against the possible workings of this flesh. This is because it will always be the believer who chooses by what he wishes to be led: by the flesh or by the Spirit—and as long as he still has to make this choice, the risk remains that he makes the wrong choice.

Please note: *he*—not just the sinful nature that dwells in him. The perfectionist cannot rescue his position by claiming that it is not *he* who still sins but only the flesh within him. To be sure, Paul makes such a distinction in Romans 7:17 and 20—in order to distinguish the new from the old nature—but much more frequently he appeals to *believers*—not just to their flesh—to sin no more.[78] If we sin, it is *we* who sin, not just some part of us. From an anthropological perspective, it is doubtful anyway to distinguish psychical, mental, or spiritual "parts" in humans that might do certain things apart from the ego.[79]

If it were true that we are able to attain the stage of perfection here on earth, why is it said, "[W]e all stumble in many ways" (James 3:2)? Why can we not find any examples of sinlessness in the New Testament (except, of course, Christ[80])? Even regarding Peter, the leader of the twelve apostles, and

---

78. Van Genderen and Velema (2008, 654).
79. See extensively, Ouweneel (2008a, 128–42).
80. See Ouweneel (2007b, §§10.4–10.6).

Barnabas, the "son of encouragement" (Acts 4:36), both mature Christians, we hear of hypocrisy at a certain moment (Gal. 2:11-14). Even regarding the mature Paul we hear that, after he criticized the high priest, he immediately had to acknowledge his error, and subsequently played off the one party in the Sanhedrin against the other (Acts 23:1-9; cf. 24:21). This is not the image of Christ. As Richard Longenecker said: "Paul's retort seems quite out of character for a follower of the one who 'when they hurled their insults at him, he did not retaliate; when he suffered, he made no threats' (1 Peter 2:23). Paul, it seems, momentarily lost his composure . . . We cannot excuse this sudden burst of anger."[81]

Actually, Paul himself says, in his very epistle of Christian maturity and experience: "Not that I have already obtained this or am already perfect, but I press on to make it my own, because Christ Jesus has made me his own. Brothers, I do not consider that I have made it my own. But one thing I do: forgetting what lies behind and straining forward to what lies ahead, I press on toward the goal for the prize of the upward call of God in Christ Jesus" (Phil. 3:12-14). Paul is perfect here in the sense of mature, spiritually adult (v. 15), but not perfect in the sense of sinless (v. 12). Maturity is not knowing Christ in perfection, but knowing the perfection of Christ: "[T]he reborn person is on earth not perfect in his knowing and loving and admiring the law of the Lord. . . . But he does learn to more and more notice the perfection of God's law and of his service."[82]

9.10.3 No Excuse

Of course, such considerations are no excuse for sinning. It remains perfectly true that, because of the indwelling Spirit, believers do not *need* to sin, and if this does happen, they have no excuse for this. But it is equally true that it does happen

---

81. Longenecker (1981, 530–31); thus many older commentaries, e.g., Grosheide (1963, 149).
82. De Groot (1952, 297).

from time to time.

In this context 1 John 1:8 is of vital importance: "If we say we have no sin, we deceive ourselves." What exactly does this entail? Does John mean to say that we should not deny that, also as Christians, we have committed sins (cf. v. 10)? Or does he refer to the Gnostic teaching that actions of Christians are by definition no longer sins?[83] In both cases, this verse strictly speaking would be no argument against perfectionism. Or does John want to say that we should not deny that the flesh is still within us? Pieter Lalleman believes that here the phrase "having sin" simply means "sinning,"[84] but others rightly distinguish between the two: the expression "having sin" refers to the flesh, whereas the verb "sinning" refers to sinful actions.[85]

Claiming that one has no sin can be valid only by denying that this flesh still produces sinful fruits, or even by claiming that the flesh has disappeared. However, none of us can deny that he sometimes falls into sin. Some people have a good conscience because they have a bad memory. John's words, "My little children, I am writing these things to you so that you may not sin," are immediately followed by the words: "But if anyone does sin, we have an advocate with the Father, Jesus Christ the righteous" (1 John 2:1). This "anyone" can definitely be a reborn Christian: "If anyone sees *his brother* committing a sin . . ." (5:16). Such a possibility always remains. If an individual Christian does sin, *we* have an advocate—*we*, because everyone of us could become this "anyone."

If John indeed intends to say that the believer must not deny his sinful nature, the verse definitely would be an argument against perfectionism. The verses that seem to be in conflict with this, and have been quoted before (3:6, 9; 5:18), are usually explained either as referring to the believer's new

---

83. Cf. Law (1914, ad loc.): "having sin" = "having guilt," that is, being responsible for our moral actions; cf. Dodd (1946, 21–22).
84. Lalleman (2005, 139).
85. Kelly (1905, 35); Smith (1979, 172); Barker (1981, 311).

nature only, or as not denying that the believer *can* sin (occasionally), but as stating that he does not *practice* sin anymore. That is, a life of sin is not his common practice anymore because he is no longer under the power of sin. If this is the right approach—and in my view it is—John would command us not to sin anymore (2:1), and would at the same time protest against those who claim that they indeed do not do so anymore, or even assert that they are no longer *able* to do so.

That this explanation of chapter 1:8 is the correct one is supported by the fact that it is immediately followed by these words: "If we confess our sins . . ." (v. 9). We still have our old and evil nature, as verse 8 indicates; we are supposed to cut off the shoots of this sinful nature in the bud, as verse 9 indicates.[86] Also compare what I said earlier about Colossians 3:5 (§9.5.2): place every working of the flesh immediately under the death of Christ, under the judgment of God. However, if we ignore these workings, and even deny their source (the flesh), "we deceive ourselves, and the truth is not in us" (1 John 1:8).

Perfectionism has been the deception of many believers, a deception that can be maintained only with a very low standard of sin.[87] That is, we can make anyone believe that we do not sin anymore only if we restrict the notion of sin to, for instance, conscious or deliberate sins. Perfectionism can be maintained only by Christians who lower their standards of sin so much that in the end they will always be right.

Sometimes, the notion of sin is limited to sinful *actions*, leaving sinful *thoughts* or sinful *inclinations* out of consideration, as long as such thoughts or inclinations are immediately suppressed. However, already Luther rightly emphasized that the inclination to sin is itself also sin.[88] A sinful thought that is suppressed is still a sin. If thought can indeed "accuse" us (Rom. 2:15), this is because thoughts can be sinful, even if

---

86. Kelly (1905, 35).
87. Ibid., 36.
88. Apology of the Augsburg Confession 2.38–41.

they do not lead to sinful acts (cf. Gen. 6:5; Job 21:27; Ps. 56:5; Prov. 15:26; Isa. 55:7; 59:7; Jer. 4:14; Matt. 15:19; Luke 1:51; 2:35; 5:22; 6:8; 11:17). It is not only the actions but also the thoughts of the righteous that are just (Prov. 12:5). The Bible does not make a distinction between the sinful quality of evil thoughts that are suppressed and that of evil thoughts that are allowed free rein; both are evil anyway. Thus, for Jesus, murderous thoughts were just as evil as murder, and adulterous thoughts were just as evil as adultery (Matt. 5:21-22, 27-28). We may manage quite well to avoid sinful actions—and still prove to have the flesh in us by our sinful inclinations and thoughts.

Jesus remains the perfect example of a truly holy person. We cannot imagine Jesus as having evil thoughts that he immediately suppressed. He was pure, perfect, holy, and righteous in his acts, in his words, in his thoughts, and in his deepest inclinations. Practical sanctification entails fixing our spiritual eyes on him, so that in the power of the Holy Spirit both our minds and our outward behavior will be transformed into his perfect image.

Appendix 1
The Time of Propitiation

1 When Was the Atonement?

IT HAS OFTEN BEEN CLAIMED that Jesus sustained the "wrath of God," or "appease[d] his Father's wrath" (Belgic Confession, Art. 21). Is this a biblical way of speaking, and if so, *when* did he sustain or appease this wrath? During his whole life on earth? During all his sufferings that he endured in the last days of his earthly life? During all the time that he was on the cross? During the three hours of darkness on the cross?

First, can we say that, at certain moments of his life or during his whole life on earth, the wrath of God was upon Jesus? We can at best conclude this in an indirect way from passages such as John 3:36 ("[W]hoever does not obey the Son shall not see life, but the wrath of God remains on him"); Romans 3:5 ("[I]f our unrighteousness serves to show the righteousness of God, what shall we say? That God is unrighteous to inflict wrath on us?"); 5:9 ("Since, therefore, we have now been justified by his blood, much more shall we be saved by him from the wrath of God"); Ephesians 5:6 ("Let no one deceive you with empty words, for because of these things the wrath of God comes upon the sons of disobedience"); Colossians 3:5-6 ("Put to death therefore what is earthly in you: sexual immorality, impurity, passion, evil desire, and covetousness, which is idolatry. On account of these the wrath of

God is coming").

All these passages speak about the wrath of God upon the wicked; one could argue that Christ has endured this wrath for us as our substitute, although we nowhere explicitly read this in the New Testament. Yet, it seems to follow naturally from his having been forsaken by a holy and righteous God (Matt. 27:46; Mark 15:34; cf. Ps. 22:1): when Jesus had been "made to be sin" (2 Cor. 5:21) and "bore our sins in his body on the tree" (1 Pet. 2:24), God, who is "of purer eyes than to see evil and cannot look at wrong" (Hab. 1:13), turned away his face from him ("forsook" him).

The next question is: *when* was this wrath of God upon Jesus? In my view, it goes much too far when, for instance, Reformed writer Aart Moerkerken says that Jesus "sustained as an innocent Child the full burden of God's wrath. When he as a boy walked in the streets of Nazareth, and labored in the workshop of his stepfather Joseph, he sustained the wrath of God against sin every day and every night."[1] We can certainly say that Jesus always suffered under the presence of sin in this world (cf. 1 Pet. 3:14), and under God's wrath against it, but can Moerkerken really maintain that Jesus already as a Child bore the *punishment* for sin? Can we say that at one and the same time both the *pleasure* of God rested on him (Matt. 3:17; 12:18; 17:5; cf. John 8:29) as well as God's *wrath*? I can image that God's wrath was upon him when he had to cry out: "My God, my God, why have you forsaken me?" But I cannot imagine that God's wrath was upon him when the Father said, "This is my beloved Son, with whom I am well pleased." And what is more important: I cannot find anywhere in the New Testament that God's wrath was upon him all his life.

Now we do have to acknowledge that Moerkerken's view ties in with the Heidelberg Catechism (Q&A 37): "[A]ll the time He lived on earth, but especially at the end of His life, He bore, in body and soul, the wrath of God against the sin of the

---

1. Moerkerken (2004, 210).

whole human race...." To support this statement, the Catechism refers to four passages. The first is Isaiah 53:4, "Surely he has borne our griefs and carried our sorrows." In Matthew 8:17, this verse is indeed applied to Jesus' ministry, and not to his sufferings on the cross. But Matthew applies the verse only to Jesus' healing ministry, *not* to his propitiatory sacrifice for sins, and even less to the wrath of God. The other passages mentioned, 1 Peter 2:24, 3:18, and 1 Timothy 2:6, do speak of Christ's work of atonement, but then unmistakably in relation to his work on the cross: Jesus bore our sins *on the tree* (1 Pet. 2:24), he suffered for our sins in the hour of death (3:18), gave himself as a ransom (1 Tim. 2:6), and this he did by his self-surrender unto death (Gal. 2:20, "crucified"). I believe that on the cross Jesus indeed sustained the wrath of God — but none of the passages referred to mentions this expression, and even less do they suggest that he sustained this wrath during his entire life on earth.

Of course, the Catechism does not stand on its own. The Reformed Form for the Celebration of the Lord's Supper says of Jesus: "From the beginning of His incarnation to the end of His life on earth, He bore for us the wrath of God, under which we should have perished eternally." Interestingly, the 1964 version of the Christian Reformed Churches' version leaves out the words "From the beginning of His incarnation to the end of His life on earth." In this way they are much more in line with what the Westminster Larger Catechism has to say (Q&A 49): "Christ humbled himself in his death ... having also conflicted with the terrors of death, and the powers of darkness, felt and borne the weight of God's wrath, he laid down his life an offering for sin, enduring the painful, shameful, and cursed death of the cross." Here, the wrath of God is explicitly linked with his sufferings during the last (night and) day of his earthly life.

2 Active and Passive Obedience

This entire problem — when did Jesus sustain the wrath of

God? — is closely linked with the Reformed distinction between Christ's *active* and *passive obedience* (or *righteousness*).[2] Allegedly, the former refers to his ministry during his walk on earth, the latter refers to his final sufferings and death. First, we asked: When did Jesus sustain the wrath of God, that is, bear God's judgment on our sins? During all the days of his earthly life, or only on the cross? Now we add the following question: When did Jesus acquire the righteousness that God would grant to believers? During all the days of his earthly life, or only on the cross?

To begin with, I find the terms "active" and "passive" rather unfortunate. Is John 10:17–18 ("I lay down my life that I may take it up again. No one takes it from me, but I lay it down of my own accord. I have authority to lay it down, and I have authority to take it up again") so very passive? And is being "led" by the Spirit (Luke 4:1, "And Jesus, full of the Holy Spirit, . . . was led by the Spirit in the wilderness") so very active?

In chapter 4 of the present study, I have discussed the doctrine of imputation, which says that the righteousness of Christ is imputed to the believers. As I have tried to show, this doctrine is in itself already doubtful enough. In my view, it becomes even worse, however, if this righteousness of Christ that is imputed is not so much the passive obedience of Christ, which entails his work on the cross, but the active obedience of Christ, that is, his Torah-observance during his life on earth. Reformed theologian Herman Bavinck was one of those who held this doctrine, although he did warn against "too sharp a distinction between Christ's passive and his active obedience."[3] Here again, I quote the Reformed Form for the Celebration of the Lord's Supper, which tells us that Jesus "[b]y His perfect obedience has for us fulfilled all the

---

2. See extensively, Berkhof (1949, 379–82); Berkouwer (1965, 319–27; I know few places in Berkouwer's work where I find his arguments weaker than here); see also Erickson (1998, 835–36, 971).
3. Bavinck (2006, 3:380; 2008, 4:224).

righteousness of God's law" *—for us*, that is, as our substitute. Reformed theologian John Piper told us that Christ suffered and died in order to fulfill for us the righteous demands of the Law.[4] I could go on like this with many more Reformed quotations.

I see several objections. First, I do not see the slightest hint in Scripture that Christ observed the Torah "for us," in our stead, as our substitute. It is nothing but the end conclusion of an involved and subtle argumentation, in which the distinct logical steps are already doubtful enough.

Second, if the righteousness that we have received is a righteousness of the *law* — what is called the "active righteousness of Christ," that is, his perfect Torah observance — then, after all, this righteousness is still nothing but "a righteousness that comes from the law (*ek nomou*)," not a "righteousness from God (*ek theou*)," as Paul says (Phil. 3:9). What Paul argues here is that he is not even *interested* anymore in whatever righteousness that "comes from the law," but only in that righteousness "from God that depends on faith."

Third, a righteousness "that comes from the law" (in the sense of the Mosaic Torah) consists only of what we ought to have done ("if a person does [my rules], he shall live by them," Lev. 18:5) *and nothing else*. Such a righteousness does not give us any right to union with the risen Christ (Rom. 6:7-8), to the glory of God (3:23-24; 5:1-2), and to eternal life (5:21), just as Adam in his innocent state had no right to these things, nor even the most Torah-faithful Israelite. Therefore, it leads to nothing if we base salvation on the God-pleasing *life* of Christ (i.e., his Torah-observance), instead of basing it exclusively on Christ's sufferings on the cross as the One forsaken by a holy and a righteous God.

In other words, salvation is not based on the *tota obedientia Christi* (the "entire obedience of Christ"), but only and exclusively on the *obedientia passionis et mortis Christi* (the

---

4. Piper (2004, 37).

"obedience of the suffering and death of Christ").[5] In the initial period of the Reformation, it was, among others, Johann Piscator (about 1600) who, following Anselm of Canterbury, taught the latter view. Johannes Bogerman (president of the Synod of Dordt) and Sibrandus Lubbertus, too, were inclined to this view.[6] David Pareus (about 1600), however, warned solemnly against this view with the argument: "For what purpose, then, served [Christ's] preceding humiliation, his assumed form of a servant, his servitude towards the law?"[7] This is a good question, to which there is a simple answer: Pareus confused atonement with the preparatory life of the One who accomplished this atonement. Christ's sufferings as well as his obedience during his life on earth formed the necessary preparation for his work of atonement—they were not part of atonement itself (see further below).

Reformed theologian Jonathan Edwards (eighteenth century) believed that the blood of Christ's circumcision (Luke 2:21) was as equally propitiatory as the blood that came out of Jesus' side (John 19:34).[8] He believed that all Christ's sufferings, during infancy and childhood, and all that trouble, contempt, scorn, and all the temptations, or whatever difficulty he experienced during his life, possessed the nature of an atonement and satisfaction. Herman Bavinck and Gerrit C. Berkouwer defended this view by referring to Galatians 4:4-5, "God sent forth his Son, born of woman, born under the law, to redeem those who were under the law, so that we might receive adoption as sons."[9] However, this passage does not say at all that Christ's living under the Torah, and his observing this Torah, as such contributed anything to redeeming those who were under the Torah. Of course, only one who had perfectly obeyed the Torah could redeem those

---

5. Cf. Thomas Aquinas, *Summa Theologiae* 3a.47, 2.
6. De Groot (1952, 68), too, seems to hold this view.
7. See Bos (1932, 10).
8. Edwards (2003, 213).
9. Bavinck (2006, 3:378); Berkouwer (1965, 322–23).

who were under the Torah. But that is very different from redeeming them *by* observing the Torah. Again, this is confusing the conditions for Jesus being our substitute with being our substitute as such.

3 No Vicarious Torah Observance

Of course, there is coherence between Jesus observing the Torah and his work of atonement. I repeat: only *this* person, who had so perfectly observed the Torah, could release the captives under the Torah (Rom. 7:6). But that does not mean that this Torah observance *as such* was part of the work of atonement. Learning English is a condition if you wish to write a book in English — but this learning is not part of the writing itself; it is only a prerequisite. Observing the Torah is a condition for releasing those who are under the Torah — but this observance is not part of the releasing itself; it is only a prerequisite.

The fact that Jesus *observed* the Torah did not contribute anything to the atonement for our *trespasses* of the Torah. Scripture never makes such a connection; we find nowhere that Christ observed the Torah in our stead, as our substitute. It is a purely human invention, unthinkingly repeated by thousands of people, but not backed up by Scripture. There is not the smallest hint whatsoever that his Torah observance as such contributed anything to our salvation. Jesus observing the Torah is an *example* to humans, it accuses and condemns wicked persons, but it does not bring them atonement. Christ did not atone our sins by showing us how we should have lived, but by undergoing the divine punishment for our trespasses. Jesus observing the Torah did not take away any guilt; on the contrary, it brought to light all the more painfully the guilt of fallen humanity. Jesus observing the Torah robs us of our excuse that God's Torah was too hard for humans to be observed. Jesus did it. But the fact that he did it does not make our guilt any less — it makes it only more horrendous. Before God's judgment seat, Jesus' Torah observance points to the sinner in an accusing way, it arraigns him, it denounces him, it condemns him, but it cannot help him.

The phrase that sounds so familiar—"Christ fulfilled the law for us"—is, in my view, totally foreign to the New Testament, according to both letter and spirit. Of course, it is perfectly true that he did observe the Mosaic Torah in a perfect way; he lived according to it, and never trespassed it.[10] However, Scripture teaches us nowhere that he did this "for us," "in our stead," as our "substitute." I repeat: Christ's Torah observance was a necessary *condition* for his being able to accomplish the work of atonement. If he had not observed the Torah himself, how could he have ever undergone the punishment for those who had broken the Torah? How could he have "borne" their trespasses if he himself had trespassed the Torah? (Heidelberg Catechism, Q&A 16: "[O]ne who is himself a sinner cannot satisfy for others").

However, this is something essentially different from his Torah observance being a *part* of the work of atonement. Therefore, we must reject the questionable sentence: "Jesus Christ, imputing to us all His merits, and so many holy works which He has done for us and in our stead, is our righteousness" (Belgic Confession, Article 22)—unless we understand by these "holy works" *only* the redemptive work that he accomplished on the cross. The fundamental error that so many Reformed theologians have committed here is that they understood the unmistakable coherence between Christ's Torah observance and his work of atonement in such a way that they made the former a part of the latter. That which qualifies someone for a task is not part of that task itself. For many professions a particular schooling is necessary; that schooling is the *condition* for exercising that profession. But it is not part of that professional work as such. In the end, maintaining the view that Christ's Torah observance had atoning significance implies a distortion of the New Testament gospel.[11]

---

10. See extensively, Ouweneel (2015a, §5.3).
11. Cf. Darby (n.d.-a, VII, 293).

4 Only on the Cross

With Joseph Ratzinger (pope Benedict XVI), we find a similar thought as the one we quoted from various Reformed sources. He drew far-reaching conclusions from Jesus' words at his baptism: "Let it be so now, for thus it is fitting for us to fulfill all righteousness" (Matt. 3:15). Ratzinger argued that in Jesus' "Yes" to the entire will of God in a world marked by sin, there was also an expression of solidarity with the people who had become guilty, but did not reach out for this righteousness. Jesus had loaded the burden of the entire humanity's guilt on his shoulders; he carried it downward to the Jordan. He opened his activity with this walking down to the Jordan in the place of the sinners.[12]

However, what proofs did Ratzinger have for the idea that Jesus during his walk on earth "bore" the sins of his own? Jesus bore them *on the tree*, that is, the cross (1 Pet. 2:24). The person who "bore" the sins of the people entered into death: he who made his soul an offering for guilt, was cut off out of the land of the living (Isa. 53:8–10). We have been reconciled to God by the *death* of his Son, not by his life on earth in any way whatever; and when Paul adds that we shall be saved by his life, he refers to Jesus' resurrection life, that is, *after* his work on the cross (Rom. 5:10). I repeat: the New Testament does not contain any clue that during his entire life on earth, or since his baptism by John, Jesus bore our sins.

To be sure, some versions of 1 Peter 2:24 say, "Christ himself carried our sins in his body to the cross" (GNT; cf. MSG, WE). And Reformed theologian Seakle Greijdanus translated the passage to read: "*Who carried our sins in his body upward to the tree* of the cross."[13] Such a rendering is certainly possible.[14] However, this does not change the fact that the actual location of the sin offering was "in his body on the tree."[15]

---

12. Ratzinger (2008, 18; cf. 19–23).
13. Greijdanus (1931, 50)
14. Brown (1992, 3:1195–96).
15. Blum (1981, 235).

Interestingly, the Geneva Catechism falls into the opposite snare (Q&A 55): " Q. Why do you leap at once from his birth to his death, passing over the whole history of his life? A. Because nothing is treated of here but what so properly belongs to our salvation, as in a manner to contain the substance of it." On the one hand, this is highly interesting because salvation is linked here exclusively with Jesus' death, *not* with his preceding life on earth. On the other hand, speaking as if "the whole history of his life" had no meaning in view of salvation is going to the other extreme. At a minimum we must say that Jesus' life was the "grain offering" without which no "burnt offering" was conceivable,[16] or something comparable. Reformed theologian Johannes Verkuyl said: "It is a fact of experience that among all nations and within all cultural circles the story of Jesus' life and activity makes a deep impression, and that this story of Jesus' life, also before the great suffering, may not be withheld from any child or adult person. Yet, it is also a fact that all roads and lines in the gospels debouch in the cross."[17]

5 God's Delight in Jesus

How could one seriously assert that Jesus endured the wrath of God during his entire life on earth? The New Testament teaches the opposite: during his entire life Jesus was in full and permanent fellowship with the Father. When Jesus was on the cross, he had to say that God had forsaken him. But during his ministry he could say: "[H]e who sent me is with me. He has not left me alone, for I always do the things that are pleasing to him" (John 8:29). Even when he was already on his way to the cross he could say: "Behold, the hour is coming, indeed it has come, when you will be scattered, each to his own home, and will leave me alone. Yet I am not alone, for the Father is with me" (16:32). He could also say: "I know that You always hear Me" (11:42 NKJV) — but at the cross he had

---
16. See Ouweneel (2009, §4.4.1).
17. Verkuyl (1992, 230).

to say: "O my God, I cry by day, but you do not answer" (Ps. 22:2; only in the resurrection he says, "You have answered Me," v. 22 NKJV).[18] How then can one claim that at the same time the wrath of God was upon him, that is, during his entire life on earth he (propitiatorily) "bore" our sins?

Reformed writer Aart Moerkerken did not discern this tension: "Yet you may never say that the Father was angry at his Son. . . . God always loved his Son, also when vicariously and substitutionarily he endured the wrath of God against the sin of the entire human race."[19] But does he not see the enormous difference between Jesus who walked here on earth in continual fellowship with the Father and was aware of the Father's pleasure, and Jesus who, during the three hours of darkness on the cross, was forsaken by a holy and righteous God? During Jesus' life, the *Father's pleasure* rested upon him, during the three dark hours on the cross *God's wrath* rested upon him. As Reformed theologian Klaas Schilder said, "[N]ow follows the essence of the sacrifice itself; now He must enter upon the darkness of night."[20] This "most proper part" was not during Jesus' life, but during the three hours of darkness preceding his death.

At the cross, Jesus said something he could never have said during his life: "My God, my God, why have you forsaken me?" If he had been bearing our sins during his entire life on earth, he ought to have been forsaken by God during all his days, for God cannot look at sins with even the smallest indulgence.[21] Bearing our sins occurred "on the tree," and nowhere else, nor ever before. Actually, it is quite astonishing that theologians ever arrived at a different idea. I cannot imagine why they ever wanted to extend Christ's atoning work to his entire life.

Lewis Sperry Chafer correctly summarized the matter as

---

18. Grant (1902, 155).
19. Moerkerken (2004, 212).
20. Schilder (1940, 372).
21. Kelly (1923, 170).

follows: "[T]he Word of God does not assign saving value to any obedience of the sufferings of Christ other than that connected with His death. . . . Salvation is based on the blood of the cross and not on the blood of circumcision or even the blood which He sweat in the garden. He provided no redemption, reconciliation, or propitiation when circumcised or when baptized."[22] At a later point Chafer wrote: "It is . . . claimed by not a few that all His sacrifice, even His leaving heaven, and every privation and rejection, was vicarious in character, that is, it was wrought in behalf of others. No doubt others were benefited; but such sacrifice was not in any sense a substitution, since no other was ever appointed to the path which He pursued. All His life was a sacrifice, but by universal Biblical usage only that sacrifice by which He gave His life on the cross is vicarious and substitutionary."[23]

At the very least, one has to acknowledge that the New Testament makes a clear distinction between Jesus' life and the sufferings at the end thereof. To be sure, Jesus suffered for righteousness' sake (cf. 1 Pet. 3:14) during his entire life on earth.[24] But not all sufferings are vicarious and substitutionary. Therefore, Jesus himself made the distinction by saying, just before the last Passover: "My time is at hand" (Matt. 26:18), and during the Passover meal: "I have earnestly desired to eat this Passover with you *before I suffer*" (Luke 22:15). Thus, he distinguished between the night and day of his final sufferings and his entire preceding life. Only in these sufferings, in this *having to* suffer at the end of his life, God's redemptive plan is carried out (cf. Matt. 16:21; 26:54, 56; Luke 9:22; 17:25; 22:53; Acts 17:3).

In Matthew 20:22, the "cup" of Jesus' sufferings was still before him: ". . . the cup that I am to drink" (NKJV: "that I am about to drink"; NIV: "that I am going to drink"). Even in Gethsemane, the "cup" was still before him: "My Father, if it

---

22. Chafer (1983, 3:42–43).
23. Ibid., 65.
24. See Ouweneel (2009, §8.3.2).

be possible, let this cup pass from me; . . . if this cannot pass unless I drink it, your will be done" (Matt. 26:39, 42). Even when he was taken captive, the "cup" was still before him, or the drinking had just begun: "[S]hall I not drink the cup that the Father has given me?" (John 18:11).

Jesus told the disciples from Emmaus: "Was it not necessary that the Christ should suffer these things and enter into his glory?" (Luke 24:26), where "these things" refer to what these disciples had been concerned about: Jesus' crucifixion and death (v. 20). Israel received deliverance through looking to the bronze serpent that had been lifted up; likewise, people are saved not through the sufferings of Jesus' entire life, but by "looking to" the Son of Man who was lifted up at the cross: "[S]o must the Son of Man be *lifted up*, that whoever believes in him may have eternal life" (John 3:14–15). At the cross, Jesus was "lifted up from the earth" (12:32; cf. 8:28) — only at that moment he paved the way for believers to receive eternal life. This is the ongoing testimony of the New Testament: we are not saved through Jesus' life on earth but through his sufferings on the cross and his death.

During his entire life on earth, the Son had glorified the Father (John 17:4; cf. 13:32; 14:13). But at the cross, the Man Jesus glorified a holy and righteous God with respect to sin through perfectly "bearing" (undergoing God's judgment over) our sins. He was, and remained, the Son of the Father, but it was necessarily as the Son of Man that he cried out: "My God, my God, why have you forsaken me?" Then, and then alone, God forsook his only unfaltering Servant, the Man Christ Jesus.[25]

6 "With His Wounds We Are Healed"

Did any of the blows that human beings inflicted upon Jesus contribute to our salvation? Jesus was scourged by wicked hands (Matt. 27:56); could any of these scourges have propitiatory value? I cannot see how. Could the pain and the

---
25. Kelly (1927, 21–22).

wounds caused by the crown of thorns (v. 29) contribute to our redemption? I do not believe so. No blow, no scourge, no pain, caused by human hands, could ever take away any guilt. On the contrary, they did nothing but *increase humanity's guilt*. How could anything that wicked humans did to Jesus ever reconcile us with God? No, it was what a holy and righteous God did to Jesus that saved us: he was "smitten by God, and afflicted . . . pierced for our transgressions . . . crushed for our iniquities . . . it was the will of the LORD to crush him; *he has put him to grief* [or, has made him sick]" (Isa. 53:4-5, 10). What *people* did to Jesus, *increased* our guilt; what God did to Jesus when he forsook him and laid the punishment on him, *took away* the guilt of all those who believe.

God said, "Awake, O sword, against my shepherd, against the man who stands next to me" (Zech. 13:7). It was the sword *of the* LORD that "awoke" against Jesus. The blows of *humans* worsened our case; the blows of *God's sword* solved our case (cf. for this term 1 Chron. 21:12; Jer. 12:12; 47:6). Jesus was "pierced for our transgression" — not by the Roman soldier (John 19:34), but by a holy and righteous God. The soldier pierced his side, God pierced his heart. Jesus was "crushed for our iniquities" — not by soldiers but by God. "With his wounds we are healed" (Isa. 53:5; cf. 1 Pet. 2:24) — not the wounds inflicted by soldiers but the wounds inflicted by God. I repeat: what humans did to him increased our guilt; what God did to him took away our guilt.

Jesus himself announced that the blood he would give would be "poured out for many for the forgiveness of sins" (Matt. 26:28; cf. 1 Cor. 10:16; 11:25, 27). The New Testament epistles take up this notion of the blood of Jesus, ". . . whom God put forward as a propitiation by his blood" (Rom. 3:25); "we have now been justified by his blood" (5:9; cf. Eph. 1:7; 2:13). It is "the blood of his cross" (Col. 1:20). Jesus "entered once for all into the holy places, not by means of the blood of goats and calves but by means of his own blood, thus securing an eternal redemption" (Heb. 9:12; cf. v. 14; 10:19; 13:12,

20; 1 Pet. 1:2; 1 John 1:7; 5:6, 8; Rev. 1:5; 5:9; 7:14; 12:11).

The blood and the water that came out when the soldier pierced Jesus' side formed an important testimony to his death (John 19:34–37). But how could this act as such have contributed to our salvation? Do we depend on the act of a Roman soldier for our redemption? Do we depend on the scourges that soldiers had inflicted on him, simply because they produced blood? Are we saved at all by the blood that dripped from Jesus' head and from his pierced hands?

We do not understand the language of Jesus' "blood" other than through the sacrificial language of the Old Testament. Jesus is compared to the sheep that was led to the slaughter (Isa. 53:7; cf. Acts 8:22). That is symbolical language, just like 1 Peter 1:19, ". . . the precious blood of Christ, like that of a lamb without blemish or spot." In the literal sense, Jesus was not slaughtered; his throat was not slit. The lamb that gives its blood *is* slaughtered; Jesus gave his blood not by being literally slaughtered but by surrendering his life into death ("the life is [in] the blood," Lev. 17:11, 14). Jesus did not give his blood by enemies inflicting wounds on his body. At best you can say that the enemies *spilled* his blood. Jesus actively *giving* his blood is metaphorical language, just as Jesus entering into the "holy places" "by means of [or, with] his blood" (Heb. 9:12; cf. 13:11), or his blood being "sprinkled" (12:24). The blood dripping from Jesus' bodily wounds has little to do with this (although God can use even wicked people to accomplish his plans; cf. Acts 2:23). These bodily wounds had been caused by evil men. Infinitely harder was what *God* did to him in those three hours of darkness: "*You* lay me in the dust of death" (Ps. 22:15).

7 Darkness

During the three hours of darkness, everything and everybody was silent on Calvary. Wicked humans did not inflict any new wounds upon Jesus. In the obscurity of that darkness, it was now a matter entirely between Jesus, the perfect sin offering, and God, the perfect Judge. Humans finally had to step back. *This* was the moment that God smote and crushed him, and inflicted the wounds upon him by which we are healed. At the end of these dreadful hours, Jesus gave up his blood (that is, his life) as a sacrifice to God. *This* was the moment that Jesus brought about atonement and that the value of his blood (his life) appeared before God in the heavenly sanctuary, and was sprinkled before the throne of God (cf. Lev. 16:14–15). No Roman soldier could have ever added anything to this work of atonement, which was entirely a matter between God and the Man Jesus Christ.

In summary: Jesus had to suffer during his entire life by the hands of wicked people, including the sufferings during his last days and hours on earth. The way he underwent these sufferings was for the glory of God, and was a testimony to humanity. But they were not vicarious and substitutionary or propitiatory. During his entire life, he enjoyed the pleasure and love of the Father, and the approval of a holy and righteous God. This pleasure and this approval were not vicarious and substitutionary or propitiatory either; they were only preparatory. On the cross, during the three hours of darkness, the innocent Jesus was made the perfect sin offering for us, and was smitten by the sword of a holy and righteous God, at the end of which Jesus gave up his human life unto sacrificial death. *These* sufferings were vicarious and substitutionary and propitiatory, and nothing else.

We remember why this conclusion is important for the present study: if we can at all say that the "righteousness of Christ" was imputed to us, this righteousness certainly did not consist of his perfect Torah observance, or of anything that he accomplished during his life on earth. On the contrary, it was the righteousness that he acquired for us during those hours in which he was the perfect sin offering. If we have "become the righteousness of God" (2 Cor. 5:21), it is because of what Jesus accomplished on the cross—not because of what he ever did during his preceding life. This is the unequivocal testimony of Scripture.

Appendix 2
The Idea of Placation in the Doctrine of Propitiation

1 God's Wrath Placated?

IN §5.8.1, I RAISED THE QUESTION concerning God's attitude toward the repentant sinner. Is God angry with him, and is Jesus the One who jumps in between in order to protect us against God's fury? What precisely is the relationship between God's wrath and our redemption? By way of introduction, let us look at the "technical" terms *expiation* and *propitiation*.[1] *Expiation* comes from the Latin verb *expio*, "to expiate," that is, "to cleanse from sin (by means of an atoning sacrifice), set free from guilt, atone, turn away evil effects (of something)." These meanings closely tie in with Hebrew *kpr* and Greek *hilaskomai*. *Expiation* indicates the meaning of a sin offering for guilty humans, whereas *propitiation* rather indicates its meaning for God. The sin offering gives satisfaction to God (*propitiation*) and implies blotting out human guilt (*expiation*): "I, I am he who blots out your transgressions for my own sake, and I will not remember your sins" (Isa. 43:25).

Sometimes, *expiate* has the meaning of placating (the wrath of) god or the gods. This latter meaning ties in closely with *propitiation*, from Latin *pro*, "for," and *peto*, "stretch out

---
1. Cf. Brown (1992, 3:151); Demarest (1997, 180).

(to something), seize, contend, strive." *Propitiation* is related to *propitious*, which is said of God or the gods, and means "graciously, favorably inclined." Hence, the Latin verb *propitio* means "to propitiate, appease, soothe (God or the gods)." Thus, *propitiation* is the act by which God or the gods are brought into a favorable mood; in this sense it is related to *reconciliation*. A common term for this is *placation*, that is, placating (appeasing, hushing, salving, soothing, softening up) God's fury. We still know this notion in expressions like making a conciliatory gesture, or speaking in a conciliatory tone, which aim at bringing an angry person to a calmer, more favorable mood.

Now the point is whether placation also played a role in the work of atonement. Did Jesus' sacrifice cause a certain change in God's mood (what the Germans so nicely call *Umstimmung*)? Did this sacrifice placate, appease, soften, quell his anger? Is this a proper way of describing what Jesus accomplished?[2] And if so, or not, what consequences do our conclusions have for the biblical doctrine of redemption? What is God's attitude toward the sinner, both before the latter's repentance, during his repentance, and after his repentance? What are the consequences for the doctrine of justification?

The Vulgate has clearly chosen the term *propitiatio* and its related forms. Thus, *propitius* ("merciful," lit. "propitiatorily inclined") occurs in Luke 18:13, *propitiatio* ("propitiation") in 1 John 2:2 and 4:10, *repropitio* ("make propitiation") in Hebrews 2:17, and *propitiatorium* ("mercy seat") in Hebrews 9:5; it is *propitiatio* or *propitiatiorium* in Romans 3:25.

2 Enmity between God and Humanity

The idea of propitiation in the sense of placation has deeply penetrated into theology. The latter term comes from Latin *placo*, "to put to rest, calm down," and from there, "to bring in a favorable mood." A good biblical example is what we find in Genesis 32:20, where Jacob wishes to "appease the face" of

---
2. Thus, e.g., Berkouwer (1965, 257–60); Hodges (1955, 45).

furious Esau (ESV margin; from *kpr*, "atone"). Is this what Jesus did: "atone" (appease the face of) the furious God in view of the sinner by means of his sacrifice?

I give here some examples of the theological application of the notion of placation. Thus, John Calvin wrote that God "was the enemy of men until they were restored to favor by the death of Christ (Rom. 5:10); that they were cursed until their iniquity was expiated by the sacrifice of Christ (Gal. 3:10, 13) . . . Christ . . . with his own blood expiated the sins which rendered them hateful to God, by this expiation satisfied and duly propitiated God the Father, by this intercession appeased his anger (Lat. *iram eius fuisse placatam*), on this basis founded peace between God and men, and by this tie secured the Divine benevolence toward them."[3] Thus, also the Canons of Dort (V.7) speak of the "grace of a reconciled God."

Likewise, the marginal note at 1 John 2:2 in the Statenvertaling (the Dutch equivalent of the King James Version) says that Jesus "soothes the wrath of God, and thus reconciles God with human beings." It refers to 2 Corinthians 5:21, although we find there, in verse 20, the very opposite: humans must be reconciled to *God*, not God to humans. The Belgic Confession says (Art. 21): "We believe that Jesus Christ is a high priest forever according to the order of Melchizedek—made such by an oath—and that he presented himself in our name before his Father, to appease his Father's wrath (Lat. *ad iram ipsius . . . placandum*) with full satisfaction."[4] From many traditional Reformed theologians, I choose Louis Berkhof, who wrote: "[T]he atonement was intended to propitiate God and to reconcile Him to the sinner."[5]

This entire presentation begins with various unilateral or exaggerated ideas.[6] In the New Testament, God is *never* an

---

3. *Institutes* 2.16.2.
4. Cf. Van Genderen and Velema (2008, 523).
5. L. Berkhof (1949, 373); also see, e.g., Lekkerkerker (1949, 67–72).
6. Cf. Brunner (1934, 470–71); Korff (1942, II, 180, 193–94); Bolkestein (1945, 95–98); Shelton (2006, 63–74), and references therein.

enemy of humans, but humans are definitely enemies of God (Rom. 5:10; 8:7; Col. 1:21; James 4:4). This is no wordplay; it is of great importance that God is hardly ever described as hostile toward humans.[7] Therefore, the New Testament *never* says that God had to be reconciled with *us* — but it does say that humans have to be reconciled to God (Rom. 5:10; 2 Cor. 5:18-20; Eph. 2:16; Col. 1:20-21). The tremendous consequence is that the New Testament knows nothing of a furious God who had to be placated by a sin offering. Not a trace of such an idea can be found in Scripture, and I hasten to add that this would even be impossible.

The initiative for the propitiatory sacrifice has not proceeded from Christ in an attempt to placate God, but precisely from the loving God himself: "He who did not spare his own Son but gave him up for us all, how will he not also with him graciously give us all things?" (Rom. 8:32). "God so loved the world that he gave his only Son" (John 3:16). God did not rage against the sinners so that Jesus had to jump in between, no, he "made his appeal" to sinners through his servants, who "implore" people "on behalf of Christ, be reconciled to God" (2 Cor. 5:20). Jesus did not need to appease a furious God, but God endeavors to appease furious sinners.

It was not a furious God who had to be reconciled, but a loving God who had to reconcile people "who once were alienated and hostile in mind, doing evil deeds" (Col. 1:21-22): "In this is love, not that we have loved God but that he loved us and sent his Son to be the propitiation for our sins" (1 John 4:10). This is what Johan A. Heyns meant when he spoke, with regard to atonement, of the both *giving* and *receiving* God: he *gave* his Son for sinners, he *received* satisfaction in regard to sin.[8] There was no question of a raging God who had to be placated, but of humans raging in their sins (cf. Ps. 2:1). Therefore, Reformed theologian Johan Verkuyl wrote perfectly correctly: "God was not moved to love by the drama

---

7. One exceptional statement is: "[Y]ou [i.e., God] hate all evildoers" (Ps. 5:5).
8. Heyns (1988, 284–85).

of Calvary, but the drama of Calvary is the deepest utterance of God's love."[9]

It is good that other theologians have implicitly contradicted such statements as the one by Calvin. It is all the more astonishing that Reformed writer Cornelis van der Waal wrote: "The Reformed confession has never stated that the Judge of heaven and earth had to be moved to another, gentle mood toward guilty, sinful humans through the bitter suffering and death of the Lord Jesus Christ on the cross."[10] The facts show differently.

3 No Placation

We may (rightly) have a lot of criticism with respect to the atonement doctrine of, for instance, Dutch theologians Herman Wiersinga and Bert Ter Schegget, but in their rejection of the placation idea they were perfectly correct.[11] Thus, the latter wrote: "Reconciliation is not that humans through religion bring God in a favorable mood. God is himself the One who comes to us and reconciles the world. It is the world that has to be renewed, not he is."[12] And a bit later: "God (subject!) is busy reconciling the world to himself [2 Cor. 5:19]. The fact that God remains subject of his reconciliation, that he is from eternity the One loving humanity, is the unrelinquishable freedom of his subjectivity. It is not the other way around: we are not busy 'reconciling' God, changing God's mood, pleasing God, getting God on our side, making God different."[13]

The New Testament does not contain the idea that Jesus has placated the wrath of God, even less the wrath of the Father. It does speak of the "wrath" of God, but this concerns rather the irreconcilable wicked ones, who consistently manifest themselves as enemies of God: "You brood of vipers!

---
9. Verkuyl (1992, 242).
10. Van der Waal (1973, 69).
11. Wiersinga (1971, 1972); Ter Schegget (1999); also see Brümmer (2005, 131–39).
12. Ter Schegget (1999, 7).
13. Ibid., 63.

Who warned you to flee from the wrath to come?" (Matt. 3:7; cf. Luke 3:7) "[W]hoever does not obey the Son shall not see life, but the wrath of God remains on him" (John 3:36). "For the wrath of God is revealed from heaven against all ungodliness and unrighteousness of men" (Rom. 1:18; cf. 2:5, 8; 3:5; 5:9; 9:22; Eph. 2:3; 5:6; Col. 3:6; 1 Thess. 1:10; 2:16; 5:9; Rev. 6:16–17; 11:18; 14:10; 16:19; 19:15). Jesus underwent vicariously the consequences of this wrath, namely, the punishment for our sins. But it is said nowhere that Jesus' sacrifice was necessary to placate (propitiate, appease, hush, salve, soothe, soften, calm down) God with respect to sinners. God already *was* in a good mood, for it was he who personally sacrificed Jesus as the sin offering.

Some[14] have tried to read the idea of placation into 1 John 2:1–2: "My little children, I am writing these things to you so that you may not sin. But if anyone does sin, we have an advocate with the Father, Jesus Christ the righteous. He is the propitiation for our sins, and not for ours only but also for the sins of the whole [or rather, for the whole] world." However, this is quite a strange argument because the passage does not refer at all to the propitiator who placates God's anger with respect to wicked sinners, but to the advocate who is with the Father in favor of God's beloved children.[15]

The whole matter is closely linked with the difference between propitiation and reconciliation. *Propitiation* is that aspect of Christ's work that is *toward God*, to put away sin by undergoing the divine judgment over it in his own person. *Reconciliation* is the aspect of Christ's work that is *toward humans*, to bring us back to God in Christ. These two aspects are equally important. If they are confused, misunderstandings arise, like suggesting that reconciliation implies placating God, as if God has to be reconciled with humans. We have to stay far away from the idea that the work of Christ would im-

---

14. Morris (1965, chapters 5–6); Hill (1967, chapter 2).
15. *Contra* Marshall (1978, 118–19), who does express himself in careful terms, though.

ply changing God from a furious Judge into a loving Father.[16]

4 Propitiation and the Wrath of God

The placation idea goes way beyond the New Testament. Yet, the propitiation idea cannot be entirely severed from the wrath of God.[17] Opinions are divided as to exactly how this relationship must be understood. Some have argued that God is not propitiated, but sin is; God must not be soothed—on the contrary, God is himself the One who furnishes the sacrifice—but sin has to be removed from before him.[18] Colin Brown has extensively dealt with the criticisms involving the notion of propitiation and the preference for the notion of expiation, referring to authors like Gustav F. Oehler, Gerhard von Rad, and Johannes Herrmann for the Old Testament, and to Charles H. Dodd and Leon Morris for the New Testament.[19] He concluded: "[I]t is clear that the authors of the Heb. OT and the LXX translators are far removed from the crude pagan idea of propitiating a capricious and malevolent deity."[20]

This is correct as far as placation is concerned; yet, we must distinguish between soothing a raging deity and bringing a holy God into a state of benevolence toward the sinner. The verb *(ex)hilaskomai* may definitely point to "propitiating God," even if this is only three times in the Septuagint: in Zechariah 7:2 ("to entreat the favor of the LORD," lit. "to soothe the face of the LORD"); 8:22 (idem); Malachi 1:9 ("entreat the favor of God," lit. "soothe the face of God"). However, these are only three cases out of many where the meaning is different. Charles Dodd therefore treats them as exceptions.[21] Moreover, there is no parallel for such a "propitiating" the Godhead in the New Testament, though it is true that Philo,

---

16. Kelly (1927, 24).
17. Cf. Berkouwer (1965, 258–61).
18. Westcott (1883, 85–87); Dodd (1935, 82–95); Verkuyl (1992, 241).
19. Brown (1992, III, 151–60).
20. Ibid., 157.
21. Dodd (1935, 86–87).

Josephus, and the Apostolic Fathers always use *hilaskomai* in the sense of "to propitiate."

Perhaps Charles Barrett has the right balance here.[22] He pointed out that expiation has, as it were, the effect of propitiation: the sin that could have aroused the wrath of God has been expiated (according to God's will), and thus no longer has this effect. Millard Erickson pointed to a passage such as Romans 3:25–26 ("God put [Christ] forward as a propitiation by his blood, to be received by faith. This was to show God's righteousness, because in his divine forbearance he had passed over former sins. It was to show his righteousness at the present time, so that he might be just and the justifier of the one who has faith in Jesus"), where the notion of propitiation does seem to loom in the background.[23] That is, in the past, God had left sins unpunished. It was conceivable that he could be accused of conniving at sin since he had not required punishment for it. Now, however, he had put Jesus forward as a *hilastērion*. This proves both that God is righteous (his wrath demanded the sacrifice), and that he is the justifier of those who have faith in Jesus (his love provided the sacrifice for them).

Perhaps John Murray has expressed all this in the most precise way.[24] He compared two related statements, the one being that the angry God through Jesus' sacrifice has been brought to an attitude of love. That would be a very wrong allegation. The other statement would be that the angry God is the one who loves. That would be perfectly true. I add to this that the propitiation that Jesus brought about did not soothe a raging God. It is no placation, and this word can therefore better be avoided. What propitiation did accomplish was that God prepared a way in which both his wrath over sins as well as his love toward sinners found perfect satisfaction. Or, to put it in more precise terms—for one cannot deny that God's

---

22. Barrett (1957, 78).
23. Erickson (1998, 829).
24. Murray (1955, 31).

wrath also pertained to the *sinners* (John 3:36; Rom. 2:8; 9:22; Eph. 5:6; Col. 3:6; 1 Thess. 1:10; 5:9; Rev. 6:16; 14:10) — Christ's work of propitiation gave satisfaction to both God's wrath toward sinners and his love toward them.

Bibliography

Aalders, W. J. 1931. *Binnen zijn lichtkring: Roeping, heiliging, handeling, spanning, menschenkennis, geleide.* Amsterdam: H. J. Paris.

Adamson, J. 1976. *The Epistle of James.* NICNT. Grand Rapids, MI: Eerdmans.

Adeyemo, T. (gen. ed.) 2006. *Africa Bible Commentary: A One-Volume Commentary.* Grand Rapids, MI: Zondervan.

Adorno, T. W. et al. 1950. *The Authoritarian Personality.* New York: Harper.

Allen, R. O. and B. Spilka. 1973."Committed and consensual religion: A specification of religion-prejudice relationships." In *Psychology and Religion*, ed. by L. B. Brown, 58–80. Harmondsworth: Penguin Books.

Althaus, P. 1938 (1963). *Paulus und Luther über den Menschen: Ein Vergleich.* 4th ed. Gütersloh: Mohn.

_____. 1952. *Die christliche Wahrheit: Lehrbuch der Dogmatik.* Gütersloh: Bertelsmann.

Anderson Scott, C. A. 1927. *Christianity According to St. Paul.* 3rd ed. Cambridge: Cambridge University Press.

Andrew, Brother and William S. DeVore. 2012. *And God Changed His Mind . . . Because His People Dared To Ask.* Harderwijk: Open Doors International.

Aune, D. E. 2006. *Rereading Paul Together: Protestant and Catholic Perspectives on Justification.* Grand Rapids, MI: Baker Academic.

Barclay, W. 1975 (rev. ed.). *The Gospel of John*, 2 vols. Edinburgh: Saint Andrew Press.

Barker, G.W. 1981. *1, 2, 3 John.* EBC 12. Grand Rapids, MI: Zondervan.

Barnett, P. 1997. *The Second Epistle to the Corinthians.* NICNT. Grand Rapids, MI: Eerdmans.

Barrett, C. K. 1957. *A Commentary on the Epistle to the Romans.* Black's New Testament Comm. New York: Harper and Row.

Barth, K. 1933. *The Epistle to the Romans.* Trans. by E. C. Hoskyns. Oxford: Oxford University Press.

_____. 1927. *Die Christliche Dogmatik im Entwurf.* Vol. 6. München: Kaiser.

_____. 1956: *Church Dogmatics.* Trans. by T. H. L. Parker et al. Vols. 1/1–4/1. Louisville, KY: Westminster John Knox.

_____. 1935. *Evangelium und Gesetz*, now in: 1998. *Rechtfertigung und Recht. Christengemeinde und Bürgergemeinde. Evangelium und Gesetz.* Zürich: Theologischer Verlag Zürich.

_____. 2008. *De brief aan de Romeinen.* Amsterdam: Boom (orig. ed. see above).

Bauer, W. et al. 2000. *A Greek-English Lexicon of the New Testament and Other Early Christian Literature.* 3rd ed. Chicago: University of Chicago Press.

Bavinck, H. 1980. *The Certainty of Faith.* St. Catharines, ON: Paideia Press.

Bavinck, H. 2002–2008. *Reformed Dogmatics.* Edited by J. Bolt. Translated by J. Vriend. 4 vols. Grand Rapids, MI: Baker Book House.

Beker, J.C. 1980. *Paul the Apostle: The Triumph of God in Life and Thought.* Philadelphia: Fortress Press.

Berger, K. 2004. *Jesus.* München: Pattloch.

Berkhof, H. 1979. *Christian Faith: An Introduction to the Study of the Faith.* Trans. by S. Woudstra. Grand Rapids, MI: Eerdmans.

Berkhof, L. 1949. *Systematic Theology.* 4th ed. Grand Rapids, MI: Eerdmans.

Berkouwer, G. C. 1952. *Faith and Sanctification.* Trans. by J. Vriend. Studies in Dogmatics. Grand Rapids, MI: Eerdmans.

_____. 1954. *Faith and Justification.* Trans. by L. B. Smedes. Studies in Dogmatics. Grand Rapids, MI: Eerdmans.

_____. 1958. *Faith and Perseverance.* Trans. by R. D. Knudsen. Studies in Dogmatics. Grand Rapids, MI: Eerdmans.

_____. 1965. *The Work of Christ.* Trans. by C. Lambregtse. Studies in Dogmatics. Grand Rapids, MI: Eerdmans.

Bernard, J. H. 1979. *The Second Epistle to the Corinthians.* EGT 3. Grand Rapids, MI: Eerdmans.

Beutel, A., K. Bornkamm, G. Ebeling, R. Schwarz, and J. Wallmann, J. 1998. "No Consensus on the 'Joint Declaration on the Doctrine of Justification': A Critical Evaluation by Professors of Protestant Theology." *Lutheran Quarterly* 12/2:193–196.

Blaauwendraad, J. 1997. *Het is ingewikkeld geworden: Pleidooi voor gewoon gereformeerd.* Heerenveen: Groen.

Bloesch, D. G. 1997. *Jesus Christ: Saviour and Lord.* Carlisle: Paternoster.

Blum, E. A. 1981. *1, 2 Peter, Jude.* EBC 12. Grand Rapids, MI: Zondervan.

Boardman, W. E. 1858. *The Higher Christian Life.* Boston: Henry Hoyt (repr. 2007. Stockton, CA: CLC Ministries).

Boice, J. M. 1986. *Christ's Call to Discipleship.* Chicago: Moody.

Bolkestein, M. H. 1945. *De verzoening.* Nijkerk: Callenbach.

Bonhoeffer, D. 1966. *The Cost of Discipleship.* New York: Macmillan.

_____. 2009. *Letters and Papers from Prison*. Trans. by C. Gremmels et al. Dietrich Bonhoeffer Works. Vol. 8. Minneapolis: Fortress Press.

Bouma, C. 1927. *Het evangelie naar Johannes*. KV. Kampen: Kok.

_____. 1937. *De brieven van den apostel Paulus aan Timotheus en Titus*. KV. Kampen: Kok.

Boyd, G. A. 2000. *God of the Possible: A Biblical Introduction to the Open View of God*. Grand Rapids, MI: Baker.

Braaten, C. E. 1990. *Justification: The Article by Which the Church Stands or Falls*. Minneapolis, MN: Fortress Press.

Brinkman, J. 1916. *De "gerechtigheid Gods" bij Paulus*. Rotterdam: T. De Vries.

Brinkman, M.E. 1996. *Justification in Ecumenical Dialogue: Central Aspects of Christian Soteriology in Debate*. Utrecht: Interuniversity Institute for Missiology and Ecumenical Research.

Brockhaus, R. n.d. *Meer dan overwinnaars: De brief aan de Romeinen*. Den Haag: J.N. Voorhoeve.

Brown, C. 1967. *Karl Barth and the Christian Message*. London: Tyndale Press.

_____, ed. (1976) 1992. *The New International Dictionary of New Testament Theology*. 4 vols. Carlisle: Paternoster.

Bruce, A. B. 1979. *The Synoptic Gospels*. EGT 1. Grand Rapids, MI: Eerdmans.

Bruce, F. F. 1982. *1 and 2 Thessalonians*. Word Biblical Commentary. Waco, TX: Word Books.

_____. 1984. *The Epistles to the Colossians, to Philemon, and to the Ephesians*. NICNT. Grand Rapids, MI: Eerdmans.

Brümmer, V. 2005. *Ultiem geluk: Een nieuwe kijk op Jezus, verzoening en Drie-eenheid*. Kampen: Kok.

Brunner, E. 1923. *Erlebnis, Erkenntnis und Glaube*. Tübingen: Mohr (Siebeck).

_____. 1934 (repr. 2003). *The Mediator: A Study of the Central Doctrine of the Christian Faith*. Trans. by O. Wyon. Cambridge: Lutterworth Press.

———. 1937. *The Divine Imperative*. Cambridge: Lutterworth Press.

———. 1949. *The Christian Doctrine of God*. Trans. by O. Wyon. Dogmatics. Vol. 1. Cambridge: Lutterworth Press.

Buber, M. (1965) 2006. *Chassidische vertellingen*. Utrecht: Servire (Eng. ed. 1991: *Tales of the Hasidim*. New York: Schocken Books).

Budiman, R. 1971. *De realisering der verzoening in het menselijk bestaan: Een onderzoek naar Paulus' opvatting van de gemeenschap van Christus' lijden als een integrerend deel der verzoening*. Delft: Meinema.

Burdick, D. W. 1981. *James*. EBC 12. Grand Rapids, MI: Zondervan.

Buri, F. 1956. *Dogmatik als Selbstverständnis des christlichen Glaubens*, 1. Tl.: *Vernunft und Offenbarung*. Bern: Paul Haupt / Tübingen: Katzmann-Verlag.

Calvin, J. 1960. *The Institutes of the Christian Religion*. Ed. by John T. McNeill. Trans. by Ford Lewis Battles. The Library of Christian Classics. Vol. 20. Philadelphia: Westminster Press.

———. 1973 (repr.). *The Epistles of Paul The Apostle to the Romans and to the Thessalonians*. Ed. by D. W. Torrance and T. F. Torrance. Trans. by R. Mackenzie. Grand Rapids: Eerdmans.

Carson, D. A. 1982. *The Sermon on the Mount: An Evangelical Exposition of Matthew 5–7*. Ada, MI: Baker Publishing Group.

———. 1984. *Matthew*. EBC 8. Grand Rapids, MI: Zondervan.

———, P. T. O'Brien, and M. A. Seifrid, eds. 2001. *The Complexities of Second Temple Judaism. Justification and Variegated Nomism*. Vol. 1. Grand Rapids, MI: Baker Academic.

_____, P. T. O'Brien, and M. A. Seifrid, eds. 2004. *The Paradoxes of Paul*. Justification and Variegated Nomism. Vol. 2. Grand Rapids, MI: Baker Academic.

Chafer, L. S. 1983. *Systematic Theology*. 15th ed. 8 vols. Dallas: Dallas Seminary Press.

Coates, C. A. [1926]. *An Outline of the Epistle to the Romans*. Newport: Stow Hill Bible Depot/London: G. Morrish.

_____. 1996. *Corinthians to Colossians*. Miscellaneous Ministry on the New Testament. Vol. 32. Lancing: Kingston Bible Trust.

_____. n.d.-a. *An Outline of the Book of Genesis*. Kingston-on-Thames: Stow Hill Bible and Tract Depot.

_____. n.d.-b. *Spiritual Blessings*. Kingston-on-Thames: Stow Hill Bible and Tract Depot.

Cohen, A., ed. 1983 (repr.). *The Soncino Chumash*. The Soncino Books of the Bible. London etc.: Soncino.

Congar, Y. 1997. *I Believe in the Holy Spirit*. 3 vols. New York: Crossroad Herder.

Cranfield, C. E. B. 1975/79. *The Epistle to the Romans*. 2 vols. ICC. Edinburgh: Clark.

Cremer, H. (1897) 1917. *Die christliche Lehre von den Eigenschaften Gottes*. 2nd ed. Gütersloh: Bertelsmann.

Darby, J. N. n.d.-a. *The Collected Writings of J. N. Darby*. Kingston-on-Thames: Stow Hill Bible and Tract Depot.

_____. n.d.-b.. *Synopsis of the Bible*. London: Morrish, repr. New York: Loizeaux.

Das, A. A. 2001. *Paul, the Law, and the Covenant*. Peabody, MA: Hendrickson.

Davids, P. H. 1990. *The First Epistle of Peter*. NICNT. Grand Rapids, MI: Eerdmans.

Davies, W. D. 1962. *Paul and Rabbinic Judaism: Some Rabbinic Elements in Pauline Theology*. London: SPCK.

_____. 1984. *Jewish and Pauline Studies*. Philadelphia: Fortress Press.

Dawkins, R. 2006. *The God Delusion.* Boston: Houghton Mifflin.

De Boer, W. 2010. *God's Twofold Love: The Theology of Jacob Arminius (1559–1609).* Göttingen: Vandenhoeck and Ruprecht.

De Chirico, L. 2003. *Evangelical Theological Perspectives on Post-Vatican II Roman Catholicism.* Bern: Peter Lang.

De Groot, D. J. 1952. *De wedergeboorte.* Kampen: Kok.

Demarest, B. 1997. *The Cross and Salvation: The Doctrine of Salvation.* Wheaton, IL: Crossway Books.

Denney, J. 1979. *St. Paul's Epistle to the Romans.* EGT 2. Grand Rapids, MI: Eerdmans.

Dennison, J. T., ed. 2008–14. *Reformed Confessions of the 16th and 17th Centuries in English Translation.* 4 vols. Grand Rapids: Reformation Heritage Books.

De Reuver, A. 1992. *'Bedelen bij de bron': Kohlbrugge's geloofsopvatting vergeleken met Reformatie en Nadere Reformatie.* Zoetermeer: Boekencentrum.

De Ru, G. 1966. *De rechtvaardiging bij Augustinus, vergeleken met de leer der iustificatio bij Luther en Calvijn.* Wageningen: Veenman.

DeSilva, D. A. 2000. *Honor, Patronage, Kinship and Purity: Unlocking New Testament Culture.* Downers Grove, IL: IVP Academic.

Diestel, L. 1859. "Über die Heiligkeit Gottes." *Jahrbücher für deutsche Theologie* 1859:3–62.

Dittes, J. E. 1969. "Psychology of religion." In: Lindzey, G. and E. Aronson, eds. *Handbook of Social Psychology.* Reading, Mass.: Addison-Wesley. 5: 602–45.

Dodd, C. H. 1932. *The Epistle to the Romans.* Moffatt New Testament Commentary. New York/London: Harper and Brothers.

———. 1935. *The Bible and the Greeks.* London: Hodder and Stoughton.

_____. 1946. *The Johannine Epistles*. Moffatt New Testament Commentary. London: Hodder and Stoughton.

Dods, M. 1979. *The Gospel of John*. EGT 1. Grand Rapids, MI: Eerdmans.

Duffield, G. P. and N. M. Van Cleave. 1996. *Woord en Geest: Hoofdlijnen van de theologie van de Pinksterbeweging*. Kampen: Kok/Rafaël Nederland (Eng.ed. 1987, 2008. *Foundations of Pentecostal Theology*. Lake Mary, FL: Creation House).

Dunn, J .D. G. 1983. "The New Perspective on Paul." *Bulletin of the John Rylands University Library of Manchester* Manchester 65.2:95–122.

_____. 1990. *Jesus, Paul, and the Law: Studies in Mark and Galatians*. Louisville, KY: Westminster.

_____, ed. 1996. *Paul and the Mosaic Law*. Tübingen: Mohr (Siebeck).

_____. 1998. *The Theology of Paul the Apostle*. Edinburgh: T.&T. Clark.

_____ and A. M. Suggate. 1993. *The Justice of God: A Fresh Look At the Old Doctrine of Justification By Faith*. Carlisle: Paternoster Press.

Ebert, K., ed. 1990. *Thomas Müntzer im Urteil der Geschichte: Von Martin Luther bis Ernst Bloch*. Wuppertal: Hammer, 1990.

Edwards, J. (1773) 2003. *A History of the Work of Redemption*. Edinburgh: Banner of Truth Trust.

Eichrodt, W. 1961. *Theology of the Old Testament*. Trans. by J. A. Baker. Philadelphia, PA: Westminster Press.

Elam, A. E., R. C. Van Kooten, and R. A. Bergquist. 2014. *Merit and Moses: A Critique of the Klinean Doctrine of Republication*. Eugene, OR: Wipf and Stock.

Ellis, E. E. 1957. *Paul's Use of the Old Testament*. Edinburgh: Oliver and Boyd.

Erickson, M. J. 1998 (rev. ed.). *Christian Theology*. Grand Rapids, MI: Baker Book House.

Erskine, E. (1730) 2010. *The Assurance of Faith Opened and Applied*. Gale ECCO.

Feiner, J. and M. Löhrer, eds. 1973. *Mysterium Salutis: Grundriss heilsgeschichtlicher Theologie*, Bd. IV. Einsiedeln: Benziger.

_____ and L. Vischer, eds. 1973. *Neues Glaubensgut: Der gemeinsame christliche Glaube*. Freuburg: Herder.

Finsterbusch, K. 1996. *Die Thora als Lebensweisung für Heidenchristen: Studien zur Bedeutung der Thora für die paulinische Ethik*. Göttingen: Vandenhoeck and Ruprecht.

Flusser, D. 1988. *Judaism and the Origins of Christianity*. Jerusalem: Magness Press.

_____. 1998. *Jesus*. Jerusalem: Hebrew University Magnes Press.

Forsyth, P. T. (1909) 1948a. *The Cruciality of the Cross*. London: Independent Press.

_____. (1910) 1948b. *The Work of Christ*. London: Independent Press.

France, R. T. 2007. *The Gospel of Matthew*. NICNT. Grand Rapids, MI: Eerdmans.

Friesen, A. 1990. *Thomas Müntzer, a Destroyer of the Godless: The Making of a Sixteenth-Century Religious Revolutionary*. Berkeley: University of California Press.

Gaebelein, A .C. 1910. *The Gospel of Matthew*, 2 vols. Wheaton, IL: Van Kampen Press.

_____. 1970. *Romans*. In: *The Annotated Bible*. Vol. 3: *Matthew to Ephesians*. Neptune, NJ: Loizeaux.

_____. 1965. *The Gospel of John*. New York: Loizeaux.

Galling, K., ed. 1986 (repr.). *Die Religion in Geschichte und Gegenwart*. 6 vols. Tübingen: Mohr (Siebeck).

Gaston, L. 1987. *Paul and the Torah*. Vancouver: University of British Columbia Press.

Glock, C. Y. 1965. "On the study of religious commitment." In *Religion and Society in Tension*. Edited by C. Y Glock and R.

Stark. 18–38. Chicago: Rand McNally.

Godet, F. (1883) 1998. *Commentary on Romans.* Grand Rapids, MI: Kregel.

Goertz, H.-J. 1993. *Thomas Müntzer: Apocalyptic Mystic and Revolutionary.* Edinburgh: T.&T. Clark.

González, A. 2005. *The Gospel of Faith and Justice.* Maryknoll, NY: Orbis Books.

Graafland, C. 1961. *De zekerheid van het geloof: Een onderzoek naar de geloofsbeschouwing van enige vertegenwoordigers van Reformatie en Nadere Reformatie.* Amsterdam: Bolland.

Grant, F. W. 1890. *The Numerical Bible: The Pentateuch.* New York: Loizeaux.

―――. 1897. *The Numerical Bible: Matthew to John.* New York: Loizeaux.

―――. 1901. *The Numerical Bible: Acts to II Corinthians.* New York: Loizeaux.

―――. 1902. *The Numerical Bible: Hebrews to Revelation.* New York: Loizeaux.

Gravemeijer, H. E. 1892–1894. *Leesboek over de gereformeerde geloofsleer.* 3 vols. Groningen: R. Boersma.

Green, J. B. 1997. *The Gospel of Luke.* NICNT. Grand Rapids, MI: Eerdmans.

Greijdanus, S. 1931. *De eerste/tweede brief van den apostel Petrus.* KV. Kampen: Kok.

―――. 1933 (repr. 1983). *De brief van den Apostel Paulus aan de gemeente te Rome.* 2 vols. CNT. Amsterdam: Van Bottenburg.

Griffith Thomas, W.H. 1946. *St. Paul's Epistle to the Romans.* Grand Rapids, MI: Eerdmans.

Grosheide, F.W. 1959. *De tweede brief van Paulus aan de kerk te Korinthe.* CNT. Kampen: Kok.

―――. 1960. *De brief van Paulus aan de Efeziërs.* CNT. Kampen: Kok.

Gundry, S. N: ed. 1987. *Five Views on Sanctification.* Grand

Rapids, MI: Zondervan.

Haitjema, Th. L. 1926. *Karl Barth.* Wageningen: Veenman.

Haldane, R. (1764) 1958. *Romans.* Geneva Series of Commentaries. London: Banner of Truth.

Han, Cheon-Seol 1995. *Raised for Our Justification: An Investigation on the Significance of the Resurrection of Christ Within the Theological Structure of Paul's Message.* Kampen: Kok.

Harinck, C. 2001. *De toeleidende weg tot Christus.* Heerenveen: Groen.

_____. 2007. *De rechtvaardigmaking.* Houten: Den Hertog.

Häring, Th. 1896. *Dikaiosynè theou bei Paulus.* Tübingen: Mohr (Siebeck).

Harris, M. J. 1976. *2 Corinthians.* EBC 10. Grand Rapids, MI: Zondervan.

Harrison, E. F. 1976. *Romans.* EBC 10. Grand Rapids, MI: Zondervan.

Heyns, J. A. 1988. *Dogmatiek.* Pretoria: NG Kerkboekhandel.

Hinrichs, C. 1952. *Luther und Müntzer: Ihre Auseinandersetzung **über** Obrigkeit und Widerstandsrecht.* Berlin: De Gruyter.

Hodge, C. A. (1864) 1972. *A Commentary on Romans.* London: Banner of Truth.

Hodges, H. A. 1955. *The Pattern of Atonement.* London: SCM.

Hodges, Z. C. 1989. *Absolutely Free!* Dallas: Redencion Viva.

Hoekema, A. A. 1989. *Saved by Grace.* Grand Rapids, MI: Eerdmans.

Holl, K. 2002. *Luther.* In: *Lexikon der theologischen Werke. Gesammelte Aufsätze zur Kirchengeschichte.* Vol. 1. Edited by M. Eckert, E. Herms, B.-J. Hilberath, E. and Jüngel. Stuttgart: Kröner.

Horton, M. ed. 1992. *Christ the Lord: The Reformation and Lordship Salvation.* Grand Rapids, MI: Baker.

Hübner, H. 1984. *Law in Paul's Thought.* Edinburgh: T.&T. Clark.

Hughes, P. E. 1962. *Paul's Second Epistle to the Corinthians.* NICNT. Grand Rapids, MI: Eerdmans.

Hultgren, A. 1985. *Paul's Gospel and Mission: The Outlook from His Letter to the Romans.* Philadelphia: Fortress.

Hunter, A. M. 1966. *The Gospel According to St. Paul.* Philadelphia: Westminster Press.

Husbands, M. and D. J. Treier, eds. 2004. *Justification: What's at Stake in the Current Debates.* Downers Grove, IL: InterVarsity Press.

_____ and _____, eds. 2005. *The Community of the Word: Toward an Evangelical Ecclesiology.* Downers Grove, IL: InterVarsity Press/Leicester: Apollos.

Jager, H. J. 1939. *Rechtvaardiging en zekerheid des geloofs.* Utrecht: Kemink.

Johnson, T. L. 2000. *When Grace Comes Home.* Fearn, Tain: Christian Focus Publications.

Jüngel, E. 2001. *Justification: The Heart of the Christian Faith.* Edinburgh: T.&T. Clark.

Käsemann, E. 1996. *Commentary on Romans.* Grand Rapids, MI: Eerdmans.

Keck, L. E. 1979. *Paul and His Letters.* Philadelphia: Fortress Press.

Kelly, W. 1898 (repr. 1966). *An Exposition of the Gospel of John.* London: C. A. Hammond.

_____. 1905 (repr. 1970). *An Exposition of the Epistles of John the Apostle.* Winschoten: H. L. Heijkoop.

_____. 1923. *The Epistles of Peter.* London: C. A. Hammond.

_____. 1927. *Selected Passages from the Writings of the Late William Kelly.* Ed. by W. J. Hocking. London: C. A. Hammond.

_____, ed. 1856-1920. *The Bible Treasury,* magazine for Bible study. Repr. Winschoten: H. L. Heijkoop.

Kennedy, H. A. A. 1979. *The Epistle of Paul to the Philippians.* EGT 3. Grand Rapids, MI: Eerdmans.

Kent Jr., H. A. 1978. *Philippians.* EBC 11. Grand Rapids, MI: Zondervan.

Kersten, G. H. 1980-1983. *Reformed Dogmatics: A Systematic Treatment of Reformed Doctrine,* Trans. by J. R. Beeke and J. C. Westrate. 2 vols. Grand Rapids: Eerdmans.

Kertelge, K. 1967. *"Rechtfertigung" bei Paulus: Studien zur Struktur und zum Bedeutungsgehalt der paulinischen Rechtfertigungslehre.* Münster: Aschendorff.

Kittel, G. et al., eds. 1964-1976. *Theological Dictionary of the New Testament.* Translated by G. W. Bromiley. 10 vols. Grand Rapids, MI: Eerdmans.

Klinghardt, M. 1988. *Gesetz und Volk Gottes.* Tübingen: J. C. B. Mohr.

Kohlbrugge, H. F. (1833) 2009. *Romans 7: A Paraphrase, and "I Believe in the Holy Spirit."* N.p.: By Faith Alone Publishing.

König, A. 2006. *Die Groot Geloofswoordeboek.* Vereeniging: Christelike Uitgewersmaatskappy.

Korff, F. W. A. 1942. *Christologie: De leer van het komen Gods.* 2 vols. Nijkerk: Callenbach.

Kraan K. J. 1974 . *"Opdat u genezing ontvangt": Handboek voor de dienst der genezing.* 3rd ed. Hoornaar: Gideon.

Kühl, E. 1913. *Der Brief des Paulus an die Römer.* Leipzig: Quelle and Meyer.

Kümmel, W.G. 1929. *Römer 7 und die Bekehrung des Paulus.* Leipzig: J. C. Hinrich.

Küng, H. 2004. *Justification: The Doctrine of Karl Barth and a Catholic Reflection.* Louisville, KY: Westminster John Knox Press.

Kuyper, A. 1873. *Uit het Woord: Stichtelijke Bijbelstudiën,* Eerste Serie, Eerste Bundel: "Heiligen." Amsterdam: J. H. Kruyt.

Lalleman, P. J. 2005. *1, 2 en 3 Johannes: Brieven van een kroongetuige.* CNT III. Kampen: Kok.

Lane, A. N. S. 2002. *Justification by Faith in Catholic-Protestant Dialogue: An Evangelical Assessment.* London: T.&T. Clark.

Lapide, P. 1979 (2003). *Der Jude Jesus*. 3rd ed. Düsseldorf: Patmos.

———. 1980 (2004). *Er predigte in ihren Synagogen*. 8th ed. Gütersloh: Mohn.

———. 1982. *Mit einem Juden die Bibel lesen*. Stuttgart: Calwer; 2011 ed.: Berlin etc.: LIT Verlag.

———. 1988. *Ist das nicht Josephs Sohn? Jesus im heutigen Judentum*. Gütersloh: Mohn.

——— and Stuhlmacher, P. 1984. *Paul, Rabbi and Apostle*. Trans. by L. W. Denef. Minneapolis, MN: Augsburg Publishing House.

Law, R. 1914. *The Tests of Life: A Study of the First Epistle of St. John*. Edinburgh: T.&T. Clark.

Lehrmann, S. M. 1980 (repr.). *The Twelve Prophets*. The Soncino Books of the Bible. London etc.: Soncino.

Lekkerkerker, A. F. N. 1947. *Studiën over de rechtvaardiging bij Augustinus*. Amsterdam: H. J. Paris.

———. 1949. *Gesprek over de verzoening*. Amsterdam: Holland.

Liebers, R. 1989. *Das Gesetz als Evangelium: Untersuchungen zur Gesetzeskritik des Paulus*. Zürich: Theologischer Verlag.

Lightfoot, J. B. 1895. *Notes on the Epistles of St. Paul*. London: Macmillan.

Locher, J. C. S. 1903. *De leer van Luther over Gods woord*. Amsterdam: Scheffer and Co.

Longenecker, R. N. 1981. *The Acts of the Apostles*. EBC 9. Grand Rapids, MI: Zondervan.

Luther, M. 1943. *Works of Martin Luther*, Vol. 6. Philadelphia, PA: Muhlenberg Press.

———. 1957. *Luther's Works*. Philadelphia: Fortress/St. Louis: Concordia.

MacArthur, J. F. (1988) 1994. *The Gospel According to Jesus*. Grand Rapids, MI: Zondervan.

McConnachie, J. 1931. *The Significance of Karl Barth*. London: Hodder and Stoughton.

McCormack, B. L., ed. 2006. *Justification in Perspective: Historical Developments and Contemporary Challenges*. Grand Rapids, MI: Baker Academic.

McGrath, A. E. 2005. *Iustitia Dei: A History of the Christian Doctrine of Justification*. 3rd ed. Cambridge: Cambridge University Press.

_____. 2010. *Christian Theology: An Introduction*. 5th ed. New York: Wiley-Blackwell.

Macquarrie, J. 1966. *Principles of Christian Theology*. London: SCM.

Manson, W. 1967. *Jesus and the Christian*. Grand Rapids, MI: Eerdmans.

Marshall, I. H. 1969. *Kept by the Power of God: A Study of Perseverance and Falling Away*. Minneapolis: Bethany Fellowship.

_____. 1978. *The Epistles of John*. NICNT. Grand Rapids, MI: Eerdmans.

Martin, B. L. 1989. *Christ and the Law in Paul*. Leiden: Brill.

Medema, H. P. 1985. *Door het geloof rechtvaardig: Bijbelstudies over de brief van Paulus aan de Romeinen*. Vaassen: Medema.

Meijering, E. P. 2004. *Geschiedenis van het vroege Christendom: Van de jood Jezus van Nazareth tot de Romeinse keizer Constantijn*. Amsterdam: Balans.

Meyer, H. A. W. 1876. *Romans*. Edinburgh: T.&T. Clark.

Moerkerken, A. 2004. *Ons troostboek: Verklaring van de Heidelbergse Catechismus*. Houten: Den Hertog.

Moffatt, J. 1979. *The First and Second Epistle to the Thessalonians*. EGT 4. Grand Rapids, MI: Eerdmans.

Moltmann, J. 1993. *The Church in the Power of the Spirit: A Contribution to Messianic Ecclesiology*. Trans. by Margaret Koh. Minneapolis, MN: Fortress Press.

Montefiore, C. G. 1900/01. "Rabbinic Judaism and the Epistles of St. Paul." *Jewish Quarterly Review* 13:161–217.

Montefiore, C. G. 1914. *Judaism and St. Paul: Two Essays.* London: M. Goschen.

Moo, D. J. 1987. "Paul and the Law in the Last Ten Years." *Scottish Journal of Theology* 40:287-307.

_____. 1996. *The Epistle to the Romans.* NICNT. Grand Rapids, MI: Eerdmans.

Moore, G. F. 1921. "Christian Writers on Judaism." *Harvard Theological Review* 14:197-254.

_____. 1927-1930. *Judaism in the First Centuries of the Christian Era: The Age of the Tannaim*, 3 vols. Cambridge, MA: Harvard University Press.

Morris, L. 1955. *The Apostolic Preaching of the Cross.* London: Tyndale Press.

_____. 1959. *The First and Second Epistles to the Thessalonians.* NICNT. Grand Rapids, MI: Eerdmans.

_____. 1971. *The Gospel According to John.* NICNT. Grand Rapids, MI: Eerdmans.

Moule, H. C. G. 1893. *The Epistle of St. Paul to the Romans.* The Expositor's Bible. London: Hodder and Stoughton.

Müller, C. 1964. *Gottes Gerechtigkeit und Gottes Volk: Eine Untersuchung zu Römer 9-11.* Göttingen: Vandenhoeck and Ruprecht.

Murray, J. 1955. *Redemption Accomplished and Applied.* Grand Rapids, MI: Eerdmans.

Murray, J. 1968. *The Epistle to the Romans.* NICNT. Grand Rapids, MI: Eerdmans.

Nee, Watchman. 1997. *The Normal Christian Life.* Carol Stream, IL: Tyndale House Publishers.

Newman, J. H. 1843 (repr. 2006). *Fifteen Sermons Preached before the University of Oxford.* Ed. by J. D. Earnest and G. Tracey. Oxford: Oxford University Press.

Noordtzij, A. 1982. *Leviticus.* Trans. by Raymond Togtman. Bible Student's Commentary. Grand Rapids, MI: Zondervan.

Nygren, A. 1978. *Commentary on Romans.* Trans. by C. C. Rasmussen. Minneapolis, MN: Augsburg Fortress.

Oepke, A. 1953. "Dikaiosyne theou bei Paulus in neuer Beleuchtung." *Theologische Literaturzeitung* 78:257–64.

Ogliari, D. 2003. *Gratia et certamen: The relationship between Grace and Free Will in the Discussion of Augustine with the So-Called Semipelagians.* Leuven: Leuven University Press/ Dudley, MA: Peeters.

Oswalt, J.N. 1998. *The Book of Isaiah, Chapters 40–66.* NICOT. Grand Rapids, MI: Eerdmans.

Otto, R. 1958. *The Idea of the Holy.* Oxford: Oxford University Press.

Ouweneel, W. J. 1981. *Glaube und Werke: Eine Auslegung des Jakobusbriefes.* Schwelm: Heijkoop Verlag.

———. 1982. *"Wij zien Jezus": Bijbelstudies over de brief aan de Hebreeën.* 2 vols. Vaassen: Medema.

———. 1994. *Godsverlichting: De evocatie van de verduisterde God: Een weg tot spiritualiteit en gemeenteopbouw.* Amsterdam: Buijten and Schipperheijn.

———. 1998. *Geestelijke strijd.* Geloofsleven. Vol. 4. Vaassen: Medema.

———. (2003) 2004a. *Geneest de zieken! Over de bijbelse leer van ziekte, genezing en bevrijding.* 4th ed. Vaassen: Medema.

———. 2004b. *Meer Geest in de gemeenten.* Vaassen: Medema.

———. 2007a. *De Geest van God: Ontwerp van een pneumatologie.* Evangelisch Dogmatische Reeks. Vol. 1. Vaassen: Medema.

———. 2007b. *De Christus van God: Ontwerp van een christologie.* Evangelisch Dogmatische Reeks. Vol. 2. Vaassen: Medema.

———. 2008a. *De schepping van God: Ontwerp van een scheppings-, mens- en zondeleer.* Evangelisch Dogmatische Reeks. Vol. 3. Vaassen: Medema.

———. 2008b. *Het plan van God: Ontwerp van een voorbeschikkingsleer*. Evangelisch Dogmatische Reeks. Vol. 4. Vaassen: Medema.

———. 2008c. *Geloof, zekerheid, groei*. Vaassen: Medema.

———. 2009. *Het zoenoffer van God: Ontwerp van een verzoeningsleer*. Evangelisch Dogmatische Reeks. Vol. 5. Vaassen: Medema.

———. 2010a. *Het heil van God: Ontwerp van een soteriologie*. Evangelisch Dogmatische Reeks. Vol. 6. Heerenveen: Medema.

———. 2010b. *De Kerk van God (I): Ontwerp van een elementaire ecclesiologie*. Evangelisch Dogmatische Reeks. Vol. 7. Heerenveen: Medema.

———. 2010c. *De kerk van God (II): Ontwerp van een historische en praktische ecclesiologie*. Evangelisch Dogmatische Reeks. Vol. 8. Heerenveen: Medema.

———. 2011. *Het verbond en het koninkrijk van God: Ontwerp van een verbonds-, doop- en koninkrijksleer*. Evangelisch Dogmatische Reeks. Vol. 9. Heerenveen: Medema.

———. 2012a. *De toekomst van God: Ontwerp van een eschatologie*. Evangelisch Dogmatische Reeks. Vol. 10. Heerenveen: Medema.

———. 2012b. *Het Woord van God: Ontwerp van een openbarings- en schriftleer*. Evangelisch Dogmatische Reeks. Vol. 11. Heerenveen: Medema.

———. 2013a. *De glorie van God: Ontwerp van een godsleer en van een theologische vakfilosofie*. Evangelisch Dogmatische Reeks. Vol. 12. Heerenveen: Medema.

———. 2013b. *Een dubbelsnoer van licht: Honderd grootse joodse en christelijke godsmannen door de geschiedenis heen – en hun moeizame relaties*. Soesterberg: Aspekt.

———. 2014a. *Wisdom for Thinkers: An Introduction to Christian Philosophy*. St. Catharines: Paideia Press.

———. 2014b. *What Then Is Theology? An Introduction to Chris-

tian Theology. St. Catharines: Paideia Press.

———. 2015a. *The Eternal Torah: An Evangelical Theology of Living Under God. An Evangelical Introduction to Reformational Theology*. Vol. 1. St. Catharines: Paideia Press.

———. 2015b. *The Eternal Covenant: An Evangelical Theology of Living With God. An Evangelical Introduction to Reformational Theology*. Vol. 2. St. Catharines: Paideia Press.

———. 2015c. *Searching the Soul: An Introduction to Christian Psychology*. St. Catharines: Paideia Press.

———. n.d. *Het boek Esther*. Alblasserdam: Stg. Boeken bij de Bijbel.

Owen, J. and R. Rushing. 2004. *The Mortification of Sin*. Edinburgh: Banner of Truth Trust.

Packer, J. I. 1961. "Introductory Essay." In *The Doctrine of Justification: An Outline of Its History in the Church and of Its Exposition from Scripture*. James Buchanan. London: Banner of Truth Trust.

———. 1970. *Evangelism and the Sovereignty of God*. Downers Grove, IL: InterVarsity.

———. 1984. "Justification." In *Evangelical Dictionary of Theology*, ed. by W. A. Elwell. Grand Rapids, MI: Baker.

Pannenberg, W. 1971. *Grundfragen systematischer Theologie*. 2nd ed. Göttingen: Vandenhoeck and Ruprecht (Eng. ed. 1970-1971. *Basic Questions in Theology*. Trans. by George H. Kehm. 2 vols. Philadelphia: Westminster Press).

Paul, M. J. 1997. *Vergeving en genezing: Ziekenzalving in de christelijke gemeente*. Zoetermeer: Boekencentrum.

Pawson, D. 1996. *Once Saved, Always Saved?: A Study in Perseverance and Inheritance*. London: Hodder and Stoughton.

Pelikan, J. 1983. *The Christian Tradition: A History of the Development of Doctrine*, Vol. 4: *Reformation of Church and Dogma (1300-1700)*. Chicago: University of Chicago Press.

Philippi, F. A. 1878. *Commentary on St. Paul's Epistle to the Romans*. Edinburgh: T.&T. Clark.

Pinson, J. M., ed. 2002. *Four Views on Eternal Security*. Grand Rapids, MI: Zondervan.

Piper, J. 2007. *The Future of Justification: A Response to N. T. Wright*. Wheaton, IL: Crossway Books.

Plass, E. M., ed. 1959. *What Luther Says: An Anthology*. 3 vols. St. Louis: Concordia.

Pohle, J. and J. Gummersbach. 1952. *Lehrbuch der Dogmatik*, Bd. I. Paderborn: Ferdinand Schöningh.

Polman, A. D. R. 1969. *In de ban der hermeneutiek. Gereformeerde katholieke dogmatiek: Een compendium*. Vol. 1. Kampen: Kok.

Pop, F. J. (1951) 1999. *Bijbelse woorden en hun geheim*. 10th ed. Zoetermeer: Boekencentrum.

Prince, J. 2008. *Bestemd voor overwinning: Leven vanuit de overvloedige genade van God*. Roermond: Dunamis.

Räisänen, H. 1983. *Paul and the Law*. Wissenschaftliche Untersuchungen zum Neuen Testament 29. Tübingen: Mohr (Siebeck).

_____. 1986. *The Torah and Christ: Essays in German and English on the Problem of the Law in Early Christianity*. Publications of the Finnish Exegetical Society 45. Helsinki: Finnish Exegetical Society.

_____. 1992. *Jesus, Paul and Torah: Collected Essays*. Journal for the Study of the New Testament, Supplement Series 43. Sheffield: JSOT Press.

Ratzinger, J. (Benedict XVI). 2008. *Jesus of Nazareth: From the Baptism in the Jordan to the Transfiguration*. Trans. by A. J. Walker. San Francisco: Ignatius Press.

Rice, J. R. (1966) 2000. *The Woman Thou Gavest Me*. Murfreesboro, TN: Sword of the Lord.

Ridderbos, H. 1959. *Aan de Romeinen*. CNT. Kampen: Kok.

_____. 1975. *Paul: An Outline of His Theology*. Grand Rapids, MI: Eerdmans.

Rietkerk, W. G. 2000. *In dubio: Handboek voor twijfelaars.* Apeldoorn: Novapres.

Ritschl, A. 1900. *The Christian Doctrine of Justification and Reconciliation.* Edinburgh: T.&T. Clark.

Robertson, O. P. 1990. *The Books of Nahum, Habakkuk, and Zephaniah.* NICOT. Grand Rapids, MI: Eerdmans.

Rokeach, M. 1969. "Religion, values, and social compassion." *Review of Religious Research* 11:3–39.

Roozemeijer, J. H. L. 1911. *De brief van Paulus aan de Romeinen.* Arnhem: G. W. van der Wiel and Co.

Ryle, J. C. 1877 (expanded 1879). *Holiness: Its Nature, Hindrances, Difficulties and Roots.* London: W. Hunt and Company (repr. 2013). CreateSpace Independent Publishing Platform.

Ryrie, C. C. 1969. *Balancing the Christian Life.* Chicago: Moody.

Salmond, S. D. F. 1979. *The Epistle to the Ephesians.* EGT 3. Grand Rapids, MI: Eerdmans.

Sanday, W. and A. C. Headlam. (1902) 1950. *A Critical and Exegetical Commentary on the Epistle to the Romans.* ICC. Edinburgh: T. and T. Clark.

Sanders, E. P. 1977. *Paul and Palestinian Judaism: A Comparison of Patterns of Religion.* Philadelphia: Fortress Press.

_____. 1983. *Paul, the Law, and the Jewish People.* Philadelphia: Fortress Press.

_____. 1985. *Jesus and Judaism.* London: SCM.

_____. 1990. *Jewish Law from Jesus to the Mishnah: Five Studies.* London: SCM/Philadelphia: Trinity Press International.

_____. 1992. *Judaism: Practice and Belief: 63 BCE – 66 CE.* Philadelphia: Trinity Press International.

Sauter, G. 1989. *Rechtfertigung als Grundbegriff evangelischer Theologie: Eine Textsammlung.* München: Kaiser.

Schilder, K. 1940. *Christ Crucified.* Trans. by Henry Zylstra. Christus in zijn lijden. Vol. 3. Grand Rapids, MI: Eerdmans.

Schlatter, A. 1995. *Romans: The Righteousness of God*. Trans. by S. S. Schatzmann. Peabody, MA: Hendrickson Publishers.

———. 1962. *Der Brief an die Römer*. Stuttgart: Calwer Verlag.

———. 1963. *Die Briefe an die Galater, Epheser, Kolosser und Philemon*. Stuttgart: Calwer Verlag.

Schlink, B. 2000. *Realities of Faith*. Phoenix, AZ: Evangelical Sisterhood of Mary.

Schmelzer, M. 1993. "Penitence, Prayer, and (Charity?)," in *Minhah le-Nahum: Biblical and Other Studies Presented to Nahum M. Sarna in Honour of his 70th Birthday*, ed. by M. Brettler and M. Fishbane, 291–99. Sheffield: JSOT Press.

Schoeps, H. J. 1961. *Paul: The Theology of the Apostle in the Light of Jewish Religious History*. Trans. by H. Knight. Philadelphia: Westminster Press.

———. 1963. *The Jewish-Christian Argument: A History of Theologies in Conflict*. New York: Holt, Rinehart and Winston.

Schreiner, T. R. 1993. *The Law and Its Fulfillment: A Pauline Theology of Law*. Grand Rapids, MI: Baker Books.

———. 2008. *New Testament Theology: Magnifying God in Christ*. Grand Rapids, MI: Baker Academic.

Schürer, E. 1885–91. *A History of the Jewish People in the Time of Jesus Christ*. 4 vols. New York: Scribner.

Schwarz, R. 1998. "Luthers Rechtfertigungslehre als Eckstein der christlichen Theologie und Kirche." *Zeitschrift für Theologie und Kirche* 10:14–46.

Schweitzer, A. 1968. *The Mysticism of Paul the Apostle*. New York: Seabury Press.

Scott, C. A. A. 1939. *Christianity According to St. Paul*. Cambridge: Cambridge University Press.

Segal, A. F. 1990. *Paul the Convert: The Apostolate and Apostasy of Saul the Pharisee*. New Haven, CT: Yale University Press.

Sevenster, G. 1946. *De Christologie van het Nieuwe Testament*. Amsterdam: Holland.

Shedd, W. G. T. (1879) 1999. *Commentary on Romans*. Eugene,

OR: Wipf and Stock.

Shelton, R. L. 2006. *Cross and Covenant: Interpreting the Atonement for 21st Century Mission*. Milton Keynes: Paternoster.

Shepherd, N. 2009. *The Way of Righteousness: Justification Beginning with James*. La Grange, CA: Kerygma Press.

Shulam, J. (with H. Le Cornu). 1998. *A Commentary on the Jewish Roots of Romans*. Baltimore: Messianic Jewish Publishers.

Siegwalt, G. 1986. *Dogmatique pour la catholicité évangélique*, I. *Les fondements de la foi*, 1. *La quête des fondements*. Genève: Labor et Fides / Paris: Cerf.

Smith, D. 1979. *The Epistles of John*. EGT 5. Grand Rapids, MI: Eerdmans.

Snodgrass, K. R. 1988. "Spheres of Influence: A Possible Solution to the Problem of Paul and the Law." *Journal for the Study of the New Testament* 32:93–113.

Sproul, R. C. 1986. *Chosen by God*. Wheaton, IL: Tyndale House Publishers.

_____. 1995. *Faith Alone: The Evangelical Doctrine of Justification*. Grand Rapids, MI: Baker Books.

Spykman, G. J. 1988. "Christian Philosophy as Prolegomena to Reformed Dogmatics." In *'n Woord op sy tijd: 'n Teologiese feesbundel aangebied aan Professor Johan Heyns ter herdenking van sy sestigste verjaarsdag*, ed. by C. J. Wethman and C. J. A. Vos, 137–55. Pretoria: NG Kerkboekhandel.

_____. 1992. *Reformational Theology: A New Paradigm for Doing Dogmatics*. Grand Rapids, MI: Eerdmans.

Stendahl, K. 1963. "The Apostle Paul and the Introspective Conscience of the West." *Harvard Theological Review* 56 (3):199–215.

_____. 1976. *Paul Among Jews and Gentiles and Other Essays*. Philadelphia: Fortress.

Stern, D. H. (1988) 1997. *Messianic Jewish Manifesto*. 3rd ed. Clarksville, MD: Jewish New Testament Publications.

_____. (1992) 1999. *Jewish New Testament Commentary.* 6th ed. Clarksville, MD: Jewish New Testament Publications.

_____. (1988) 2009. *Restoring the Jewishness of the Gospel,* 3rd ed. Clarksville, MD: Messianic Jewish Publishers.

Stewart, J. S. (1936) repr. 2002. *A Man in Christ: The Vital Elements of St. Paul's Religion.* Vancouver: Regent College Publishing.

Stott, J. R. W. 1959. "Must Christ Be Lord to Be Saviour? Yes." *Eternity.* Sept. 1959: 37.

Strack, H. L. and P. Billerbeck. 1922–1928 (repr. 1986–1997). *Kommentar zum Neuen Testament aus Talmud und Midrasch.* 6 vols. München: Beck.

Stuart, C.E. n.d. *Tracings from the Gospel of John, or, Records of the Incarnate Word.* London: E. Marlborough and Co.

Stuhlmacher, P. 1966. *Gerechtigkeit Gottes bei Paulus.* Göttingen: Vandenhoeck and Ruprecht.

_____ (with D. Hagner). 2001. *Revisiting Paul's Doctrine of Justification: A Challenge to the New Perspective.* Downers Grove, IL: InterVarsity Press.

Stumme, W. C., ed. 2006. *The Gospel of Justification in Christ: Where Does the Church Stand Today?* Grand Rapids, MI: Eerdmans.

Swidler, L., L. J. Eron, G. Sloyan, and L. Dean. 1990. *Bursting the Bonds? A Jewish-Christian Dialogue on Jesus and Paul.* Maryknoll, NY: Orbis Books.

Tavard, G. H. 1983. *Justification: An Ecumenical Study.* New York: Paulist Press.

Tenney, M. C. 1981. *The Gospel of John.* EBC 9. Grand Rapids, MI: Zondervan.

Ter Schegget, G. H. 1999. *De menslievendheid van God: Gedachten over de verzoening.* Baarn: Ten Have.

Thielman, F. 1994. *Paul and the Law: A Contextual Approach.* Downers Grove, IL: InterVarsity Press.

Tholuck, F. A. G. (1824) 2008. *Exposition of Paul's Epistle to the Romans.* Charleston, SC: BiblioLife.

Thomas, R. L. 1978. *1, 2 Thessalonians.* EBC 11. Grand Rapids, MI: Zondervan.

Tozer, A. W. 1991. *I Call It Heresy.* Ed. by G. B. Smith. Camp Hill, PA: Christian Publications.

Trench, R. C. (1880) repr. 1976. *Synonyms of the New Testament.* Grand Rapids, MI: Eerdmans.

Trevethan, T. L. 1995. *The Beauty of God's Holiness.* Downers Grove, IL: InterVarsity Press.

Trillhaas, W. 1972. *Dogmatik.* 3rd ed. Berlin: W. de Gruyter.

Troost, A. 1977. *Theologie of filosofie?* Kampen: Kok.

_____. 1982/83. "Theologische misverstanden inzake een reformatorische wijsbegeerte." *Philosophia Reformata* 47:1-19, 179-192; 48:19-49.

_____. 2004. *Vakfilosofie van de geloofswetenschap: Prolegomena van de theologie.* Budel: Damon.

Van de Beek, A. 2008. *God doet recht: Eschatologie als christologie.* Zoetermeer: Meinema.

Van de Pol, W. H. 1948. *Het Christelijk dilemma: Katholieke kerk–Reformatie.* Roermond/Maaseik: J. J. Romen and Zonen.

Van der Meer, F. G. 1941. *Catechismus, dat is onderrichting in het ware geloof.* Utrecht: Spectrum.

Vander Stelt, J. C. 1980. "Theology or Pistology?" In *Building the House: Essays on Christian Education*, edited by J. A. De Jong and L. Y. Van Dyke, 115-35. Sioux Center, IA: Dordt College Press.

Van der Waal, C. 1973. "De rechtvaardiging." In *De religie van het belijden,* by H. Goedhart et al. 65-78. Kampen: Kok.

Van der Zwaag, K. 2003. *Afwachten of verwachten? De toe-eigening des heils in historisch en theologisch perspectief.* Heerenveen: Groen.

_____. 2008. *Augustinus, de kerkvader van het Westen: Zijn leven, zijn werk, zijn invloed.* Heerenveen: Groen.

Van Genderen, J. 1988. *Gerechtigheid als geschenk: Gedachten over de rechtvaardiging door het geloof.* Kampen: Kok.

_____ and W. H. Velema. 2008. *Concise Reformed Dogmatics.* Trans. by Gerrit Bilkes and Ed M. van der Maas. Phillipsburg, NJ: P&R Publishing.

Van Leeuwen, J. A. C. 1953. *De brief aan de Colossenzen / De brieven aan de Thessalonicenzen.* KV. Kampen: Kok.

_____ and D. Jacobs. 1952. *De brief aan de Romeinen.* 3rd ed. KV. Kampen: Kok.

VanLandingham, C. 2006. *Judgment and Justification in Early Judaism and the Apostle Paul.* Peabody, MA: Hendrickson Publishers.

Van Spanje, T. E. 1999. *Inconsistency in Paul? A Critique of the Work of Heikki Räisänen.* Wissenschaftliche Untersuchungen zum NT 2. Reihe 110. Tübingen: Mohr (Siebeck).

Van 't Spijker, W. 1993. *De toeëigening van het heil.* Amsterdam: Buijten and Schipperheijn.

Verkuyl, J. 1992. *De kern van het christelijk geloof.* Kampen: Kok.

Vermes, G. 1983. *Jesus and the World of Judaism.* Minneapolis, MN: Fortress Press.

_____. 1993. *The Religion of Jesus the Jew.* Minneapolis, MN: Fortress Press.

_____. 2003. *Jesus in his Jewish Context.* Minneapolis, MN: Fortress Press.

_____. 2010. *Jesus in the Jewish World.* London: SCM Press.

Vine, W. E. 1985 (repr.). *The Collected Writings.* 4 vols. Glasgow: Gospel Tract Publications.

Von Rad, G. 2001. *Old Testament Theology.* Trans. by D. M. G. Stalker. Vol. 1. Louisville, KY: Westminster John Knox Press.

Warfield, B. B. (1931) 1958. *Studies in Perfectionism.* Phillipsburg: Presbyterian and Reformed Publ. Co.

Weber, F. 1880. *System der altsynagogalen palästinischen Theologie oder Die Lehren des Talmud;* repr. 1897 *Jüdische Theolo-*

gie auf Grund des Talmud und verwandter Schriften, ed. by F. Delitzsch and G. Schnedermann. Leipzig: Dörffling Franke.

Weber, O. 1981. *Foundations of Dogmatics*, Vol. 1. Grand Rapids, MI: Eerdmans.

Wendland, H.-D. 1935. *Die Mitte der paulinischen Botschaft.* Götttingen: Vandenhoeck and Ruprecht.

Wenham, D. 1995. *Paul: Follower of Jesus or Founder of Christianity?* Grand Rapids, MI: Eerdmans.

Wentsel, B. 1987. *God en mens verzoend: Godsleer, mensleer en zondeleer. Dogmatiek.* Vol. 3a. Kampen: Kok.

Wesley, J. (1848) 2013. *A Plain Account of Christian Perfection.* www.theclassics.us.

Westcott, B. F. 1883. *The Johannine Epistles.* London: Macmillan.

Westerholm, S. 1988. *Israel's Law and the Church's Faith: Paul and His Recent Interpreters.* Grand Rapids, MI: Eerdmans.

_____. 2003. *Perspectives Old and New on Paul: The "Lutheran" Paul and His Critics.* Grand Rapids, MI: Eerdmans.

White, J. R. 2001. *The God Who Justifies.* Minneapolis: Bethany House Publishers.

White, N. J. D. 1979. *The First and Second Epistles to Timothy and the Epistle to Titus.* EGT 4. Grand Rapids, MI: Eerdmans.

Wiersinga, H. 1971. *De verzoening in de theologische diskussie.* Kampen: Kok.

_____. 1972. *Verzoening als verandering: Een gegeven voor menselijk handelen.* Baarn: Bosch and Keuning.

Wiersinga, W. A. 1952. *Gods werk in ons.* Kampen: Kok.

Willis, D. 2002. *Notes on the Holiness of God.* Grand Rapids, MI: Eerdmans.

Winger, M. 1992. *By What Law? The Meaning of* Nomos *in the Letters of Paul.* Atlanta: Scholars.

Wisse, P. M. 2003. "Habitus Fidei: An Essay on the History of a Concept." *Scottish Journal of Theology* 56:172–89.

Woelderink, J. G. 1941. *De rechtvaardiging uit het geloof alleen.* Aalten: De Graafschap.

Wood, A. S. 1978. *Ephesians.* EBC 11. Grand Rapids, MI: Zondervan.

Wrede, W. (1907) 1962. *Paul.* Lexington, KY: American Theological Library Association.

Wright, N. T. 1991. *The Climax of the Covenant: Christ and the Law in Pauline Theology.* Minneapolis, MN: Fortress Press.

_____. 1997. *What Saint Paul Really Said: Was Paul of Tarsus the Real Founder of Christianity?* Grand Rapids, MI: Eerdmans.

_____. 2002. *The Letter to the Romans.* New Interpreter's Bible X. Nashville, TN: Abingdon Press.

_____. 2005. *Paul in Fresh Perspective.* Minneapolis, MN: Fortress Press.

_____. 2006. *Simply Christian: Why Christianity Makes Sense.* New York: HarperCollins.

_____. 2009. *Justification: God's Plan and Paul's Vision.* SPCK Publishing.

_____. 2013. *Pauline Perspectives: Essays on Paul, 1978–2013.* Minneapolis, MN: Augsburg Fortress.

_____. 2014. *Paul and His Recent Interpreters.* Minneapolis, MN: Augsburg Fortress.

Wuest, K. S. (1953) 1977. *Ephesians and Colossians in the Greek New Testament.* Grand Rapids, MI: Eerdmans.

Young, E. J. 1972. *The Book of Isaiah*, Vol. 3: *Chapters 40–66.* Grand Rapids, MI: Eerdmans.

Youngblood, R. F. 1992. *1 and 2 Samuel.* EBC 3. Grand Rapids, MI: Zondervan.

Zahn, Th. 1925. *Der Brief des Paulus an die Römer.* 3rd ed. Leipzig/Erlangen: Deichert.

Ziesler, J. A. 1972. *The Meaning of Righteousness in Paul: A Linguistic and Theological Enquiry.* Cambridge: Cambridge University Press.

Scripture Index

OLD TESTAMENT

Genesis
1:26-27 243
2:3 396
2:17 117
5 88
5:22 63
5:24 63, 87
6:5 514
6:9 63, 84, 87
8:1-13 268
11:10-26 88
12:3 361
15 91, 92, 361
15:6 55, 79, 88, 89, 90, 91, 94, 158, 166, 169, 170, 171, 248, 253, 259, 282
15:9-10 93
17 92
17:1 85
17:1-2 64
17:6 361
17:17 92, 361
18:23-32 373
18:25 4, 54
19:27 120
22 92, 253
22:1-18 93
24:1 361
24:27 287
24:40 64
24:63 120
28:11 120
30:33 54
32:20 534
38:15 170
38:26 54, 55
39:3 80
39:23 80
44:16 21
48:15 64

Exodus
3:2-6 395
4:31 281, 283, 288
9:27 30
12:13 125
13:2 416
14:30-15:18 268
14:31 281, 283
15:11 428
19:6 402, 425
19:9 283, 288
19:21 416
20:2 139
20:7 110
20:12 61, 109, 211
20:22 396
21:17 109
22:31 416
23:7 54, 55
23:11 78
29 418
29:4 418
29:18 204
29:21 418
29:25 204
29:36-46 119
29:40-41 204
29:41 204
29:44-45 395
29:45 403
30:35 432
32:14 373

Leviticus
1 213
1:2 204
1:4 204
1:9 204
1:12 204
1:13 204
1:17 204
2 119, 213
2:11 391

8	418	6:14	117	19:15	70
8:6	418	6:16	117	22:7	264
8:12	417	8:16–18	416	23:12–14	464
8:30	418	12:13	371	23:14	425
10:3	427, 429	14:11	370	23:18	396
11:4	108	14:20	374	24:10–13	78
11:20–23	108	14:21	96	24:19–21	78
11:44–45	398, 425, 455	15:38	363	25:1	54, 55
12:6–8	117	15:40	425	26:12–13	78
14:19	117	16:7	417	26:19	402
15:25–33	363	20:12–13	396	27:16	109
16	278	21:8–9	330	27:19	78
16:6	417	25:7–8	89	27:26	126
16:8–10	278			28:4	76
16:11	417	**Deuteronomy**		28:9	403
16:14–15	530	1:17	54	28:11	76
16: 15	278	4:1	61, 262, 264	30:6	262, 264
16:20	278	4:8	150	30:11–14	150
16:21	278	4:10	62	30:12	151
16:29	119	4:24	427	30:15–16	262
16:31	119	4:37	416	30:19–20	262
17:4	179	5:6	139	32:4	30
17:11	118, 204, 529	5:10	264	32:35	70
17:14	529	5:12	396	32:36	70
18:5	60, 126, 261, 519	5:16	61, 109	32:37	262
		5:33	62, 264	33:3	416
19:2	397, 398, 425, 455	6:2	61		
		6:5	80	**Joshua**	
19:10	78	7:6	402	5:15	395
19:15	78	7:6–7	416	22:5	264
19:18	138, 249	7:6–8	139	24:19	420
20:3	396	7:9	264		
20:9	109	8:1	264	**Judges**	
20:26	398, 425	9:3	427	5:11	43
21:8	398, 425, 455	11:9	61, 264	7	369
22:2	396	11:11	264		
23:22	78	11:13	264	**1 Samuel**	
25:23	78	14:1	132	1:15	170
26:11	403	14:2	402, 416	3:19	80
		14:21	402	10:6	382
Numbers		14:29	78	10:9	382
3:11–13	416	15:11	78	12:7	44
3:40–51	416	16:20	264	15:22	120
5:1	363	17:6	70	16:14	382
5:1–4	363	18:13	85	17:50–54	268

Scripture Index

18:12 80	5:2-4 368	1:9-19 365
18:14 80	5:10-14 356	1:21 365
20:15 272	5:11-12 368	2:3 84
20:17 272	5:14 368	2:6-7 365
24:18 54	13:14 359	2:10 365
28:16 382	17:28 51	4:17 9, 64
31:4 382	18:7 80	9:2 9
		9:14-15 54
2 Samuel	**1 Chronicles**	9:19-20 54
5:8 271	9:20 80	9:32-33 54
5:10 80	11:9 80	11:2 55
9:1 271	12:27 417	13:15 21
9:1-3 271	16:10 396	13:24 170
9:3 271	16:35 396	15:14 64
9:6 271	21:12 528	19:15 170
9:8 272	21:14-17 374	21:27 514
9:11 272	29:3 395	25:4 9, 64,
9:13 271, 272		32:2 21
15:4 55	**2 Chronicles**	33:10 170
19:19 169, 179	1:1 80	36:3 21
19:24 272	12:6 30	36:22 51
19:28 272	15:9 80	40:8 25
21:7 272	20:17 248	42:5-6 503
22:14 84	20:20 281, 283, 288	
24:16 373	33:12-13 147	**Psalms**
24:25 373		1 74
	Ezra	1:1-3 63
1 Kings	7:10 74, 110	1:2 110
3:6 86, 287	9:15 30	1:3 74, 126, 249
3:14 61		2:1 536
8:27-30 395	**Nehemiah**	2:6 395
8:32 22, 55	1:5 264	4:1 42
8:46 64	9:8 30	5:5 536
14:8 88	9:29 261	5:7 395
17:17-24 369	9:33 32	5:8 42
18:1 359	11:1 395	7:9 30
18:20-40 353	11:18 395	7:11 30
18:41-45 359		7:17 42
21:27-29 329	**Esther**	9:8 4
22:11 391	4:11 269	11:7 30
	4:16 270	15 84
2 Kings		15:1-5 464
4:6 357	**Job**	15:2-5 82, 263
4:9 417	1:1 84	16:11 264
4:18-37 369	1:8 84	18:22 283

573

18:23	84, 85	51:11	396	104:8	345
19:7	62	51:12	331	104:28	326
19:8	110	51:14	42	105:42	396
19:8–10	63	55:2	498	106:12	281, 283, 288
19:9	55	56:5	514	106:30–31	79
19:11	224	57:5	96	106:31	89
19:13	85	57:11	96	107:20	348
22	43	62:12	68	111:9	432
22:1	516	64:10	86, 97	112:4	30
22:2	525	66:18	371	115:12	417
22:15	529	67:4	4	116:5	30
22:22	525	71:2	42	116:10	283, 336
22:30–31	43	71: 15–16	42	118:3	417
22:32	98	71:19	42	118:22	148
24:3–4	82, 464	71:24	42	118:26	96
24:5	42, 98	72:19	96	119:7	86
25:10	287	73:24	362	119:14–16	62
27:13	282, 283	75:7–8	54	119:16	110
31:1	42	78:22	283, 291	119:24	63
31:15	365	78:32	370	119:25	62
32:1–5	359	79:1	395	119:30	97
32:2	169, 173, 179	82:6	42	119:35	63
33:5	42	84:6	51, 498	119:37	62
33:21	396	84:7	436	119:40	42, 62
34:22	97	84:8	498	119:47	63, 110
35:27	21	85:10	42	119:50	62
35:28	42	85:10–13	42	119:70	63, 110
36:5–6	42	86:5	85	119:77	63, 110
36:10	86	89:5	414	119:88	62
36:9	62, 75	89:14	32, 42	119:92	63, 110
36:10	42	89:14–16	98	119:93	62
37:39–40	97	89:15–16	42	119:97–98	62
40	43	92	75	119:107	62
40:7–8	124	92:12–13	75	119:123	42
40:9–10	43, 98	94:2	54	119:137	30
43:3	395	94:15	86	119:138	32
44:17–18	85	95:7	385	119:143	63, 110
48:10	42, 98	96:10	4	119:149	62
50:6	4	96:13	4, 32	119:154	62
50:8–9	120	97:11	86	119:159	62
50:23	120	98:1–2	42, 98	119:174	63, 110
51	233	98:2	44	129:4	30
51:4	21, 233	98:9	4, 44	130:3	64
51:4–7	85	103:1	396	130:3–4	85, 329
51:6	25, 233	103:17	42	130:4	427

131:1-2 452	1:26 252	43:10 283
132:9 187	1:27 42	43:25 533
132:16 187	5:16 396	43:26 54
133:1 62	5:23 55, 85	45 44
133:3 62	6:3 396, 426, 431, 432	45:8 44, 101
138:2 395		45:19 45
138:8 377	6:5 85	45:21 42, 45, 98
143:2 64	6:7 85	45:23 68
145:7-8 42	7:9 283	45:23-25 45
145:17 30	8:12-13 430	45:25 21, 52, 59, 98, 251
	8:14 148	
Proverbs	9:7 252	46:12 85
2:19 264	9:15 51	46:12-13 42, 98
3:5 95	11:5 32	48:1 85
3:22 62	11:9 96, 395	48:2 395
5:6 264	16:5 32, 43	50:8 42, 55
6:23 264	26:2 87, 252	50:8-9 54
8:7 110	26:3 98	51:1 70, 86, 256
10:28 97	26:9-10 85, 99	51:1-2 88
11:19 29	27:9 251	51:4 63
11:31 406	27:13 395	51:5 4
12:5 514	28:16 148, 283	51:5-8 42, 98
14:34 82	28:17 252	51:7 63
15:9 70, 86	30:20 51	52:1 395
15:24 264	32:1 252	53:4 517
15:26 514	32:16-17 252	53:4-5 528
17:15 21, 55	33:5 252, 263	53:5 192, 528
18:10 97	33:14 263	53:7 529
20:4 364	33:14-15 59, 464	53:8-10 523
20:20 109	33:14-16 339	53:10 528
21:21 70	33:15 83, 85	53:11 42, 52, 55, 98
24:16 86	33:15-16 263	54:10 380
24:30-31 364	33:15-17 253	55:1 325
26:11 70	33:24 253	55:3 399
28:13 119, 233, 307	37:3 496	55:7 514
	38:2-5 372	56-66 253
Ecclesiastes	38:5 374	56:1 42, 85, 98, 263
3:17 4	40-55 253	
7:20 64	40:9-10 99	56:7 120, 395
12:14 68	40:10 69	57:15 432
	41:8 248	58:2 85
Isaiah	41:14 428	58:6-7 83
1-39 253	41:16 428	58:8 99
1:4 420	41:20 428	59:7 514
1:11 120	43:9 54	59:20 251

60:21	52, 99, 252, 253	**Lamentations**		9:14	30, 268
		1:18	30	9:16	42, 395
61:3	85			9:24	395
61:10	85, 187	**Ezekiel**		11:28	396
61:11	102	6:9	449	11:30	396
62:1-2	99	8	330	11:33	52
62:12	416	8:8-9	330	11:35	52
63:10-11	396	8:12-13	330	12:2	62
63:15	432	13:10-15	391	12:3	52, 59
63:18	403, 416	13:18	388	12:7	416
64:6	82, 146, 332, 492	16:6	264	12:10	52
		16:8	188		
64:11	395, 432	18:5-9	83, 263, 465	**Hosea**	
65:24	372	18:31	382	2:19	43
66:3	120	18:32	264	6:6	108, 120
		20:11	60, 261	10:12	43
Jeremiah		20:13	60	11:9	396, 429
4:14	514	20:41	396	14:2	120, 418
5:24	504	20:43	449		
6:20	120	22	345	**Joel**	
9:24	43	22:28	391	2:23	51
11:20	4	22:29-31	346	2:32	326
12:12	528	28:22	396		
17:6	74	28:25	396	**Amos**	
17:6-8	249	28:36	396	4:2	397
17:7-8	74	36	448	5:4	263
17:9	296, 390	36:20-23	396	5:6	263
21:8	264	36:23	396, 430	5:14	263
23:1	101	36:25-26	449	5:22	120
23:5	101	36:25-27	66	6:8	397
23:5-6	51	36:26	382		
23:6	186	36:27	449	**Jonah**	
26:19	373	36:31	449	3:5	283
28:2	391	37:27	403	3:10	373
29:12-13	372	38:16	396		
30:11	101	39:27	396	**Micah**	
31:1	403	42:20	395	6:1-5	42
31:14-15	100	47:7-12	75	6:8	64, 263, 465
31:30	100			7:19	332
31:33-34	100	**Daniel**			
33:14-16	101	3	369	**Habakkuk**	
33:15	51	6	369	1	95
33:16	186	6:22	84	1:13	47, 226, 271, 516
47:6	528	7:9-10	54		
		9:4	264	2	259

Scripture Index

2:3-4	96	
2:4	29, 30, 37, 52, 90, 94, 95, 97, 126, 259, 263, 283, 295, 369	
2:14	96	

Zephaniah
2:3	69, 450
3:5	30

Zechariah
3:4-5	188
7:2	539
8:8	32
8:22	539
13:7	528
14:5	409
14:20	396

Malachi
1:9	539

NEW TESTAMENT
Matthew
1:18	397
1:19	29, 76
3:2	7, 307
3:7	538
3:8	66
3:10	313
3:15	23, 523
3:17	516
4:5	395
4:17	7, 15, 307
4:23	7, 143, 304
5-7	290
5:6	23, 235, 254, 256
5:7	108
5:8	459
5:10	23, 254, 256
5:12	69
5:16	67, 223
5:17	128
5:20	23, 254
5:21	109
5:21-22	514
5:22	130
5:27-28	514
5:33-36	110
5:39	465
5:43-44	110
5:45	29
5:48	408, 467, 508
6:1	23, 256
6:1-4	79
6:2	129, 466
6:3	465
6:4	69
6:5	129, 466
6:6	69
6:9	396, 398, 429
6:12	510
6:14	465
6:16	129, 466
6:16-18	82
6:18	69
6:30	329
6:30-32	339
6:30-33	333
6:31	465
6:33	23, 46, 254, 339
6:33-34	340
7:3	109
7:5	129, 466
7:7	345
7:9-12	109
7:12	41
7:17-19	314
7:21	138, 381
7:22-23	330
8	349
8-9	290
8:5-10	372
8:5-13	348
8:8	362
8:10	290, 350, 357
8:11-12	351
8:12	7
8:13	290, 293, 348, 352, 357
8:17	517
8:24-26	339
8:26	329
9:1-8	368
9:2	290, 348, 357, 359
9:10-17	146
9:12	365, 504
9:13	30, 108, 223
9:20	363
9:22	291, 292, 348, 356
9:27-30	343
9:28-29	291
9:28-30	341
9:29	91, 293, 348
9:32-33	359
9:35	7, 143, 304
10:1	348
10:8	365
10:22	317, 384
10:26	427
10:28	427
10:29	504
10:31	427
10:40-42	69
10:41	29
11:3	96
11:19	21, 25, 146
11:28	326
11:29	450
12:3	52
12:5-6	399
12:7	108
12:18	516
12:25-28	335
12:28	304
12:33	314
12:37	21, 26
13:8	330
13:17	29
13:23	330

13:38	351	21:31	22	27:24	30, 77
13:39	365	21:42	283	27:29	528
13:43	29, 52	22:18	129	27:46	516
13:49	29	22:36–40	105, 264, 462	27:51–54	268
13:58	350, 357	22:40	41	27:52	414
14:22	7	23:1–33	254	27:53	395
14:28–29	362	23:1–36	146	27:56	527
14:29–31	340	23:2–4	108	28:18–19	143
14:31	329, 362	23:13–14	331	28:23	7
15	349	23:13–29	129	28:31	7
15:1–9	107	23:16–17	399		
15:7	129	23:17	398	**Mark**	
15:19	514	23:19	398	1:14	304
15:21–28	357	23:23	108, 254, 285, 348	1:15	308
15:22–28	350, 372			1:24	397, 419
15:27	362	23:23–24	108	1:40–41	352, 360
15:27–28	334	23:24	254	1:41	363
15:28	291, 293, 329, 348, 352	23:28	30	2:5	291
		23:29	29	3:10	363
16:5–8	340	23:35	29, 87	4:30	300
16:8	329	23:39	96	4:40	291
16:8–9	339	24:13	317, 378, 384, 386	5:22–23	372
16:21	526			5:26–28	363
16:27	68	24:14	143, 304	5:27	363
17:5	516	24:23	289	5:34	291, 345, 363, 365
17:16–20	367	24:26	289		
17:17	338, 350, 367	25:21	285	5:35	342
17:19–20	340, 341	25:23	285	5:36	291, 342, 357, 368
17:20	300, 329, 337, 338, 342, 345	25:31	409		
		25:31–46	69	5:39–40	358
17:21	291	25:34	62	5:41	363
18:35	466	25:35–36	83	6:5	345, 366
19:8	7	25:37	29	6:5–6	357
19:16	62, 211	25:46	29, 62, 103, 211	6:12	307
19:17	62, 262			6:20	29, 417, 432
19:17–19	129	26:10	67	6:56	363
19:21	407	26:18	526	7:1–23	107
19:24	109	26:28	194, 528	7:22	466
19:29	211, 407	26:39	527	7:31–37	368
20:22	526	26:42	527	7:32	357
20:25	7	26:54	526	7:32–33	358
20:34	307	26:56	526	8:23	358
21:9	96	26:59	130	9:14	367
21:21	291, 340, 345	26:61	399	9:19	356
21:28–32	146	27:19	30, 77	9:22–24	352

9:23	94, 342, 348, 368	2:21	520	11:14	359
		2:24	117	11:17	514
9:23-24	291, 357	2:25	29, 76	11:37-52	146
9:24	336, 342	2:29-32	76	11:42	108, 254
9:25	359	2:35	514	12:28-31	339
9:50	265	2:36-38	77	12:29	498
10:27	342, 348	3:7	538	13:3	307
10:39	474	3:11	504	13:5	307
10:46-52	347	4:1	518	13:10-17	359, 365
10:51	372	4:34	397, 419	13:19	341
10:52	291, 292, 345, 356, 365	4:43	304	13:23-24	406
		5:14	117	13:31	147
11:22	95, 291	5:17	80	14:11	448
11:22-24	336, 346	5:20	291, 364	14:14	30
11:23	341, 367, 369	5:22	514	14:26-27	303
12:28-34	147	5:32	307	14:33	303
13:19-20	406	6:8	514	15:1-2	146
14:36	266, 348, 360	6:36	467	15:7	30
15:34	516	6:46	381	15:18-19	497
16:11	289	7:2-9	348	15:20-24	22
16:13-14	289	7:9	291	15:22	332
16:16	142, 293	7:29	21, 167, 429	15:22-23	497
16:17-18	365	7:34	22	16:8	29
		7:35	25	16:10	29
Luke		7:36-50	146	16:10-12	285
1:5-6	11	7:37-50	363	16:11	293
1:6	23, 29, 63, 75, 128, 147	7:47	448	16:15	21, 30
		7:50	283, 291, 292, 345	16:16	41, 304
1:7	76			16:31	370
1:9	399	8:1	304	17:5	300, 337, 341
1:17	29	8:12	291	17:5-6	291, 329, 333
1:20	288	8:13	289, 330	17:6	341
1:35	397, 419	8:15	377	17:10	69
1:38	76	8:25	291	17:16	307
1:43	302	8:48	291	17:19	291, 292, 345, 357, 365
1:46	429	8:50	291		
1:46-55	76	9:22	526	17:25	526
1:51	514	9:51	64	18:6	29
1:66	80	10:9	365	18:7	358
1:68-71	147	10:25	407	18:8	358
1:68-75	66	10:28	211	18:7	358
1:68-78	76	10:29	21, 26	18:8	358
1:74-75	413	11:2	396, 398, 429	18:9	30, 145
1:75	399	11:9	345	18:9-14	223
2:11	283	11:13	479	18:11-12	107, 110, 148

18:13	117, 147, 534	3:3	65, 66	6:27	407
18:13-14	26, 55, 158	3:5	65	6:33	96
18:14	5, 21, 156, 448	3:6	408	6:37	48, 285
		3:7	222, 329	6:39	379
18:18	407	3:10	65	6:40	407
18:20	75	3:14-15	527	6:47	407
18:42	364	3:15	292	6:56	473
19:2-5	364	3:15-16	407	6:63	297
19:7	146	3:16	38, 103, 267, 283, 295, 328, 536	6:69	397, 419
19:8	364			6:70-71	77
19:9-10	364			7:5	291
19:17	285	3:17	143	7:24	29
19:42	152	3:19-21	129	7:31	289
20:20	30	3:31	96	7:38-39	74, 81
21:18	504	3:35	102	7:48	291
21:19	317, 377, 378	3:36	37, 284, 311, 329, 407, 515, 538, 541	7:50-51	77
22:15	526			7:52	50
22:32	336, 379			8:11	484, 508
22:53	526	4:1-30	306	8:28	527
22:69	217	4:21	289	8:29	516, 524
23:16	502	4:22	283	8:31	474
23:22	502	4:24	425, 432	8:31-36	508
23:40-42	460	4:29	307	8:56	360
23:47	30	4:41	291	9:2-3	359
23:50	30, 77	4:42	103	9:6-7	344
23:56	75	4:46-53	343	9:18	289
24:11	289	4:46-54	357	9:25	303
24:20	527	4:47-49	372	9:31	426
24:26	527	4:48	291, 369,	9:35-38	344
24:44	41	4:50	288, 343,	10:14	292
24:47	143	4:53	291	10:17-18	201, 216, 518
		5	356	10:18	205
John		5:1-18	354	10:27-28	304, 326
1:7	291	5:3-4	354	10:28	376
1:12	329	5:6	354	10:28-29	71, 379, 386
1:18	217	5:7	354	10:34	42
1:29	102, 273	5:8	355	10:36	398, 418
1:46	41	5:14	354, 359, 484, 508	11:25-26	240
1:47	77			11:27	291
2:11	370	5:24	267, 326, 379, 405, 407	11:42	524
2:23	289			12:24	213
2:23-25	290, 330	5:30	4, 29, 103	12:32	527
2:24	293	5:39	407	12:37-38	291
2:24-25	390	6	13	12:49-50	216
3:1-21	77	6:25-40	13	12:50	205

13	461	17:3	211	3:14	30, 77, 267, 397, 419, 432
13:1	216	17:4	215, 527		
13:3	102	17:4–5	49, 50, 475	3:14–15	50
13:8	461	17:5	216, 476	3:16	291, 356
13:10	461	17:8	289	3:17	130
13:31	50	17:11	387, 397, 432	3:19	307
13:32	50, 216, 527	17:15	379, 387	3:21	102
13:34	308, 462, 490	17:17	398, 456	4:4	283, 291
14:2	216	17:19	398, 419, 456	4:12	143, 329
14:6	234, 264	17:19	398	4:27	397
14:13	527	17:22	475	4:30	397
14:13–14	370	17:22–23	473	4:33	451
14:15	63, 105, 264, 308, 462, 490	17:24	379	4:36	390, 511
		17:25	30, 50, 432	5:1	390
14:16	380	17:26	473	5:1–11	386
14:20	473	18:11	527	5:30–31	460
14:21	63, 264, 308, 462, 490	19:30	50	5:31	194, 283, 307
		19:34	520, 528	5:32	311
14:21–24	105	19:34–37	529	5:33–39	130
14:23	63, 462, 473	19:39	77	5:34–39	147
14:31	205	20:8	291	6:7	147, 283, 284, 291, 299, 311, 329
15	338	20:13	302		
15:1–7	476	20:17	474		
15:1–8	74, 247	20:28	302	7:2	361
15:2	338	20:29	291	7:22	502
15:2–5	75	20:31	284	7:52	30, 77, 267
15:2–7	473			8	438
15:3	473	**Acts**		8:4–17	260
15:5	338, 463	1:3	7, 304	8:12	304
15:6	338, 383	1:6	304	8:12–13	283, 289
15:7	370, 383	1:14	377	8:13	390
15:8	338	1:24	390	8:19	348
15:10	205, 215, 264, 383, 462, 490	2	438	8:20–23	390
		2:21	326	8:21	461
15:10–17	308	2:23	529	8:22	307, 529
15:14	383	2:27	419	8:26–39	260
15:16	370	2:28	264, 460	9:1–19	260
15:20	474	2:36	302, 305	9:2	64
16:8–11	49	2:37–41	260	9:10	390, 438
16:10	216	2:38	194, 307	9:13	414
16:14	216	2:42	377	9:17	438
16:23	370	2:44	283	9:32	414
16:32	524	3	356, 359	9:36	67, 223
16:33	500	3:1	117	9:41	414
17:1	216	3:12	426	9:42	283

581

10	438	15:40	451	22:14	30, 77, 267
10:2	390, 427	16:1	390	22:16	460
10:20	366	16:5	300	22:19	283
10:22	30, 427	16:14	426	23:1	127
10:35	256	16:14–15	260	23:1–9	511
10:36	302	16:15	285	23:9	147
10:38	349, 359, 490	16:27–34	260	24:14	41, 64
10:43	194	16:30–31	143	24:15	30, 267
10:43–44	283	16:31	283, 291, 292, 293	24:16	127
10:44–48	260			24:21	511
10:46	429	16:34	283	24:22	64
11:17	283	16:35	326	24:24	283
11:18	307	17:3	526	24:25	267
11:21	283	17:4	426	25:26	302
11:23	451	17:7	304	26:18	194, 283, 398, 413, 414
12:22	302	17:12	283, 291		
13:10	267	17:17	426	26:20	66, 307
13:12	283	17:28	476	26:27	283
13:15	41	17:30	284, 307, 321, 329	28:4	20
13:16	427			28:23	7, 41, 304
13:23	283	17:31	4, 103, 267	28:24	289
13:26	427	17:34	283, 291	28:31	7, 304
13:34	399, 432	18:7	426		
13:35	419	18:8	283	**Romans**	
13:38	194	18:27	451	1:1	255
13:39	26, 221, 222, 283, 291	19:2	283	1:2	396
		19:4	283	1:4	241, 398
13:43	451, 474	19:8	7, 304	1:5	235, 284, 302, 311, 329
13:48	283, 321	19:9	64		
13:50	426	19:12	359	1:7	32, 414, 457
14:1	283, 321	19:18	283	1:8	302
14:8–10	357	19:23	64	1:11	451
14:9	291, 300	19:27	172, 399	1:16	221, 260, 293
14:22	304, 474	20:19	450	1:16–17	1, 267
14:22–23	283	20:20	300	1:17	16, 29, 30, 32, 33, 34, 37, 38, 42, 46, 47, 95, 153, 186, 224, 230, 259, 286, 287
14:26	451	20:21	283, 308		
14:27	283, 291	20:25	7, 304		
15:5	147, 283	20:30	381		
15:7	291	20:32	398, 413, 422, 451		
15:8	390			1:18	37, 538
15:9	283, 291	21:8	390	1:32	23
15:10	65, 110, 137, 462	21:20	283	2:5	29, 103, 53
		21:26	117	2:5–10	69
15:11	283, 291, 293	22:10	303, 307, 471	2:6–7	377
15:14	402	22:12	390		

Ref	Pages
2:7	211, 236
2:7–10	66
2:8	311, 538, 541
2:12	106, 113, 207
2:13	21, 26, 61, 64, 111, 126, 128, 146, 214
2:14	207
2:15	513
2:15–16	447
2:17	106, 113
2:17–27	146
2:23	106, 113
2:26	23, 177
2:29	447
3	167, 174, 265, 266, 273
3:1	175
3:2	293
3:3	153, 286
3:4	21, 25
3:4–5	167, 233
3:5	29, 32, 37, 38, 45, 46, 515, 538
3:5–7	440
3:8	21, 315
3:9	222, 241, 273
3:10–18	42
3:13	466
3:19	42, 106, 113, 207
3:19–20	168
3:19–31	146
3:20	10, 61, 64, 73, 222, 229, 273
3:20–26	34
3:21	32, 38, 46, 47, 153, 206, 211
3:21–22	1, 16, 32, 41, 186
3:21–26	185
3:21–4:25	48
3:22	34, 46, 48, 52, 64, 95, 153, 166, 194, 224, 230, 231, 234, 286
3:22–25	219
3:22–26	234, 284
3:22–30	287
3:23	51, 234
3:23–24	4, 211, 222, 224, 519
3:24	22, 149, 156, 223, 231, 313
3:24–25	121, 202, 225
3:24–26	38, 40, 364
3:25	34, 41, 166, 201, 223, 224, 231, 234, 273, 286, 528, 534
3:25–26	32, 33, 46, 186, 226, 540
3:26	30, 34, 35, 39, 40, 47, 48, 56, 95, 100, 118, 153, 166, 174, 177, 187, 227, 234, 267
3:27	222, 286
3:27–28	126, 286
3:28	10, 61, 64, 73, 140, 149, 173, 202, 222, 224, 227, 231
3:29–30	222
3:30	224, 227, 232, 286
3:31	106, 113, 224, 231
4	87, 91, 93, 158, 166, 167, 171, 172, 174, 182, 237, 273, 508
4–8	265
4:1–12	158
4:2	64, 222
4:2–6	91
4:3	55, 89, 171, 172
4:3–5	90
4:3–8	171
4:3–13	32
4:4	126, 140, 172, 223, 224
4:5	3, 18, 21, 27, 29, 38, 46, 47, 64, 126, 140, 141, 142, 156, 166, 172, 177, 178, 182, 223, 224, 227, 235, 242, 430
4:6	65, 171, 172, 179, 196, 222
4:7	273, 451
4:8	172, 179, 273
4:9	89
4:9–10	172, 223
4:10–11	171
4:11	65, 172, 177, 179, 196
4:11–12	88
4:12	48
4:13	65
4:13–15	146
4:14–15	106, 113
4:15	106, 113
4:15–16	91
4:16	48, 153, 223
4:17	92
4:18	89, 94
4:19	92, 93
4:22	32, 89, 172
4:23	171
4:23–24	172, 179, 196
4:24–25	94, 166, 188, 202, 208, 210, 221, 226, 266
4:24–26	51
4:24–5:1	41, 197
4:25	23, 50, 158, 166, 211, 237,

5	255, 265, 268 205, 215, 237, 243, 265, 266, 269	5:15 5:15–16 5:15–17 5:16	274, 275, 277 275 225 23, 24, 27, 274, 276	6:7–11 6:8 6:8–11 6:9–14 6:10	168 236 241 255 238
5–8	251	5:16–18	24	6:10–11	217
5:1	46, 158, 166, 228, 244, 256, 266, 273, 313	5:17 5:17–18	24, 236, 244, 275 32, 236	6:10–23 6:11	241 236, 237, 435, 459, 472, 481, 483
5:1–2	211, 519	5:18	23, 24, 173,		
5:1–5	255		200, 201, 236,	6:12	189, 436, 508
5:1–11	269		275, 276, 277,	6:12–14	242, 444
5:2	51, 237, 244, 265, 266, 269	5:18–21	278, 279, 328 255	6:12–23 6:13	508 32, 236, 255, 445, 447, 478
5:3	269	5:19	32, 181, 195,		
5:3–4	377		198, 199, 200,	6:14	106, 113, 214,
5:5	38, 269, 459, 462		201, 203, 205, 276, 277, 278,	6:14–15	331, 436 146
5:6	167, 239		279	6:15	315
5:6–11	237	5:19–20	205, 215	6:16	32, 235
5:7	30	5:20	106, 113, 205,	6:16–17	311
5:8	19, 22, 38,		215	6:16–22	444
	189, 239, 266,	5:21	32, 211, 236,	6:17	302
	269, 290, 391, 493		237, 241, 244, 450, 519	6:17–19 6:18	441 189, 391, 423,
5:8–9	71	6	237		435, 436, 442,
5:8–10	202	6:1	315		443, 493
5:9	41, 121, 156,	6:1–2	241	6:18–19	32
	158, 166, 201,	6:2	236	6:19	398, 445, 447,
	223, 226, 231,	6:3–4	241, 255		457, 478
	244, 269, 515,	6:3–6	28	6:22	189, 247, 391,
	528, 538	6:4	169, 216, 221,		398, 423, 435,
5:9–10	260, 269, 335		236		436, 442, 443,
5:9–11	255	6:4–11	238, 268		457, 459, 493
5:10	210, 236, 237, 523, 535, 536	6:5 6:5–11	265 227, 472	6:22–23	211, 236, 239, 255
5:10–11	269	6:6	214, 216, 239,	6:23	117, 210
5:11	92, 244, 266, 269	6:6–7	241, 380, 481 197, 241, 255	7	81, 238, 274, 394, 434, 435,
5:12	273, 275	6:7	18, 27, 28, 41,		436, 437, 438,
5:12–13	241		141, 142, 240,		440, 441, 442,
5:12–14	274		241, 391, 435,		444, 446, 447,
5:12–21	274		442, 443, 493,		449, 450, 494,
5:13	172, 179		508		495, 499
5:13–14	205, 215	6:7–8	211, 519	7:1–8:4	146
5:13–17	274				

Reference	Pages
7:2	106, 113
7:4	106, 113, 212, 214, 217, 238
7:4–6	441
7:6	106, 113, 214, 217, 437, 521
7:7–13	436
7:7–14	433
7:7–16	394
7:7–24	440
7:7–26	441
7:8–9	241
7:10	433
7:11	241
7:12	215, 433
7:13–14	241
7:13–25	274
7:14	433, 434, 443
7:14–16	436
7:14–25	434
7:14–26	422, 433, 434, 436, 439, 443, 445, 500
7:14–8:4	443
7:15–17	435
7:16	443
7:17	241, 510
7:17–26	437
7:20	241, 510
7:21	442, 443
7:22	110, 435, 443
7:23	241, 442, 443
7:24	423, 433, 436, 448, 498
7:24–25	498
7:25	241, 436, 449
7:26	443
8	238, 269, 271, 274, 435, 440, 442, 443, 444, 445, 449
8:1	472
8:1–2	238, 441, 472
8:1–6	479
8:2	106, 113, 189, 236, 391, 423, 437, 442, 443, 444, 493, 508
8:2–3	241
8:3	238
8:3–4	261, 443, 509
8:4	23, 122, 146, 208, 212, 248, 249, 261, 308, 315, 331, 444
8:4–5	445
8:4–14	297
8:6	236, 445
8:6–7	481
8:7	536
8:9–11	472
8:10	32, 236, 239, 241, 262, 477
8:11	238, 408
8:12–13	236
8:13	445, 449, 480, 481, 482, 493
8:14	408, 445, 509
8:15	266, 408, 497
8:16	325, 326
8:23	408
8:23–25	406
8:24	260
8:25	377
8:26	273
8:26–27	371
8:27	414
8:28	365, 503
8:29	320, 470, 486
8:29–30	265
8:30	211, 265
8:31	355
8:31–34	220, 266, 271
8:32	56, 227, 268, 536
8:33	158
8:34	238
8:35	380
8:35–37	351
8:35–39	38
8:37	436, 498
8:38–39	380
9–11	251
9:8	172
9:11	222, 380
9:22	538, 541
9:30	65, 171, 177, 228
9:30–31	88
9:30–32	146
9:30–10:3	251
9:31–10:4	148
9:32	126, 224
9:32–33	148
9:33	283
10:3	33
10:3–6	171
10:4	128, 146, 214
10:5	61, 210, 261
10:5–8	150, 206
10:6	151, 210
10:8–10	289, 301
10:9	305, 310, 326
10:9–10	293
10:10	149, 171, 326
10:11	283
10:12	493
10:13	326
10:16	311
11:6	313
11:7	416
11:12	493
11:18	447
11:20–22	384
11:22	474
11:25–27	251
11:29	380
11:33	493
11:36	102
12:1	433, 479
12:2	423, 447, 470, 471, 489
12:3	344, 450
12:6	344
12:6–8	451

12:12	358	16:19	276, 302	6:1-8	465
12:13	414, 465	16:26	284, 302, 311	6:5-8	414
12:16	450			6:9	30
12:17-18	276	**1 Corinthians**		6:9-10	7, 466
12:18	265	1:2	398, 414, 471	6:9-11	27, 158
12:19	465	1:4	302	6:11	5, 149, 156,
13	250	1:4-5	451, 472		221, 258, 393,
13:1	228	1:7	451		398, 412, 461
13:2-5	250	1:9	313	7:7	451
13:8	212	1:18	414	7:14	397, 398, 415
13:8-10	105, 122, 138,	1:21	293	7:19	138
	146, 212, 249,	1:29-31	447	7:25	286
	261, 308, 315,	1:30	51, 101, 104,	7:34	479
	462		159, 163, 171,	8:6	305
13:9	264		174, 186, 197,	8:11	382
13:10	212		198, 212, 398,	9:12	461
13:11	260, 335		413, 468, 471	9:13	399
13:12-14	468	2:4-5	349	9:17	293
14	108, 465	2:6	408, 423	9:20-21	146
14:2	276	2:14	241	9:21	104, 105, 212,
14:5	376	2:16	468, 490		248, 256, 308,
14:8-9	303	3:1	471		315, 461
14:9	305	3:1-3	332, 490	9:22	404
14:10	149	3:1-4	481	9:27	382
14:10-12	68	3:6-7	480	10:12	385, 509
14:11	45	3:10	451	10:16	528
14:15	382	3:13	68	10:17	461
14:17	254, 304	3:14	69	10:21	461
14:17-18	7, 108, 304	3:15	414	10:28	399
14:21	108	3:21	447	10:29-30	440
14:23	224	4:1	255	10:33	404
15:4-5	316	4:2	286	11:1	303
15:5	377	4:4	26	11:25	528
15:10	451	4:5	68	11:27	528
15:15	228, 451	4:7	447	11:32	502
15:16	398, 403	4:15	486	12:3	303
15:18	302, 311	4:17	286, 477	12:4	451
15:18-19	267	4:20	7, 304, 349	12:6	404
15:25-26	414	5:5	414, 503	12:8-10	451
15:26	504	5:6	447	12:9	300, 365
15:30	501	5:7	125	12:28-30	365
15:31	414	5:11	382	12:28-31	451
16:2	414	6	414	12:31	452
16:7	471	6:1	30	13:2	341, 345, 351,
16:15	414	6:1-2	414		369

13:4–7	466		468, 497	9:12	414
13:13	300	4:2	493	10:3–5	501
14:1	452, 458, 459	4:4	467	10:5	311
14:12	452	4:5	309	10:17–18	447
14:20	423, 493	4:10–12	262	11:2	397
14:34	414	4:16	423	11:22	222
14:39	452	4:20–21	2	11:23	255
15:1–2	283, 293, 383	5:2–3	383	12:7	365, 503
15:3	103, 194	5:7	96, 408	12:7–9	371
15:17	241	5:10	68, 149	12:7–10	359
15:18	472	5:15	303	12:9	451, 472
15:22	472	5:17	29, 472, 508	12:12	377
15:27–28	102	5:18–20	100, 536	12:21	302
15:28	404, 456	5:19	179, 537	13:4	477
15:56	146	5:19–21	165	13:5	299, 327, 385, 477
15:58	67	5:20	48, 535, 536		
16:1	414	5:21	5, 46, 49, 51, 101, 103, 159, 163, 175, 176, 185, 186, 187, 189, 199, 212, 213, 264, 413, 472, 516, 530, 535	13:13	414
16:9	356				
16:10	67			**Galatians**	
16:13	299, 509			1:3–4	294
16:15	414			1:4	103, 194, 255
				1:6–9	305
2 Corinthians				1:10	256
1:1	414, 457			1:15	451
1:12	398, 426, 450	6:7	257, 456	1:22	471
1:19–20	92	6:9	502	1:23	299
1:21–22	349, 490	6:10	493	2:4	472
1:22	438	6:16–18	403	2:7	293
1:24	254	7:1	398, 420, 422, 427, 453, 457, 462, 479	2:9	451
2:14	477			2:10	504
2:15	414			2:11–14	511
2:16	230	7:5	500	2:15–16	149
3	100	7:9–11	426	2:16	10, 61, 65, 73, 95, 126, 153, 222, 228, 234
3:2–3	151	8:1	451		
3:3	100	8:4	414		
3:6	100	8:5	307	2:16–17	221
3:7	106, 113	8:6–7	451	2:16–19	126, 146
3:8	100	8:9	185, 493	2:19	106, 113, 214
3:9	100, 106, 113	8:19	451	2:20	95, 153, 234, 239, 262, 290, 294, 436, 472, 517
3:9–11	126	8:22	337		
3:14–15	153	9:1	414		
3:14–16	124	9:7	465		
3:15	117	9:8	67, 451	2:20–21	217
3:16	131, 153	9:9	504	2:21	214, 222
3:18	230, 313, 423,	9:10	256	3:1–5:4	146

587

3:2	73, 126	5:16–23	73	2:4–8	405
3:3	408	5:17	499	2:5	66, 335, 408
3:3–14	100	5:18	396	2:5–6	472
3:5	73, 126	5:19	247	2:6	474, 476
3:6	55, 89, 172	5:19–21	466	2:7	323, 472
3:6–8	90	5:19–22	253	2:8	154, 230, 232, 284, 293, 335
3:8	228	5:22	74, 254, 286, 300, 315, 465	2:8–9	65, 222
3:10	73, 106, 113, 535	5:22–23	235, 247, 458, 459	2:8–10	316, 405
3:10–12	126			2:9	447
3:11	29, 65, 95, 222, 259	5:24	239, 449, 481, 494	2:10	67, 223, 247
				2:13	472, 528
3:11–12	210	5:26	466	2:15	380, 403, 456
3:12	61, 206, 224, 261	6:1	385, 509	2:16	536
		6:2	104, 105, 146, 155, 212, 235, 248, 256, 308, 315, 461	2:19	414
3:13	185, 215, 535			2:20	283
3:18	146			2:21	480
3:19	205			3:7–8	451
3:22	95, 153, 234	6:7–8	68	3:8	323, 414
3:23	299	6:13	447	3:17	74, 477
3:24	228	6:14	470	3:18	414
3:25	299	6:15	29, 508	3:19	7
3:28	403			3:22–24	447
4:4	54, 215	**Ephesians**		4:1–2	450
4:4–5	520	1:1	414	4:5	305
4:5	408	1:1–14	472	4:7	451
4:6	266	1:4	433	4:10	102
4:9	470	1:5	408	4:10–12	439
4:19	216, 313, 468, 469, 477, 486, 497	1:6	215, 472, 474	4:11	84
		1:7	208, 323, 528	4:12	7, 67, 84, 414
		1:13	283, 293, 325, 438, 456, 490	4:13	313, 408, 423, 468, 480, 497
4:21	216			4:13–14	486
5	247	1:15	414	4:14	301
5:4	222, 224	1:18	382, 414	4:15–16	423, 480
5:6	9, 155, 223, 235, 250, 300, 310, 315, 400, 405	1:20	217	4:17–5:6	466
		1:20–23	302, 474	4:21	234, 477
		1:20–2:6	265	4:21–24	482, 483
		1:21	312	4:23	423
5:7	311	1:22	102	4:23–24	380
5:13–14	105, 462	1:23	404	4:24	29, 176, 187, 212, 242, 399, 403, 404, 413, 456, 481, 508
5:14	146	2:1	92, 408		
5:14–16	437	2:2	312		
5:15	138, 509	2:2–3	61		
5:16	396, 499, 509	2:3	140, 538		
5:16–22	297	2:4–6	472	4:25	466

Reference	Pages
4:25–5:20	476
4:25–6:9	476
4:28	67
4:31	466, 493
4:32	465
5:1–2	467
5:2	109, 294
5:3	414
5:6	515, 538, 541
5:8	467
5:8–9	248
5:9	257
5:18	261, 460, 490, 508
5:21–6:4	476
5:25–27	402
5:26	398
5:27	433
6:2–3	146
6:4	502
6:5–9	476
6:12–20	500
6:14	257
6:17	391
6:18	377, 414

Philippians

Reference	Pages
1:1	256, 414, 471
1:3	302
1:6	379
1:9–11	256
1:11	235, 247, 459
1:19	376, 406
1:20	429
1:21	468, 486
1:25	254
1:27	299, 501
1:29	284
1:30	501
2:3	447
2:5	468
2:6–8	469
2:8	200, 201, 205, 210
2:9–11	302, 305
2:10	45
2:12	311, 318, 367, 452
2:12–13	154, 285, 318, 384, 406
2:13	318, 367
2:20	286
2:30	67
3:4–6	65
3:4–9	127
3:5	222
3:5–6	128
3:6	84, 146, 211, 478
3:8	302, 468
3:8–10	496
3:9	5, 9, 46, 49, 65, 95, 128, 146, 153, 171, 178, 186, 187, 200, 210, 211, 224, 232, 234, 519
3:10	468
3:10–11	474
3:12	285, 408, 452, 511
3:12–14	458, 511
3:14	452, 506
3:15	408, 423, 511
3:18–19	505
3:19	296
3:20–21	406
3:21	102
4:5	465
4:6	339, 360, 465
4:7	387, 477
4:8	397
4:13	472
4:19	302
4:21	471
4:22	414

Colossians

Reference	Pages
1:2	414, 471
1:4	414
1:5	456, 467
1:6	456
1:7	286
1:9–11	313
1:10	67, 480
1:11	316, 377
1:12	332, 408, 414
1:13	7, 304
1:14	194
1:19–20	102, 103
1:20	528
1:20–21	536
1:21	536
1:21–22	103, 536
1:22	433
1:22–23	320, 383
1:23	474
1:26	414
1:27	472, 477
1:28	408, 423, 468, 477, 486, 497
1:29–2:1	501
2:2	493
2:6	309, 329
2:6–7	477
2:7	74, 299
2:8	470
2:9–10	468
2:10	312
2:11–13	472
2:13	66, 408
2:13–14	199
2:15	302
2:16–17	125
2:18	447
2:19	313, 480
2:20	470
2:23	448
3:1–4	216
3:2	505
3:4	216, 472, 476
3:5	480, 482, 483, 513
3:5–6	515

3:5-8	466	5:10	290	3:16	21, 26, 426
3:6	538, 541	5:14	465	4:1	299, 386
3:8	482, 493	5:15	88, 452, 458	4:4	504
3:9	466, 481	5:17	358	4:5	398
3:9-10	483	5:23	387, 398, 420,	4:6	299
3:9-11	380		457	4:7-8	426
3:10	403, 423, 456,			4:10	501
	508	**2 Thessalonians**		4:14	451
3:11	404	1:3	423, 480	4:16	509
3:12	414, 433, 450,	1:4	316, 378	5:4	426
	465	1:5	7, 304	5:8	299, 300
3:13	465	1:5-6	29	5:10	67, 223, 414
3:16	460	1:7	409	5:22	387, 397
3:23-24	67	1:7-9	103	5:25	67, 223
4:1	29	1:8	311	6:3	426
4:2	358, 501	1:9	20	6:5-6	426
4:12	408, 423, 489	1:10	409, 414	6:8	339
4:14	365	1:11	67, 235	6:9-10	466
		2:3	386	6:10	299
1 Thessalonians		2:13	396, 398, 431,	6:11	70, 85, 88,
1:3	67, 72, 235,		457		256, 300, 317,
	378	2:17	67		378, 412, 426,
1:4-6	328	3:2	286		452, 458, 459
1:5	349	3:3	286, 387	6:12	235, 264, 407,
1:6	303, 329	3:5	316, 378		501
1:10	538, 541			6:18	67, 223
2:2	501	**1 Timothy**		6:19	264
2:4	293	1:2	486	6:21	299, 300
2:10	433	1:7-10	146		
2:11-12	486	1:8-10	215	**2 Timothy**	
2:12	7, 304	1:11	293	1:1	472
2:13	329	1:12	286	1:2	486
2:14	471	1:13	130	1:6	451
2:16	538	1:18	486, 501	1:7	339
2:18	365	1:18-20	300	1:9	54, 65, 222,
3:13	398, 409, 414	1:19	299, 376		422
4:3	398	1:20	386, 503	1:10	283
4:3-4	457	2:2	426	1:12	294
4:3-7	466	2:3-4	328	2:1	451
4:4	398	2:6	517	2:1-2	504
4:7	398, 457	2:10	67, 223, 426	2:2	293
4:7-8	396	2:15	398	2:10	335
4:16	472	3:11	286	2:13	286, 428
5:8-9	406	3:13	337	2:15	391, 456
5:9	335, 538, 541	3:14	426	2:17	386

Scripture Index

2:18	153, 300	3:14	67, 223	6:5–6	318
2:19	292			6:10	414, 457
2:21	398, 479	**Philemon**		6:20	295, 502
2:22	70, 85, 88,	1:4	302	7:11	407
	254, 256, 300,	1:5	414	7:25	379, 399
	412, 452, 458,	1:7	414	7:26	194, 399
	459	1:10	486	8:1–2	418
2:25	502	1:18	173	8:5	125
3:1–5	381, 466	1:20	477	8:7	123
3:5	107, 426			8:13	123
3:8	300	**Hebrews**		9:1	23
3:10	316, 378	1:2	102	9:1–25	397
3:12	426, 477	1:3	194, 467	9:5	534
3:14	474	2:2	21	9:9	407
3:15	293, 396	2:5	335, 361	9:10	23
3:16–17	67, 256	2:9	278, 295	9:12	150, 528, 529
4:7	300, 501	2:10	295	9:13	398
4:8	4, 29, 30	2:11	398, 413, 417,	9:13–14	417
4:10	335, 376, 386		418, 457	9:14	72, 528
		2:14	459	9:22	118, 121, 204
Titus		2:17	117, 194, 286,	9:24	417, 418
1:1	256, 300, 426		534	9:28	237, 242
1:2	53	2:17–18	194	10	417
1:3	293	3:1	295, 414, 457	10:1	125
1:4	283, 300, 486	3:1–6	417	10:1–2	407
2:2	316, 378	3:2	286	10:2	417, 499
2:5	397	3:5	286	10:4	124
2:7	223	3:6	320, 383	10:5–10	125
2:10	286	3:12–13	385	10:10	295, 398, 413,
2:11	328	3:13	509		417, 457
2:11–12	154	3:14	70, 320, 383,	10:12	194
2:11–14	451		417	10:14	393, 398, 407,
2:12	426, 470, 502	4:1	385		413, 417, 457
2:13	283	4:6	312	10:18	238
2:13–14	67, 247, 294	4:11	385, 509	10:19	528
2:14	223, 402, 416	4:14	295	10:19–22	417, 418
3:2–3	466	5:7	295	10:24	67, 223
3:3	312	5:8	205	10:26	499
3:3–7	158	5:12–14	332	10:26–27	318
3:4–5	222, 405	5:13–14	256	10:26–29	383
3:5	65, 423, 461	5:14	408, 423	10:26–31	70, 502
3:6	460, 493	6:1	72, 308, 423	10:29	398, 415, 422
3:7	5, 224, 231,	6:4	416	10:31	271, 427
	239	6:4–6	70, 383, 389	10:32	500
3:8	67, 223	6:5	361	10:35	69

10:35-36	384	12:23	30, 408	2:19	289, 310
10:36	97, 377	12:24	529	2:20	459
10:37-38	96	12:25	385	2:20-24	220, 303
10:38	29, 95, 259, 295, 369	12:28	361	2:21	28, 334
		12:29	427	2:21-24	61
11	353, 508	13:2	465	2:21-25	5
11:1	300, 325	13:11	238, 529	2:21-26	248
11:3	300	13:12	295, 398, 413, 457, 528	2:22	235, 310, 408
11:4	30, 87			2:23	55, 89, 90, 172
11:5	87	13:14	361		
11:6	69, 313	13:15	120, 417, 418	2:24	65, 104, 149, 224
11:7	88	13:20	529		
11:9-10	361	13:24	414, 457	2:24-25	28
11:9-16	325			2:25	334
11:10	66	**James**		2:26	72, 305, 459
11:11	92, 286	1:1	256	3:2	85, 444, 484, 510
11:13-16	66	1:2-4	503		
11:16	361	1:3	235	3:13	67
11:19	92	1:4	377, 508	3:17	397
11:27	325	1:6-7	346	3:17-18	235
11:33	257, 351	1:6-8	340, 367	3:18	247, 248
11:33-35	369	1:18	456	4:1	500
11:33-38	354	1:20	46, 257	4:2	345
11:40	295, 408	1:21	406, 493	4:4	536
12	499	1:25	105, 110, 212, 248, 462	4:6	450
12:1	377, 502, 504			4:10	448
12:2	295, 360, 502, 506	1:27	250, 387	4:12	54
		2	10, 72, 155, 158, 248, 250, 303, 334, 405	5	356
12:3	499, 502			5:6	30
12:4	499, 500			5:7-9	97
12:5-11	502, 505	2:1	95, 153, 234	5:11	377
12:5	505	2:3	504	5:14-16	365, 504
12:6	506	2:5	7, 493	5:15	345, 356
12:9	505	2:6	504	5:15-16	307, 359
12:10	398, 415, 458, 501, 503, 506	2:8	105, 212, 248, 462	5:16	30, 77, 372, 374
12:11	235, 247, 459, 505, 506	2:8-12	65	5:19-20	391
		2:12	105, 110, 212, 248, 462	5:20	19
12:14	265, 398, 404, 412, 422, 447, 452, 453, 458, 459, 462, 478, 506	2:14-24	112	**1 Peter**	
		2:14-26	65, 149, 315, 459	1:1-2	221, 393, 414
				1:2	311, 396, 398, 431, 529
		2:15-16	504		
12:15	325, 376, 466	2:17	294, 305, 459	1:3	65
12:22	361	2:17-26	246	1:3-5	335

Scripture Index

1:4–5	380	4:10	451	1:3	313, 475
1:6–7	503	4:13	503	1:3–4	473
1:7	235	4:17	311, 416	1:5	425, 432, 467
1:9	284, 293	4:18	30, 378, 406	1:7	506, 508, 529
1:14	470	4:19	355	1:8	424, 444, 484,
1:14–16	453	5:5	450		491, 494, 510,
1:15–16	397, 461	5:6	448		512, 513
1:16	398, 424, 455	5:7	339, 498	1:9	26, 30, 32,
1:17	69	5:8	385, 509		39, 46, 47, 56,
1:18–20	125	5:9	299		100, 118, 119,
1:19	529	5:10	380, 471		153, 187, 226,
1:19–20	54	5:14	471		233, 273, 307,
1:22–2:1	297				326, 329, 331,
1:23–25	406	**2 Peter**			450, 513
2:1	466, 493, 500	1:1	46, 197, 256,	1:10	512
2:2	406, 423, 447,		283, 300	2:1	30, 77, 331,
	480	1:3	426		424, 485, 494,
2:2–3	451	1:4	7		508, 510, 512,
2:4	283	1:5–7	317		513
2:5	399, 417	1:6–7	426	2:1–2	538
2:6	283	1:10	484, 508	2:2	194, 534, 535
2:9	399, 417	1:11	7, 283, 406	2:3	105, 383
2:9–10	403, 416	2:1	381	2:3–6	489
2:11	509	2:5	88	2:3–8	308
2:12	67, 223	2:7–8	30	2:4	137
2:19–20	451	2:9	426	2:5	407
2:21	303	2:20	283	2:5–6	473
2:23	4, 511	2:20–21	385	2:6	488
2:24	29, 53, 103,	2:20–22	70	2:7–8	490
	192, 194, 208,	2:21	256	2:8	264
	256, 278, 516,	3:2	283	2:9–11	84, 490
	517, 523, 528	3:9	328	2:10	474, 488
3:2	397	3:11	426, 479	2:12	485
3:5	414	3:13	102, 103, 456	2:12–14	485
3:8	450	3:16	315	2:12–17	495
3:14	257, 516, 526	3:17	386	2:12–27	485
3:15	303, 309, 310,	3:18	423, 447, 450,	2:13	485, 487
	398, 430		468, 480, 486,	2:13–14	313, 486, 495
3:16	477		496	2:14	485, 487, 488
3:18	30, 77, 194,			2:15–17	488, 500
	517	**1 John**		2:17	488
3:21–22	302	1:1	456	2:18	485, 488
4:1–2	239	1:1–3	486	2:18–19	381, 386
4:2	489, 508	1:1–4	211	2:18–27	500
4:9	465	1:2	102	2:19	489

593

2:20	349, 397, 419	4:15	491	1:7	20
2:23	491	4:15–16	488	1:14	409
2:24	383, 473, 488	4:16	268, 426, 432,	1:20	300, 346, 347,
2:25	53		467, 488		396, 397
2:26	489	4:17	39, 237, 264	1:20–21	384, 387
2:27	349, 488, 490	4:17–18	408		
2:27–28	473, 488	4:18	507	**Revelation**	
2:28	485, 488	4:19	154	1:5	103, 194, 529
2:29	30, 190, 256, 489	4:19–5:3	105	1:9	316
		4:20	383	2	416
3:3	397	4:20–21	490	2:2	67, 316
3:4–9	494	4:20–5:2	84	2:4–5	72
3:6	190, 473, 484, 491, 506, 508, 512	4:21	490	2:10	286
		5:1	284, 491	2:13	95
		5:2	490	2:19	67, 316
3:7	30, 190, 256, 489	5:2–3	264, 308	2:20–23	381
		5:3	462, 489	2:21	72
3:9	71, 190, 484, 488, 491, 506, 512	5:4–5	235, 351, 500	2:23	69, 71
		5:5	491	3	416
		5:6	529	3:1–3	71
3:9–10	491	5:8	529	3:7	397, 419
3:10	84, 190, 256	5:11–12	474	3:8	67, 356
3:14	84, 490	5:11–13	476	3:10	316
3:14–15	488	5:13	292	3:15–16	72
3:15	262	5:14	345, 360	3:15–17	381
3:17	488, 504	5:14–15	353, 371	3:19	502
3:18–19	490	5:16	512	4:8	431
3:21–22	371	5:18	190, 387, 488, 491, 494, 507, 512	5:4	399
3:22	489			5:8	414
3:22–24	308			5:9	529
3:23	292			6:10	397, 432
3:24	473, 488, 490	**2 John**		6:16	541
4:1–6	489	1:5–6	490	6:16–17	538
4:2	491	1:6	105, 264, 462	7:14	529
4:4	487	1:7	489, 491	8:3–4	414
4:7	63	1:8	69, 509	11:2	395
4:7–8	490	1:9	474	11:15	144
4:8	268, 426, 432, 467			11:18	69, 414, 538
		3 John		12:10	336
4:9	38	1:5	286	12:11	339, 529
4:10	103, 194, 534, 536			13:7	415
		Jude		13:8	54
4:12	488	1:1	256	13:10	316, 415
4:13	473, 488, 490	1:3	300, 346, 376, 414, 501	14:4	303
4:14	103, 283			14:10	409, 538, 541

14:12	95, 153, 234, 316, 415
14:13	69
15:2	339
15:4	23, 24, 427
16:5	4, 30, 399, 419, 428
16:6	415
16:19	538
17:6	415
18:4	403
18:20	414
18:24	415
19:2	4
19:8	23, 24, 257, 414, 492
19:11	4
19:15	538
20:6	433
20:9	414
21:1–7	103
21:1–8	103
21:2	395
21:3–4	403
21:5	102
21:7	339
21:8	103, 339
21:9	467
21:10	395
21:11	467
22:2	75
22:11	29, 257, 398, 478
22:17	325
22:19	395

Subject Index

A

Aalders, Willem 430, 454, 467
Aaron 288, 417, 418
Abana 368
Abel 87, 88
Abigail 356
Abraham 48, 60, 61, 64, 79, 85, 86, 87, 88, 89, 90, 91, 92, 93, 94, 96, 111, 120, 153, 158, 166, 167, 170, 171, 176, 219, 220, 222, 223, 248, 249, 253, 259, 334, 351, 353, 356, 360, 361, 362, 372
Abram 55, 63, 87, 89, 166, 282, 353
Adam 121, 144, 198, 201, 205, 211, 213, 214, 215, 216, 225, 273, 274, 275, 277, 519
Adamson, James 10, 500
Adeyemo, T. 47, 73, 173, 260, 339, 341, 370, 390
Adorno, T. W. 296
Ahasuerus 269, 271
Alexander 300, 386
Allen, R. O. 296
Althaus, Paul 36, 432, 433, 434, 436, 437
Ambrosiaster 32
Ananias 77, 386, 390
Andria, S. 73
Anglicans 12, 476
Anna 76
Anselm 239, 520
Antichrist 386, 487
Antichrists 381, 386, 500
Apostasy 375, 376, 378, 380, 383, 384, 386, 388, 389, 390, 502, 505
Apostles 7, 84, 87, 113, 118, 122, 152, 284, 307, 333, 338, 339, 341, 365, 493, 510
Apostles' Creed 8, 289
Aquinas, Thomas 31, 431, 520
Arminian trauma 318, 319

Arminianism 183, 319, 375
Arminians 19, 381
Arminius, Jacob 285, 320, 378
Asa 80
Ashby, Stephen M. 379
Atlas 4
Atonement 6, 7, 55, 103, 118, 119, 192, 204, 225, 227, 278, 402, 497, 515, 517, 520, 521, 522, 530, 534, 535, 536, 537
Augsburg Confession 10, 513
Augustine 8, 9, 11, 15, 32, 33, 34, 144, 175, 321, 362, 422, 433, 434, 436, 501
Augustinus 230
Aune, David E. 12

B
Babylon 403, 415
Balaam 43
Balak 43
Baptism 8, 9, 14, 15, 169, 223, 241, 251, 255, 323, 390, 420, 421, 472, 474, 476, 523
Barbarians 403
Barclay, William 361
Barker, G.W. 512
Barnabas 511
Barnett, P. 360, 383
Barrett, Charles 540
Barth, Karl 12, 17, 34, 35, 36, 48, 136, 173, 175, 189, 199, 231, 286, 287, 412, 431, 433, 436, 458, 496
Bartimaeus 347, 356
Bauer, W. 478
Bavinck, Herman 3, 17, 31, 36, 54, 56, 69, 73, 182, 183, 185, 191, 198, 241, 316, 321, 396, 397, 412, 431, 436, 518, 520
Beautiful Gate 356, 359
Beker, J.C 36
Belgic Confession 69, 72, 114, 164, 182, 224, 228, 245, 257, 375, 400, 411, 469, 475, 492, 515, 522, 535
Ben Levi, Rabbi Joshua, 119
Benedict XVI 9, 13, 523
Bengel, Johannes 433
Berakoth 119
Berger, Klaus 427
Bergquist, R. A. 202, 203
Berkhof, Hendrikus 3, 12, 17, 32, 35, 36, 221, 315, 327, 451, 478, 480
Berkhof, Louis 190, 195, 209, 213, 316, 401, 402, 455, 478, 480, 518, 535
Berkouwer, Gerrit C. 17, 18, 19, 36, 42, 69, 72, 73, 91, 113, 176, 182, 183, 189, 190, 200, 229, 232, 248, 253, 316, 336, 346, 375, 379, 381, 383, 384, 386, 387, 412,

Subject Index

433, 434,
435, 447,
448, 460,
462, 479,
496, 497,
498, 518,
520, 534,
539
Bernard, J. H.
186
Berrouard, M. F.
49
Beutel, A. 14
Bible 3, 4, 6, 10,
36, 65, 74,
77, 85,
102, 107,
121, 134,
135, 153,
160, 177,
180, 182,
196, 197,
199, 203,
205, 208,
210, 220,
221, 231,
232, 289,
296, 298,
305, 319,
330, 353,
374, 378,
381, 390,
391, 414,
441, 442,
467, 499,
514
Billerbeck, P.
34, 263,
361
Blaauwendraad,
Johan
323
Blocher, H. A.
13
Bloesch, Donald G.

Blood
3, 455
21, 37, 38,
39, 41, 70,
71, 77, 87,
88, 118,
121, 122,
124, 125,
150, 166,
167, 168,
187, 194,
200, 202,
204, 205,
208, 219,
220, 221,
223, 224,
225, 226,
231, 237,
238, 243,
244, 245,
264, 269,
273, 278,
284, 301,
335, 356,
362, 363,
384, 389,
393, 412,
413, 414,
415, 416,
418, 439,
473, 492,
499, 506,
515, 520,
526, 528,
529, 530,
535, 540
Blood of Christ
39, 121,
122, 125,
167, 168,
187, 224,
225, 243,
264, 273,
389, 412,
413, 529
Bloody sacrifice

121, 124,
139
Blum, E. A.
315, 523
Boardman, W. E.
424
Body of Christ
7, 9, 212,
441, 475
Bogerman, Johannes
520
Boice, J. M.
303
Bolkestein, M. H.
535
Bonhoeffer, Dietrich
136, 138,
315, 451
Bos 520
Bouma, C.
300, 361
Bounds, Chris
423
Boyd, G. A.
374
Braaten, C. E.
3
Brakel, Wilhelmus à
319
Brinkman, M.E.
12
Brinkman, J.
36
Brockhaus, R.
36
Brother Andrew
373
Brown, Colin
20, 36,
172, 282,
395, 407,
523, 533,
539
Bruce, A. B.
340

Bruce, F. F.
    230, 457,
    482
Brümmer, V.
    537
Brunner, Emil
    36, 294,
    431, 432,
    462, 535
Buber, Martin
    249, 250
Buddhists 298
Budiman, Rudy
    36, 173
Burdick, Donald W.
    406, 500

C
Cain   87
Calvary   481, 529,
    537
Calvin, John
    3, 12, 33,
    73, 113,
    139, 163,
    165, 192,
    193, 194,
    195, 197,
    230, 253,
    276, 354,
    535, 537
Calvinism 7, 374
Calvinists 12, 16,
    193, 374,
    379
Cana   370
Canaan   336
Canaanite woman
    349, 352,
    357, 362
Canadian Reformed
    Churches
    323
Canons of Dort
    71, 229,
    292, 316,
    321, 326,
    327, 330,
    375, 376,
    410, 535
Capernaum
    342, 347
Carson, Donald A.
    113, 134,
    135, 145,
    147, 184,
    224, 338
Catechism of the
    Catholic Church
    14
Catholics   2, 11, 12,
    13, 14, 19,
    314, 381,
    421, 476
Chafer, Lewis Sperry
    188, 525,
    526
Chaldeans 95
Children of God
    84, 105,
    256, 325,
    329, 475,
    487, 491
Christ's blood
    220, 223,
    225, 269,
    492
Christ's redemptive
    work
    36, 275,
    276, 277
Christian Reformed
    Churches
    322, 517
Christianity
    4, 5, 8, 11,
    107, 122,
    128, 135,
    299, 386,
    416, 501

Christians 2, 15, 69,
    70, 72,
    116, 130,
    140, 157,
    294, 297,
    298, 304,
    319, 327,
    334, 352,
    378, 379,
    381, 388,
    389, 390,
    394, 402,
    404, 406,
    414, 416,
    422, 428,
    445, 448,
    449, 454,
    465, 466,
    470, 476,
    492, 494,
    497, 502,
    505, 509,
    511, 512,
    513
Chrysostom, John
    130, 300
Church fathers
    16, 32, 433
Church of the
    Nazarene
    421
Circumcision
    106, 113,
    133, 138,
    177, 196,
    223, 472,
    520, 526
Clarke, Adam
    421
Coates, Charles
    36, 37, 43,
    91, 93,
    100, 167,
    221, 233,
    244, 254,

Subject Index

255, 267,
268, 272,
323, 447,
477, 502
Cohen, A. 62
Commandments
26, 60, 61,
62, 63, 66,
75, 79, 84,
86, 87, 88,
105, 107,
108, 109,
111, 116,
129, 136,
137, 138,
145, 147,
150, 196,
199, 205,
209, 212,
215, 216,
234, 246,
249, 261,
262, 263,
264, 301,
308, 371,
400, 415,
425, 462,
465, 484,
489, 490,
492
Comrie, Alexander
318, 319,
320, 438
Condemnation
23, 106,
113, 126,
127, 165,
192, 225,
236, 238,
270, 274,
275, 441,
472
Confessionalism
112, 161
Confessions

5, 16, 165,
182, 203,
245
Congar, Y. 49
Consecration
155, 395,
398, 409,
416, 417,
418, 424,
454, 463
Conversion
14, 15, 32,
119, 127,
130, 156,
168, 211,
284, 301,
303, 304,
306, 311,
316, 328,
330, 388,
394, 402,
408, 409,
410, 412,
435, 461,
463, 482,
491
Corneliu 260, 366,
438
Cosmos 102, 103
Council of Trent
46, 312,
313, 322
Counter-
Remonstrants
376, 377
Covenant of grace
143, 144,
318
Covenantal nomism
112, 115,
116, 118,
121, 122,
134, 135,
145, 147,
148, 149

Covenants 4, 116,
121, 123,
143, 144,
150, 151
Cranfield, C. E. B.
34, 227,
236, 263,
436
Creeds 5, 8, 203,
316
Cremer, Hermann
396
Cross of Christ
16, 42,
200, 449

D
Da Costa, I.
496
Damascus 132, 368,
438
Darby, John N.
36, 103,
153, 423,
449, 457,
483, 486,
495, 506,
522
Darmstadt 94
Das, A. A. 139
David 51, 61, 63,
76, 80, 84,
85, 88,
101, 164,
171, 222,
233, 252,
263, 268,
271, 272,
343, 347,
349, 356,
372, 373,
374
Davids, P. H.
406

601

Davies, William
　5, 6, 139
Dawkins, Richard
　501
Day of Atonement
　278
Day of Pentecost
　260
De Boer, W.
　378
De Chirico, Leonardo
　14
De Groot, D. J.
　16, 506,
　511, 520
De Montefiore,
　Claude
　115
De Reuver, A.
　16
De Ru, Gerrit
　8
Death of Christ
　37, 41,
　150, 166,
　191, 192,
　199, 212,
　215, 241,
　242, 265,
　266, 449,
　482, 500,
　513, 520,
　535
Deborah　356
Deification
　7, 455, 467
Deism　463
Deliverance
　6, 13, 42,
　76, 99,
　147, 359,
　442, 448,
　527
Demarest, Bruce
　3, 17, 19,
　34, 73,
　173, 175,
　200, 204,
　305, 316,
　366, 397,
　412, 420,
　424, 458,
　475, 476,
　481, 507,
　533
Demas　386
Dembele, Y.
　260
Demons　289, 310,
　330, 348,
　359, 365,
　386, 419
Denney, James
　34, 37,
　201, 230,
　232, 236,
　240, 276
DeSilva, D. A.
　154
Diestel, L.　431
Discipline　247, 382,
　454, 501,
　502, 503,
　504, 505,
　506
Dittes, J. E.
　296
Doctrine of
　justification
　2, 3, 4, 5,
　6, 7, 8, 9,
　11, 12, 13,
　14, 16, 56,
　89, 116,
　160, 164,
　169, 171,
　176, 178,
　179, 190,
　191, 203,
　239, 248,
　250, 251,
　315, 534
Dodd, Charles H.
　36, 230,
　512, 539
Doddridge, Philip
　441
Dods, M.　456
Dordrecht　375
Duffield, Guy P.
　3, 22, 191,
　381, 483
Duncan, J. Ligon
　160
Duncan, John
　446
Dunn, James
　106, 112,
　132, 133,
　134, 135,
　139, 201,
　203

E
Eastern Orthodox
　tradition
　409, 455
Eastern Orthodoxy
　7
Eastern theology
　8
Ebert, K.　251
Edwards, Jonathan
　199, 520
Egypt　139, 147,
　353, 425
Egyptians　281, 428
Eichrodt, W.
　31, 53,
Elam, A. E.
　202, 203
Eleazar　80
Election　139, 143,
　144, 317,
　318, 320,

Subject Index

Elijah 321, 327, 328, 380, 388, 484, 508
Elijah 353, 356, 359
Elisha 359, 368
Elizabeth 63, 72, 75, 111, 128
Ellis, E. E. 383
Emmaus 527
Enoch 63, 87, 88
Enosh 87
Epistle of Mathetes to Diognetus 185
Erasmus 436
Erickson, Millard 518, 540
Erskine, E. 321
Esau 535
Esther 220, 269, 270, 271
Eternal life 7, 15, 32, 53, 62, 66, 68, 71, 159, 165, 198, 202, 205, 211, 216, 236, 239, 240, 244, 246, 247, 255, 262, 264, 283, 284, 294, 295, 304, 321, 326, 377, 379, 389, 390, 407, 409, 423, 439, 450, 457, 519, 527
Eternity 19, 53, 144, 244, 290, 291, 294, 317, 319, 334, 373, 374, 405, 426, 431, 537
Ethiopian eunuch 260
Ethnocentrism 105, 106, 112, 113, 114, 123, 133, 146
Evangelicals 12, 191, 379, 381
Expositors 30, 34, 36, 48, 95, 96, 153, 201, 286, 287, 338, 414, 456

F
Faithfulness 2, 30, 31, 32, 35, 48, 53, 96, 97, 98, 108, 153, 155, 231, 235, 247, 254, 272, 285, 286, 287, 302, 332, 348, 371, 383, 397, 458
Federalists 4, 144
Feiner, J. 12
Finsterbusch, K. 139

Flusser, David 135
Forgiveness 6, 8, 11, 15, 26, 35, 39, 46, 47, 60, 70, 76, 85, 86, 116, 117, 118, 119, 121, 122, 139, 143, 144, 147, 148, 149, 167, 169, 193, 202, 208, 238, 239, 265, 266, 290, 304, 307, 325, 329, 331, 363, 411, 427, 450, 485, 528
Forsyth, Peter T. 38, 39
Fountain of life 62, 75
France, Richard T. 109, 337, 338, 348, 350, 357
Francke, August Hermann 433
Frankfurt am Main 135
Free Reformed Churches 323
Freedom 15, 105, 110, 137, 248, 388, 423, 462,

603

537
Friesen, A. 251

G
Gaebelein, A. C.
  36, 50,
  304, 361
Galilee 370
Gamaliel 130, 147
Gaston, L. 139
Geisler, Norman L.
  379
Geneva Catechism
  524
Gentiles 67, 81, 88,
  90, 133,
  206, 207,
  211, 222,
  228, 232,
  251, 311,
  320, 338,
  349, 350,
  351, 398,
  402, 403,
  404, 451,
  456
Gerhard, Johann
  32
Germans 135, 466,
  534
Germany 94, 135,
  251
Gethsemane
  360, 526
Gilgal 43, 395
Gill, John 338, 351
Glock, C. Y.
  296,
Glorification
  50, 265
God the Father
  220, 221,
  229, 250,
  298, 318,
  387, 393,
  414, 535
God's grace
  8, 13, 15,
  50, 118,
  121, 124,
  144, 146,
  152, 154,
  178, 220,
  223, 224,
  225, 232,
  274, 282,
  323, 324,
  325, 388,
  422, 424,
  427, 431,
  451, 455,
  460, 496
God's love 2, 38, 42,
  44, 46, 47,
  105, 153,
  267, 268,
  428, 431,
  432, 459,
  488, 537
God's Word
  63, 326,
  327, 415,
  488, 493
God's wrath
  37, 71,
  250, 516,
  517, 525,
  533, 541
Godet, Frederick L.
  201, 276
Godhead 220, 469,
  475, 539
Godliness 107, 114,
  223, 256,
  317, 322,
  376, 381,
  426, 452,
  479, 496
Goertz, H.-J.
  251
Goliath 268, 369
Gomarus, Francis
  285
González, A.
  19
Gospel 1, 3, 5, 6,
  7, 15, 32,
  34, 36, 38,
  40, 42, 47,
  64, 95,
  136, 142,
  143, 144,
  148, 151,
  159, 160,
  201, 221,
  230, 246,
  259, 267,
  275, 278,
  282, 283,
  285, 293,
  299, 301,
  302, 304,
  305, 306,
  307, 309,
  310, 311,
  320, 321,
  324, 325,
  328, 329,
  349, 351,
  360, 383,
  386, 389,
  414, 437,
  438, 451,
  483, 486,
  501, 522
Graafland, C.
  321
Grace of God
  4, 39, 150,
  154, 167,
  217, 223,
  224, 244,
  246, 254,
  255, 274,
  275, 282,

Subject Index

323, 324, 325, 328, 363, 394, 450, 451, 474
Grant, Frederick W. 36, 47, 50, 93, 204, 232, 443, 525
Gravemeijer, Henricus 4
Great Tribulation 304
Greeks 222, 308, 321, 403
Green, Joel B. 64, 76, 108, 460
Greijdanus, Seakle 36, 46, 436, 523
Griffith Thomas, W.H. 440
Grosheide 48, 230, 383, 482, 511
Gundry, Robert H. 184
Gundry, S. N. 420

H
Habakkuk 60, 87, 94, 95, 96, 220, 259
Haitjema, Theodorus 17
Haldane, R. 276
Han, Cheon-Seol 166
Harinck, Cornelis 4, 5, 319, 438, 449
Harper, J. Steven 379
Harris, M. J. 186
Harrison, Everett 36, 47, 436, 437, 440, 442
Häring, Th. 36
Headlam, A. C. 36, 236, 276
Heaven 8, 15, 22, 67, 69, 79, 87, 96, 102, 103, 106, 110, 132, 137, 143, 144, 150, 151, 157, 199, 202, 224, 254, 262, 304, 331, 335, 351, 353, 362, 380, 381, 385, 388, 417, 459, 497, 504, 526, 537, 538
Heidelberg Catechism 70, 101, 102, 154, 155, 164, 181, 182, 224, 229, 245, 288, 301, 325, 364, 375, 399, 410, 423, 428, 434, 439, 445, 446, 448, 469, 477, 480, 484, 492, 498, 504, 516, 522
Heresies 298, 315, 381
Herrmann, Johannes 539
Heyns, Johan 173, 185, 301, 316, 411, 455, 463, 480, 536
Hezekiah 80, 371, 372
Hindus 298
Hinrichs, C. 251
Hodge, C. A. 276
Hodges, Zane C. 306, 307, 308, 309, 310, 312, 314, 315
Hodges, H. A. 534
Hoekema, A. A. 506
Holiness 29, 76, 123, 164, 176, 181, 187, 194, 229, 242, 246, 257, 313, 317, 393, 394, 395, 396, 397, 398,

399, 401,
403, 404,
409, 410,
411, 412,
413, 415,
416, 419,
420, 421,
422, 423,
424, 425,
426, 427,
428, 429,
430, 431,
432, 445,
447, 452,
453, 454,
456, 457,
458, 459,
461, 462,
463, 464,
465, 466,
467, 468,
478, 479,
480, 482,
495, 502,
506
Holl, Karl 17, 18
Holy Ghost
    11, 325
Holy Spirit
    13, 14, 15,
    26, 49, 59,
    65, 66, 74,
    75, 76,
    106, 108,
    113, 123,
    129, 151,
    157, 159,
    178, 207,
    208, 212,
    222, 245,
    246, 254,
    255, 259,
    262, 269,
    274, 293,
    297, 298,

303, 304,
311, 318,
325, 326,
328, 329,
331, 348,
349, 353,
366, 376,
378, 380,
383, 384,
387, 388,
389, 390,
394, 396,
397, 400,
403, 405,
409, 411,
412, 415,
416, 418,
419, 421,
424, 432,
435, 436,
437, 438,
439, 440,
442, 444,
445, 446,
447, 448,
449, 450,
454, 455,
460, 462,
463, 466,
476, 479,
480, 481,
483, 484,
487, 489,
493, 496,
500, 501,
506, 507,
508, 509,
514, 518
Holocaust 81
Horton, Michael S.
    310, 379
Hübner, H.
    131
Hughes, P. E.
    186

Hulda   356
Hultgren, A.
    36
Human
    responsibility
    122, 152,
    282, 285,
    292, 317,
    318, 320,
    321, 363,
    377, 384,
    387, 388,
    416, 422,
    424
Humanists
    436
Humanity 4, 17, 93,
    122, 167,
    211, 213,
    229, 233,
    275, 278,
    396, 521,
    530, 534,
    537
Humans 2, 16, 18,
    29, 35, 36,
    37, 38, 39,
    46, 122,
    155, 209,
    211, 214,
    231, 233,
    241, 284,
    286, 298,
    364, 365,
    427, 430,
    458, 467,
    510, 521,
    528, 529,
    530, 533,
    535, 536,
    537, 538
Humility 322, 332,
    447, 448,
    449, 450,
    452, 495,

Subject Index

496, 497
Hunsinger, G. 13
Hunter, Archibald 7
Huntington, William 388
Husbands, M. 5, 184
Hymenaeus 300, 386
Hyper-Calvinism 344, 484, 496
Hyper-Calvinists 16, 327, 328, 498
Hypocrites 79, 82, 108, 122, 129, 147, 331

I
Ibn Ezra 51, 62
Imputation 2, 16, 17, 28, 159, 160, 163, 164, 165, 166, 169, 170, 175, 178, 179, 180, 181, 182, 183, 184, 187, 190, 191, 193, 197, 198, 202, 203, 213, 253, 319, 399, 518
Incarnation 7, 360, 491, 517

Indiana 12
Institutes of the Christian Religion 3, 73, 165, 193, 194, 535
Isaac 61, 64, 88, 90, 92, 93, 111, 120, 219, 248, 263, 334, 351, 361
Isaak, P. J. 341
Israel 21, 43, 44, 45, 51, 59, 60, 61, 62, 63, 72, 74, 76, 80, 83, 85, 88, 95, 98, 99, 101, 106, 108, 112, 114, 127, 129, 130, 131, 133, 138, 139, 148, 149, 152, 153, 205, 207, 211, 251, 252, 261, 264, 268, 275, 281, 290, 304, 330, 334, 348, 350, 353, 368, 369, 373, 396, 402, 403, 416, 420, 425, 428, 429, 464, 527
Israelites 66, 82, 288, 351,

398, 416, 428
Italy 14

J
Jacob 64, 88, 120, 251, 285, 351, 378, 428, 534
Jacobs, D. 36, 230, 232, 436
Jael 356
Jager, Harm Jan 36, 182, 183
Jairus 342, 357, 368
Jansenists 436
Jehoshaphat 288
Jerusalem 64, 77, 81, 101, 110, 130, 152, 186, 272, 281, 290, 361, 374, 395, 467
Jesuits 436
Jesus Christ 1, 5, 10, 14, 15, 27, 30, 34, 41, 46, 48, 52, 67, 70, 71, 77, 92, 125, 126, 128, 140, 142, 149, 154, 155, 157, 158, 159, 160, 164, 166, 170, 182, 186, 191,

607

Jews 197, 200, 202, 221, 222, 225, 228, 231, 234, 236, 244, 247, 256, 258, 266, 269, 274, 275, 284, 294, 298, 308, 309, 311, 318, 331, 335, 376, 379, 385, 387, 393, 406, 412, 413, 414, 417, 420, 431, 436, 449, 450, 451, 457, 467, 468, 475, 486, 491, 494, 496, 498, 503, 512, 522, 530, 535, 537, 538 34, 77, 81, 108, 112, 113, 115, 116, 117, 118, 124, 129, 130, 131, 132, 134, 135, 136, 137, 138, 144, 145, 146, 147, 148, 149, 152, 168, 207, 214, 221, 222, 232, 260, 270, 289, 293, 304, 308, 321, 403, 404, 438, 456

John the Baptist 7, 76, 273, 291, 307, 313

John Paul II 420

Johnson, Terry L. 373, 446

Joint Declaration on the Doctrine of Justification 13, 14

Jonathan 272, 273

Joseph 76, 117, 516

Joseph of Arimathea 77

Josephus 540

Judah 51, 52, 99, 101, 149, 281

Judaism 19, 31, 59, 76, 112, 113, 114, 115, 116, 117, 118, 121, 122, 123, 128, 131, 132, 133, 134, 135, 139, 145, 146, 147, 148, 152

Judaizers 123

Judgment of God 33, 70, 108, 194, 513

Judgment seat of God 4, 68, 149, 157, 193, 194, 197, 253

Jüngel, E. 3

Justification by faith 3, 4, 5, 9, 10, 25, 89, 91, 101, 104, 133, 149, 220, 221, 250, 253, 305, 307, 313, 314, 315, 438

Justification by works 15, 104, 220, 249, 250, 251, 305

Justice 2, 10, 15, 20, 21, 22, 31, 34, 40, 42, 43, 51, 52, 53, 54, 55, 56, 64, 78, 83, 88, 98, 100, 101, 108, 132, 138, 142, 146, 160, 240, 242, 251, 252, 254, 263, 267, 276, 278, 324, 353, 358, 395, 404, 465

K

Kapolyo, J. 339

Subject Index

Kasali, D. M. 47, 173
Käsemann, E. 36, 227
Kassa, T. 390
Keck, Leander 41
Kelly, William 36, 50, 231, 232, 441, 442, 457, 512, 513, 525, 527, 539
Kennedy, H. A. A. 407
Kent, Homer 407
Kersten, G. H. 19, 25, 299, 410
Kertelge, K. 36
Kingdom of God 7, 27, 65, 66, 103, 108, 143, 158, 248, 253, 254, 282, 304, 307, 333, 336, 340, 349, 350, 362, 407
Kingdom of heaven 15, 254, 331, 351, 381
Kittel, G. 20, 30, 36, 53, 56, 172, 276, 282, 395, 407
Klinghardt, M. 139

Kohlbrugge, Hermann F. 16, 17, 434, 478, 479, 496
König, Adrio 17, 18, 36, 386
Korah 498
Korff, F. W. A. 535
Kraan, K. J. 342
Kühl, E. 36
Kümmel, Werner 433, 440
Küng, Hans 12
Kuyper, Abraham 17, 461

L
Lalleman, Pieter 512
Lane, A. N. S. 12, 13
Lapide, Pinchas 134, 135, 136, 137, 138
Laodicea 71
Law, R. 512
Law of Christ 248, 256, 308, 315
Law of God 136, 195, 248, 274, 435
Law of Moses 26, 221, 222, 291
Law of sin 238, 274, 423, 437, 441, 442,

443, 444, 446
Laws 31, 196, 199, 207, 248, 442
Lechler, Gotthard V. 201, 203
Legalism 105, 106, 107, 109, 112, 113, 114, 123, 133, 146, 310, 462, 466
Legalists 144
Lehrmann, S. M. 51
Lekkerkerker, A. F. 3, 9, 535
Leuenberg Concord 5
Levites 416
Liberation theology 420
Liebers, R. 139
Lightfoot, J. B. 236, 276
Locher, J. C. S. 10
Löhrer, M. 12
Lombard, Peter 431
Longenecker, Richard 201, 511
Lord's Supper 195, 223, 323, 476, 517, 518
Love of God 15, 38, 39, 105, 108, 136, 254, 255, 267, 318, 380,

609

384, 387,
462, 505,
507
Lubbertus, Sibrandus
520
Luther, Martin
3, 4, 10,
11, 12, 16,
31, 32, 33,
113, 136,
137, 139,
174, 175,
185, 188,
189, 192,
193, 197,
250, 251,
266, 282,
294, 312,
313, 314,
434, 436,
493, 499,
507, 513
Lutheranism
7
Lutherans 12, 13, 16,
193, 314,
381, 476
Lydia 260
Lystra 357

M
MacArthur, J. F.
303, 306,
314
Macquarrie, John
6
Manson, William
441
Marshall, Howard
386, 485,
538
Martin, B. L.
139
Martyr, Justin
31, 90

Mary 76, 94,
117, 419,
421
McConnachie, J.
412
McCormack, B. L.
13
McGrath, Alister
9, 12, 19,
28, 33,
175, 188,
189, 312,
314
Medema, H. P.
36
Meijering, E. P.
8
Melanchton, Philip
16, 19, 28,
287
Melchizedek
535
Mephibosheth
220, 271,
272
Messiah 43, 44, 51,
52, 96, 98,
101, 123,
150, 151,
152, 186,
252, 302,
305, 350,
361, 460
Messianic Kingdom
62, 64, 66,
96, 98,
122, 129,
137, 144,
211, 252,
335, 336,
362, 396
Methodist Churches
421
Meyer, Frederick B.
424

Meyer, Heinrich A.
34, 201,
203, 276
Moab 43
Moerkerken, Aart
192, 325,
411, 480,
498, 516,
525
Moffatt, J. 457
Moltmann, Jürgen
138
Montefiore, Claude
115, 131,
134
Moo, Douglas
11, 12, 20,
22, 36, 42,
48, 49, 95,
139, 172,
201, 203,
227, 230,
231, 232,
236, 240,
241, 265,
266, 276,
284, 311,
433, 434,
436
Moore, George Foot
115, 131
Mordecai 269
Morris, Leon
20, 36, 55,
180, 360,
456, 457,
538, 539
Mosaic Torah
76, 116,
117, 123,
126, 128,
134, 139,
159, 164,
169, 192,
193, 195,

Subject Index

	196, 197,	**N**	130, 131,
	198, 205,	Naaman 356, 368	135, 138,
	206, 207,	Nachmanides	141, 143,
	209, 211,	62	144, 145,
	212, 213,	Nathanael 77	147, 163,
	214, 215,	Nations 43, 44, 81,	164, 169,
	216, 274,	99, 102,	172, 175,
	275, 519,	248, 284,	177, 178,
	522	403, 427,	179, 180,
Moses	26, 61, 70,	430, 524	181, 194,
	108, 109,	Nee, Watchman	207, 210,
	122, 150,	436	219, 247,
	151, 153,	Nemesis 20	250, 253,
	211, 221,	Neo-Platonists	254, 256,
	222, 231,	475	261, 283,
	264, 281,	Nero 250	288, 292,
	288, 291,	Netherlands	294, 295,
	330, 353,	5, 16, 285,	301, 304,
	356, 369,	319, 323,	305, 307,
	370, 371,	438	308, 334,
	373, 374,	Netherlands	335, 356,
	416, 443	Reformed	378, 382,
Moule, Handley		Churches	385, 386,
	39, 40, 424	323	391, 397,
Mount Carmel		New Covenant	398, 399,
	353	99, 100,	403, 404,
Mount Sinai		144, 149,	407, 414,
	42, 123,	150, 152	417, 418,
	151, 211	New Perspective on	421, 424,
Müller, C. 36		Paul	448, 449,
Müntzer, Thomas		19, 132,	454, 465,
	250, 251	133	468, 471,
Murray, Andrew		New Testament	476, 479,
	424	2, 3, 5, 7,	480, 481,
Murray, John		17, 20, 21,	484, 493,
	34, 48, 55,	23, 24, 31,	494, 495,
	172, 200,	44, 46, 55,	498, 499,
	203, 209,	60, 65, 68,	501, 504,
	231, 232,	74, 75, 80,	508, 509,
	236, 240,	84, 85, 87,	510, 516,
	276, 436,	91, 92, 93,	522, 523,
	540	95, 104,	524, 526,
Muslims 298		113, 114,	527, 528,
Mysteras, Lambertus		115, 116,	535, 536,
	401	117, 118,	537, 539

611

Newman, John H.
　　7
Ngewa, S. 370
Nicene Creed
　　8, 294
Nicodemus
　　65, 77,
　　222, 283
Noah　63, 84, 87,
　　88, 268,
　　353
Noordtzij, Arie
　　425
North America
　　319, 323
Nouwen, Henri
　　14
NPP　112, 132,
　　133, 134,
　　135, 139,
　　153, 157,
　　160
Nygren, Anders
　　34, 433,
　　434

O
O'Brien, Peter T.
　　134
Obedience of Christ
　　165, 174,
　　175, 181,
　　187, 192,
　　194, 196,
　　197, 198,
　　200, 201,
　　202, 203,
　　208, 209,
　　210, 215,
　　518, 519
Obedience of faith
　　235, 284,
　　302, 311,
　　317, 355
Oehler, Gustav F.

　　539
Oepke, A. 34
Ogliari, Donato
　　8, 9
Old Covenant
　　100, 123,
　　150, 152
Old Perspective on
　　Paul
　　132
Old Testament
　　2, 41, 43,
　　52, 55, 60,
　　62, 63, 64,
　　74, 75, 80,
　　82, 84, 85,
　　87, 88, 97,
　　98, 118,
　　120, 124,
　　125, 186,
　　204, 238,
　　254, 258,
　　271, 282,
　　291, 362,
　　368, 369,
　　379, 382,
　　394, 395,
　　397, 398,
　　402, 425,
　　463, 507,
　　529, 539
Onesimus 486
Osiander, Andreas
　　16
Oswalt, John N.
　　52, 88,
　　251, 252,
　　253
Othello　107
Otto, Rudolf
　　431
Owen, John
　　481

P
Packer, J. I.
　　4, 200, 310
Pagans　82, 142
Pannenberg, W.
　　31
Pareus, David
　　520
Pascal, Blaise
　　152
Passover 526
Passover Feast
　　290
Passover Lamb
　　125
Paul　2, 6, 7, 9,
　　10, 11, 19,
　　25, 26, 27,
　　34, 37, 38,
　　39, 41, 42,
　　43, 44, 45,
　　46, 47, 49,
　　61, 64, 71,
　　72, 73, 87,
　　90, 91, 93,
　　95, 96,
　　100, 104,
　　105, 106,
　　108, 111,
　　112, 113,
　　114, 115,
　　117, 118,
　　122, 123,
　　126, 127,
　　128, 130,
　　131, 132,
　　133, 134,
　　137, 138,
　　139, 140,
　　142, 144,
　　146, 148,
　　149, 150,
　　151, 152,
　　153, 154,
　　155, 157,

Subject Index

160, 164,
166, 167,
171, 176,
180, 186,
189, 195,
196, 198,
200, 201,
202, 206,
207, 210,
211, 215,
221, 224,
225, 228,
230, 232,
236, 247,
248, 251,
253, 255,
258, 259,
260, 261,
264, 267,
273, 274,
277, 283,
284, 285,
286, 289,
300, 302,
304, 308,
315, 320,
327, 337,
344, 349,
357, 359,
367, 371,
379, 382,
383, 406,
407, 412,
413, 433,
436, 437,
439, 440,
441, 444,
445, 446,
447, 450,
452, 454,
457, 468,
469, 470,
471, 472,
477, 481,
486, 489,

492, 493,
494, 503,
510, 511,
519, 523
Paul, M. J.   367
Pawson, D.
  381
Pelagius   436
Pelikan, Jaroslav
  11
Pentecostals
  191
Perfectionism
  394, 423,
  446, 454,
  484, 506,
  507, 508,
  509, 512,
  513
Perseverance
  71, 97,
  282, 316,
  317, 321,
  322, 334,
  375, 376,
  377, 378,
  384, 385
Pesch, Otto H.
  12
Peter   65, 77,
  117, 125,
  130, 256,
  284, 293,
  302, 303,
  315, 329,
  336, 340,
  356, 362,
  366, 390,
  414, 419,
  461, 471,
  510
Pharisaism
  466
Pharisees   107, 108,
  109, 146,

147, 254,
331, 340
Pharpar   368
Philetus   386
Philippi, F. A.
  34, 231,
  276
Philippian jailer
  260, 283
Philo   539
Phinehas   79, 80, 89
Photius   130
Pilate   77
Pinson, J. M.
  379
Piper, John
  138, 139,
  140, 141,
  142, 143,
  149, 160,
  170, 175,
  184, 199,
  519
Piscator, Johann
  520
Placation   270, 533,
  534, 535,
  537, 538,
  539, 540
Plass, E. M.
  3, 507
Polycarp   507
Pop, F. J.   20, 36, 282
Prayer of Manasseh
  88, 147
Predestination
  8, 144,
  320, 327,
  328, 376,
  380, 470
Priests   147, 187,
  284, 299,
  311, 353,
  416, 417,
  418

613

Prince, Joseph 379
Promised land 61, 211, 335, 369
Prophets 1, 41, 42, 43, 66, 69, 84, 147, 206, 264, 281, 283, 288, 351, 370, 391, 415
Propitiation 6, 38, 102, 116, 118, 121, 194, 202, 219, 225, 238, 284, 515, 526, 528, 533, 534, 536, 538, 539, 540, 541
Protestant Church in the Netherlands 5
Protestant theologians 11, 12, 14, 131, 229, 315, 431
Protestant theology 114
Protestantism 4, 5, 11, 159
Protestants 2, 9, 11, 12, 14, 15, 131, 132, 133, 260, 314, 322, 423

Pseudo-Clement 130

Q
Quakers 421
Quickening 6, 75, 92, 229, 408

R
Rab Judah 81
Rabbi Aqiva 146
Rabbi Eliezer 81
Rabbi Hillel 130
Rabbi Joshua 81
Rabbi Simlai 263
Rabbis 52, 61, 115, 118, 119, 137, 361
Rahab 248, 249, 334, 356
Räisänen, Heikki 131, 132, 139, 145
Rashi 51
Ratzinger, Joseph 13, 14, 523
Rebirth 6, 322, 437, 463, 470
Reconciliation 6, 11, 100, 102, 103, 204, 244, 255, 266, 386, 409, 526, 534, 537, 538
Red Sea 369, 428

Redeemer 70, 268, 301, 302, 428
Redemption 6, 22, 38, 40, 43, 44, 45, 76, 77, 97, 99, 101, 103, 116, 118, 121, 122, 139, 143, 144, 145, 150, 154, 163, 186, 191, 198, 199, 202, 208, 215, 219, 220, 222, 224, 225, 239, 253, 278, 361, 394, 396, 397, 402, 406, 409, 410, 411, 413, 427, 428, 429, 487, 526, 528, 529, 533, 534
Redemptive history 124, 152
Reformation 2, 5, 8, 9, 10, 11, 13, 16, 17, 31, 32, 132, 174, 175, 181, 189, 251, 305, 312, 314, 520
Reformed Christians

Subject Index

319, 327
Reformed Churches
  Liberated
  323
Reformed circles
  322, 480,
  484
Reformed doctrine
  16, 90,
  160, 164,
  169, 171,
  178, 190,
  195, 203,
  375
Reformed
  theologians
  15, 16,
  132, 143,
  160, 164,
  180, 182,
  184, 200,
  209, 319,
  321, 364,
  374, 438,
  476, 522,
  535
Reformed theology
  5, 60, 86,
  101, 143,
  180, 181,
  196, 208,
  209, 210,
  220, 316,
  394, 402,
  404, 408,
  409, 410,
  421, 434
Reformed tradition
  18, 33,
  182, 184,
  190, 191,
  257, 375,
  378
Reformers 5, 10, 11,
  16, 19,

113, 114,
176, 190,
197, 294,
401, 434
Regeneration
  6, 28, 59,
  60, 63, 65,
  66, 68, 71,
  74, 75, 86,
  102, 103,
  156, 157,
  159, 168,
  222, 259,
  284, 301,
  304, 306,
  316, 319,
  331, 335,
  380, 389,
  402, 405,
  407, 408,
  409, 412,
  413, 416,
  438, 442,
  448, 460,
  461
Rehabilitation
  22, 239,
  257, 258
Remonstrantism
  183, 375
Remonstrants
  19, 375,
  376, 377
Repentance
  39, 66, 87,
  115, 116,
  117, 119,
  139, 143,
  146, 233,
  267, 284,
  306, 307,
  308, 309,
  310, 313,
  314, 318,
  323, 328,

329, 376,
383, 435,
534
Resurrection
  18, 28, 41,
  92, 93, 94,
  141, 164,
  166, 167,
  168, 169,
  174, 178,
  180, 188,
  198, 199,
  202, 207,
  210, 211,
  212, 213,
  214, 216,
  227, 237,
  238, 240,
  241, 242,
  243, 255,
  265, 305,
  353, 369,
  401, 405,
  471, 472,
  474, 523,
  525
Rice, John R.
  188, 189
Ridderbos, Herman
  6, 18, 34,
  35, 172,
  200, 203,
  230, 231,
  232, 240,
  260, 261,
  276, 433
Rietkerk, W. G.
  366
Righteousness of
  Christ
  2, 16, 17,
  18, 19, 32,
  33, 101,
  141, 159,
  160, 163,

615

164, 165,
171, 172,
174, 175,
177, 179,
180, 181,
182, 184,
185, 188,
190, 191,
192, 193,
194, 195,
196, 199,
202, 208,
209, 212,
319, 518,
519, 530
Righteousness
 of God
1, 2, 14,
15, 16, 32,
33, 35, 37,
38, 39, 40,
41, 42, 43,
46, 47, 50,
52, 53, 56,
95, 98,
101, 148,
163, 175,
176, 177,
178, 184,
185, 186,
187, 188,
189, 206,
213, 230,
231, 233,
253, 259,
264, 267,
284, 440,
515, 530
Ritschl, Albrecht
 17, 55
Robertson, O. Palmer
 90, 94, 97
Rokeach, M.
 296
Roman Catholic

Church
 10, 14, 19
Roman Catholicism
 5, 11, 114
Roman Catholics
 11, 12, 13,
 14, 19,
 381, 476
Roman centurion
 290, 352
Roman Empire
 130
Roman law
 31, 257
Rome 2, 9, 11,
 14, 16,
 189, 282,
 289, 302,
 314
Römerbrief 17, 175,
 189, 286
Roozemeijer, Jean,
 33, 34
Rushing, R.
 481
Ryle, John 424, 498
Ryrie, Charles C.
 305, 309,
 310, 312,
 314, 315

S
Sabbath 125, 196,
 439
Sacks, Jonathan
 77, 78
Sadducees 340
Salmond, S. D. F.
 230, 482
Salvation 1, 3, 4, 5,
 6, 7, 8, 9,
 13, 14, 17,
 43, 44, 45,
 46, 65, 68,
 71, 73, 76,

97, 98, 99,
101, 102,
103, 104,
106, 112,
113, 128,
137, 142,
143, 144,
145, 146,
147, 148,
154, 157,
159, 187,
189, 195,
199, 209,
210, 214,
221, 229,
237, 244,
255, 260,
268, 279,
282, 283,
284, 285,
289, 292,
293, 294,
301, 304,
305, 306,
307, 309,
311, 313,
318, 322,
324, 325,
327, 328,
329, 331,
332, 335,
336, 367,
378, 379,
380, 383,
384, 388,
402, 404,
405, 406,
407, 409,
421, 429,
437, 438,
442, 448,
449, 451,
452, 457,
471, 496,
501, 519,

616

Subject Index

521, 524, 526, 527, 529
Salvation Army 421
Samaritans 260, 438
Sanctification 4, 6, 15, 16, 28, 101, 102, 103, 156, 163, 186, 198, 220, 221, 239, 247, 255, 257, 258, 306, 311, 316, 322, 393, 394, 395, 397, 398, 399, 400, 401, 402, 403, 404, 405, 406, 409, 410, 411, 412, 413, 414, 415, 416, 417, 418, 419, 420, 421, 422, 423, 424, 433, 434, 435, 439, 440, 441, 442, 445, 447, 450, 451, 453, 454, 455, 456, 457, 458, 459, 460, 461, 463, 465, 466, 467, 468, 470, 471, 476, 477, 478, 479, 480, 485, 489, 490, 491, 496, 497, 501, 502, 503, 504, 505, 506, 514

Sanday, W. 36, 236, 276
Sanders, Ed 112, 115, 116, 123, 125, 127, 128, 131, 132, 134, 135, 138, 139, 145, 148
Sapphira 386, 390
Sarah 88, 92, 93
Sardis 71
Satan 49, 300, 318, 351, 359, 365, 375, 376, 487, 500
Saul 271, 272, 382
Saul of Tarsus 77, 84, 260, 307, 438, 471
Sauter, G. 12
Savior 45, 46, 67, 70, 98, 103, 114, 155, 157, 158, 159, 197, 222, 247, 282, 283, 303, 304, 305, 328, 385, 405, 406, 450, 451, 460, 468, 486, 496

Schilder, Klaas 525
Schlatter, A. 36, 231, 482
Schlink, Basilea, B. 94
Schmelzer, M. 119
Schoeps, Hans-Joachim 11, 132, 134, 135
Schreiner, Thomas 7, 139
Schrenk, Gottlob 30, 31
Schürer, Emil 114, 115
Schwarz, R. 3
Schweitzer, Albert 5, 6
Scott, C. Anderson 36, 180, 181
Scribes 108, 146, 147, 254, 331, 338
Scroggie, William Graham 424
Scythians 403
Second Helvetic Confession 165, 181
Second Reformation 16

617

Second Temple
    Judaism
        121, 131,
        132, 133,
        134, 135,
        145, 147
Seebass, H.
        36
Segal, A. F.
        139
Seifrid, Mark A.
        134
Septuagint
        94, 96,
        399, 418,
        539
Sermon on the Mount
        109, 290
Seth   87
Sevenster, G.
        36
Shakespeare
        107
Shedd, W. G. T.
        276
Shelton, R. L.
        6, 36, 535
Shem   87
Shepherd, Norman
        202, 203
Shittim   43
Shulam, Joseph
        36, 48, 51,
        52, 231,
        261, 263
Siloam   344
Simeon   76
Simon the Magician
        348, 390
Sin offering 117, 118,
        238, 278,
        523, 529,
        530, 533,
        536, 538
Sinaitic covenant

        124, 139
Singapore 379
Sinners   3, 19, 22,
        40, 46, 47,
        54, 55, 56,
        63, 71, 73,
        143, 144,
        146, 149,
        164, 177,
        179, 181,
        185, 189,
        198, 200,
        202, 204,
        214, 221,
        223, 239,
        266, 269,
        271, 273,
        274, 277,
        282, 304,
        391, 400,
        423, 435,
        445, 447,
        454, 484,
        492, 493,
        494, 495,
        497, 498,
        499, 523,
        536, 538,
        540, 541
Slaves   32, 158,
        235, 239,
        247, 255,
        302, 311,
        403, 404,
        423, 441,
        445, 447,
        457, 459,
        466, 478,
        508
Smith, D.   512
Smith, Robert P.
        424
Snodgrass, K. R.
        139
Sodom   372

Solomon   61, 80, 86,
        95, 145
Son of David
        101, 343,
        347, 349
Son of God
        7, 70, 92,
        186, 217,
        234, 241,
        262, 268,
        284, 294,
        351, 383,
        384, 416,
        468, 469,
        475, 486,
        491, 497
Son of Man 50, 68,
        217, 330,
        344, 358,
        527
Soteriology
        103, 158,
        407
Spilka, B.   296
Spirit of God
        370, 408,
        439, 509
Springer, K.
        354
Sproul, R. C.
        3, 18, 176,
        200, 374
Spykman, G. J.
        12, 175,
        316, 433
Statenvertaling
        33, 173,
        178, 372,
        382, 385,
        386, 535
Stendahl, Krister
        115, 131
Stern, David H.
        34, 48, 72,
        135, 151

Stewart, James
  7, 471
Stott, J. R. W.
  303
Strack, H. L.
  34, 263,
  361
Strickland 462
Stuart, C.E.
  457
Stuhlmacher, Peter
  4, 36, 135
Stumme, W. C.
  13
Suggate, A. M.
  133
Supersessionism
  131
Susa 270
Swidler, L.
  139
Synod of Dordt
  520
Synod of Dordrecht
  375

T
Talmud 51, 81, 82,
  115, 119,
  146, 240,
  363
Tanakh 42, 65,
  206, 263,
  399
Targum 51
Tavard, George H.
  12
Ten Commandments
  196, 212
Tenney, Merrill
  361, 456
Ter Schegget, G. H.
  537
Textus Receptus
  248, 303

Theologians
  6, 10, 11,
  12, 14, 15,
  16, 32, 55,
  113, 131,
  132, 133,
  139, 141,
  143, 150,
  160, 164,
  175, 180,
  182, 184,
  190, 193,
  200, 209,
  229, 305,
  314, 315,
  319, 321,
  323, 364,
  374, 381,
  421, 431,
  432, 436,
  437, 438,
  446, 475,
  476, 496,
  497, 501,
  522, 525,
  535, 537
Theology 3, 5, 7, 8,
  13, 14, 17,
  19, 60, 86,
  101, 114,
  132, 142,
  143, 158,
  161, 180,
  181, 183,
  196, 208,
  209, 210,
  220, 258,
  278, 306,
  316, 322,
  382, 386,
  394, 402,
  404, 408,
  409, 410,
  420, 421,
  434, 484,

  534
Theosis 7, 409,
  454, 455,
  456, 466,
  467
Thessalonica
  304
Thielman, Frank
  113, 116,
  139, 145,
  151, 152
Tholuck, F. A. G.
  344
Thomas, R. L.
  457
Thyatira 71
Torah obedience
  163, 171,
  187, 196,
  197, 210,
  213
Torah observance
  16, 61, 76,
  116, 137,
  139, 145,
  178, 198,
  199, 202,
  203, 204,
  208, 210,
  212, 213,
  214, 215,
  216, 222,
  518, 519,
  521, 522,
  530
Torah of Christ
  104, 122,
  155, 212,
  235, 461,
  462
Tosefta 81
Tozer, Aiden W.
  310
Traditionalists
  154, 157,

Subject Index

619

159, 177
Translators
276, 286,
287, 408,
539
Treier, D. J.
5, 184
Trench, R. C.
469
Trevethan, T. L.
424, 428
Trinity 53, 197
Tsaddiq 20, 22, 29,
30, 52, 59,
60, 74, 76,
77, 78, 79,
80, 81, 82,
83, 84, 85,
86, 87, 88,
94, 95, 96,
97, 105,
106, 107,
108, 110,
129, 130,
131, 148,
156, 158,
167, 207,
208, 220,
224, 239,
249, 258,
259, 260,
261, 262,
306, 372,
430
Tsaddiqim 27, 60, 66,
75, 76, 77,
80, 87, 96,
97, 99,
112, 128,
129, 156,
158, 189,
248, 277

U
Ulpianus, Domitius
31
Unbelief 37, 73,
130, 311,
321, 332,
334, 336,
337, 338,
339, 342,
350, 351,
352, 354,
356, 357,
358, 366,
384
University of Leyden
285
University of Notre
Dame
12
Unrighteousness
32, 37, 38,
47, 88,
188, 215,
226, 233,
242, 255,
326, 440,
444, 445,
478, 515,
538

V
Van Cleave,
Nathaniel
3, 22, 191,
381, 483
Van de Beek, A.
103
Van de Pol, Willem
11
Van der Groe,
Theodorus
319
Van der Kooi, C.
175
Van der Meer, F. G.
421
Van der Waal,
Cornelis
3, 4, 537
Van der Zwaag,
Klaas
9, 19, 433,
501
Van Genderen, Jan
3, 16, 18,
19, 32, 36,
69, 173,
175, 180,
182, 192,
229, 239,
284, 288,
316, 322,
326, 420,
455, 460,
480, 507,
510, 535
Van Kooten, R. C.
202, 203
Van Leeuwen, J. A. C.
36, 230,
232, 436,
457
Van Spanje, T. E.
131
Van 't Spijker,
Willem
321, 323
VanLandingham,
Chris
139, 148,
149
Vatican 13
Velema, Willem H.
3, 18, 19,
32, 36, 69,
175, 192,
229, 239,
284, 288,
316, 322,
326, 420,
455, 480,
507, 510,

Subject Index

535
Verkuyl, Johan
 91, 412,
 484, 485,
 496, 524,
 536, 537,
 539
Vermes, Géza
 135
Vine, William E.
 36, 42,
 201, 202,
 203, 226,
 227, 231,
 236, 240,
 276, 300,
 456, 457,
 483
Vischer, L. 12
Von Hofmann,
 Johann
 201, 203
Von Rad, Gerhard
 395, 539
Vulgate 51, 273,
 362, 534

W
Warfield, B. B.
 506
Weber, Ferdinand
 114, 115
Weber, O. 36
Wendland, H.-D.
 3, 36
Wenham, D.
 139
Wentsel, B.
 36
Westerholm, Stephen
 139
Wesley, John
 421, 433,
 506
Westcott, B. F.

539
Western Christianity
 5, 501
Western theology
 8, 484
Westminster
 Confession
 80, 164,
 181, 195,
 245, 257,
 317, 400,
 426, 480
Westminster Larger
 Catechism
 164, 181,
 517
Westminster Shorter
 Catechism
 160
Westminster
 Standards
 17, 160,
 161, 171,
 203
White, J. R.
 3, 36, 175
White, N. J. D.
 300
Wiersinga, Herman
 36, 537
Wiersinga, W. A.
 69, 366,
 480, 506
Williams, Susan
 DeVore
 373
Willis, D. 424
Wimber, John
 354
Winger, M.
 139
Wisdom 21, 25, 67,
 85, 101,
 103, 163,
 186, 198,

233, 349,
 371, 413,
 431, 448,
 468
Wisse, P. M.
 320
Woelderink, Jan
 Gerrit
 182, 183,
 184, 240
Wood, A. S.
 230, 482
Word of God
 15, 35,
 109, 326,
 327, 383,
 391, 487,
 488, 526
Wrath of God
 195, 202,
 226, 244,
 260, 269,
 284, 311,
 335, 502,
 515, 516,
 517, 518,
 524, 525,
 533, 535,
 537, 538,
 539, 540
Wrede, Wilhelm
 5, 6
Wright, N. T.
 112, 116,
 134, 135,
 138, 139,
 140, 141,
 142, 143,
 149, 156,
 158, 160,
 170, 184,
 289, 302,
 465
Wuest, K. S.
 482

Y

Yad Vashem
 81
Yancey 450
Yom Kippur
 119, 278
Young, E. J.
 34
Youngblood, R. F.
 272

Z

Zacchaeus 364
Zahn, Th. 34, 231
Zechariah 63, 66, 72,
 75, 76,
 111, 128,
 288
Ziba 272
Ziesler, John
 36, 44, 52
Zion 42, 98,
 148, 251,
 252, 263,
 283, 395,
 464, 498
Zook 182

www.ingramcontent.com/pod-product-compliance
Lightning Source LLC
Chambersburg PA
CBHW060646150426
42811CB00086B/2442/J